® BAR REVIEW

D1249837

Director
Steven R. Rubin, Esq.

Associate Directors
Robert W. Cohen, Esq.
Erica B. Fine, Esq.

Table of Contents

New York Testing

NYT

To be used in conjunction with the Summer 2007 and Winter 2008 BAR/BRI Bar Review Courses

THOMSON
BAR/BRI

Celebrating XL years one million students

BAR REVIEW

ESSAY GRADING KEY

DATE RECEIVED _____

Name _____

Address _____

_____

BAR/BRI ID #_____

ESSAY QUESTION #_____

COURSE LOCATION _____

SESSION: AM / AFT / PM   (circle one)

ESSAY GRADE _____

GRADER NUMBER _____

GRADER'S COMMENTS

GRADER'S COMMENTS

BAR REVIEW

ESSAY GRADING KEY

DATE RECEIVED _____

Name _____

Address _____

_____

ESSAY GRADE _____

BAR/BRI ID #_____

ESSAY QUESTION #_____

COURSE LOCATION _____

SESSION: AM / AFT / PM   (circle one)

GRADER NUMBER _____

GRADER'S COMMENTS

GRADER'S COMMENTS

ESSAY GRADING KEY

DATE RECEIVED _____

Name _____

Address _____

_____

BAR/BRI ID # _____

ESSAY QUESTION # _____

COURSE LOCATION _____

SESSION: AM / AFT / PM   (circle one)

ESSAY GRADE _____

GRADER NUMBER _____

_____
_____
_____
_____
_____

GRADER'S COMMENTS

GRADER'S COMMENTS

ESSAY GRADING KEY

DATE RECEIVED _____

Name _____

Address _____

_____

ESSAY GRADE _____

BAR/BRI ID # _____

ESSAY QUESTION # _____

COURSE LOCATION _____

SESSION: AM / AFT / PM   (circle one)

GRADER NUMBER _____

_____
_____
_____
_____
_____
_____

	GRADER'S COMMENTS

GRADER'S COMMENTS

BAR REVIEW

ESSAY GRADING KEY

DATE RECEIVED _____

Name _____

Address _____

_____

BAR/BRI ID # _____

ESSAY QUESTION # _____

COURSE LOCATION _____

SESSION: AM / AFT / PM   (circle one)

ESSAY GRADE _____

GRADER NUMBER _____

_____
_____
_____
_____
_____

GRADER'S COMMENTS

BAR REVIEW

ESSAY GRADING KEY

DATE RECEIVED _____

Name _____

Address _____

_____

ESSAY GRADE _____

BAR/BRI ID # _____

ESSAY QUESTION # _____

COURSE LOCATION _____

SESSION: AM / AFT / PM   (circle one)

GRADER NUMBER _____

_____
_____
_____
_____
_____

GRADER'S COMMENTS

GRADER'S COMMENTS

BAR REVIEW

NEW YORK BAR EXAM SUGGESTED ESSAY TECHNIQUE

1.   Read the *call of the question*.

2.   Spend the first *10-15 minutes outlining the issues* in the essay and framing your answer. Spend the remaining *25-30 minutes writing your answer*.

3.   *IRAC*—each issue presented:

   I   *Issue*. State the issue presented by the facts.
   R   *Rule*. State the applicable rule of law.
   A   *Analysis*. For each element of the rule of law, state the fact(s) that apply or the absence of any fact(s) that would make the rule applicable.
   C   *Conclusion*. Restate your conclusion.

4.   Write *concise sentences*. Run-ons, fragments, and dangling participles make it difficult for the grader. Graders should not have to "search" for the answer. Remember, you want the grader to "like" you.

5.   Write *clearly*. If the grader cannot read your paper, the grader cannot grade your paper. Using print rather than script and double spacing may make it easier for the grader.

6.   *Do not argue both sides* unless the facts warrant. Take a position and stick to it. Follow through with the best support for the argument based upon your knowledge of the applicable law. Being indecisive makes the bar examiners think you do not know the law at all.

7.   Only deal with *the issue(s) presented*. For example, if you are dealing with one particular hearsay exception, you should not list all the hearsay exceptions. It is not necessary to tell the bar examiners what *does not apply* to the facts presented.

8.   *Do not overemphasize* (*i.e.*, by underlining, capitalizing, etc.) so many words that the effect is lost. Only "buzz words" should be highlighted.

9.   Always *complete the discussion of one issue* before moving to another. Do not combine two or three issues into one paragraph and one thought. Discussion of each issue should be viewed as a "mini essay" and should be able to stand by itself.

10.   *Develop your analysis fully*. A mere conclusion without legal reasoning and fact application is worthless. For each element of each rule of law, you must state how a fact (or the absence thereof) applies or does not apply.
Examples: There was an entering *because* he put his hand through the window.
           It is a dwelling *because* people live there.
           The defendant was armed *because* he had a gun.

11.   *Do not interject your personal opinion* as to how a court should rule based upon your sense of "fairness, justice, and decency" rather than on the applicable legal principles.

12.   If a statute is applicable to your answer, you should *mention the broad name of the statute*, *e.g.*, UCC, CPLR, BCL, etc. However, *do not mention statute numbers or case names* unless they are extremely significant and recognizable, *e.g.*, *Miranda*.

13. Finally, we suggest that you **_write on the right-hand page only_**. By doing this, if you want to add something as an afterthought, all you have to do is draw an arrow to the left-hand page and make your insert. You will be given as many 8½ × 11 "bluebooks" as you need.

barbri®

BAR REVIEW

Essay Questions

ESSAYS TABLE OF CONTENTS

Please note: Because of the addition of the MPT in 2001, recent bar exam essays contain one to two fewer issues than in previous exams. Therefore, all essays marked with an asterisk have been edited to reflect those changes. The issues that were removed from these questions have been made into multiple choice questions so that you can still review these issues. (*See* Multiple Choice Questions by Subject.)

*41	Evidence
*42	Criminal Law/Criminal Procedure
43	Partnership
*44	N.Y. Practice/Torts/Equity/Contracts
45	Corporations/Contracts (Sales)
46	Criminal Law/Criminal Procedure
47	Domestic Relations/N.Y. Practice
48	Wills/Torts
49	N.Y. Practice/Torts
50	Real Property
51	Domestic Relations
52	Domestic Relations/N.Y. Practice
*53	N.Y. Practice/Real Property/Mortgages
54	Wills
55	Criminal Law/Criminal Procedure
56	Wills
*57	Domestic Relations/Real Property
58	Real Property/N.Y. Practice/Contracts
59	Criminal Law/Criminal Procedure/Evidence
*60	Domestic Relations
*61	Wills/Trusts
62	N.Y. Practice
63	Contracts (Sales)/N.Y. Practice
64	Real Property/N.Y. Practice
*65	Domestic Relations
*66	Contracts (Sales)
*67	Wills/Trusts/Future Interests
68	Commercial Paper/Fed. Jur. & Pro.
*69	Contracts (Sales)
70	Wills/Trusts
71	Conflict of Laws/Fed. Jur. & Pro./N.Y. Practice
*72	Corporations
*73	Domestic Relations
*74	Contracts (Sales)
75	Criminal Law/Criminal Procedure/Constitutional Law
*76	Commercial Paper/Criminal Procedure/Evidence
*77	Criminal Law/Criminal Procedure
*78	Domestic Relations
79	Criminal Law/Criminal Procedure/Evidence
80	Real Property/Mortgages
81	Corporations/Contracts/N.Y. Practice
82	Domestic Relations/N.Y. Practice
83	Commercial Paper/Conflict of Laws
*84	Fed. Jur. & Pro./N.Y. Practice/Torts
85	Evidence
*86	Contracts (Sales)
*87	Criminal Law
88	Corporations
89	Evidence
90	Wills

91	Contracts (Sales)
92	Criminal Law/Criminal Procedure/Constitutional Law
93	Domestic Relations
94	Criminal Law/Criminal Procedure/Evidence
95	Wills
*96	Torts
*97	Torts/Wills/N.Y. Practice
*98	Contracts (Sales)
*99	Real Property/Domestic Relations
*100	Torts/N.Y. Practice/Conflict of Laws

Released Questions

R-1	Professional Responsibility/Domestic Relations
R-2	Wills/Professional Responsibility
R-3	Wills/Professional Responsibility
R-4	Contracts/Professional Responsibility/Corporations
R-5	Evidence/Criminal Law
R-6	Domestic Relations/Mortgages/Wills
R-7	N.Y. Practice/Torts/Evidence
R-8	Wills/Partnership
R-9	Contracts/Agency/Professional Responsibility/Corporations
R-10	Criminal Law/Commercial Paper
R-11	Wills
R-12	Torts/N.Y. Practice/Evidence
R-13	Domestic Relations/Mortgages
R-14	Sales/Contracts
R-15	Evidence/Criminal Law/Criminal Procedure/ Professional Responsibility
R-16	Domestic Relations
R-17	Workers' Compensation/Torts/N.Y. Practice
R-18	Wills
R-19	Torts/Conflict of Laws/N.Y. Practice
R-20	Professional Responsibility/N.Y. Practice/Conflict of Laws
R-21	Domestic Relations/Real Property
R-22	Domestic Relations/Professional Responsibility/Real Property
R-23	Domestic Relations/Real Property/N.Y. Practice
R-24	Contracts
R-25	Corporations
R-26	Torts/N.Y. Practice/Contracts
R-27	Corporations/Contracts
R-28	Constitutional Law/Criminal Law/Criminal Procedure
R-29	Criminal Procedure/Criminal Law
R-30	Criminal Procedure
R-31	Professional Responsibility/Wills

QUESTION 1

In preparation for a visit to F Bank, where W maintained her checking account, W wrote and signed a check to be drawn against her account, payable to "cash" in the amount of $100. As she was about to leave her apartment, she received a phone call from S, one of her creditors, who demanded that W immediately pay him an overdue debt that amounted to $300. Therefore, W wrote and signed a second check, also against her account at F Bank, payable "to the order of S" in the amount of $200. She then put both checks in an envelope addressed to S and mailed them.

Thieves confiscated the mail and divided it up among themselves. H, one of the thieves, obtained W's letter and took the checks to F Bank, where he indorsed them as follows: "Pay to the order of H. [Signed] S." He then presented them for payment and received $300 in cash, which he used the following day to purchase a new horse from T.

Meanwhile, W was struck by lightning and was admitted to the hospital with a case of temporary amnesia. On the 11th business day after H's presentation of the checks at F Bank, W remembered herself and went home. As soon as she arrived at her apartment, she received an irate telephone call from S, who said, "I've been trying to call you all week. Where's my $300?" W said she had mailed it, and S replied that he had not received any letter from her.

W therefore went to F Bank, where a teller told her that the checks had been cashed. W, who was an attorney, immediately advised the teller that the bank had improperly made payment on the basis of a forged indorsement.

Assume that H cannot be apprehended.

(a) What are S's rights against W?

(b) What are W's rights against T?

(c) What are W's rights against F Bank?

QUESTION 2

A, B, and C set up X Corp., each purchasing 100 shares of the corporation's 500 authorized shares, without par value. As shareholders, they unanimously pass several bylaws, two of which are:

> No shareholder shall sell his shares to any third party without first offering
> them to the corporation at the price agreed to by said third party.

> A unanimous vote of the directors shall be required to authorize the sale of
> any shares by any shareholder.

A, B, and C elect themselves as the three directors, and, as directors, elect A as president, B as vice president, and C as secretary. The certificate of incorporation made no reference to the two quoted bylaws or their subject matter, nor did the share certificates. The certificate of incorporation and the bylaws were silent on preemptive rights.

Later, at a duly noticed and held meeting of the directors, the following resolution was adopted by A and C (with B dissenting): It was decided to issue 100 shares to O to purchase a piece of real property that O was willing to sell to the corporation.

Upset at this development, B attempted to sell his shares for $10,000 to D. D paid B, and B indorsed his certificates to D. D then went to the offices of X Corp. and demanded that C record his ownership. C refused, and quoted the above bylaw provisions. C then served a demand on B and D that the shares be sold to X Corp. for the $10,000.

B hires you as his attorney and asks you the following questions:

(1)   What are B's rights with regard to the shares issued to O?

(2)   What are B's rights with regard to the shares sold to D?

(3)   What are D's rights with regard to the shares bought from B?

QUESTION 3

D and P were domiciliaries of New York. On June 1, while driving in New Jersey, their vehicle collided with that of O, a domiciliary of New Jersey. D was driving, and P was a passenger. Immediately after the accident, P told D that D was a rotten driver, whereupon D severely beat P, adding to P's considerable injuries from the auto accident.

P died on December 1. On the following June 30, H, P's surviving spouse and executor, brought an action against D in the Supreme Court for Nassau County, the county of H's residence, alleging three causes of action: H, as executor of the estate of P, sued D for personal injuries resulting from D's negligence, and also sued D for battery. H, individually, sued D for wrongful death, seeking recovery for grief, heartache, and sorrow; for loss of consortium; for H's pecuniary loss as a result of the death of P; and for punitive damages.

D immediately moved through his lawyer to dismiss H's causes of action, claiming that H's actions were variously time barred, and/or failed to state a cause of action. The court (1) denied D's motion in toto.

Also on June 30, H (through his lawyer) brought suit alleging $100,000 in damages against O in the United States District Court for the Eastern District of New York. O was personally served at his home by a U.S. Marshal. O promptly moved (through his lawyer) to dismiss the cause of action for lack of jurisdiction. The court (2) granted O's motion.

Discuss the court's rulings.

QUESTION 4

A, B, C, and S as partners each contributed capital to form V Co., a partnership. A, B, and C put up $10,000 each, and S put up only $100 and then retired to Florida shortly after the company commenced, in 1986, with its business of selling and leasing jukeboxes and vending machines. The partnership agreement provided for the equal sharing of profits among the partners, and provided that in the event of the death of one or more partners, the partnership would be continued by the survivors, with the surviving spouse of any deceased partner receiving what would have been that partner's share of the profits. V Co.'s business was highly profitable until January 1999, when B was killed by an explosion in his automobile and C died of multiple gunshot wounds. B was unmarried and C was survived by a spouse, D.

A thereupon assumed complete responsibility for the business, which began to fall into debt. In February 1999, E lent V Co. $50,000 and took a promissory note in that amount signed by A on behalf of V Co. In March 1999, A was sentenced to prison for reasons unrelated to the partnership business, and A and S both asked D to take over the business for the duration of A's prison term. D agreed to do so, and until A was released in March 2000, D held herself out as a partner and performed all the work that was necessary to manage V Co. while A contributed no services to the partnership.

In January 2000, with V Co.'s debts continuing to accumulate, D was persuaded to accept an additional $50,000 loan to V Co. from E, who took a note in that amount signed by D on behalf of V Co. In April 2000, when A had resumed an active role in the management of V Co. together with D, A and D approached F to request a loan in the amount of $30,000 in order to pay some of V Co.'s creditors. F told them he was afraid to become involved in any transactions with V Co., but would be willing to make a personal loan to D. D thus received from F a suitcase containing $30,000 and gave F a note that recited that she owed F that amount payable on demand. In consultation with A, she has since used all of the $30,000 to pay various debts of the partnership, including half of the February 1999 loan to V Co. from E, but none of the January 2000 loan to V Co. from E. E has returned the February 1999 promissory note to A and D, and has taken a new note signed by D on behalf of V Co. in a reduced amount to reflect the fact that he has received partial payment.

V Co.'s assets now amount to $20,000, and the remaining creditors have strongly suggested that they be paid. A has ordered you, as his attorney, to advise him on the liabilities of the various parties. Tell A the extent to which each party may be liable for any sums due to any party.

QUESTION 5

P was employed by E Corp. on a piecework basis, as an operator of its punch press. The punch press, which was built in 1985, had been purchased from M Co., its designer and manufacturer. The machine was constructed with a guard plate that protected the operator from coming into contact with the moving parts of the machine. If the guard plate were to be displaced, the punch press would automatically shut off.

P believed that he could increase his output by removing the guard plate. In June 1989, P removed the guard plate and rewired the machine so that it would function without the guard plate.

On July 1, 1989, P caught his arm in the machine while he was operating it; the power did not shut off according to the original design, and P's arm and hand were crushed and severely injured.

S, a surgeon, performed emergency surgery on P that day. During the operation, S severed P's ulnar nerve, causing P to lose all use of his hand. S continued to treat P with short hospital stays until March 15, 1990.

In June 1992, P sued S and M Co. P alleged against M Co. that the punch press was unreasonably dangerous and negligently designed. P alleged in his complaint that S, through his negligent treatment, had aggravated his injuries.

M Co. timely served an answer which claimed for an affirmative defense that M Co. was not liable for the original injuries to P because P had removed the guard plate and rewired the machine.

M Co.'s answer also contained a cross-claim against S stating that if M Co. was liable for any of P's injuries, S was liable to M Co. for that portion of P's injuries caused by S's own negligence.

S moved to dismiss P's complaint on the ground that it was not timely. (1) The court denied the motion.

On the eve of trial, S settled with P and P gave S a release. S then moved to dismiss M Co.'s cross-claim. (2) The court granted the motion.

P continued his suit against M Co. At trial, P called two expert witnesses. To the surprise of P's attorney, the first expert testified that P's injuries would not have occurred if the guard plate had not been removed.

The first expert further testified that the machine had been subsequently redesigned in 1991, so that it could be operated safely, at higher speeds, without the guard plate. At this point, the attorney for M Co. objected to the testimony, but (3) the court overruled the objection.

P's second expert witness stated that M Co. could not have manufactured the machine with the 1991 improvements in 1985; that the new technology was still in the experimental stage and was not the state of the art at the time the accident occurred; and that the machine had been designed and constructed in accordance with the state of the art in 1985. At the close of P's case, M Co. moved to dismiss, claiming that P failed to establish a prima facie case. The trial judge (4) denied the motion. Thereafter, the case went to the jury, which returned a verdict in favor of P for $945,000.

Discuss the numbered rulings.

QUESTION 6

Pursuant to an oral agreement with A, B was employed as a salaried salesman for A's dress company, A Co. B was responsible for selling merchandise to small high-priced and well-known boutiques. Several months after B began working for A, he signed a brief written agreement which stated that:

> In the event B's employment with A Co. is terminated, B agrees not to work
> for any competitor of A Co. for one year from the date of termination.

After B had been working at A Co. for some time, A approached B and said that if B were, through his sales efforts, to acquire Super Huge Retailer as a customer for A Co., A would then pay B 10% of all future sales to Super Huge Retailer, even if B were no longer employed by A Co. when those sales were made.

Soon after that conversation, in June, B made a presentation to Super Huge Retailer and received a commitment to order during the pre-Christmas buying season.

One month later, in July, B left A Co. to work for C Co., A Co.'s largest competitor. Before leaving A Co., B copied and kept lists of customers with whom he had a close business relationship.

At an industry convention in October, B learned that A Co. had just doubled production of winter dresses as the result of a tremendous order from Super Huge Retailer.

In November, B commenced a lawsuit against A Co. In his complaint, B alleged that A Co. owed him 10% commission on the sales of dresses by A Co. to Super Huge Retailer.

A Co. served a timely answer to the complaint. In the answer, A Co. asserted two counterclaims, the first of which sought to enjoin B's use of the customer lists, and the second of which sought to enjoin B's continued employment at C Co. B served a timely reply which denied the counterclaims.

A Co. moved for summary judgment (a) dismissing B's complaint with prejudice and (b) awarding A Co. summary judgment on both counterclaims. In A Co.'s affidavit in support of the motion, A alleged that B's solicitation of Super Huge Retailer was done in the ordinary course of his salaried duties, and therefore, B was entitled to no commission. In his opposing affidavit, B alleged that soliciting a huge retailer was not part of his regular employment, and thus he was entitled to the commission. Both parties agreed that B had signed the agreement restricting his future employment and that B had taken and used the customer lists of well-known specialty shops.

The court (1) denied A Co. summary judgment on the branch of its motion to dismiss B's complaint with prejudice; (2) denied A Co. summary judgment on its first counterclaim, and awarded B summary judgment dismissing the counterclaim with prejudice; and (3) denied A Co. summary judgment on its second counterclaim and awarded B summary judgment, dismissing the counterclaim with prejudice.

B pressed his cause of action for the commission to trial. During the trial, A Co. attempted to raise a Statute of Frauds defense. (4) The trial judge denied A Co.'s motion to interpose that defense.

Discuss the numbered rulings.

QUESTION 7

On June 2, 1994, Stevie, 17 years old, and his younger brother Joey, age 15, were walking in a residential neighborhood bordering a private airport. The airport is surrounded by a barbed wire fence erected by the airport security department. The fence is controlled exclusively by the airport. On the fence were signs that read, "Danger, No Trespassing."

Joey and Stevie climbed over the fence, along a portion of the fence that was missing its barbed wire, to watch planes land. They started to run across one runway to get to a culvert where they could stay out of sight while watching the planes. Stevie made it across but Joey tripped and twisted his ankle. Stevie started to head back to help Joey, but then saw a plane that had landed on that runway heading toward them in excess of 150 miles per hour. Mark, the pilot, saw Joey at the last second but was unable to avoid him. Joey had his back to the plane and was struck by one of the engines on the plane's wing and propelled through the air.

Stevie ran to Joey, who was conscious for a few moments before dying in Stevie's arms. Stevie and Joey's parents as guardian on behalf of Stevie and as administrator of Joey's estate sued the airport's owner/manager ("Airport").

As the law clerk for the judge, prepare a memorandum discussing the potential causes of action against each party. Identify the party, the factual and legal issues, each potential defense, and cross-claim.

QUESTION 8

Mike and Frances have a child, Cora. At the age of two, Cora was removed from their custody by appropriate county social services department proceedings. She lived with her foster parents for seven years, at which time the family court directed the department of social services to develop a plan to reintegrate her into her natural family. Pursuant to this plan, Mike and Frances had brief visits with Cora every other week; they rented a more suitable home in which to raise children; and they eliminated several other problems that had led to the initial loss of custody. Nevertheless, following an interview with a psychologist, in which Cora stated a preference against living with Mike and Frances, the department initiated a proceeding to terminate parental rights based on permanent neglect, so that the foster parents could adopt Cora.

(a) At the fact-finding hearing, a social worker from the department wants to introduce her entire case file, which includes statements from neighbors and co-workers. Alice, the lawyer for Mike and Frances, objects to the admission of this evidence. The court sustained the objection. Was the court's ruling correct?

(b) The judge takes Cora into chambers, without attorneys or anyone else, and talks with her over objections by both attorneys. The judge refuses to make this conference part of the record. Are the judge's actions proper?

(c) The judge decides, based exclusively upon his conversation with the child, to terminate the parental rights of Mike and Frances (because the foster parents are wealthier, better educated, and able to give Cora a better start in life). Is this standard proper?

(d) Mike and Frances have been renting Sam's house. Wishing to buy the house, Mike directs his bank to issue a cashier's check to his order. He indorses it to Sam and tenders it with a written offer to buy the house. Sam accepts in writing. Two days later, Mike learns of the court's ruling. No longer interested in the house, he tells the bank to stop payment. The bank pays, knowing that it received a stop order. Were the actions of the bank proper?

QUESTION 9

Father ("F") and Mother ("M") brought their son ("S") outside to play. M went inside to get refreshments for everyone. Momentarily distracted, F failed to notice S wander off by the road. A, a driver, swerved to avoid a car driven by P and hit the child, maiming him. M, standing in the kitchen, saw S get hit and had a heart attack.

In Rochester Supreme Court, F, on behalf of S, timely brought suit against A. A impleaded P and also initiated a suit against F for negligence. F moved to dismiss A's claim.

(1)   The court dismissed A's claim against F. While the action was pending, A left the jurisdiction for a year and a half. During that time, M knew of A's out-of-state residence. Four years after the accident, M brought suit against A in tort for damages suffered when she saw the child get hit. A moved to dismiss. (2) The court dismissed the action by M.

After trial but before judgment in the action between F, A, and P, P settled with F for $30,000. F prevailed in the judgment. The court awarded $100,000, finding P and A each 50% liable. A's assets equal only $10,000.

(A)   Were the court's numbered rulings correct?

(B)   How much can F collect from A?

QUESTION 10

For the past two years, H regularly beat his wife, W. In June, H was involved in an automobile accident. H spent three months in the hospital. During the period of time he was in the hospital, he commenced a lawsuit based on his injuries in the accident and eventually recovered $100,000 for the pain and suffering.

Upon H's release from the hospital, W cared for him at home until he regained 50% of his strength. At that point, fearing for her safety, she moved out and immediately commenced a divorce action based on the ground of cruel and inhuman treatment. In her complaint, she alleged the specific incidents of her various beatings at the hands of H, and demanded equitable distribution.

After being properly served with the summons and complaint, H made a motion to dismiss for failure to state a cause of action based on the premise that W cohabited with him after the beatings.

(1)   The court denied H's motion on both grounds. H then timely served his answer generally
      denying all of W's allegations.

W submitted affidavits of herself, the police who responded to several of her calls after being beaten by H, and doctors who treated her after the beatings. Each of these affidavits was specific and enumerated the dates and events of each occurrence and W's specific injuries. Based on these affidavits, W made a motion for summary judgment. H did not respond to this motion.

(2)   The court granted W's motion for summary judgment.

(3)   The court then provided for distribution of H and W's property. Among the property that the court distributed between the parties was H's damage award for pain and suffering and the advances that W received for a book on "How to Succeed in Marriage," which she wrote while married to H.

Fully discuss each of the numbered rulings or actions of the court.

QUESTION 11

On July 30, 1995, A, B, and C formed a corporation to design and manufacture children's clothing. The corporation was incorporated pursuant to the laws of the state of New York and was authorized to issue 200 shares, no par value. A owned 25%, B owned 45%, and C owned 30%, and the three became the corporation's sole officers and directors.

In January 1996, D offered to purchase all of the assets of the corporation, and, at validly noticed and held meetings of the directors and shareholders of the corporation, A and C voted to accept the offer. B voted against it.

In preparation for the sale, A and C executed an agreement with D, wherein they agreed not to compete with D in the county of Nassau, where the corporation maintained its facilities, for a period of 10 years. The agreement provided for liquidated damages in the sum of $10,000 in the event of a breach by A or C as a nonexclusive remedy.

In February 1996, after compliance with all of the statutory requirements, B instituted an action against A and C, in their corporate capacities. X, the attorney representing A and C, immediately brought a motion to dismiss.

Also in February 1996, A and C opened a new business in Nassau, in direct competition with their former corporation and D. D sought injunctive relief.

(1)   Will A and C prevail in their motion to dismiss? What are B's rights?

(2)   Will D receive an injunction?

QUESTION 12

A and B are Canadian citizens who reside in a town close to the New York border. While driving in A's motor vehicle in New York, they consumed the contents of two six-packs of a well-known malt beverage and, thoroughly inebriated, picked up H, a hitchhiker and a New York resident. Half a mile from the point at which they had made their unscheduled stop, A failed to make a turn because of his slowed reflexes, and the vehicle struck a bridge abutment. H, who was sitting in the back seat, and B, who was sitting in the front seat, were both severely injured.

H duly sued A in the proper federal district court situated in New York, using New York's service of process rules. H sought $80,000 in damages. A moved to dismiss the complaint on the ground that the court lacked jurisdiction. The court (1) denied A's motion.

After trial, a verdict was entered in favor of H. A moved for costs. The court (2) awarded costs to A.

B subsequently caused a summons and complaint to issue against A in the Supreme Court for New York County. A asserted in his answer an affirmative defense that the Canadian guest statute prohibiting suits against motor vehicle owners by their passengers in the absence of gross negligence should apply. B moved to strike the defense as insufficient as a matter of law. The court (3) granted the motion.

A thereupon moved to dismiss B's complaint on the ground of forum non conveniens. The court (4) denied the motion.

B timely moved for summary judgment on the ground that the issues had been decided in the *H v. A* suit. The court (5) denied the motion. Were the numbered rulings correct?

QUESTION 13

An undercover police officer, P, approached D in a bar and offered him a plan to join him in robbing a liquor store. P said he would meet D at the store at 10 p.m. with a gun. D agreed and said he would meet P and rob the store. D went to the store. When he arrived, P arrested him and advised D of his *Miranda* rights.

P took D to the police station and again advised D of his rights. D said, "Look, I know my rights, and you and I know that I planned to rob that liquor store with you. That's why I went there." P asked D if D would sign a statement to that effect, and D said, "I ain't signing nothing until I can talk to my attorney, A." P took D to the phone, where D tried to call A, but A was not home, and so D left a message. Then P took D to another part of the building and asked D again to sign a written statement. This time, D agreed.

While the police were taking D's written confession, A arrived at the station house, spoke to the desk sergeant, and asked to speak to his client, D. The desk sergeant tried to locate D and the police who had him in custody, but could not locate them.

The police taking D's written confession did not know of A's attempt to reach his client, D.

Before trial, A made a pretrial motion to suppress the oral and the written confessions.

(A) (i)   Can the defendant's oral confession be admitted?

    (ii)   Can the defendant's written confession be admitted?

(B)   Can the defendant be convicted of conspiracy?

QUESTION 14

On May 1, T, a widower, executed a will in his lawyer's ("L") presence. The will, which was signed and witnessed in proper form, contained the following bequests: (i) $140,000 to a specific charity; (ii) $30,000 to his father ("F"); and (iii) the residue of his estate to his daughter ("D").

Thereafter in July, after a long discussion with L, T decided to have a new will drawn up. In accordance with T's wishes, L drafted a new will changing the bequest to the charity to $30,000 and omitting the bequest to F. On July 29, T read over the new document in L's office and signed it. L then witnessed his signature and told T that because his secretary was out to lunch, T would have to get a second witness on his own. He then explained to T the procedure he should follow with the witness.

In December, T called L to make an appointment to discuss other matters. L told T to bring the original July will with him when he came so that the copies could be conformed.

When T showed up, L examined the will and discovered that T had failed to get a second witness. T claimed that he forgot and that he did want the bequests as set forth in the July will. L then drew up a codicil simply stating that the July will was valid and had T sign it. L and his secretary witnessed T's signature on the codicil.

T died three months later. When his safe deposit box was opened, his executor found the May will, the July will, and the December codicil. All the documents were submitted to surrogate's court, which ruled that the May will was to be admitted to probate.

Thereafter, F renounced his bequest. D, the daughter, instituted a proceeding contesting the May will because of the bequest to the charity.

Discuss the correctness of the surrogate's ruling and the rights of F, D, the charity, and B, a brother of T who was not named in either will. Can D sue L for L's negligence?

QUESTION 15

H was the sole shareholder in S Co., a manufacturing firm with its principal place of business in Albany, New York, and incorporated in New York for the purpose of manufacturing yellow lapel buttons inscribed with a neo-abstractionist representation of a happy, smiling face. U Co. was a more diversified New York corporation, also with its principal place of business in Albany, engaged in the manufacture of buttons bearing happy faces as well as buttons inscribed "Win."

In June, U Co., S Co., and H executed a contract effective July 1, whereby U Co. would acquire all the shares of S Co. in return for paying H a monthly salary of $3,000. The contract further provided that the filing of a certificate of merger in the office of the secretary of state was a condition precedent to performance by U Co., and that H would be employed at U Co. for five years in "an executive and supervisory capacity" as director of U Co.'s research bureau, which consisted of 12 psychiatrists engaged in smile studies.

The certificate of merger was duly filed. From July 1 until the following February 1, H worked diligently, and the bureau, largely as a result of his direction, made great advances. Due to adverse economic conditions, however, demand for U Co.'s products virtually disappeared. In order to stave off insolvency, U Co.'s directors resolved to make major organizational changes, which included the elimination of H's bureau and the reassignment of H to a position as a night watchman. When H asserted that he would not perform the duties of a night watchman because the assignment was a violation of his contract, U Co. refused to offer him any alternative assignment. Therefore, on February 1, he carried out his warning by reporting to the factory each night but spending his time reading detective stories instead of making rounds. In addition, he posted signs on the open doors bearing smiling faces and the legend "Thieves and arsonists welcome here." As a result, a number of crimes and fires occurred in the plant and U Co. dismissed H and terminated his salary in March.

H, who had begun searching for a new job as of February 1, soon found that no other research supervisory positions were available in the Albany area at a salary greater than $1,500 per month, although comparable jobs were being offered in New York City for $3,000 per month and more. Not wishing to relocate or to suffer a diminution of income, H commenced an action against U Co. on June 1, to recover the amount of salary he would have received had he been employed by U Co. for five years, less the $27,000 he already had received.

U Co.'s responsive pleading asserted (1) that H rather than U Co. had initially breached the employment contract; (2) that even if U Co. committed the breach, H was entitled to less than the amount demanded because of his failure to accept comparable employment; and (3) that no cause of action for the amount demanded would accrue until the end of the contract's five-year term. How should the court rule on each of U Co.'s numbered pleas? Specify the amount of damages, if any, to which H is entitled.

QUESTION 16

On January 1, 1981, Tessie, a widow, executed a will in the presence of her neighbor Buddy and her daughter Chrystal, who signed at Tessie's request as witnesses. The will read as follows:

(1) To my son, Allan, I leave $20,000;

(2) To my daughter, Betsy, I leave $50,000;

(3) I leave the rest and residue of my estate to my daughter, Chrystal;

(4) If anyone should bring an action against my will or my estate for any reason, in that case that person shall take nothing under my will; and

(5) I appoint Buddy as my executor.

Tessie signed the will at the bottom; Buddy and Chrystal signed below Tessie's signature.

On March 11, 1982, Tessie gave Betsy $50,000 for a trip around the world. When she gave the money to Betsy, Tessie said, "Consider this money to be part of what you're going to get when I die." Betsy agreed.

Tessie died on December 21, 1984. She was survived by all three of her children. With Tessie's will, a letter was found in which Tessie wrote that she had given the $50,000 to Betsy as an advancement, to be credited against Betsy's share in the estate. The letter was dated June 21, 1982.

Allan objected when Buddy offered the will for probate, on the grounds that neither Buddy nor Chrystal was a competent witness to the will. Over Allan's objection, Buddy and Chrystal testified to the due execution of the will. The surrogate admitted the will to probate in its entirety. Tessie's estate is worth $75,000.

What will Allan, Betsy, and Chrystal take under the will?

QUESTION 17

C, a retail pharmacist, sent a letter dated March 1, 1993, to the state department of education. In the letter he accused P, one of his more effective competitors, of permitting E, his unlicensed assistant, to dispense prescription drugs in P's absence to six persons named in the letter.

The letter was routinely processed and investigated.

The department, two weeks later, sent P notice of formal charges of "professional misconduct," specifying the sale of prescription drugs to six persons named in the letter from C.

At the hearing, the investigator testified to conversations he had had with the six persons named in C's letter, to the effect that they had in fact dealt only with E in filling their last prescriptions at P's store. P requested the department to produce the six persons and allow him to cross-examine them. The department denied the request.

The department made a finding of facts. It issued the finding to P along with the following notification of its decision, labeled "Decision: P is guilty of permitting an unlicensed person to dispense prescription drugs in his absence." The department therewith suspended P's license as a pharmacist for six months.

(1)   Was the department's denial of the request to cross-examine the six persons named in the letter correct?

(2)   What are the rights and remedies of P?

QUESTION 18

Darryl owned a garbage truck rental company, from which he rented his garbage trucks out to various contractors. On March 10, 1996, Darryl rented a truck to Mel, a general contractor who was engaged in sewage work in midtown Manhattan. As part of the agreement, Darryl included the services of Lorraine, his assistant, who was well trained in the operation of all the garbage trucks. Darryl and Mel had a good working relationship and had engaged in similar transactions in the past. Therefore, Darryl rented Mel a brand new truck which Darryl recently purchased from Yoram, a well known manufacturer of garbage equipment. The truck had arrived on March 9.

On June 10, 1996, while readying one of the waste sites for pickup, Mike, an employee of Mel, became caught in the truck's compactor. The compactor severed Mike's right ankle before shutting down. Upon inspection of the truck, which had been operated by Lorraine, it was discovered that a safety mechanism designed to turn off the compactor if it made contact with objects larger than seven inches caught on the side, was not working properly.

On May 15, 1999, Mike commenced an action against Darryl in the Supreme Court for New York County. The complaint alleged that Mike's injuries were caused by a defect in the safety mechanism on the garbage truck as well as by Lorraine's negligent operation of the truck. Darryl's answer consisted of a general denial.

On July 1, 2000, Darryl commenced a third-party action against Yoram, alleging that the accident was a result of a manufacturing defect of the safety mechanism. Darryl demanded indemnification by Yoram for any monetary damages awarded to Mike. Yoram's answer consisted not only of a general denial, but also an affirmative defense that Darryl commenced this action after the statute of limitations expired.

At the consolidated trial, Darryl proved that Lorraine was qualified to use the garbage truck and was thoroughly familiar with all of Darryl's trucks. Lorraine testified that she had used the truck in accordance with the operating manual and that the safety mechanism simply did not work. Mike, of course, offered his medical bills, injuries, and loss of wages into evidence. Darryl and Mike stipulated that Darryl leased the truck to Mel and that Lorraine was Darryl's employee and was operating the truck at the time of the injury. Yoram offered no evidence at all.

Darryl moved for summary judgment on the ground that (1) Mike failed to prove a prima facie case against him. Yoram moved for summary judgment against Darryl on the grounds that (2) Darryl's third-party action was barred by the statute of limitations, and (3) the evidence offered at trial was insufficient to establish a prima facie case against Yoram. The court denied Darryl's motion and denied Yoram's motion in its entirety.

However, before submission to the jury, Mike and Darryl settled the case for $700,000, and Mike discontinued his case against Darryl on its merits. As a result, Yoram moved for dismissal of Darryl's third-party complaint against him on the ground that the settlement terminated all of Darryl's rights against him (4). The court granted the motion.

Were the court's rulings for the numbered motions correct?

QUESTION 19

A, B, and C were duly licensed physicians practicing as a partnership in the city of Utica, New York. In their fifth year as a successful partnership, they decided to accept D, another duly licensed physician, into the partnership. A clause of the partnership agreement signed by D read as follows:

> In the event of termination of this partnership by reason of the dissatisfaction of a majority of partners with the performance by D of his professional duties, D will not, and hereby agrees that he will not, engage in the practice of medicine within the boundaries of the city of Utica for a period of five years from the date of such termination. In the event of termination, D's share of profits to the date of termination will be computed, pursuant to this agreement, and paid in full to him.

The A, B, C, and D partnership functioned smoothly for four months, until repeated complaints about D's missed appointments, irregular hours, unorthodox billing practices, and abusive manners convinced A, B, and C to dissolve the partnership according to the agreement and to inform D of their intention. D attempted to persuade A, B, and C that he would reform, but to no avail. A week after moving out of his former offices, D opened a new office under his own name in another part of Utica, about three miles from the A, B, and C partnership's offices. His practice suffered by the move, but the partnership's practice did not in fact suffer in the least. A, B, and C, however, as a matter of principle, have decided to hold D to his bargain and have come to you for advice on the following questions:

Can the partnership enforce the restrictive covenant against D?

If they can, what defenses to enforcement can D raise?

Who would prevail?

QUESTION 20

On January 18, the home of B, an aged widow, was burglarized. Cash, jewelry, and securities worth $15,000 were taken. D was seen and recognized while exiting the scene of the crime. On the basis of this information, D was subsequently arrested a few blocks away by P, a policeman who knew D personally. D was advised of his rights and taken to the police station, where P again advised him of his rights. D indicated that he understood his rights and wished to waive them. P then proceeded to question D, and obtained a written statement, signed by D, wherein D confessed to burglarizing B's home and stealing her property.

D then asked for and received permission to call his lawyer, L. L immediately came to the station house and ordered all questioning to cease.

D was then arraigned on a charge of burglary and released on bail.

While D was out on bail, on February 3, he approached F in a local bar and suggested that they rob X's drugstore. F agreed and obtained a layout of the store, as well as a gun, which he gave to D.

On February 14, the night before the robbery was to be executed, F changed his mind and decided to abandon the scheme. He vigorously urged D to give up the plan. D refused. F demanded the gun back. D refused to turn it over. F departed.

On February 15, D entered X's drugstore, pointed the gun at a clerk, and demanded the contents of the cash register. While handing D the cash, the clerk tripped a silent alarm, which was hooked up to the precinct. After D had all the money and was walking out of the store, P arrived and arrested him. P advised D of his rights. As he had done previously, D waived his rights and gave P an oral statement regarding his plan with F to rob the drugstore. P searched D and found securities, which were later identified as part of the loot taken from B's home in January.

(1)   At the pretrial hearing on the burglary charge, L moved to suppress (i) the written statement and (ii) the securities found in D's pockets.

(2)   At the trial of D and F on the conspiracy charge, L moved to suppress the oral statement obtained on February 15.

Decide the motions.

(3)   Can F be found guilty of conspiracy? If so, what defenses, if any, are available to him?

QUESTION 21

Automobiles driven by A and B collided at night on the unlit New York State Thruway in a remote area. A's vehicle had crossed the median strip, jumped the guardrail on B's roadway, and plowed into B's vehicle from the side and rear. There were no witnesses to the accident apart from the drivers.

Several minutes after impact, B was able to locate A in the wreckage of A's vehicle. A, seriously injured, gasped to B, "I know I'm dying; sorry—it wasn't your fault, it was mine." At this moment, A expired.

B was prosecuted for criminally negligent homicide. He took the stand in his own defense and sought to testify to A's statement that it was not B's fault. The court (1) excluded the testimony.

On cross-examination, the district attorney asked B how fast he had been driving, and B refused to answer. The court (2) sustained B's refusal to answer.

The district attorney then asked B whether he had ever stolen money, in the amount of $1,000, from an employer. B vehemently denied ever having done such a thing. The district attorney, on rebuttal, called E, B's former employer, who sought to testify that $1,000 had been discovered missing and had never been accounted for, although under B's sole control as employee at the time. The court (3) excluded this testimony. B was acquitted.

W, A's widow, duly commenced a wrongful death action at this point against B. B sought to introduce as evidence the court record of his acquittal. The court (4) excluded the offered evidence. B then sought to testify about the movement of the vehicles at the time of the accident, including the collision. Over W's objection, the court (5) allowed the testimony. B then sought to testify to the statement made to him by A immediately following the accident. The court (6) admitted the testimony.

Were the numbered rulings correct?

QUESTION 22

A's 1970 will included a provision as follows:

> $300,000 in trust to be held by T as trustee, to pay the income of the trust to my son B for his life, and at his death the trust principal to be paid to such person or persons as B shall appoint in trust or otherwise, or if B does not exercise this power of appointment by will, to his issue.

The income of the trust amounted to $3,500 per month, which T duly paid to B for the first several months after A's death in 1970.

C then loaned $10,000 to B, for which B gave C a written note, assigning $100 per month of the trust income to C "until the loan and interest are fully repaid." T was duly notified of the assignment. Two weeks later, however, B had a change of heart and wrote T and C, revoking the assignment and directing T not to pay C anymore. T held up the first month's payment until C sent him a copy of an unsatisfied valid judgment entered against B on the note. T then released a check to C.

B died in 1975, leaving a will that read, in part:

> Exercising the power of the appointment granted to me by my father, A, in his will, I appoint T to hold the trust principal in trust and to pay the income to my three sons in amounts that seem suitable in T's sole discretion, then on the death of the survivor of my sons, to pay to the issue of my sons.

At B's death, he left three sons: D, age 15; E, age 12; and F, age two.

Did T act properly as trustee by disregarding B's direction to stop paying C? How should the trust be dealt with at B's death?

QUESTION 23

A owned Blackacre, an undeveloped tract in New York valued at $50,000.

In exchange for a loan in the amount of $30,000, A gave B a deed that stated, "I, A, hereby deed Blackacre to B" and was dated January 6, 1992. B then wrote a letter to A stating that if A repaid the loan within one year, B would return the deed to A. B then recorded the deed. B's loan to A was not mentioned on the deed. A did not record B's letter.

As a result of nearby land development, Blackacre greatly appreciated in value. Meanwhile, A failed to pay the loan by the due date. On March 7, 1993, B appointed C, a licensed real estate broker, in writing, to be his "exclusive agent" for three months in order to sell Blackacre for a minimum purchase price of $110,000. C's commission was stated to be 7%. The document was silent as to how C would earn his commission.

On March 12, 1993, C obtained a written offer from F to purchase Blackacre for $100,000. B rejected the offer, although F had the funds to buy Blackacre. On March 14, B sold Blackacre to X for $100,000. X recorded his deed, but he did not know about the loan to A nor the agreement with C.

On May 20, 1993, A tendered payment to B of the loan, together with interest to date. B refused the tendered payment and informed A of the sale to X.

A brought suit against B and X, demanding reconveyance of Blackacre from B or X, or its fair market value, together with damages.

(1) What rights, if any, does A have against B?

(2) What rights, if any, does A have against X?

(3) C sued B for his commission. In his answer, B asserted the following affirmative defenses: (a) Blackacre was sold to X solely as a result of B's efforts; and (b) there was never any sale to F. What rights, if any, does C have to a commission?

QUESTION 24

On November 10, Shop, the owner of a retail contractors' supply business, sold six sticks of dynamite to Thug. Shop sold Thug the dynamite knowing that Thug, on many previous occasions, had threatened the owners of local businesses by offering them a choice between paying for his "protection" or having Thug destroy their property with dynamite. Later that night, Thug used the dynamite to blow up a truck owned by Cab, an independent trucker who had refused Thug's offer of "protection." Cab's truck, which he used in his trucking business, was unoccupied and was parked on a public street. Vic, who had just gotten off a public bus at a well-lighted and designated bus stop adjacent to where Cab's truck had been parked, was killed in the explosion.

On November 12, Shop, who was unaware of the dynamiting, came to a nearby police station and informed Dick, a detective, of the sale of the dynamite to Thug. Dick, who was investigating the dynamiting and Vic's death, then learned that Thug was under arrest on a separate and unrelated drug charge and went to the police station where Thug was being held awaiting arraignment.

Dick informed Thug that he was investigating the dynamiting which had resulted in Vic's death, and he then duly advised Thug of all of Thug's legal rights, including his right to counsel. Thug told Dick that he fully understood his rights and was willing to answer any questions. In response to Dick's questions, Thug gave and signed a written confession admitting the dynamiting of Cab's truck, but stating that he had not been aware of anyone in the vicinity and that he had not intended to injure or kill anyone.

(1) What crimes, if any, were committed by:

   (a) Thug in threatening Cab and in dynamiting Cab's truck?

   (b) Shop?

(2) On motion duly made, is Thug entitled to an order suppressing the use in evidence of the written confession which Thug gave to Dick?

QUESTION 25

P, the owner of a dress manufacturing concern whose liabilities exceeded its assets, sought advice from A, his attorney. A, who was also an arsonist, suggested that P have the dress factory burned down in order to collect the insurance proceeds, and offered to set the fire if P would pay him his customary fee of $10,000. P agreed, and A drew up a contract that recited that P would pay A $10,000 upon A's performance of "professional services."

> conspiracy to commit arson

When the contract had been signed and acknowledged by both parties, A set fire to P's factory. The factory was destroyed. P, who had remained inside the building under the misapprehension that the fire was to be set the following night, was seriously burned and died in a hospital several days later.

A subsequently demanded payment of the $10,000 from W, P's widow and the executor of his estate. W retained B as her attorney, and B advised W to ignore A's demand. A, by his attorney M, thereupon commenced an action against P's estate in the supreme court. The complaint alleged that P's estate was liable to A for the $10,000 debt arising under the contract, and B filed an answer in which the estate through W claimed that the contract was for an unlawful purpose and therefore void.

void contract.

In the course of a jury trial, after A had completed his direct testimony, he was asked by B whether the "professional services" to be performed under the contract included arson. Relying on the Fifth Amendment privilege against self-incrimination, A refused to answer. B immediately moved for dismissal of the complaint. The court (1) denied B's motion.

Continuing the cross-examination, B then asked A whether A shared an apartment with Z, a woman who was not A's wife. M objected, and the court (2) sustained the objection. In an additional attempt to introduce evidence regarding A's living arrangements, B later called as a witness S, the superintendent of the building in which A's apartment was located. S testified over M's objection that "there must be a woman in there because if there isn't, then A sure has a squeaky voice sometimes." The court (3) ordered that S's statement be struck from the record.

[handwritten margin note: impeachment on collateral issue]

W's next witness was C, a dress cutter who had been employed in P's factory. Over M's objection, the court (4) permitted C to testify that A visited P at the factory the day before the fire and said to C, as A was leaving, "If you think today was hot, you're really going to need air conditioning tomorrow. It's going to be an absolute scorcher!" *[handwritten: → admission by party opponent]*

Finally, B called as a witness N, a claims investigator for the company that had issued the fire insurance policy on P's factory. N testified that she had visited P in the hospital shortly before P's death and filed a report of her conversation with P. P has stated "I had to, business was lousy." B asked N whether P had admitted conspiring with A to burn the factory. M objected and the court (5) sustained the objection.

[handwritten margin note: declaration against interest]

[handwritten: YES/NO - no inference can be drawn from taking 5th in civil action]

The judge instructed the jury that an unfavorable inference may be drawn by A's invoking the Fifth Amendment privilege. M objected. (6) The court overruled M's objection.

Were the numbered rulings correct?

QUESTION 26

In 1990, W, a widow, executed a will. L and N acted as witnesses. The will was typed and read (in part) as follows:

   (1)   To my daughter, A, I leave $10,000.

   (2)   To my son, S, I leave my stamp collection.

   (3)   All the rest and residue of my estate I leave to be divided equally between my friend F and my daughter B.

   (4)   I appoint E as my executor.

After W's signature, there appeared the following language:

> On the above date, W declared to us that the foregoing instrument was her last will and testament, and she asked us to witness her signature. She then signed the will in our presence, and each of us then signed the will in W's presence and in the presence of each other.

L's and N's signatures were affixed below this paragraph and in no other place.

In 1991, W executed a valid codicil to her will in which she revoked paragraph (1) and in all other respects reaffirmed the will. Later that year, W's stamp collection was destroyed by fire. When her insurance company sent her a check representing the value of the collection, W put the funds in the bank in a savings account in her name. The account contained no other funds.

In 1992, B died. She was survived by her daughter G.

W died in 1995. When her will and the codicil were found, it appeared that W had added a new paragraph to the will in her own handwriting. This clause stated that W revoked the codicil and reinstated the gift to A. The clause was signed by W, but was not witnessed. Also, W's signature on the codicil had been crossed out.

E moved to admit the will and codicil to probate, on the face of the documents themselves. The court (1) denied E's motion. E thereupon produced N, who testified that L had died; that she recognized her signature and L's signature on the will; and that she distinctly remembered that L and she had witnessed the will before W signed it, and that she had never in fact seen W sign it. The court then (2) admitted the will to probate, but (3) denied effect to the additional clause in W's handwriting. The court also (4) denied effect to the codicil.

(a)   Were the numbered rulings correct?

(b)   What are the rights of the interested parties under the will?

QUESTION 27

On May 10, 1989, A and B commit a burglary at X Corp.'s warehouse. They take furs valued in excess of $50,000. On the way to their getaway car, B asks A, "Where do we unload these furs?" A replies, "I know a fence, F, who specializes in hot furs. I mentioned to him last week that we intended to do this fur heist. Let's go to his wholesale fur shop and see if he will make a deal."

A and B approach F, who agrees to buy the stolen furs for cash, and pays A and B $250 each. The transaction between A, B, and F is secretly viewed and heard by G, F's disgruntled employee, who promptly informs the police that F possesses stolen furs. The police go to F's shop without a search warrant, knock down the front door, find the stolen furs, and arrest F. The police do not give F his *Miranda* rights, nor do they let him consult an attorney. After a prolonged interrogation punctuated by physical abuse, they obtain a full confession from him. On the basis of F's confession, the police arrest A and B. A and B are given their *Miranda* rights and given the opportunity to consult an attorney. A says, "I'm telling you nothing. Get me a lawyer." B says, "Well, you've got me. I might as well spill the beans." B answers questions and gives a complete admission as to his part in the caper.

The prosecutor offers to grant F immunity if he testifies before the grand jury, which F agrees to do. In his grand jury testimony, F testifies to a conversation he had with A prior to the burglary in which A told F of his intent to burglarize X Corp. with a friend. F testifies that A and B delivered the stolen furs to him. B's confession is introduced into evidence before the grand jury.

O, the owner of X warehouse, testifies before the grand jury that A and B did not have permission or authority to enter or remain on the premises. O also testifies to the value of the furs.

The grand jury returns indictments charging A and B with grand larceny in the second degree and burglary in the third degree.

(1)   The attorneys for A and B, and L and M, respectively, (a) move to have F's testimony suppressed, and (b) move to dismiss the indictments on the ground that the evidence before the grand jury was insufficient as a matter of law as to (i) A, and (ii) B. The court denies both motions.

M, B's attorney, and the prosecutor negotiate a plea bargain whereby B will plead guilty to petit larceny in full satisfaction of the complete indictment on June 1. F dies in a car accident on May 25. The prosecutor learns of the death of F on May 28, but fails to tell this fact to M. (2) On discovering this fact, M moves to withdraw the guilty plea. The court denies M's motion.

Were the court's numbered rulings correct?

QUESTION 28

Bonnie and her husband Clyde were tenants in "The Keyhole," a rent-stabilized apartment complex owned by Frank Howard Associates in Westchester County. Unsatisfied with conditions at "The Keyhole," Bonnie organized the Keyhole Tenants Association, with herself as president. She then organized a rent strike to protest the conditions in the complex.

On March 13, Bonnie convinced three other tenants to file applications with the New York State Division of Housing and Community Renewal ("DHCR") for refunds of alleged rent overcharges. Bonnie helped the three tenants to complete the applications. Each application alleged that the owner, Frank Howard Associates, misrepresented the base rents used by DHCR to calculate the rents for the three tenants, resulting in a rent overcharge. This allegation of misrepresentation was false. However, Bonnie and each of the three tenants believed it to be true. The DHCR applications were signed by the individual tenants and Bonnie as "President, Keyhole Tenants Association."

On March 25, after learning of the rent overcharge applications, Frank Howard went to the apartment shared by Bonnie and Clyde. In Clyde's presence, he said, "Bonnie, you are a liar and a rabble-rouser; I don't want your kind in my building." Clyde got angry and shouted, "If you ever say anything like that again to my wife, I'll beat you up." Frank became frightened and ran out of the apartment.

On May 1, Bonnie and Clyde moved to Hartford, Connecticut. One year later, on May 1, Frank caused Bonnie and Clyde to be personally served with a summons and complaint by his attorney in Connecticut. He sued Bonnie for maliciously injuring his reputation in filing the applications with the DHCR. He sued Clyde for assault. Each action was brought in the Supreme Court of Westchester County. Immediately prior to serving the defendants, the summons and complaints were filed in the county clerk's office and index numbers were obtained by the plaintiff. Immediately after serving the defendants, proof of service was properly filed in a timely manner.

Without answering the complaint, Clyde and Bonnie each moved to dismiss the complaint (a) on grounds of lack of jurisdiction and (b) on grounds that the statute of limitations had run. The court denied the motions.

(1) Were the court's rulings correct?

(2) What are Frank's rights against each of the parties? What defenses are available to each party?

QUESTION 29

On November 10, 1998, Alan and Ben, who did not know each other, started drag racing on Maple Road, a two lane road in a suburban community. As Alan, driving at 60 m.p.h., attempted to pass Ben at a blind curve in the road, he struck and killed Vic, a pedestrian who was crossing the road. Alan remained at the scene. Ben, who did not see the collision, drove away.

Police arrived at the scene almost immediately. Jerry, a police officer, placed Alan under arrest and then gave Alan the *Miranda* warnings. Alan was thereafter indicted for criminally negligent homicide.

About an hour after the incident, while investigating drug trafficking, Frank, an undercover police officer, saw Ben on a street corner, receiving what appeared to be drugs in exchange for money. Frank radioed Debra, another police officer, told her that he had observed what appeared to him to be a drug sale, and gave Debra a detailed description of Ben and his location. Debra, who had no personal knowledge of the drug sale, proceeded to the scene and arrested Ben for possession of illegal drugs. After giving Ben his *Miranda* warnings, and questioning him about his activities during the preceding hours, Ben stated that he had earlier been in a drag race on Maple Road. Thereafter, Ben was indicted for criminal possession of drugs and for the criminally negligent homicide of Vic.

Prior to the start of their trials, and based on the foregoing facts, Alan duly moved to dismiss his indictment for criminally negligent homicide, on the ground that his conduct did not constitute that crime. The court (1) denied Alan's motion to dismiss.

Ben then duly moved to dismiss the indictment against him for criminally negligent homicide, on the ground that he was not criminally liable for Alan's conduct, and to dismiss his indictment on the drug possession charge, on the ground that Debra's arrest of him lacked probable cause and was therefore illegal. The court (2) denied Ben's motion to dismiss his indictment for criminally negligent homicide and (3) denied Ben's motion to dismiss his indictment on the drug possession charge. Thereafter, based on proof of the foregoing facts, Alan and Ben were tried and convicted of the charges against them.

Were the numbered rulings of the court correct?

QUESTION 30

On March 15, 1998, Green formed a New York corporation to own and operate a large furniture store. Green was the sole incorporator and sole holder of the 1,000 authorized and issued shares. The bylaws adopted at the organization meeting provided for a four-member board of directors. Green and three friends (Black, White, and Blue) were elected. The bylaws also provided that any director could call a special directors' or shareholders' meeting. Some months thereafter, Green sold 150 of his shares each to Black, White, and Blue. Green, Black, and White then entered into a written agreement, some of the provisions of which were that:

(i) Each of the three parties should be a director and an officer;

(ii) The number of directors would not be increased without the unanimous consent of the three;

(iii) No amendment of the bylaws could be adopted without an affirmative vote of two-thirds of the outstanding stock; and

(iv) Each of the three would vote as director and as shareholder so as to enforce this agreement.

Blue was not a party to the agreement. A properly called meeting of the shareholders was then held, at which the bylaws were amended to provide for a two-thirds vote for any future amendment. Black was elected president by the board of directors, Green became vice president, and White became secretary-treasurer.

In early 1999, Green learned that another furniture store in a nearby city could be bought at a bargain price. Without passing this information on to any of the officers or directors of the corporation, Green purchased the store for himself.

In late 1999, the following occurred: Black and White learned of Green's purchase of the store and they demanded that Green assign the new property to the corporation at the same price he had paid for it. Upon Green's refusal, at a properly called directors' meeting, Black and White moved to sue Green for the property or for damages. The motion failed upon a tie vote (yes: Black and White; no: Green and Blue).

A properly called shareholders' meeting then took place, at which Green moved for the adoption of the shareholders' resolution to increase the number of directors from four to five, effective at the next annual meeting. The resolution passed by a vote of 550 (Green) to 450 (Black, White, and Blue). Nevertheless, Black, as president of the corporation, commenced a lawsuit demanding that Green turn over the new store to the corporation, and seeking an accounting for all profits from the new store. Green moved to dismiss on the ground that Black lacked the power to bring the suit on behalf of the corporation. The court (1) granted the motion. White then, as a director and shareholder, sued Green making the same demands. Green moved to dismiss on the ground that White had failed to comply with the requirements for a derivative suit (especially the requirement of demand upon the board). The court (2) denied the motion.

Were the above-numbered rulings correct? At the next annual meeting, how many directors should be elected?

QUESTION 31

On January 6, 1987, H and W, husband and wife, were window shopping in Buffalo, New York, where they resided. H espied a snow cleaning machine in a hardware store window and, surmising that it was probably the only such machine left in the vicinity, went inside to purchase it. Although it was only a floor sample, R, the owner of the store, offered to sell it for $1,000, explaining that its value had increased substantially in direct proportion to the snowfall that winter. H knew a bargain when he saw one, and gave R his personal check in that amount, dated that day, even though he knew that he did not have enough money in the bank to cover the check and that the check would be dishonored upon presentation to the bank.

Still flush from his bargaining, H took W to see their friend, G, who lived two blocks away. After a few drinks to drive away the cold, H informed G that he needed money and that he was willing to pay a "bonus" of $100 if G would lend him $500 for one month. G, also knowing a good deal when he saw one, thereupon presented H with five new $100 bills, and H in return gave him his personal check for $600, dated February 6, 1987. G warned H that he would deposit the check on February 6, and that H had better have enough money in the bank to cover it.

After leaving G, H and W were picked up by S, their son, who was driving the family car. H insisted on driving home. While driving down a main thoroughfare, H's vehicle was sideswiped by another vehicle that continued on without stopping. No one was injured, but the automobile was demolished. The identity of the owner or operator of the vehicle that struck H's vehicle was never determined. The police officer who investigated the accident arrested H at the scene because of his apparent drunken condition. At the police station, H was informed without elaboration that he must submit to an immediate blood test. H thereupon refused to submit to the test. At a subsequent trial, H was acquitted of the drunken driving charge.

H notified his automobile insurance company of the accident and claimed that although he had no collision coverage, he was entitled to recover under his policy for the property damage to his automobile caused by the hit-and-run driver. The liability insurance policy made no reference to hit-and-runs. H's checks to R and G were both dishonored upon presentation because of insufficient funds. H was recently notified by the Commissioner of Motor Vehicles that his motor vehicle operator's license was subject to revocation because of his refusal to take the blood test. What are H's rights and liabilities with respect to (1) his check to R; (2) his check to G; and (3) the threatened revocation of his operator's license? (4) What crimes, if any, did G commit?

QUESTION 32

H and W were married in Boston in 1978, but shortly thereafter moved to Yorkville in New York City. In 1983, W suspected that H had committed adultery and brought an action for separation against H in the New York Supreme Court. During the pendency of the action, H and W agreed upon and executed a separation agreement that provided that H pay W $200 per week for her support and maintenance. The agreement was silent as to its survival after the entry of a decree of divorce or separation. At the trial of the separation action, W was awarded a judgment of separation. The judgment, dated June 1, 1984, explicitly incorporated the separation agreement by reference.

H made the weekly payments to W until January 1993, when he moved to the state of Minnsylvania and embarked on a new business venture, whereupon he ceased making any payments to W. W continued her residence in Yorkville. In August 1993, H instituted an action for divorce in the appropriate local court and properly effected service of the summons and complaint by registered mail in accordance with Minnsylvania law. W received the summons and complaint, but did not appear in the action. H obtained a default judgment in the latter part of the year.

Shortly thereafter, W commenced an action against H in the New York Supreme Court to recover judgment for the accrued and unpaid installments due her for support that H had failed to pay. H interposed the following affirmative defenses: (i) that the judgment of divorce that he had obtained in Minnsylvania terminated his marriage to W; (ii) that the judgment of divorce terminated his obligation to support W; and (iii) that W had for the past year been engaging in adultery with X during weekend visits to X's beach house in New Jersey. W moved to dismiss H's affirmative defenses on the ground that they were insufficient as a matter of law. Over H's objection, the court (1) granted W's motion for dismissal of the affirmative defenses, and (2) awarded W counsel fees of $500.

Assume that under the law of Minnsylvania, a judgment of divorce terminates all rights and obligations under a prior separation agreement or judgment of separation, and that Minnsylvania has a six-month residency requirement before an action for a divorce may be brought. Were the numbered rulings correct?

QUESTION 33

C, who had become a resident of Switzerland after being paroled from a Swiss prison, went to Greece for business discussions with O, a famous heiress who was a Greek resident. C's purpose for making the trip was to secure O's permission to prepare and publish her memoirs in the form of a book to be written by C and published by R Co., a New York corporation whose principal place of business was in New York City.

During C's visit, which lasted several days, C and O executed a contract which provided that C would interview O, write the book subject to O's authority to revise the manuscript, and represent O in negotiations with R Co. It was understood that C and O would share in the royalties from the book.

C then went to New York and commenced negotiations with R Co. The negotiations were lengthy and required C's presence in New York for four months, during which C and R Co. regularly exchanged correspondence with O concerning the terms of the agreement. Eventually it was decided, among other things, that C and O would share the royalties equally. After signing a publishing contract with R Co., on behalf of O and himself, C received a cash advance on behalf of O and himself and returned to Switzerland. C did most of the writing in Switzerland but made occasional forays to Greece and New York in order to interview O and perform research tasks, respectively. The manuscript, in various stages of refinement, was circulated among Switzerland, Greece, and New York together with comments appended by R Co., C, and O.

The book was published in New York and distributed nationwide. F, a well-known attorney who resided in Michigan, read a chapter entitled "Embarrassing Moments of Famous People" and concluded that he had been libeled, inasmuch as the chapter contained a statement by C that when F was attempting to alight from an airplane in Austria, he had fallen down the steps because he was unable to walk and chew gum at the same time.

F commenced an action against R Co., C, and O in the Supreme Court of New York by causing each defendant personally to be served properly with a summons in the countries of their respective residences. Immediately prior to serving the defendants, the summons and complaints were filed in the county clerk's office and index numbers were obtained by the plaintiff.

All the defendants made timely appearances by counsel. R Co.'s attorney moved to have the complaint against R Co. dismissed on condition that R Co. submit to service of process in Michigan, on the ground that most of the witnesses who could testify regarding the truth of C's statements resided either in Michigan or Austria, and it would be unduly burdensome to bring them to New York. The court (1) denied R Co.'s motion on the ground that R Co., as a New York resident, was not entitled to invoke the doctrine of forum non conveniens in a New York court. C's attorney moved for dismissal on the ground that C was not subject to personal jurisdiction, and the court (2) denied the motion. O's attorney moved for dismissal on the same ground, and the court (3) denied the motion.

Were the court's numbered rulings correct?

QUESTION 34

A, B, and C, as equal partners, form Abco, a produce distributorship. The partnership is to run 20 years according to a written agreement. In May 1992, A, B, and C agree to take on D as a partner in consideration of his making a substantial capital contribution to the partnership. In June 1992, A assigns his partnership interest to E to satisfy a personal loan. E calls B, C, and D, sends them copies of the assignment, and advises that he is replacing A in the partnership. Moreover, E demands that he participate in all management decisions of Abco. B, C, and D refuse to allow E any management authority.

In July 1992, A, B, C, and D decide to make F a new partner. In August 1992, F files a lawsuit against Abco which alleges that he is owed $20,000 from a single business transaction which arose in 1989. He serves A, B, C, and D individually and Abco.

In April 1992, Farmer makes delivery of produce to the partnership under a contract. In November 1992, Farmer demands payment by Abco. Abco refuses to pay. In December, Farmer decides to sue for his money.

(1) What rights, if any, does E have with respect to Abco?

(2) What will be the outcome of F's suit against A, B, C, D, and Abco?

(3) What are Farmer's rights against Abco and against each of the partners?

QUESTION 35

S is the Buffalo franchisee for the T-G Lawn Mower Co. B operates a local landscaping and gardening company. On May 1, 1988, S sold B 10 Model 100 golf course lawn mowers for $2,500 apiece. The total purchase price was $25,000. B paid $5,000 down and agreed to pay the balance of $20,000 in four equal monthly installments, beginning on June 1. B executed and delivered to S a security agreement and financing statement covering the lawn mowers to secure the balance of the purchase price. S duly filed the financing statement.

On May 15, B discovered that the lawn mowers that S had sold him were not Model 100s but Model 80s. Nevertheless, B was sufficiently pleased with their performance and made no mention of the discrepancy to S. B made the installments due in June, July, and August, but on August 15, he learned from one of his customers that a Model 80 retailed for only $2,000. B tendered the lawn mowers to S, demanding that S return the $20,000 that B had already paid to S. S refused tender and demanded that B pay the last installment of $5,000 or return the lawn mowers to him as provided in the security agreement. B refused and told S, "You set foot on my property after these lawn mowers and my boys will break your body." B kept the lawn mowers and locked them in his warehouse.

S now seeks your advice. He states that he can use the lawn mowers in his own business or, perhaps, resell them for the balance due under the contract of sale. S also tells you that the word in the trade is that B is in poor financial condition and that B now has few assets other than the lawn mowers. S has just learned that B is planning to immediately remove the lawn mowers and sell them in Ohio.

What advice would you give S?

QUESTION 36

M, a manufacturer of fluorescent orange vests, was about to go out of business. C, a close friend and retail customer of M, entered into a valid agreement with M in which C loaned M $50,000 on a promissory note and agreed to lend him another $50,000 six months later, if M would continue in business and supply all of C's retail needs. M stayed in business, filled C's needs, and used the first $50,000. The second $50,000 was never asked for nor advanced.

On April 15, J, a jobber and retailer of specialty vests, wrote to M as follows:

> I offer to buy 500 vests, style No. 13, from you at $40 per; offer irrevocable until May 10; payment in full due on delivery July 15, your premises.

On April 16, M replied to J's letter by signing a form letter of acceptance approved by the industry trade association that disclaimed all warranties of merchantability. On May 17, M received a report from a reputable credit agency, stating that J was more than 90 days behind in several of his business obligations. M then wrote to J, requesting a financial report within 30 days. There was no further communication until July 15, when J tendered the contract price in the form of a certified check for $20,000. M, who had the vests, rejected the tender, stating that J's failure to respond to his letter within 30 days constituted a breach of contract. The vinyl used in the vests has skyrocketed in cost, and the vests are currently selling on the wholesale market for $50 per. M has no other contract to sell the vests. J has also learned of C's loan arrangement and the fact that C failed to make the second loan even though M is in financial difficulty now. J has not been able to buy vests on the open market.

What rights does J have against M? Against C?

QUESTION 37

Jake, a successful physician, is 35 years old and married to Wanda, his second wife. Two years ago Jake divorced his first wife, Marilyn, with whom he had a son, Ned, age eight. Jake seeks your advice regarding the following:

Jake's father, Papa, died 20 years ago. Under his will, Papa established a $1.5 million trust with income payable to Mama for life. Papa's will additionally provided that Mama may appoint anyone to be the beneficiary of the trust principal during her life or by her will.

Mama recently died, having not exercised her power of appointment during her life. However, upon review of Mama's will, you discover the following with respect to the exercise of her power of appointment:

(1) The principal of the trust shall be distributed to Trustco as trustee.

(2) The income from the trust shall be paid during Jake's life, 80% to Jake and 20% to the Home for Wayward Boys.

(3) Upon Jake's death, Trustco shall continue as trustee with the income payable to Jake's children until the youngest attains age 35, at which time the principal shall be paid to Jake's children equally.

In addition, Jake has his own will in which he intends to leave $1 million in trust income to Wanda for life, with the principal paid to Ned upon Wanda's death. There is also a paragraph by which Jake bequeathes his ranch "The Bar XM" to his family forever.

Prepare a memorandum addressing the following questions.

(1) Has Mama properly exercised her power of appointment?

(2) Can creditors of Mama's estate reach the assets that are subject to the power of appointment?

(3) Assuming at his death Jake's estate is worth $4.5 million, what rights will Wanda have if she survives Jake?

QUESTION 38

Braves Inc. is a New York corporation and a manufacturer of "autobus." The three shareholders of Braves Inc. are Allison and Brian (wife and husband), who each own 50 shares of stock, and Carl, who owns 10 shares of stock. Allison, Brian, and David (a nonshareholder) are the three directors on the board of Braves Inc.

Braves Inc.'s articles of incorporation limit the liability of the board of directors. The bylaws of Braves Inc. state that if the corporation liquidates, Allison and Brian receive $250,000 each (the money Allison and Brian each paid for their 50 shares of stock), before any other persons or debts are paid.

On March 15, 1991, the board of directors decided that Braves Inc. should invest some of its money in real estate. On March 16, 1991, the board of directors visited Scumacre, a five-acre plot with a structure standing on its center. Allison and Brian fell madly in love with the simple character and charm of the property and wanted to buy it on the spot. David, however, was convinced that he remembered reading in the local newspaper that Scumacre had structural and environmental problems. Because Allison and Brian were afraid of losing Scumacre to another buyer, they purchased this property for $300,000, over the stern objection of David.

As luck would have it, Scumacre is neither structurally sound nor environmentally safe and is a useless and valueless piece of land. A proper inspection of Scumacre would have revealed these problems.

(1) Do the shareholders of Braves Inc. have any action against the board of directors for buying Scumacre?

(2) Is the provision in the bylaws valid regarding Allison and Brian receiving the first $500,000 if Braves Inc. liquidates?

In April 1991, Dodger Inc. purchased an "autobus" from Braves Inc. Evan, an employee of Dodger Inc., was killed while using the "autobus." Evan's estate sues Braves Inc. for the negligent manufacture of the "autobus." Braves Inc. needs to determine how Dodger Inc. instructs its employees to operate the "autobus" and how the "autobus" was being used when Evan was killed.

(3) Assuming that Braves Inc. must respond to a motion of Evan's estate within 30 days, how can Braves Inc. get the needed information from Dodger Inc. in time to respond to the motion?

QUESTION 39

T, in 1972, established a funded inter vivos, irrevocable trust with income to his son, S, for life and at S's death to either or both of S's two children then living, namely D and G (twins), as S should appoint by will for their lifetime; with the principal to vest in T's six-month-old nephew, N, on the death of the survivor of the twins.

N died in 1998 while T was still alive and left his interest in the trust by will to his best friend, F. Two weeks later, T died, leaving all he had by will in trust for D for life, remainder to D's children, A and B. N and T were buried in the family plot alongside G, who had died of an acute identity crisis in 1994.

S, D, and F were all at T's funeral. Upon finding out that you are a lawyer, they related the above facts to you and asked what interests, if any, they have in the trust, and in T's estate. Tell them.

QUESTION 40

Alan is driving a car in which Burton is a passenger. While driving in New York, they are involved in an accident with a car driven by Daniel, a New York resident and citizen. Alan and Burton are citizens and residents of State X, which has a law barring recovery by a contributorily negligent plaintiff. Alan brings suit against Daniel in the New York Supreme Court for damages in the amount of $77,000.

(1)   Assume that Alan was negligent with respect to the car accident. In the lawsuit, Daniel moves that the law of State X (referred to above) be applied. What result and why?

(2)   Daniel is found not negligent, based largely upon testimony of his expert witness. After the trial, Alan learns that an expert, whom he had wanted to call at trial, has just returned to the United States from a one-month vacation in Europe. The expert's testimony would be the opposite of Daniel's expert. Alan moves for a new trial based upon newly discovered evidence. What result and why?

(3)   Assume that in the first suit, Daniel had filed a petition to remove the suit to a federal court. Should a motion by Alan to remand the case to the New York Supreme Court be granted? Give reasons.

QUESTION 41

On April 1, while A was proceeding through Syracuse on his way to Ithaca, his automobile collided with a motor home operated by B. A had been traveling south and B north on a two-lane highway. The night before, there had been a severe storm and the road surface was covered with ice and slushy snow. Nobody other than A and B saw the accident, and each claimed that the collision was caused by the other's failure to keep to his side of the highway.

B sued A to recover damages for his serious personal injuries and property damage. B's complaint alleged that A's car had skidded across the center line of the road because of the defective tires on A's car.

At the trial, X, B's attorney, offered a certified copy of an accident report made by S, a New York highway patrolman, which read substantially as follows:

> I arrived at the scene of the accident with my assistant shortly after the impact. We saw the tire tracks of both vehicles in the northbound lane, location of the vehicles after the collision in northbound lane, and debris from same vehicles in northbound lane.

> These facts demonstrated to us that A's vehicle had crossed the center line into the northbound lane and collided with B's motor home.

> [Signed] S

On the objection of Y, A's attorney, the court (1) excluded the report.

X then offered a photograph that B identified as a photograph of the tires that were on A's automobile at the time of the collision. On examination by Y, B admitted that the photograph had been taken several days after the collision and that the tires had been severely damaged by the collision. The court (2) sustained the objection of Y to the admission of the photograph.

X then called A as a witness, and A admitted that the photograph did show the worn treads on his tires at the time of the collision. X then offered it into evidence for the sole purpose of showing the worn treads, admitting that the other defects in the tires had been caused by the collision. The court, on objection by Y, (3) again excluded the photograph.

X also offered proof showing that A, on his plea of guilty, had been convicted in the City Court of Syracuse of the traffic offense of driving with unsafe tires at the time and place of the accident, in violation of the Vehicle and Traffic Law. The court, over Y's objection, (4) admitted this evidence.

Were the above-numbered rulings correct? Discuss.

QUESTION 42

Karen, a neighborhood girl, decided to rob a local bodega to help support her marijuana habit. She needed a lookout for the job and convinced 15-year-old Stacey to participate in the hold-up.

Karen drove Stacey to the bodega and instructed Stacey to contact Karen by cell phone if the police arrived. Karen then pulled a small caliber revolver from her purse and checked to make sure that it was loaded. Satisfied, she entered the bodega, drew her gun, and ordered the cashier to hand over the cash. Little did Karen know that this bodega had been held up on numerous occasions, and the owner had therefore installed a state of the art alarm system. Immediately upon Karen's uttering the words "this is a stickup," a computer recognized the phrase, recorded it, and sent an alarm to the local police station. The cashier handed Karen a bag of money and Karen fled the store.

Upon leaving the bodega, Karen was met by four police cars. Upon seeing Karen, the police officers immediately emerged from their cars with their guns drawn. Karen fired her gun, and a fierce firefight erupted, leaving one police officer dead and Karen under arrest.

Stacey watched the entire sequence of events unfold and simply drove away undetected. Karen was charged with first degree murder and first degree robbery.

Shortly after Karen's arrest, the police received information that Stacey was also involved in the robbery, and they proceeded to Stacey's house to question her. Stacey was home alone; her mother was at work. Stacey agreed to accompany the officers to the police station to answer some questions.

Upon arriving at the police station, officers advised Stacey of her rights, and she responded that she did not want to hire an attorney, but that she did want to speak with her mother. At about the same time, Stacey's mother, Mary, discovered that Stacey was at the police station. Mary called the station, advised them that her daughter was only 15 years old, and demanded to speak with Stacey. Mary was told that she could speak with Stacey soon. Meanwhile, despite the fact that her mother was on the telephone, the police told Stacey that they would try to locate her mother. The officers continued to question Stacey and ultimately secured a confession that Stacey had acted as the lookout for Karen. Stacey was then put in contact with her mother.

An autopsy revealed that the police officer killed during the robbery was actually killed by a bullet fired from a fellow officer's gun.

Stacey was charged with first degree robbery.

Stacey moved to have her confession suppressed, but the court denied the motion. Was the court correct?

Assuming the above facts were proven, can Stacey and Karen be convicted of the crimes for which they were charged?

QUESTION 43

Gus is a buyer for the Family Department Store, a partnership in Rochester, New York. N, O, and P are the partners of the Family Department Store. There is no written partnership agreement among the partners. N instructs Gus to go to a trade show in Utica. The trade show is to run from May 9 to May 12 from 9 a.m. to 10 p.m. Gus is to use his own car and keep track of his expenses so that he can be reimbursed.

Gus is to view the latest styles the clothing manufacturers are offering this season and order what he thinks will sell. On May 10, Gus stops by the Elegant Clothes booth to place an order with Mr. Funk. Mr. Funk is busy with another customer and so suggests that they meet for dinner that evening at 6 p.m. at the Yummy Restaurant, five blocks away, to discuss the order. Gus was to meet a friend for dinner but canceled in order to meet with Mr. Funk.

That evening, Gus gets into his car (vehicle 1) to go to dinner. He starts driving with his lights off. Vehicle 2 is coming in the opposite direction, driven by X. Gus crosses the center line and collides with vehicle 2.

After exchanging the necessary information, Gus proceeds to the Yummy Restaurant and has dinner with Mr. Funk. Mr. Funk leaves after Gus places an order with him. Gus goes to the bar and starts drinking. After a while, he becomes rowdy and B, a bouncer, asks him to leave. Gus refuses and so B physically throws Gus off the premises, breaking his arm.

(1)   Can X recover from Family Department Store?

(2)   Can Gus recover from Yummy Restaurant?

In May, P went to Florida for a three-month vacation.

On June 25, P drowned in the Bahama Islands after his deep-sea fishing boat collided with a coral reef.

On June 26, N, who normally negotiates contracts for the partnership with suppliers, entered into a contract with a longtime supplier, R, a rayon manufacturer, to purchase 300 rayon suits worth $10,000, with delivery to be made in six weeks. On June 27, N received a telegram from P's bereaved widow in Nassau, Bahamas, notifying N of P's death.

On July 3, a new supplier, S Silk Co., entered into an agreement with N to sell the store $5,000 worth of new silk dresses, with delivery to be made in four weeks. Before executing the contract, S received oral and written assurances from N that N could act as the store's representative and bind the partnership to the contract. On July 11, the Family Department Store Partnership sent letters to R and S notifying them that P died on June 25, and that the partnership could not be responsible for any contracts made after that date.

(3)   What are the rights and liabilities of S and R with respect to the partnership, N, O, and P?

QUESTION 44

After 30 years of service, F, a well-known key engineer on P Inc.'s staff, retired and moved to Florida. F had been primarily responsible for the initial design and manufacture of P Inc.'s Polar Bear line of heavy duty refrigerators, which were sold only to restaurants, caterers, and hospitals. Over the years, F had become intimately familiar with P Inc.'s operations. X Inc., a newly formed Connecticut corporation which has just entered the heavy duty refrigerator business on a national scale, contacts F in Florida and hires him as a consultant for its manufacturing operation. After hiring F, X Inc. notified many of P Inc.'s customers by mail that X Inc. would soon be selling refrigerators in New York and that F had become a consultant. X Inc. has not transacted any business in New York nor contracted with any New York customers. P Inc. then sued X Inc. to permanently enjoin X Inc. from employing F and sued F to enjoin him from revealing P Inc.'s customer list and trade secrets to X Inc. F was duly personally served in Florida with a summons and complaint naming X Inc. and F as defendants, and the president of X Inc. was likewise served in Connecticut. Immediately prior to serving the defendants, the summons and complaints were filed in the county clerk's office and index numbers were obtained by the plaintiff. X and F hired A, a New York lawyer, who moved to dismiss under CPLR 3211 for lack of jurisdiction.

The court denied the motion.

(1) Was the court's ruling on the motion correct?

(2) What are P Inc.'s rights with respect to the injunction sought against F and X Inc., regarding trade secrets, customer lists, and employment?

QUESTION 45

D Inc., a corporation chartered under New York law, held a meeting of the board of directors, at which all of the seven directors attended after receiving statutory notice of the meeting. One of the directors, S, was a controlling shareholder in L Corp., a lumber supplier. At the meeting, the board adopted a contract with L Corp. under which L Corp. would provide D Inc. with all the wood D Inc. would need in the manufacture of its line of golf clubs. The vote to adopt the contract was unanimous, except for the abstention of S, who did not disclose to the board that he had an interest in L Corp. Prior to the vote, S refrained from participating in the discussion of the contract.

D Inc.'s board subsequently learned of S's interest in L Corp. and now asks you, the general counsel, what the board's options are. (1) How should the board be advised?

G Corp., which owned 7% of the common shares of D Inc., seeks to inspect the books of D Inc. to determine whether D Inc. would be worth taking over. G Corp. made a duly written demand to inspect the shareholder lists of D Inc. D Inc., afraid that G Corp. was contemplating a takeover, denied the request. You are general counsel to G Corp. (2) What are G Corp.'s rights?

On August 31, D Inc. contracted to supply R, a country club, with all the golf clubs R needed for the next four years. D Inc. shipped golf clubs in monthly shipments, each shipment paid for separately. On December 5, D Inc. received notification that R was insolvent. On December 1, D had shipped golf clubs that were scheduled to be delivered by common carrier to R on December 20. (3) What are the rights and remedies of D Inc. as to the shipment in transit and the rights for future shipments?

Discuss the numbered questions.

QUESTION 46

It was the evening of December 31. A and B knew that V would be at a party that evening. They agreed that this would be the perfect opportunity for them to obtain V's valuable coin collection as their own.

At the stroke of midnight, A and B broke into V's home. N, a neighbor of V who was walking his dog, observed A and B in V's home and phoned the police. However, before the police arrived, N attempted to stop A and B. In the struggle that followed, A broke N's arm. During the struggle, N recognized B as a bartender at a local pub. The police arrived. B managed to get away, taking the coin collection with him. A was taken to the police station and questioned without a *Miranda* warning. A then signed a written confession.

Based on N's identification of B, P, a police officer, went to B's apartment without obtaining a warrant. P tricked B into opening his door by claiming that he was with the gas company and had come to inspect a gas leak. Once P was inside B's apartment, he saw the coin collection. P then arrested B and seized the collection.

(1)   Based solely on N's testimony, the grand jury indicted B for burglary in the third degree. B moved to dismiss the indictment. The judge denied B's motion.

(2)   The judge ruled that the coin collection is admissible against B.

(3)   A and B were given separate trials. At A's trial, the prosecutor introduced the coin collection that P found in B's apartment. A moved to suppress the collection. The judge denied A's motion.

(4)   At his trial, A took the stand and denied all allegations against him. The prosecutor then introduced A's confession. A made two objections, the first being that the confession may not be used to incriminate him, the other that the confession may not be used to impeach him. The judge overruled both of A's objections.

Discuss the judge's rulings.

QUESTION 47

John and Mary married in 1993. They both had jobs with very good salaries. In 1997, after four years of a childless marriage, they executed a valid separation agreement which provided that neither party was to provide support for the other. After a few months of separation, John and Mary decided that they could not live without each other, so they resumed their marital relationship, pledging eternal devotion. After three weeks, they realized that they could not live with each other, and they separated again. After 12 months, John brings suit for divorce in New York.

The sole basis of John's suit is the separation agreement. Mary moves to dismiss for failure to state a cause of action upon which relief can be granted. (1) Should the court grant or deny the motion?

John moves to State X, which has adopted all of New York's laws as its own. Mary has never been to State X. After John has resided in State X for two years, on August 1, 2000, he commences a divorce action and serves process on Mary in New York by giving the summons and complaint to a lawyer with whom Mary is acquainted. Mary does not appear. In October 2000, State X grants John a divorce decree that does not provide for any support for Mary. (2) Was the court's ruling correct?

John moves back to New York in November 2000. In September 2000, Mary had lost her job. She now has only a part-time job and does not earn nearly as much as she did before. However, Mary is not in danger of becoming a public charge. (3) Is Mary entitled to receive an award in the New York courts for maintenance or support?

Discuss the issues raised in the numbered questions.

QUESTION 48

Mr. H was a citizen of Buffalo. While en route to Albany, H was seriously injured when his plane crashed. He suffered in a hospital for one week and then died.

According to H's will, which was executed after January 1996, his spouse is to receive 50% of his estate; his son, 40%; and his daughter, 10%. His daughter did not depend on him for her support.

The will names Mr. A, H's attorney, as executor. A and one of H's friends, F, were witnesses to the will. A had recommended himself to H when H was indecisive about whom to name as executor. H did not sign any other documents other than his will.

H's daughter objected to the will's being admitted to probate since A was both witness and attorney. H's spouse objected to the will's being admitted since A was both attorney and executor. The court found that the will should be admitted to probate.

A, as executor to the will, brings suit for wrongful death and pain and suffering of H.

(1) Discuss both arguments for denying the will in probate.

(2) How are the proceeds from the wrongful death suit to be distributed? How should any awards that may be given to the estate be distributed with respect to the spouse, son, and daughter?

QUESTION 49

P works for X. X rented a lift machine from C. C supplied X with employee E to operate the machine. The machine was manufactured by M and bought by C in 1986. On June 1, 1987, P was injured when the machine cable gave way and the heavy steel bar that was being lifted fell upon him. E said, "That stupid machine was defective, since I had my hand on the brake controls at all times."

On May 1, 1990, P sued C for his injuries under theories of negligence and strict liability in tort. Immediately prior to serving the defendant, the summons and complaint were filed in the county clerk's office and an index number was obtained by the plaintiff. C moved to dismiss P's suit for failure to state a cause of action and for failure to bring a timely action. (1) The court granted the motion as to the strict liability claim but denied the motion with respect to the negligence claim.

On July 1, 1990, C impleaded M by serving a third-party summons and complaint upon M. M moved to dismiss on the grounds that (a) the statute of limitations had run, and (b) the complaint failed to state a cause of action. (2) The court denies M's motion.

On August 15, 1990, C settled with P for $50,000, and thereafter M moved to dismiss C's third-party action. (3) The court granted M's motion.

Were the numbered rulings correct?

QUESTION 50

P, owner of Blackacre, leased the entire premises to D on January 1, 1989, at a rental fee of $15,000 per annum, plus an additional 2% of D's gross sales over $2 million in any given year. D's accountants submitted estimates that D would gross $2.1 million in 1989 with a potential for higher numbers in the future. These estimates were reviewed by P's accountants and approved. By January 1, 1992, D had not grossed even $1.5 million in any year. Also contained within the lease was an option clause giving the lessee the right to purchase Blackacre and the right of first refusal, upon the same terms, conditions, and purchase price that P could get from another bona fide purchaser. No mention was made in the lease of assignment.

On January 1, 1992, D assigned the lease to X, a specialty boutique with no potential to gross in excess of $2 million in any given year. P objected to the assignment as being improper, insofar as X's inability to achieve gross sales of $2 million rendered it ineligible as an assignee of the lease. (1) Was P correct? Was the assignment by D to X proper?

With X in possession of Blackacre on January 1, 1993, P enters into a contract for the sale of Blackacre to Y, a bona fide purchaser, for the purchase price of $1 million. Y agrees to indemnify P for brokerage fees attendant to the sale to Y. X offers the sum of $1 million to P relying upon the option and rights in the original lease between P and D. There would be no brokerage fee in a sale to X. (2) Can X enforce the option?

A wind storm damages 40% of Blackacre. (3) Y retains you as his counsel. Advise him as to his rights and obligations relating to any purchase of Blackacre.

QUESTION 51

H and W were married in New York on May 20, 1982. Four years later their son S was born.

The parties lived happily until 1988, when they mutually decided that they had grown in different directions and that perhaps they should separate.

They attempted marriage counseling, but nonetheless on February 15, 1989, H and W, each represented by their respective attorneys, entered into a separation agreement which provided, among other things, for maintenance and child support for W and S. That afternoon H removed his belongings from their Long Island residence and moved to Manhattan.

In August 1989, H and W ran into each other at a party given by a mutual friend. After spending an enjoyable evening together, they decided that they would go away for a week to their favorite resort with the intent of reconciling their marital relationship. H and W did go away together a few weeks later to a honeymoon resort, where they stayed together and resumed all the incidents of marriage. Nevertheless, they mutually agreed after the experience that it would be better if they remained apart, and thus they did not see each other again or repeat the experience.

H and W abided by all the terms of their separation agreement into 1990; in April, H filed for divorce in the supreme court alleging that he and W had lived separate and apart pursuant to the separation agreement and that he had substantially complied with all the terms of the agreement.

W, in her answer, set forth an affirmative defense based on their week-long stay at the resort. Additionally, W counterclaimed for divorce, setting forth several allegations of acts of adultery by H, which took place on specific dates from January 1989 up to and through the commencement of the divorce action. H thereafter made a timely motion to strike the affirmative defense (1) and to dismiss the counterclaim (2). The court granted both motions.

In May 1991, after H and W were duly divorced, W discovered that S was being beaten up at school. W was fully aware that their neighborhood had been deteriorating but also knew that the child support that she had been receiving from H in accordance with their divorce decree along with her $10,000 per year salary was not enough for her and S to move. For the past year, W had been having to borrow money from her father so that she and S could live in even a modest fashion.

W was aware that H had taken a new job and was now making approximately $60,000 a year, whereas at the time of their divorce, he had had a salary of $35,000.

W decided to make a motion in family court to increase the amount of support for her son. H moved to dismiss on two grounds. First, the family court did not have jurisdiction (3); second, the relief sought by W was beyond the court's discretion (4). The family court agreed with H and dismissed W's action.

Discuss the numbered motions and the correctness of the courts' rulings as to each.

QUESTION 52

Evelyn and Joseph Smith met in Manhattan in 1989 and were married in the chambers of a New York Supreme Court justice at Foley Square, Manhattan, in 1990. They resided in a very small studio in Greenwich Village since they could afford nothing else.

In 1991, Joseph inherited $20,000 from his late uncle, Harry. He deposited the money in a savings account entitled "Joseph Smith in trust for Evelyn Smith."

In the spring of 1992, Evelyn became frustrated with living in the studio and with Joseph's ineffective efforts in finding a better job. On May 25, 1992, Evelyn told Joseph, "I want you to get a better job so we can move out of this dump and I can have children." Joseph replied, "I don't feel like getting another job, I was never crazy about having kids, especially YOUR kids, and as a matter of fact, I'm not particularly crazy about you." Upon hearing this, Evelyn gathered her personal possessions and moved back to her mother's house on Long Island.

In June 1992, Joseph surrendered the studio to his landlord and moved to Cleveland, Ohio, to start a new job.

In July 1993, Evelyn consulted a matrimonial lawyer who prepared a summons and complaint for annulment of the marriage. The lawyer told Evelyn, "It will take a little time to serve the complaint because I have to find Joseph's address in Cleveland. In any case, here is a copy of the summons and complaint for your personal files." Evelyn took her copy of these papers, and the next day she encountered Joseph's friend, Andrew, who told her his address in Cleveland. Immediately, Evelyn filed the summons and complaint in the county clerk's office, obtained an index number, boarded a Cleveland-bound plane at LaGuardia Airport, and personally served Joseph in Cleveland with her copy of the summons and complaint.

Evelyn's cause of action for annulment alleged that Joseph had fraudulently induced her to marry him by misrepresenting that he wanted children. Joseph hired a New York attorney, who served a timely motion to dismiss the action. (1) The court dismissed the action.

In September 1993, Evelyn's lawyer had the summons and complaint reserved upon Joseph in Cleveland by an Ohio attorney. Joseph's New York attorney again moved to dismiss the action. (2) The court denied the motion.

Joseph served a timely answer, which contained a counterclaim for divorce based on abandonment, and a demand for equitable distribution of the marital property. Evelyn served a timely reply to the counterclaim, demanding equitable distribution of the savings account.

At trial, the only evidence which Evelyn offered on the annulment was her personal testimony on the argument she had had with Joseph on May 25, 1992. At the close of her case, Joseph moved to dismiss Evelyn's complaint and (3) the court granted the motion.

During his case, Joseph testified that Evelyn left on May 25, 1992. Moreover, he testified that the savings account contained the proceeds of his uncle's inheritance. Evelyn did not contradict this testimony. The court (4) awarded Joseph judgment of divorce and (5) held that the savings account proceeds belonged solely to Joseph.

Discuss the court's rulings.

QUESTION 53

On November 10, 1992, S and B executed a written contract under which S agreed to sell B Blackacre for $100,000. The payment terms were $10,000 upon execution of the contract,

$10,000 to be paid at closing on December 1, 1992, and the balance of $80,000 was to be evidenced by B's promissory note to be delivered by him at the closing. The note was payable on May 1, 1993, with interest. B paid S $10,000 upon execution of the contract. The closing was held on December 1, 1992, at which time B paid S $10,000 and executed and delivered his promissory note to S for the $80,000 balance due, and S gave B a bargain and sale deed which B duly recorded that day.

On January 18, 1993, B told S that he probably would not be able to pay S on May 1, 1993. Accordingly, S agreed to extend the payment date to May 15, 1993, provided B did the following:

(a) Give S a new note, at the same interest rate, payable on May 15, 1993; and

(b) Give S a deed to Blackacre which S would hold for "safekeeping" until the new note was paid.

On January 20, 1993, B gave S the new note and a deed to Blackacre. S canceled B's old note and gave B a letter stating that S was holding the deed for Blackacre until the new note was paid.

On April 20, 1993, B told S that he would not be able to pay the entire balance on May 15, 1993. After further discussion, S and B agreed that on May 1, S would accept the accrued interest then due and a principal reduction of $40,000 with the balance of $40,000 plus interest at the same rate to be paid by B on November 1, 1993. On May 1, 1993, B paid S the accrued interest then due and $40,000.

On May 28, 1993, B fell asleep smoking in bed and a fire resulted. B escaped without injury, but Blackacre was burned to the ground.

Since B's house on Blackacre no longer existed, he failed to make his November 1, 1993, payment for the balance due on the note. B also claimed that as of January 20, 1993, he was no longer the legal owner of Blackacre since he was no longer in possession of the deed. On November 10, S's attorney filed a notice of pendency against Blackacre in the office of the clerk of Westchester County, the county where Blackacre is located. On December 14, S's attorney served a summons and complaint on B. Immediately prior to serving the defendant, the summons and complaint were filed in the county clerk's office and an index number was obtained by the plaintiff. The complaint set forth the foregoing facts, and the prayer for relief demanded (i) judgment against B for $40,000, together with interest from January 20, 1993, and (ii) that an equitable lien be imposed against Blackacre for that amount.

On December 16, B made a motion to cancel the notice of pendency. The court denied the motion.

(1) Was S entitled to file a notice of pendency with the Westchester County clerk?

(2) Was the court's ruling on B's motion to cancel the notice of pendency correct?

(3) Advise B as to his rights and liabilities on monies owed to S on the outstanding promissory note.

QUESTION 54

Elyse and Frank were passengers aboard U.S.A. Air flight 440 when it was shot down by a terrorist's missile. Both were killed, and there was no evidence of who had died first. Elyse and Frank were survived by their two children: Jerry and Teddy.

In Elyse's will, she left her entire estate to Frank if he survived her, and if not, to Jerry. Jerry was also one of two witnesses to Elyse's will. Marvin, a close family friend, was the other witness but had died years earlier.

In Frank's will, he left his entire estate to Elyse if she survived him, and if not, to his sister, Debbie. His two witnesses were close friends of the family and both were available. Upon Frank's death, his will was discovered in his safe deposit box with the word "REVOKED" scribbled across the document. Two of Frank's friends testified that Frank was joking the night he wrote "RE-VOKED" on the will, and he had no true intention of revoking the will.

Neither will contained a clause directing the executor what to do in the case of simultaneous deaths.

A month before their deaths, Elyse had announced, at Teddy's birthday party, that she had just transferred her summer home to Teddy, and that the transfer was an advance of any inheritance from Elyse's will. This transfer and the notion that it was an advance of any inheritance was included in subsequent letters from Elyse to Teddy and Jerry.

The decedents' estates consisted of, among other things, a house that was owned by Elyse and Frank as tenants by the entirety.

Both wills were offered for probate and admitted after all available witnesses testified as to the due execution of the wills. The surrogate received testimony from numerous witnesses at Teddy's birthday party that Elyse had announced the advance to Teddy, and Teddy testified as to the letter sent to him by his mother. The surrogate ruled that the transfer of the summer home was not an advance against Teddy's inheritance.

(1)   Did the surrogate correctly admit the wills to probate?

(2)   What should Jerry receive as his inheritance?

(3)   Did the surrogate correctly rule with respect to the advance?

(4)   Who should inherit the family home?

QUESTION 55

A and B agree to burglarize W, a warehouse. A tells B that he will get a vehicle for the burglary. B states that he will get a gun. The next day, B obtains the gun. A subsequently steals a van for use in the burglary and tells B that he stole the van because he did not want to use his own vehicle in case it was seen at the scene of the crime.

A and B go to the warehouse and try to break into the building by opening a side window. The window is locked and they cannot get it open. They go around to the other side of the warehouse and try to gain entry through a door. They cannot get the door opened. They then proceed to the rear and break a window. A and B climb through the window and grab two televisions. X, a security guard patrolling the outside of the premises, spots A and B exiting the building through the side door and begins to chase them down the alley. A panics, stops and begins to run away and pushes X out of the way. As a result of the push X loses his balance and falls to the ground. In the fall X fractures his skull and dies. A and B then leave the area. E, a bartender of the local bar located across the street, observes this whole scene, recognizes A and B, and gets the license number from the stolen van. E easily recognizes A and B because they are frequent patrons of his bar.

A short time later, A and B are arrested by the police and taken to the station house. No *Miranda* warnings are given. A and B are advised that they are to be in a lineup. A and B request a lawyer but none is provided, and they are made to participate in the lineup. E easily identifies A and B as the two men who were at the warehouse and A as the person who struck the security guard. No accusatory instrument has yet been filed against A and B. A and B are subsequently indicted for burglary, murder, and conspiracy.

At the pretrial hearing, A and B move to suppress the identification made by E at the lineup, arguing that their constitutional rights were violated.

(1)   Will the lineup be suppressed?

(2)   (a)   Will A be convicted of murder?

     (b)   Will B be convicted of murder?

     (c)   Will A and B be convicted of conspiracy?

QUESTION 56

On January 10, 1986, Alf duly executed a will, prepared by his attorney, Fred, which included the following provisions:

> FIRST: I revoke all wills previously made by me.

> SECOND: I give to my wife, Bev, if she survives me, one-third of my net estate.

> THIRD: I give to my children, Cal and Deb, the residue of my estate.

> FOURTH: I nominate my trusted secretary, Eve, as executor of this will.

The execution of the will was duly witnessed by Fred and by Gert, Fred's partner. Alf kept the original of the will in a safe in his office. Fred kept a photocopy of the will in his office safe.

In 1994, Alf and Bev separated, and Alf directed Fred to prepare a new will. On January 10, 1995, Alf duly executed a will, prepared by Fred, which included the following provisions:

> FIRST: I revoke all wills previously made by me.
>
> SECOND: I give to my trustee, if my wife, Bev, survives me, that share of my estate to which my wife would be entitled if she were to exercise her right of election, in trust, with the income to be paid quarterly to my wife during her life. Upon the death of my wife, Bev, I give the principal and unexpended income of the trust to Save The Birds, Inc., a New York Not-For-Profit Corporation.
>
> THIRD: I give the residue of my estate to Save The Birds, Inc.
>
> FOURTH: I make no provision for my children, Cal and Deb, for good and sufficient reasons.
>
> FIFTH: I nominate my trusted secretary, Eve, as executor of this will, and as trustee of the trust created in paragraph SECOND above.

The execution of Alf's new will was duly witnessed by Fred and Gert. At Alf's direction the original of the will was kept in Fred's office safe. Fred gave Alf a receipt for the will, together with a photocopy of the will. Alf placed both in his office safe with the 1986 will.

On July 10, 1996, Alf died in Warren County, New York, where he was domiciled, leaving a substantial estate. Surviving him are Bev, from whom he remained separated without having executed a separation agreement, and Cal and Deb, his two adult children, all of whom are domiciled in Warren County.

When Eve opened Alf's office safe she found the original of the 1986 will, the receipt for the 1995 will, and the photocopy of the 1995 will. Eve then contacted Fred regarding probate of the 1995 will. After making a thorough search of his office, Fred informed Eve that he was unable to find the 1995 will. Fred told Eve that he concluded that the 1995 will had been lost when Fred had moved his office to a new location in the summer of 1995.

(1)   Should the 1995 will be admitted to probate?

(2)   If the 1995 will is admitted to probate, what are the rights, if any, of Bev, Cal, Deb, and Save The Birds, Inc.?

(3)   If the 1995 will is denied probate, what are the rights, if any, of Bev, Cal, and Deb?

QUESTION 57

After Beth and Pat were married in 1981, they moved to Whiteacre, property in Broome County, which Beth had inherited from an uncle. Beth then conveyed Whiteacre to Beth and Pat as tenants by the entirety. Pat was a computer analyst employed by the Technology Group, a small technology company, and Beth worked in an area flower shop.

Lisa, their only child, was born in 1982, and thereafter Beth became a full-time homemaker. She regularly entertained Technology Group customers at Whiteacre and frequently accompanied Pat on business trips. In 1990, Pat became an officer and director of the Technology Group, which experienced rapid growth over the next several years.

In April 1998, Beth and Pat agreed to separate. Pat then moved into an apartment within Broome County, and Beth and Lisa stayed at Whiteacre. Beth and Pat, each represented by counsel, met to discuss a separation agreement.

At the meeting, Pat represented in writing that his annual salary was $200,000 and that he owned 40,000 shares of the Technology Group worth $800,000, which he acquired during the marriage. Whiteacre had been substantially renovated by Beth and Pat since they moved there. Its value in 1981 was $300,000 and its value in 1998 was $600,000.

On May 1, 1998, a written agreement providing that Pat and Beth would live separate and apart was duly executed by Beth and Pat. The agreement provided that Beth and Pat would have joint custody of Lisa and Lisa would live with Beth. After Pat and Beth duly agreed not to be bound by the Child Support Standards Act, Pat agreed to pay $2,000 per month to Beth for the support and education of Lisa until Lisa reached the age of 21 or completed college. Pat also agreed to pay $5,000 per month to Beth for her maintenance during Pat's or Beth's life or until her remarriage. The agreement identified Whiteacre and the 40,000 shares of Technology Group stock acquired by Pat as marital property. The parties agreed that the marital property would be divided 60% to Pat and 40% to Beth, and that Pat would convey his interest in Whiteacre to Beth and pay her $300,000 in full satisfaction of her interest in their marital property. Finally, the agreement included a representation by Pat and Beth that each had made complete and accurate disclosure of their respective assets and the value of such assets. The agreement was duly filed in the Broome County Clerk's Office. Pat made the monthly payments to Beth as required by the agreement.

Last month the local newspapers reported that all of the outstanding shares of the Technology Group have been acquired for cash at $100 per share by SPR, a huge corporation. Pat, now the president of the Technology Group, was accurately quoted in a statement released by the Technology Group. "We are gratified that 18 months of negotiations have happily concluded in our joining the SPR family of companies." Pat never disclosed to Beth that negotiations for the sale of the Technology Group at $100 per share had been ongoing for several months prior to the execution of their separation agreement.

Lisa, who has recently graduated from high school, has been accepted as a first year student at an excellent but expensive college where tuition, room, board, and fees will be $30,000 a year.

On September 10, 1999, Beth was properly served at Whiteacre with a summons and complaint in an action by Pat against Beth. The complaint alleged the foregoing pertinent facts and sought a divorce on the grounds that Pat and Beth had been living separate and apart for more than a year pursuant to the separation agreement, and that Pat had complied with the terms and conditions of the agreement.

(1) Was Whiteacre properly considered marital property in the separation agreement, and if so, was Beth entitled to any credit for its value in 1981?

(2) May the provisions of the separation agreement relating to the valuation and the distribution of the 40,000 shares of the Technology Group stock be modified?

(3) May Beth obtain an increase in support for the cost of Lisa's college education?

QUESTION 58

Obie owned all of Mayberry Acres, a 20-acre parcel of property. Mayberry is bounded on the north by State Highway No. 88, on the west by Avenue A, on the east by Avenue B, and on the south by the Sticks River. On November 17, 1977, Obie conveyed the southeastern quarter of Mayberry to Andy in fee simple absolute. On the same date, he conveyed the southwestern quarter of Mayberry to Don, also in fee simple absolute. Obie had a private road going from the southern half of his property to the state highway. At the beginning, Andy and Don used this road for access to the state highway, although they could get to Highway No. 88 by the less direct route of Avenue A or Avenue B.

On February 20, 1985, Obie had an argument with Andy, and told Andy that he could not use the private road anymore for access to the state highway. Don was present, and Obie told Don that he could continue to use the road. Andy did not stop using the road, even though Obie protested.

On April 20, 1992, Obie built a chain fence across the road. He told Don that Don could have a set of keys to the locked gate if Don agreed to let Obie use Don's dock on the Sticks River. Don said that the deal was okay with him, and they shook hands on it. But a week later, Obie called Don and said that he had changed his mind and the deal was off.

On May 4, 1992, Andy filed a notice of pendency together with a copy of his complaint with the clerk of the Supreme Court of Niagara County, where Mayberry is located. The complaint asked the court to declare that Andy had a right to use the road. On June 6, upon learning of the notice of pendency from a friend in the courthouse, Obie made a motion in the Erie County court to have the notice of pendency vacated. Erie County adjoins Niagara County. The court (1) granted the motion and entered an order vacating the notice of pendency.

On June 21, 1992, Obie was personally served with the summons and complaint prepared by Andy. Service was accomplished by a New York process server at Mayberry. On that date, Obie was also served with a summons and complaint by a process server hired by Don, who alleged (i) that he was entitled to specific performance on the agreement of April 20, 1992, respecting use of the road; and (ii) that in any event, Don had acquired the right to use the road.

(1)   Was the court's ruling correct?

(2)   What are the rights of Andy? Of Don? What defenses does Obie have?

QUESTION 59

On July 24, 1994, Detective Danger, the officer on duty, received a phone call early in the morning from Vivian Victom, who said that she had just been raped by a stranger. Vivian gave Danger an excellent description of the assailant, which, she explained, was based on the 20 minutes she had been forced to spend with the stranger. After making the phone call, Vivian went to the hospital on Danger's advice, where she was examined and released.

From Vivian's description, Danger recognized Luke Skydiver, a man whom Danger had arrested a week before on other rape charges, and who was presently out on bail. Danger called Luke at home, and after a short conversation, Luke volunteered to come to the police station for questioning. Danger also called Vivian and said, "I think that I have the man who raped you. Please come right down."

When Vivian arrived, she was shown into Danger's office. Danger brought Luke out of another room. "That's the man," screamed Vivian, "That's the man who raped me!" Luke was indicted for rape forthwith.

Before the trial, Luke (through his attorney) moved to suppress all identification of him. The court (1) granted his motion as to the identification made in the police station but limited the suppression to that one instance.

At the trial, Vivian testified that she had been asleep on July 24 at dawn, when, as she got up to get bottles for her twin daughters, Cagnie and Lacie, who lived with her in her studio apartment, a man whom she had never seen before appeared, armed with a knife. He grabbed her and demanded that she have sexual relations with him. If not (he said), he would kill her daughters. Vivian testified further that the man had sexual intercourse with her. She stated that she neither screamed nor made any resistance, for fear of the danger to herself and her children. When asked if the man who raped her was in the courtroom, Vivian said yes, and pointed to Luke. When asked how she was able to identify him, she stated that she recognized him from the attack, when she was in his presence for more than 10 minutes. The prosecution put forth no further testimony.

At the close of the People's case, the defense moved to dismiss on the ground that the People had failed to meet their burden of proof. The court (2) denied the motion. Then, out of the hearing of the jury, the defense offered proof that Vivian was known as "an easy woman" who had had sexual relations with at least 10 men in the past month; that Cagnie and Lacie were illegitimate; and that Vivian was a prostitute. The court (3) refused to allow the proof to be put before the jury. At the close of the trial, Luke was found guilty.

Discuss the court's rulings.

QUESTION 60

Billy and Christie were married in New York on November 3, 1990. Their only daughter, Madonna, was born shortly thereafter. They lived together in New York until March 19, 1995. At that time, they separated and entered into a separation agreement, which they duly executed and filed with the clerk of the supreme court in the county of their residence. The agreement provided that Christie would have custody of Madonna; that Billy would pay her $200 per week for child support; and that Billy would further pay Christie a lump sum of $20,000 in settlement of any claims Christie might have against Billy for support. At the time the parties separated, Billy was making $40,000 per year as a piano player, and Christie was making $15,000 a year as a photographer's assistant. The separation agreement further stated that all the "marital property" would be equally divided between the parties. Finally, the agreement stated that it would be incorporated but would not merge into any divorce that either party might obtain in the future.

On March 19, 1999, Billy started a divorce action in the New York Supreme Court in the county of his residence, based upon the separation agreement. Billy submitted an affidavit which alleged that the parties had lived separate and apart for a period of one year in accordance with the terms of the agreement.

Christie filed an answer to Billy's complaint within the period provided by law, in which she raised the defense that the separation agreement should be declared void because it was against public policy for Billy to avoid further liability by making a lump sum settlement to her. In the time since the separation, Christie had gotten a raise and now made $30,000 per year. The court (1) held that the defense was without merit and awarded a divorce to Billy. Billy then moved for an award of custody of Madonna. In an affidavit in support of his motion, Billy alleged that during the period of separation, Christie had moved into the home of John Z, a bachelor, and that Christie and John Z were holding themselves out to the public as man and wife. Christie did not controvert these allegations. (2) Over the objections of both parties, the court took Madonna into chambers and interviewed the child out of the presence of parties and counsel. The court (3) denied Billy's motion to award him custody of Madonna.

Were the court's rulings correct? Discuss the court's actions.

QUESTION 61

A was married to F. In 1990, A and F were divorced. In 1995, A married S. In 2000, A and S duly executed an agreement whereby they agreed from then on to live separate and apart. Subsequently, S moved to Vermont.

In 1998, A, having testamentary capacity, executed a will which designated F as his executor and left his entire estate to F. P and V, employees of B Bank, where A conducted his banking, witnessed A's signature on the will and signed a standard attestation clause after the signatures.

In 2000, A purchased Whiteacre, a piece of real property located in New York state, for $50,000. The deed was made "to A in trust for N," his nephew. At that time, A and N agreed in writing that N would live on Whiteacre and pay $500 per month rent to A. Thereafter, N lived on Whiteacre in accordance with this agreement.

A died in December 2001, survived by all other parties mentioned and by no other heirs or issue. When F offered the will of A for probate, S lodged an objection, claiming that there was insufficient proof of due execution of the will. At the hearing, P and V testified that they were employees of B Bank; that in their capacity as employees, they commonly acted as witnesses to wills of customers of the bank; and that they had witnessed many wills in this fashion. P and V were able to identify their own signatures, but they could not remember witnessing the will of A nor could they identify A's signature as his own, nor could they testify as to the manner in which the will was executed. B, A's business partner, testified that the signature on the will was that of A. In addition, F produced an expert who testified over the objection of S that in his opinion the signature was that of A. The surrogate admitted the will to probate, whereupon S moved to exercise her right of election.

(1)   Was the court's ruling correct?

(2)   What are the rights of F, S, and N in the estate of A?

QUESTION 62

B was driving a car owned by O, who had given B permission to use it. P was a passenger in the car. While driving down Elm Street in the village of X, B collided with a car owned and driven by D, due to the negligence of both B and D. A contributing cause of the accident was the poor state of repair of Elm Street. P was injured. W, a passenger in the car driven by D, was killed.

W died leaving no will. He was survived by S, age 15, and by T, age 19. No administrator was appointed for the estate of W. When S turned 18, he applied for and was granted letters of administration over the estate of W. S, acting as the administrator of the estate of W, then commenced an action against D for the wrongful death of W. More than two years had elapsed between the date of W's death and the date upon which S commenced suit. Within 20 days after service of S's complaint, D served a third-party summons and complaint upon the village of X, claiming that the village was responsible for any injuries to W due to the poor condition of Elm Street. The village of X moved to dismiss, claiming that under CPLR 9804, no claim for injury against the village could be upheld unless the village had notice in writing of the defective condition. D opposed the motion on the ground that his claim was not for injury, but for contribution. The court (1) granted the motion and dismissed D's third-party complaint. D moved to dismiss the action, based upon the statute of limitations. The court (2) granted the motion to dismiss.

P then commenced an action against B, D, and O. Before the verdict was reached, P settled with B for $10,000. After trial, P was awarded a judgment in the amount of $50,000 against D and O. The jury found that D and O were each 50% negligent in causing the injuries to P. The judgment was satisfied.

O then commenced an action against B for indemnification. B moved to dismiss O's cause of action, upon the grounds (a) that the statute of limitations had run, and (b) that in any event, B had settled and thus could not be sued for indemnification. The court (3) dismissed O's suit on both grounds.

Immediately prior to serving the defendants, the plaintiffs filed the summons and complaints with the clerk of the county court and obtained index numbers.

Discuss the numbered rulings.

QUESTION 63

S was a manufacturer of clothing; B was a retailer who had not previously done business with S. B telephoned S on November 1, 1994, and asked S to manufacture 200 suits for him at $75 per suit, to be delivered on December 13, with payment 10 days after delivery. S agreed. On November 8, S sent to B a document entitled "Confirmation of Sale" on S's letterhead, confirming B's order, which also added the following terms: (1) in the event payment was not made 10 days after delivery, there would be a 1.25% per month interest charge on the unpaid balance; and (2) any dispute under the contract would be settled by arbitration according to the rules of the American Arbitration Association. B received the memorandum, but made no response.

On November 21, B called S and said that because he had overestimated his sales, he was canceling his order. S said that the suits had already been manufactured, and that if B did not take them, he would be liable for all of S's damages. B said that there was no contract between them and he owed S nothing. S immediately tried to find another purchaser for the suits. After using his best efforts, S was able to sell the suits on January 15, 1995, to X for $50 each. In addition, S incurred some expense in storing the suits before X bought them.

On January 22, 1995, S demanded in writing that B make S whole for the damages he suffered. B again replied that, because there was no contract, he owed S no money.

(1)   Was there an enforceable contract between B and S?

On February 1, 1995, S served B with a "notice of intention to arbitrate" with the American Arbitration Association.

(2)   What actions, if any, may B take with respect to this notice?

(3)   Assuming that the dispute does not proceed to arbitration, what remedies, if any, are available to S?

QUESTION 64

O was the owner of Blackacre and Whiteacre, adjacent parcels of real property in Albany County. X was the owner of a parcel of property adjacent to Whiteacre. In 1983, X built a house and garage upon his parcel. The garage protruded 10 feet over the property line dividing X's property from Whiteacre. Neither X nor O was aware of the encroachment.

In 1983, O duly executed a deed granting his interest in Blackacre and Whiteacre to his son, S, who resided in France. O delivered the deed to L, S's attorney, together with written instructions to hold the deed in escrow until the death of O, and then to deliver the deed to S. L agreed in writing to comply with O's instructions.

In July 1993, O borrowed $15,000 from X, giving X his note promising to repay the sum upon demand. In July 1994, when O had failed to repay the note, X recovered a judgment against O. X duly docketed the judgment with the clerk of Albany County on November 4, 1994. X knew nothing about the deed given by O to L. The judgment has never been satisfied.

On November 1, 1994, O died. S returned from France that same day, whereupon L delivered to S the deed from O to S in Whiteacre and Blackacre. S recorded the deed on November 5, 1994.

After the death of O, S had Blackacre and Whiteacre surveyed, and discovered X's garage encroached upon Whiteacre. S promptly demanded that X remove the garage forthwith. X refused, and in turn demanded that S honor the $15,000 outstanding note of O. S refused.

In December 1994, S and Y agreed in writing to the sale of Whiteacre for the sum of $30,000. Y paid to S the sum of $3,000 as a down payment. Upon conducting a search of the title to Whiteacre, Y discovered the judgment against O, whereupon Y contacted S and stated that he would not honor his contract with S to purchase Whiteacre because the judgment by X against O constituted a lien on Whiteacre, and demanded the return of his $3,000 down payment. S refused and commenced an action against Y for specific performance of the sales contract.

(1)   What are the rights of S and Y regarding the sales contract for Whiteacre?

(2)   Can S compel X to remove the garage?

(3)   What are the rights of X and S regarding the judgment?

QUESTION 65

H and W were married in 1980 in Buffalo, New York, where they resided together. In 1985, W gave birth to a child, D. In January 1994, H's employer transferred him to State X. W refused to accompany H to State X and remained in Buffalo with D when H moved.

On June 1, 1994, having satisfied the 90-day residency requirement of State X, H commenced an action in State X for divorce from W on grounds of irreconcilable differences, which were proper grounds in that state. W was personally served in New York with the summons and complaint by a New York attorney. On August 1, 1994, after W failed to appear or respond, H procured a decree of divorce in State X. The court's order was silent with respect to custody or support of D. W was served with a copy of the divorce decree.

In October 1994, W commenced an action in the New York State Supreme Court for divorce based upon grounds of abandonment, claiming that H had failed to provide any support for W or D since January 1994, and that H had left the marital home without justification. W also moved for an order providing for maintenance for her and support for D, as well as for custody over D. H was personally served in New York by a New York attorney. H duly appeared and moved to dismiss W's cause of action upon the grounds (i) that W had failed to state a claim upon which relief could be granted, and (ii) that the action for divorce was barred by the decree and order of State X. The court (1) denied H's motion to dismiss. After trial, the court entered a decree of divorce against H, which provided that W would have custody of D, subject to H's right to have D visit with him during D's regular school vacations.

D visited H in State X over the Christmas and New Year's holidays in December 1994. While D was visiting with H, W was severely injured in an automobile accident, which left her disabled for a period of six months. Upon learning of W's accident, H enrolled D in a school in State X and refused to return D to W. H then filed a petition in a court of competent jurisdiction in State X for custody over D, and caused W to be served with a copy of the petition in New York by a New York attorney. W appeared by counsel and opposed H's petition on the ground that the court did not have jurisdiction over D. W further petitioned the court of State X for an order returning D to her in New York. The law of State X relating to custody is the same as the law of New York. The court of State X (2) granted H's petition for custody.

Were the numbered rulings correct?

QUESTION 66

C, a contractor in Buffalo, New York, prepared a bid on an office building to be built for X Inc. In connection with his bid, C asked T, a tile manufacturer, for a quote on tile to C's specifications. On October 1, 1994, T returned a statement on his letterhead with a quote of $8,000 based on C's specifications and said that the quote was irrevocable.

On February 15, 1995, after the price of tile had gone up, T delivered a note to C, revoking his offer. On February 16, C was notified that he had been awarded the job to build the office building. C demanded that T deliver tile as per T's offer, but T refused. C thereupon purchased tile to his specifications from another manufacturer for $9,000. C seeks $1,000 from T.

C also needed doors and windows for the office building. He contacted G, a manufacturer in

Utica, New York, and placed an order for the doors at a cost of $6,000, F.O.B. Utica. G entered into a contract that was reasonable in all respects with a common carrier for the transportation of the doors from Utica to Buffalo. While the doors were en route, the truck in which the doors were being transported was struck by lightning. The doors were completely destroyed. C refused G's demand for payment. C obtained replacement doors from another manufacturer for a cost of $7,200, which was then the current market value for doors meeting C's specifications. C seeks $1,200 from G.

G and C entered into a separate written agreement whereby G agreed to provide windows to C's specifications no later than May 30, 1995, for a cost of $12,000. G's profit on the sale to C was $2,000. On May 15, 1995, G delivered windows to C; however, the windows did not conform to C's specifications. C refused the windows and notified G in writing that day. Three days later, G wrote C that he was going to send a new shipment of windows by May 30 which would conform to C's specifications. On May 28, 1995, G delivered new windows which conformed to C's specifications, but C had already purchased the windows he needed from another supplier for $11,500, and refused to accept G's second shipment.

(1)   May C recover from T?

(2)   What will be the outcome of the claims of C and G against one another (a) for the doors? (b) for the windows?

QUESTION 67

F, a widower, died in 1985. In his duly executed last will and testament, he left his entire estate in trust, to pay the income to his son H for his lifetime, and upon the death of H, to pay the principal to whomever H should appoint by will, whether in trust or otherwise.

H died on January 1, 2000, survived by his widow W and two sons, X and Y, who were respectively 21 and 10 at the time of H's death. H's duly executed last will and testament, dated 1995, contained the following provisions:

> 1.   Exercising the power vested in me by the will of my father, F, I direct that the principal of the trust be paid to E, my trustee, to pay the income therefrom to my son Y until he shall reach the age of 35, and then to pay the principal over to Y if Y lives to attain the age of 35.

> 2.   I leave the sum of $200,000 to E, as trustee, to pay the income therefrom to my wife W in annual installments, until her death, and thereafter to pay the principal over to X and Y in equal shares.

> 3.   All the rest, residue, and remainder of my estate, I leave to my trustee, E, to divide the income between my wife W and my son X in such shares and at such times as he shall deem appropriate, and upon the death of my wife, to pay the principal to my son X.

> 4.   I appoint E as my executor.

H's estate upon his death was worth $600,000; in addition, the trust created by the will of F had a value of $300,000. In a timely manner, W duly exercised her statutory right of election.

What are the rights of W, X, and Y?

QUESTION 68

X bought goods from Y and gave to Y in payment therefor his check drawn on B Bank in the amount of $1,500. Y altered the check so that it read $81,500 and indorsed the check over to Z in settlement of an existing debt Y owed to Z. Z indorsed the check in blank and cashed it at B Bank. All the parties are residents of Albany, New York. B Bank is chartered in New York state and has its principal office in Albany.

B Bank then sent a statement to X which showed that B Bank had debited X's account by $81,500. The statement also contained the canceled check that Y had altered. X did not review his statement until 31 days later. As soon as he saw the statement and the check, X notified B Bank of the error, but B Bank refused to make any adjustment. Neither B Bank nor Z was negligent in failing to notice the alteration of the check, nor was X negligent in preparing the check. Y has disappeared.

Subsequently, X established a new domicile in Vermont, for the sole purpose of instituting suit against B Bank in the United States district court, because he would receive a speedier adjudication of his claim in federal court than in the New York State Supreme Court. X commenced his action in the United States District Court for Vermont, claiming (in good faith) a judgment of $81,500. B Bank moved to dismiss X's action for lack of subject matter jurisdiction. The court (1) denied B Bank's motion.

B Bank then duly commenced a third-party claim against Z on two grounds: (i) for indemnification on the check; and (ii) on a $60,000 overdue loan taken out by Z from B Bank. Z moved to dismiss the third-party complaint against him as to both claims. The court (2) denied the motion as to B Bank's first claim, but (3) granted the motion as to the second claim.

After trial, the court (4) gave judgment to X against B Bank in the amount of $81,500, and (5) dismissed the claim against Z.

Were the numbered rulings correct?

QUESTION 69

On January 1, P, the owner of Blackacre, real property with a jewelry store located thereon, bought a burglar alarm from M, a manufacturer and distributor of security systems. The burglar alarm was installed by M. M's standard contract for sale, which was signed by P, stated:

> M will not act as an insurer under this contract. He has no responsibility for any losses arising from failure of the burglar alarm system.

On March 15, P's store was broken into, and P sustained a loss of $50,000. At that time, the burglar alarm system failed to operate properly. P commenced an action against M for the sum of $50,000. M interposed an affirmative defense based upon the terms of the agreement between P and M. P moved to dismiss the affirmative defense. (1) The court denied P's motion.

On April 1, P entered into a contract with X for the sale of Blackacre. Under the terms of the agreement between P and X, at the closing X would give to P a down payment of $50,000, with the balance of $50,000 to be given as a 25-year bond with 10% interest per annum, and a purchase money mortgage to secure the bond. Closing was set for May 15.

On May 1, X assigned his right in the contract for sale of Blackacre to Y. Y assumed all the rights of X, but did not assume X's obligations. X and Y gave notice to P of the assignment. Y paid $2,000 to X for the assignment.

On the appointed date set for closing, Y appeared and tendered to P $50,000 cash and a bond made by himself but otherwise in accordance with the agreement. Thereafter, Y commenced a suit against P for specific performance. P moved to dismiss, claiming (a) that there was no privity of contract between P and Y; (b) that the contract was not assignable; and (c) that Y failed to perform in accordance with the contract terms. (2) The court granted P's motion.

Discuss whether the court's rulings in (1) and (2) were correct.

QUESTION 70

In 1988, W, who has two daughters, A and B, both adults, duly executed her will which read:

1.   I give the painting "City" to my sister, S;

2.   I give the residue of my estate to my daughter, A; and

3.   I appoint T Trust Co. as executor.

In 1990, W married H and in 1991, H and W had a daughter, C. W then transferred $200,000 to T Trust Co., as trustee under a trust agreement, which provided that the trustee was to invest the principal and pay the income to W during her lifetime, and on W's death to pay the income to W's daughter A, and on A's death "to pay the principal to W's heirs." The trust agreement was silent concerning W's rights to revoke the trust.

In June 1993, W borrowed $30,000 from P and gave P a note due on February 11, 1994. W did not pay the note when due and on May 1, 1994, P recovered a judgment against W for $30,000. P petitions the court for an order requiring T Trust Co. to apply both the principal and the income of the trust created by W to satisfy P's judgment. The court denied P's petition in all respects, and thereafter, W paid P.

In June 1995, W delivered to T Trust Co. a writing signed and acknowledged by W and by A, which recited that W revoked the trust and that A consented to the revocation. T was advised by L, its attorney, that the trust was validly revoked and despite objections of H and B, T delivered the principal and accumulated income to W.

A short time later, H and S died. W thereafter dies in a fire in which the painting "City" is destroyed. A, B, and C and nephew N, who is the only child of S, survive W. The net estate equals $500,000 including $90,000 paid to the executor in January 1996, representing the proceeds of W's fire insurance policy covering the painting. In addition, G, C's duly appointed guardian, has received $25,000 representing proceeds of a life insurance policy on W's life which was purchased in 1993 and named C as beneficiary.

(1)   Is the ruling on P's petition correct?

(2)   Is L's advice to T regarding the revocability of the trust correct?

(3)   What are the rights of N, A, B, and C regarding W's estate?

QUESTION 71

E, a resident of New York, was driving in State X when his vehicle collided with a vehicle driven by D, a resident of New York, and in which P, a resident of New York, was a passenger. The car driven by D was owned by O, a resident of New York. In all respects, the laws of State X are the same as the laws of New York, except that State X has a statute that states:

> The owner of a motor vehicle will not be held liable for the negligent acts of any driver of that motor vehicle, unless the driver of the vehicle is an employee of the owner, acting within the scope of his employment.

P sued O and E in New York for $150,000. O moved to dismiss the action based upon State X's law which did not provide for vicarious liability on the part of the owner. The court (1) denied O's motion. E made a motion in federal District Court for the Southern District of New York to remove the action to federal court. The federal court (2) denied the motion for removal. E then commenced a third-party action against D, and P amended his complaint to assert a claim against D as well. D and E cross-claimed against each other.

P settled with O for $25,000 after the jury retired but before a verdict was reached. The jury found for P in the amount of $100,000 and found that D and E were 50% negligent. After the entry of judgment for P, O commenced an action against D for the $25,000 paid by O to P in settlement. O moved for summary judgment, and D moved to dismiss O's action, based on the provisions of General Obligations Law section 15-108. The court (3) denied D's motion and granted O's motion for summary judgment.

(a) Were the numbered rulings correct?

(b) How much may P collect from D? From E?

QUESTION 72

Grant purchased the Richmond Office Building ("ROB") for $500,000 in cash on April 1, 1996. At the closing Grant conveyed his entire interest in the building to Richmond Inc. Richmond Inc. had been formed by Grant for this purpose. Richmond Inc. was authorized to issue 100,000 shares of common stock at $100 par value per share.

Richmond Inc. then issued to Grant 5,000 shares of its common stock as payment for his work in the formation of the corporation. Richmond Inc. also issued a promissory note for $700,000 in consideration for conveyance of the office building. As recorded in the corporate minutes, Grant, the sole shareholder and director, approved of these transactions on behalf of Richmond Inc.

Shortly thereafter, Grant issued 1,000 shares each to Manny, Moe, and Jack who, after examining the corporate books and records, paid $100,000 respectively for these stocks. The proceeds from this sale were used to upgrade ROB, and Manny, Moe, and Jack were each made a director.

Richmond Inc. then proceeded to rent all of the office space in ROB. After expenses, including payments on the promissory note, ROB's cash flow was $500,000.

Grant, one of the four directors of Richmond Inc., entered into a contract on behalf of Richmond Inc. with Maint Co. Maint Co. was wholly owned by Grant. This contract provided that Maint Co. would clean and maintain ROB for an annual fee of 5% of gross receipts. The customary fee for maintenance contracts in the area was 2.5%.

Grant then purchased the Excelsior, a luxury building with office suites. Grant used Maint Co. to provide special maid service for the Excelsior, including its executive dining room. Due to this added benefit, Excelsior was rented to its capacity, including most of the tenants of ROB whose leases had expired. Consequently, ROB started to lose money.

Manny, Moe, and Jack have retained an attorney who has written to Grant demanding: (1) that Grant's promissory note be reduced by $200,000, which represents Grant's profit on his sale of ROB to Richmond Inc.; (2) cancellation of the 5,000 shares of Richmond Inc. issued to Grant at the closing of ROB; (3) cancellation of the maintenance contract providing a 5% fee to Maint Co.; and (4) damages resulting from the loss of tenants by ROB to Excelsior.

What rights, if any, do Manny, Moe, and Jack have in regard to each of the numbered demands?

QUESTION 73

H and W were married in New York in January 1976 and have continuously resided there. In April 1991, following marital differences, H and W separated and each retained an attorney. Later that month, H and W entered into a separation agreement that was duly signed, acknowledged, and filed with the clerk of the county in which W resided. At that time, H was earning $50,000 a year from a computer business that he started in 1985. W was employed as a school teacher at a salary of $17,000 per year.

The agreement was fair and reasonable in all respects to W and H when it was made. H was obligated to pay the sum of $300 per week to W, and the agreement also provided it would survive any subsequent judgment of divorce.

H made the required support payments until January 1, 1994. Thereupon, H informed W that he would no longer pay her $300 a week. At that time, H's income from his computer business was $75,000 a year, and W's salary as a teacher was $20,000 per year.

On June 1, 1994, W duly instituted an action against H in the New York Supreme Court for a judgment of separation on the grounds of nonsupport. The complaint alleged the foregoing facts and asserted that H's conduct constituted a repudiation by H of the separation agreement.

Following a trial at which uncontroverted evidence of the foregoing pertinent facts was presented, but despite H's objections, (1) the court granted W a judgment of separation together with an award of support in the amount of $350 a week. The resulting judgment was entered on September 10, 1994, and no appeal was taken by H.

Thereafter, H and W continued to live separate and apart in New York, and H made the required payments of $350 a week to W until June 1999, when H and W effected a reconciliation and resumed living together as husband and wife. However, the reconciliation lasted only until December 1999, when the parties separated again; they have lived separate and apart since then. H has not made any support payments to W since December 1999.

In June 2000, W lost her job as a school teacher due to a budgetary cutback. Since then, W has been able to obtain only part-time work as a substitute teacher although she is not in danger of becoming a public charge. H's computer business has continued to prosper, with the result that its value is now markedly greater than it was in 1994, when W instituted the separation action. H's income has also increased and is now $150,000 per year. W has demanded that H make support payments to her sufficient to meet her needs, but H has refused to do so.

(1)   Was the court's ruling correct?

(2)   Would W be entitled to obtain a divorce against H on the ground that H and W lived separate and apart for more than one year?

(3)   Assuming that W was properly granted a divorce, would the court have power to award W, in addition to maintenance, an equitable share of the value of H's computer business?

QUESTION 74

C Corp. manufactures camera lenses. On October 1, 1995, A and C Corp. entered into an oral contract for A's employment for one year, to begin on November 1, 1995, and terminate on October 31, 1996. A worked for and was paid by C Corp. for 10 months, at which point C Corp.'s business went sour and A was fired. A was unable to find other employment.

On January 2, 1996, during the course of A's employment, the president of C Corp., Y, said to A, "If you can get business from S Corp., we will give you 15% commissions on each sale. You will receive your commission whether or not S Corp. purchases through you or calls C Corp. directly. The commissions are to be paid indefinitely." S Corp. continuously ordered products from C Corp., and A got paid commissions for business received until the day he was fired.

(1)   Can A collect salary for the last two months of his employment contract?

(2)   Is A entitled to continued commissions from S Corp.'s business?

C Corp. also made a written agreement with Z, a retailer of camera equipment, whereby C Corp. will deliver 30 lenses to Z on June 1, 1996. Z agreed to either purchase the units at $100 each or return them by August 31, 1996. C Corp. timely delivered the lenses to Z's store. However, on July 28, 1996, Z's store burned down. All the camera lenses were completely destroyed, and C Corp. demands to be paid.

(3)   Discuss the rights and liabilities of C Corp. with respect to Z.

QUESTION 75

The New York state legislature was in session, debating whether nuclear power should be allowed in the state. Several protest groups gathered in the area. S parked his van on a street near the Albany capitol building. There were banners on the van which said:

"CHERNOBYL NUKES KILL"
"BUSH IS A WARMONGER"
"NO MORE NUKES"

S was besieged by an angry crowd that surrounded and began to rock the van. S locked himself in the van and began making obscene gestures at the people outside.

X went to the local police and swore to the above facts. X described S's van, and gave the police a physical description of S. A magistrate issued a warrant on the basis of what X told the police. The warrant was made out for "John Doe, whose name is not otherwise known" and was for disorderly conduct pursuant to a state statute prohibiting "inciteful behavior."

P, a police officer, took the warrant to the area where S was parked and with some difficulty dispersed the crowd. P then knocked on the rear door of the van, and S opened the door and invited P in. P identified himself, showed S the warrant, and arrested S for disorderly conduct.

As P and S were leaving the van, P saw approximately 200 copies of a photograph depicting a young child engaging in explicit sexual acts with an adult. P took the pictures and further charged S with violation of a section of the Penal Law which states: "A person is guilty of the crime of obscenity if he knowingly promotes or possesses with the intent to promote or distribute obscene material."

S hired L as his attorney. L moved as follows in court:

(1) To dismiss the disorderly conduct charge as unconstitutional.

(2) To dismiss the obscenity charge under the Penal Law as unconstitutional as applied.

(3) To suppress the photographs from evidence.

How should the court decide?

QUESTION 76

Harriet Hoctor was an accountant for "Allways Corp." for four years. As Allways's accountant, Harriet was expressly authorized to sign and issue Allways Corp. checks solely for payment of corporate obligations up to $20,000. Recently, Harriet was experiencing financial difficulties and decided that Allways would not miss $1,500. Accordingly, she wrote a check on the Allways account payable to Aristocrat Caterers for a party Harriet was giving. The check was properly dated and imprinted with the legend "Allways Corp." Allways had never done business with Aristocrat Caterers, but had leased office furniture from Aristocrat Office Supplies. Aristocrat Caterers had no knowledge that Harriet was improperly using Allways corporate accounts to satisfy a personal debt. Allways's bank paid Aristocrat and charged Allways's account for the $1,500.

Eleven months later, Allways auditors discovered the $1,500 missing from the account and Harriet was discharged from her position. A grand jury subsequently indicted Harriet for larceny of "Allways Corp." funds.

Upon learning of the indictment, Harriet drove to the nearest liquor store and purchased two quarts of gin. She sat in her car a block away from the store and consumed both quarts in quick order. Harriet then decided to go over to see her former employers to give them a piece of her mind. As Harriet pulled away from the curb, she was observed by a police officer.

The officer followed Harriet in her patrol car and noticed Harriet driving so erratically that she almost jumped the curb and nearly hit a man walking his dog.

The officer turned on her siren and signaled Harriet to pull over. Harriet ignored the officer. With the police officer following behind her, Harriet drove home and pulled into her garage and entered her apartment located over the garage.

The police officer knocked on the door of Harriet's apartment. When there was no response, the officer turned the knob, found the door unlocked, and entered. Once inside, the officer saw Harriet passed out on the couch. Harriet smelled of alcohol. The officer arrested Harriet for driving while intoxicated, a misdemeanor, and took her to the police station. The officer did not have either an arrest or search warrant.

At the station house the police officer advised Harriet of the law that her driver's license would be suspended if she refused to take a breathalyzer test. Harriet consented and took the test. The test established that Harriet's blood alcohol level was well above what was needed to establish that Harriet had been driving while intoxicated.

The officer then asked Harriet to perform physical coordination exercises, such as walking a straight line. Harriet was not given *Miranda* warnings prior to these tests being administered. She was unable to successfully complete this battery of tests.

As Harriet's attorney you make the following pretrial motions: (1) to suppress the results of Harriet's breathalyzer test on the ground that it was the product of an unlawful arrest in violation of Harriet's Fourteenth Amendment rights; (2) to suppress the results of the physical tests on the grounds that they violated Harriet's rights under the Fifth and Fourteenth Amendments; and (3) to preclude the prosecution from cross-examining Harriet in regard to the larceny charge for the purpose of impeaching Harriet's credibility if Harriet testifies on her own behalf. The court granted each of your motions.

(a) May Allways force its bank to recredit its account for the $1,500 check to Aristocrat Caterers?

(b) Was the court correct in granting each of the numbered rulings?

QUESTION 77

New York City police officers John and Ponch had a local storefront under surveillance for approximately two months. After satisfying himself that the store was being used solely for the purpose of selling unlawful firearms, John submitted an affidavit to the district attorney's office, which in turn applied to a supreme court judge for a video and audio surveillance warrant.

The affidavit stated, among other things, that John and Ponch had observed known gang members entering and leaving the building, that there is no listing of the business in the New York telephone directory, and that there is no evidence of any legitimate business transactions occurring at the store. John further stated that, based on his experience as a weapons specialist in the New York City Police Department, as well as his and Ponch's gang experience while working for the California Highway Patrol in the early 1980s, he believed the store was being used to sell firearms and explosives to local gangs and organized crime figures. In fact, on one occasion he observed Teddy "Squeaky" Dapolito, a known weapons dealer with the Colombo crime family, enter the premises carrying military satchels over his shoulder. He believed that the satchels carried by Squeaky contained small arms, and the small packages being carried out by customers contained explosives. On the strength of John's affidavit, the warrant was granted, and the surveillance equipment was covertly installed.

Shortly after installation of the surveillance equipment pursuant to the warrant, John and Ponch observed Dinky, a local gang member, enter the store and discuss the purchase of two AR-15 assault rifles and a pound of plastic explosives. Squeaky advised Dinky that he had the guns and explosives in stock, and the price would be $3,500. Squeaky's associate, Jerry "the Knife" Milano, was also present in the room, but he was involved in paperwork cataloguing the guns. Dinky handed over the cash, and Squeaky handed over the guns and explosives.

As soon as Dinky left the store, John and Ponch stormed through the front door to arrest Squeaky and "the Knife." However, "the Knife" drew an Uzi submachine gun and sent a burst of armor-piercing bullets through Ponch's bullet-proof vest, killing him. John was then able to disarm and arrest Squeaky and "the Knife."

Both men were indicted separately for the illegal sale of weapons and conspiracy to sell illegal weapons to Dinky. "The Knife's" indictment also contained a charge of first degree murder. Squeaky and "the Knife" were tried separately. Before either trial, the district attorney notified each defendant that the video surveillance tape would be used. Both defendants moved to suppress the tape based on allegations that the warrant had been improperly granted. The court (1) denied both motions.

At trial, although Squeaky was convicted of the illegal sale of weapons, he was acquitted on the conspiracy charge. As a result, "the Knife" moved to dismiss his conspiracy charge since there was no one with whom he could conspire. The court (2) denied the motion.

"The Knife" notified the district attorney that he would be introducing psychiatric evidence of his long history of mental illness, claiming that he lacked responsibility by reason of mental disease or defect.

The judge charged the jury as follows:

1.   The burden is on the prosecution to prove every element of the crime. Because the defendant offered evidence of his mental condition, the prosecution also has the burden of proving beyond reasonable doubt the defendant's mental capacity to commit the crime.

2.   If you find that the defendant, by reason of mental disease or defect, was unable to resist doing wrong or did not know his conduct would cause harm to the police officer, you must acquit him.

(a)   Were the court's rulings correct?

(b)   Were the court's charges to the jury correct?

QUESTION 78

H and W were married in New York. They had two children, S (a son) and D (a daughter). After 17 years of marriage in New York, H moved out of the marital residence due to marital difficulties and never returned. Thirteen months later, W commenced a divorce action for abandonment by properly serving H with a summons and complaint.

While the action was pending, W moved for temporary maintenance. H answered and submitted affidavits stating that W had just received an inheritance which was enough to support her. H further defended on the grounds that (i) W has not shown the probability of success on the merits, and (ii) W has not shown need. H was making $60,000 a year and had not paid any support or maintenance to W or the children from the day he had left the house.

The court decided in favor of H on both grounds.

(1) Was the court correct?

The court granted W a divorce on the grounds of abandonment. W was awarded $400 a month maintenance and $100 a week child support per child until each child's emancipation.

H paid both the maintenance and the child support for a while but then found out his 19-year-old son was working full-time and was self-supporting. H ceased paying the child support for S, but continued for D. H further found out that W had moved in with F, her boyfriend, and that S and D were living with them. H immediately stopped paying maintenance.

Three months later, W made a motion in court for arrearages for both her and S. H cross-moved for retroactive termination of maintenance and support.

(2) How should H's and W's motions with respect to arrearages be decided?

QUESTION 79

On September 20, at 11 p.m., B entered a one-story building owned by V in Albany for the purpose of stealing anything of value he found there. The building contained a sporting goods store and an apartment in which V lived. B gained entry to the building by raising a partially open window in V's bedroom and then proceeded into the store part of the premises. B took a .38 automatic pistol from a display case in V's store and placed it in a duffle bag he had brought with him.

V, who had returned from a movie, unlocked the front door and entered the store. B grabbed the duffle bag and ran past V towards the door, accidentally knocking V down as he fled. V, an elderly man, struck his head on the floor and sustained a skull fracture. B ran to his car and drove away.

P, an Albany police officer driving a patrol car, observed B go through a stop sign at an intersection a block from V's store at a speed in excess of the city speed limit.

P stopped B a short distance away and asked B to produce his license and registration. While B was looking in the glove compartment of the car for the license and registration, P observed the duffle bag on the back seat. P opened the unlocked rear door, unzipped the duffle bag, and discovered the pistol. When B could not produce a pistol permit, P placed B under arrest, charging B with criminal possession of a weapon and with the traffic infractions of speeding and passing a stop sign.

Meanwhile, a neighbor found V and took V to a hospital where V was interviewed by D, an Albany detective. V, before he lapsed into a coma, told D that he had surprised an intruder who had knocked him down while fleeing from V's store. V further stated that he recognized the intruder as B, who until recently had worked at a nearby diner. V's last words were, "I know I'm dying. Don't let B get away with it." V died later that night.

Thereafter, B was charged in a felony complaint with the burglary and second degree murder. B retained L as his lawyer and at the arraignment in Albany Police Court on September 22 pleaded not guilty. L demanded a preliminary hearing. The court ordered a hearing held on September 26. On September 24, a grand jury returned an indictment for burglary in the first degree and murder in the second degree. No preliminary hearing was held on September 26, and on September 27, L moved to dismiss the indictment on the grounds that B had been deprived of his right to a preliminary hearing. The court (1) denied the motion.

L then moved to suppress the use of the pistol as evidence. The evidence addressed at the suppression hearing established the foregoing pertinent facts. Following the hearings, the court (2) denied the motion.

On the trial of the indictment in January:

(i)   P testified as to his observation and acts on September 20, in relation to B;

(ii) V's ownership of the pistol was duly established through its serial number;

(iii) Over L's objection, the court (3) permitted D to testify to the statements which V made at the hospital shortly before he died; and

(iv) The death of V as a result of the head injury was established by medical proof.

The prosecution then rested and L moved for a trial order of dismissal on the ground that the evidence was not legally sufficient to establish either of the crimes charged in the indictment. The court (4) denied the motion.

Were the numbered rulings correct?

QUESTION 80

In 1970, O, a farmer, purchased Blackacre, a 30-acre farm in the western part of New York, and constructed a house in which he still lives on the southerly half of the property. A state highway runs east and west along the northern boundary of Blackacre. In 1971, in order to travel between O's house, which is near the southern boundary of Blackacre, and the state highway, O constructed a private paved road that runs south from the state highway across Blackacre to O's house. A private dirt road along the southern boundary of Blackacre also provides access to a county highway that runs north and south along the eastern boundary of Blackacre. O rarely uses the private dirt road because it is in poor condition and is a less convenient route from O's house to almost all destinations.

In 1986, O sold and conveyed the northerly half of Blackacre to A for $60,000. At the closing, A paid O $40,000 in cash and gave O a bond and purchase money mortgage for the balance of $20,000, payable in monthly installments of $500 principal plus interest at 8%. The mortgage provided that at O's option, the entire balance of principal and interest would become due upon 30 days' default in the payment of any monthly installment.

A immediately recorded his deed, but O failed to record his mortgage until December 1988.

The deed from O to A was silent as to O's right to use the private paved road across the parcel conveyed to A, but O continued, without objection by A, to use the private paved road as passage to the state highway to and from his house.

Meanwhile, in September 1988, A conveyed the northerly half of Blackacre to B for $48,000. B paid A $40,000 in cash, and the deed conveying the parcel to B stated that it was "subject to O's mortgage upon which there is now due the sum of $8,000 plus interest." The deed also provided that B assumed and agreed to pay the $8,000 mortgage debt. The deed was signed and acknowledged only by A. B promptly recorded the deed.

No payments were made on the bond and mortgage after September 1988. In January 1989, O notified A and B that he elected to declare the entire $8,000 plus interest due. In February 1989, O commenced an action to foreclose the mortgage, naming A and B as defendants. Both A and B were personally served with the summons and complaint. Immediately prior to serving the defendants, the plaintiff filed the summons and complaint with the clerk of the county court and obtained an index number. The complaint included a demand for a deficiency judgment for any balance remaining unpaid on the bond after the foreclosure sale.

A's answer pleaded, as an affirmative defense, that he was no longer liable to O because B had assumed and agreed to pay the mortgage debt due to O. B's answer pleaded, as affirmative defenses, that O's mortgage was not a lien on the northerly half of Blackacre because it had not been recorded until after B had recorded his deed, and, in the alternative, B was not liable for any deficiency because he had never assumed or agreed to pay the mortgage debt to O.

O moved to dismiss (1) A's affirmative defense, and (2) B's affirmative defenses on the ground that each of these defenses was insufficient as a matter of law.

In May 1994, B commenced construction of a fence along the southern border of his property and has advised O that he will no longer permit O to use the private paved road across B's property.

(a)   How should the court decide O's motions (1) and (2)?

(b)   What rights, if any, does O have to use the private paved road across B's property?

QUESTION 81

ABC Corp., a manufacturer of outdoor furniture, is a New York corporation with its office and plant in Albany. Its president, A, and his wife, B, each own 20% of the outstanding shares of the corporation. The other shareholders are C, who is B's sister, and D, who is C's husband, each of whom owns 30% of the shares of the corporation.

In May 1999, A and B, who were nearing retirement age, decided to sell the business and move to Florida. After negotiations, X, a wealthy investor, agreed to pay $1 million for all of the assets of ABC Corp., including its name. Thereupon, a written agreement was prepared for the sale by ABC Corp. of its assets to X and was executed on June 1, 1999, by A, as president of ABC Corp., and by X.

The agreement included the following paragraphs:

> 33. This agreement shall become effective and binding upon the parties only if authorized and approved as required by the New York Business Corporation Law.

> 34. Any dispute arising out of a claimed breach of this agreement shall be submitted to arbitration pursuant to the rules of the American Arbitration Association.

A and B told X that they planned to sell their home in Albany. After some discussion, X agreed to purchase the home for $150,000, pursuant to a written contract of sale, dated June 2, 1999, and executed that day. The contract provided for a down payment of $15,000, which X paid to A and B upon signing the contract, and included the following paragraph:

> Buyer shall have the absolute right to cancel this contract upon written notice to Sellers within 10 days of the date hereof, in which event the down payment will be returned.

On June 5, 1999, a meeting of the board of directors of ABC Corp. was held. A, B, and C, who together constitute the entire board, attended the meeting and each executed a waiver of notice of the meeting. A, B, and C then unanimously adopted a resolution authorizing the sale of ABC Corp.'s assets to X pursuant to the June 1, 1999, agreement and directing submission of the proposal for such sale to a vote of the shareholders at a meeting to be held on June 12, 1999.

A, B, C, and D attended the shareholders' meeting on June 12. Each executed a waiver of notice of the meeting. During the discussion of the proposed sale, C stated that she had serious second thoughts about the adequacy of the purchase price. A vote was then had on a motion to approve the sale. A and B voted "yes" and C and D voted "no."

Immediately after the shareholders' meeting on June 12, A telephoned X and told him: "I am sorry, but the sale is off. C and D did not go along." That same day, X wrote a letter to A, as president of the ABC Corp., stating that X considered ABC Corp.'s refusal to proceed with the sale to be a breach of the June 1 agreement and demanding arbitration of the dispute between the parties.

X also wrote a letter to A and B on June 12 stating: "I am canceling the contract for the purchase of your home, and I demand return of the $15,000 down payment."

Both letters were sent by certified mail on June 12 and were received by their respective addressees on June 15.

A, as president of ABC Corp., replied to X by return mail rejecting the demand for arbitration. A and B also replied to X by return mail, advising X that they considered X to have breached the contract for the sale of their home and that they were retaining the $15,000 as liquidated damages. On June 20, A and B sold their home to Y for $160,000.

What are the respective rights, if any, of:

(1)   ABC Corp. and X with respect to (a) the June 1, 1999, agreement for the sale of ABC Corp.'s assets to X, and (b) X's demand for arbitration?

(2)   A and B and X with respect to the June 2, 1999, agreement for the sale by A and B of their home to X?

QUESTION 82

In January 1980, H, a corporate executive, and W, a registered nurse, were married in New York, where they lived until January 1984, when they moved to New Jersey. H and W thereafter lived together in New Jersey until November 15, 1994, when H left W upon discovering that she had engaged in sexual relations with another man, M, in October 1994, while H was overseas on a business trip. Shortly thereafter, H moved to Connecticut. H and W did not have any children. W continued to reside in New Jersey until January 15, 1995, when she moved to Suffolk County, New York. She has continuously resided in Suffolk County since that time.

In June 1995, W caused her attorney, L, to prepare a summons and complaint in an action for separation by W against H in the New York Supreme Court, Queens County, the county in which L maintains his law office. The complaint alleged that W had been residing in New York continuously since January 1995, and that W and H had been married in New York in 1980 and had resided together in New York from 1980 to 1984. The complaint also alleged that H had left W without justification in November 1994 and sought a judgment of separation on the ground of abandonment and an award of maintenance of $1,000 per month. On June 20, 1995, copies of the summons and complaint were personally served on H in Connecticut by a Connecticut attorney. Immediately prior to serving the defendant, the attorney filed a copy of the summons and complaint in the county clerk's office and obtained an index number.

Thereafter, H timely moved to dismiss W's complaint on the grounds (a) that the court did not have jurisdiction of H's person; (b) that the court did not have jurisdiction of the subject matter of the action; and, in the alternative, (c) that the complaint failed to state a cause of action. In support of ground (a) of this motion, H submitted uncontroverted proof that he was a resident of Connecticut, where he had been served with the summons and complaint, and that he had not resided in New York since January 1984. The court (1) rejected grounds (a) and (b) of H's motion, but granted H's motion to dismiss W's complaint on ground (c). No appeal was taken by W.

In December 1996, H became a resident of Albany County, New York. In January 1997, W commenced a new action against H in the New York Supreme Court, Queens County. W's complaint in that action contained the same allegations as those set forth in W's complaint in her prior action for separation, except that it sought a judgment of divorce on the ground of abandonment and equitable distribution of the marital property, in addition to an award of maintenance of $1,000 per month.

On January 20, 1997, personal service of the summons and complaint was duly made on H in Albany County, New York. Immediately prior to serving the defendant, the attorney filed a copy of the summons and complaint in the county clerk's office and obtained an index number. On February 2, H served an answer consisting of a general denial and a counterclaim for a judgment of divorce, alleging that W had committed adultery with M in October 1994.

With his answer, H served a written demand for a change of place of trial from Queens County to Albany County on the ground that Queens County was not a proper county for trial. W did not respond to H's demand, and on February 13, H made a motion in the Supreme Court, Albany County, for an order changing the place of trial from Queens County to Albany County. W objected to the motion on the grounds (a) that the motion could not be made in Albany County, and (b) that, in any event, there was no basis for changing the place of trial. The court (2) granted the motion.

At the subsequent trial, the undisputed evidence established that W had committed adultery with M on three separate occasions in October 1994 while H was overseas on a business trip. The evidence also established that H earned $75,000 a year; that W earned $25,000 a year; and that H had a net worth of $500,000, of which $400,000 had been acquired by H while H and W had lived together, between January 1970 and November 15, 1994.

The court granted H a judgment of divorce against W and ruled (3) that, as a matter of law, because of W's adultery, she was not entitled to either maintenance or any share of the marital property.

Were the numbered rulings correct?

QUESTION 83

On October 1, Larry, an attorney living in Garden City, New York, drew a check for $600 on his account in Bogus Bank in Hempstead, New York, to the order of Nancy, his 16-year-old niece, and delivered it to her as a birthday present. The next day, Nancy indorsed and delivered the check to Otis, the owner of a music store, in full payment of Nancy's purchase of records and CDs reasonably worth $600. Nancy did not look like the average 16-year-old, and due to her poise and demeanor Otis believed she was over 18 years old.

On October 3, while standing in line at the teller's window in Bogus Bank, Larry collapsed and died. That afternoon, Otis was in Bogus Bank depositing his weekend receipts and presented Larry's check bearing Nancy's indorsement for payment. Bogus Bank refused to honor the check on the ground that Larry had died. The next morning, Otis gave notice to Nancy and Evan, the duly appointed executor under Larry's will.

Larry's death was determined to have been directly related to injuries Larry had received in a motorcycle accident in the state of Franklin. On May 20, Larry had gone from his house in Garden City to Franklin to meet his friend Rose, a resident of Franklin. While Larry and Rose were riding Larry's motorcycle to a nearby movie theater, they were involved in an accident with Steve, a New York resident in Franklin on business. Both Larry and Rose were seriously injured in the accident. Larry's motorcycle and Steve's car were each registered and insured in New York. The accident was caused by the negligence of both Larry and Steve.

The relevant Franklin statute provides that neither the owner nor the driver of a vehicle would be liable for injuries sustained by a guest passenger unless the owner or driver was guilty of gross negligence. In all other aspects, the relevant law of Franklin is the same as New York's. Although Larry and Steve were each negligent, neither was grossly negligent as defined by either Franklin or New York.

In July, Rose commenced an action in New York Supreme Court, Nassau County, against Larry and Steve to recover damages resulting from Rose's injuries. Rose's complaint alleged the above facts about the accident and Rose's injuries. Larry filed an answer, which was a general denial, and pleaded the Franklin guest statute as an affirmative defense. Rose moved by CPLR 3211 to strike Larry's affirmative defense as insufficient as a matter of law. Evan has subsequently been substituted for Larry as a party defendant in the action. At this time Rose's motion to strike is still pending.

(1)   What are Otis's rights, if any, versus Evan and Bogus Bank?

(2)   How should the court rule on Rose's CPLR 3211 motion to strike Larry's affirmative defense?

QUESTION 84

Steve owned the Border Club, a nightclub located in State A just across the border from New York State. On April 4, Steve read in a local paper that an unnamed "surprise" guest star would appear on May 6, at Club Mystique, a popular nightclub on the New York side of the border. Although Steve did not know who would be appearing at Club Mystique on May 6, he decided that he would also offer special entertainment on May 6 to ensure the Border Club's regular patrons would not be attracted to Club Mystique.

On April 5, Steve telephoned Rocker, a popular rock singer, at Rocker's home in State B. Steve asked Rocker to headline the May 6 program at the Border Club and offered Rocker a payment far in excess of his usual fee. Rocker agreed to perform at the Border Club, although he had previously signed a contract with Melanie, the owner of Club Mystique, to appear as Club Mystique's "surprise" guest star on May 6, for his usual fee. Rocker did not tell Steve of his contract with Melanie, and Steve did not learn until May 7 that Rocker had agreed to appear at Club Mystique.

On the evening of May 6, Rocker appeared before a sellout crowd at the Border Club. Club Mystique was also filled to capacity that evening. Arguments and fighting broke out among Club Mystique's patrons when Melanie announced late that evening that she had just learned that the guest star would not appear. Club Mystique sustained substantial losses because all of the entrance fees that had been paid that evening were refunded, and because Club Mystique's property and equipment were damaged during the fighting.

Sheryl, a patron of Club Mystique who was not involved in the fighting, was stabbed on the club's dance floor by Tony, a patron who had entered the club with a metal switchblade concealed in his jacket.

On May 21, Melanie duly commenced an action against Rocker and Steve in federal district court in New York, alleging that Rocker had breached his contract with Melanie and that Steve induced Rocker to do so. Melanie caused the summons and complaint to be served personally on Steve at his home in State A by a State A attorney, and on Rocker at his home in State B by a State B attorney.

Rocker timely moved to dismiss the complaint as against him for lack of personal jurisdiction. The uncontroverted proof at the hearing on Rocker's motion established that Rocker's contract with Melanie had been negotiated and executed in State B and that Rocker neither resided nor did business in New York. The court (1) granted Rocker's motion.

Steve interposed a timely answer to Melanie's complaint, consisting of a general denial. Melanie then moved for summary judgment against Steve, and uncontroverted proof of the foregoing pertinent facts was presented by affidavits offered by Melanie and Steve. The court (2) granted Melanie's motion.

On July 6, Sheryl duly commenced an action against Melanie in the New York Supreme Court, seeking $62,000 damages for personal injuries. In her complaint, Sheryl alleged that (a) Club Mystique is located in a high-crime area, (b) Melanie had failed to provide adequate security at Club Mystique on the night of May 6, (c) Melanie had removed metal detectors from the club's entrance to make room for a ticket window shortly before the events of May 6, and (d) Sheryl had suffered serious injuries when she was stabbed by Tony at Club Mystique. On July 22, Melanie moved to dismiss the complaint for failure to state a cause of action, contending that she could not be held responsible for injuries caused by Tony. The court (3) granted Melanie's motion.

Were the numbered rulings correct?

QUESTION 85

In January, Paula was injured when a car that she owned and operated collided with a truck owned and operated by David. The accident occurred at an intersection controlled by traffic lights. The police were called to the scene and, after investigation, charged David with driving under the influence of alcohol, a misdemeanor. David entered a plea of not guilty. At the trial in March 1990, Paula testified against David, and David testified on his own behalf. David was found not guilty of the charge.

In April, Paula retained an attorney who, on Paula's behalf, duly instituted an action in New York Supreme Court against David to recover damages for Paula's injuries. Paula's complaint alleged that David's truck had entered the intersection against a red traffic light and that David was intoxicated at the time of the accident. David retained an attorney who interposed an answer on David's behalf, consisting of a general denial.

Later in April, David died of natural causes unrelated to the accident, and Paula's attorney caused Evelyn, the duly appointed executor of David's estate, to be substituted as the defendant in the action. The action was reached for trial last week.

On Paula's direct case, her attorney sought to have Paula testify as to the color of the traffic signal as David entered the intersection and to David's intoxication at the time of the accident. Evelyn's attorney objected, and the court (1) sustained the objection. The court (2) permitted

Wayne, a witness to the accident, to testify that (a) Wayne saw David's truck enter the intersection against the red light, (b) immediately after the collision, Wayne spoke to David and noticed that David's speech was slurred and David's gait was unsteady, and (c) it was Wayne's opinion that David was intoxicated.

On Evelyn's case, her attorney called Cathy, the court reporter who had transcribed the testimony at the trial on the misdemeanor charge against David. Over the objection of Paula's attorney, the court (3) permitted Cathy to testify that David had stated under oath at the earlier trial that he was not intoxicated at the time of the collision, that the traffic light was green in David's favor, that David had bitten his tongue when the accident occurred, which made it difficult and painful for David to speak, and that David had consumed only one bottle of beer several hours before the incident.

Over the objection of Paula's attorney, the court (4) permitted Evelyn's attorney to call Neil, who testified that he was a neighbor of Wayne and that Neil knew Wayne's reputation for veracity in the community and knew it to be bad. But, over the objection of Evelyn's attorney, the court (5) refused to admit Neil's proffered testimony that Wayne had lied to Neil on several occasions in the past.

On rebuttal, Paula's attorney again offered Paula's testimony, which the court had excluded in ruling (1). On the objection of Evelyn's attorney, the court (6) again refused to admit Paula's proffered testimony.

Were the numbered rulings correct?

QUESTION 86

Rose owned a small flower shop which specialized in tulip arrangements. She was concerned about maintaining a steady supply of tulips in her shop because a nationwide plague on tulip bulbs had recently decimated the domestic supply. To guarantee her tulip supply, Rose met with her largest distributor, Daisy, and asked for assurances that her tulip requirements would continue to be met. Daisy replied that she would look into the matter.

A week later, Daisy wrote to Rose, informing her that Lily had sold her a tulip nursery along with her entire stock of healthy domestic tulip bulbs. Consequently, Daisy offered to supply Rose's tulip requirements for the upcoming year at a price that was specified in the letter. At the bottom of the letter, Daisy wrote as follows: "If the above accords with your understanding, please execute the signature line below and return this letter to me immediately." Rose immediately signed the "letter agreement" in the appropriate place and returned it to Daisy.

Several months later, Daisy learned that the tulip bulbs she had acquired from Lily were, in fact, a rare hybrid strain of tulip that could only be found in Southern Mongolia. As a result, the tulips Daisy was selling to Rose were actually worth 20 times the price that she had agreed to accept in the letter agreement and the subsequent contract with Daisy.

When Rose sent her next tulip order, Daisy refused to deliver tulips from her own nursery, but offered to supply Rose with domestic tulips from Violet's tulip nursery. Rose refused, contending that the agreement they had executed specified that the tulips to be delivered to Rose were to be grown in the tulip nursery that Daisy had acquired from Lily.

Rose has contacted you to represent her in this matter. You have spoken with Daisy's attorney who claims that:

(1) The letter agreement is unenforceable due to indefiniteness.

(2) The contract is void due to:

    a. Unconscionability.

    b. Mutual mistake.

How would you evaluate each of these defenses?

QUESTION 87

Joe was a farmhand on Ed's cattle and horse ranch. He worked from 9 to 5 on Mondays through Fridays. In addition to feeding and exercising Ed's horses, Joe was responsible for cleaning the barn where Ed's prize cow, Elsie, was kept. Elsie was Ed's pride and joy and had recently been valued at $999.99.

One Saturday afternoon, Joe approached his friend Hal with a plan to steal Elsie and sell her to the nearest local butcher. Hal agreed to participate in Joe's plan on the condition that no violence at all would be involved in the theft. Joe assured Hal that the cattle and horse ranch was always deserted on the weekends. The two friends therefore agreed to drive out to the ranch the next day (Sunday) and steal Elsie. They both agreed that they would carry no weapons and avoid violence at all costs.

On Sunday morning, Hal and Joe drove to the cattle and horse ranch in Joe's van. Joe opened the barn door and, together, both men entered it. However, after searching all the stalls they discovered that Elsie was nowhere to be found. Hal and Joe returned to the van, which was parked in the ranch parking lot, and began driving. Just before they reached the gate of the parking lot, they saw Ed running after them. To Hal's surprise, Joe pulled a gun out from his jacket and shot Ed at close range, killing him instantly. Hal and Joe thereafter returned to their separate apartments.

(1) What charges can be brought against Joe and Hal?

(2) What affirmative defense does Hal have?

QUESTION 88

Bump Corp. and Frump Corp. are each incorporated in the state of New York in June 2003, and have their principal place of business in New York County. Ed, the president of Bump, made an offer to Don, the president of Frump, on behalf of all the Bump Corp. shareholders. He informed Don that the shareholders would be willing to buy all of the stock in Frump for $500 per share. Frump's issued and outstanding stock consisted of 160,000 common shares owned in different amounts by 10 people.

Don told Ed that he would only consider selling his own stock as well as that of the other three directors sitting on Frump's board of directors (a total of 80,000 shares), at a price of $550 per share. Ed agreed, and Bump bought the directors' 80,000 shares of Frump. The six Frump shareholders who were not directly involved with the sale were not informed of the sale until after the purchase was completed.

After learning of the deal with Bump, two other Frump shareholders, owning 5,000 shares of stock each, informed Don that they wanted to sell all their shares. Don, with the approval of the Frump board, arranged for Frump to buy the additional 10,000 shares at the price of $500 per share for Frump's treasury.

Bump's board of directors thereupon agreed to acquire sole ownership of Frump in order to reduce the aggregate number of shareholders in Frump. The board of directors of Bump and Frump each unanimously voted to approve a merger of Frump into Bump. The shares in Frump that had not yet been acquired by Bump were to be purchased by Bump at $450 each.

The merger was unanimously approved by the Bump shareholders. At the Frump shareholders' meeting, Bump voted its 80,000 shares of Frump in favor of the merger. The 10,000 shares that were in its treasury were not voted, and 30,000 shares were voted against the merger.

Action I: One of the Frump shareholders brought an action against Don and the three other Frump board members who had sold their shares at $550, seeking a court order that they disgorge the profit they received on the sale of their shares.

Action II: Another shareholder in Frump Corp. brought an action to invalidate the merger on the ground that (i) the 10,000 shares that had been purchased by Frump at $500 per share were unlawfully purchased; (ii) the merger had not been approved by a sufficient number of shareholders since it would not have occurred but for an unlawful stock purchase; and (iii) the merger served no lawful purpose.

There are no relevant provisions in the certificate of incorporation and the bylaws of the two corporations involved.

How should Action I and Action II be resolved? Do not discuss procedural issues.

QUESTION 89

Jack and Don decided to go out for a drink after work one Friday afternoon. After having a few drinks at "The Neighborhood Bar," they discovered that they were both dating the same woman, whom they had met several weeks earlier at a conference they attended together. Both men became enraged at this discovery and soon began throwing punches at each other. It did not take very long for a full scale barroom brawl to break out. The police were called, and upon arriving, arrested several patrons of the bar, including Jack. Don, however, was seriously injured and was taken to the hospital.

At the precinct house, Jack was charged with the assault of Don. He was released on bail. Jack appeared at his pretrial hearing without counsel and entered a plea of guilty. The court adjourned the case for sentencing. On the return date, Jack appeared with an attorney, and on his attorney's application was granted leave to withdraw his guilty plea and enter a plea of not guilty. Following a jury trial, Jack was acquitted of assaulting Don. Thereafter, Don commenced a civil action against Jack in supreme court to recover damages for the injuries he sustained in the barroom brawl.

At the trial of Don's action, Don testified that Jack instigated the fight in "The Neighborhood Bar" by throwing the first punch of the evening at him. Don also testified that to the best of his recollection, most of his injuries were caused by Jack. Don then offered into evidence a duly certified transcript of the docket book of the criminal court, which showed that Jack had initially pleaded guilty to the assault on Don. Jack objected on the ground that he had withdrawn his original plea of guilty. The court (1) sustained Jack's objection. Don then introduced into evidence portions of the hospital record relating to his injuries, after establishing that the record had been kept in the regular course of business.

Jack offered into evidence another portion of Don's hospital record, wherein Don's doctor, Lance, made an entry stating that upon admittance to the hospital Don had told him that he had instigated the fight with Jack and that Jack had inflicted Don's injuries while acting in self-defense. On Don's objection, the court (2) excluded this portion of the hospital record.

Jack then called Lance as a witness. Lance identified the foregoing entry in Don's hospital record as having been written and signed by him. However, he testified that he had no independent memory of the incident and believed that the entry was an accurate description of what Don told him. Jack offered the hospital record entry into evidence again. On Don's objection, the court (3) excluded it.

Jack offered into evidence the duly certified transcript of the portion of the criminal court docket book which showed that after a jury trial, Jack was acquitted of assaulting Don. On Don's objection, the court (4) excluded this evidence.

Jack then took the stand and testified that Don had instigated the fight, and that any injuries that he had inflicted on Don were inflicted in self-defense. On cross-examination, Jack was asked whether he had been involved in two other barroom brawls in the past month. The court (5) sustained Jack's objection to the question.

Were the numbered rulings correct?

QUESTION 90

On February 5, 1996, Tessa, a widow, duly executed this will:

(i) I bequeath to my brother Marcus all the money deposited in my savings account in the Spendthrift Savings & Loan.

(ii) I bequeath to my brother Paul my two original Monet paintings.

(iii) I bequeath to my brother John 300 shares of common stock in the Monumental Corporation.

(iv) I bequeath to my son-in-law Leon the sum of $75,000.

(v) I bequeath the residue of my estate to my son Sidney and my daughter Debbie in equal shares.

(vi) I appoint my attorney, Simon Saez, as executor.

Tessa died on December 1, 1999, leaving an estate valued at $750,000. Tessa was survived by Sidney, Debbie, Marcus, Paul, and John. Tessa was also survived by Leon, Debbie's former husband. Debbie and Leon had been married in 1994, but Debbie had obtained a judgment of divorce against Leon in July 1998 on the grounds of abandonment.

Tessa's will of February 5, 1996, was duly admitted to probate, and Saez duly qualified as executor.

Tessa's only account in the Spendthrift Savings & Loan was a savings account in the name of "Tessa in trust for Sidney." Tessa had opened the trust account in April 1994 and maintained it until her death, at which time there was a balance of $35,000. Sidney learned of that account after Tessa's death. Both Sidney and Marcus have asserted claims thereto.

Paul demanded that Saez deliver to Paul the two original Monet paintings bequeathed to Paul. However, Debbie claims that Tessa gave the paintings to Debbie in June 1994. It is undisputed that on June 10, 1994, Debbie, who was then studying art in France, received the following letter from Tessa:

June 3, 1994

Dearest Debbie:

I know how much you admire my two Monet paintings, and I want to make a gift of them to you, which I am doing now by this letter. But meanwhile, and so long as I live, I will keep possession of these paintings.

(signed) Tessa

There was no other communication between Tessa and Debbie with respect to the paintings, and they remained in Tessa's possession until Tessa's death.

At the time of her death, Tessa owned 650 shares of common stock in the Monumental Corporation, consisting of 300 shares purchased by Tessa in November 1994, 300 shares received by Tessa in October 1996 as a result of a stock split, and 50 shares received by Tessa in November 1998 as a stock dividend. John demanded that Saez deliver to him all 650 shares of the Monumental Corporation. Sidney and Debbie contend that John is entitled to only 300 shares.

Sidney and Debbie also contend that Leon does not have the right to receive the bequest of $75,000 mentioned in Tessa's will.

What are the rights of Sidney, Debbie, Marcus, Paul, John, and Leon?

QUESTION 91

On July 16, Fashion Coordinates, Inc., a New York corporation and manufacturer of women's dresses, received an order from X, a New York resident and owner of a local basketball team. The order was for 12 specially designed sweat suits. X gave Fashion the exact height and weight of his players and specified that due to an allergic reaction of the star player, only a special blend of cotton, wool, and cashmere was to be used on all sweat suits. The price agreed upon was $750 per sweat suit, and delivery was to be before October 16. Fashion Coordinates calculated that the cost to manufacture each sweat suit would be $500, making for a profit of $250 on each suit.

Fashion Coordinates ordered the necessary quantity of the special blend from Y, the only importer of the blend in the United States. Y did not have any of the material in stock, but expected a shipment by September 25.

On July 18, Fashion Coordinates sent a letter to X confirming the order of 12 sweat suits made of the special blend at $750 per suit. Fashion also stated that delivery would be made by October 16.

X received the letter the next day.

On July 26, Fashion sent a letter to X stating that Y's shipment of the special blend would be delayed two weeks. Fashion promised to deliver the sweat suits by October 30.

X received the letter that day but made no reply.

On August 20, Fashion received the special material from Y and paid Y $3,000. Fashion then cut the material to X's specifications.

On October 18, Fashion called X and told him that eight of the sweat suits were finished and that the others would be done by October 25.

X replied: "I don't need them anymore; the players are on strike, so my order is canceled."

On October 19, Fashion notified X that the four remaining sweat suits would not be manufactured and that the eight suits already made would be sold.

Fashion then sold the eight sweat suits to a volleyball team for $4,000, the highest obtainable price. Fashion incurred shipping costs of $500 in connection with the resale.

By not completing the last four sweat suits, Fashion saved $2,000. Fashion sold the remaining special blend for $100.

Fashion sued X for breach of contract and moved for summary judgment.

X argued that Fashion is not entitled to summary judgment because: (1) an enforceable contract between X and Fashion Coordinates did not exist, and (2) Fashion is not entitled to recover damages because it breached the contract by not delivering the sweat suits by October 16.

You have been asked to prepare a memorandum of law on the following issues: (a) X's arguments that Fashion Coordinates is not entitled to summary judgment, and (b) what damages Fashion will be able to recover if summary judgment is granted in favor of Fashion.

QUESTION 92

Tom, an employee of Ace Burglar Alarm Company, joined with Ned and Peter to steal paintings and cash from the New York Art Museum.

On April 20, Tom, Ned, and Peter drove to the museum in Peter's car. Peter remained in the car as lookout while Tom and Ned opened a window and deactivated the burglar alarm. Tom had memorized the alarm code while at work. Tom and Ned overpowered Wally, the night watchman, injuring him when they tied him up.

Tom and Ned removed five paintings and a bag full of cash from the museum. They placed the bag in the back seat of Peter's car and put the paintings and Wally in the trunk.

The three then drove away only to be stopped at a roadblock set up to stop every vehicle to check driver sobriety, driver licenses, and vehicle registrations.

The policeman, Jack, asked to see Peter's license and registration. Jack, having already been alerted that the New York Art Museum had been burglarized, noticed the leather bag, marked "New York Art Museum," on the back seat. Jack reached through the window and removed the bag. Jack opened the bag and found the cash.

He then placed Tom, Ned, and Peter under arrest. Jack removed the keys from the ignition and opened the trunk, where he found Wally and the paintings.

Tom, Ned, and Peter were indicted on the following charges: burglary in the second degree, robbery in the second degree, and kidnapping in the second degree.

As an assistant district attorney, you are asked to prepare a memorandum on the following questions:

(1)   Is there sufficient evidence to satisfy the elements of the three crimes?

(2)   Should the court suppress the following evidence:

   (a)   The bag from the back seat of the car; and

   (b)   The five paintings taken from the trunk?

QUESTION 93

In 1972, Tom and Jane were married in Manhattan, where they still reside. Their son Joe was born in 1989. In June 1997, Tom moved out and Tom and Jane agreed to separate. Tom made payments to Jane for the support of Jane and Joe. In 1997, Tom ran his own delicatessen and made $100,000 a year, while Jane worked in an employment agency and made $30,000 a year.

In October 1997, Jane brought an action for annulment, claiming that Tom had defrauded her. At the trial, Jane argued that Tom had promised to convert to her religion and that she relied on this when she married him. Tom kept postponing the conversion and finally in July 1995, he told Jane that even though he had intended to convert when he made the original promise, he later changed his mind and would never convert.

At the end of the trial, Tom moved to dismiss Jane's complaint, and Jane cross-moved for a judgment of annulment and for equitable distribution of the marital assets. The court (1) dismissed Jane's complaint, and (2) denied Jane's motion for equitable distribution.

In December 1997, Tom and Jane agreed upon a duly executed separation agreement in which Tom would pay Jane $200 a week for her maintenance and $100 a week for Joe's support. The agreement also stated that the marital property would be divided equally and that if either party sought a divorce, the agreement would be incorporated but not merged into any judgment of divorce.

In January 1999, Jane brought an action for divorce based upon their having lived apart for over one year pursuant to the separation agreement. Tom opposed the action. Jane also brought a motion pendente lite for an order granting her temporary maintenance of $350 per week, claiming that she was in serious financial need. Tom opposed this, claiming that he had complied with the separation agreement by paying her the agreed-upon amounts. The court (3) denied Jane's motion.

At the trial it was shown that Jane and Tom lived separate and apart since December 1997. Jane and Tom substantially complied with the separation agreement except that on January 18, they cohabited. At the end of the trial, the court (4) granted Jane a judgment of divorce.

In July 1999, Jane made a motion to increase the amount Tom was obligated to pay for the support of Joe from $100 per week to $300 per week. Jane's affidavit alleged the following:

(i)   Tom had sold his delicatessen for $400,000.

(ii)   Tom had a contract to run the delicatessen at an annual salary of $85,000 for five years.

(iii)   Tom has made timely payments to Jane for her support and the support of Joe.

(iv)   Jane continues to work for the employment agency and still makes $30,000 a year.

While Tom did not contest the above facts, he opposed Jane's motion to increase Joe's support.

(a)   Were rulings (1), (2), (3), and (4) correct?

(b)   How should the court rule on Jane's motion?

QUESTION 94

In August, Betty and Jerry, wife and husband, marketed themselves in Queens County as "great gardeners." They went door to door showing pictures of household lawns and gardens before they worked on them and after they allegedly worked on them. One hundred people in Queens gave Betty and Jerry $1,500 in advance, and upon completion of the lawn work, the client would pay the remaining $500 balance to them. Betty and Jerry then ran off with this money without ever doing any of the promised work. Betty and Jerry had successfully pulled this same scam on 50 people in Brooklyn at an earlier date.

In October, while driving through Manhattan, Jerry was arrested for reckless driving. Jerry hired Alan, an attorney, to represent him in this matter. Alan was able to get Jerry cleared of the reckless driving charge. However, the Queens police, having heard of Jerry's arrest for reckless driving, went to the Big Apple and brought Betty and Jerry back to Queens in separate police vehicles. After each was properly read *Miranda* rights, both gave written confessions to the Queens scam. Neither Betty nor Jerry requested counsel at any time. They were both placed in lineups and were identified as the two who ran the "Queens lawn scam."

Betty and Jerry then were both charged with grand larceny. Thereafter Jerry again hired Alan to represent him in this matter.

The Queens County District Attorney is threatening to use evidence of the "Brooklyn lawn scam" at Jerry's and Betty's trials. The Queens D.A. has accurately stated that the Brooklyn police have plenty of evidence against Betty and Jerry for the Brooklyn scam, but the Brooklyn police had not been able to locate Betty or Jerry to charge them with this crime.

Alan moves to suppress (1) the written confessions, (2) the lineups and identifications, and (3) the Brooklyn scam from evidence.

You are the trial judge on this case. What are your rulings on Alan's motions based on the above?

QUESTION 95

In February 1995, Thomas decided to make his will and visited the office of his lawyer and close friend, Larry. Thomas's will provides the following wishes, gifts, and bequests:

(1)   Larry shall serve as executor of the estate;

(2)   Larry shall receive $25,000 cash;

(3) $200,000 cash into a trust, the income to my wife Sue for life; remainder to the Red Cross;

(4) $100,000 cash outright to Sue; and

(5)   The remainder and residue of my estate to Danny, a close friend, since Sue and I have no children or living relatives.

Thomas signed his signature at the end of the will, in front of Larry, and then Larry signed the will as a witness. Thomas then walked down the street to an auto parts store, folded the will in such a way that only Thomas's name was visible, and had two delivery drivers sign the document.

Thomas died on December 5, 2000, of a heart attack. At the time of his death, Thomas's net estate was valued at $600,000. The will was found in Thomas's safety deposit box on December 8, cut neatly into two pieces. Along with the pieces of the will was an intact, properly executed attorney/executor disclosure form signed by Thomas and acknowledged by two witnesses.

Stanley, a friend of Thomas, stated that Thomas told him that he accidentally cut the will in half but did not redraft it because it would unnecessarily infringe upon Larry's time.

On December 10, Donna's guardian came forward with a letter dated June 5, written to Donna from Thomas. Thomas stated in the letter in part, "I know that you are my daughter, and I am sorry that we had never spent any time together. I know that you will grow to be a fine young person. I am sorry that you were raised without a father."

You are the presiding judge over this matter and must decide how Thomas's estate should be allocated. (1) Discuss all relevant issues. (2) Assume that the will is admitted to probate as is; who takes what under the will?

QUESTION 96

Daff Duck, the mayor of New York, purchased a two-seat mini-car for his son Porky on his 13th birthday. The mini-car's top speed is 35 miles per hour. Porky has never driven any type of motor vehicle, and his father believed that it was time for him to learn. A day after receiving the mini-car, Porky and his 12-year-old buddy, Elmer, were carefully operating the vehicle in Porky's backyard. Without any negligence on their part, the mini-car raced at top speed into the side of Daff's house, seriously injuring both boys. The accident was caused by the grossly negligent design of the gas pedal. Acme Corporation designed, manufactured, and sold the mini-car.

Bugs, Daff's wife and Porky's mother, instituted a suit against Daff for Porky's injuries. Elmer's father, Yosemite, sued Acme for Elmer's injuries.

(1)   Should the trial judge hold the defendants liable? Explain.

Will, a writer for the *New York Lamp* newspaper, wrote an article stating that Daff has close ties to the mob and is an unloved father. Will got his information from an undisclosed source. A year and a half later, another newspaper, the *Day*, bought the rights to Will's story from the *Lamp* and republished Will's article without Will's knowledge or consent.

The story is false, and Daff is now so mad that he timely sued the *Day* for defamation.

(2)   What are the rights and liabilities of Daff and the *Day*?

QUESTION 97

Hap, a New York state domiciliary, age 20, was a brilliant student at a college in Vermont and had a promising career as a professional athlete.

In December, while driving to school along a New York highway, Hap was struck in his car by a vehicle operated by John, a New Jersey resident. John's vehicle was owned by Mary, also a New Jersey resident, who insured and registered the vehicle in her home state. John drove Mary's car with her permission.

The force from the collision knocked Hap's car into a guardrail, which was installed, owned, and maintained by New York State. Due to erosion, the guardrail gave way, resulting in Hap's car hitting a nearby tree.

Hap was transported to a hospital in Albany where he handwrote a will. After signing the will, Hap died.

Prepare a memorandum addressing the following issues:

(1) Is Hap's will valid, and should it be admitted to probate?

(2) What causes of action can be instituted on behalf of Hap?

(3) Are Mary and John subject to legal action instituted in New York?

(4) In what court(s) should the actions be brought?

QUESTION 98

On October 15, Bill, a manufacturer of toy missiles in Albany, New York, telephoned Hillary, a large volume plastics wholesaler who was also located in Albany. During this conversation Bill ordered 6,000 sheets of plastic at an agreed-upon price of $2 per sheet, for a total of $12,000. Delivery was to be made by truck at Bill's Albany plant on December 15. Bill then proceeded to immediately send out a form purchase order which stated the agreed-upon terms. He received a signed confirmation from Hillary a few days later. On October 15, Hillary could have purchased the required plastic at a market price of $1.50 per sheet.

By November 15, the cost of purchasing plastic had risen to $2.50 per sheet. At that time, Hillary telephoned Bill and informed him of the increase in cost to her of the purchase of the material. She further informed Bill that due to the increased price she might not be able to fill Bill's order at $2 per sheet. Hillary asked Bill to agree to a price increase to $3 per sheet. Bill told Hillary, "I'm not happy about this, but I'm really in a bind and need that plastic, so I agree to $3 per sheet." Neither Bill nor Hillary put this new agreement in writing.

In anticipation of her need for plastic sheeting to fill Bill's order, Hillary purchased a large quantity of plastic sheeting from her supplier at $2.50 per sheet.

During the last week of November, the market price of plastic declined sharply. This event prompted Bill to call Hillary and complain that: "You got me to agree to a higher price, and now I see that the market price has gone down." Hillary replied that she was very sorry, but when Bill had agreed to pay $3 per sheet she had purchased the necessary material for $2.50 per sheet and now could not afford to sell it for less than the $3 per sheet that they had agreed upon. Bill replied that he had been forced into the higher price by Hillary, and that since she "had nothing in writing" he was not going to purchase the plastic from her. Hillary made no attempt to deliver the plastic to Bill.

Hillary's attorney wrote to Bill to notify him that he was in breach of contract.

Bill's attorney replied that Bill was not bound to buy the plastic at $3 per sheet because: (1) Hillary had coerced Bill into agreeing to the price adjustment; (2) there was no consideration for the price adjustment; and (3) the Statute of Frauds bars recovery of the $3 price. Bill's attorney further contended that even if the modified contract was valid, (4) Hillary cannot recover due to her failure to tender delivery of the plastic.

Discuss the validity of each of the numbered assertions made by Bill's attorney.

QUESTION 99

In 1976, three months after their marriage, Bruce and Patty purchased a home in Queens County, New York. They took title to this property, Fairacre, as husband and wife.

Patty, who had been an associate in a law firm, decided to start her own practice in 1979. Needing office space, she entered into a written lease with Larry, who owned an office building in Queens. The lease period was for 10 years beginning June 1, 1979, and ending May 31, 1989. The rent was to be paid monthly at $1,500 per month. The lease also included an option to renew for another 10-year period upon written notice mailed to Larry at a specified address no later than one year prior to the expiration of the lease. The rent for the renewal term would be $2,000 per month. The lease stated that any improvements made to the office space would become the sole property of Larry at the end of the lease term.

Patty set about her law practice and in so doing built floor-to-ceiling mahogany bookcases attached to the office walls, installed new electrical systems for computers and other office equipment, and added a full kitchen and bath due to the long hours she and her staff worked.

Happy with her surroundings, on May 15, 1988, Patty sent, by certified mail, a written notice of her intent to exercise her option to renew the lease. Patty sent this notice to Larry's attorney whom she knew professionally and to whom she had sent all other communications regarding the lease for the past several years. Upon reviewing her lease in June, Patty realized her error and sent written notice directly to Larry, who refused to renew the option, stating that it had not been exercised on time.

Due to the refusal, Patty commenced an action in supreme court, Queens County, seeking a declaratory judgment that she had effectively exercised her option to renew.

In the bench trial that followed, the above facts were established along with the fact that no other comparable office space was available and that Larry had made no efforts to relet the office. The court (1) ruled that despite Patty's failure to give timely notice in the manner specified, she had effectively exercised her renewal option.

Due to Patty's long hours of devotion to the law, she and Bruce found themselves increasingly unhappy in their marriage. Because of this they entered into a written separation agreement, and in May 1987, Patty moved into her own apartment. In March 1990, Bruce was granted a divorce based on the 1987 separation agreement. In the divorce, the court granted Bruce exclusive possession of Fairacre until March 1992, at which time Fairacre was to be sold, with the proceeds of the sale to be divided between Patty and Bruce.

Several months after the decree, Patty wished to purchase a condominium. She asked Bruce if he would consider selling Fairacre so that she could make the down payment on the condominium. Bruce refused. Patty then began an action for partition of Fairacre in supreme court,

Queens County. Bruce moved for summary judgment on the ground that Patty was not entitled to partition until the expiration of Bruce's two-year period of exclusive possession. The court (2) denied Bruce's motion.

Were the numbered rulings correct?

QUESTION 100

Mary owned a home in Rockland County, New York. The home was surrounded by a tremendous lawn, half of which was located in Rockland County and the other half of which was located in adjoining State A. On May 1, 1995, Mary purchased a new riding lawn mower from Hal's Lawn Mower Company ("HAL") in Suffern, New York. HAL is a New York corporation. Mow N' Ride Inc. ("MOW") manufactured the lawn mower and is incorporated in State B. Mary used the mower for the next two years for cutting her lawn without a mishap.

On July 1, 1998, Mary was operating the mower on the portion of her lawn located in State A when the blade on the machine spun out of control and severely injured Mary.

On October 1, 1998, Mary began an action against HAL and MOW in the supreme court, Rockland County, claiming damages for personal injuries in the amount of $1 million. Mary alleged in her complaint causes of action against MOW for manufacturing and marketing defects and against HAL for selling a mower containing a design defect that caused injury. Negligence was not alleged against either HAL or MOW.

HAL's answer contained a general denial and the affirmative defense that the suit was barred by a four-year statute of limitations in New York. MOW's answer contained only a general denial.

HAL made a timely motion to dismiss Mary's complaint on the grounds that HAL, as a retail seller, could not be held liable for a design defect; Mary moved to strike HAL's affirmative defense. The court (1) denied HAL's motion and (2) granted Mary's motion.

At trial, MOW moved the court to take judicial notice of and apply the law of State A, which would limit Mary's recovery to $200,000. Mary opposed MOW's motion, stating that New York law should apply. The court (3) denied MOW's motion and ruled that New York law applied.

Were the numbered rulings correct?

QUESTION R-1

Molly and Joe were married in 1983 in Niagara Falls, New York. In 1987, Molly conceived a child, fathered by another man, with whom she had a brief affair. After the child was born,

Molly admitted to Joe that he was not the child's father. Joe forgave Molly and agreed to raise the child as his son. They decided to name the child Tim and to keep secret the fact that Joe was not Tim's biological father. They listed Joe as Tim's father on his birth certificate.

In 1995, Molly and Joe began to have matrimonial problems and decided to separate. They entered into a separation agreement which recited that Tim was a child of their marriage and provided that Joe would have custody of Tim and that Molly would have regular visitation with Tim three days a week, and on designated holidays. The agreement provided that Joe would not move beyond 40 miles from Niagara Falls, New York, where they both resided, without court approval, until Tim was 18. The agreement was signed and acknowledged in January 1996.

→ separation agreement valid.

In March 1997, Molly went to see Parker, an attorney, in order to get a divorce. She gave Parker the original signed separation agreement and told him that both she and Joe had abided by its terms and that they had been separated since it was signed. Parker told her that his fee would be $150 per hour, and that there would be a $4,000 nonrefundable retainer. Molly orally agreed to the terms of the retainer and gave Parker $4,000. *→ retainer must be in writing.*

In April 1997, Parker filed the separation agreement in the Niagara County Clerk's Office. In June 1997, Parker commenced an action for divorce by Molly against Joe based on the separation agreement. Joe did not contest the divorce. Upon due proof of the above relevant facts, a judgment of divorce was granted. The judgment incorporated the terms of the separation agreement and referred any future issues as to custody, visitation, or support to Family Court.

Parker sent Molly a bill, marked paid in full, which showed that he had spent 10 hours working on her divorce. No portion of the retainer was returned to Molly. *→ must return unused part of retainer*

After he and Molly separated, Joe returned to school, and he has now received a master's degree in finance. In June 2000, Joe was offered a high paying job as an analyst at an investment firm in Florida.

Joe filed a petition in Family Court for modification of the divorce judgment to allow him to move to Florida and take Tim. Molly opposed Joe's petition, asserting that Joe is not Tim's biological father, and seeking an order requiring blood testing to disprove Joe's paternity. Molly has never before told anyone that Joe is not Tim's biological father, and Molly and Joe have always held Tim out as Joe's son in every way. The court precluded Molly from offering any evidence contesting Joe's paternity and denied Molly's request for blood testing. *→ Parent by estoppel*

A hearing was then conducted on Joe's petition. At the hearing, Joe testified that he has made arrangements for Tim to attend an excellent school in Florida. Tim presently attends a school where funding is low and the academic achievement of the students is below the state average. He further testified that he is planning to remarry, and that his fiancee, an attorney who already lives and works in Florida, has developed a close relationship with Tim and has two sons who have become good friends with Tim.

Joe acknowledged that the proposed move will disrupt Molly's visitation with Tim and will deprive her of the regular and meaningful access to him she has always enjoyed. He testified, however, that he is willing to send Tim for frequent visits with Molly and that the income he will be earning will allow him to do that. He also indicated that he will send Tim to visit Molly on all holidays and school vacations during which she wishes to have visitation, and will cooperate fully in ensuring Molly's continuing nurturing relationship with Tim.

Joe admitted that there is no health or economic necessity for the move, and acknowledged that he would have employment opportunities in the Niagara Falls area. He testified, however, that the jobs available to him in the Niagara Falls area would not offer him the same economic advantages as the job he has been offered in Florida, and staying in the Niagara Falls area will disrupt his marriage plans.

Molly testified that she has been an active participant in decisions regarding Tim's care and upbringing. She further testified that Tim is very close to her parents and to her siblings and their children, who all live in the Niagara Falls area.

The court denied Joe's petition on the ground that no exceptional circumstances were presented justifying the relocation. Joe has now appealed from that ruling.

(1) Was the retainer agreement Parker made with Molly proper, and was Parker entitled to retain the $4,000?

(2) Was the judgment of divorce properly granted?

(3) Did the court correctly preclude Molly from denying Joe's paternity of Tim and deny Molly's application for blood testing?

(4) Should Joe succeed on his appeal?

QUESTION R-2

Cole, a wealthy widow, called one of her closest friends, Attorney Walker, an experienced probate attorney, to have him prepare a will on her behalf. When Walker went to Cole's home to discuss the terms of her will, he learned that Cole wanted him to receive a specific bequest of $100,000 from her $10 million estate because of their longtime friendship. Walker told Cole that he could not ethically accept a bequest from her under any circumstances because he was her attorney. Cole acceded to Walker's wishes, and the will which Walker drafted for her review and signature made no bequest to Walker. The will provided that after certain specific bequests were made, the residue of Cole's estate was bequeathed to CO, a properly qualified charitable organization. Cole executed the will immediately after stating to Walker and two of his secretaries that the instrument she was about to sign was her will. Walker signed the attestation clause while Cole and the two secretaries were still in his office. Two days later, both secretaries signed attestation clauses.

Two years later, Cole had occasion to speak with her cousin, Nelson, who was also a lawyer. Cole shared with Nelson her disappointment that her friend Walker believed that he could not be a beneficiary of any portion of her estate. Nelson advised Cole that he did not agree with Walker's conclusion. Nelson said that he would be happy to prepare a codicil to her will which included a bequest to Walker. Cole requested that Nelson do so, and shortly thereafter she went to Nelson's office, where he presented a codicil to Cole for her review. The codicil provided for a specific bequest of $100,000 "to Walker, or his issue in equal shares *per stirpes*" and $10,000 to Nelson himself. The codicil specifically affirmed every other provision of the first will drafted by Walker. When Cole reviewed the codicil, she questioned Nelson about the bequest to himself, and he indicated that he included the bequest in lieu of submitting a bill to her for his services in drafting the codicil. After hearing Nelson's explanation, Cole agreed to sign the codicil. Cole declared to Nelson and two of his paralegals that she intended the document to be a codicil to her will. The two paralegals, one of whom was a notary public, duly executed the attestation clauses in the presence of Cole. Nelson did not sign an attestation clause.

Following the death of Cole in New York, her will and codicil were offered for probate by her nominated executor in the county where she had been domiciled. A true copy of the will and codicil were provided to all of the beneficiaries and to all of Cole's distributees. Walker died before Cole. Walker was survived by two sons, Dick and Bryan, and a daughter, Diane. His other son, Ira, predeceased him. Ira left three daughters surviving him.

An officer of CO, the residuary legatee, knowing that both Walker and Nelson were attorneys, contacted the office of the attorney general to see if the attorney general could look into the probate application which had been submitted. The attorney general's office objected to the bequests to both attorneys in the codicil. Dave, a distributee who was not a beneficiary, objected to the probate of the will because of the absence of contemporaneous signature of the attestation clause and to the codicil because the codicil was witnessed by only two persons.

Attorney Nelson, appearing *pro se* at the return of the probate petition, objected to the standing of the attorney general to raise objections to the bequests to Walker and Nelson.

You are the law clerk to the Surrogate, and she has asked you to comment on the following questions:

(1) Should Dave's objections to the probate of the will or the codicil be sustained?

(2) Is there any issue concerning the propriety of the bequest to:

(a) Walker?

(b) Nelson?

(3) Does the attorney general have standing to raise objections in this Surrogate's Court proceeding?

(4) What share, if any, will Ira's children receive from Cole's estate?

QUESTION R-3

In 1997, Luke, a lawyer, prepared wills for Herb and Wendy, husband and wife, which they duly executed. In those wills Herb and Wendy each named the other as primary beneficiary and executor.

In 2000, Herb and Wendy, by mutual agreement, began living separate and apart, but they did not sign a written separation agreement.

In 2001, Herb duly executed a new will, prepared by Luke at Herb's request. The new will gave Herb's entire estate to his son, Seth, and named Luke as executor and Seth as alternate or successor executor.

Herb and Wendy continued to live separate and apart until Herb died on January 25, 2002, survived by Seth and Wendy. Luke plans to present a petition to the Surrogate's Court asking that Herb's 2001 will be admitted to probate and that Luke be appointed executor. Wendy, having learned of the existence and provisions of the 2001 will, has asked Luke what rights she might have in Herb's estate.

Herb's estate, after payment of all debts, administration expenses, and funeral expenses, consists of (i) investments in Herb's name alone valued at $300,000; (ii) investments purchased by Herb in the names of Herb and Wendy as joint tenants with right of survivorship valued at $120,000; (iii) money deposited in a savings account in the name of Herb in trust for Seth with a balance of $90,000; and (iv) a life insurance policy payable to Seth as the named beneficiary having proceeds of $120,000.

(1) May Luke advise Wendy regarding her rights in Herb's estate?

(2) Assuming Herb's 2001 will is admitted to probate, what rights, if any, will Wendy have in Herb's estate?

(3) If Luke serves as executor of Herb's estate, may he receive a full executor's commission in addition to receiving attorneys' fees?

QUESTION R-4

Mal and Sal formed Mal and Sal, P.C. ("the P.C."), for the purpose of conducting a law practice. The P.C. hired Bonnie as an associate in 1995. In 2000, Mal was indicted for his role in an insurance fraud scheme and entered into a misdemeanor plea agreement with the district attorney. Mal anticipated that a disciplinary proceeding resulting from his criminal conduct would likely result in a suspension from the practice of law for at least one year. On May 1, 2001, Mal asked Bonnie to continue working for the firm at an annual salary of $60,000 until the conclusion of any disciplinary proceeding against Mal and then during the period of any suspension. Bonnie orally agreed to do so.

Mal was suspended for two years beginning January 1, 2002. After commencement of the suspension, Mal continued to be involved in the law practice by coming into the office and meeting with clients. On February 1, 2002, Bonnie told Mal that such conduct by Mal was unlawful and that she would not participate in it. Mal then told Bonnie that her employment was terminated.

Bonnie commenced an action against Mal and the P.C. for breach of contract by filing and serving a summons and complaint alleging the foregoing pertinent facts. In her complaint, Bonnie specifically alleged that the contract was breached (i) because her employment was terminated before the expiration of its term and, in the alternative, (ii) because the basis for the termination of her employment constituted a breach of an implied term that both parties would comply with the prevailing ethical standards of the legal profession. Mal and the P.C. both timely moved to dismiss the action on the grounds that (a) the complaint failed to state a cause of action on either alleged theory of breach of contract, and (b) the statute of frauds was a defense. The court (1) denied the motion.

After timely serving the answer, Mal moved for summary judgment dismissing the action as to him on the ground that he was not personally liable on the contract. When the motion was heard, the parties provided the court with proof of the foregoing pertinent facts. The court (2) denied Mal's motion.

Were the numbered rulings correct?

QUESTION R-5

In the early morning of May 20, 2002, a fire destroyed a restaurant owned by Chef. Detective Drake of the arson squad investigated the fire, and determined that the fire had been deliberately set using gasoline. An empty gasoline can was found on the premises, and the fingerprints of Arnie, a known arsonist, were found on the can.

Detective Drake picked Arnie up for questioning. Arnie admitted to Detective Drake that he set the fire. He told Detective Drake that Chef had hired him to burn down the restaurant and had paid him $5,000 after he did so.

Arnie agreed to testify against Chef in exchange for a plea to a reduced charge. Arnie then appeared and testified before the grand jury. Thereafter, Chef was indicted for the crime of arson in the third degree.

At trial, the prosecution presented Arnie, who testified that he set the fire; that he was hired and paid $5,000 to do so by Chef; and that he was testifying in exchange for a reduced plea. The prosecution also presented proof that Chef sold some of his restaurant equipment for $5,000 a few days before the fire and that he had recently increased the insurance on the restaurant. Out of the presence of the jury, the prosecution offered the testimony of Owl, an undercover officer, who testified that Chef had recently approached him and attempted to hire him to burn down Chef's home. Chef has not been charged with any crime with respect to those allegations. On Chef's objection, the trial judge ruled that the proposed testimony of Owl was inadmissible.

At the close of the prosecution's case, Chef moved to dismiss the indictment on the grounds that (a) even if the facts testified to at trial were accepted as true, he could not properly be convicted of the crime of arson because no proof was offered that he set the fire; and (b) in any event, he could not be convicted on the evidence presented by the prosecution.

(1) Was the court's ruling excluding the testimony of Owl correct?

(2) How should the court rule as to grounds (a) and (b) of Chef's motion to dismiss the indictment against him?

QUESTION R-6

Ann and John had been married for 25 years at the time of their separation in 1994. They had two children, both of whom were over 21 years of age at the time Ann and John separated.

In September 1996, Ann and John entered into a valid separation agreement which required John to make maintenance payments of $1,500 per month "until the death or remarriage of the wife." The agreement provided that it was to be "binding upon the heirs, legal representatives and assigns of both parties." Both parties expressly waived "any right of election" with respect to the estate of the other. The separation agreement, by its express terms, was to survive, and not merge with, any subsequent divorce decree.

The agreement also provided that Ann receive a $100,000 mortgage from John on Greenacre, a parcel of real property owned by John individually, as security for John's maintenance obligation. The agreement provided that the mortgage was to "survive the death of John." In November 1996, in accordance with the agreement, John signed a duly drawn mortgage which contained no acknowledgment. A year later, John borrowed $50,000 from Lender, and as security for the loan gave a duly executed mortgage on Greenacre to Lender, which was recorded in November 1997.

John and Ann were duly divorced in 1998. John died in June 2002. His last will, executed in 1982, named Ann as his executrix and as the residuary beneficiary of his estate.

Ann has come to your office inquiring about her rights and has posed the following questions to you:

(1)   Does she have a right to maintenance payments after John's death?

(2)   Assuming she has a right to maintenance payments after John's death, what rights does she have with respect to Greenacre as related to: (a) John's estate; and (b) Lender?

(3)   Can she serve as John's executrix and/or inherit from his estate?

QUESTION R-7

On June 6, 2000, Paul and his wife, Mary, checked into the new Lazy Day Motel, in the Town of Erie, New York. In the afternoon, Mary left the motel to visit a nearby shopping center. Paul remained in their room at the motel to take a nap.

When Mary returned from the shopping center, the motel was in flames, and the Erie Fire Department was trying to put out the fire. Mary told the fire captain that her husband was asleep in their room, whereupon two firemen broke into Paul's room and rescued Paul, who sustained serious and disfiguring injuries from the fire.

An investigation by the Erie Fire Department established that the fire started because the motel's electrical wiring had been defectively installed in the Lazy Day Motel in violation of the Town of Erie Building Code. The Town of Erie building inspector, who was charged by statute with the duty of inspecting the motel's electrical wiring, had failed to discover the defective installation and had issued a certificate of occupancy which permitted the motel to operate. In addition, the alarm system, which would have warned motel occupants of the fire in time to escape injury, did not function because it had been defectively manufactured.

The alarm system had been purchased from Fire Corp., a Nevada corporation, which had its only place of business in Nevada. Dave, the owner of the Lazy Day Motel, on a trip through Nevada, saw the system at Fire Corp.'s showroom and told representatives of Fire Corp. that he would consider using it in a motel then under construction in Erie, New York. Shortly thereafter, a representative of Fire Corp. called Dave to inquire whether he was still interested in using Fire Corp.'s alarm system, and upon receiving an affirmative answer, Fire Corp. sent a purchase order to Dave. The purchase order, which provided for a cash price of $15,000, was executed by Dave and sent back to Nevada, where it was countersigned by a representative of Fire Corp. A month later, Fire Corp. shipped its alarm system to Dave, F.O.B. Nevada, and upon receipt it was installed in the Lazy Day Motel.

After duly serving a notice of claim on the Town of Erie, Paul commenced an action in Erie County Supreme Court against Dave, the Town of Erie, and Fire Corp., to recover damages for his injuries. Dave and the Town of Erie were served with the summons and complaint in New York. Fire Corp. was served with the summons and complaint by an authorized process server at Fire Corp.'s office in Nevada.

Prior to answering Paul's complaint, Fire Corp. timely moved to dismiss the complaint against it based upon lack of jurisdiction. The court (1) denied the motion. The Town of Erie moved to dismiss the complaint against it for failure to state a cause of action. The court (2) denied the motion.

At the start of the jury trial, Paul's attorney moved for an order precluding the defendants from offering any proof before the jury that Paul's medical expenses had been fully paid by Paul's insurance company. The court (3) granted the motion.

Were the numbered rulings correct?

QUESTION R-8

Pat, Iz, and Pete, New York residents, were equal partners in PIP Manor, a catering business. PIP Manor had no written partnership agreement. It owned a building and three cars, one of which was used exclusively by Iz. Iz also worked individually as a party planner, operating "Izquisite Affairs", a sole proprietorship.

In January 2002, Iz died intestate, survived by his wife, Win, and his adult son, Sam, an attorney. Neither Win nor Sam had ever worked with Iz in either of his two businesses. At the time of his death, Iz's assets consisted of $10,000 in the "Izquisite Affairs" checking account, $150,000 in a personal savings account, and his interest in PIP Manor.

In February 2002, Sam and Win both filed petitions for letters of administration of Iz's estate. Sam claimed that he was best qualified to administer the estate. Win claimed that she, rather than Sam, should be appointed administrator of the estate. The surrogate granted letters to Win.

In her capacity as administrator, Win continued to operate "Izquisite Affairs". Due to her lack of business experience, Win used all the money in the Izquisite Affairs checking account and an additional $50,000 of the personal savings account in an unsuccessful attempt to operate "Izquisite Affairs".

Pat and Pete continued to operate PIP Manor after Iz's death and demanded that Win return Iz's car to them. Win refused to return the car and demanded that they allow her, as administrator of Iz's estate, to be substituted for Iz as a partner in PIP Manor or immediately turn over one-third of the partnership assets to the estate.

(1)   Was the Surrogate's ruling granting letters of administration to Win correct?

(2)   What are the respective rights and liabilities, if any, of Sam and Win with respect to Iz's estate?

(3)   What are the respective rights of Pat, Pete, Win, as administrator, and Iz's estate in the partnership and its assets?

QUESTION R-9

Dressco, Inc., ("Dressco") a manufacturer of dresses, is a closely held New York corporation. Until March 2002, Major, Min, and Dan were Dressco's only directors and shareholders. Major, the owner of 100 shares, was responsible for sales and business operations, while Min, who owned 50 shares, was in charge of designing the Dressco collections. Dan, the owner of the remaining 50 shares, was not involved in the day-to-day operations of Dressco but attended regularly scheduled director and shareholder meetings.

On January 2, 1990, Dressco, Major, Min and Dan signed a written agreement that provided in pertinent part:

> Upon the written request of any shareholder, Dressco shall, within sixty days of receipt of such request, purchase the shares of the requesting shareholder for $1,000 per share.

In March 2002, Dan decided to move to Florida and made a written request on Dressco for Dressco to purchase his 50 shares pursuant to the agreement. Major then reminded Dan that at the time the agreement was signed, the parties had orally agreed that the buyback provision would only apply if the corporation was making a profit on the date of the shareholder's request. As of March 2002, Dressco had not made a profit for the preceding three years. For this reason, Major told Dan that the corporation would not buy his shares.

PER

Dan duly commenced an action against Dressco for breach of contract, seeking to recover $50,000 for his shares. At trial, Al, Dan's attorney, objected when Major and Min sought to testify about the oral agreement limiting the buyback provision. The court overruled the objection and permitted the testimony. After hearing their testimony, Al decided that it would be in Dan's best interest to settle the case. Although Dan was not present in court and Al was not able to reach Dan to discuss the settlement, Al entered into a written stipulation with Dressco's attorney, settling the case for $7,000.

can't settle w/o client's consent

Co-mingling In October, Major started to neglect Dressco's business, wrote company checks to pay his personal expenses, and stopped paying Dressco's rent and electric bills. When Min questioned Major about his actions, Major told Min that Dressco belonged to him and that he could do whatever he wanted with the business. Since that time Major has refused to discuss company business with Min, to give Min any financial statements, or to hold any director or shareholder meetings. On February 3, 2003, Min filed a petition alleging the foregoing facts and seeking (a) a preliminary injunction preventing Major from wasting any corporate assets, and (b) the dissolution of Dressco.

Min owns 50 shares = 25%

Major breached duty of care.

(1) Was the court's ruling allowing the testimony of Major and Min concerning the oral agreement correct? *Parol Evidence Rule*

(2) Is Dan bound by the stipulation of settlement? *—No*

(3) Is Min entitled to (a) the preliminary injunction she seeks; or (b) the grant of her petition for dissolution of Dressco?

QUESTION R-10

Duke purchased a motorboat from Earl for $10,000. When the boat was delivered, Duke paid for it by giving Earl a $10,000 check drawn on his personal account at B Bank. At the time Duke gave Earl the check, Duke knew he had only $7,000 in his account, but he hoped to be paid on an outstanding insurance claim in time to cover the check. Earl immediately deposited the check in Earl's account at C Bank, and several days later was advised by C Bank that the check was being dishonored and returned for insufficient funds. Earl complained to Duke, and Duke explained that some funds he had expected had not arrived, but that he could make the check good in two weeks. Earl agreed to wait for two weeks before redepositing the check.

Duke was employed as an accounts payable clerk in the bookkeeping department at Acme Corp. Within a week after Duke assured Earl that he would make the check good, Duke prepared an Acme Corp. check drawn on its account at B Bank payable to Duke Corp., a nonexistent entity, in the amount of $3,000. Because Duke did not have check signing authority, he obtained by deception the signature of Acme's treasurer on the check. Duke took the check, endorsed it payable to the order of Duke, signed the endorsement, "Duke Corp., by Duke, President," and deposited the check in his personal account at B Bank.

Duke then realized that other checks he had written might clear before the check he had given to Earl so that the $3,000 deposit would not be sufficient. Duke prepared another Acme Corp. check drawn on its account at B Bank payable to Duke in the amount of $2,000. This time Duke signed the name of Acme's treasurer to the check. Duke endorsed the check and deposited it in his personal account at B Bank.

After waiting the agreed two weeks, Earl redeposited Duke's check and it cleared.

(a) Based on proof of the foregoing facts, may Duke properly be convicted of the crimes of (1) issuing a bad check, (2) larceny, or (3) forgery?

(b) May B Bank be held liable to Acme Corp for paying (1) the $3,000 check or (2) the $2,000 check?

QUESTION R-11

On December 1, 1998, in the presence of two attesting witnesses, Ted duly executed a will that contained the following provisions:

   (1) I bequeath the sum of $400,000 to my wife, Wendy.

    (2)   I bequeath my 100 shares of C Corp. to my brother, Bob.

    (3)   I bequeath my Tiffany lamp to my aunt, Ann.

    (4)   I give all the residue of my estate to my wife, Wendy.

    (5)   I appoint my friend, Ed, executor.

Immediately after Ted duly executed his will, he realized that he had inadvertently omitted a $25,000 bequest he intended to make to his mother, Mary. While still in the presence of the witnesses, Ted, in his own handwriting, inserted the bequest to Mary above his signature and above the signed attestation clause of his will.

Ted died on January 1, 2003. Ted was survived by Wendy and his only child, Debra, who was born in 2001. He was also survived by Bob, Ann, Mary, and Ed.

At his death, Ted's net estate consisted of assets worth $800,000, which included a bank account with B Bank titled, "Ted in trust for Debra," in the amount of $75,000. B Bank has paid $75,000 to Debra's duly appointed guardian.

Ted's will of December 1, 1998 was duly admitted to probate and Ed qualified as executor.

At the time of his death, Ted owned 200 shares of C Corp., consisting of 100 shares purchased by Ted in 1995 and 100 shares received by Ted in 2002 as a result of a 2-for-1 stock split. Bob has demanded the 200 shares of C Corp. Ed contends that Bob is entitled to receive only 100 shares.

Debra's guardian has asserted that Debra is entitled to receive her intestate share of Ted's estate, because she was not provided for in her father's will.

At Ted's death, it was discovered that one month earlier, Ted sold the Tiffany lamp to a local art dealer and was paid $50,000. Ann has asserted that, in lieu of the Tiffany lamp, she is entitled to receive $50,000 from Ted's estate. It is undisputed that the Tiffany lamp had a fair market value of $50,000 at Ted's death.

(a)   Is Ted's mother, Mary, entitled to receive the $25,000 bequest under Ted's will?

(b)   Is Ted's brother, Bob, entitled to receive the 200 shares of C Corp.?

(c)   Is Ted's aunt, Ann, entitled to receive $50,000 from Ted's estate?

(d)   Is Ted's daughter, Debra, entitled to receive her intestate share of Ted's estate?

QUESTION R-12

On April 15, 2000, Nathan sustained internal injuries when the car he was operating collided with a truck operated by Martin. Nathan was speeding at the time of the accident and was not wearing a seat belt. Martin received a ticket for crossing over the center line of the road, a violation of the New York State Vehicle & Traffic Law. He was found guilty of that violation after trial.

As a result of the accident, on April 20, 2000, Nathan underwent surgery performed by Dr. Scalpel ("Scalpel") for removal of his spleen. Scalpel saw Nathan for several post-surgical office visits, and discharged him on June 20, 2000. Six months later, in December 2000, Scalpel saw Nathan for an outpatient visit, at which time he removed a benign cyst from Nathan's arm which was unrelated to the accident.

In October 2002, Nathan began to experience abdominal pain and went to visit Dr. Smith ("Smith"). Smith made a provisional diagnosis, based on an x-ray, that there was a mass in Nathan's abdomen that should be removed. With Nathan under general anesthesia, Smith performed an exploratory procedure that confirmed his provisional diagnosis and removed a sponge, which had been left there by Scalpel during the April 20, 2000, surgery.

Nathan has contacted the office where you work to explore his legal rights. Yesterday (February 21, 2003), you sat in on the conference with a partner in your office. Following the conference, you are asked by the partner to provide her with a memorandum of law in which you are to focus on the following questions:

(1) (a) What are the necessary elements of any causes of action Nathan may assert against Martin?

     (b) What are the merits of any affirmative defenses that may reasonably be asserted by Martin?

(2) (a) What are the necessary elements of any causes of action Nathan may assert against Scalpel?

     (b) What are the merits of any affirmative defenses that may reasonably be asserted by Scalpel?

(3) At the trial of a personal injury action by Nathan against Martin, is Martin's traffic conviction admissible?

QUESTION R-13

Ben and Bonnie were married in Buffalo, New York, in 1975. In 1999, Ben took a new job in Albany, and he moved there with Bonnie. Ben purchased Blackacre, a one-family residence in Albany, from Owen for $200,000. Ben paid Owen $50,000 cash and orally agreed to assume the existing mortgage on the property which was held by Mort. Owen had given a note and the mortgage to Mort when Owen purchased the property in 1995. The mortgage was valid in all respects and was duly recorded. The note and mortgage were silent as to any right of Mort to accelerate the balance due upon any default. The deed to Ben, which was signed only by Owen, stated that the conveyance was subject to Mort's mortgage.

Bonnie did not like Albany and, shortly after they moved there, she commenced a course of verbal abuse toward Ben consisting of criticism, mean-spirited remarks, and belittling comments in front of family and friends. This behavior continued until July 2002 when Bonnie moved back to Buffalo, where she has since resided. She has refused Ben's requests that she return to Albany and has advised Ben that she will not live there. Ben's and Bonnie's differences are irreconcilable and irremediable. In December 2002, Ben duly commenced an action against

Bonnie for divorce on the ground of cruel and inhuman treatment or, in the alternative, for a separation on the ground of abandonment.

Ben has continued to support Bonnie, and the financial burden of maintaining two households has caused Ben to fall behind in the mortgage payments to Mort. No payment has been made to Mort since July 2002. Owen left New York after selling Blackacre to Ben, and his whereabouts are unknown. Mort duly commenced an action against Ben to foreclose the mortgage. As part of the relief sought in the complaint, Mort is demanding payment of the entire principal balance of the mortgage, alleging that the default had the effect of accelerating the mortgage debt, and that Ben is personally liable on the mortgage, in the event of any deficiency upon the foreclosure sale. No judgment of foreclosure has, as yet, been entered.

(1)   Is Ben likely to prevail at trial on (a) his cause of action for divorce based on cruel and inhuman treatment or (b) his cause of action for a separation based on abandonment?

(2)   Is Mort correct in alleging (a) that the default had the effect of accelerating the mortgage debt, and (b) that Ben is personally liable on the mortgage in the event of any deficiency upon the foreclosure sale?

QUESTION R-14

On June 3, 2003, Sarah, a shoe manufacturer located in Farmingdale, Suffolk County, entered into the following written agreement with Linda, a wholesale supplier of leather heels:

June 3, 2003

Linda agrees to sell to Sarah, and Sarah agrees to buy from Linda, 10,000 leather heels, delivery to be made on June 5, 2003, at Sarah's shoe factory, located in Farmingdale. The price shall be agreed upon by Linda and Sarah after delivery of the heels to Sarah.

(Signed) Linda
(Signed) Sarah

On June 5, Linda delivered 10,000 heels to Sarah at Sarah's shoe factory, along with a $5,000 invoice. Later that day, Sarah telephoned Linda and stated that she was accepting the heels, but she believed that the $5,000 price was excessive, and offered to pay Linda $4,000. Linda refused to accept less than $5,000.

On June 16, 2003, Sarah entered into a written contract with Anne, who owned a retail shoe store located in Albany, for the sale by Sarah to Anne of 1,000 pairs of shoes for $20,000, F.O.B. Farmingdale. On June 16, Sarah delivered the shoes to a licensed carrier in Farmingdale, notified Anne of the shipment of shoes, and sent Anne all of the necessary documents to enable Anne to obtain possession of the shoes from the carrier.

While in route to Albany, the carrier's truck was involved in an accident that totally destroyed the shoes. Upon learning of the accident, Anne immediately purchased 1,000 pairs of the identical shoes from another shoe manufacturer for $25,000, the market value of such shoes at the time, and asserted a claim against Sarah for $5,000 damages. Sarah rejected Anne's claim and demanded that Anne pay her the $20,000 contract price of the shoes. Anne refused Sarah's demand. *→ Anne is wrong.*

Sarah not a merchant w/regard to warehouse.

On May 1, 2003, Sarah entered into a duly executed written contract to sell a warehouse to Beth for $500,000. The contract provided for a down payment of $50,000, which Beth paid to Sarah upon signing the contract. The contract set a closing date of June 9, 2003, and provided that "time is of the essence." The contract contained the following provision:

→ 1/10 no consideration?
1/10 of purchase

> Buyer shall have the absolute right to cancel this contract at any time prior to closing, and, in such event, the down payment of $50,000 shall be returned to Buyer.

gives buyer lots of power, no power to seller

The contract did not grant the seller a similar right to cancel the contract, and was silent concerning remedies or damages in the event of breach. *→ no liquidated damages. —must be a reasonable forecast of damages*

On May 3, Beth learned that another warehouse was available for sale for $400,000 from a different seller, and, therefore, she decided not to buy the warehouse from Sarah. On May 9, Beth notified Sarah in writing that she was canceling the contract and demanded that Sarah promptly return the $50,000 down payment. Sarah replied that she did not consider the contract to be cancelled. On June 9, Beth did not appear at the closing, and Sarah notified Beth that she was retaining the $50,000 down payment as liquidated damages. On June 20, Sarah sold the warehouse to another buyer for $50,000.

(1)   Is there a contract between Linda and Sarah for the sale of 10,000 heels and, if so, what is the price?

(2)   What are the rights and obligations of Sarah and Anne with respect to the June 16, 2003, contract for the sale of the shoes?

(3)   (a)   In the May 1, 2003, contract for the sale of the warehouse, does the provision granting Beth the exclusive right to cancel make the contract illusory? *Yes, @ no mutuality of obligation*

      (b)   If the May 1, 2003, contract did not contain the cancellation provision, would Sarah be entitled to retain the entire $50,000 down payment? *— may be not could . excess*

QUESTION R-15

Cal was the building superintendent of an apartment building. On January 2, 2003, Cal telephoned the T Town police to report a "strange odor" coming from one of the apartments. Officer Opie responded to the call and met Cal outside the apartment building. Cal told Opie that for the past several days he had smelled a foul rotting odor coming from apartment 2A.

Cal escorted Opie into the building where Opie immediately confirmed the rotting smell that intensified as they approached apartment 2A. Opie knocked on the door, but got no response. Cal could not provide Opie with a key to the apartment but told Opie that the apartment was rented to Max and Veda Anabel. Unable to find another way in, Opie forced the apartment door open and discovered the partially decomposed body of a woman in the bedroom and a bloody knife on the floor.

The police investigation determined that the woman was Veda and that the fingerprints found on the knife belonged to Max. Shortly thereafter Max was arrested and indicted for murder. Max hired Al Attorney to represent him. Al and Max entered into a written retainer agreement that provided in pertinent part that Al's fee was $10,000, and that an additional $25,000 would be payable to Al if "Max was acquitted or found not guilty by reason of insanity."

At his arraignment, Max pled not guilty by reason of insanity. After Max's arraignment, Al timely served a motion to suppress both the knife and any testimony from Opie regarding his observations while in apartment 2A.

At the suppression hearing, Opie testified to the aforesaid pertinent facts. At the end of the hearing, Al argued that Opie's entry into the apartment without first obtaining a search warrant violated Max's Fourth Amendment rights, requiring the suppression of the knife and Opie's observations. The court (a) denied the motion.

During jury selection, Al requested that the court ask the prosecutor why she used her first seven peremptory challenges to excuse panel members who were of the same race as Max. The court refused, advising Al that the prosecutor is not required to provide reasons for exercising her peremptory challenges.

At trial, the prosecution offered testimony from Cal and Officer Opie. Over Al's objection, the court admitted the knife into evidence.

The prosecution also presented expert testimony that only Max's fingerprints were on the knife, that Veda's blood was on the knife, and that the cause of death was multiple stab wounds.

After the prosecution rested, Al moved for a trial order of dismissal based upon the prosecution's failure to offer any psychiatric evidence that Max was sane at the time of the commission of the crime. The court (b) denied the motion on the ground that Max had the burden of proof with respect to his mental condition. The defense rested without presenting any evidence.

Max was convicted of murder and timely filed a notice of appeal. Max hired a new attorney who has asserted on appeal that Max's conviction should be reversed because:

(1) The court incorrectly denied:

    (a) The motion to suppress; and

    (b) The motion to dismiss.

(2) The court failed to question the prosecutor about the use of her peremptory challenges; and

(3) Max was denied effective assistance of counsel because of the contingent retainer agreement.

How should the appellate court rule on each assertion?

QUESTION R-16

Win and Hal were married in 1990. In January 2002, Win and Hal discovered that they each had fallen in love with another person and mutually agreed to separate. Since then they have

separate living arrangement

lived separate and apart from one another. Win has been living with her boyfriend in his house, and Hal has been living with his girlfriend in her apartment. Their only child, Carl, resides with Win, who allows frequent visitation by Hal. On February 1, 2002, each signed and gave to the other a letter stating only: "To whom it may concern: My spouse and I have separated. From this day forward my spouse will not be liable for my expenses or debts, and I will not hassle my spouse about living arrangements." The parties signed no other document relating to their separation. *may not be proper, ⊕ both must sign the document*

Prior to their marriage, Hal had acquired title to Parcel A, a vacant tract of land, which he continues to own. *↗ non-marital property* *as long as spouse does not become a public charge. ↗ active appreciation)*

Also prior to their marriage, Hal had acquired title to Parcel B, which is improved by an apartment building. During their marriage, Hal and Win occupied one of the apartments as their marital residence. While they were living together, Win handled telephone calls from tenants and collected and deposited rent payments. Title to Parcel B remains in Hal. *↗ active participation by W — marital*

the building is marital

Last week Hal was personally served with a summons and complaint in a divorce action commenced by Win. The complaint alleges adultery and living separate and apart for more than one year as grounds for divorce and seeks equitable distribution of marital property and child support. *OK*

Hal has visited Lou, a lawyer, and explained the foregoing facts. In their discussion, Hal has asked Lou the following questions: *↗ condonation*

(1)   Are the grounds for divorce alleged by Win valid, and if so, does Hal have any defenses to them?

(2)   If Hal is agreeable to a divorce and defaults in answering the complaint, how might that affect him in any determination regarding (i) distribution of marital property, and (ii) child support?

(3)   To what extent, if at all, will Parcels A and B be considered marital property?

How should Lou advise Hal?

QUESTION R-17

Apple, the owner and operator of a cider mill in upstate New York, hired Renee to renovate a section of the mill to create a store to sell apple products. Renee hired Carp to lay the carpet required for the renovations. Renee supplied the carpet, but Carp selected and supplied the adhesives to be used on the job and utilized his own tools. In order to coordinate laying the carpet with other parts of the job, Renee determined what hours and where in the store Carp would work. Carp determined the methods to be utilized in preparing the premises and laying the carpet.

In May 2003, while renovations were ongoing, an explosion occurred in the mill. Evan, who was employed by Apple as a maintenance mechanic working in the mill, was knocked against a cider press by the force of the explosion, striking his head. Evan died instantly from his injuries.

An investigation revealed that Carp had carelessly knocked over a can of explosive and highly flammable carpet adhesive that he had left open in the area where he was laying the carpeting. The explosion occurred when fumes from the spilled adhesive were ignited by a space heater in the store. The fire investigator determined that the pilot light on the space heater should have been extinguished by Carp while preparing the premises before the adhesive was used. Apple told the investigator that Carp had asked him to extinguish the pilot light, but that he forgot to do so.

Evan was survived by his wife, Willie, two adult children, and a sister, Sara. Sara is disabled, and she was dependent on Evan for her support. Although Evan's children were financially independent, he often assisted them with household maintenance and car repairs.

Evan's duly executed will left his estate one-half to Willie and one-half to Sara. Willie was appointed executrix of Evan's estate.

Willie, as executrix of Evan's estate, has commenced an action against Apple, Renee and Carp seeking to recover damages for Evan's wrongful death. In her complaint, Willie asserts the foregoing facts and alleges that Apple and Carp were negligent in causing Evan's death and that Renee is liable for Carp's negligence.

Renee and Carp each answered Willie's complaint and asserted cross-claims for contribution against Apple. Apple moved to dismiss Willie's complaint and the cross-claim of Renee and Carp, alleging that, as Evan's employer, no claim could be stated against him. The court granted the motion.

(1) Were the court's rulings dismissing (a) the complaint and (b) the cross-claims for contribution against Apple correct?

(2) Is Renee liable for Carp's negligence?

(3) If Willie succeeds in recovering damages for Evan's wrongful death, what elements of damages may be recovered and to whom would such damages be paid?

QUESTION R-18

Theresa executed a will on June 11, 1990. First, she directed payment of all her outstanding debts and administrative expenses. Second, she made a specific bequest of an original portrait of her grandmother to her first cousin, Denise. Third, her residuary clause provided as follows:

All the rest, residue and remainder of my estate, real, personal or otherwise and wheresoever situate, including any bank accounts and insurance benefits (hereinafter called my "residuary estate"), shall be disposed of as follows:

> (a) If Mother shall survive me, I give, devise and bequeath my entire residuary estate to my Trustee hereinafter named, in trust, to apply so much of the income therefrom to the support and maintenance of Mother as my Trustee, in her absolute discretion, deems necessary, accumulating any balance of the income and adding the same to principal.

(b) Upon the death of Mother, the then principal shall be paid over absolutely to my longtime friend Mary, or if she shall not survive me, to her
issue surviving me, per stirpes."

Finally, the will nominated Abe as the executor and cousin Denise as trustee. Denise was also
one of the three witnesses who attested to the execution of the will by Theresa.

Mother died on July 2, 1995, predeceasing Theresa.

Theresa died on January 5, 2003, leaving her cousin Denise and another first cousin, Robert, as
her only surviving distributees.

On May 1, 2003, the will was admitted to probate. After being granted Letters Testamentary,
Abe petitioned the court for a construction of Theresa's will. Abe contends that Theresa's intent,
under subpart (a) of the residuary clause, was to create a trust for the benefit of Mother, only if
Mother survived her, and that the residuary estate should be paid over to Mary because Mother
predeceased Theresa.

Cousin Robert filed an answer to the construction petition, alleging that subpart (a) of the residuary clause created a trust if, and only if, Mother survived Theresa and that any remainder interest
Mary had in the principal of the trust was contingent upon Mother's survival of Theresa. Robert
asserts that the residuary should therefore be distributed pursuant to the laws of intestate succes-
sion. Robert also asserts that Denise, as a witness to the will, is disqualified from receiving any
benefit under the will.

Theresa owned a life insurance policy insuring her life. The named beneficiary on the policy was
Robert. Abe contends that because Theresa specifically included "insurance benefits" as part of
her residuary estate, the proceeds of that policy should be payable to Mary. Robert claims the
proceeds are payable entirely to him. The policy provided that policyholders could change their
beneficiary designations "by written request filed at the Home Office of the Insurance Company." Theresa never filed her will or any form designating a change of beneficiary with the
Insurance Company.

You are a law clerk for the surrogate court judge who asks you to write a memorandum outlining the principles to be applied and the decision that should be reached on the following questions:

(a) How should Theresa's residuary estate be distributed?

(b) To whom should the proceeds of the life insurance policy be paid?

(c) What, if anything, is Denise entitled to receive from Theresa's estate?

QUESTION R-19

Paul, a New York resident, was driving through an intersection in New York City when his car
was struck by a car driven by Dan. At the time of the collision, Dan was speeding and had run a
red light. As a result of the collision, Paul's car was pushed onto the sidewalk, striking Walker, a
pedestrian.

Shortly after the accident, Officer Ike interviewed Paul, Dan, and Walker. Officer Ike's accident report noted that Dan's vehicle was registered in State X and insured by AutoCo, a State X company that does business in New York, but that Dan's driver's license listed a New York address.

Walker declined medical assistance at the scene, but later went to her doctor complaining of a headache. The doctor examined Walker, ran some medical tests, and charged Walker $500. Walker had no health insurance and paid the doctor $500 in cash. Walker has timely filed a claim with Paul's automobile insurance carrier, seeking reimbursement for her medical expenses.

Complaining of neck and back pain, Paul was taken by ambulance to the hospital, where he was examined and released. No diagnostic tests were performed on Paul. He later went to his doctor for treatment. Paul did not miss any time from work as a result of the accident.

In his application to AutoCo for insurance, Dan misrepresented that he resided at, and would garage his car at, his mother's State X address. AutoCo always sent Dan's insurance premium bills to the State X address. Upon receipt of the police accident recport, AutoCo retroactively canceled Dan's insurance based on the misrepresentations made by Dan in his application. Dan commenced an action in New York against AutoCo seeking a declaratory judgment that his policy was in effect at the time of the accident, because New York law does not permit retroactive cancelation of automobile insurance policies. AutoCo's defense is that State X law permits retroactive cancelation, if the cancelation is based on a misrepresentation that was material to the risk when assumed. During discovery, Dan admitted that although he was a New York resident, he stated in his application for insurance that he was a State X resident who would garage his car in State X.

In January 2004, Paul duly commenced an action against Dan in supreme court to recover damages for his personal injuries caused by Dan's negligence. Dan's attorney had Paul examined by a physician retained by Dan, who submitted an affidavit which stated that although Paul complained of neck and back pain, there were no objective physical findings to corroborate those complaints.

After discovery was complete, Dan moved for summary judgment on the ground that Paul had not suffered a serious injury as defined by New York law. Dan's motion papers included the affidavit of the physician retained by Dan, and Paul's deposition testimony that he missed no time from work as a result of the accident. In opposition to Dan's motion, Paul submitted an affidavit from his doctor, which noted Paul's complaints of pain, and provided a diagnosis of back and neck sprain, for which he prescribed a continuing course of therapy from the date of the accident to the present time. The affidavit did not reference any objective testing to support the doctor's diagnosis or include any indication that Paul's daily activities were limited in any way because of his injuries.

(1)   Is Walker entitled to recover $500 from Paul's insurance company?

(2)   In Dan's declaratory judgment action, should the New York court apply the law of New York or the law of State X?

(3)   How should the court rule on the summary judgment motion?

QUESTION R-20

Wild World, Inc. ("WW") owns and operates Wild World, a wildlife preserve in northern New York State. Fred, a New York resident, was a regular visitor to Wild World.

On May 5, 2001, while hiking on a well-marked trail, Fred decided to leave the trail to see a beaver dam. While attempting to climb down the steeply sloped and muddy riverbank, Fred suffered severe injuries when he lost his footing and fell. As Fred was being taken to the hospital, Don, the ambulance driver, gave Fred the business card of Anne, a lawyer, and told him that Anne could help him get money for his injuries.

After his release from the hospital, Fred discovered that his car had been stolen from the garage at his home, and he immediately made a claim under his Acme Insurance Co. automobile insurance policy. Acme, a State X corporation, denied coverage and retroactively canceled Fred's insurance policy based on misrepresentations in his insurance application. In order to pay lower premiums, Fred had stated in his application that he resided in State X and that the car would be principally garaged in State X. However, Acme's investigation revealed that from the time Fred applied for the policy, which had been issued and delivered in State X, Fred has resided and garaged the car in New York.

Fred consulted Anne and Anne told him that for a flat fee of $1,000 she would get the cancelation of his insurance policy rescinded. Fred paid Anne $1,000 and gave her the cancelation notice that he had received from Acme. Anne also said she would file a negligence action against WW. She told Fred not to worry about the cost of the lawsuit and that her fee would be "a fair percentage" of any recovery. Fred did not sign a written retainer agreement. Anne sent Don a check for $500 for referring Fred to her.

Anne commenced an action against WW to recover damages for Fred's injuries, alleging that WW's negligent operation of the wildlife preserve and its failure to warn of a dangerous condition had caused Fred's accident. Fred testified at his deposition that he knew that the riverbank was steep and saw that it was muddy before he began to climb down. After the completion of discovery, WW moved for summary judgment dismissing the complaint. The parties stipulated that WW had neither fenced off the area where Fred was hurt nor posted any warning signs in the area.

Anne also commenced an action against Acme Insurance Co. to rescind the cancelation of the automobile insurance policy based on New York law, which prohibits such retroactive cancelation. In its answer, Acme asserted as an affirmative defense that the court should apply State X law, which permits retroactive cancelation of such an insurance policy.

(1) What are the ethical considerations, if any, raised by (a) Anne's payment to Don and (b) her fee arrangements with Fred?

(2) On WW's motion for summary judgment, what arguments should the parties make and how should the court rule?

(3) In the action against Acme Insurance Co., what law should the court apply?

QUESTION R-21

Grant owned Black Acres, a subdivision of 100 lots in Westchester County. In 1992, Mary and Fred were married and immediately bought one of the Black Acres lots. A year later, Deb, their daughter, was born.

The deeds from Grant for every lot, including Mary's and Fred's, contained a restrictive covenant setting forth that only one single-family house could be built on each lot, and that the covenant would be binding on all successors in interest. Mary's and Fred's deed was duly recorded in the Westchester County clerk's office.

Mary and Fred built a single-family house on their lot and lived there with Deb until April 1996, when Fred moved out. Mary and Fred then sold the house and lot to Mary's brother, Jeff. The deed conveying the property to Jeff did not contain the restrictive covenant.

Mary and Fred each retained counsel and entered into a duly executed separation agreement. The agreement provided in pertinent part that Mary would have custody of Deb, but that Fred would be entitled to liberal visitation. The agreement also provided that, until Deb reaches age 21, Fred would pay $1,000 per month for child support, an amount that both Mary and Fred acknowledged was correct under the Child Support Standards Act, and that the agreement would be incorporated but not merged into any judgment of divorce. In August 1997, Mary was granted a judgment of divorce.

In February 2003, Mary unexpectedly lost the job that she held for 10 years and started to experience financial difficulties. Despite her best efforts, she has been unable to find a job for the last year. Mary has informed Fred that she cannot afford to care for Deb without an increase in child support payments of an additional $500 per month. Fred has refused to pay the additional $500 per month, citing the terms of the separation agreement, and has told Mary that in order to make sure that Deb's financial needs are met, he is going to seek custody of Deb. Deb has expressed a preference to live with Fred.

Jeff has decided to convert his home into a two-family residence by adding a second floor and renting it out as an apartment. The local building code allows such a conversion, and Jeff's application to convert the second story of the house was approved. Jeff was about to begin construction when he received a letter from Phil, who owns a lot in Black Acres, threatening to sue to prevent Jeff from converting the house into a two-family house in violation of the restrictive covenant.

Mary has consulted you for advice and wants to know:

(1)   If she can get more child support from Fred;

(2)   Whether Fred can get custody of Deb; and

(3)   Whether Phil can successfully sue to stop Jeff from converting the house into a two-family residence.

How should you advise Mary?

QUESTION R-22

In January 1989, Harry and Wanda were engaged to be married. After pooling their savings, they decided to purchase Blueacre, improved real property located in the Bronx. In June 1989, at the closing of title to the premises, Harry and Wanda paid one-half of the purchase price by certified check and both signed the mortgage documents for the balance due. The deed delivered to them was made to Harry and Wanda, "as husband and wife." Shortly thereafter, Harry and Wanda both moved to Blueacre and began to live together.

In June 1990, one year after they purchased Blueacre, Harry and Wanda were married. In 1991, Harry and Wanda planted a vegetable garden on a 50-foot strip of the property adjacent to a stream which they believed to be the boundary line to their property. Harry and Wanda installed several posts and a six-foot-high fence around the garden to protect it from small animals and to clearly delineate the boundary line between what they thought was Blueacre and the property of their neighbor, Nancy. From time to time, at Wanda's invitation, Nancy would pick vegetables from the garden for her use.

In June 2002, Nancy decided to sell her home. In preparation for the sale, she hired a surveyor to perform a survey of her property. The survey revealed that the 50-foot strip where Harry and Wanda had planted the garden was not on Blueacre but was actually located on Nancy's property.

Nancy approached Harry and Wanda and asked that they remove the garden and fence. Harry and Wanda refused. Nancy convinced them to meet with a common neighbor, Art, an attorney, who had represented Nancy in the purchase of her property, to discuss a possible solution to the problem of the garden and the fence. At the meeting, Art advised the parties that he would act neutrally to mediate the dispute. After two lengthy mediation sessions, Art's attempts to get the parties to agree upon a settlement were unsuccessful. When Harry and Wanda refused to stop using the property, Art told them that he would see to it that Nancy "got her land back."

In January 2003, Art, as attorney for Nancy, commenced an action to quiet title to the 50-foot strip of land. In their answer to Nancy's complaint, Harry and Wanda asserted the affirmative defense of adverse possession. Harry and Wanda filed a motion to disqualify Art from representing Nancy on the ground of his prior role as a mediator. The court (1) denied the motion.

After trial of Nancy's action, the court found that Nancy was the fee simple owner of the 50-foot strip and that (2) Harry and Wanda had failed to establish that they were owners of the 50-foot strip by adverse possession.

In April 2004, Harry decided to seek a divorce from Wanda, quit his job, and travel around the world. He moved out of Blueacre and consulted with an attorney who advised Harry that he had no cause of action for a divorce. However, Harry needed money to accomplish his dream of world travel, and Blueacre was his only asset. In May 2004, Harry commenced an action against Wanda seeking the partition and sale of Blueacre and half of the proceeds. In Harry's action, the court found: (3) that as a result of their marriage, Harry and Wanda owned Blueacre as tenants by the entirety, and (4) that Harry is not entitled to the partition and sale of Blueacre.

Were the numbered rulings correct?

QUESTION R-23

In 1990, Ann and Bill were married in State X, where they both resided and where they were employed by Crash.com, a computer consulting company. There were no children of the marriage.

In 1991, Bill became an officer of Crash.com, with a very large increase in income. That same year, Ann and Bill purchased Blackacre, a substantial residence in Washington County, New York, with 200 feet of frontage on the easterly shore of a large lake. The deed conveying Blackacre was to "Ann and Bill, grantees, as tenants by the entirety." Ann and Bill then moved to Blackacre, and Bill continued to be employed by Crash.com in State X, commuting each weekday from Blackacre. Ann did not work again after moving to Blackacre.

Greenacre, the property adjoining Blackacre on the south, was owned by Carl. Carl became concerned about the privacy of his property after Ann and Bill moved into Blackacre, and in 1993, Carl erected a six-foot-high wood fence along what he believed to be the boundary line between Blackacre and Greenacre. In fact, the fence erected was five feet southerly of the northerly boundary of Greenacre as it was described in the deed to Carl. Ann and Bill then proceeded to use the five-foot strip northerly of the fence for their own purposes by constructing a tool shed, planting a garden, and mowing that portion of the strip that was lawn. This use continues to date. Ann and Bill never discussed the fence or the five-foot strip with Carl, the owner of Greenacre.

In 2005 Ann discovered that Bill was having an affair with Dawn, a co-worker at Crash.com, and Ann and Bill agreed to separate. Bill and Dawn moved into a one-bedroom apartment in State X. Ann and Bill, each represented by counsel, entered into a separation agreement which was duly executed, acknowledged, and filed on December 30, 2005. The agreement provided, *inter alia*, for the division of marital property, with Ann receiving sole ownership of Blackacre, and provided for maintenance for Ann of $1,000 per month for her life or until she remarries. In the quitclaim deed conveying Blackacre from Ann and Bill to Ann, the southerly boundary of Blackacre is described as "along the wood fence erected in 1993." The deed was duly executed and recorded on December 30, 2005.

In April 2006, Carl conveyed Greenacre to Ed. Ed had an engineer survey Greenacre, and the survey revealed that the fence erected by Carl was five feet south of the north line of Greenacre as described in the deed from Carl to Ed.

Ed went to Ann and told her she was trespassing on his property. Ed offered to "rent" the five-foot strip to Ann for $1,000 per year. Ann, without consulting an attorney, agreed and paid Ed $1,000 for the year 2006. In 2007, Ann consulted Fred, a lawyer in Washington County, by whom you are employed as an associate. Fred has relayed the above facts to you and asked you to prepare a memorandum addressing the following issues:

(1) Does Ann have a valid cause of action against Bill for divorce in New York and, if so, on what grounds?

(2) What jurisdiction is necessary, and how may it be obtained for a New York court:

   (a) to grant Ann a judgment of divorce; and

   (b) to incorporate the separation agreement into the judgment?

(3) (a) What interest, if any, does Ann have in the five-foot strip?

   (b) What effect, if any, did Ann's agreeing to pay rent to Ed have?

QUESTION R-24

In August 2000, Mindy entered into a written contract with Ben, a builder, to construct an addition to her family's residence. One of Mindy's reasons for building the addition was to provide a practice gym for her son, Mike, a 21-year-old college student, who wanted to become a professional basketball player. Thus, the contract between Mindy and Ben provided, in part, that the gym would have a hardwood floor and a basketball hoop while the remainder of the addition would be carpeted. The contract price was $100,000, one-half of which was paid upon execution of the contract, with the balance to be paid upon completion of the job.

In September 2000, while Mike was playing basketball at a local sports center, Alice, a well-known sports agent, approached Mike and invited him to have dinner with her to discuss his career. At dinner, Alice told Mike that he could be a professional basketball player. Alice offered to be Mike's agent, and she handed him a proposed 20-page typewritten contract. When Mike asked Alice if he could review the contract with his mother, Alice said that this was Mike's "golden opportunity" and that if he did not sign the contract then, it would be withdrawn. Mike signed the contract immediately.

The next day, when Mike was reviewing the contract with his mother, they realized that it gave Alice the exclusive right to represent Mike for the next 10 years, as well as 60% of all of Mike's gross income from employment in the field of basketball during that period. Shortly thereafter, Mike learned that the standard percentage for a basketball agent is 20% and that the usual term of such a contract if three years. Mike then promptly advised Alice that he would not comply with the terms of their contract.

On December 18, 2000, Ben notified Mindy that the addition to her residence was completed. When Mindy inspected the work, she realized that Ben had installed carpeting in the gym, as well as all of the other rooms, and had failed to install a practice hoop. Ben said that his failure to install the hardwood floor and hoop in the gym was inadvertent, but the value of the addition was unchanged by the error. The cost to remove the carpet and install a hardwood floor and hoop has not yet been determined. On December 20, 2000, when Ben asked Mindy for the $50,000 balance of the contract price, she refused to pay.

In January 2001, in response to New School District's advertisement for bids for the construction of a high school gym, Ben prepared a preliminary bid proposal in accordance with the plans and specifications of the school district. Before submitting the bid, Ben decided that he would be able to reduce his bid by $25,000. In transposing this reduction from his worksheet to the actual proposal however, $250,000 was inadvertently deducted instead of $25,000, and the bid submitted was therefore $225,000 lower than Ben had intended. When the bids were opened by the school district, Ben discovered his error. Ben promptly advised the district of his error and asked it to withdraw his bid. Ben provided his worksheet, which confirmed his error, but the district nonetheless awarded the contract to Ben based upon his submitted bid. Ben refused to perform the contract.

(1) Can Alice enforce her contract with Mike?

(2) What are the rights and liabilities of Ben and Mindy with respect to payment of the balance of the contract price?

(3) Is Ben bound by the bid he submitted to the New School District?

QUESTION R-25

In 1995, Builder, Inc. ("Builder") was incorporated by Al and Bob, two carpenters experienced in the construction business. Builder was authorized to issue 200 shares of common stock, of which 50 were issued to Al, and 50 were issued to Bob. In accordance with the bylaws of Builder, Al, Bob, and Bob's wife, Sue, were duly elected as the directors and officers of Builder.

In 1999, Builder decided to hire another carpenter. When Builder approached Cal, an experienced carpenter, Cal agreed to join Builder for an annual salary of $75,000, provided he could acquire shares in Builder and participate in its management. After Builder agreed to Cal's salary demand, it voted to issue 45 shares of it stock to Cal for $20,000, which Cal paid. At a duly held meeting of the shareholders of Builder, Sue tendered her resignation as a director and officer, and Cal was duly elected as a director of Builder. At the same time, Builder and Cal entered into an agreement which provided, in relevant part:

> If, at any time, Cal voluntarily terminates his employment with Builder, Builder shall have the option, for a period of 30 days after such employment ceases, to repurchase Cal's shares in Builder for the purchase price of $20,000 originally paid by Cal.

Although Builder's business continued to be profitable, Al and Bob soon found that they were unable to get along with Cal and that they were dissatisfied with the quality of his carpentry work. Accordingly, just a year after Cal joined Builder, Al and Bob decided to hold a special meeting of the directors for the purpose of terminating Cal as an employee and director of Builder. Without giving any formal notice of the meeting or its purpose, Al and Bob met at Builder's offices. As the meeting was about to begin, Cal, who by coincidence was at Builder's offices, learned of the meeting. Cal walked into the meeting room, and Al called the meeting to order. Al and Bob then resolved and voted to terminate Cal as an employee and director of Builder, and to reelect Sue as Builder's third director. Cal voted against the Board's actions, reminding Al and Bob that the only reasons that he had agreed to join Builder were for the salary and the right to participate in its management.

A week after the meeting, Cal consulted his attorney and asked the following questions:

(1) Was the special meeting of the board of directors validly held?

(2) Was Cal's employment by Builder validly terminated?

(3) What action or proceeding can Cal maintain as a shareholder against Builder?

(4) In such action or proceeding:

   (a) Can Cal be compelled to sell his shares in the corporation back to Builder?

   (b) Can Cal be required to accept $20,000 for his shares?

Prepare a memorandum answering Cal's questions.

QUESTION R-26

In 2001, Punch, the owner of a metal stamping plant, purchased a used conveyor system from Usedparts, Inc., a distributor of refurbished industrial equipment. The conveyor system, consisting of a hydraulic lift and several moving platforms, was sold "as is." Punch contracted with Gen Installation Co. ("Gen") for Gen to install the conveyor system in the plant for $350,000. Installation drawings showing the layout of the system, and the structural modifications that were required to be made to the plant by Gen in order to install the system, were made a part of the contract.

Prior to the installation of the conveyor system, Punch determined that the system would move products more efficiently if it were reconfigured. Gen drew new installation drawings, incorporating Punch's revisions. A revised contract, which provided for the change in the work, was prepared and signed by Punch and Gen. The revised contract did not provide for any change in the contract price, although the revisions would require more labor to install the system than would have been required under the original plans.

Gen subcontracted with Sub for Sub to do the installation work in accordance with the revised plans. Punch closed the plant for one month so that the conveyor system could be installed. When Sub's work crew installed the conveyor system, they did not follow the revised plans, but mistakenly installed the conveyor system in accordance with the original drawings. The error was not discovered until after the work was completed. Both Gen and Sub refused Punch's request that they reinstall the conveyor system in accordance with the revised plans. Punch then hired another contractor to reinstall the conveyor system in accordance with the revised plans at a cost of $150,000.

Once the plant reopened, Punch put the newly installed conveyor system into operation. Shortly thereafter, in January 2002, the hydraulic lift on the conveyor system failed due to a defective cylinder, causing a raised conveyor platform to fall to the floor. The accident caused significant damage to the conveyor system.

Usedparts, Inc. is now out of business. The conveyor system, including the hydraulic lift, was originally manufactured by Move-It Inc. in 1990. Punch commenced an action against Move-It Inc. for the cost of repairing the conveyor system, asserting a cause of action in tort for strict products liability. Punch's complaint alleged that the damage caused to the conveyor system was the result of the defective cylinder. Move-It Inc. moved to dismiss the action on the grounds that (a) as a matter of law, it could not be held liable in strict products liability for the cost of repairing the conveyor system, and (b) in any event, the action was barred by the statute of limitations.

(1)   How should the court rule on Move-It Inc.'s motion?

(2)   Is the contract revision enforceable against Gen, despite the lack of consideration for the revision?

(3)   Can Punch recover against Sub for breach of contract?

QUESTION R-27

You are a law clerk for an appellate division justice. There is a pending appeal from an order granting summary judgment in favor of the defendant dismissing the complaint in the action. The decision below contained the following accurate recitation of the facts:

> The defendant, No Comparison, Inc. ("Comparison"), was incorporated under the laws of the state of New York as a catering business on July 31, 2001. Prior to the incorporation, on June 1, 2001, Edward Early, a co-owner of the business, entered into a verbal agreement for payroll services with plaintiff, Best Office Services, Ltd. ("Best"), which was memorialized in a letter

from an officer of Best dated June 15, 2001, referencing the agreement between her company and Comparison. On June 20, 2001, Early submitted to Best a credit application in which he referenced "our agreement" and set forth the assets of Comparison. The application stated that "No Comparison, Inc." was the business name of the entity, that he was its president, and that Sharon Jones was it chief financial officer.

Pursuant to the agreement, Best was to provide services for the period July 1, 2001, to June 30, 2002. Consistent with the agreement, Best submitted monthly invoices through February 1, 2002, covering, as was customary, the immediately preceding month. Out of the seven invoices submitted by Best, only the first applied to the period prior to Comparison's incorporation.

Comparison promptly paid the first three invoices.

The payments were made in the form of checks signed by Sharon Jones, which contained the reference "for payroll services." Thereafter, Comparison made no further payments. The president of Best, without consulting the board of directors of Best, authorized Best's counsel to commence this Action to recover damages for Comparison's breach of contract. The certificate of incorporation and bylaws of Best are silent on the question of who has authority to commence a legal action on the part of the corporation. In its answer, Comparison raised as affirmative defenses that (1) the action was not duly authorized by the board of directors of Best, (2) the agreement between the parties was unenforceable because it was entered into before the existence of the corporation, and (3) the agreement violated the Statute of Frauds.

Following the joinder of issue, Comparison moved for summary judgment dismissing the complaint based on the affirmative defenses. The court granted the motion, holding that although board authorization was not required for Best to bring the action, the agreement itself was not enforceable for the reasons set forth in the other affirmative defenses asserted by Comparison.

Best has duly filed and perfected its appeal. The appellate division justice has asked you to prepare a memorandum analyzing the merits of the three affirmative defenses.

QUESTION R-28

Clare was the leader of "SUFFER," Students Undertaking Full Fledged Educational Reform, an organization dedicated to the elimination of all standardized testing of students. On January 3, 2001, without having obtained a permit, Clare led approximately 100 SUFFER members in a march through the streets of Albany to the state capitol. When the police became aware of the marchers' destination, several dozen uniformed officers were stationed in front of the capitol building and barricades were erected to ensure that the demonstrators would not block pedestrian or vehicular traffic around the building.

When they reached the barricades, Clare and the other marchers began chanting, "No tests or no peace." Officer Paul told Clare and the marchers to disperse because they did not have a permit and were causing a public disturbance. Clare then climbed on top of one of the barricades and screamed to the crowd, "Don't let the cops stop you. We have the right to march and we will fight if they try to stop us." Clare then pushed over one of the barricades and yelled to the crowd, "Let's go. We have the right to march on the state capitol. Fight the cops if you have to." While Clare continued to loudly urge them on, about 20 demonstrators started to climb over the barricades while others threw rocks and bottles at the police.

Officer Paul then approached Clare and told her that she was under arrest for inciting to riot. When he placed one handcuff on her, Clare screamed, "No way, cop" and pulled away, causing the other handcuff to fly up and cut Officer Paul in the head. Officer Paul then placed Clare under arrest, removed the backpack she was wearing, transported her to the police station, and placed her in a holding cell. While Clare was in the cell, Officer Paul searched her backpack and discovered marijuana.

Upon presentation of the foregoing pertinent facts to the grand jury, Clare was indicted on charges of assault in the second degree, inciting to riot, resisting arrest, and possession of marijuana. Penal Law section 240.08 provides that: "A person is guilty of inciting to riot when he urges 10 or more persons to engage in tumultuous and violent conduct of a kind likely to create public harm." Penal Law section 120.05(3) provides that: "A person is guilty of assault in the second degree when . . . with intent to prevent a police officer . . . from performing a lawful duty, he causes physical injury to such . . . police officer." Clare's attorney timely filed an omnibus motion:

(a) To dismiss the inciting to riot charge, on the ground that her words were protected by the First Amendment to the Constitution;

(b) To dismiss the assault charge, on the ground that she did not intend to cause injury to Officer Paul; and

(c) To suppress the marijuana found in her backpack.

The court denied the motion in its entirety.

At trial, the prosecution proved the foregoing pertinent facts. Clare testified in her defense that she pulled away from Officer Paul in an attempt to protect herself from what she believed to be an unlawful arrest. After both sides rested, over the prosecution's objection, Clare's attorney requested that the court charge the jury on the defense of justification with respect to the charge of resisting arrest.

(1) Did the court decide each branch of Clare's omnibus motion correctly?

(2) Should the court instruct the jury on the defense of justification?

QUESTION R-29

In September 2003, Udall, an undercover police officer, noticed that Drew often drove his car into an area known to be frequented by several cocaine dealers. On several occasions Udall approached Drew's car and offered to purchase cocaine from Drew. Drew continuously refused Udall's offers until October 21, 2003, when Udall again approached Drew's car and offered to purchase a packet of cocaine. Drew asked how much Udall would pay, and Udall replied, "One hundred bucks." Drew agreed to the sale. Udall gave Drew $100, whereupon Drew handed Udall a packet of cocaine weighing 600 milligrams.

Drew was immediately placed under arrest by Udall, removed from the car, and handcuffed. Udall then frisked Drew and felt the outline of what he believed to be two bullets in Drew's left

[handwritten margin note: *unilateral conspiracy OK*]

[handwritten note at bottom: *Search incident to arrest in a car — Can search Weapon, Not Trunk*]

rear pocket. Udall reached into the pocket and removed two .38 caliber bullets. At that point, Udall inspected the interior of the car where he saw nothing incriminating. However, upon discovering that the glove compartment was locked, Udall took the keys from the ignition, unlocked the glove compartment, and found a loaded .38 caliber handgun.

Shortly thereafter, Drew was indicted for the crimes of criminal possession of a weapon, criminal sale of a controlled substance, and criminal possession of a controlled substance in the fifth degree. Under Penal Law section 220.06(5) a person is guilty of criminal possession of a controlled substance in the fifth degree: "when he knowingly and unlawfully possesses . . . cocaine and said cocaine weighs 500 milligrams or more."

In a pre-trial motion, Drew moved to suppress the handgun on the ground that the search of the locked glove compartment violated his rights against unreasonable search and seizure. The court (1) denied Drew's motion to suppress the handgun.

At Drew's trial, Udall testified to the foregoing facts involving the undercover operation and Drew's arrest. At the close of the prosecution's case, Drew moved to dismiss the indictment on the ground that the prosecution failed to establish that Drew knew the weight of the packet of cocaine which he allegedly possessed. The court (2) denied Drew's motion.

Drew then testified and denied that he sold any drugs to Udall or that he had any drugs in his possession at the time of his arrest. He further testified that Udall had approached him on 10 different occasions in a harassing manner asking to buy drugs, and he had consistently refused. He further denied that Udall gave him any money or that he gave drugs to Udall.

In rebuttal, the prosecution introduced evidence that Drew was convicted of criminal possession of cocaine the previous year.

Drew requested that the court charge the jury on entrapment with respect to the charge of criminal sale of a controlled substance. The prosecution objected, asserting that the defense was not available to Drew (a) because he denied the underlying crime, (b) because he had a prior conviction for a drug related offense, and (c) because the proof presented as to the elements of the defense was insufficient to require the charge.

1.   Were the rulings numbered (1) and (2) correct?

2.   Should Drew's request to charge the defense of entrapment be granted?

QUESTION R-30

Nick asked Dom if he could store a tractor on Dom's property. A few days later, Dom overheard Nick tell a mutual friend that the tractor was stolen. Unbeknownst to Nick, Dom was a reliable police informant, who advised the local sheriff's office of Nick's statement. Dom told the sheriff that the tractor was now located on Dom's property, but that Nick had kept an ignition key. He told the sheriff that Nick was actively trying to sell the tractor by phoning potential buyers.

With Dom's consent, the sheriff inspected the tractor. By tracing an identification number stamped on the tractor, the sheriff located the owner who confirmed that his tractor had recently been stolen. The sheriff obtained a warrant authorizing a search of Nick's house for the stolen tractor's ignition key, as well as "any other property which would be considered contraband."

During a search of a closed cabinet in Nick's house, the sheriff found a gun wrapped in clear plastic and adjacent to it, an ignition key for the tractor. Later, another gun wrapped in cloth was found hidden underneath Nick's bathroom sink. Both guns were unregistered.

The sheriff also obtained a warrant to place a wiretap on Nick's telephone line. The warrant application specified Nick's home address and the phone number for the telephone line, the only one which serviced his residence. It also set forth the reasons for believing Nick committed a crime and the type of communications sought to be intercepted, which included admissions of his theft of a tractor and his efforts to sell it by telephone. No other representations appeared in the application for the warrant. Between the time of the issuance of the warrant, which specified the phone number set forth in the application, and installation of the wiretap, the phone number for the line was changed, although the line continued to be listed in Nick's name. After 40 days, the sheriff intercepted a telephone communication by Nick that he stole the tractor. The following day, Nick was arrested and charged with grand larceny and possession of unlicensed firearms.

Nick pled not guilty to the charges, and his counsel moved to suppress the evidence seized in the search and any admissions recorded during the phone wiretap. As the newest member of the district attorney's office, you are asked to prepare a memorandum for the district attorney outlining the likely outcome of the motion to suppress. You are asked to focus on the following questions:

(1)   Was the search warrant valid?

(2)   Should any of the evidence gathered during the search be suppressed?

(3)   Was the wiretap warrant properly issued?

(4)   Assuming the court concludes that the wiretap warrant was properly issued, should the admission obtained during the wiretap be suppressed?

QUESTION R-31

Hub and Win were married in 2002. Prior to their marriage, Hub and Win orally agreed that each would execute a will naming the other a sole beneficiary. Shortly after their marriage, Win executed a will prepared by her lawyer. The will named Hub as the sole beneficiary but did not refer to the oral agreement.

Hub died in June 2004, a resident of New York, survived by Win and his mother, Mona. The only will discovered among Hub's effects upon his death was a will which his lawyer, Len, had prepared and Hub had executed in 2001. In the will, Hub named Mona as sole beneficiary and Len as sole executor.

Hub's estate, after payment of all debts, administration expenses, and funeral expenses, consists of (a) a condominium at a Vermont ski resort in Hub's name alone free of any liens, valued at $180,000; (b) a joint savings account in the names of Hub and Mona, the only deposit into which was made by Hub when he opened the account in 2001, having a balance of $90,000; (c) a joint checking account in the names of Hub and Win, having a balance of $30,000, all of which had been provided by Hub; and (d) a savings account in the name of Hub, in trust for Mona, the only deposit into which was made by Hub when he opened the account in 2001, having a balance of $120,000.

Win has inquired of Len as to her rights in Hub's estate.

(1) To what extent may Len advise Win about her rights?

(2) To what extent, if any, does Win have rights in Hub's estate under the agreement to execute mutual wills?

(3) Assuming Win has no rights under the agreement, and the 2001 will is admitted to probate, what rights, if any, does she have in Hub's estate?

BAR REVIEW

Essay Answers

ANSWER 1—COMMERCIAL PAPER/TORTS

(a)   RIGHTS OF S AGAINST W

The issue is whether the checks were duly negotiated to S. **1/2 point**

Negotiation of bearer instruments (*i.e.,* the check made payable to "cash" for $100) is accomplished by delivery of the instrument to the transferee. Once the transferee has possession, he qualifies as a "holder." Under the facts, the check made out to "cash" never reached S, and so it was not negotiated to him. **1-1/2 points**

For order instruments (*i.e.,* the check made payable to S for $200), negotiation is accomplished by delivery of the instrument to the payee named on the instrument. Any further negotiation requires that the payee indorse and deliver the instrument to the transferee. Here, the check made out to S also failed to reach him, and so it was not negotiated to him. **1-1/2 points**

Consequently, W would have no defense to an action by S for the $300, and W still owes that sum to S.

(b)   RIGHTS OF W AGAINST T

The issue is whether a person who receives cash has good title to it. Anyone with possession of cash has good title to it. **1/2 point**

According to the facts presented, H gave T $300 cash. Therefore, T has title to the $300 he received from H, and W has no right to recover from him. **1/2 point**

(c)   RIGHTS OF W AGAINST F BANK

The issue is whether the $100 check made payable to "cash" is bearer paper. **1/2 point**

Bearer paper is payable to anyone in possession of the instrument. Unlike cash, this does not mean that anyone with possession has good title to it; but bearer paper is freely negotiable, like cash. The U.C.C. specifically allows a bank to honor bearer paper and charge the drawer's account, whether or not the person who negotiated the paper to the bank had rightful possession of it. **1 point**

Under the facts, H was in possession of the $100 check payable to cash (bearer paper). Thus, the bank is protected from liability with respect to the $100 check made out to "cash." **1/2 point**

The bank is liable to W for the $200 check made payable to S, which was negotiated to the bank with a forged indorsement. The issue is whether a bank is liable when it honors an instrument with a forged indorsement when the instrument is payable to the order of a specific payee. **1/2 point**

The U.C.C. imposes upon drawee banks the duty to honor a check as drawn. "As drawn" refers to the original draft as written by the drawer, as distinguished from any changes made by one other than the drawer. Specifically, a bank is not allowed to charge the account of its customer where the bank pays the wrong person—*i.e.,* the forger of payee's or indorser's signature. **1 point**

Thus, F Bank could not properly pay out over H's forged indorsement; even though H signed S's name, the bank cannot claim protection thereby. Bank's action was a breach of the contractual relationship between F and W. W is entitled to a chargeback on her account in the amount of $200. **1 point**

F Bank's only possible defense is to claim that W failed to notify F Bank of the theft of the checks within a reasonable time. The U.C.C. imposes on the drawee the duty to notify the bank of such unauthorized use with "reasonable promptness." In this case, 11 days is not an unreasonably long delay. Thus, F's defense will fail, and W will recover the $200. **1 point**

ANSWER 2—CORPORATIONS

(1) B'S RIGHTS WITH REGARD TO THE SHARES ISSUED TO O

The issue is whether B has preemptive rights and, if so, whether he can exercise them so as to block the issuance of the shares to O. **1/2 point**

For corporations formed before February 22, 1998, the rule is that a shareholder who holds shares with either an unlimited dividend right or voting rights is entitled to maintain his relative rights by the use of preemptive rights, unless preemptive rights are limited or denied by the certificate of incorporation. For corporations formed on or after February 22, 1998, a shareholder is entitled to preemptive rights only if provided for in the certificate of incorporation. In this fact pattern, there is no indication of when the corporation was formed or whether there is any mention of preemptive rights in the certificate of incorporation. Therefore, in the case of formation **on or after** February 22, 1998, B would not have preemptive rights. **1 point**

In the case of formation before February 22, 1998, because there is only one class of shares and the certificate of incorporation is silent as to preemptive rights, B is a holder of preemptive rights. As a holder of preemptive rights, B is entitled to purchase any new shares issued by the corporation in the amount necessary to maintain his relative rights where the issuance of the shares would otherwise affect his dividend or voting rights. Therefore, as a holder of preemptive rights, B is entitled to protect his relative dividend right and voting right status. **1 point**

Regardless of whether B is *entitled* to preemptive rights, B is not entitled to *exercise* preemptive rights. The New York Business Corporations Law ("BCL") limits preemptive rights in several situations, of which two are relevant here: (i) preemptive rights do not attach to shares authorized in the original certificate of incorporation and sold or optioned within two years of the filing of the certificate; and (ii) preemptive rights do not attach to shares offered for consideration other than cash. **1 point**

In this case, although the facts do not give specific dates for all the activities, it is more likely than not that the meeting where the shares were voted to be issued to O took place within two years of incorporation. If this is so, B is prohibited from exercising his preemptive right because the 100 shares issued to O are from the original 500 shares authorized by the certificate of incorporation. In any event, B is prohibited from exercising his preemptive rights because the shares were issued to O in exchange for real property, not cash. Therefore, even though B is a preemptive right holder, he may not exercise that right. **1 point**

Finally, B may object to the issuance of shares to O on the ground that the shares are worth far more than the value of the land. This fails, however, because the BCL provides that where the board issues shares of no par stock in exchange for real property, there is a conclusive presumption that the shares were exchanged for good value, absent a showing of fraud, and the facts indicate no fraud on O's part. Therefore, B may not challenge the issue to O on the basis of lack of adequate consideration. **1 point**

Thus, B cannot stop O from acquiring 100 shares of X Corp.

(2) B'S RIGHTS WITH REGARD TO THE SHARES SOLD TO D

The issue is whether B is liable for breaching the bylaws restricting the transfer of shares. **1/2 point**

New York has held that reasonable restrictions on the sale of shares of stock are valid and will be upheld by the courts. [Allen v. Biltmore Tissue Corp., 2 N.Y.2d 759 (1957)] A restriction requiring the selling shareholder to first offer his shares to the corporation or other shareholder is a reasonable restriction on alienation and not "prohibitive," provided that there is no restriction on price. However, a restriction requiring unanimous consent before sale is a prohibition on sale, for it allows the sale of shares to be restricted for any reason or no reason at all, and thus is unreasonable. [Rafe v. Hinde, 29 A.D.2d 481, *aff'd,* 23 N.Y.2d 759 (1968)] These restrictions may be contained in the bylaws, the certificate of incorporation, or in a separate agreement. **1 point**

In this case, the first restriction merely provides that a shareholder must first offer his shares to the corporation before selling them to a third party and is therefore reasonable and enforceable. The second restriction, however, requires the unanimous vote of the directors before any shareholder may sell shares. This restriction is a restriction on alienation which is not reasonable and cannot be enforced. Therefore, B has breached the first restriction on transfer but not the second, and may be held liable for provable damages resulting from his failure to offer his shares to X Corp. before selling them to D. **1 point**

(3) D'S RIGHTS WITH REGARD TO THE SHARES BOUGHT FROM B

The issue is whether the restrictions are binding on D. Restrictions on alienation of shares are binding on all persons with actual notice and are binding universally if noted conspicuously on the shares themselves. However, restrictions imposed by the issuer are not binding on a bona fide purchaser without actual knowledge, unless the restrictions are noted on the shares. **1 point**

In this case, the shares themselves are silent as to the restrictions on alienation, therefore, D as a bona fide purchaser without notice, was not bound by the restrictions on the sale of the shares. D is therefore entitled to the ownership of the shares, and C as secretary can be compelled to record the transfer of the shares to D. **1 point**

ANSWER 3—TORTS/NEW YORK PRACTICE/FEDERAL JURISDICTION & PROCEDURE

(1)(a) The first issue is whether the negligence cause of action was timely. Rule 215 of the CPLR provides a three-year statute of limitations for causes of action arising out of negligence. H, as executor, sued D for P's personal injuries arising from D's negligence within three years. Therefore, this cause of action is timely. **1/2 point**

The second issue is whether the battery cause of action was timely. The statute of limitations for intentional torts under CPLR 215 is one year. The suit here was instituted more than one year after the cause of action arose. However, CPLR 210 provides that where a person entitled to commence an action dies before the expiration of the time within which the action must be commenced and the cause of action survives, an action may be commenced by his representative within one year of the date of death. In this case, the statute of limitations would have expired on June 1. P's death on December 1, however, extended the time in which P's representative (H) might institute the suit until the following December 1. Thus, H's suit is not time-barred as to the battery cause of action. **1-1/2 points**

The third issue is whether H's individual wrongful death action is timely. A wrongful death action is timely if it is brought within two years of the date of death. The action here was brought seven months after the date of death. Therefore, this suit is not barred by the statute of limitations. (*Note:* H may bring the wrongful death action within two years of P's death only if the statute of limitations has not yet run on the underlying personal injury claim.) [EPTL §5-4.1] **1/2 point**

(b)   The issue is whether H has stated valid claims. In making this determination, the court must look at each cause of action, take all of H's allegations as true, and determine whether in fact H has stated a claim upon which relief may be granted. **1 point**

The facts state that D was driving the car that got into the accident that injured P. Therefore, a negligence action is proper. Additionally, the facts tell us that D beat P. Thus, a battery cause of action is present. Hence, under the facts, H may maintain claims against D for negligence and for battery, acting as P's executor. The survival of causes of action lying in tort is provided by EPTL section 11-3.2. **1 point**

(c)   The issue is what may be recovered under a wrongful death cause of action. EPTL section 5-4.3 limits damages for wrongful death to pecuniary losses and punitive damages. Grief, sorrow, and heartache, as well as loss of consortium are not compensable in a wrongful death action. [Liff v. Schildkraut, 49 N.Y.2d 622 (1980)] H may maintain his individual wrongful death action only insofar as he seeks to recover for pecuniary losses and punitive damages. Thus, insofar as H has stated a claim for grief, sorrow, and heartache, or for loss of consortium, H has not stated a claim upon which relief may be granted, and the court incorrectly denied D's motion to dismiss that part of H's action. **1-1/2 points**

(2)   The issue is whether the federal district court may exercise jurisdiction under the facts.

The court must have both subject matter jurisdiction and personal jurisdiction. District courts have original subject matter jurisdiction of all civil actions where (i) the matter in controversy exceeds the sum or value of $75,000, exclusive of interest and costs, and (ii) there is complete diversity among the parties. The legal representative of the estate of a decedent is deemed to be a citizen only of the same state as the decedent. Because the amount in controversy exceeds $75,000, (i) above is met. We are told that P is a domiciliary of New York, while O is a domiciliary of New Jersey. Hence, (ii) above is also met. Thus, the court has subject matter jurisdiction over this case. **2 points**

The next issue is whether the court has personal jurisdiction over this defendant. This turns on whether the defendant was properly served. The Federal Rules of Civil Procedure provide that service is proper if made either within the state in which the district court is located, or if made under the long arm statute of the state in which the district court sits. New York's long arm statute [CPLR 302] does not subject out-of-state residents to the jurisdiction of New York courts when the accident occurred outside of New York, the defendant is a resident and domiciliary of a state other than New York, and there is no showing that the defendant could reasonably expect his acts to have consequences in New York. Here, O was served at home in New Jersey, while the district court sits in New York. Furthermore, none of the above requirements have been met. Thus, the United States district court does not have personal jurisdiction over O and therefore may not exercise jurisdiction over him. Hence, the court was correct in dismissing H's suit on motion of O. **2 points**

ANSWER 4—PARTNERSHIP/AGENCY

LIABILITIES OF A

The issue is for what debts A, as general partner, is liable. **1/3 point**

A general partner is personally liable for all debts of a partnership whether or not the partner contributed services to the partnership. A remained a general partner throughout all transactions (*e.g.,* loans, etc.), including the time he spent in prison. Thus, A is liable for all V Co. debts. **1/2 point**

LIABILITIES OF S

The issue is for what debts S, a retired general partner, is liable. Simply because a general partner retires, he is not released from partnership liability. A retiring partner remains liable until he withdraws from the partnership and proper notice is given of withdrawal. Since S gave no notice of withdrawal from V Co., he is still liable for V Co.'s debts. **2/3 point**

Even though S contributed only $100 as compared to the $10,000 contributed by the other partners, S was entitled to the equal sharing of profits and the equal sharing of losses (since losses follow profits), because there was no agreement to the contrary. Therefore, S is liable for all obligations of V Co. **1/2 point**

LIABILITIES OF D

The issue is D's liability. **1/3 point**

In New York, when a person, by words or conduct, represents himself as a partner, he will be liable to third persons who extend credit to the partnership in reliance on the representation. This is known as "partnership by estoppel." The doctrine of partnership by estoppel applies to D. Although not a partner and therefore not liable as a general partner, D held herself out to be a general partner of V Co. Consequently, she will be estopped to deny that she is a general partner as to partnership liabilities that arise as a consequence of her representation. Having privately represented to E that she was a partner, and E having lent funds to the partnership based on the representation, D cannot now deny that she is a partner, and she will be personally liable to the extent of the $50,000 loaned to V Co. on the fact of her representation. **1 point**

D is also personally liable to F for $30,000. A person is liable for her debts. The facts state that F loaned $30,000 to D as a personal loan, and not as a loan to V Co. Thus, D's liability arises from her personal transaction with F, and not from her status as agent (or partner by estoppel) of V Co. **1/2 point**

Neither V Co. nor A nor S is liable to F for the $30,000. F insisted on dealing with D personally and specifically refused to deal with the partnership. Therefore, no liability attaches to the partnership nor to any general partner. **1/2 point**

Thus, D is liable on both the $50,000 loan (to E) and the $30,000 loan (to F).

LIABILITIES OF B AND C

The issue is whether deceased partners are liable for future partnership debts. **1/3 point**

In New York, a deceased partner does not become liable for new partnership debts. In our facts, V Co.'s debt arose *after* both B and C died. Hence, neither B nor C is liable for any of this post-death debt. **1/2 point**

Note: Although the partnership agreement provided that the surviving spouse of any deceased partner shall receive what would have been that partner's share of the profits, such a surviving spouse does not become a partner of the partnership. **1/3 point**

Also note: B and C's financial interest in the partnership continued as per agreement until there was a loss. A deceased partner does *not* become liable for new debts—so only capital contributions are at stake to be lost. **1/3 point**

LIABILITIES OF V CO.

The issue is V Co.'s liability. A partnership is liable for its debts. V Co. owes E the following: $50,000 arising from the February 1999 promissory note; $50,000 from the January 2000 promissory note; less $25,000 paid after April 2000, out of the funds provided by F through D; so V Co. now owes E $75,000. **1/2 point**

Note: A and S are personally liable to E for the unpaid $75,000. Under the law affecting partnerships in New York, a general partner is personally liable for all debts of the partnership. **1/2 point**

LIABILITIES TO D

The first issue is whether an agent is entitled to compensation. In New York, an agent is entitled to compensation for her services rendered. If there is no agreement setting the rate of compensation, the rate will be the fair market value. **1/3 point**

As D was not a partner, but rather an agent, she is entitled to compensation for her services at their fair market value, absent an agreement setting a rate of compensation. The facts show no agreement here, so D may recover the fair value of her services to the partnership. **1/3 point**

The second issue is whether D can recover from V Co. the $30,000 she owes to F. A person who lends money to a partnership is entitled to recover this money.

Had D borrowed the funds in her capacity as agent for V Co., she would have incurred no personal liability, and thus would have no right of recovery. However, D borrowed from F in her personal capacity, and then in turn loaned the funds to V Co. Thus, she is a creditor of V Co. and is entitled to recover the $30,000. **1/2 point**

D may recover the $30,000 and the value of her services from V Co., A, or S for the reasons discussed above. **1/2 point**

SETTLEMENT OF LIABILITIES IN EXCESS OF PARTNERSHIP ASSETS

The issue is how losses are shared when the partnership agreement is silent on this topic. The rule of partnership law is that where no agreement is made among partners respecting sharing of losses, losses will be shared in the same proportion that profits are shared. **1/2 point**

In this instance, the agreement is silent with regard to sharing losses but provides that profits will be shared equally. Therefore, losses are shared equally among the partners, and S and A, as surviving partners, must divide the loss equally. **1/2 point**

The partnership assets amount to $20,000, while liabilities exceed $105,000. Note that while any claimant may seek recourse against either A or S (once the assets of V Co. are exhausted), each partner will have a right of contribution against the other for any amount paid by him in excess of his 50% share. **1/2 point**

Hence, S and A are equally liable for V Co.'s losses.

ANSWER 5—TORTS/NEW YORK PRACTICE/EVIDENCE

(1)   The issue is whether P's action for medical malpractice is timely. **1/2 point**

Under the CPLR, the statute of limitations for medical malpractice is two years, six months. The cause of action accrues when the complained-of act occurs *or* if there is a continuous course of treatment of the patient by the physician, from the last date of such treatment. **1 point**

Under the facts, S treated P continuously from the date of the accident until March 15, 1990. P instituted suit in June 1992, which is less than two years, six months from the last date of treatment. Thus, the action was commenced within the statutory period. Therefore, the court properly denied the motion. **1 point**

(2)   The issue is the effect on co-defendants for contribution and indemnification when the plaintiff executes a release to one of the defendants. **1/2 point**

A party released by the plaintiff may neither seek nor be subject to a claim for contribution from any other party defendant. [N.Y. Gen. Oblig. Law §15-108] Since P released co-defendant S, the other co-defendant, M Co., may not seek contribution from S as a matter of law. Nor may M Co. seek indemnification against S. Indemnification is no longer available between parties in a comparative negligence situation, although indemnification remains available in contractual and vicarious liability situations. Thus, if P obtains a judgment against M Co., its liability will be reduced by either the amount of S's release or S's proportionate share of the total damages, whichever is greater. **1-1/2 points**

On these facts, S and M Co. do not have a contractual relationship upon which to base M Co.'s cross-claim. Nor could M Co. assert that it has been held vicariously liable for S's negligence. Therefore, because contribution is barred by statute and indemnification does not apply, the given facts no longer support M Co.'s cross-claim against S. The court's ruling was correct. **1 point**

(3)   The issue is when a post-accident design modification may be admissible as evidence. **1/2 point**

Under New York law, evidence of a post-accident design modification is admissible in a manufacturing defect/products liability case, but *not* in a design defect/products liability case. In this case, P sued solely on the theory of a defect in design in his product liability action. The testimony introduced concerns a post-accident design modification. Thus, the court erred; the testimony should have been stricken. **1-1/2 points**

(4)   The issue is what is required to maintain an action in strict liability in tort or in negligence. **1/2 point**

With regard to P's cause of action arising out of strict liability in tort, P must show that either: (i) the manufacturer produced a product that was dangerous beyond the expectation of the ordinary consumer; or (ii) a safer alternative or modification was economically feasible. **1 point**

Here, the testimony unequivocally shows that but for P's removing the guard, the accident would not have occurred, ***and*** the machine was in accord with the state of the art at the time of manufacture. Thus, it is clear that the machine was not unreasonably dangerous, and P has not made out a cause of action grounded in strict liability in tort. **1/2 point**

Furthermore, with regard to P's action in negligence, the testimony shows no breach of M Co.'s duty of care to users of the machine. Thus, P cannot make out a prima facie case in negligence. **1/2 point**
Therefore, the court should have granted M Co.'s motion and dismissed P's action.

ANSWER 6—EQUITY/CONTRACTS/NEW YORK PRACTICE

(1) The issue is when summary judgment may be granted.

A motion for summary judgment may be made by any party after issue has been joined (*i.e.,* service of an answer or reply). The only ground that will support a motion for summary judgment is that upon the affidavits, documents, depositions, and other submitted proofs, the court must conclude as a matter of law that there is no material issue of fact requiring trial. Where there is a material issue of fact that requires a trial, the motion must be denied. **1 point**

Here, A Co. is alleging that B's solicitation of Super Huge Retailer was part of his duties, and B was not entitled to receive additional compensation for duties that he was already obligated to perform. Supporting A Co.'s position is the New York view that performance of a preexisting legal duty is not an adequate detriment for purposes of consideration. However, contrary to A Co.'s position, B, a salaried salesman selling to well-known boutiques, alleged that a new employment relationship was created whereby he would solicit huge retailers for commissions. Thus, the conflicting positions regarding the nature and extent of B's duties create a material issue of fact regarding those duties and compensation for them. Thus, the court properly denied A Co.'s motion to dismiss B's complaint with prejudice. **1-1/2 points**

(2) The issue is whether a court may grant summary judgment to a nonmoving party when there is failure to state a cause of action to enjoin the use of customer lists as unfair trade competition. **1/2 point**

The general rule is that only a party who has made a motion or cross-motion may be accorded relief. However, CPLR 3212 specifically provides that if the court concludes that someone other than the moving party is entitled to summary judgment, the court may grant such relief in the absence of a cross-motion. **1 point**

Here, the first counterclaim sought to enjoin use of the customer lists as unfair trade competition. In New York, former employees may solicit their former employer's customers in the absence of an express contract to the contrary or any secret or confidential character of the employment. This is especially so where the former employer's customers are openly engaged in business in advertised locations. The facts show there was no agreement prohibiting B's use of customer lists, and both parties agreed in their motion papers that B kept lists of well-known specialty shops. Since there was no material issue of fact as to the nature and use of the customer lists, and since, as a matter of law, B did not commit unfair trade competition by using them, the court correctly "searched the record" and awarded summary judgment in favor of B. **1-1/2 points**

(3) At issue is when a court may grant summary judgment when the underlying claim is a noncompete clause. **1/2 point**

In order to enforce a covenant not to compete, the employer must show that (i) the services to be performed under the contract are unique, thus rendering any legal remedy inadequate; (ii) the covenant is reasonable as to both geographic scope and duration; and (iii) the covenant is reasonably necessary to protect the employer. Covenants tending to restrain a person from engaging in his lawful vocation are disfavored and are sustained only if they are not unduly burdensome on the person restrained and only to the extent that they are reasonably necessary to protect the legitimate interests of the employer. **1-1/2 points**

Here, A Co. is seeking to enforce, by the equitable remedy of injunction, the employment restriction signed by B; *i.e.*, enjoining his employment with C Co. Nothing in the facts indicates that B's services as a salesman are unique, or that the covenant is reasonably necessary to protect A Co.'s interests. Furthermore, although time limits of one year are usually considered reasonable, the covenant contains no limitation as to its geographic scope, thus rendering it unenforceable on its face. Accordingly, the court properly dismissed the counterclaim by awarding B summary judgment. **1 point**

(4) The issue is when a Statute of Frauds defense may be asserted.

Under CPLR 3018(b), a defendant is required to affirmatively plead the Statute of Frauds defense in his first responsive pleading. If he fails to so plead the defense, the defense is waived. [CPLR 3211(e)] Here, A Co. has moved to amend its pleadings at trial by adding the Statute of Frauds defense. Having failed to assert this defense in its answer, A Co. has waived it. **1-1/2 points**

Accordingly, the trial judge correctly refused to permit A Co. to interpose the Statute of Frauds defense at trial.

ANSWER 7—TORTS/NEW YORK PRACTICE

JOEY v. AIRPORT

The issue is whether Airport's failure to adequately maintain the fence was negligent. The elements of negligence are: (i) duty, (ii) breach of the duty, (iii) the breach is the actual cause of injury/death, (iv) the breach is the proximate cause of injury/death, and (v) damages. **1 point**

Joey's parents must prove that Airport had a duty to reasonably maintain a fence that would keep trespassers from entering the runway. Airport obviously did not adequately maintain the fence and therefore breached the duty. But for the damaged fence and the breach of the duty to adequately maintain the fence, Joey would not have been injured. Airport's failure to adequately maintain the fence was the proximate cause of Joey's death, as it was reasonably foreseeable that by not adequately maintaining the fence, someone may enter the runway and be killed by an airplane, which was the exact danger that the fence was installed to prevent. **1 point**

Moreover, in New York, the plaintiff's legal status no longer determines the duty owed him. The single standard of reasonable care under the circumstances governs all injuries on land. The plaintiff's status, while no longer determinative, remains relevant in connection with the foreseeability of his presence and the amount and nature of precautions required to meet the standard of reasonable care under the circumstances. As a result of Airport's negligence, Joey suffered damages in that he was killed. As administrators of Joey's estate, Joey's parents can sue Airport for wrongful death under a negligence theory. **1 point**

STEVIE v. AIRPORT

The issue is whether Stevie suffered a physical injury. **1 point**

Generally, there is a duty to avoid causing emotional distress to another, and this duty is breached when the defendant creates a foreseeable risk of injury to the plaintiff through physical impact or threat thereof and the plaintiff suffers a physical injury from the distress. In New York, recovery is limited to a plaintiff who is an immediate family member, exposed to immediate harm, who suffers physical injury. *Note:* Most courts do not require that the plaintiff actually be subjected to physical impact in order to recover, but the plaintiff must have been within the "target zone" or "zone of danger" of physical injury from the defendant's negligent conduct. **1-1/2 points**

In this case, Stevie was Joey's brother. Stevie was present at the scene and watched Joey get struck by the plane. More importantly, Joey died in Stevie's arms. However, there is no evidence of a physical injury to Stevie; Stevie will state a prima facie case for negligent infliction of emotional distress only if a physical injury is established. **1 point**

DEFENSES

The defendant will prove that Joey and Stevie were contributorily negligent. New York is a pure comparative negligence state, in which each party is liable for the damage caused by his conduct, and a plaintiff may recover even if his conduct is more culpable than the defendant's. Moreover, since Joey and Stevie are minors, the standard of care applied is that of a reasonable child of that age, intelligence, and experience. Since New York is a pure comparative negligence state, some damages will be recovered, but they will be reduced by the amount the victim contributed to his own injury. **1-1/2 points**

Airport may also prove that Joey and Stevie assumed the risk of being struck by an airplane when they actively chose to climb over the fence onto the runway. Generally, a plaintiff may be denied recovery if he assumed the risk of any damage caused by the defendant's act. The plaintiff must have (i) known of the risk, and (ii) voluntarily proceeded in the face of the risk. This too is not an absolute bar to recovery and falls within the doctrine of comparative negligence to reduce any damage award. In this case, it is likely that the damage award will be reduced based on the conduct of Joey and Stevie. **1 point**

DAMAGES

Joey's parents will be able to bring a survival action against Airport for Joey's pain and suffering before he died, and receive pecuniary damages in a wrongful death suit for Joey's death and recover damages for Stevie's psychological trauma. Of course, all damage awards will reflect the comparative negligence of Joey and Stevie. **1 point**

ANSWER 8—DOMESTIC RELATIONS/EVIDENCE/COMMERCIAL PAPER

(a)   The issue presented here is whether hearsay evidence is admissible in a judicial hearing covered by the Family Court Act. **1/2 point**

The Family Court Act provides that only competent, material, and relevant evidence may be admitted in a fact-finding hearing. **1/2 point**

The problem here is that the case file is hearsay. That is, it is a record of out-of-court statements offered for the truth of the statements contained therein. It will be inadmissible unless it falls within a recognized exception to hearsay. The only possible exception under which the case file may gain entry into the record is the business records exception. The business records exception in New York law is grounded in statute [CPLR 4518], which states that the record will be admissible if it was made in the regular course of business. But New York case law [Johnson v. Lutz, 253 N.Y. 124 (1930)] has limited the statute insofar as statements in the business records are admissible only if made by someone in the ordinary course of business. In other words, it is necessary that the statements in the case file have been made by witnesses whose job it was to evaluate the fitness of Mike and Frances to keep Cora. Clearly, this is not the case. Therefore, although the social worker was pursuing the ordinary course of her business when she compiled the case file, its contents may not be admitted in toto; it will be necessary to determine the admissibility of each item in the file individually. Thus, the court acted properly. **1-1/2 points**

(b)   The issue is whether a judge may interview a minor in chambers without putting the conference on the record.

Family Court Act section 152(b) specifically empowers a judge to take the unsworn testimony of a minor. Because the best interests of the child are at stake, the judge may take the child's testimony in camera, even over the objections of both parties. [Matter of Lincoln v. Lincoln, 24 N.Y.2d 270 (1969)] The only record that need be made is a stenographic record of the interview. [CPLR 4019(a)] The judge's failure to enter some account of the child's testimony into the record is reversible error only if, on appeal to the appellate division from a judgment or order of the court on any such action or proceeding, the stenographic record of any such interview was not made part of the record sent to the appellate division. This lack of a record makes intelligent review of the judge's decision by an appellate court impossible, and necessitates reversal and remand. [*See* Romi v. Hamdan, 417 N.Y.S.2d 523 (1979); Matter of Erlich v. Ressner, 391 N.Y.S.2d 152 (1977)] **1 point**

Here, the judge's actions were not improper in and of themselves. Unless, upon appeal to the appellate division, a stenographic record of the in camera interview was not produced, the judge's actions do not amount to reversible error. **1 point**

(c)   The issue presented here is whether the standard to be applied in a hearing to determine whether parental rights should be terminated is "the best interests of the child." **1/2 point**

While "the best interests of the child" is the standard applied when determining the rights of the child, in this case we are dealing with the rights of the parents. The termination of parental rights requires that the court satisfy the requirements of the Social Service Law section 384-b, which provides that termination may be ordered for one of the following reasons: (i) abandonment, (ii) inability to care for the child due to mental illness or retardation, (iii) permanent neglect, or (iv) severe or repeated child abuse. The Supreme Court has held that parental rights may be terminated only upon showing one of the above reasons by a standard of clear and convincing evidence. [Santosky v. Kramer, 455 U.S. 745 (1982)] **1 point**

Under these facts, only (i) or (iii) might arguably apply. Abandonment has been defined as failure to visit or communicate with the child for a period of six months, although able to do so. Permanent neglect consists of failure to substantially and repeatedly maintain contact with or plan for the future of the child although able to do so, following placement outside the parental home. Both abandonment and permanent neglect contemplate facts where it can be shown that the parents' actions evidence little or no effort to provide a home for the child, or to provide a relationship between the child and the parents. **1 point**

The facts make it clear that Mike and Frances have not permanently neglected Cora (nor have they abandoned her). Thus, the court's decision was improper, not only as an application of an improper standard, but also as a failure to meet the requisite burden of proof. (The status of the foster parents is never an issue in the termination of parental rights.) **1/2 point**

Finally, the termination of parental rights should be contrasted with the denial of custody. In any fight for custody, the best interests of the child are paramount; however, parental rights continue and are given great weight. Under New York case law, a parent with custody may not be denied custody absent a showing of some unfitness or extraordinary circumstances; even then, the court will invoke the "best interests of the child" test only after there has been a showing of unfitness or extraordinary circumstances. **1/2 point**

(d)   The issue is whether a bank must honor a stop payment order on a cashier's check.

It is necessary to characterize the negotiable instrument at issue here. A cashier's check is a draft drawn on the bank, where the drawer is also the bank. The payee here is Mike. He has indorsed the draft to Sam. In other words, Mike's bank account is not involved at all. Mike holds paper representing an unconditional promise to pay from the bank to him. Thus, the normal contractual relationship between drawer (depositor) and drawee (bank) does not exist in the case of a cashier's check. **1 point**

Consequently, the bank is under no obligation to honor Mike's stop payment order. The U.C.C. as adopted in New York reflects this rule. [U.C.C. §4-403] Thus, the bank acted within its rights, and Mike has no right of relief. **1 point**

(*Note:* First, a bank may be compelled to stop payment on an uncollected cashier's check either on order of a court, or upon posting of an indemnity bond. Second, the bank might be liable were it to cash the check for a thief, or improperly to cash it over a restrictive indorsement. But as none of these situations appears here, the bank acted properly.)

ANSWER 9—TORTS/NEW YORK PRACTICE

(A)(1)   The issue is whether A's claim that F negligently supervised S should be dismissed. **1/2 point**

To dismiss A's claim, the court must take all the allegations of the claim as true and determine that A has stated no cause of action upon which relief may be granted. **1/2 point**

Although New York has eliminated the defense of intrafamily immunity for negligent torts, it has been held that a child may not recover against his parent for negligent supervision. [Holodook v. Spenser, 36 N.Y.2d 35 (1974)] The court in *Holodook* also disallowed "a counterclaim or third-party complaint against a parent for negligent supervision of his child." Accordingly, a party may not maintain a claim based upon a parent's negligent supervision of S. **1 point**

Our facts state that F failed to notice S wander to the road. A then claims that F negligently supervised his child, S. As stated above, the Court of Appeals has disallowed this cause of action. Thus, the court correctly dismissed A's counterclaim. **1/2 point**

(2)   At issue are (i) whether a proper cause of action for negligent infliction of emotional distress has been stated, and (ii) whether M's action for personal injuries is time-barred. **1/2 point**

(i)   To dismiss M's cause of action, the court must take all of M's allegations as true and determine that M has stated no cause of action upon which relief may be granted. **1/2 point**

Under the facts, the only theory of recovery M could ground her claim in would be a theory of negligent infliction of emotional distress. The only harm that A could have caused M must have derived from M's seeing S's injury. **1/2 point**

New York law does not recognize recovery for negligent infliction of emotional distress under these facts. For M to have a cause of action grounded in this theory under New York law, it is necessary that M had actually been within the "impact zone" or "zone of danger" at the time of the injury, and that M had also viewed injury to an immediate member of her family. [Bovsun v. Sanperi, 61 N.Y.2d 219 (1984)] Because M was distant from the "zone of danger," having been inside the house while the accident occurred in the street, so that she was in no danger herself, she may not recover for her injuries. The court correctly dismissed her complaint. **1-1/2 points**

(ii)   M's action was also subject to dismissal on the basis of the statute of limitations. Claims for personal injuries are time-barred three years after the cause of action accrues [CPLR 214], and M is suing four years after the event. The fact that A was absent from New York for a year and a half does not entitle M to toll the statute during the defendant's absence because A's conduct in New York (an alleged tortious act) subjects him to long arm jurisdiction, thus allowing for service of process on A outside New York. Even if M had not been aware of A's out-of-state residence, the benefit of the toll was lost because of the theoretical availability of long arm jurisdiction. [Yarusso v. Arbotowicz, 41 N.Y.2d 516 (1977)] Thus, the court correctly dismissed M's cause of action. **1-1/2 points**

(B)   The issue is the effect of a settlement between a plaintiff and defendant on the remaining co-defendants. **1/2 point**

General Obligations Law section 15-108(a) provides that when the plaintiff settles with one tortfeasor, recovery against a remaining tortfeasor will be reduced by the highest of the following figures: (i) the amount stipulated in the release; (ii) the amount actually paid for the release; or (iii) the apportioned share of damages that the settling tortfeasor would have paid but for the settlement. **1 point**

In the instant case, we take the highest of these three figures: (i) $30,000 (the amount P agreed to pay in settlement of F's claim); (ii) $30,000 (the amount P actually paid); (iii) $50,000 (the apportioned damages that P would have had to pay had he not settled). Thus, we reduce the $100,000 award by $50,000, and A's liability is limited to the $50,000 remaining. However, A actually has only $10,000 under the facts. Therefore, F can collect no more than the $10,000 and can seek no additional contribution from P, notwithstanding the reduction in his recovery caused by the settlement and A's impoverished condition. **1-1/2 points**

Thus, F can collect $10,000 from A.

ANSWER 10—DOMESTIC RELATIONS/NEW YORK PRACTICE

(1)(A)   The issue here is whether the grounds of cruel and inhuman treatment exist. This situation involves a divorce action, which is governed by both the Domestic Relations Law and the Civil Practice Law and Rules. **1/2 point**

In a divorce action, the plaintiff's complaint is required to plead the nature of circumstances of the defendant spouse's alleged misconduct, and the time and place of each act complained of must be specified. In this instance, W's action for divorce is based on the grounds of cruel and inhuman treatment. Cruel and inhuman treatment is defined by New York courts as conduct by the defendant spouse which so endangers the plaintiff's physical or mental well being as to render it unsafe or improper for the plaintiff to cohabit with the defendant. New York courts use a standard of serious misconduct, as distinguished from minor incidents, in determining whether cruel and inhuman treatment is in fact evidenced. In her complaint, W alleged specific beating incidents. It appears that W's complaint does in fact state a cause of action for cruel and inhuman treatment. Therefore, the court was correct in refusing to dismiss W's complaint for failure to state a cause of action for cruel and inhuman treatment. **2 points**

(B)   The issue here is whether cohabitation is a defense in a divorce action for cruel and inhuman treatment. **1/2 point**

Cohabitation in itself is not a defense to an action for divorce based on cruel and inhuman treatment especially in a situation such as the present, where the husband suffers an accident and is incapacitated and the wife first cares for him until he is partly recuperated and then moves out to protect herself. Moreover, H's affirmative defense is an assertion of condonation. The defense of condonation is not available in an action for divorce based on cruel and inhuman treatment; it is available only on a cause of action based on adultery. The fact that H and W cohabited after the alleged beatings will be weighed by the court in determining whether cruel and inhuman treatment actually occurred. Hence, the court was correct in refusing to dismiss W's complaint based on H's contention that W cohabited with him after the beatings. **1-1/2 points**

(2)   The issue is whether a material issue of fact remains for trial.

Under CPLR 3212, a motion for summary judgment may be made in any action, including a matrimonial action, once issue has been joined (*e.g.*, after service of an answer). Summary judgment will be granted only if upon all the affidavits, documents, depositions, and other submitted proofs, the court can conclude that there is no issue of fact requiring trial. **1 point**

In this situation, W submitted affidavits of herself, the police who responded after the beatings, and the doctors who cared for her. Additionally, the doctors enumerated her injuries from the beatings. H did not submit any reply or opposition to W's motion. It is also important to note that police and doctors are credible witnesses. Accordingly, it appears that after all documentation and pleadings were submitted, the facts appear straightforward and uncontroverted. H was required to establish either that there was a triable issue of fact or that W was not entitled to summary judgment. H failed to do so. Hence, the court was correct in granting W's motion for summary judgment. **1-1/2 points**

(3)(A)   The first issue is whether personal injury claims earned during marriage are marital property subject to "equitable distribution." The division of property in divorce actions after July 19, 1980, is governed by the "equitable distribution" law contained within the Domestic Relations Law. Under equitable distribution, marital property is distributed equitably between the parties to a divorce action considering the circumstances of the particular case. Marital property is defined as all property acquired during marriage by either or both spouses and before either the execution of a separation agreement or the commencement of a matrimonial action. There are a number of statutory exceptions to the term "marital property," including "compensation for personal injuries," which is considered separate property under the equitable distribution scheme. **1-1/2 points**

The facts state that H recovered $100,000 as compensation for personal injuries. Therefore, H's proceeds from his personal injury claim are not marital property. Hence, the court was incorrect in distributing H's award. **1/2 point**

(B)   The second issue is whether advances during marriage are marital property subject to "equitable distribution." The advances are marital property as defined by the Equitable Distribution Law because they were acquired as a result of work W performed during the marriage and before the execution of the separation agreement [N.Y. Dom. Rel. Law §236(b)] Thus, the court was correct in distributing W's advance for the book she wrote while married to H. **1 point**

ANSWER 11—CORPORATIONS/CONTRACTS/EQUITY

(1)   The issue is whether B has any grounds to bring an action against the corporation and, if so, what may B recover. **1/2 point**

When the defendant's motion is to dismiss on the ground of the plaintiff's failure to state a claim upon which relief may be granted, the court must determine the adequacy of the claim stated in the complaint. If the court finds that the grounds for dismissal are established, it will order dismissal of the claim. **1 point**

At the threshold, it must be determined whether B has standing to maintain the suit. Under the facts, it appears that B is suing in his own name and not in the name of the corporation. Thus, B is not maintaining a shareholder's derivative action, although he might have been able to maintain such an action if he had sued on behalf of and in the name of the corporation. B may, however, maintain an action in his own name and right. Section 720 of the Business Corporations Law authorizes an officer, a director, or a shareholder of a corporation to maintain an action to enjoin an illegal transfer of corporate assets. While a shareholder must sue in the name of the corporation, an officer or director may sue in his own name and in his capacity as officer or director. Thus, B was entitled to bring suit in his own name, without complying with the requirements of a shareholder's derivative suit (demand upon the board, posting a bond, or minimum stock ownership, etc.). **2 points**

Since B's complaint passed the threshold inquiry, the complaint must next be analyzed to determine whether B has stated a valid claim upon which relief may be granted. For a corporation formed on or before February 23, 1998, section 909 of the Business Corporations Law sets out specific procedures that a corporation must follow before it can sell all or substantially all of its assets, if such sale is not within the usual course of business. First, the sale must be approved by the board of directors. Then, the sale must be submitted to the shareholders and approved by a vote of at least two-thirds of the shares in order for the sale to be valid. In this instance, two-thirds of the shares were not voted to approve the sale—only 55% of the outstanding shares approved. Thus, the sale is invalid, and B may block it. Consequently, B has stated a claim upon which relief may be granted, and the court should deny the motion of A and C. (If this were a corporation formed after February 22, 1998, the sale would be valid. Under revised section 909, there need only be a simple majority of the shareholders, not a two-thirds vote. Therefore, in that scenario, B could not block the vote and there would be no claim upon which relief could be granted.) **2 points**

Finally, it should be noted that B may elect to receive the fair market value of his shares from the corporation, if he filed a written objection to the sale before the shareholders' vote, including a statement of intent to demand his "appraisal" rights if the vote went against him. [N.Y. Bus. Corp. Law §§623, 910] However, it is B's duty as a director to object and to sue to compel the other directors to invalidate the sale. **1 point**

(2)   A restrictive covenant is generally enforceable by injunction, as long as the covenant: (i) is necessary for the protection of the purchaser; (ii) is reasonable in time, distance, and extent; and (iii) represents part of a bargained-for exchange. Covenants not to compete have been enforced for periods as long as 10 years in the absence of a showing that enforcing the covenant would preclude the covenanting party from pursuing its business. [Karpinski v. Ingrasci, 28 N.Y.2d 45 (1971)] **1-1/2 points**

A and C are not restricted to such a degree in terms of geographic area or type of work as to preclude them from doing any business whatsoever. Since D purchased the covenant not to compete as part of the overall transaction with A and C, to refuse to allow the injunction would act to deprive D of the benefit of his bargain. Thus, it is clear that D will receive an injunction preventing A and C from competing. **1 point**

ANSWER 12—CONFLICT OF LAWS/NEW YORK PRACTICE/FEDERAL JURISDICTION & PROCEDURE

(1)   The issue is whether the federal court has subject matter jurisdiction over the case and personal jurisdiction over the parties. **2/3 point**

A federal court has subject matter jurisdiction over a particular case if the cause of action arises out of (i) a federal question; or (ii) complete diversity among the parties, and the amount in controversy exceeds $75,000. Lack of subject matter jurisdiction is a basis for a motion to dismiss that may be raised at any time. **2/3 point**

Since the plaintiff is a citizen of the United States, and the defendant is a citizen of Canada, 28 U.S.C. section 1332(a)(2) applies. Furthermore, the amount in controversy exceeds $75,000, the required jurisdictional amount in diversity cases. As to personal jurisdiction, federal law requires plaintiffs to use state jurisdictional bases for obtaining jurisdiction over parties in federal district court. CPLR 302(a)(2) (tortious act within the state) provides ample basis for exercising jurisdiction over the defendant because the defendant engaged in tortious conduct in the state. Thus, the court correctly denied A's motion to dismiss. **2/3 point**

(2)   The issue is when a losing party may recover costs.

The general rule is that costs are awarded to the prevailing party, unless to do so would be inequitable. Costs may be awarded to the losing party only if the losing party has won some part of the suit; *i.e.,* she has won in part and lost in part. Therefore, the court erred; at best, the court could have awarded no costs to either party, but even then it would have been necessary to cite equitable considerations supporting such an action. **1 point**

(3)   The issue is whether the Canadian guest statute should be applied by the New York court.

When faced with a conflict of law regarding loss distribution rules in a tort case, the New York Court of Appeals has rejected the old vested rights approach, which would mandate the automatic application of the law of the situs where the tort occurred. Now, New York courts apply the *governmental interest analysis*. This is to ensure that the jurisdiction with the greatest interest in the suit has its law apply. In order to make the determination, the court will look at the factual contacts of each jurisdiction, the differing laws, and the underlying policies for each law; apply the facts to the policies; and apply the greater governmental interest. For tort cases, New York refined the interest analysis in *Neumeier v. Kuehner*, 31 N.Y.2d 121 (1972). The *Neumeier* rules are a product of the analysis. Under the first *Neumeier* rule, if parties are from a particular jurisdiction, then the law of that jurisdiction will apply. **1 point**

In this case, the Canadian guest statute should be applied. While the accident took place in New York, each litigant is from Ontario. New York has very little interest in the litigation because no New York parties are involved. Under Ontario law, these suits should not be allowed, to prevent insurance collusion to the detriment of Canadian insurers. Because each party is from Canada, the Canadian interest is furthered if the guest statute is applied. At the same time, no New York interest is harmed. Accordingly, the court should apply the Canadian guest statute. Therefore, the court erred in granting the motion. **2 points**

(4)   The issue is when a motion may be dismissed on the grounds of forum non conveniens.

A's motion is timely even though made after service of the answer. No time limit is specified in CPLR 327 for the making of a motion to dismiss on the ground of forum non conveniens; the courts merely apply a test of reasonableness. Furthermore, CPLR 327 provides that, upon motion of a party, if the court finds that the interests of justice require an action to be stayed or dismissed so that the action may be heard in a more appropriate forum in another state, the court may "stay or dismiss the action in whole or in part on any conditions that may be just." Since the rationale of the doctrine is that New York is an inconvenient forum in which to litigate, a defendant's chances for success on the motion will decrease as pretrial proceedings progress. Here, A's motion is made at a very early stage of the lawsuit, so it is timely, even though made after service of the answer. **1 point**

In evaluating the court's denial of the motion, one may only inquire whether the court abused its discretion. As that is not true here, the ruling was correct. Although both A and B are Canadian citizens, the accident occurred in New York and at least one witness (H), and probably others, are New York residents. **1 point**

(5)   The issue is whether collateral estoppel applies and whether the court may award summary judgment.

A court may award summary judgment to either party whenever the court finds as a matter of law that there is no material question of fact to be determined. For the court to make such a determination here, it is necessary for the court to apply the principle of collateral estoppel—to find that all issues in the *B v. A* action are identical to the issues presented in *H v. A;* that the issues were necessarily decided in *H v. A* (*i.e.,* that no issue was peripheral to *H v. A* but central to *B v. A*); and that A had a full and fair opportunity to litigate each issue in *H v. A,* so that precluding him from litigating the same issue in *B v. A* does not deprive A of the right to a hearing. **1 point**

There is no identity of issues here. In *H v. A,* the district court would not have applied the Canadian guest statute. Rather, it would have allowed H the benefit of New York law, which does not preclude a suit by a guest against a host. This is because of the operation of *Neumeier* rule 2, which provides that where the law of the plaintiff's domicile provides for recovery, and the accident occurs in that jurisdiction, it will be the law of that jurisdiction that applies. Thus, because H was a New York resident and the accident occurred there, the law of New York applies. But in *B v. A,* the court would apply the Canadian guest statute (*see* ruling (3), *supra*). Thus, collateral estoppel does not apply, and the court correctly denied the motion to dismiss. **1 point**

ANSWER 13—CRIMINAL LAW/CRIMINAL PROCEDURE

(A)(i) D'S ORAL CONFESSION

The issue is whether D validly waived his *Miranda* rights.

For a confession to be admissible under the Fifth Amendment's privilege against self-incrimination, a person in custody must be informed of his *Miranda* rights prior to interrogation.

For D's oral statement to be used against him in the state's case, it is necessary that D have been advised of his rights, and that D made a valid waiver of his rights before making a statement. Under the facts, it is clear that D was informed of his rights before questioning began. D's statement that he knew his rights is a strong indication that he made a voluntary, knowing, and intelligent waiver of his rights prior to making a statement. **1 point**

Questioning had not actually begun when D made his oral statement. Thus, even had D not expressly waived his rights, it may be argued that this statement was "blurted out." D's oral statement relating to the planned robbery is admissible. It does not matter that D refused to sign his statement. **1 point**

(ii) D'S WRITTEN CONFESSION

The issue is whether D had revoked his *Miranda* waiver.

If D requests the presence of counsel before making any written statements, all questioning must cease. **1 point**

D's statement that he would not sign a statement without speaking to his attorney constituted a revocation of his *Miranda* waiver. At that point, it was necessary that all questioning cease until the attorney arrived or until D himself initiated further conversation. Thus, under federal constitutional law, D's written statement will be excluded. In addition, under New York constitutional law, once a criminal defendant in custody requests an attorney, all questioning must cease until the attorney is present. Any waiver of rights made out of the presence of the attorney after such a request is invalid, and any statement taken after such a request is barred. This is the *Arthur-Hobson* rule. Consequently, once D requested to speak with his attorney, his statements could no longer be used against him. His written confession is thus inadmissible against him. **1-1/2 points**

It is irrelevant that A actually went to the police station and attempted to see D. It is D's request, and not A's presence, that protects D from interrogation. **1 point**

(B) CRIME OF CONSPIRACY

The issue is whether the elements of conspiracy have been met.

The elements of conspiracy are: (i) intent; (ii) agreement; and (iii) an overt act in furtherance of the conspiracy. **1-1/2 points**

D's intent can be shown by his statement of agreement and his arrival at the store at the time the robbery was supposed to take place. Here also is the overt act. D may argue that there could have been no agreement, as P was a police officer and thus could not agree to the conspiracy. However, New York has held that lack of intent or capacity on the part of a co-conspirator is no defense to the charge of conspiracy, including the situation where the sole co-conspirator is a police officer. [People v. Schwimmer, 420 N.Y.2d 218 (1979)] **1 point**

D may attempt to raise the defense of entrapment. Under New York law, entrapment is an affirmative defense that must be affirmatively pleaded and proved by the defendant. The defendant must prove by a preponderance of the evidence that he lacked the predisposition to commit the crime, and was induced to commit the crime solely by the acts of a police officer or other public servant. Since conduct by the police that affords the defendant the opportunity to commit the crime is not entrapment by itself, and since once the defendant raises the defense, the prosecution may introduce evidence to show the defendant's past criminal acts, D has very little chance to prevail. Thus, D may be convicted of conspiracy. **2 points**

ANSWER 14—WILLS

THE SURROGATE'S RULING REGARDING THE MAY WILL

The issue is whether the May will was revoked by the July will or the December codicil. **1/2 point**

A will or any part thereof may be revoked by another will, by a writing of the testator clearly indicating an intention to effect the revocation, or by an alteration executed with the formalities prescribed for the execution and attestation of a will. These formalities include the requirement of two attesting witnesses. Also, under New York law, a document cannot be incorporated by reference into a testamentary instrument unless the document was executed with testamentary formalities (with certain exceptions not applicable here). **1 point**

Under the facts, the May will was validly executed. Therefore, that will should be given effect unless it was later revoked. A will may be revoked by a subsequent will as T attempted to do here. However, T's attempts were unsuccessful because the July will was not validly executed and that problem could not be fixed by the December codicil. **1 point**

As noted above, a will must have two attesting witnesses. Here, the July will had only one witness; therefore, it was invalid. T tried to remedy this problem by executing a codicil that incorporated the July will's terms by reference. However, as noted above, New York generally does not recognize the doctrine of incorporation by reference. Thus, the codicil did not solve the witness problem of the July will. Therefore, the court was correct in ruling that the May will should be admitted. **1-1/2 points**

F'S RENUNCIATION AND ITS EFFECT

The issue is the effect of F's renouncing his bequest. **1/2 point**

To renounce his bequest effectively, F must (i) file an irrevocable renunciation (ii) which is notarized (iii) within nine months of the death of T. In addition, F must file a separate affidavit that he received no consideration for his renunciation. **1 point**

Assuming that F complied with this procedure, the effect of F's renunciation is that F will be treated as having predeceased the testator. F's bequest will lapse, and the anti-lapse statute does not apply because F is neither a sibling nor issue of T. Thus, given that B was not named in his brother's (T's) will and that the anti-lapse statute does not apply to save the gift to F (who is also presumably B's father), B will take nothing from T's estate, and the bequest will pass through the residuary clause to D. **1-1/2 points**

D'S CHALLENGE TO THE CHARITABLE BEQUEST

The issue is whether testamentary gifts to charity will be limited.

The limitation on testamentary gifts to charity has long been abolished. Neither the date of the will nor the date of T's death determines D's rights; she is barred from challenging the bequest. **1 point**

L'S LIABILITY

The issue is whether a potential will beneficiary can recover for an attorney's negligence in drafting a will. **1/2 point**

L's failure to reexecute the July will and his improper drafting of the December codicil were both negligent acts. Under these facts, while the EPTL would allow T's executor to maintain a suit against L based on L's failure of duty to T, damages would probably be nonexistent. New York's courts still hold to the theory that under the privity of contract doctrine a lawyer's duty runs only to the client. For any other party to recover, she would have to show that L breached a duty to her, which resulted in harm. D certainly can show such harm—she lost $110,000—however, she cannot show a duty owing to her. Thus, D has no right of relief under current New York law. **1-1/2 points**

ANSWER 15—CONTRACTS

(1)   The issue is what constitutes a breach of an employment contract. **1/2 point**

A breach of contract occurs when there is an absolute duty to perform and such duty has not been performed. A material breach is deemed to have occurred when the nonbreaching party does not receive the substantial benefit of his bargain due to such nonperformance or defective performance. **1/2 point**

In this case, H sold his interest in S Co. in exchange for a five-year employment contract in which he would receive a monthly salary of $3,000 and hold an "executive and supervisory" position. Those two elements, salary and position, were the "benefit" that H bargained for in exchange for his interest in S Co. By removing H from his position as an executive, half of the benefit of the bargained-for exchange was not realized by H. This is a material breach of the contract by U Co. **1/2 point**

When a material breach of contract occurs, the nonbreaching party may consider the contract at an end, meaning that no further performance by the nonbreaching party is due under the contract. The nonbreaching party has the immediate right to all remedies available for breach of the entire contract, including damages. In employment contracts, if the employer breaches, the employee is entitled to the full contract price, regardless of when the breach occurred. To recover, the nonbreaching party must show that he is willing and able to perform but is unable to do so as a result of the breaching party's failure to perform. **1 point**

In this case, at the moment that U Co. relieved H of his duties as an "executive and supervisor," a breach of the contract occurred. At that point, the contract was at an end and no further performance by H was owed to U Co. Here, H displayed his willingness to perform by staying on with U Co. in the lesser position while he sought similar employment elsewhere. That H acted negligently in the performance of his duties as night watchman does not diminish or eliminate U Co.'s liability under the contract. **1 point**

Thus, H did not breach the contract and U Co.'s first plea should be denied.

(2)   The issue is whether H had a duty to mitigate damages. **1/2 point**

In an employment contract, if the employer breaches the contract, the nonbreaching employee has the duty to mitigate damages by using reasonable care in finding a position of the same kind, rank, and grade in the same area. The fact that the like position does not pay the same amount does not remove the requirement of mitigation by the nonbreaching party. The employer has the burden of proof to show that such an available position exists. Thus, under the ordinary rules governing breach of employment contracts, H would be held to have breached his duty of mitigation since there were positions of the same kind in the Albany area but not of the same pay level. However, this is not an ordinary employment contract, because the consideration here was not simply salary for performance. In this case, H's employment contract was the basis for the sale of his interest in S Co., and thus the salary represented more than just compensation for services. Hence, H is not under a duty to mitigate damages because this employment contract is part of a bargained-for exchange, and H's interest is greater than simply compensation for personal services. Therefore, U Co.'s second plea should be denied. **2 points**

(3)   The issue is whether a nonbreaching party can bring an action prior to a contract's termination if the contract is materially breached. **1/2 point**

When one party materially breaches a contract, the nonbreaching party may consider the contract at its end and may *immediately* recover all remedies for breach of the *entire* contract. There is no need to wait until the termination date of the contract. **1 point**

U Co. materially breached its contract with H on February 1. Soon thereafter, H properly brought an action to recover all monies owed to him under the contract. Thus, U Co.'s third plea should be denied because when it materially breached its contract with H, the contract ended, and H became entitled to an immediate action on the full amount due under the contract. **1 point**

H'S DAMAGES

The issue is the amount of damages to which H is entitled.

The amount of damages is calculated by determining the contract amount—in this case, $180,000 ($36,000 per year for five years). Any amount that has been paid to H will be credited against the contract amount. In this instance $27,000 has already been paid; therefore, the amount of damages due to H is the contract amount ($180,000) less any amount already paid ($27,000), or $153,000. In addition, H may be liable to U Co. on a counterclaim for any damages proximately caused by H's negligence, and that amount would be deducted from H's award. **1-1/2 points**

Therefore, H is entitled to $153,000 in damages, less any damages proximately attributable to H's negligence.

ANSWER 16—WILLS

ALLAN

The issue presented is whether his objection to probate of the will may bring the fourth clause into play, depriving him of a share. **1 point**

The fourth clause of Tessie's will is a no-contest (also called an in terrorem) clause. Most states hold that if the beneficiary had reasonable cause for bringing the contest, the no-contest forfeiture clause is not given effect. However, New York's EPTL section 3-3.5 specifically provides that such clauses shall be given full effect. Allan's objection is not covered by the exceptions to EPTL section 3-3.5. Challenges based upon improper execution are not excepted from the operation of a no-contest clause. Thus, Allan's objection will bring the no-contest clause into play, and he will take nothing. **2-1/2 points**

BETSY

The issue presented with regard to Betsy is whether the money given to her by Tessie two years before Tessie's death will reduce Betsy's bequest under the will, so that she gets nothing. **1 point**

EPTL section 2-1.5 states that an advancement made to a donee under a will may reduce the gift to the donee, but only where the advancement can be proven by a contemporaneous writing signed by either the donor or the donee which demonstrates the donor's intent. In this case, Tessie made an oral statement to Betsy at the time the money was advanced but did not put the statement into writing. Three months after making the advancement, Tessie did make a writing which made her intention clear; however, that writing was not contemporaneous. **2-1/2 points**

Consequently, Tessie's efforts to reduce Betsy's share under the will were ineffective. Betsy will take $50,000.

CHRYSTAL

The issue presented is whether Chrystal's bequest is affected by her status as a witness to the will.

Under EPTL section 3-3.2, while an interested witness does not invalidate the will, a disposition to an interested witness may be void. But if the interested witness is also an intestate distributee, the witness will take the lesser of her legacy and her intestate share. **1 point**

In this case, Chrystal, as issue of Tessie, is an intestate distributee. Because Tessie is survived by three children and no spouse, Chrystal would take one-third of the estate if Tessie had died intestate, in which case she would have taken $25,000. As the residuary legatee, she also takes $25,000. Consequently, she is entitled to $25,000. **2 points**

ANSWER 17—CONSTITUTIONAL LAW/NEW YORK PRACTICE/TORTS

(1) The issue is whether due process is applicable in an administrative proceeding. **1/2 point**

The Due Process Clauses of the Fifth Amendment (applicable to the federal government) and the Fourteenth Amendment (applicable to the states) provide that the government shall not take a person's life, liberty, or property without due process of law. Due process contemplates fair process and procedure, and requires at least an opportunity to present objections to the proposed action to a fair, neutral decisionmaker. **1 point**

As a matter of due process, P is entitled to a "trial type" hearing (as opposed to the "argument type" hearing conducted here) where (i) the order will be based on adjudicative facts, (ii) the number of parties to whom notice and opportunity to be heard would have to be given is not impractically large, and (iii) agency action deprives the party of liberty or property. Adjudicative facts are in issue here because of the necessity to decide who did what, when, where, how, and with what motive or intent. The number of parties is not unduly burdensome. P has a property interest in retaining his license because it allows him to pursue his livelihood. A "trial type" hearing includes the right of cross-examination. The agency has the ability to subpoena witnesses. Refusing to do so, resulting in P being denied his right to cross-examination, is an abuse of discretion. Therefore, the ruling denying P's request to cross-examine the persons named in C's letter was incorrect. **1-1/2 points**

(2) The issues are whether and how P may appeal the decision of the administrative hearing. **1/2 point**

(a) The first issue is what is the appeal process of an administrative hearing. P may commence an Article 78 proceeding in the supreme court to obtain review of the administrative action against him. The Article 78 proceeding is in the nature of certiorari; that is, the court will determine only whether the department's determination is, on the record, supported by substantial evidence. P must file his petition for review within four months of the department's determination in order to preserve his right to judicial review. The appellate division will hear the case on transfer from the supreme court. The burden of proof in the proceeding will be on P, the petitioner. Therefore, P may appeal the decision of the department of education. **1-1/2 points**

(b) The second issue is whether the administrative agency's decision was based on substantial evidence. **1/2 point**

P's best argument in his petition is that the department's decision is not based upon substantial evidence. The only reasonable evidence given at the hearing was (i) C's letter, and (ii) conversations between S and the six persons named in C's letter, and this evidence is not substantial under the circumstances. **1/2 point**

The two pieces of evidence would constitute hearsay, *i.e.,* out-of-court statements intended to prove the truth of the matter asserted therein. Hearsay is admissible at an administrative hearing, unless the agency's rules specifically state otherwise, as long as it is relevant and material. To determine whether hearsay constitutes substantive evidence, it is necessary to review its reliability and probative value. (Although largely discredited, some courts have required that hearsay be corroborated, which was not done here. [Skyline Inn v. S.L.A., 44 N.Y.2d 695 (1978)] However, this would not change the outcome.) C's letter may not be very reliable as it was written by a competitor who would like P to have his license suspended. The conversations between S and the six persons would seem to be more reliable, although their names were supplied by C, who was seeking to discredit his competitor. The reliability of the evidence is further diminished by P's not being afforded the opportunity to cross-examine these six persons. As discussed above, this was an abuse of discretion. Therefore, there should be a reversal of the agency's decision. **1-1/2 points**

(c) The third issue is whether an action lies in defamation. P may bring an action for defamation, but the action will not succeed because C has a viable defense. **1/2 point**

Defamatory language is language that tends to adversely affect one's reputation. At issue here is libel, which is a defamatory statement in written or other permanent form. **1/2 point**

P's effort here may fail for two reasons: (i) Truth is an absolute defense to defamation. The facts appear to support the statements in C's letter; thus, C has an absolute defense to P's defamation action. (ii) In addition, C's letter was sent to an appropriate authority, respecting licensure of a type regulated by the department to which the letter was sent. New York recognizes a qualified privilege in such cases—C has the limited right to make defamatory statements in a letter written to such an authority, provided the letter is written in good faith and C believes the contents to be true. As it happens, the contents are true, so that C need not avail himself of the qualified privilege. Therefore, a defamation action by P would be unsuccessful. **1-1/2 points**

ANSWER 18—TORTS/NEW YORK PRACTICE/AGENCY

(1)   The issue here is how much Mike needed to prove to establish a prima facie case against Darryl under two theories: (i) that the truck rented by Mike had a manufacturing defect, and (ii) that Lorraine was negligent in her operation of the truck. **1/2 point**

A manufacturing defect arises when a product emerges from manufacturing different from and more dangerous than properly made products. A defendant will be liable under this theory if the product failed to perform as safely as an ordinary consumer would expect. It is important to note that the defect must have existed when the product left the defendant's control, and retailers may be liable even if they had no opportunity to inspect the product. This will be inferred if the product moved through normal channels of distribution. **1 point**

Liability may be based on either strict liability or negligence. Under strict liability, the plaintiff must prove a strict duty to supply safe products from a commercial supplier (which includes commercial lessors), a breach of that duty which was the actual and proximate cause of the injury, and the damage resulting. In New York, the CPLR dictates a three-year statute of limitations. **1 point**

To prove liability under a negligence theory, the plaintiff must prove that the defendant owed a duty, there was a breach of that duty, the breach was the actual and proximate cause of the injury, and damages. In New York, the CPLR dictates a three-year statute of limitations. **1/2 point**

In this case, Darryl, as a commercial lessor, was a commercial supplier of the garbage truck and owed a duty of strict liability to all foreseeable plaintiffs, including Mike, an employee of the person leasing the truck. Breach of duty is established by showing that the product supplied by the defendant was so defective as to be unreasonably dangerous, and here, the evidence at trial showed that the truck's safety mechanism failed to work, creating an unreasonable danger. The evidence also established that the failure of the safety mechanism was the actual and proximate cause of Mike's injuries, and he presented evidence of all of his damages. Consequently, Mike established a prima facie case against Darryl under a theory of strict liability sufficient to withstand a summary judgment motion. It should be noted that Mike's claim falls within the statute of limitations. **1 point**

Mike has not established a prima facie case based on negligence, either for the supplying of a defective product or for the negligent conduct of Darryl's employee, Lorraine. To establish breach of duty in a products liability action based on negligence, Mike must show negligent conduct by the defendant leading to the supplying of a defective product. Using res ipsa loquitur, a manufacturer can be found to have acted negligently just by evidence of the defect; however, other defendants in the chain of supply need only make a cursory inspection of the product to avoid liability for manufacturing defects. Here, Darryl supplied Mel with a brand new garbage truck from a reputable manufacturer; Mike has presented no evidence that Darryl acted negligently in doing so. **1 point**

Mike has also presented no evidence of negligent conduct by Lorraine. While Darryl would be vicariously liable for any negligence on the part of Lorraine because she was his employee and acting within the scope of her employment, the undisputed testimony shows that Lorraine was qualified to use the garbage truck and followed the operating manual instructions. Thus, there was no evidence of negligence by Lorraine. **1/2 point**

Since Mike was able to establish a prima facie case under a theory of strict liability, the court's ruling was correct.

(2) The issue is, under the CPLR, what is the statute of limitations for an action of indemnification, which is the duty to pay debts on behalf of another. **1/2 point**

In New York, the CPLR provides for a six-year statute of limitations to implead a third party for indemnification purposes. The period is measured from the date the payment is made. In this case, Darryl impleaded Yoram roughly 14 months after the case was commenced by Mike. Therefore, the second ruling denying Yoram's affirmative defense was correct. **1 point**

(3) The issue is whether the evidence was sufficient to establish a prima facie case against Yoram. **1/2 point**

The manufacturer is strictly liable for defects in its products. Since Darryl offered undisputed evidence that Lorraine was not negligent in handling the truck, and the product failed to perform as safely as an ordinary consumer would expect, a prima facie case against Yoram was established. There is also an undisputed inference that since the product moved through normal channels of distribution, the defect existed when the product left Yoram's control. Consequently, an indemnification case has been established and the court was correct in its ruling. **1 point**

(4) The issue is whether a joint tortfeasor may be subject to a claim for indemnification subsequent to a settlement. **1/2 point**

In New York, pursuant to the CPLR, while a settling tortfeasor may not seek or be subject to a claim for contribution, here, Yoram is not a joint tortfeasor seeking contribution; he is seeking indemnification. He is not being sued by Mike and was impleaded solely for indemnification purposes of Darryl. Under the CPLR, the release statute does not apply to the release of a party who is entitled to complete indemnification from another. In this case, Darryl is seeking such indemnification from Yoram, and his decision to settle the case does not bar any attempts to continue seeking monies from Yoram. Thus, the court was incorrect. **1 point**

ANSWER 19—EQUITY/CONTRACTS

The issue is whether the restrictive covenant against D is enforceable by the partnership, and if so, whether specific performance is available as a remedy.

Specific performance is available for breach of a covenant not to compete if the following conditions are met: (i) there is a valid contract; (ii) the conditions have been satisfied; (iii) the legal remedy is inadequate; (iv) the decree is enforceable; (v) mutuality of remedy is present; and (vi) no defenses are available. **1 point**

(i) There is a valid contract here. A contract is valid if it contains all of the necessary elements: mutual assent, valid consideration, and no existing defenses to the contract. Such defenses include mutual mistake, lack of consideration, misrepresentation and fraud, illegality, incapacity to contract, unconscionability, and the Statute of Frauds. In this case, the partnership of A, B, and C offered D a position as equal partner, which he accepted. The consideration passed was D's promise to perform in exchange for a share in the profits of the partnership. Additionally, all of the partners consented to the agreement. There do not appear to be any of the defenses available to either party. Thus, from the facts, it can be concluded that a valid contract exists because all of the elements of a contract are present. **1 point**

(ii) All conditions have been satisfied here. The conditions that must be satisfied are those of a covenant not to compete in an employment contract. To be valid and enforceable, such a restrictive covenant must be reasonable. To determine whether the covenant is reasonable, the court looks to see if: (i) the covenant is reasonably necessary to protect the employer; (ii) the duration of the restriction is reasonable; (iii) the scope of the geographic ambit is reasonable; (iv) there is not an unreasonable burden on one of the parties; and (v) the general public will not be harmed by such restriction. Furthermore, the services to be performed under the contract must be unique so that money damages would not be an adequate remedy. **1 point**

Here, the contract clause restricts D from practicing medicine for five years within the city of Utica. It has been held that a restrictive covenant requiring no competition within a five-mile radius for five years is reasonable. Thus, the scope and duration elements are satisfied in this case. **1/2 point**

Since the partnership has not suffered and D is having such a difficult time with his new practice, it may be argued that D is unduly burdened by the restriction. However, D's difficulties are not, based on these facts, directly related to the restriction, and thus are not relevant to the court's consideration of the issue of a person's right to practice his profession. D freely entered into the contract. The court will not change the intentions of the contracting parties if the terms "work no undue penalty or unjust forfeiture, overreaching, or other violation of public policy." **1 point**

The general public is not harmed by the restrictive covenant placed upon D. D's services are still available to the general public; D is merely restricted from practicing medicine within the city of Utica or at least within a five-mile radius of the office of the partnership. **1/2 point**

Finally, the restriction is needed to protect the partnership from bad will being attributed to it due to D's poor professional behavior. The restriction also will limit D's use of the partnership's goodwill, which he derived while associated with the partnership. Thus, the covenant is reasonably necessary to protect the partnership. **1/2 point**

Therefore, the covenant not to compete is valid and enforceable because it is not overreaching in its duration and geographic scope, there is no undue burden upon either party, the general public is not harmed by the restriction, and it is reasonable for the protection of the partnership. **1/2 point**

(iii) The legal remedy in this case would be inadequate. The goodwill of the partnership is intangible, and money damages generally do not compensate for its loss. Therefore, a showing of the potential loss of the partnership's goodwill will suffice for specific performance. **1 point**

(iv) The decree is enforceable. Equity will not act where it is not feasible to enforce the decree. Here, the decree would be enforceable because all of the parties are within the state and are amenable to service of process. Thus, they are under the jurisdiction of the courts of this state. Also, it is not difficult for the court to enforce this decree since no supervision by the court is required. **1 point**

(v) Mutuality of remedy existed under this contract. Mutuality of remedy means that each party to the contract would have a right to enforce it should the occasion arise. Because D would have been entitled to his share in the profits of the partnership and could have brought an action to enforce this right had it been breached by A, B, and/or C, mutuality exists here. **1 point**

(vi) It does not appear from the facts of this case that any of the defenses mentioned earlier would be available to D. **1 point**

Therefore, the partnership will prevail in this action and the court will grant the order for specific performance of the covenant not to compete because the covenant is reasonable and all of the elements for the remedy of specific performance exist.

ANSWER 20—CRIMINAL LAW/CRIMINAL PROCEDURE

(1) D'S WRITTEN STATEMENT

The issue is whether D properly waived his *Miranda* rights.

For a confession to be admissible under the Fifth Amendment privilege against self-incrimination, a person in custody must, prior to interrogation, be given his *Miranda* warnings and in effect waive such rights. Such a waiver must be knowing, voluntary, and intelligent. In New York, the waiver must be obtained in the presence of counsel if the defendant is known to be represented by counsel. **1 point**

The facts indicate that D was advised of his *Miranda* rights (the right to remain silent/privilege against self-incrimination) and that he understood his rights and wished to waive them. The fact that D requested counsel after providing the confession does not render it inadmissible as long as he made his statement after receiving the warnings and he fully understood his rights. Thus, the court should deny D's motion to suppress the written statement. **1 point**

THE SECURITIES FOUND IN D'S POCKETS

The issue is whether the securities were found during an illegal search.

Evidence found during a search incident to a lawful arrest is admissible. The police may search one in custody in order to ensure their safety and to protect evidence from being destroyed. The facts indicate that P made a valid warrantless arrest of D, since all that was necessary was a reasonable belief that D was the one robbing the drugstore. The fact that the police found evidence of a crime different from the one that occasioned the arrest is irrelevant. The search and seizure were proper, and the evidence is therefore admissible. L's motion to suppress the securities should be denied. **1-1/2 points**

(2) D'S ORAL STATEMENT OF FEBRUARY 15

The issue is whether D can waive his right to counsel on the present case if the police know that D is being represented by counsel on a pending unrelated charge.

As indicated above, a confession will be admissible only if the defendant properly waives his *Miranda* rights. If the defendant is known to be represented by counsel *in the pending case,* waiver must be in the presence of counsel. If the defendant is not known to be represented in the present case, he can waive his right to counsel himself, even if he is represented by counsel on an unrelated case and the police are aware of that representation. [People v. Bing, 76 N.Y.2d 331 (1990)] **1-1/2 points**

Here, although D was represented by counsel on his pending unrelated case, and P was aware of the representation, D properly waived his rights and the oral statement given to P regarding the plan to rob the drugstore is admissible since P had no indication that D was represented by counsel with respect to this case. L's motion to suppress the oral statement should be denied. **1 point**

(3)   F CAN BE FOUND GUILTY OF CONSPIRACY

The issue is whether F properly withdrew from the conspiracy.

For F to be found guilty of conspiracy, three factors must be present: (i) intent, (ii) agreement, and (iii) an overt act. F's intent can be shown clearly by his agreement, which is given in the facts, as well as by the overt acts committed by him, namely obtaining the layout of the store and a gun. (Note that it is not necessary for F to have committed the crime for him to be guilty of conspiracy; any overt act in furtherance of the scheme is sufficient, even if committed by another co-conspirator.) **1-1/2 points**

The crime of conspiracy does not merge into the completed offense. Thus, the actual commission of the crime does not free F of guilt for conspiracy. The conspiracy charge stands apart from the underlying crime. Note, however, that F can be found guilty only if D's evidence against F is corroborated. The uncorroborated evidence of a co-conspirator alone is insufficient to support a finding of guilt. **1-1/2 points**

F has no defense to the charge of conspiracy (assuming corroboration of D's testimony). Once the crime contemplated by the conspiracy takes place, no defense of renunciation or withdrawal is available to the conspirators. Under New York law [P.L. §40.10], the affirmative defense of renunciation is available only to a defendant who shows that he renounced the criminal scheme and prevented the commission of the crime. He must show that he actually prevented the crime by his actions, not simply that the crime did not take place. Note also that the affirmative defense must be pleaded by the defendant and then proved by a preponderance of the evidence. **1 point**

Therefore, F can be found guilty of conspiracy.

ANSWER 21—EVIDENCE

(1)   The issue is whether an out-of-court statement made immediately prior to death is admissible.

Hearsay is a statement, other than one made by the declarant while testifying at a trial or hearing, offered into evidence to prove the truth of the matter asserted. Hearsay evidence must be excluded upon appropriate objection unless the statement falls under one of the recognized exceptions to the hearsay rule. **1 point**

There is a recognized exception for dying declarations. To qualify as a dying declaration, the statement must meet the following tests: (i) the statement was made by the victim of a homicide; (ii) the declarant was dying when he made the statement and knew that he was dying; (iii) the declarant would have been a competent witness, and the statement is pertinent to the action; and (iv) the action in which the testimony is offered is a prosecution for the homicide. Since the offered testimony meets those conditions, it is admissible and the court erred in its ruling. **2 points**

(2)   The issue is whether a defendant who takes the stand in his own defense may claim Fifth Amendment protection.

B's refusal to answer can be grounded only in his Fifth Amendment right against self-incrimination. However, B has taken the stand as a witness in his own defense, *i.e.,* in support of his case. The Fifth Amendment may not be used as both a shield and as a sword—B may not testify as to those facts that are in his favor and refuse to testify about potentially incriminating facts. Having voluntarily taken the stand, B has waived his Fifth Amendment protection and may be compelled to answer questions on cross-examination. The court's ruling was wrong. **1 point**

(3)   The issue is whether the prosecutor may use collateral evidence to prove prior bad acts of the defendant.

A specific act of misconduct relevant to impair credibility can be elicited only on cross-examination of the witness. If the witness denies the act, the cross-examiner cannot refute the answer by introducing extrinsic evidence. The prosecution's question about B's alleged thievery was proper as a test of B's credibility. However, once B answered negatively, the prosecutor was barred from attempting to introduce collateral evidence on the point. Thus, the court properly excluded the proffered testimony. **1 point**

Note that there is one exception to the above rule: Had B been convicted of the theft, the prosecutor could then introduce the record of B's conviction to impeach B's testimony. Absent proof of conviction, prior bad acts cannot be proved by collateral evidence. **1/2 point**

(4)   The issue is whether a defendant's acquittal in a criminal case can be used to show nonliability in a civil case.

The record of B's acquittal is irrelevant to a civil action against him. The burden of proof in the civil action is lower than in the criminal action. Thus, B could be liable in civil court even though he was not guilty in the criminal action. Thus, proof of his innocence does not bear on his liability in the civil action, and the court ruled correctly. **1 point**

(5) and (6)   The issue is whether the "Dead Man Act" precludes all testimony by a party to litigation against the estate of a deceased person.

CPLR 4519—also known as the "Dead Man Act"—provides that a party who is interested in the outcome of litigation (here, B) may not testify against the interest of the representative of a deceased person (A) concerning any personal transaction or communication between them. In other words, B is incompetent to testify about any aspect of the auto accident, with the following exception. **1-1/2 points**

New York case law allows the survivor (or survivors) of an automobile accident to testify as to facts of negligence arising out of ownership or operation of an automobile, the "Dead Man Act" notwithstanding. [Rost v. Kessler, 267 App. Div. 686 (1944)] Thus, B may testify as to the facts of the accident, even though his testimony is in his own interest and against the interest of A's representative (his widow). Thus, ruling (5) was correct. **1 point**

However, the conversation between A and B after the accident does not fall within the *Rost v. Kessler* exception outlined above. The conversation is not a fact of negligence arising out of ownership or operation of an automobile involved in the accident. Thus, the "Dead Man Act" applies to this portion of B's testimony. B sought to testify in his own interest and against the interest of A's widow. It is irrelevant that B's testimony is otherwise competent and admissible as the admission of a party (and thus an exception to hearsay). Therefore, ruling (6) was incorrect; B's testimony should have been excluded. **1 point**

ANSWER 22—FUTURE INTERESTS/TRUSTS

T'S ACTION IN MAKING PAYMENTS TO C

The issue is whether a trustee may assign trust income to a creditor on direction from the beneficiary. **1/2 point**

New York's statutory spendthrift protection [EPTL §7-1.5(a)ff] prohibits the assignment of trust income interest absent an express provision in the trust document. B had no authority to direct T to pay C, and T had no authority to make any such payment on B's order. Neither could T pay C after receiving a copy of an unsatisfied valid judgment from C. Although CPLR 5205(e) would allow C to levy up to 10% of B's trust income after judgment, in such a case T would have received an order of execution from the sheriff and not a mere copy of the judgment sent by C himself. Thus, the judgment did not empower T to transfer funds to C. **1-1/2 points**

While the EPTL provides that C could reach B's income interest if the income was "excess income" to B, C would first have to prove that the income was indeed excess, and that C had exhausted all other remedies. C has made no showing and has no court order, so this exception to the statute's spendthrift protection does not empower T to release funds to C. T's action was improper. **1 point**

TRUST ON B'S DEATH

The issue is whether the testamentary power of appointment violates the Rule Against Perpetuities.

New York follows the common law rule that the validity of the interests created by the exercise of a ***testamentary*** power of appointment ("POA") is determined by the date of the instrument creating the power and ***not*** from the date that the power is exercised. (This is also true of a presently exercisable special POA; but the validity of interests created by a presently exercisable general POA is determined by the date of exercise.) B is treated as though he merely "filled in the blanks" of A's will. New York also applies "the second look doctrine" to an interest that appears to fail at its inception. This doctrine allows review of a gift after both the initial grantor and the first grantee pass away. If a gift that would have otherwise failed for perpetuity reasons at the time it was made will satisfy all future interest requirements at the time the first grantee passes away, the gift will stand. So we must consider whether the gifts to B's children, and then to their issue, are valid. **2 points**

We can classify the interests created by B: D, E, and F have life estates, and their issue have contingent remainders, since the issue were unborn at the time the interest was created. B holds a reversion in fee that passed to B's issue on B's death. The life estates violate both the Rule Against Suspension of the Power of Alienation and the Rule Against Perpetuities. For perpetuities purposes, the life estates are treated as powers of appointment exercisable by the trustee in his discretion in favor of the sons. F could outlive D and E by more than 21 years, and the trustee could then exercise his discretionary power by appointing and distributing the income to F. Such a distribution would be violative of the Rule Against Perpetuities. (*Note:* The trustee cannot be considered a life in being for Rule Against Perpetuities purposes. Similarly, F could not join in a conveyance of his interest in the trust within lives in being plus 21 years since he could outlive D and E by more than 21 years.) **2 points**

To determine whether the gift to the issue of D, E, and F violates either rule, we then apply the "second look doctrine"; that is, we consider the facts as they stand at the date of B's death, and not at A's death. Under the facts, it is clear that the gift to the issue of D, E, and F violates both the Rule Against Perpetuities and the Rule Against the Suspension of the Power of Alienation. F was two years old when B died in 1975, and thus was unborn when A died in 1970; so he cannot be used as a measuring life. But if F dies more than 21 years after the death of D and E, the interest of the issue will vest more than 21 years after lives in being; in addition, persons in being will not be able to join to create an absolute fee or estate, for issue might be born more than 21 years after lives in being. The Perpetuities Reform Statute does not apply in this situation. **2 points**

The effect of the violation of the rules is that the gift to the issue of D, E, and F fails. D, E, and F will receive the trust corpus, divided equally among them. **1 point**

ANSWER 23—REAL PROPERTY/MORTGAGES/CONTRACTS

(1)   The issue is whether transfer of a deed without intent to create a conveyance automatically conveys real property.

Where it is intended that a mortgage be created, Real Property Law section 320 provides that a legal mortgage exists if there is a transfer of a deed "intended only as a security in the nature of a mortgage." The fact that the mortgagee records the deed will give him no advantage unless he simultaneously records all other written instruments that show the intent of the transfer to be a mortgage. Additionally, in the absence of other written instruments showing the intention to create a mortgage, an equitable mortgage can be created upon a showing by parol evidence of such an intention. **1-1/2 points**

In this case, A transferred Blackacre to B intending the deed to be security for the loan to A. B's letter to A is a written instrument which is evidence of the parties' intention. The deed, coupled with the parties' intent, creates a legal mortgage. The fact that B recorded the deed is of no value. B had the duty to record the deed along with "every writing" that indicates that a mortgage was created and not a fee interest. A was under no obligation to record the letter; only "the person for whose benefit the deed is made" has that burden. **1 point**

Thus, A, by transferring the deed to B, did not make an absolute conveyance, but only created a mortgage. However, as explained below, X's purchase of Blackacre cut off all of A's rights in the property. A can only recover damages from B in the amount of the fair market value of Blackacre at the time of the trial less a setoff for the loan plus interest. **1/2 point**

(2)   The issue is who prevails when several parties make a claim to the same real property.

In race-notice jurisdictions, such as New York, when a bona fide purchaser ("BFP") purchases for value and without notice, the BFP will prevail over those who make a claim to the property. **1 point**

In this example, X purchased Blackacre for value. Upon searching the records, X would have found that A held title until January 6, 1992, when he transferred title to B. Since B did not record the writings that evidenced the mortgage, X was not on notice that the deed represented only a mortgage and was not an absolute transfer to B. Additionally, the deed made no reference to the mortgage. Had there been language in the deed that referred to another document, X would have been under a duty to inquire into the nature of the unrecorded instrument and thus would have been deemed to have been on inquiry notice. However, in this case, the deed neither contained a reference to any other instruments nor made any statement that it was merely security for the debt from B to A. **1 point**

Therefore, A cannot recover Blackacre from X because, as a BFP for value and without notice of the unrecorded transaction, X takes the property free and clear of all claims. As stated above, A's sole remedy is an action for damages against B. X, the bona fide purchaser of Blackacre, takes Blackacre free and clear of A's claim. **1 point**

(3)   The issue is when a real estate broker is entitled to a commission.

A real estate broker is entitled to his commission upon the procurement of a buyer who is ready, willing, and able to purchase the premises, restricted only by the terms of the agency agreement. The facts of this case state that B appointed C to be his "'exclusive agent' . . . to sell Blackacre." Whether C is entitled to collect a commission turns on the interpretation of the phrase "exclusive agent." By itself, that phrase could mean that either an exclusive agency was created, whereby either the seller or the agent may sell the property, or an exclusive right to sell was created, whereby only the agent is permitted to sell. **1-1/2 points**

Under article 12a of the Real Property Law, in an exclusive agency contract, if the seller procures his own purchaser, the agent is not entitled to a commission. In the exclusive right to sell, the agent collects his commission even if the seller procures the purchaser on his own. **1/2 point**

According to these facts, it would be held that an exclusive agency contract had been established. Thus, C did not have the exclusive right to sell, and B retained the right to sell the property on his own. B exercised that right and found X; therefore, C is not entitled to a commission. C also has no claim for recovery based on his procurement of F. The terms of the exclusive agency provided that C must procure a ready, willing, and able buyer at a minimum purchase price of $110,000. F's offer was not in accordance with those terms. It is irrelevant that B accepted an offer similar to F's. C failed to meet the terms of his agency. The terms clearly require C to fully perform in order to earn his commission; without such performance, C is not entitled to any recovery. **2 points**

ANSWER 24—CRIMINAL LAW/CRIMINAL PROCEDURE

(1)(a)   CRIMES COMMITTED BY THUG

At issue are the crimes committed by Thug. **1/2 point**

Thug committed arson when he blew up Cab's truck. Under the New York Penal Law, a person commits arson in the first degree if he (i) intentionally damages a building or motor vehicle, (ii) by intentionally starting a fire by using an incendiary or explosive device, (iii) with the knowledge that a nonparticipant is present in the building or motor vehicle or if circumstances are such that a person's presence is a reasonable possibility. The nonparticipant need not be injured. **1 point**

Here, Thug intentionally blew up Cab's Truck by using dynamite, an explosive device. Cab's truck was parked on a public street. The street was well lit and there was a designated bus stop adjacent to the truck. Although Thug believed that the truck was unoccupied, it was reasonable to believe that there would be a person in the truck or present in the area when the truck exploded. In this case, Vic was killed when he stepped off the public bus at the designated bus stop adjacent to the explosion. Therefore, Thug has committed the crime of arson in the first degree. **1 point**

Thug also committed second degree murder (felony murder). Under New York law, a person is guilty of felony murder when he commits any of certain enumerated felonies and a nonparticipant is killed in the course of commission of the felony or in the defendant's immediate flight therefrom. The death of the nonparticipant must be independent of the felony committed. Arson is included among the felonies enumerated in the felony murder statute. Here, Vic was killed while Thug's arson was in progress. The killing was not part of the intended crime, but rather was incidental to it. Therefore, Thug has committed felony murder. **1 point**

Thug might also have committed extortion, but the facts are not completely clear on this. A person commits extortion when he obtains property from another by means of threats to physically harm the victim or his property. Here, the facts state that Thug blew up Cab's truck for Cab's refusal to pay "protection" money and that Thug has been known to offer business persons a choice between paying him protection money and having their property destroyed by dynamite. If Thug threatened such conduct when he asked Cab for the protection money, the threats would constitute the crime of extortion. He probably made such threats and is guilty. **1 point**

Therefore, Thug has committed arson, felony murder, and probably extortion.

(1)(b)   CRIMES COMMITTED BY SHOP

At issue are the crimes committed by Shop.

Shop has committed the crime of criminal facilitation. Under the New York Penal Law, a person commits criminal facilitation when he knowingly aids in the commission of a crime but his culpability does not reach accomplice level. The facilitator need only believe that it was probable that he was rendering aid, and the conduct alleged must have aided in the commission of the object felony. The facilitator may not be convicted on uncorroborated testimony of the person facilitated. The facilitator has an affirmative defense if he takes steps to prevent the felony. **1 point**

Here, Shop aided Thug in the arson when he sold Thug the dynamite. Shop knew that he was probably rendering aid to Thug in the commission of arson since he knew that Thug had previously threatened the owners of local businesses by offering them a choice between paying for his "protection" and having Thug destroy their property with dynamite. **1 point**

It is arguable whether Shop may successfully assert the affirmative defense. He went to the police station to inform them of the sale of dynamite to Thug, and this act can be construed as an attempt to prevent the felony. However, he went to the police two days after Thug used the dynamite. A court will probably find Shop's act to be too little, too late. To encourage swifter remedial action by others in the future, it would be better policy to limit the defense to cases where the attempted remedial action is undertaken before the crime is actually committed. Thus, it is doubtful that Shop will be successful in raising the defense, and he will be liable for criminal facilitation. **1 point**

(2)   SUPPRESSION OF EVIDENCE: WRITTEN CONFESSION

The issue is whether a confession is admissible when it was obtained from a person who: (i) was being held, but had not yet been arraigned, on another charge; (ii) was informed of his rights; and (iii) waived them. **1/2 point**

Thug's confession is admissible because it was not illegally obtained. Under the exclusionary rule, a confession that was obtained illegally generally is not admissible into evidence. Thus, a confession obtained in violation of a defendant's right to counsel will be suppressed. A defendant has two distinct rights to counsel. The Sixth Amendment (applicable to the states through the Fourteenth Amendment) provides a right to counsel after judicial proceedings have begun. Under federal case law, this right is offense specific, meaning that a defendant who claims the right with respect to one crime does not thereby invoke the right as to other crimes; the right must be claimed for each crime individually. A defendant also has a Fifth Amendment right to counsel that arose out of *Miranda v. Arizona.* The Fifth Amendment right arises whenever there is custodial interrogation by the police. This right is not offense specific; once claimed, a defendant cannot be questioned about any crime absent counsel. New York law goes even further to protect the right to counsel. New York provides an indelible right to counsel (i) whenever the defendant is in custody, there is overwhelming police activity, and the defendant requests counsel; (ii) at arraignment; (iii) upon the filing of an accusatory instrument; or (iv) whenever there has been any significant judicial activity. Once the New York right to counsel attaches, it may not be waived by anyone known to be represented by counsel unless counsel is present. **1 point**

No right to counsel was violated here when Thug was questioned. Although Thug had been in custody on an unrelated drug charge for a short time before being questioned about the murder, charges were not filed and no significant judicial activity had occurred. Thus, at the time of the questioning, Thug did not have a Sixth Amendment right to counsel with respect to any crime. Thug did have a Fifth Amendment right to counsel, since he was being questioned by the police, but he validly waived that right since he was informed of the right and chose to speak. Finally, none of the conditions were present under which the New York indelible right to counsel would attach. Therefore, Thug's confession would be admissible evidence and his motion to suppress his written confession would be denied. **1 point**

ANSWER 25—EVIDENCE

(1)   The issue is whether a plaintiff's action may be dismissed for properly invoking the Fifth Amendment privilege against self-incrimination.

A plaintiff in a civil action for breach of contract has the burden of proving that a valid contract existed and that there was a breach thereof. The elements of a valid contract are offer, acceptance, and consideration; although a contract will be void, even if it contains these elements, if the subject matter or consideration is illegal. **1 point**

Here, A has brought an action against P's estate for breach of contract, *i.e.,* not paying for services rendered. Therefore, A must prove the existence of a valid contract. A's refusal to testify as to the nature of the contract negates proof of a material element of the contract in question. While A has the right—even in a civil action—to refuse to answer any question that would be self-incriminating (and testifying that he has committed arson would certainly be self-incriminating), he cannot use the Fifth Amendment privilege as both a "shield" and a "sword." If he uses it as a "shield" to protect himself from criminal liability, he cannot use it as a "sword" for obtaining affirmative relief. By invoking the privilege against self-incrimination, A cut off his ability to make his case. Therefore, the court should have dismissed A's claim. **1 point**

Additionally, P's contract was to commit the crime of arson. Thus, the contract was created for an illegal purpose and is void. Therefore, even if A had testified as to the nature of the contract, the case would be dismissed because A could not prove that he had a valid contract. **1/2 point**

(2)   The issue is whether a witness may be questioned as to extrinsic facts.

Generally, evidence must be relevant to be admissible. Evidence is relevant if it tends to prove any fact of consequence to the action. That is, the evidence must tend to prove or disprove a material issue, or render it more probably true or untrue than it would have been in the absence of such evidence. Evidence must also be legally relevant. Legal relevance means that the evidence being offered does not unfairly prejudice a party, confuse the issue, or mislead the jury. **1 point**

In this case, the fact that A shared an apartment with a woman to whom he was not married would not tend to prove or disprove the issue of whether A's "professional services" meant the commission of arson. Furthermore, the question is unfairly prejudicial to A. It neither tests his credibility nor lays the groundwork for further, relevant questions. Therefore, the court properly sustained the objection. **1/2 point**

(3)   The issue is whether opinion testimony is admissible.

The general rule is that a witness should testify only to those facts to which the witness has personal knowledge. It is for the trier of fact to draw conclusions from the facts presented by a witness. Therefore, opinion testimony by a witness, except in cases where, in the opinion of the court, the witness's opinion is necessary or helpful in deciding the issue, is not admissible. **1 point**

Here, the issue of A's living arrangements has already been determined to be irrelevant and should not be admitted on those grounds. In addition, S's further testimony on this issue is not even firsthand knowledge of the matter asserted; it is a mere conclusion of fact. S does not know that A shares his apartment with Z; he has only heard a "squeaky voice" coming from the apartment. Therefore, S's statement was properly stricken from the record. **1/2 point**

(4)   The issue is whether A's statement is hearsay.

Generally, hearsay evidence is inadmissible. Hearsay is generally defined as "a statement, other than one made by the declarant while testifying at the trial or hearing, offered in evidence to prove the truth of the matter asserted." However, hearsay will be admitted into evidence if it falls under one of the exceptions to the hearsay rule. An admission by a party-opponent is an exception to the hearsay rule. Such an admission is an act or statement made by the party which shows that the party had prior knowledge of one of the relevant facts. **1 point**

In this case, C testified that she heard A make a statement about how it was going to get "hot" at the factory. C's testimony is hearsay because she is repeating the out-of-court statement of another (A), and her testimony is being presented to prove that A committed the arson. This testimony will be allowed into evidence, however, because it falls under the admission by a party-opponent exception to the hearsay rule. Therefore, C's testimony was properly admitted. **1/2 point**

(5)   The issue is whether an out-of-court adverse statement is admissible as evidence.

As indicated above, hearsay is inadmissible unless it falls within an exception. N was asked whether, in her conversation with P, P had made any statement pertaining to a conspiracy with A to commit arson to the factory. N's testimony would be hearsay. However, there is an exception to the hearsay rule for a statement against interest. When a person who is unavailable to testify at trial made a declaration that he knew was against his interest *at the time it was made,* the declaration will be admissible as an exception to the hearsay rule. **1 point**

According to the facts, at the time P made the statement here, he knew that it was against his interests to make such a statement. Therefore, N should be permitted to testify. **1/2 point**

The Dead Man Act does not apply in this case. A witness cannot testify to the declarations of a deceased person if that witness has an interest in the outcome of the case. A person is considered "interested" if she stands to gain or lose by the outcome of the case or if the testimony could be used against her in a subsequent trial. The witness here, N, is not "interested" in the outcome of the case and so the statute does not apply. **1/2 point**

(6)   The issue is whether assertion of a Fifth Amendment privilege in a civil case can lead to adverse inference by the jury.

In a civil proceeding, when the plaintiff bears the burden of proof, it is up to the plaintiff to prove each and every element of the case. Failure to testify on an issue in the case when the plaintiff was able to testify gives rise to an inference adverse to that plaintiff's interest. **1/2 point**

In this case, A invoked his Fifth Amendment right and in doing so failed to present evidence necessary to put the case forward; *i.e.,* he failed to prove that a valid contract existed. A was capable of testifying but for his invoking the privilege. Therefore, the judge was correct in overruling M's objection. **1/2 point**

ANSWER 26—WILLS

(a)(1)   The issue is the effect of an attestation clause in proving a will. **1/2 point**

The person offering a will for probate has the burden of proving that it was duly executed. The paragraph quoted in the question is an attestation clause; as such, it is prima facie evidence of the valid execution of the will. But unlike a self-proving affidavit, it is not a substitute for formal proof of the will. The proponent of the will must bring witnesses to prove the signatures of the witnesses and the testator. The court properly denied probate to the will and codicil on the face of the documents themselves. **1 point**

(2)   The issue is whether the will was properly proved. **1/2 point**

It is well settled that a will that contains a completed attestation clause may be admitted to probate even though the witnesses cannot remember or are actively hostile, if the court is otherwise satisfied from all the evidence that the will was properly executed. An attestation clause that recites the facts of due execution establishes a prima facie case for probate. The combination of proof of the signatures, plus the attestation clause, is sufficient. In addition, failure of the witnesses to sign the will twice, once as witnesses and again to the attestation clause, will not bar admission of the will to probate. It is therefore of no great consequence that N now claims she never witnessed W's signing of the will. Based on the evidence of N and E, the court properly admitted the will to probate. **1 point**

(3)   The issue is whether handwritten additions appearing after the testator's signature in a will are valid. **1/2 point**

Testamentary dispositions must be executed with testamentary formalities, which include: (i) a signature (ii) at the end (iii) in the presence of witnesses; (iv) that the testator publish the disposition; and (v) that she obtain the signatures of two witnesses. Holographic wills, which are not executed with such formalities, are not valid in New York. The addition here was not executed with any testamentary formalities except W's signature. Thus, the addition will be disregarded. **1 point**

(4)   The issue is whether the codicil was validly revoked. When W crossed out her signature, she revoked through "cancellation" or physical act. Such revocation is recognized in New York. Wills or codicils may be revoked by changed circumstances, subsequent writing, or physical act. Striking out a signature is a valid revocation by physical act. Thus, as W crossed out her signature on the codicil, she effectively revoked it. The court was correct in denying effect to the codicil. **1 point**

(b)(1)   The issue is the effect of revocation of a codicil partially revoking an existing will. **1/2 point**

New York applies the "no revival of revoked wills" doctrine, and this applies to parts of wills. The first clause was validly revoked by the codicil when the codicil was validly executed. Subsequent cancellation of the codicil does not revive the clause. There is an exception where a later codicil incorporates the prior-revoked terms by reference, but the handwritten clause here was ineffective to revive the first clause, because it was improperly executed. Thus, the first clause is revoked, and A takes nothing. **1 point**

(2)   The issue is the status of a specific devise if the subject matter no longer exists. **1/2 point**

The doctrine of ademption applies to the gift to S: A specific bequest which is not in the estate at the death of the testator fails, and the devisee takes nothing. Here, the stamp collection was destroyed before W's death, so ademption applies. Although the EPTL provides that casualty insurance proceeds will be paid to a specific devisee in spite of the doctrine of ademption, the statute covers only proceeds paid *after* the death of the testator. Here the proceeds were paid before W died, so the statute does not apply, and S takes nothing. **1 point**

(3)   The issue is the effect of a beneficiary of the residuary estate predeceasing the testator and leaving issue. **1/2 point**

The EPTL provides that in the event of the death of a residual legatee (here, B), the residue will pass to the surviving residual beneficiaries. Thus, normally F would take the entire estate. Here, however, B was issue of W. Consequently, New York's "anti-lapse" statute (also part of the EPTL) comes into play. The statute relating to residual beneficiaries gives way to the anti-lapse statute: B's devise passes to her daughter G, who shares the residuary estate equally with F. **1 point**

ANSWER 27—CRIMINAL PROCEDURE/CRIMINAL LAW/EVIDENCE

(1)(a)   The issue is whether a nonwitness for the defendant may raise a witness's immunity or violation of a witness's constitutional rights as ground for suppression of testimony.

To have standing, the claimant must have suffered or must presently suffer a direct impairment of his own constitutional rights. F's constitutional rights were violated, those rights were personal to him, and accordingly A and B have no standing to assert the violation of those rights. [Wong Sun v. United States, 371 U.S. 471 (1963)] **1 point** Thus, the "fruit of the poisonous tree" doctrine does not afford A and B any ground for suppression. The court was correct.

(b)(i)   The issue is whether there is legally sufficient evidence presented to the grand jury against A.

Under New York law, a grand jury may indict a person for an offense when the evidence before it is legally sufficient to establish that such person committed the offense. [N.Y. Crim. Proc. Law §190.65] This means that the evidence before the grand jury must be the equivalent of prima facie proof that the defendant committed the crime for which he is charged. **1 point**

A and B have been charged with burglary and grand larceny. A person is guilty of burglary in the third degree when he knowingly enters or remains unlawfully in a building with the intent to commit a crime therein. [N.Y. Penal Law §140.20] A person is guilty of grand larceny in the second degree when he steals property in excess of $50,000. [N.Y. Penal Law §155.40] To determine whether either indictment should be quashed, it is necessary to look at the evidence adduced before the grand jury with respect to each defendant. **1 point**

The evidence introduced to show a prima facie case against A consists of the following: F's testimony about the conversation between A and F before the burglary. B's confession is not evidence of A's wrongdoing. A close reading of the facts shows that B's confession did not directly implicate A. B did not testify before the grand jury, so B has made no other statement implicating A. While B's statement might have been used against A had the conspiracy still been in existence (as admissible hearsay of a co-conspirator (*see* below)), B made his statement after arrest, and thus after the conspiracy had come to an end. Thus, B's statement does not bear on the case against A. **1 point**

Also, O's testimony is not evidence of the crime charged against A. At most, O's testimony tends to show that A possessed stolen goods. However, A is not charged with possession. O cannot place A at the scene of the crime. **1/2 point**

F only testified that A made a statement of future criminal intent and that A delivered the stolen goods. F was incompetent to testify whether A unlawfully entered O's premises, had intent to commit a crime therein when he entered, or stole the property of O—all essential elements of the crimes with which A is charged. **1 point**

Thus, there is no legally sufficient evidence before the grand jury for it to have indicted A, and the indictment should have been quashed.

There is an additional issue of whether F is an accomplice of A. If F were the accomplice of A, it might be argued that the evidence before the grand jury would be stronger: F could be said to have testified as to the common criminal purpose of A and F, and his testimony could be said to tend to show A's participation in the conspiracy. Although A could not be indicted (or convicted) on the uncorroborated testimony of an accomplice [N.Y. Crim. Proc. Law §60.22], one might argue that O's testimony now shows A's actions to be illegal and acts as corroborative testimony "tending to connect the defendant with the commission" of the offense. (The quote is from the statute.) But F is not an accomplice. There is no showing that F "took part in the preparation or perpetration of the crime with the intent to assist therein, or that the witness counseled, induced, or encouraged the crime." [People v. Wheatmen, 31 N.Y.2d 12 (1972)] Moreover, it has been held that a receiver of stolen goods (a fence) is an accomplice to a thief only where there is proof of a prior agreement between them. [People v. Brooks, 34 N.Y.2d 475 (1974)] Here there was no agreement, only a statement of intent by A to F. **1-1/2 points**

Therefore, the court erred in denying A's motion.

(b)(ii)   The issue is whether there was legally sufficient evidence presented to the grand jury against B.

B's statement provides the elements of each of the crimes with which B is charged. However, under New York law, a person may not be convicted based upon his admission alone, absent additional proof that the offense was actually committed. [N.Y. Crim. Proc. Law §60.50] The testimony of F and that of O provide the necessary proof that a crime was committed. Furthermore, although A's statements to F are hearsay, they are nonetheless admissible under the "co-conspirators" exception to the hearsay rule, as statements made during the course of and in furtherance of a conspiracy of which B was a co-conspirator. [People v. Salko, 47 N.Y.2d 230 (1979)] Thus, there is legally sufficient evidence to support an indictment of B for burglary and larceny, and the court was correct in its ruling. **1 point**

(2)   The issue is whether a defendant may withdraw a plea upon learning that the prosecutor withheld favorable evidence from the defendant.

A defendant is not denied due process when the prosecutor fails to disclose during plea negotiations that he has received information that the principal witness died. [People v. Jones, 44 N.Y.2d 76 (1978)] The doctrine of *Brady v. Maryland,* 373 U.S. 83 (1963), which holds that suppression by the prosecution of evidence favorable to an accused who has requested it violates due process where the evidence is material either to guilt or to punishment, irrespective of the good faith or bad faith of the prosecution, is inapplicable here because (i) the fact that the witness died is not evidence, and (ii) even if proof of the fact of the witness's death were admissible on trial, it would not constitute exculpatory evidence—*i.e.,* evidence favorable to an accused where the evidence is material either to guilt or to punishment. [People v. Jones, *supra*] Finally, the extent of the prosecutor's duty is directly proportional to the specificity of the defendant's request. Here, no request about witnesses was made by the defendant. Thus, the court's ruling was correct. **2 points**

ANSWER 28—NEW YORK PRACTICE/TORTS

(1)(a)   The first issue is whether the court has jurisdiction over Bonnie and Clyde, both out-of-state defendants.

The court lacked jurisdiction over Bonnie. To assert jurisdiction in a particular case, the court must have jurisdiction over the subject matter and the defendant, and the method of service must have been proper. In this case, there is no question that the supreme court has subject matter jurisdiction over the two causes of action, as its jurisdiction is general. Similarly, the method of service on both Bonnie and Clyde was proper. Under CPLR 313, a defendant may be served out-of-state in any manner in which service may properly be made within the state. Personal delivery by a nonparty over the age of 18 would be proper within the state; thus, service was proper as to method. **1 point**

As to Bonnie, however, there is no basis upon which the court may assert personal jurisdiction. New York's long arm statute [CPLR 302(a)(2)] provides for service on out-of-state defendants in tort actions arising within the state, except as to a cause of action for defamation of character. As Frank's claim against Bonnie is grounded in libel, he may not obtain personal jurisdiction over her by service outside of the state. **1/2 point**

Therefore, the court incorrectly denied Bonnie's motion to dismiss for lack of jurisdiction.

[*Note:* While Frank may argue that Bonnie was transacting business within the state when she assisted in the filing of the DHCR applications, such that he might assert jurisdiction under CPLR 302(a)(1), this argument will fail. New York courts have not extended the definition of "transacting business" to encompass voluntary, nonprofit activities grounded in noncommercial relationships (here, landlord-tenant). Another argument Frank might make is that his cause of action arises out of Bonnie's "use or possession" of real property [CPLR 302(a)(4)], since her false statements relate to alleged overcharges on real property she was renting from Frank. A defendant may be reached under the long arm statute only when the lawsuit arises out of New York activity. CPLR 302(a)(4) provides for long arm jurisdiction for a New York court to exercise personal jurisdiction over any nondomiciliary who owns, uses, or possesses any real property situated within the state. However, this argument will fail because the statute in question was intended to cover actions for personal injuries arising from accidents on New York realty and actions for economic damages for such matters as nonpayment of rent or breach of contract to sell.]

As to Clyde, the court may properly assert personal jurisdiction. The long arm statute provides for personal jurisdiction over out-of-state defendants who commit a tortious act within the state; the limitation on assertion of jurisdiction in defamation actions does not extend to assault. Thus, Clyde may be personally served under CPLR 302(a)(2), as he allegedly committed a tortious act within the state. **1/2 point**

(b)   The second issue is whether Bonnie and Clyde, out-of-state defendants at the time of service, were properly served within the applicable statutes of limitation for defamation and assault.

The court correctly dismissed Bonnie's motion to dismiss based on the statute of limitations. While it is true that the statute of limitations for defamation is one year, and that under the facts presented the cause of action arose on the date of the alleged defamation—March 13—the action filed about 14 months later on May 1 was nevertheless timely because the statute of limitations was tolled by Bonnie's absence. The CPLR provides that when a defendant is absent from the state for four months under circumstances preventing the exercise of jurisdiction over the defendant, that absence operates to toll the statute of limitations during the period of the defendant's absence. Bonnie's moving out of state prevented the exercise of jurisdiction over her because, as stated above, under the long arm statute there is no means of obtaining personal jurisdiction over a defamation defendant while outside of the state. Therefore, the court correctly denied Bonnie's motion to dismiss as barred by the statute of limitations. **1-1/2 points**

The court was incorrect, however, in failing to dismiss the cause of action against Clyde as being time-barred. The cause of action against Clyde is for assault. The statute of limitations for intentional torts is one year under the CPLR. The cause of action arose when the harm occurred—on March 25. Thus, Frank had until March 25 of the following year to effect service. The statute of limitations was not tolled by Clyde's absence from the state because jurisdiction and service could still be obtained under the long arm statute. Thus, the statute ran out before Frank effected service, and the cause of action against Clyde should have been dismissed. **1 point**

(2)   BONNIE

The issue is whether Frank can make a prima facie case for defamation, and if so, whether Bonnie has any defenses available.

The elements Frank must prove are: (i) defamatory language by the defendant; (ii) that the defamation was "of or concerning" the plaintiff; (iii) publication to a third party; (iv) damage to the plaintiff's reputation; and probably (v) fault on the part of the defendant, whether intentional or negligent, since illegal rent increases are arguably a matter of public concern where Bonnie lived. **1 point**

Under the facts, Frank can prove a prima facie case in defamation. There was a defamatory statement made by Bonnie, "of or concerning" Frank, that was published to a third party. We cannot tell whether Frank can prove injury to reputation, but it seems more likely than not (his reputation with other tenants was damaged). Frank need only prove general damages. He need not prove specific pecuniary loss. Frank can sustain proof of libel per se, that is, that Bonnie's statement was libelous on its face (damage to business reputation) and thus damages need not be proved by extrinsic means. **1/2 point**

Since Frank is not a public figure within the meaning of *New York Times v. Sullivan,* Frank would be able to recover at least his actual damages by proving negligence on the part of Bonnie. However, because Bonnie may raise the defense of qualified privilege, Frank must prove malice—knowing or reckless falsehood. As Frank could, at best, show negligence on the part of Bonnie, his case will fail. **1/2 point**

Bonnie will be able to successfully raise the defense of qualified privilege. A qualified privilege is recognized in New York whenever one person makes a confidential communication to another concerning a third party in which both have a legitimate interest. The privilege extends only to defamatory state-ments made negligently, not maliciously. Therefore, the privilege would apply here, where the libelous statements were made in good faith, without knowledge of their falsehood and were related to the applications to the DHCR for rent rebates. **1/2 point**

The burden is on the defendant to prove the qualified privilege; then the burden shifts to the plaintiff to show that the privilege was exceeded. In this case, Bonnie had a legitimate interest, shared by the DHCR; in Frank and his acts. Thus, Bonnie had a qualified privilege with respect to the statements in issue, as long as the statements were made negligently and not maliciously. As such, Frank's action for defamation will fail. **1/2 point**

CLYDE

The issue is whether Frank can present a prima facie case for assault. **1/2 point**

To make out a prima facie case for the tort of assault, the plaintiff must allege: (i) an act by the defen-dant which created a reasonable apprehension of immediate harm or offensive contact to the person of the plaintiff; (ii) intent by the defendant; and (iii) causation (that the defendant's act was the actual and proximate cause of the plaintiff's reasonable apprehension). Damages need not be proved to assert a prima facie case for the intentional tort of assault. **1-1/2 points**

Under the facts, Frank cannot make out a prima facie case for assault because Frank cannot allege that Clyde's act created in Frank reasonable apprehension of *immediate* harm or offensive contact. Clyde's threat was directed exclusively toward the future. Thus, Frank's prima facie case fails and he has no right to relief. **1/2 point**

ANSWER 29—CRIMINAL LAW/CRIMINAL PROCEDURE

(1)   The issue is whether Alan's conduct was culpable and Vic's death foreseeable. **1/2 point**

Under the New York Penal Law, criminally negligent homicide arises where one person causes the death of another due to the failure to perceive a substantial and unjustifiable risk of death. The defen-dant's conduct must have been culpable (mere failure to perceive risk is not enough) and the death-producing event foreseeable. **1 point**

Here, Alan's conduct satisfies the standard. It is foreseeable that in a suburban neighborhood, on two-lane roads, there would be pedestrians crossing the streets. It is also foreseeable that driving 60 miles per hour and attempting to pass on a blind curve will likely cause the death of any pedestrian unlucky enough to be in the street when the car goes racing by. Alan failed to perceive the substantial and unjustifiable risk of death created by his conduct that an ordinary and reasonable person would have perceived. Therefore, the court was correct in denying Alan's motion to dismiss the indictment of criminally negligent homicide. **1-1/2 points**

(2)   The issue is whether Ben can be held liable as an accomplice. **1/2 point**

Although Ben did not actually hit Vic, Ben is still a party to the crime as an accomplice. A person who aids, counsels, or encourages the principal in committing a crime is also guilty of the crime as an accomplice. As discussed above, Alan's conduct constituted criminally negligent homicide. Ben encouraged Alan's conduct by participating in the drag race with Alan that resulted in Vic's death.

Therefore, Ben can be held liable as an accomplice. Thus, the court was correct in denying Ben's motion to dismiss his indictment for criminally negligent homicide. **2 points**

(3)   The issue is whether a police officer may arrest a suspect based on probable cause created by the observations of another police officer. **1/2 point**

The Fourth Amendment of the United States Constitution provides individuals protection from unreasonable searches and seizures by the government. To be reasonable, arrests, which are seizures of the person, must be based on probable cause. Probable cause to arrest is present when at the time of the arrest, the officer has within his knowledge reasonably trustworthy facts and circumstances sufficient to warrant a reasonably prudent person to believe that the suspect has committed or is committing a crime. Under some circumstances, an arrest will be reasonable only if made pursuant to a warrant. However, a police officer generally does not have to obtain a warrant before arresting a person in a public place, even if the officer has time to obtain a warrant. A police officer may arrest a person without a warrant when he has reasonable grounds to believe that a felony has been committed and that the person before him committed the crime. In addition, a police officer must have probable cause in order to arrest an individual. **2 points**

Here, Frank, an undercover police officer, observed Ben on a street corner, receiving what appeared to be drugs in exchange for money. Frank radioed Debra, another police officer, with a detailed description of Ben and his location. Debra, who had no personal knowledge of the drug sale, proceeded to the scene and arrested Ben for possession of illegal drugs. Although Debra did not observe the transaction herself, she arrested Ben based on reasonably trustworthy facts sufficient to warrant a reasonably prudent person to believe that Ben had committed a crime. Debra's actions were a result of her knowledge; therefore she had sufficient probable cause to arrest Ben. Thus, the court was correct in denying Ben's motion to dismiss his indictment for criminal possession of drugs. **2 points**

ANSWER 30—CORPORATIONS

(1)   The issue is whether a corporate president has standing to bring an action under the corporate opportunity doctrine. **1/2 point**

Under Business Corporation Law ("BCL") section 720, an action may be brought against an officer or director to compel an accounting for neglect or violation of duties in management and disposition of assets or for waste or misappropriation (to himself or others) of corporate assets, due to neglect or other violation of duty. The action may be brought by, among others, the corporation itself, an officer or director of the corporation, or a shareholder. **1-1/2 points**

Here, Green violated his duties in management by diverting a corporate opportunity to himself—the furniture store. Under the corporate opportunity doctrine, neither directors, officers, nor controlling shareholders may acquire or divert property or opportunities to themselves which the corporation needs or is seeking, or as to which it has a tangible expectancy, without first offering the opportunity to the corporation. Since Green did not first present the furniture store opportunity to the corporation, he breached his management duties and violated section 720. Therefore, Black, as an officer, has standing and the court improperly dismissed Black's action. **1 point**

(2)   The issue is whether White was required to make a demand upon the board prior to commencing a suit. **1/2 point**

Under New York's Business Corporations Law section 720, a director is entitled to sue on behalf of a corporation to compel an accounting for neglect or other violations of duty in management. Section

720 does not require any demand to be made on the board of directors in order for the suit to proceed. **1 point**

In this case, White can sue as a director of the corporation based on his allegation that Green usurped a corporate opportunity. In White's capacity as a director of the corporation, which is one basis he is suing under, there is no need to seek board approval. **1/2 point**

Section 626 of the BCL provides that a shareholder's derivative action requires the shareholder to make a demand on the board to take action before the lawsuit may be commenced. However, section 626(c) provides that the demand requirement may be excused if such a demand would be futile. The reasons for futility must be set forth with particularity in the pleading. **1 point**

Here, White can claim that the demand requirement should be excused because any demand would have been futile. The board had already refused to require Green to assign the new property to the corporation and it is therefore unlikely that the board would permit a lawsuit by White which was premised on an action that the board has already refused to act upon. **1 point**

ELECTION OF DIRECTORS

The issue is whether the requirements of the shareholders' agreement will be specifically enforced. **1/2 point**

For corporations formed *after* February 22, 1998, absent a provision to the contrary in the certificate of incorporation, the number of directors authorized can be amended by a majority vote of the share-holders. Here, a majority of the shares were voted in favor of the increase, so the increase was properly adopted. **1 point**

The voting agreement among Black, White, and Green does not change the above result. Even though the voting agreement requires increases in the board to be unanimously agreed upon, such a requirement must be in the certificate of incorporation or bylaws to be enforceable. The requirement that a bylaw shall not be adopted without approval of two-thirds of the outstanding stock is similarly unenforceable. The requirement that the three shall vote to enforce the agreement is not specifically enforceable in New York; it will be enforced only at law, and the only remedy available is damages. Thus, five directors should be elected at the next annual meeting. **1-1/2 points**

ANSWER 31—CRIMINAL LAW/COMMERCIAL PAPER

(1) H'S CHECK TO R

The issue is what the liabilities are of a person who knowingly issues a check for which he has insufficient funds. The giving of a no-account or insufficient funds check with the intent to defraud is similar to the common law crime of false pretenses and the statutory crime of issuing a bad check, both of which are considered larceny in New York. In this regard, the crime consists of obtaining title to the property of another by an intentional (or knowing) false statement of a past or existing fact with intent to defraud the other. **1/2 point**

The check that H gave to R meets all of the requisite elements constituting the common law crime of false pretenses. H obtained the property of R (the snow blower) by an intentional false statement (the insufficient funds check) with the intent to defraud R.

Because H obtained the property by issuing a bad check, his crime is larceny under both theories.

When H gave his check to R in the amount of $1,000 for the snow blower, he negotiated a negotiable instrument to R, who thereby became a holder in due course ("HDC"). The check, of course, is a draft. There is nothing to indicate that R did not take for value and in good faith. The fact that both H and R believed the snow blower to be worth $1,000 at that time in that place is dispositive on the question of value. As a holder in due course, R takes the check subject only to real defenses and free of personal defenses. The real defenses are infancy, incapacity, illegality, duress, fraud in factum, discharge in insolvency, discharges known to HDC, suretyship, material alteration, forgery, and persons HDC has dealt with. None of these real defenses are applicable in this situation; therefore, there are no defenses available to H. Thus, H is liable to R for the face amount of the check. **2 points**

(2) H'S CHECK TO G

The issue is whether G is a holder in due course. **1/2 point**

A holder in due course is a holder who takes the instrument for value, in good faith, and without notice of any real defenses against or claim to it on the part of any person. **1 point**

As above, H negotiated a negotiable instrument to G when he gave G his check in the amount of $600. The $100 bonus is actually interest on the loan at a usurious rate. That being the case, illegality is a real defense to any action on the draft. The illegality of the underlying contract between G and H denies G or anyone else the status of an HDC. H is protected even though he was a party to the usury. Thus, H does not have to pay G on the draft. **2 points**

Furthermore, H has not issued a bad check here, as he did above. The difference is that here H cannot be said to have known when he wrote the check that it was bad. Unlike the check to R, the check to G was payable 30 days later. Thus, H lacks the requisite intent to be guilty of larceny in this case (H took property for the check here as above). **1 point**

(3) THREATENED REVOCATION OF H'S LICENSE

The issue is whether H was properly warned of the consequences of refusing a blood test. **1/2 point**

Vehicle and Traffic Law section 1194(2) and the required automobile liability insurance policy state that a driver's license can be revoked for refusal to submit to a blood test, but only where the suspect has been warned of this consequence of his refusal to submit. Where, as here, no warning is given, no revocation is possible. Thus, H will not lose his license. **1 point**

(4) CRIMES OF G

The issue is whether the interest rate agreed upon by H and G was usurious. **1/2 point**

In New York, it is a felony to loan money at an annual rate exceeding 25%—provided the lender is not a bank. Under the facts, G has lent H $500 at a monthly rate of 20%; this works out to an annual rate of 240%, which is clearly usurious. Thus, G is guilty of the crime of usury. In addition, G may not legally compel H to repay the loan. **1 point**

ANSWER 32—DOMESTIC RELATIONS

(1)(i)   The first issue is whether the Minnsylvania court had jurisdiction to award a divorce. **1/2 point**

The court incorrectly dismissed H's first affirmative defense pertaining to lack of jurisdiction. The state where either party to a marriage is domiciled has, by virtue of the domicile, the power to grant a judgment of divorce. According to the facts presented here, H became a domiciliary of Minnsylvania in 1993; therefore, the Minnsylvania court had jurisdiction to award H a divorce. Hence, the court was incorrect in dismissing this defense. **1 point**

(ii)   The second issue is whether the court had jurisdiction to terminate support. Although the court has the power to grant the divorce, as detailed above, the court did not have the jurisdiction necessary to decide support issues. Personal rights such as the right to support are, under the doctrine of "divisible incidents of divorce," personal to each party and cannot be affected unless the court has jurisdiction over the person entitled to the support. **1-1/2 points**

In this case, there is no possible argument for the Minnsylvania court's exercise of jurisdiction over W. W never became a resident or a domiciliary of Minnsylvania and therefore was not subject to the necessary jurisdiction. Absent such jurisdiction, the court could not cut off W's support rights notwithstanding Minnsylvania's law to the contrary. **1 point**

Furthermore, a separation agreement is presumed to be incorporated and survives a divorce decree unless the agreement specifically directs a merging of the decree. "Incorporated and survives" essentially means that the agreement can stand by itself notwithstanding that it is read with the divorce decree. Under the equitable distribution doctrine of the Domestic Relations Law, if a separation agreement is incorporated and survives the divorce decree, the court may modify the provision relating to maintenance only if the petitioning party makes a showing of extreme hardship. **1-1/2 points**

Unless H could prove fraud, duress, etc., and thus set the separation agreement aside completely, a court could not reduce arrears due under an agreement that has been incorporated merely because of changed circumstances or inability to pay. The arrears judgment must be entered unless there is "good cause" for the supporting spouse's failure to seek a modification prior to the application for enforcement. The court correctly dismissed H's second affirmative defense. **2 points**

(iii)   The third issue is whether H's support obligations will be affected if W committed adultery. New York Domestic Relations Law section 248 states that if a party is habitually living with another person and they are holding themselves out as husband and wife, the court may annul or modify support provisions. However, in this case, H alleged mere adultery on the part of W. Adultery in and of itself is not enough to warrant modification of support. The court was correct in dismissing the third affirmative defense. **1-1/2 points**

(2)   The issue is whether W is entitled to counsel fees in her action to compel payment under the matrimonial judgment.

Domestic Relations Law section 238 states that counsel fees may be awarded in an action to compel payment of any sum of money required to be paid by a matrimonial judgment. Here, W is enforcing a sum due under the judgment of separation and is therefore entitled to counsel fees. Hence, the ruling was correct. **1 point**

ANSWER 33—NEW YORK PRACTICE/AGENCY/PARTNERSHIP

(1)   The issue is whether a complaint against a New York corporation may be dismissed on the ground of forum non conveniens. **1/2 point**

CPLR 327 provides that if, upon motion of any party, the court finds that the interests of substantial justice require an action to be heard in the court of some other state (including a foreign country), the court "may stay or dismiss the action in whole or in part on any conditions that may be just." Substantial justice refers to dismissal on the grounds of convenience of the court, convenience of the plaintiff, or convenience of the defendant. A New York court may dismiss the action on such ground regardless of the fact that the action is one over which the court has subject matter and specific jurisdiction. **1-1/2 points**

In the present situation, the court may find that substantial justice would be better served in Michigan since all of the essential witnesses are there and the plaintiff is a resident. Furthermore, to bring the witnesses to New York to testify would be an extraordinary expense to the defendant R Co. CPLR 327 permits any party to use the doctrine of forum non conveniens, whether or not the party is a resident of New York, and the court's ruling regarding the doctrine need not be based solely on the moving party's residence. Hence, the reason for the denial was incorrect. **1 point**

(2)   The issue is whether long arm jurisdiction exists over C in New York. **1/2 point**

Under the long arm statute [CPLR 302], personal jurisdiction can arise out of certain actions by the defendant. One qualifying action is that the defendant transact any business within the state and the suit arises out of that in-state transaction. **1 point**

Here, C had transacted business in New York through negotiations of a substantial character, requiring C's presence in New York for four months. This nexus with New York is statutorily and constitutionally sufficient for a finding that the court had personal jurisdiction over C because the cause of action "arose out of" C's transacting business in New York. Thus, the court was correct. **1-1/2 points**

(3)   The issue is whether one transacting business in New York through an agent is subject to New York jurisdiction. **1/2 point**

As stated above, under the long arm statute [CPLR 302], a person who transacts business in New York is subject to personal jurisdiction as to causes of action arising out of the business transacted. Furthermore, a court may exercise personal jurisdiction over a nondomiciliary who, in person or through an agent, is involved in conduct falling under the long arm statute. Transacting business includes not only the personal transaction of business, but also transaction of business through an agent. **1 point**

C was O's agent via their partnership. The Uniform Partnership Act defines a "partnership" as a voluntary association of two or more competent persons to carry on a business as co-owners for profit. Partners are agents of one another. **1 point**

The business relationship between O and C is a partnership. This can be demonstrated by the fact that they executed a contract and agreed to share in the profits of their enterprise. Therefore, New York may exercise jurisdiction over the person of O based upon the fact that the alleged defamation arises out of business transacted in New York by O through her agent C. Thus, the court's ruling was correct. **1 point**

Note that F could not base his assertion of jurisdiction over C and O on the commission of a tort in New York [CPLR 302(a)(2)] since causes of action for defamation are specifically excepted from coverage under that statute. **1/2 point**

ANSWER 34—PARTNERSHIP

(1)   The issue is what are a partner's rights with respect to assigning his interest in the partnership to a third party.

Each partner has an interest in the partnership. This interest is personal property and may be sold or assigned by her. A partner's partnership interest consists of her right to a share of profits, a share of any distributed surplus, and a share of proceeds after dissolution. Therefore, A's assignment of his partnership interest to E was valid and proper. **1 point**

Each partner also owns an interest in specific partnership property, such as the partnership's bank account. But each partner holds this interest as a tenant in partnership with all other partners. No partner may possess partnership property for other than the partnership purposes without the consent of all the other partners. A partner's interest as tenant in partnership is nontransferable. **1 point**

Additionally, each partner has a right to participate in the management of the partnership, which is equal to the rights of all the other partners—one partner, one vote. As with the interest held in tenancy in partnership, a partner's right to participate in management of the partnership is not assignable. **1 point**

Thus, E may assert an interest only in A's partnership interest. E is entitled to A's share of all distributions of profits or surplus, and may be entitled to A's share of proceeds upon dissolution. But E may not participate in management of the partnership, nor may E assert any interest in any partnership property. **1 point**

(2)   The issue is whether F may sue the partnership on a claim that arose before F acquired his partnership interest. The general rule is that a partner may not sue the partnership. The sole remedy of a partner who has a claim against the partnership or another partner is an action for an accounting. **1-1/2 points**

There are few exceptions to this rule. One exception concerns disputes over one fully completed, but unadjusted transaction. [*Cf.* Schuler v. Birnbaum, 405 N.Y.S.2d 351 (1978)] This is the case presented by the facts. The transaction that gives rise to the lawsuit is a single business transaction. Thus, no complex accounting is necessary in order to adjust the rights of the parties. Abco dealt with F as though he were a third person—in point of fact, he was not a partner at the time of the transaction. Therefore, F may maintain an action at law against the partnership and may collect a judgment from the partnership, and from such partners as he serves personally. **1-1/2 points**

It is important to note that D's liability will be limited to his contribution to the partnership, while the other partners may each be held personally liable for the total sum. Under the Partnership Law of New York, each partner is personally liable for the entire amount of all partnership debts. However, a partner who is admitted after the cause of action arises will be held liable only to the extent of his interest in partnership property. Thus, D's liability is limited, while the liability of A, B, and C is not. **1 point**

Thus, assuming that F's cause of action is valid, he will be entitled to judgment in his favor against Abco, A, B, and C; but as to D, his recovery will be limited to partnership property.

(3)   The issue involves who is liable for partnership obligations.

As before, not only is the partnership liable for obligations duly incurred in the course of partnership business, but also all of the partners are jointly liable on contractual obligations. Farmer may sue any partner individually, or the partnership; he may collect the full amount due from any partner whom he serves personally; but he may not collect more from D and F than the amounts of their interests in the partnership, for they were not partners when the partnership incurred the obligation, and neither has affirmatively incurred any obligation to pay preexisting debts of the partnership. **2 points**

Therefore, Farmer may recover the sum owed him from Abco, A, B, or C; but from D or F he may recover only their interest in the assets of the partnership.

ANSWER 35—SECURED TRANSACTIONS/CONTRACTS (SALES)/NEW YORK PRACTICE

At issue are the remedies available to a secured creditor when a debtor defaults.

B has defaulted on his loan from S and has few viable defenses. (*See infra.*) Thus, S has the right to sue B on the contract for the $5,000 owing. However, according to the facts, B's assets consist primarily of the mowers, and a suit for damages might not yield a meaningful judgment. Therefore, S's best remedy is to use his rights as a secured creditor to replevy the mowers. **1 point**

S has a perfected purchase money security interest ("PMSI") in the mowers. A PMSI arises where, as here, the vendor of the collateral sells it to the debtor-purchaser on credit. For a security interest to be valid it must attach, and for it to give maximum protection against other third-party creditors of the debtor, it must be perfected. **1 point**

According to the facts, both steps were taken here: the security interest attached by the written security agreement, and the security interest was perfected by filing the financing statement. [Note that the PMSI was not automatically perfected here because the mowers are equipment, which requires filing for perfection.] **1 point**

Upon default of a debtor, the secured party has a right to take possession of the collateral, either by self-help or by an action for replevin. Self-help may be used only where it will not involve a breach of the peace. Upon repossession, the secured party may keep the goods if the debtor makes no objection within 20 days, or resell the goods and obtain a deficiency judgment if the amount recovered in the sale is insufficient to cover the amount owed plus the costs of replevin and sale. **2 points**

Here, it is clear that B is in default, since he refuses to pay the last $5,000 installment under the contract. It is not a defense that the mowers were nonconforming goods under the contract. (*See infra.*) It is also clear that S will not be able to use self-help to repossess, given B's threats. Thus, S must replevy the mowers. **1 point**

Since B is planning to immediately remove the mowers from the state, S should seek a prejudgment, ex parte seizure under CPLR 7102(d). A plaintiff may obtain an ex parte order of seizure to be executed by the sheriff upon showing the court by affidavit: (i) that the plaintiff is entitled to possession of the chattel that the defendant wrongfully holds; (ii) the value of the chattel; (iii) that there is no defense against the plaintiff; (iv) that the plaintiff will probably prevail on the merits; and (v) that the chattel may become unavailable or be impaired. The plaintiff must post an undertaking of twice the value of the chattel to obtain this remedy, and a motion to confirm the seizure must be made within five days after the seizure, with notice to the defendant. If the seizure is not confirmed, the defendant is entitled to damages. **1 point**

On the facts presented here, S would prevail if he sought this equitable remedy: B wrongfully holds the goods—which have value—while he has not paid for them; there are probably no defenses that would succeed against him (*see* below); S will probably succeed on the merits based on these facts; and the chattel is in danger of becoming unavailable because B is planning to move the mowers out of state. **1 point**

S should be advised of B's possible but weak claims against him. The lawn mowers delivered were nonconforming goods because they were not those ordered (they were Model 80s instead of Model 100s). B could have revoked his acceptance of the goods on this ground under U.C.C. section 2-608. B could also have claimed that S breached his warranty by delivering the wrong goods. The breach of warranty claim could be asserted as a separate suit by B against S or as an offset against the $5,000 balance due on the sale. S must be further advised that the law provides that a buyer is barred from any remedy unless he has notified the seller of the breach within a "reasonable time." In this case, B discovered the faulty delivery on May 15 but did not advise S of his objection until three months later, after he had used the goods for that period. Thus, it appears that B did not give S the required notice within a reasonable time pursuant to U.C.C. sections 2-607(3)(a) and 2-608(2). **2 points**

In sum, of the remedies available to S, the remedy of replevin appears to be the one most suited to achieve the enforcement of his rights.

ANSWER 36—CONTRACTS (SALES)

J'S RIGHTS AGAINST M

The issue is whether M's reply to J's letter constitutes a contractually binding acceptance of J's offer. **1/2 point**

Under U.C.C. section 2-207, applicable because the sale was one of goods and was between merchants, an acceptance can be expressed to an offer despite the fact that it contains terms different from those in the offer, unless acceptance is expressly made conditional on assent to the different terms. J's letter of April 15 was clearly an offer, containing the necessary terms such as quantity, price, and time for performance. M, by giving a written and signed reply to this letter on April 16, accepted the offer well before the May 10 deadline. **1 point**

The disclaimer of the warranty is also at issue in this situation. U.C.C. section 2-207(2) states that between merchants, additional terms become part of the contract unless: (i) the offer expressly limits acceptance to its terms, (ii) the additional terms materially alter the contract, or (iii) objection has already been given or is given within a reasonable time. **1/2 point**

According to the facts given, J's offer was not expressly limited to its terms, and J made no objection to M's disclaimer. The warranty disclaimer was part of a form approved by the industry; thus, it can be inferred that the practice is customary in the trade and that the disclaimer does not materially alter the contract. Therefore, this was a proper offer and acceptance sufficient to form a valid contract between J and M. **1 point**

The next issue is whether there was repudiation of the contract and whether this repudiation was retracted. **1/2 point**

When reasonable grounds for insecurity arise, a party may demand in writing adequate assurance of due performance under U.C.C. section 2-609(1). After receipt of this demand, the party whose performance is being questioned must provide adequate assurances within 30 days. However, this time limit is not relevant where the aggrieved party has not canceled, materially changed his position, or otherwise considered the repudiation to be final. Instead, the questioned party may retract the repudiation before performance is due, if he makes known his intention to that effect and includes assurances. **1-1/2 points**

The facts indicate that the credit report gave grounds for justifiable apprehension on M's part, and J did miss the 30-day deadline. But J did retract his repudiation properly under U.C.C. section 2-611 by tendering the certified check, which was effective as payment under the agreement, on the date of performance. There are no facts that indicate that M canceled, changed his position, or otherwise considered the repudiation final; instead, M waited until the day of performance to refuse tender and incorrectly cited the failure to give assurances as a breach of contract entitling M to refuse performance himself. **1-1/2 points**

Inasmuch as M was not excused from performance and J suffered damages despite his attempt to cover, J can recover the difference of $5,000 plus incidental damages. **1/2 point**

J'S RIGHTS AGAINST C

The issue is whether a party to a contract with a particular individual has any rights against a third party who, in a second, unrelated action with that individual, promised to make the individual a loan, but failed to do so. Under New York law, J could only succeed in such circumstances if there was a surety agreement, if he was a third-party beneficiary to the other contract, or if he held a negotiable instrument. **1 point**

First, there is no suretyship agreement. A surety transaction involves three parties: the creditor or obligee, the debtor or obligor, and the surety. For there to have been a surety arrangement, the creditor must have extended credit to the debtor in consideration of the surety's promise. Here, there is no suretyship agreement because J, as theoretical creditor, did not extend credit to M, debtor, in consideration of C's (surety's) extension of $50,000 to M. **1 point**

Second, J is not a promisee under a third-party arrangement. For J to have benefited under this legal theory there would have to have been clear intention manifested in the agreement between C and M to have benefited J. Since this intent was absent, J cannot claim to be a third-party beneficiary. **1/2 point**

Last, the facts do not indicate that J held any commercial instrument, so that the law of negotiable instruments provides no basis for relief. Hence, there is no theory by which J can assert rights against C. **1/2 point**

ANSWER 37—WILLS/TRUSTS

(1)   The first issue is what appointments Mama could make. **1/2 point**

Mama held a general, presently exercisable power of appointment. A general power of appointment can be exercised wholly in favor of the donee, her estate, her creditors, or the creditors of her estate. A power is deemed presently exercisable if it can be effected during the holder's life or by her will. In New York, trust income interests are given spendthrift protection by statute. Thus, any income beneficiary cannot sell or otherwise transfer her trust interest, and the beneficiary's creditors cannot reach that interest. However, because the donee of a presently exercisable general power of appointment can appoint to herself at any time, property covered by this power is subject to the payments of the claims of the donee's creditors or her estate. Statutory spendthrift protection is therefore not afforded to the property covered by the presently exercisable appointment. Thus, Mama's testamentary appointment in trust with the payment of income of 80% to Jake and 20% to the Home for Wayward Boys was proper. **1-1/2 points**

However, in exercising the power, Mama violated the Rule Against Perpetuities as to principal. The rule in pertinent part provides that no estate shall be valid unless it must vest, if at all, within the period of a "life in being plus 21 years." Mama's instructions provide that the trust principal will be paid to Jake's children when the youngest attains age 35. Because Jake may still have children and a child not yet born may reach age 35 more than 21 years after the deaths of all lives in being at the time the interest was created, the gift might not vest within the perpetuities period. The fact that the power is presently exercisable, and thus the perpetuities period begins to run on the effective date the power is exercised does not eliminate the perpetuities problem. At common law, this defect would have voided Mama's exercise of the power with respect to the trust principal. However, the New York perpetuities reform statute automatically reduces all age contingencies to 21 years, thereby saving Mama's appointment. **2 points**

Mama's appointment also violated the suspension rule but is saved by the "wait and see" doctrine. The suspension rule provides that every present or future interest is void in its creation if it suspends the absolute power of alienation for a period longer than lives in being plus 21 years. The power of alienation is suspended where there are no persons in being who can transfer a fee simple absolute. Thus, the suspension rule is violated if the trust beneficiaries are a class that may include unborn children, because even if there is a child alive (in being) at the trust's creation, that child could not convey a fee simple (as he has a vested remainder subject to open) for possibly longer than lives in being plus 21 years. However, the "wait and see" doctrine, generally rejected in New York except when applied to powers of appointment, permits a look at the facts as they exist on the date the donee exercises the power to determine the validity of the appointed interests under the suspension rule. **1 point**

Here, Mama's appointment created an income interest in Jake's children to take effect on Jake's death. Although this is an income interest in "unborn beneficiaries," by using the "wait and see" doctrine, we can see that Jake, as the measuring life of Mama's appointment, obviously cannot have any additional children upon his death. Although the trust provides for income to be paid to Jake's children until the age of 35, by using the perpetuities reform statute to reduce the age contingency for distribution of the principal to age 21, all beneficiaries will, in theory, be able to join together within "lives in being" in order to convey a fee simple absolute. Thus, the suspension rule is not violated. **1 point**

(2)   At issue is whether creditors of the decedent's estate can reach the property covered by a power of appointment. **1/2 point**

Property covered by a presently exercisable general power of appointment is subject to the claims of creditors of the donee or her estate, since the donee of such a power of appointment can appoint to herself at any time. Since Mama is treated as absolute owner so far as her creditors are concerned, the statutory spendthrift protection is therefore not afforded to the property covered by the general power of appointment. Thus, creditors of Mama's estate can reach the property covered by the presently exercisable general power of appointment. **1 point**

(3)   The issue is whether Jake's bequest to Wanda will satisfy her right of election. **1/2 point**

The elective share is one-third of the net estate. Here, Jake left a net estate of $4.5 million. Accordingly, Wanda has the right to elect to take one-third of the net estate, or $1.5 million. This right is limited to the difference between the spouse's actual bequest and the spouse's rightful elective share.

Jake's will provided Wanda with $1 million in an indefeasible trust. This trust does not satisfy Wanda's elective share right, and Wanda, upon filing a notice of election, would be entitled to outright ownership of one-third of Jake's net estate, or $1.5 million. **2 points**

ANSWER 38—CORPORATIONS/NEW YORK PRACTICE

(1) The first issue is whether Allison and Brian breached their fiduciary duty of care by hastily buying Scumacre. Directors and officers of a corporation must exercise the diligence, care, and skill that an ordinarily prudent person would exercise under similar circumstances in like positions. [BCL §§715(h), 717(a)] Since Allison and Brian did not investigate Scumacre for defects, did not conduct an inspection of its premises, and ignored David's warnings against buying the property, Allison and Brian did not act as ordinary prudent persons and hence breached their duty of care. (It is important to note that since David voiced his objection against the purchase, he did not breach his fiduciary duty.) **1-1/2 points**

Allison and Brian will argue that the business judgment rule protects them from this breach since courts will not second-guess the business judgments of directors if exercised in good faith on available information. However, since Allison and Brian made no good faith effort to gather all relevant information, the business judgment rule is of no help to them. **1 point**

The second issue is whether the articles of incorporation shield Allison and Brian from liability for their breach of duty of care. **1/2 point**

The certificate of incorporation may limit the liability of directors to shareholders for breaches of duty where the breach is not found to (i) be in bad faith; (ii) be due to intentional misconduct or knowing violation of the law; (iii) result in a financial profit or other advantage to which the director was not legally entitled; or (iv) violate statutory liabilities of directors. **1 point**

Since the facts indicate that Allison and Brian did not intentionally or in bad faith buy Scumacre, and did not profit from its purchase, the articles' provision limiting liability of the board will protect Allison and Brian. It is important to note that there is no evidence of bad faith by Allison and Brian merely because they failed to exercise good faith, as stated above. Therefore, the shareholders cannot successfully hold Allison and Brian liable for the losses resulting from the purchase of Scumacre. **1 point**

(2) The issue is the priority of claims when a corporation dissolves. **1/2 point**

After dissolution, the corporation must wind up its affairs and liquidate all of its assets. The first to get paid from the liquidation funds are the outside creditors of the dissolved corporation. Then the remaining money, if any, is distributed to shareholders according to their respective rights. Since the bylaws are merely an agreement between the corporation and its shareholders, outsiders dealing with the corporation are not charged with knowledge of the bylaws. Therefore, Allison and Brian take *after* all outside creditors are paid. Then, since the bylaws have the force and effect of a contract among shareholders, Allison and Brian will receive $500,000 before Carl receives anything. Thus, the bylaw provision is not valid. **2-1/2 points**

(3) The issue is how Braves Inc. can get its required information in time to respond to the estate's motion. **1/2 point**

A nonparty may be subpoenaed to take an oral deposition at least 20 days prior to the date of the deposition. Hence, since Braves Inc. needs to know within 30 days how Dodger Inc. told Evan to use the "autobus," and how Evan used the "autobus" on the date of his death, an oral deposition of a nonparty works well in this time limit. Therefore, Braves Inc. should subpoena Dodger Inc., a non-party, to produce a person with relevant information of the facts at issue, for an oral deposition. **1-1/2 points**

ANSWER 39—TRUSTS/WILLS/FUTURE INTERESTS

EFFECT OF THE WILL

The first issue presented is what rights D has in light of the will.

A trust may be created during the settlor's lifetime (inter vivos) or by will (testamentary trust). If the settlor has clearly established a trust, but failed to name a trustee, the trust will not fail. Rather, the court will appoint a trustee. *Rationale:* The settlor's primary intention was to create a trust to carry out the specified objectives; the naming of the specific trustee was incidental to this primary objective. Also, the EPTL sets forth statutory fiduciary powers, and thus it is not necessary for the settlor to specify the trustee's powers. **1 point**

T's will is fully effective. The will established a testamentary trust for D and D's children: D will receive the trust income for life. At his death, the principal will pass to A and B. Although it is not clear from the facts whether T appointed a trustee or set forth specific administrative provisions, the court will appoint a trustee and the statutory powers will govern. **1 point**

TREATMENT OF THE INTER VIVOS TRUST

The second issue is what the rights of the parties are in connection with the inter vivos trust. As stated above, a trust created during the settlor's lifetime is known as an inter vivos trust. **1/2 point**

(a)   S's Interest

T's irrevocable inter vivos trust survives his death. The income interest created by T will continue. S will receive the trust income until his death. **1 point**

(b)   D's Interest

A power of appointment is an authority created in or reserved by a person enabling that person to designate, within the limits prescribed by the creator of the power, the person(s) who shall take the property and the manner in which they shall take it. **1 point**

Here, S was given a testamentary power of appointment ("POA") by T, since it was exercisable only by S's will. Furthermore, it is a special power of appointment (rather than a general POA) because it is exercisable only in favor of a specified class of persons *not* including the testator, his estate, his creditors, or his estate's creditors. **1 point**

In this case, the specified class of persons is D and G and therefore S may only appoint the trust income to one of them. Since G predeceased S, S can only appoint the income to D. Since T made no gift in case S failed to exercise his POA, the courts will infer an "imperative" POA in order to carry out T's intent as creator of the trust should S neglect to appoint. Therefore, whether or not S exercises his power of appointment, D will receive the trust income upon S's death, provided D survives S. **1-1/2 points**

(c)   F's Interest

At the death of the survivor of S and D, the trust principal will pass to F via N's will. EPTL section 6-5.1 provides that future interests may be devised, alienated, or passed by descent in the same manner as estates in possession. N had a remainder interest in the trust, which is a future interest. Thus, he could properly bequeath it to anyone. **1 point**

Although income interests are given statutory spendthrift protection prohibiting the transfer of the right to the income, the devise of N's future interest to F is not prohibited by this protection, for N has given an interest in principal, not income. Only income interests fall within the purview of statutory spendthrift protection. In fact, while income interests cannot be transferred unless a provision is inserted expressly authorizing such transfers, remainder interests in the corpus can be transferred unless a provision is inserted expressly prohibiting such transfers. **1-1/2 points**

Finally, there is no perpetuities problem, because all interests vest within lives in being at the time the estates were created. There are no unascertained beneficiaries to require perpetuities analysis. **1/2 point**

ANSWER 40—FEDERAL JURISDICTION & PROCEDURE/EVIDENCE/CONFLICT OF LAWS/NEW YORK PRACTICE

(1) At issue is which state's law the New York court should apply. When faced with a conflict of law regarding loss distribution rules in a tort case, the New York Court of Appeals has rejected the old vested rights approach, which would mandate the automatic application of the law of the situs of the tort. Now, New York courts apply the ***governmental interest analysis***. This is to ensure that the jurisdiction with the greatest interest in the suit has its law apply. In order to make the determination, the court will look at the factual contacts of each jurisdiction, the differing laws, and the underlying policies for each law; apply the facts to the policies; and apply the greater governmental interest. For tort cases, New York has refined the interest analysis in *Neumeier v. Kuehner*, 31 N.Y.2d 121 (1972). The *Neumeier* rules are a product of the governmental interest analysis. Since under the *Neumeier* rules, the present case is an unprovided-for situation, the law of the situs will control unless that would frustrate or significantly undermine an important policy of the outside jurisdiction. **2 points**

In this case, the accident occurred in New York, the plaintiff is from State X, and the defendant is from New York. New York provides for a comparative negligence rule, and State X has a rule that contributory negligence by the defendant is a complete bar to recovery. The policy of State X's rule is that citizens in State X should not profit from their wrongs, no matter how slight the wrong may be. It is likely that the rule was enacted in order to protect defendants in State X from having to pay when the plaintiff has engaged in some degree of culpable conduct. New York's rule of comparative negligence is grounded in the view that there should be apportionment of damages based on the relative degree of fault between the parties. **2 points**

Here, applying the law of New York greatly helps the policies of New York because it is a New York defendant who will bear the brunt of damages, even if there is culpable conduct on the part of the State X plaintiff. Second, the policies of State X will not be harmed because the defendant is not from State X. If anything, the plaintiff from State X is helped because he will still be able to recover even if he was at fault to some degree. Accordingly, since there is no great violation to the interest of State X, the New York court will utilize the third *Neumeier* rule and apply the law of New York. Daniel's motion should be denied. **1 point**

(2) The issue is whether a court has power or discretion to order a new trial on the basis of newly discovered evidence, where the evidence consists of expert testimony which was not available at the time of trial. **1 point**

CPLR 5015(A)(2) provides that a party may obtain relief from judgment upon application to the court that rendered the judgment "upon such terms as may be just," provided that there is **newly discovered** evidence which "probably" would have produced a different result if introduced at trial, and which **could not** have been discovered in time to move for a new trial when the verdict was entered. **1 point**

The facts indicate that Alan knew of the existence of this expert and that he presumably could have sought a delay until the expert returned from Europe. It is apparent that the evidence is therefore not newly discovered, merely newly available. Thus, Alan's motion falls outside the bounds of grounds upon which a relief from judgment after trial may be granted, and the motion will fail. **1 point**

(3) The issue is whether Alan can have this case remanded to the New York Supreme Court. **1/2 point**

Section 1441(b) of the United States Code provides that where complete diversity exists between parties, and the amount in question exceeds $75,000, then an action begun in state court may be removed to the appropriate United States district court, **unless** one of the defendants is a citizen of the state in the courts of which the action was originally brought. **1 point**

Here, Daniel, the defendant, is a citizen of New York, so he may not remove the case to federal court. The motion for remand should be granted. **1/2 point**

ANSWER 41—EVIDENCE

(1) The issues are whether the report is hearsay, and if so, whether it is admissible pursuant to a recognized exception to the hearsay rule. **1/2 point**

Hearsay is a statement, other than one made by the declarant while testifying at the proceeding, offered in evidence to prove the truth of the matter asserted. If a statement is hearsay, and no exception to the rule is applicable, the evidence must be excluded upon appropriate objection to its admission. Here, S's report is an out-of-court statement being offered for its truth; thus, it is hearsay. The fact that the copy of the report was certified makes it prima facie authentic and satisfies the "best evidence rule," but the report is still hearsay. The next issue is whether it falls within a recognized exception. **1 point**

CPLR 4518 creates a business records exception to the hearsay rule. Any writing or record made as a memorandum or record of any act, transaction, occurrence, or event is admissible in evidence as proof of that act, if made in the regular course of business, and it was the regular course of such business to make it at that time or within a reasonable time thereafter. The first paragraph of S's report falls within the hearsay exception stated above. It is a writing that was made in the regular course of S's business as proof that an accident occurred and of what he witnessed when he arrived at the accident shortly after it occurred. However, a foundation for satisfaction of this hearsay exception is lacking. The fact that the record was made in the regular course of business, at or about the time of the recorded event, must be established by a person in the police department who is knowledgeable about the record-keeping practices. The second paragraph, on the other hand, is not covered by the business record exception because it fails to state what was observed and merely states conclusions that S made based upon his findings as set forth in paragraph one of his report. Opinions are not admissible under the business record exception to the hearsay rule. Generally, for opinions to be admissible, they must come from expert testimony. It must first be established that expert testimony is necessary to draw useful conclusions about the facts. It seems likely that such testimony would be helpful to the trier of fact in this case. If so, the expert must be qualified as such. Since it has not yet been determined that expert testimony is needed, and particularly since S has not been qualified as an expert, the second paragraph was properly excluded. In conclusion, no portion of the police report is admissible. **1-1/2 points**

Similarly, no portion of the police report is admissible under the public documents exception to the hearsay rule. The issue is what are the requirements for a document to qualify as a public record. New York's public document exception is more restrictive than the common law rule. New York has a statutory exception that requires: (i) the record be made by a public officer; (ii) the record be in the form of a certificate or affidavit; (iii) the record be authorized or required by special provision of law; (iv) the record be made in the course of the officer's official duty; (v) the record be of a fact ascertained or act performed by the officer; and (vi) the record be filed with a public records division. [CPLR 4520] If the document satisfies these requirements, the entire document will be admitted, without the need for foundation testimony. Because this rule is narrowly construed, and difficult to satisfy, most police reports of accidents are admitted, if at all, under the business records exception to the hearsay rule. The New York Court of Appeals "has not delineated the contours of the common law hearsay exception for public records" nor has it defined the scope of CPLR 4520. Here, there are not enough facts given to satisfy the public records exception. Therefore, the court was correct. **1 point**

(2)   The issues are whether the photograph is relevant and whether it has been properly authenticated. Photographs are admissible if they are identified by a witness as a portrayal of the facts relevant to the issue in question and they are verified by the witness as a correct representation of those facts. **1/2 point**

Relevant evidence is evidence having any tendency to make the existence of any fact of consequence to the determination of an action more probable than it would be without the evidence. One issue in this case is whether A's tires were defective at the time of the accident. There is nothing in the facts to indicate that B knew what A's tires looked like at the time of the accident, which is the only relevant time. Whenever evidence offered relates to a time other than the time involved in the controversy being litigated, the relevance of that evidence is suspect and should be examined very carefully. Moreover, there has been no demonstration that the condition of the tires several days after the accident is relevant. Showing that the tires were defective after the accident, without more, does not make it more probable that they were defective at the time of the accident. It has not been established that B can properly authenticate the photograph. Therefore, the court was correct in refusing to admit the photograph on B's testimony. **1-1/2 points**

(3)   The issue is whether the photograph is relevant and whether it was properly authenticated by A. **1/2 point**

A photograph showing the level of wear of the tire treads *at the time of the accident* tends to make the existence of the fact that the tires were defective more probable than it would be without the evidence; thus, the photograph is relevant if it is demonstrated that it shows the condition of the tires at the time of the accident. Once A, a person familiar with the objects in question (the tires), authenticated the photograph as accurately representing the wear on the treads at the time of the accident, the photograph became relevant evidence. Even where changed conditions have occurred because of the lapse of time between the event and the photograph so that the photograph is not a completely accurate depiction of the object, it may be admitted if it is not misleading. If the jury is cautioned to consider only the worn tread and not the other damage to the tires, there seems to be little danger of unfair prejudice. Therefore, the court should have allowed the photograph into evidence, and its ruling was incorrect. **1-1/2 points**

(4)   The issue is whether A's guilty plea is hearsay and, if so, whether it is admissible under a statutory hearsay exception. **1/2 point**

A's guilty plea is hearsay because it is an out-of-court statement offered to prove the truth of the matter asserted therein. Nevertheless, it is admissible because it is an admission by a party, and therefore is within an exception to the hearsay rule. Thus, the court ruled correctly. Note that this is not a record of criminal conviction, within the meaning of the hearsay exception. Records of prior criminal conviction do not include traffic infractions. **1-1/2 points**

ANSWER 42—CRIMINAL LAW/CRIMINAL PROCEDURE

SUPPRESSION OF THE CONFESSION

The issue is whether a Fifth Amendment right against self-incrimination—specifically the right to counsel—is violated when an infant is denied access to her mother prior to questioning. **1/2 point**

The Fifth Amendment provides suspects a right against self-incrimination during custodial police interrogation. In *Miranda v. Arizona*, the United States Supreme Court held that all suspects being interrogated by the police in a custodial setting must be advised of their right to remain silent and their right to an attorney. A waiver of these rights must be knowing, intelligent, and voluntary. Nevertheless, to invoke the rights, a suspect generally must specifically ask to speak with an attorney; merely asking to speak with someone else, such as a probation officer, does not invoke the suspect's Fifth Amendment rights. However, in New York there is an exception—attempts to keep parents from their infant children held by police may invalidate a confession. **1 point**

The exception will apply here. First, Stacey will be considered an infant. Stacey is 15 years old. Under New York law anyone under age 16 is considered an infant for purposes of Criminal Law. Moreover, Stacey's mother attempted to contact her, and the police intentionally delayed the contact. Stacey also requested to see her mother, and the police deceitfully advised that they would try to find her, despite the fact that Stacey's mother was already in contact with the police. Finally, although Stacey said that she did not want to speak with an attorney, it is questionable whether a minor can waive this right knowingly, intelligently, and voluntarily. As a result, the confession elicited by the police must be suppressed. **1-1/2 points**

POSSIBILITY OF STACEY'S AND KAREN'S CONVICTIONS

(a)   Robbery

The first issue is whether Stacey and Karen committed first degree robbery. **1/2 point**

Robbery consists of: (i) a taking of personal property of another; (ii) from the other's person or presence; (iii) by force or threats of immediate death or physical injury to the victim, a member of the victim's family, or some person in the victim's presence; (iv) with the intent to permanently deprive the victim of it. In New York, a defendant is guilty of first degree robbery if she: (i) caused a nonparticipant serious physical injury; or (ii) was armed, threatened the use of a dangerous instrument, or displayed what appeared to be a firearm. In this case, Karen robbed the bodega and threatened the storekeeper with a firearm. She took personal property from the storekeeper's person or presence by threatening immediate death or physical injury, with the intent to permanently deprive him of it. Therefore, Karen should be convicted of first degree robbery. **1-1/2 points**

With respect to Stacey, New York law allows the prosecution of defendants ages 14 or 15 who are responsible for serious offenses against person or property. They need not be brought up on juvenile delinquency charges in Family Court. **1/2 point**

Under the general rule of modern accomplice liability, a person who intentionally aids or encourages a principal to commit a crime is liable for the principal crime. Moreover, in New York, an accomplice is not absolved of liability merely because the principal has a defense, the state has failed to prosecute the principal, or the offense is defined so that the accomplice cannot commit the offense in an individual capacity. However, withdrawal can be raised as an affirmative defense if the accomplice voluntarily and completely renounces her criminal purpose, withdraws prior to commission of the offense, and makes a substantial effort to prevent the crime. In this case, Stacey was an accomplice. She was an integral part of the crime, despite her failure to warn Karen. Although she left the scene of the crime, she did not affirmatively withdraw in any manner recognized in New York. Consequently, Stacey should be held liable for the substantive offense. **1-1/2 points**

Upon proof of the facts of this case, Stacey and Karen should be convicted of first degree robbery.

(b)   Murder

The issue is whether Karen committed murder. Murder is the unlawful killing of a human being with malice aforethought. Under New York law, a defendant who is 13, 14, or 15 years of age may be prosecuted for second degree murder. Any death caused in the commission of, or in an attempt to commit, a felony is felony murder. In felony murder, malice is implied from the intent to commit the underlying felony. The killing must have been a foreseeable result of the felony, and the death must have been caused during the commission of the felony or the defendant's immediate flight from the felony. Felony murder applies to all participants, and robbery is included in the list of felonies to which the felony murder rule applies. The defendant need not be convicted of the underlying felony; there need only be sufficient evidence to support the conclusion that the defendant committed the crime. A felony murder conviction is possible even if the underlying felony is dismissed. **1-1/2 points**

Karen cannot be convicted of first degree murder. While the New York felony murder rule applies to first degree murder as well as second degree murder, for first degree murder, the victim must have been intentionally killed by the defendant during the course of the robbery or immediate flight therefrom. That is not the case here. The autopsy showed that Karen did not actually kill the police officer; instead, the officer was killed by a bullet from a fellow officer's gun. Consequently, Karen cannot be convicted of first degree murder. However, she can be convicted of second degree murder, a lesser included charge. **1-1/2 points**

ANSWER 43—PARTNERSHIP

(1)   The issue is whether Gus stands in some special relationship to Family Department Store ("Family"), so that Family will be responsible for Gus's negligence. **1/2 point**

The relationship between Gus and Family is that of employee/employer—in other words, it is a master/servant relationship. Under the common law of torts in New York, a master will be liable for the tortious acts of his servant if the tort occurs within the scope of employment. This is the doctrine of respondeat superior. (Note that for full credit, the student must define the term, not just use it.) **1 point**

Thus, the question turns on whether Gus was acting within the scope of his employment at the time of the accident. Under the facts, Gus is a buyer who is sent to Utica on instructions from his employer. He is required by his employer to use his own vehicle. The stated purpose of his traveling to the restaurant at the time of the collision is to meet with a clothing manufacturer to place an order. Thus, under the facts, Gus is certainly acting within the scope of his employment, and X will be entitled to recover from Family under the doctrine of respondeat superior as defined above. **1 point**

(2)   The issue is whether the doctrine of respondeat superior as discussed above extends to an employer's liability for his employee's intentional tort, committed within the scope of the employee's occupation. **1/2 point**

In general, an employer is not liable for intentional tortious acts of his employees. However, under New York law, intentional tortious conduct is considered to be within the scope of employment either when force is authorized beforehand or when the employee furthers the employer's business by his acts. **1 point**

In the instant case, both of these conditions are present. First, B is described as a bouncer; *i.e.,* someone who is expected to eject customers from the establishment, using force if necessary. Thus, while Yummy Restaurant certainly did not specifically authorize B to break Gus's arm, it did authorize the use of force; so Yummy will be liable for all such use of force, if excessive, even though B acted intentionally. Second, B's tortious act was in furtherance of his employer's business. Even if B were not expected to use force in the performance of his duties, his actions were solely motivated by the carrying out of his employer's wishes. Under such circumstances, New York courts will hold the employer liable for his acts. Thus, Gus will recover from Yummy. **1-1/2 points**

(3)   The issue is the effect of a partner's death on partnership contracts. **1/2 point**

Under New York law, a partnership dissolves on the death of any partner, unless the partnership agreement provides to the contrary. The facts show that there was no written partnership agreement. Therefore, the partnership was dissolved by P's death. **1/2 point**

R's contract with N is binding on the partnership and each partner individually. Generally, all partners are liable for debts of the partnership incurred by any partner in the course of partnership business. However, once the partnership dissolves, a partner may not bind the partnership to new business; he may only wind up old business. An exception exists, however, when the partner does not have notice of the dissolution, in which case he may continue to bind the partnership until he receives notice of the facts requiring dissolution. **1-1/2 points**

Here, N entered into a contract with R for partnership purposes before N had notice of P's death. Thus, N had actual authority to enter into the contract, and the contract is binding and enforceable by both sides. Since both the partnership and the individual partners are liable on partnership obligations, R could look to Family, N, O, and/or P's estate for performance. **1 point**

S may look only to N to recover on their contract. N entered into the contract with S after N had notice of the dissolution. Thus, N lacked actual authority. **1/2 point**

N also lacked apparent authority. Although the contract apparently was for partnership purposes (and partners have apparent authority to bind their partnership to such contracts), the partnership was dissolved, so N lacked even apparent authority. A third party may not rely on representations as to agency from an agent without prior course of dealing and without seeking acknowledgment from the principal. Where the third party does so, as here, and the agent lacks authority, the third party may look only to the agent to recover. Therefore, S may look only to N for recovery. **1/2 point**

ANSWER 44—NEW YORK PRACTICE/TORTS/EQUITY/CONTRACTS

(1) The issue presented by X Inc. and F's motion to dismiss is whether a New York court may exercise jurisdiction over them. In order to answer this, three other issues must first be addressed.

First, does the court have personal jurisdiction over X Inc. and F? **1/2 point**

The court may exercise personal jurisdiction over X Inc. The facts make it clear that P Inc. can recover, if at all, on a theory of tortious interference with business relationships, or a theory of misappropriation of trade secrets. Clearly, the cause of action is grounded in tort. Therefore, New York may assert jurisdiction over X Inc. by using CPLR 302(a)(3)(ii), which enables personal jurisdiction to be asserted whenever the defendant commits a tortious act outside the state which causes injury within the state, if the defendant "expects or should reasonably expect the act to have consequences in the state and derives substantial revenue from interstate or international commerce." Clearly, X Inc.'s mailing indicates that X Inc. expects its (allegedly tortious) acts to have consequences in New York; and X Inc. does business "on a national scale." The injury in New York is the loss of sales to New York customers. [Sybron Corp. v. Wetzel, 46 N.Y.2d 197 (1978)] Thus, jurisdiction over X Inc. is proper. **1-1/2 points**

Likewise, the court has personal jurisdiction over F. F has allegedly committed separate tortious acts against P Inc., which will have consequences within the state. Arguably, CPLR 302(a)(3)(i), which applies to anyone who commits a tortious act outside the state that causes harm within the state and who "derives substantial revenue from goods used . . . within the state," applies to F on the theory that (assuming tortious conduct) F stands to derive substantial revenue from goods sold by X Inc. within the state. Also, if F carried P Inc.'s trade secrets or customer lists with him out of New York, he has committed a tortious act within the state under CPLR 302(a)(2). **1-1/2 points**

Second, does the court have jurisdiction over the subject matter of the dispute? **1/2 point**

The court has subject matter jurisdiction if it has the constitutional or legislative authority to grant the relief that a party is seeking. Under section 1314 of the BCL, actions against a foreign corporation by a New York resident are permitted in the New York courts. In this situation, P Inc., a domestic New York corporation, is suing X Inc. and F to enjoin them from participating in competitive activities in New York. Since the New York court could grant this relief to P Inc., the court has subject matter jurisdiction. **1 point**

Finally, the method of service on X Inc. and F was proper under the CPLR. The issue regarding X Inc. is whether service is proper if executed out of state on a corporate officer of a foreign corporation. Since a basis of personal jurisdiction existed over X Inc. under New York's long arm statute, it does not matter that its president was served in Connecticut. **1/2 point**

Likewise, F was properly served. As explained above, F's tortious acts will have an effect within New York. Therefore, since the court had jurisdiction and F was properly served in all other regards, as was X Inc., the court properly dismissed the motion. **1/2 point**

(2) The issue is what burden of proof P Inc. has to bear to prevail on its action to obtain a preliminary injunction against F and X Inc., and whether it can do so. **1/2 point**

P Inc.'s theory of recovery (*see* above) is grounded in unfair competition, a tort theory of recovery. To recover, P Inc. must be able to show that X Inc. has misappropriated a right or a res belonging to P Inc., or (with regard to F) that F has misappropriated a trade secret belonging to P Inc. **1/2 point**

As to trade secrets, any trade secrets in the possession of X Inc. must have come from F, so that both would be liable. But P Inc. must show that F took some plan, process, formula, or other information which gave P Inc. a competitive advantage only as long as it was kept a secret. The facts show only that X Inc. is sending announcements to P Inc.'s customers. A customer list is secret only if it can be shown that the list is proprietary information. Here, there is nothing to indicate that the list was derived from a secret list, rather than the phone book or some other generally available source. Absent such a showing, P Inc. will not recover on this ground. Thus, P Inc. has no right to relief on either of the first two grounds. **1-1/2 points**

As to employment, P Inc. must show either that X Inc. interfered with a contractual right P Inc. had in F, or that F violated a restrictive covenant of some sort. But the facts show neither a continuing contractual relationship between P Inc. and F, nor any restrictive covenant. P Inc. retains no continuing contractual rights in F's work—he has retired. The courts construe restrictive covenants regarding employment very narrowly. Where, as here, there is no such covenant, the courts will not imply one. Thus, P Inc. has no right of recovery, and its causes of action will fail. **1-1/2 points**

(*Note:* The material tested in the last portion of this essay is in the Equity outline.)

ANSWER 45—CORPORATIONS/CONTRACTS (SALES)

(1)   The issue is whether S's interest in L Corp. renders D Inc.'s contract with L Corp. void or voidable under the "interested directors" doctrine. **1 point**

All corporate directors owe a duty of loyalty to the corporation. The Business Corporations Law specifically requires that directors act in good faith. [N.Y. Bus. Corp. Law §717] Where a director has a personal stake in the outcome of corporate business, the Business Corporations Law provides specific criteria that must be met for the corporation to be bound by a contract involving the "interested director." The statute [N.Y. Bus. Corp. Law §713] provides that interested director transactions are voidable unless the director shares all the material facts of his extracorporate interest before any corporate action is taken. Unless such material facts are made known to the corporation before the directors vote on the transaction, the corporation cannot approve the transaction within the criteria of the Business Corporations Law. However, where the terms of the statute are not met, the parties to the transaction may still enforce the contract if they affirmatively establish that the transaction was fair and reasonable to the corporation at the time it was made, notwithstanding the failure to comply with the statutory requirements concerning interested director transactions. **2 points**

In this case, S failed to disclose his interest in L Corp. to his fellow directors in D Inc. Thus, the directors of D Inc. could not approve the transaction with L Corp., within the requirements of the statute; and D Inc. may avoid the contract with L Corp., unless L Corp. affirmatively establishes that the transaction was fair and reasonable to D Inc. at the time it was made. **1 point**

(2)   The issue is whether the prevention of a takeover constitutes valid ground for the denial of inspection rights, and whether G Corp. had the right to inspect the books of D Inc. **1/2 point**

Under Business Corporations Law section 624, any shareholder may demand inspection for any purpose reasonably related to such person's interests as a shareholder. However, before permitting inspection, the corporation may require the shareholder to furnish an affidavit that his purpose is not other than in the interest of the corporation and that he has not participated in any attempt to sell a shareholder list within the past five years. The right of inspection may not be denied even if the purpose of the inspection is to solicit shareholders for tender offers. Under this statute, a corporation must deliver to such shareholder information in written form or in any form to such extent information is kept by the corporation. In this case, G Corp., as a shareholder, is entitled to inspect the records. **1-1/2 points**

(3)   Remedies of D Inc. under the Uniform Commercial Code

The issue is what rights and remedies D Inc. has upon receipt of notification that R is insolvent and how R's insolvency affects future shipments from D Inc. to R. **1/2 point**

(a)   Goods in Transit

Under U.C.C. section 2-705, a seller may stop delivery of goods in the possession of a carrier if he discovers that the buyer is insolvent. **1/2 point**

Here, D Inc. received notice on December 5 that R was insolvent. Thus, D Inc. had good reason to want to recover the goods sent to R on December 1. D Inc. would be justified in stopping the golf clubs in transit and recovering them from the carrier. **1 point**

(b)   Future Shipments

Under U.C.C. section 2-609, if reasonable grounds for insecurity arise with respect to the performance of either party, the other party may in writing demand adequate assurance of due performance. If the assurance is not given within 30 days of demand, the party requesting the assurance may treat the contract as repudiated. In this situation, D Inc., after receiving notification that R was insolvent, certainly had reasonable grounds for insecurity as to R's ability to perform. Accordingly, if after assurance is requested R does not comply within 30 days, D Inc. may treat the contract as repudiated and would not be obligated to make any future shipments to R. **2 points**

ANSWER 46—CRIMINAL LAW/CRIMINAL PROCEDURE

(1)   The issue presented is whether the grand jury may indict solely on N's testimony. **1/2 point**

To indict, the grand jury must have legally sufficient evidence presented before it. Thus, N must be able to testify as to each element of burglary in the third degree, the crime with which B was charged. The elements are: (i) knowingly entering or remaining unlawfully (ii) in a building (iii) with intent to commit a crime therein. **1 point**

N cannot prove unlawful (*i.e.,* unpermitted) entry; only V could do that. Therefore, N's testimony is legally insufficient to support the indictment, and the motion should have been granted. **1/2 point**

(2)   The issue presented is whether the search of B's apartment was a lawful warrantless search and seizure. **1/2 point**

The search and seizure of B's apartment was unlawful. The general rule is that an officer must have a warrant to conduct a search and seizure, unless the search and seizure fall within one of several exceptions. **1 point**

There was no consent to the search; P tricked B to gain entry, and trickery cannot give rise to voluntary consent. Nor is the seizure within the plain view exception because P was not legitimately on the premises, where he viewed the evidence (*i.e., coin collection*). **1 point**

Furthermore, the search was not incident to a lawful arrest, for the arrest was unlawful. P may not arrest B at home without a warrant, absent an emergency. Here, no emergency existed. The nonemergency arrest of an individual in his own home requires an arrest warrant. Where the arrest is unlawful, the search is unlawful, and the seized evidence must be excluded. **1 point**

Finally, it should be obvious from the facts that there was no hot pursuit, nor was the evidence evanescent. **1/2 point**

Thus, the search and seizure come within none of the recognized exceptions to the requirement of a warrant, and the court ruled incorrectly.

(3) The issue is whether A has standing under the Fourth Amendment to challenge the lawfulness of the search of B's apartment. **1/2 point**

A must show ownership or possession of, or residence at, B's house, in order to assert his rights under the Fourth Amendment. But the facts do not point to any of these situations. A had no possessory interest in the coin collection seized and was not present when the search took place at B's house. Therefore, A has no standing to challenge the lawfulness of the search, and the coin collection was properly admitted into evidence. **1-1/2 points**

(4) The issue is to what extent a confession taken in violation of *Miranda* may be used. **1/2 point**

At the time A was taken into custody, he should have been given his *Miranda* warnings. Because he was not given the warnings, no statement made by A may be introduced to prove his guilt. This is not an occasion when A's statements may be used even though no warnings were given; *i.e.,* "blurted out" statements. Thus, the court was incorrect as to this point. However, a confession taken in violation of *Miranda* but otherwise voluntary may be used to impeach A if he testified at trial. A may not commit perjury with impunity just because his *Miranda* rights were violated. Here, the court was correct. **1-1/2 points**

ANSWER 47—DOMESTIC RELATIONS/NEW YORK PRACTICE

(1) The issue is whether the separation agreement survived for purposes of a conversion divorce after John and Mary resumed their marital relationship. **1/2 point**

After establishing a duly executed separation agreement, a spouse can obtain a "conversion divorce" (*i.e.,* a separation agreement "converted" into a divorce decree) if it can be shown that the parties actually lived apart continuously for one or more years. Occasional cohabitation by the parties during the period of separation is, by itself, insufficient to rescind the agreement and defeat a conversion divorce claim. It must be shown that the parties cohabited together with the intention to reconcile and abandon the agreement. **1-1/2 points**

The facts here demonstrate John and Mary's intention to reconcile and resume married life together, thereby voiding their separation agreement. **1/2 point**

Where a separation agreement is nullified by an intended reconciliation, the agreement is not revived when the parties separate again. Since no separation agreement was in effect, John has failed to state a cause of action upon which relief can be granted, and Mary's motion to dismiss should be granted. **1/2 point**

(2)   Since the facts indicate that State X has adopted all of New York's laws as its own, the first issue is whether State X has subject matter jurisdiction over the divorce action and whether John has satisfied State X's durational residency requirements. **1/2 point**

When process is served on a defendant out of state, the basis for matrimonial jurisdiction is the presence of "property" within the state. The marriage itself is regarded as a res and, for jurisdictional purposes, is deemed located in the jurisdiction where either party is domiciled. Here, John is domiciled within State X. This provides the court with a jurisdictional basis to determine the status of the marriage. **1/2 point**

Furthermore, durational residency requirements may be imposed in addition to personal and in rem jurisdictional requirements. The durational residency requirements are merely substantive elements of the matrimonial cause of action and do not limit the subject matter jurisdiction of the court to adjudicate the dispute. The durational residency requirements of New York (and therefore State X) can be satisfied in alternative ways. One acceptable method is when either party, here John, has been a resident of the state for a continuous period of at least two years preceding the commencement of the action. **1 point**

The next issue is whether there was proper service on the defendant in the ex-parte divorce action. **1/2 point**

New York will give full faith and credit to a divorce decree issued by another state, if the state has a statutory basis for jurisdiction and if the defendant has been properly served. In an ex parte matrimonial action, the defendant must be served in accordance with the laws of the forum state, and such methods must be constitutionally reasonable. **1 point**

Again, the facts state that the laws of State X are the same as those of New York. Therefore, personal service must be made upon the defendant, his appointed attorney, or by court order. Here, service upon an attorney who was only an acquaintance of the defendant was improper. **1/2 point**

Furthermore, even if State X did have jurisdiction, the court could grant only the ex parte divorce decree and may not affect the "incidentals" to the marriage. The rights to support and maintenance are personal and cannot be cut off by a court that lacks in personam jurisdiction over the party seeking to enforce those rights. **1/2 point**

Therefore, the court did not have jurisdiction.

(3)   The issue is whether a party is entitled to a maintenance award when the divorce decree granted in another state does not provide for support and the party is not in danger of becoming a public charge. **1/2 point**

The court will consider the case in light of the Equitable Distribution Law and will award maintenance according to the reasonable needs of the parties. The fact that the State X decree does not provide for maintenance will not abrogate Mary's right to have the issue of maintenance decided, de novo, by a New York court. Since Mary is not asking for modification of a previous decree or agreement, she does not have to show that she is in danger of becoming a public charge, nor even extreme hardship, to qualify for an award. Since John returned to New York, the New York court has personal jurisdiction over all the parties and can therefore impose maintenance obligations on John. **2 points**

ANSWER 48—WILLS/TORTS

(1) DENIAL OF WILL TO PROBATE

The issue is whether the fact that A is attorney, executor, and attesting witness defeats the will or interferes with its admission to probate. **1/2 point**

Under the EPTL and the SCPA, which govern testamentary dispositions, there is no rule that prohibits the same individual from acting as both attorney and witness of a will. Furthermore, the fact that a person is the attorney, executor, and witness of a Last Will and Testament will not affect the probate of the will. In New York, an attesting witness who is also named as executor is a competent witness to the will's execution. **1 point**

A "beneficial disposition or appointment" to an attesting witness may be void. The term "beneficial disposition or appointment" does not apply to appointment as an executor. It only applies to beneficial dispositions and appointments that bestow a financial benefit. Appointment as an executor is not considered a beneficial disposition, as the executor earns his commissions. Therefore, the will is not defeated and should be admitted to probate. However, by statute, if an attorney drafts a will that names the attorney as executor, he must disclose to the client that (i) any person, not just an attorney, can be named executor, (ii) executors are entitled to statutory commissions, and (iii) the attorney also will be entitled to attorney's fees for any legal services rendered to the estate. The client must sign a written acknowledgment of the disclosure. Absent compliance with the statute, the commission of an attorney who serves as executor shall be one-half of the statutory commission. **2 points**

Here, the fact that A is the attorney, executor, and witness will not defeat the probate of the will. However, as there is no indication that A complied with the attorney/executor disclosure statute, he will be entitled only to half the statutory commissions. **1/2 point**

(2)(a) WRONGFUL DEATH ACTION

The issue is who is entitled to wrongful death proceeds. **1/2 point**

In a wrongful death action, the recovery is based on pecuniary loss by the distributees for whose benefit the action has been brought, and any damages recovered are not included as part of the decedent's estate. The amount of recovery should be based on loss of support, medical and funeral expenses, voluntary assistance, and the possibility of the diminishment of an inheritance due to the premature death. The proceeds should be distributed proportionately, based on the pecuniary loss to the beneficiaries. **2 points**

It is clear that H's wife and son are entitled to respective shares of the damages. H's daughter's financial independence in and of itself does not necessarily preclude her from sharing in the recovery. The possibility of voluntary financial assistance by H or the possibility of an inheritance are other factors to be considered in addition to the daughter's lack of dependence, although the latter factor will be highly determinative of the amount of D's recovery. The wrongful death proceeds should be distributed among H's wife, son, and daughter. **2 points**

(b) PERSONAL INJURY ACTION

The issue is the distribution of any award to H's estate. Any damages recovered in the action for pain and suffering are included in H's estate and will be divided among his spouse, son, and daughter as provided in his will. Accordingly, H's spouse will get 50% of the damages, his son will get 40%, and his daughter will get 10%. **1-1/2 points**

ANSWER 49—NEW YORK PRACTICE/TORTS

(1)   The first issue is whether the actions were brought within the statute of limitations. **1/2 point**

Under New York law, both the negligence and strict products liability claims are governed by a three-year statute of limitations, running from the date of injury. P's action was brought within three years of the accident and is therefore timely. **1/2 point**

The second issue is whether a cause of action was stated in each of the claims. Each of P's claims stated a cause of action. The negligence claim against C stated a cause of action, since a lessor has a duty to inspect the leased goods to ensure their safety and, in addition, C, through its employee, E, was exercising control over the equipment at the time of the accident. Fault might lie in the manner in which E operated the machine or in his failure to take protective steps to warn P to move when the cable gave way. **1 point**

A claim in strict products liability is probably also stated on these facts. To establish a prima facie case in products liability based on a strict liability theory, it must be proven that there was a strict duty owed by a commercial supplier who breached that duty and that his breach was the actual or proximate cause of the damages suffered. This theory of recovery was originally designed to protect persons injured by products sold by distributors and manufacturers of defective products despite the absence of privity, in part, because merchants and manufacturers can spread their losses for harm from injury-causing products through pricing and insurance. The same rationale should apply to persons in the business of *leasing* a particular product, and at least one court in New York has so indicated. [Nastasi v. Hochman, 58 A.D.2d 564 (1977); *see* Samaras v. GATX Leasing Corp., 75 A.D.2d 890 (1980)] At the same time, however, strict products liability should *not* apply to "the casual or isolated lease." Thus, the outcome here will turn on whether C's lease of the machine to X was an isolated transaction or whether C was a commercial supplier of leasing equipment of the type that was involved in the accident. The facts do not provide enough information to give a definitive answer. Thus, the court was incorrect in dismissing P's claim. **1-1/2 points**

(2)   The issue is whether C has a cause of action for indemnity or contribution against M. **1/2 point**

A basis for impleader exists against M on the theory that M may be liable to C for all or part of P's claim against C. [CPLR 1007] Such liability on the part of M to C could be grounded on either indemnity or contribution. Any tortfeasor may seek indemnification or contribution from joint tortfeasors who participated in the tort. Contribution involves a sharing of responsibility based on relative degrees of culpability, while indemnification involves a 100% shifting of responsibility for that conduct that exposed defendant to liability. If C is held liable to P for C's own negligence, M would have a statutory duty to make contribution to C for M's relative share of culpability if M's conduct was a contributing factor. Such contribution could be based on strict products liability, negligence, or breach of warranty. [CPLR 1401-1403] **1 point**

If C's liability to P turns solely on strict products liability—leasing a defective product in the absence of negligence by C—C's claim over against M would lie in indemnity, an implied-in-law obligation. **1/2 point**

As to timeliness, regardless of whether C's impleader claim is based on indemnity or contribution, the statute of limitations is six years from the date of payment of a judgment or settlement by C to P. The underlying theory of liability for contribution or indemnity, whether based on negligence, strict products liability, or breach of warranty, becomes irrelevant. Thus, the fact that M sold the machine to C more than four years ago or that the impleader claim is asserted more than three years after the accident does not make C's claim untimely. **1-1/2 points**

The cause of action for contribution or indemnity technically has not accrued yet because no judgment or settlement has occurred. The impleader claim is, in effect, a permissible premature suit. Thus, C stated a timely cause of action against M. **1/2 point**

(3)   The issue is whether C's settlement with P bars C from bringing an action against M for contribution or indemnity. **1/2 point**

General Obligations Law section 15-108 provides that when a tortfeasor such as C settles an action prior to trial, he thereby relinquishes any right to contribution from any other joint tortfeasor, such as M. Thus, to the extent C's impleader claim against M is based on **contribution** for shared responsibility (*e.g.,* C's negligence in inspecting and using the machine coupled with M's sale of a defective product), it is now barred as a matter of law because of the settlement. However, section 15-108 does **not** apply to claims for 100% **indemnification**. [McDermott v. City of New York, 50 N.Y.2d 211 (1980)] Thus, if C's liability to P is based solely on strict products liability for leasing a defective product, such liability would be the result solely of M's sale of a defective product. Such a 100% shifting of responsibility to M constitutes indemnification; a settlement, therefore, would have no effect on C's rights against M. C could seek full reimbursement of the $50,000 settlement from M. In that event, M would have a right to assert against C whatever defenses C would have had against P, *i.e.,* in effect seek to disprove P's case against C. The court might find, for example, that P had no cause of action against C to begin with, thereby rendering the settlement improvident in retrospect. In any case, since it is impossible to state whether C's claim against M sounds in contribution or indemnity, C's third-party action should not be dismissed at this time. **2 points**

ANSWER 50—REAL PROPERTY

(1)   The issue is whether leases that do not contain a "no assignment" clause are assignable. **1/2 point**

New York courts will construe covenants restricting the free alienation of property strictly. Where such covenants are not express, the courts generally will not imply one, as restraints on alienation of real property are particularly disfavored. A covenant against assignment will not be implied in favor of a landlord, unless it can be shown that the covenant was material to the landlord's bargain and expectations. **1-1/2 points**

Because the lease is silent as to assignment, P must prove an implied covenant against the assignment. The only evidence that points to an implied covenant against assignment is the percentage clause. It will not suffice, for there was no clause in the lease providing for termination should D fail to reach the necessary gross. Thus, P did not negotiate the lease requiring the percentage clause as a material part of the consideration, but rather as a bonus. Therefore, P's argument fails, and the assignment by D to X was proper. (Note that the percentage clause is personal to D and not a covenant that runs with the land. If D makes over $2 million in any location during the term of the lease, P should have a right of relief.) **1-1/2 points**

(2)   The issue is whether the option "runs with the land." **1/2 point**

In New York, a legitimate assignee is entitled to the benefit of all terms of the lease that run with the land—that is, which touch and concern the land. X, as stated in (1) above, is a legitimate assignee under the lease. The option clause runs with the land, for it concerns ownership. Thus, X has all the rights obtaining under the option clause. **1 point**

X has met the terms of the option clause with his offer. The brokerage fee indemnification by Y is not a term of the purchase agreement, but incidental. If P were to sell to X under the option clause, he would incur no broker's fee directly thereby. Hence, X has met the terms offered by Y, and may exercise the option. **1 point**

(3)   The issue is what rights and obligations Y has with regard to the purchase of Blackacre. **1/2 point**

As to the damage caused by the windstorm, New York will apply the Uniform Vendor and Purchaser Risk Act if the contract between P and Y is silent as to risk of loss. The Act provides that the risk of loss passes to the purchaser only when legal title passes or the purchaser takes actual possession. Since neither of these events has taken place, the risk falls on P, who must bear the burden of the loss. **1-1/2 points**

P may not obtain specific performance of the contract against Y, for a material part of Blackacre (40%) was damaged. Thus, Y may avoid the contract should he so choose. In the alternative, if Y chooses, he may compel enforcement of the contract. In that case, Y is entitled to a setoff representing the diminution in value of the property as a result of the loss. **1 point**

Additionally, Y must be advised that he has no rights to Blackacre if X exercises the option. In such a case, Y is entitled only to incidental damages from P. **1 point**

ANSWER 51—DOMESTIC RELATIONS

(1)   The issue here is whether W raised a valid affirmative defense to H's application for a "conversion" decree of divorce based upon the February 1989 separation agreement. **1/2 point**

Under the Domestic Relations Law of New York, a decree of divorce is available where the spouses have lived separate and apart for a period of one year, pursuant to a written separation agreement. For the separation agreement to serve as grounds for the divorce, the spouses may not cohabit after the agreement is executed and before the decree is granted. **1 point**

The facts indicate that the parties cohabited with intent to reconcile. While mere sexual relations will not vitiate a separation agreement, actual cohabitation with intent to reconcile will effect a rescission of the agreement. The separation agreement was rescinded by the parties' actions, and the divorce should not have been granted on the basis of the agreement. Thus, the court's ruling was in error. **1-1/2 points**

(2)   The issue is whether W's counterclaim for divorce based on adultery is proper. **1/2 point**

A counterclaim for adultery based on acts committed after the date of separation is improper in an action for divorce based upon a separation agreement, unless the separation agreement has been rescinded. To state a claim for divorce on grounds of adultery, it is necessary to allege opportunity, inclination, and intent to commit adultery. **1-1/2 points**

W has alleged her cause of action with sufficient particularity to meet the requirements of the cause of action. In addition, her allegation that the separation agreement was rescinded by voluntary cohabitation removes the statutory bar to a counterclaim grounded in adultery. Thus, W should be allowed to present her proof on the merits. The court erred in its ruling. **1/2 point**

(3)   The issue is whether the Family Court has jurisdiction to modify the support terms of a supreme court divorce. **1/2 point**

The Family Court does not have jurisdiction over divorces, separations, or annulments. These matters must be brought in the supreme court. The Family Court generally has concurrent jurisdiction with the supreme court in support proceedings with some exceptions. In a post-divorce support modification proceeding where the original divorce decree is issued by the supreme court and contains a clause specifying that the decree be enforced or modified only in the supreme court, the Family Court will not have jurisdiction. Here, nothing indicates that the supreme court specifically retained jurisdiction. Thus, the Family Court has proper jurisdiction in the case, and the dismissal of W's entire action was improper. **1-1/2 points**

(4)   The issue is whether the Family Court has discretion to modify support orders. **1/2 point**

The Family Court Act enables the court to modify support orders. In determining whether to modify a child support order, a New York court will assess whether: (i) there has been a change of circumstances warranting the increase, and (ii) the modification is in the best interest of the child. The factors that the court may consider include increased needs of the child due to special circumstances or additional activities, and a parent's loss of income or improved financial condition. The court will always consider the best interest of the child in determining whether a total change in circumstances is warranted. **1-1/2 points**

Here, the facts show that there are special circumstances and the father's ability to pay has increased. Therefore, the court improperly dismissed W's action. **1/2 point**

ANSWER 52—DOMESTIC RELATIONS/NEW YORK PRACTICE

(1)   The issue is whether a plaintiff herself can serve process on a defendant out of state. **1/2 point**

Under the CPLR, service outside of the state may be made in the same manner as service within the state. [CPLR 313] Service within the state cannot be made by one who is a party to the action. [CPLR 2103(a)] Since Evelyn is the plaintiff in this action and she served the summons and complaint on Joseph personally, this service was improper. Therefore, the court's ruling to dismiss was proper due to Evelyn's improper service on Joseph. **1 point**

(2)   The issue is whether the court had jurisdiction over Joseph and the divorce action. **1/2 point**

For the court to have jurisdiction, the defendant must have properly been served and there must be a statutory basis for jurisdiction, meaning compliance with the durational residency requirement. Service out of state may be made by any method proper for service in the state. Proper service of papers can be made by any person not a party to the action, who is of the age of 18 or older. Therefore, service by Evelyn's attorney was proper. **1 point**

A court in any matrimonial action may exercise personal jurisdiction over the defendant regardless of whether the defendant is a nonresident or domiciliary of the state, if the party seeking support is a resident or domiciled in the state and New York was the matrimonial domicile of the parties shortly before their separation. Since Evelyn lived in the state for two years prior to commencing the action and it was the matrimonial domicile of the parties before they separated, the durational residency requirement was complied with. Therefore, the court properly denied the defendant's motion to dismiss. **1 point**

(3)   The issue is whether a party's testimony alone is sufficient to prove annulment. **1/2 point**

Evelyn's cause of action for an annulment represents a claim that the marriage is voidable because of some fundamental defect in the marriage—in this case, fraudulent inducement. If she is successful, the marriage will be considered void from the time a decree of annulment is entered. Under the CPLR, there is a three-year statute of limitations for causes of action for annulment based upon fraud. [CPLR 214] The statute begins to run from the date of discovery of the facts constituting fraud by the defrauded party. **1 point**

Evelyn's action is timely because it was brought less than three years after the argument, which provides the basis for her allegation. However, a cause of action of annulment cannot be sustained merely by the unsupported declarations of a party. The law clearly states: "the declaration or confession of either party to the marriage is not alone sufficient as proof, but other satisfactory evidence of the facts must be produced." [N.Y. Dom. Rel. Law §144] Evelyn has offered only her personal testimony concerning the argument of May 25, 1982. This is insufficient as a matter of law; therefore, the court correctly dismissed Evelyn's cause of action at the close of her proof. Also, it is well settled in New York that the fraudulent representation of an intention to have children must have been made at the time of the marriage as an inducement to marry. There is no such showing here. **1 point**

(4)   The issue is whether Evelyn's actions constituted abandonment. **1/2 point**

To make out a cause of action for divorce based upon abandonment, Joseph must show: (i) that Evelyn willfully and voluntarily abandoned him, (ii) without justification, (iii) without intent to return, and (iv) for a period of more than one year before the commencement of the lawsuit. The intent element may be inferred from the length of the absence. While the facts do not contain conclusive information regarding the element of justification, certainly Joseph's uncontradicted testimony would more likely than not meet all of the required elements. Therefore, the court could easily find a basis for granting Joseph a decree of divorce based on abandonment. **1 point**

(5)   At issue are: (i) whether the savings account constituted marital property or separate property; and (ii) whether in fact Joseph had made a gift of the proceeds of the savings account to Evelyn before the parties separated. **1/2 point**

As to the first question, the New York Equitable Distribution Law clearly provides that property acquired by bequest is separate property not subject to equitable distribution, irrespective of the date of receipt (whether before or after the marriage). [N.Y. Dom. Rel. Law §2368] Thus, Evelyn has no claim on the savings account based upon the Equitable Distribution Law. As to the second question, the type of savings account opened by Joseph in 1981 is known as a "Totten" trust. Under the case law of New York, such a trust remains the property of the creator until the creator dies without having revoked the disposition. Therefore, Evelyn has no right to the proceeds of the account on the second ground, and the court correctly awarded the account to Joseph. **1-1/2 points**

ANSWER 53—NEW YORK PRACTICE/REAL PROPERTY/MORTGAGES

(1) FILING OF NOTICE OF PENDENCY

The issue is whether S's underlying claim "affected" title to Blackacre. **1/2 point**

CPLR 6501 provides that a notice of pendency (lis pendens) can be filed in any action in which the judgment demanded would affect the title to, or possession, use, or enjoyment of real property. The basic function of the device is the placing of a record impediment on the title to the realty involved in the action, thus preventing acquisition of a title free and clear of the claim being asserted in a lawsuit. This is accomplished by filing the "notice of pendency." Thereafter, any purchaser or subsequent lienor "is bound by all proceedings taken in the action after such filing to the same extent as if he were a party." The notice of pendency (if appropriate) can be filed automatically without a court order. **1 point**

For a notice of pendency to be appropriate, the claim upon which it is based must affect title or possession to real property. The title is "affected" only where a successful suit by the plaintiff will create a lien or encumbrance upon the title. Examples of real property actions in which this procedure may be used are specific performance actions, mortgage foreclosures, and actions to enforce a vendee's lien. **1 point**

Here, the notice of pendency filed by S's lawyer is appropriate because the action in which it was filed seeks, in essence, foreclosure of a mortgage held by S on Blackacre to secure B's payment of the note. S holds a mortgage on Blackacre because section 320 of the Real Property Law provides that a deed conveying real property will be construed as a legal mortgage if there is "any other written instrument" which makes it appear that the deed was intended to create a mortgage. Here, S took the deed to Blackacre as collateral for B's payment of the note and gave B a letter clearly indicating that intent. Thus, S's lawyer was entitled to file the notice of pendency with the Westchester County Clerk. **1-1/2 points**

(2) RULING ON NOTICE OF PENDENCY

The issue is whether commencing suit more than 30 days after filing a notice of pendency renders the notice void. **1/2 point**

Although under CPLR 6511 a notice of pendency may be filed prior to suit, CPLR 6512 provides that service of the suit must be accomplished within 30 days of the filing or the notice of pendency is void. Upon motion, the court must cancel it when service has not been made within the 30-day period. Here, the notice of pendency was filed on November 10, 1993. However, the summons and complaint were not served until December 14, more than 30 days thereafter. Therefore, the court should have granted B's motion to cancel, and its decision to the contrary was incorrect. **1-1/2 points**

(3) The issue is whether B or S bears the risk of loss. **1/2 point**

Section 320 of the Real Property Law provides that a deed conveying real property will be construed as a legal mortgage if there is "any other written instrument" that makes it appear that the deed was intended to create a mortgage. [*See* Corcillo v. Martut, Inc., 45 N.Y.2d 878 (1978)] Therefore, on January 20, 1993, when B gave S the new note and a deed to Blackacre, he did not "convey" Blackacre back to S. In fact a legal mortgage was created. **1-1/2 points**

The new promissory note coupled with the deed made it clear that a mortgage, *i.e.,* security interest, was being created rather than an absolute conveyance. Thus, B remained the legal owner of Blackacre since the December 1, 1992, closing. **1/2 point**

Risk of loss passed to B when legal title passed to him. Legal title passed on December 1, 1992, when the closing was held. The fact that at closing the property was not yet fully paid for did not change the shifting of the risk of loss to B. In addition, the creation of a legal mortgage on January 18, 1993, did not affect the risk of loss. **1 point**

Thus, on May 28, 1993, when Blackacre was destroyed by fire, B bore the risk of loss. Further, B's liability to S on the promissory note in the amount of $40,000 still exists. **1/2 point**

(*Note for the student:* The Uniform Vendor & Purchaser Risk Act does not help B because such would only take effect where legal title and possession were still with S.)

ANSWER 54—WILLS

(1)(a) ADMISSION OF ELYSE'S WILL TO PROBATE

The issues are whether there are enough witnesses available to prove the will was properly executed and whether an interested witness may testify as to the proper execution of the will. **1/2 point**

Pursuant to the New York EPTL, the burden of proving that a will was properly executed is on the will proponent. The testimony of two witnesses to the will's execution is required. However, if one witness is deceased, the testimony of the other witness will suffice. Additionally, an interested witness (*i.e.,* a person left a gift in the will) may testify as to the proper execution of the will, but that witness may not take under the will unless he would otherwise receive an intestate share. Specifically, in New York, if an interested witness would otherwise be eligible for an intestate share of the decedent's estate, the witness may take the lesser of the gift under the will or the intestate share. Notably, a self-proving affidavit signed contemporaneously with the will allows the will to be admitted without the testimony of any witnesses. **1 point**

In this case, assuming there was no self-proving affidavit, Jerry is available to testify, and the will should be admitted to probate. As a result, he will not be permitted to take more than the lesser of his intestate share or the gift under the will. Consequently, the surrogate's decision was correct. **1/2 point**

(b) ADMISSION OF FRANK'S WILL TO PROBATE

The issue is under what circumstances New York recognizes revocation by physical act. **1/2 point**

Pursuant to the EPTL, if the testator has the intent to revoke, a will may be revoked by an act of burning, tearing, cutting, canceling, obliterating, mutilating, or other destruction by the testator or another person in the presence of, and by direction of, the testator. Accidental destruction or partial revocation of a will does not revoke it. The presumption of revocation may be overcome by proof that the will was revoked by accident. However, declarations of the decedent designed to show that the will had not been revoked are not admissible unless they are made in connection with the act, "under circumstances as to become part of the res gestae." In this case, Frank wrote the word "revoked" on the will, which is a sufficient act of revocation if coupled with the intent to revoke. However, what appears to be a revocation here can be overcome by testimony of Frank's friends that he had no intention of revoking the will at the time he did the act. Consequently, the surrogate was correct in admitting the will to probate. **1-1/2 points**

(2)   JERRY'S LEGACY

The issue is how to determine who died first. **1/2 point**

A will should contain a simultaneous death clause that instructs what to do if it cannot be determined who died first. In New York, if such a clause is not included, the Uniform Simultaneous Death Act governs. The Act applies to the distribution of property by any means and specifies that the property of each person is disposed of as if each survived the other. **1/2 point**

In this case, Jerry will take as if Frank predeceased Elyse and therefore, should inherit Elyse's entire estate, other than the home held in tenancy by the entirety. However, as noted above, because Jerry is also an interested witness, he will take the lesser of his intestate share or his legacy. His intestate share will clearly be less than the entire estate. He is one of two siblings and his intestate share is therefore half. The other half will go to Teddy. **1 point**

(3)   TEDDY'S ADVANCE

The issue is whether the gift is considered an advancement. **1/2 point**

An advancement is a payment or gift to an heir during one's lifetime. At common law, a lifetime gift to a child was presumed to be an advancement of part of his intestate share. In New York, such a gift is not treated as an advancement unless proved by a writing: (i) made contemporaneously with the gift, (ii) signed by the donor, and (iii) evidencing his intention that the gift be treated as an advancement. In this case, the house was transferred to Teddy prior to the letter from Elyse setting out the arrangement. Since the letter was not written contemporaneously with the transfer, the summer home is not considered an advance of Teddy's inheritance. **1-1/2 points**

(4)   THE FAMILY HOME

The issue is how tenancy by the entirety property is divided upon the simultaneous death of the tenants. **1/2 point**

Division of property held in tenancy by the entirety when the tenants die simultaneously is governed by the Uniform Simultaneous Death Act since, as discussed above, the act applies to distribution of property by any means. In the case of property held in tenancy by the entirety, the Act provides that one half of the property passes as though one party survived and the other half passes as though the other party survived. The property interests are converted into tenancies in common. Here, under the terms of the will Jerry should inherit Elyse's undivided one-half interest in the house. However, because he is an interested witness to the will (*see* above) he will inherit only one-half of the half, his intestate share. Teddy will inherit the other half of Elyse's half as the other intestate beneficiary. **1-1/2 points**

Under Frank's will, Debbie will receive Frank's undivided one-half interest in the family house. In sum, Teddy and Jerry each receive a 1/4 interest as tenants in common, and Debbie receives a 1/2 interest as a tenant in common.

ANSWER 55—CRIMINAL LAW/CRIMINAL PROCEDURE

(1)   The issue is whether the Fifth or Sixth Amendment right to counsel applies to a precharge lineup. **1/2 point**

The lineup did not violate *Miranda*. *Miranda* requires that a defendant be advised of his constitutional rights whenever he is in custody (*i.e.,* not free to leave) and subject to interrogation. The warnings are intended to protect defendants against self-incrimination. Here, there is no doubt that the defendants were in custody; however, there was no interrogation. There is no Fifth Amendment right against self-incrimination that prevents the taking of physical evidence, such as is taken at a lineup (physical makeup). Therefore, the failure to give *Miranda* warnings before the lineup is irrelevant. **1 point**

Neither was the defendants' right to counsel violated. A defendant has a right under the Sixth Amendment to be represented by counsel at adversarial proceedings. The right does not extend, however, to a **precharge** lineup, even if the lineup is held after arrest. In New York, the right is more expansive than is constitutionally required; it indelibly attaches as soon as there has been significant judicial activity. However, even in New York, absent significant judicial activity or a court order, the right does not apply at an investigatory lineup. Here, the facts clearly state that no accusatory instrument had been filed and neither was there significant judicial involvement. Therefore, the defendants had no right to counsel at the lineup. **1 point**

Finally, due process standards were not violated. The Due Process Clause prevents a lineup that is unduly suggestive. However, the facts here do not suggest that the lineup procedure was unduly suggestive or prejudicial. Therefore, the lineup will not be suppressed because it did not violate *Miranda,* the defendants' right to counsel, or due process standards. **1/2 point**

(2)(a)   The issue is whether A will be liable under New York's felony murder statute. Under New York law, a person is guilty of felony murder when he commits an enumerated felony, of which burglary is one, and in the course of or in the immediate flight therefrom, he or another participant causes the death of a person other than a participant. Burglary is defined as the unlawful entering or remaining in a building with intent to commit a crime therein. Under New York law, felony murder is considered murder in the second degree. **2 points**

Here, A and B entered the warehouse with intent to commit larceny therein. Thus, they are guilty of burglary. During the course of the burglary they encountered X, and while in immediate flight from the premises, A caused the death of X without justification. Under the felony murder statute, the killing is not required to be intentional. Since the killing was committed during the course of the burglary, it was felony murder under New York law. **1 point**

Thus A is guilty of murder in the second degree.

(*Note:* Since the facts indicate that A did not intend to kill X (*i.e.,* he just pushed X; it is unlikely that he was trying to kill X with the push), A could not be convicted of murder in the first degree. One of the several scenarios in which a person may be convicted of first degree murder is when during the commission of an enumerated felony, of which burglary is one, the perpetrator *intentionally* kills a nonparticipant in the course of the felony or in the immediate flight therefrom. Since during the course of burglary A did not intentionally kill X, murder in the first degree does not apply.)

(b)   The issue is whether a person can be convicted of felony murder when the death was caused by the co-felon. Under New York law, liability for felony murder will extend to co-felons unless they have a defense. To defeat a prosecution for felony murder, a defendant must show that: (i) he did not commit, cause, or aid in the killing; (ii) he reasonably believed that his accomplice was not armed with a deadly weapon; (iii) he reasonably believed that his accomplice had no intent to engage in conduct likely to result in death or serious physical injury; *and* (iv) he was not armed with a deadly weapon. Since the facts indicated that B was armed with a gun which he obtained for the burglary, he cannot make out a valid defense to felony murder. Accordingly, B will be convicted of murder in the second degree. **2 points**

(c)   The issue is whether the elements of a conspiracy are present.

To be guilty of conspiracy, it is necessary to show: (i) an intent to commit a crime; (ii) an agreement; and (iii) an overt act in furtherance of the conspiracy. All are present in these facts: A and B agreed to burglarize the warehouse, and this shows an agreement and intent to commit the burglary. Both A and B stole the van and obtained the gun in furtherance of the conspiracy. (Note that any act will support the third requirement, whether or not the act is performed by the party sought to be held.) **1-1/2 points**

In addition, conspiracy does not merge into the substantive crime. Therefore, both A and B may be found guilty of both conspiracy and the crimes of burglary and murder. **1/2 point**

ANSWER 56—WILLS

(1)   The issue is whether a copy of a will can be probated when the original will has been lost. **1/2 point**

In New York, a lost or destroyed will may be admitted to probate only if: (i) it is established that the will has not been revoked, (ii) execution of the will is proved in a manner required for the probate of an existing will, and (iii) all of the provisions of the will are clearly and distinctly proved by each of at least two credible witnesses or by a copy or draft of the will proved to be true and complete. The proof submitted must be sufficient to overcome the presumption that the reason the will cannot be found is that the testator destroyed the will with intent to revoke. **1 point**

In this case, it can be established that the 1995 will was not revoked. Although a presumption of revocation arises if a will cannot be found after a testator's death and the will was last seen in the testator's possession, no such presumption arises where the will was last seen in a third party's possession. Here, the receipt and the attorney's statement show that the will was in the attorney's possession and that the attorney lost the will; Alf did nothing to revoke it. Furthermore, the copy of the 1995 will in Alf's office safe is sufficient to satisfy the other statutory requirements: It shows that the will was properly executed by Alf and witnessed by Fred and Gert; it shows clearly the provisions of the will; and it shows two witnesses (the witnesses to the will) who can testify that the copy is a true copy. Thus, the copy of the 1995 will can be admitted to probate. **1 point**

(2)   RIGHTS OF BEV

The first issue is whether a spouse is disqualified from exercising the surviving spouse's right of election when the spouses are not divorced but living separate and apart from each other at the time of the decedent's death. **1/2 point**

Under the EPTL, a surviving spouse of a decedent can relinquish rights under the decedent's will and take a statutory share instead. However, for purposes of this right of election, a spouse is not considered a surviving spouse if: (i) a final decree of divorce or annulment recognized as valid in New York has been issued; (ii) the marriage was bigamous, incestuous, or a prohibited marriage; (iii) the surviving spouse procured an invalid divorce or annulment; (iv) a valid final decree of separation was rendered against the surviving spouse; (v) the surviving spouse abandoned the deceased spouse; (vi) the surviving spouse failed or refused to support the deceased spouse; or (vii) the surviving spouse openly and notoriously cohabitated with another. The burden of establishing that the surviving spouse is disqualified lies with whomever is opposing the right of election. **1 point**

Here, Alf and Bev were living separate and apart, but a final decree of separation had not been issued. Furthermore, Bev does not fall within any of the other classifications that would render her incapable of exercising a right of election. Therefore, Bev has not been disqualified as a surviving spouse and may still exercise her right of election against Alf's estate. **1/2 point**

Since Bev is not disqualified from taking an elective share, the second issue is how much she can take. Under the EPTL, a surviving spouse is entitled to take the greater of $50,000 or one-third of the decedent's net estate. However, in an effort to preserve the decedent's testamentary scheme as much as possible, the surviving spouse takes any outright gifts that are given to the spouse under the will, and the elective share amount is reduced by the value of such gifts. Terminable interests, such as life estates, do not constitute outright gifts and their value is not applied to reduce the elective share. **1 point**

In this case, Alf's will leaves Bev the share of Alf's estate that Bev would receive if she were to exercise her right of election. However, the will leaves the gift in the form of a trust, with the income being paid quarterly to Bev and that interest terminating on Bev's death. Because such terminable interest trusts are not outright gifts, if Bev elects to take the surviving spouse's elective share, she will forfeit her entitlement to the terminable interest and the trust will be read as though Bev predeceased Alf. However, Bev will be entitled to receive the greater of $50,000 or one-third of the value of the estate. **1 point**

CAL AND DEB

The issue is whether a negative bequest is recognized in New York. In New York, a parent is not compelled to leave property to his children. New York recognizes the validity of provisions in a will that direct how property shall not be disposed, with any property passing by partial intestacy being distributed as though the disinherited person had predeceased the decedent. Absent any proof of lack of capacity, fraud, or undue influence, the disinheritance is valid and enforceable. Cal and Deb take nothing under the 1995 will. **1/2 point**

SAVE THE BIRDS, INC.

After Bev exercises her right of election, Save the Birds, Inc. is entitled to the residuary estate. **1/2 point**

(3) The issue is whether Alf's estate will be distributed under the laws of intestacy or pursuant to the terms of the 1986 will. **1/2 point**

The laws of intestacy apply when (i) the decedent did not leave a will; (ii) the decedent's will is denied probate; or (iii) the decedent left a will, but the will does not make a complete disposition of the estate. **1/2 point**

Here, the laws of intestacy will apply because it can be shown that Alf died without a valid will. A will may be revoked by a subsequent writing executed with testamentary formalities. Once a will is revoked, it cannot be revived unless it is reexecuted with testamentary formalities. Merely revoking the later will, including the language that revoked the earlier will, does not revive the earlier will. **1/2 point**

Here, the 1995 will was executed with proper formalities (signed by the testator and two witnesses) and it revoked the 1986 will since it provided: "I revoke all wills previously made by me." Thus, even though the copy of the 1995 will was denied probate, it can be used to show that Alf revoked his 1986 will. This being the case, Alf's estate would be distributed based on the laws of intestacy. **1/2 point**

Under the laws of intestacy, when a decedent dies leaving a spouse and children, the spouse takes the first $50,000 and one-half of the remainder. The children take the remaining half. Here, Bev and her children, Cal and Deb, would be the distributees of Alf's estate. Bev would receive $50,000 plus one-half of the balance of Alf's estate. Cal and Deb would be entitled to the remaining one-half. **1/2 point**

ANSWER 57—DOMESTIC RELATIONS/REAL PROPERTY

(1) The issue is whether property inherited by one spouse, but then conveyed to both spouses as tenants by the entirety, should be considered marital property and whether the spouse who inherited the property should be given a credit for its original value. **1/2 point**

Unless otherwise provided by an agreement of the parties, marital property includes all property acquired by either spouse during the marriage, regardless of the form of title prior to the commencement of any matrimonial action. Separate property includes: all property acquired before marriage; property acquired by bequest, devise, descent, or as a gift to one spouse; compensation for personal injuries; property acquired in exchange for or by increase in value of separate property (less the contribution by the other spouse); and property described as separate by written agreement of the parties. **1 point**

Whiteacre was considered separate property when Beth inherited Whiteacre prior to her marriage. However, Whiteacre became marital property when Beth conveyed the property to herself and her husband as tenants by the entirety. A tenancy by the entirety is a marital estate akin to a joint tenancy between husband and wife. The estate contains a right of survivorship, with the surviving spouse retaining an undivided right in the property. Originally, one spouse could not convey property to herself and another spouse as tenants by the entirety because the unities of time, title, interest, and possession would be disrupted. Therefore, parties would convey the property to a third party (a straw person) who would then re-convey the property to the husband and wife in order to maintain the four unities. However, New York's Real Property Law permits a spouse to convey land to herself and her spouse as tenants by the entirety without the use of a straw person. Here, Whiteacre would have remained Beth's separate property but for her conveyance. Because of the conveyance, the property became marital property. **1-1/2 points**

Beth is not entitled to a credit for the prior value of the property. A spouse retains her separate property, while an increase in the value of separate property of one spouse, due to direct or indirect contribution of the other spouse, will become marital property. This allows the original value to remain separate property. However, Whiteacre did not remain separate property. It became marital property immediately subsequent to the marriage, when Beth conveyed the property to herself and her husband as tenants by the entirety. Moreover, the value of the property did not increase until after it became marital property. Therefore, the property was properly considered marital property, and Beth is not entitled to a credit for its value in 1981. **1 point**

(2) The issue is whether the separation agreement was entered into freely and with full disclosure. Separation agreements are valid if they are freely made, they do not violate the statutory public policy provisions (*i.e.*, altering or dissolving marriage or support obligations of the spouse), and the parties are separated when they enter into the agreement or become separated immediately thereafter. Separation agreements are governed by ordinary contract principles to the extent that there is no conflict with public policy, and they are enforceable in any court having jurisdiction over contract actions. Separation agreements have the permanency of contracts except in extreme cases. Since separation agreements are governed by ordinary contract principles, there are three elements necessary for the formation of the agreement: (i) mutual assent; (ii) consideration or a substitute; and (iii) no defenses to formation. Defenses to formation include mistake, misrepresentation, and fraud. Fraud in the factum occurs when one of the parties was tricked into giving assent to the agreement under circumstances that prevented her from appreciating the significance of her action. **1-1/2 points**

Both Beth and Pat entered into the agreement freely: They were both represented by counsel when the separation agreement was executed, and they both signed the agreement. However, Pat did not give full financial disclosure. Pat was fully aware of the negotiations between his company, Technology Group, and SPR. Pat, as president of Technology Group, was aware that a merger of the companies would increase the value of his shares. With full knowledge of the ongoing negotiations, Pat did not disclose this information to Beth. Pat had a duty of the utmost good faith in contracting with his wife. Had Beth been aware of the negotiations, she probably would have included a clause in the separation agreement in case the negotiations were successful. Beth would not have agreed to the terms of the stock provisions had she been aware that she was potentially forfeiting $1,280,000 (40% of $3,200,000). Therefore, the valuation of shares was based on fraud and Beth can get the provisions of the separation agreement relating to the valuation modified. **1-1/2 points**

Note: Credit would also be given for arguing that because Beth was represented by counsel, an investigation into the future value of the shares should have been made.

(3) The issue is whether a support provision in a separation agreement can be modified. Custody and support provisions can be annulled, amended, or modified on notice motion. The child should not, and is not, bound by the terms of the parents' separation agreement. The court must take into account the child's best interests; the assets, earnings, and liabilities of the father; and the financial situation of the mother. However, when a modification of support is sought for reasons other than because it is inadequate to meet the child's needs, the party seeking the change must demonstrate that there are unforeseen and unreasonable changes in circumstances warranting modification. **1-1/2 points**

With due regard for the parents' circumstances and the best interest of the child, the court may award educational expenses, including those for college. However, the court should not freely disregard the child support provisions in a separation agreement. Here, the separation agreement expressly provided for an amount that the parties felt was adequate for child support, including for Lisa's college education. In the separation agreement, it was determined that Pat would pay $2,000 per month for the support and education of Lisa until she reached the age of 21 or completed college. Although Lisa is not bound by her parents' separation agreement because she was a minor, she cannot show that there were any unforeseen changes in circumstances or that the agreement was not fair and equitable when her parents entered into it. Beth and Pat provided for Lisa's college education and determined that the amount was fair and adequate for her educational needs. Pat is paying $24,000 a year toward Lisa's education and support. Furthermore, there was no stipulation that Pat would be the sole provider for Lisa's college education. The fact that Lisa was accepted to an expensive college is neither an unforeseen nor unreasonable change. Given Lisa's academic ability and her parents' standard of living and financial ability, Lisa has a right to a college education. However, there is no right to receive the most expensive education. Since Beth cannot show that the child support amount is inadequate or that there has been an unforeseen change in circumstances, the support provisions of the agreement should not be disturbed. Therefore, Beth is not entitled to a modification of support for Lisa's college education. **1-1/2 points**

ANSWER 58—REAL PROPERTY/NEW YORK PRACTICE/CONTRACTS

(1) At issue are the jurisdiction of a county court and the durational requirements of a notice of pendency. **1/2 point**

New York Judiciary Law section 190 limits the jurisdiction of a county court to actions for the recovery of less than $25,000 where all the defendants are residents of the county; or actions respecting real property located within that county. As the property was located in Niagara County and not in Erie County, the court lacked subject matter jurisdiction, and any order issued by it is void. Therefore, the court's ruling was incorrect. **1 point**

Nevertheless, the lis pendens is void. The CPLR provides that any notice of pendency is automatically canceled if the plaintiff fails to serve the summons and complaint upon the defendant within 30 days after the notice of pendency is granted. [CPLR 6514] The facts state that Obie learned of the notice of pendency from a friend 32 days after the notice was filed. Hence, Andy did not serve a summons and complaint on Obie within 30 days. Thus, Obie may have the notice of pendency vacated by applying to the proper court. **1 point**

(2) At issue is whether Andy and/or Don have acquired an easement over Obie's road. **1/2 point**

Under the law of New York respecting real property, an easement by prescription may be acquired by one who uses the property of another for the required period, where such use is open, notorious, adverse, continuous, and under claim of right. The CPLR provides a 10-year statute of limitations for actions to recover real property, so this is the necessary period for acquiring an easement by prescription. [CPLR 212] **1 point**

Under the facts, Andy's use meets these requirements. Andy's use was open and hostile, even before he had the argument with Obie, in that Andy did not seek permissive use, and his use was actionable (Obie could have sued him before the period ran, in order to prevent Andy's use). Andy's use was open, and not covert; it was continuous and under a claim of right, in that Andy's use indicated to the world that he asserted the right to use the road. Andy's use met these conditions for at least 10 years, from November 1977 to April 1992. Thus, Andy is entitled to an easement by prescription to use the road across Obie's land, and Obie may not prevent the court from entering an order to this effect. **2 points**

Don has failed to acquire an easement by prescription. Don's use has not been adverse and hostile for the required period. Once Obie specifically gave Don permission to use the road, in 1985, Don's use ceased to be a hostile use, so as to create an easement by prescription. Therefore, Don will fail in this argument. **1 point**

Don may attempt to prove an easement by necessity, but this argument will also fail. An easement by necessity arises when the seller conveys a tract of land which has no outlet to a public road except over the remaining estate of the seller, in which case a right-of-way is created by implied grant. But here, Don has access to the state highway via Avenue A. Thus, no easement by necessity can arise. **1 point**

Don's last claim, for specific performance of the oral agreement between Obie and him on April 20, 1992, will also fail. The problem here is that Obie can interpose the Statute of Frauds, which states that enforcement of an oral contract respecting an estate in land will be barred by law. Obie may properly interpose the Statute of Frauds as an absolute defense to Don's suit. Thus, Don has no right to use the road, as he was a mere licensee who held only a privilege, revocable at the will of the licensor. **2 points**

ANSWER 59—CRIMINAL LAW/CRIMINAL PROCEDURE/EVIDENCE

(1)   The issue is whether the identification violated Luke's right to counsel or due process rights. **1/2 point**

Luke's right to counsel was not violated. An accused has a right to have counsel present at a post-charge lineup. From the facts, it is clear that Luke was not in custody at the time of the out-of-court identification by Vivian. He had not yet been charged with this crime or put under arrest, nor had a court ordered his presence at a lineup. Therefore, no right to counsel had attached, whether by operation of federal constitutional law, *i.e.*, the Sixth Amendment [*cf.* Moore v. Illinois, 434 U.S. 220 (1977); United States v. Wade, 388 U.S. 218 (1967)], or by operation of New York State law [*cf.* People v. Hawkins, 55 N.Y.2d 474 (1982)]. Consequently, it was not improper for Danger to have produced Luke for identification out of the presence of counsel, even if Danger knew in fact that Luke was represented by counsel, whether by virtue of Danger having previously arrested Luke or for some other reason. **2 points**

Luke's due process rights were not violated. Luke will not succeed in suppressing the identification on grounds that his right to due process was denied, unless he can show that the identification was conducted in such manner as to create a substantial likelihood of misidentification. There is no question that the procedure at the identification was improper, insofar as it was unnecessarily suggestive. Danger said to Vivian, "I think I have the man who raped you. Please come right down." However, Luke cannot show such substantial likelihood of misidentification, given that the identification occurred the same day as the crime, and that Vivian gave Danger an unusually detailed description. Therefore, the court erred in its first ruling. **2 points**

If the pretrial identification was suppressed, the in-court identification would be admissible if the prosecution could prove by clear and convincing evidence that it was not tainted by the prior identification, but derived independently. **1/2 point**

(2)   The issue is what must be proved to make out a prima facie case.

Rape occurs in New York when any person engages in sexual intercourse with another person by forcible compulsion. The New York Penal Law does not require any corroboration in cases of forcible rape. **1 point**

Applying these two points of law to the facts, it is clear that the prosecution met its burden of proof based exclusively on the testimony of Vivian. Her testimony showed that intercourse occurred, and that there was force, or the threat of force (which comprises forcible compulsion). It is not necessary for the People to have adduced any additional evidence, including the hospital report, if any was made. Thus, the evidence was prima facie sufficient, and the court ruled correctly. **1 point**

(3)   The issue is what evidence of a victim's character may be introduced to rebut a charge of rape. **1 point**

The law of evidence as applied in New York to cases of rape provides that the defense may introduce evidence tending to prove that the victim was convicted of prostitution within the last three years, but that the defense may not introduce evidence that challenges the character of the victim, except to impeach her veracity. Here, the offered testimony as to Vivian's "easiness" and the illegitimacy of her children was immaterial and prejudicial. It did nothing to disprove her veracity and is thus inadmissible, so the court was correct. The facts do not specify, however, if Vivian was convicted of prostitution within the last three years. Assuming that she was, the offer of proof as to her prostitution should have been allowed. Therefore, if there was a conviction within three years, the court erred. **2 points**

ANSWER 60—DOMESTIC RELATIONS

(1)   The issue is whether a lump sum settlement of support obligations is enforceable. **1/2 point**

New York recognizes no general ban on lump sum settlements of support obligations. General Obligations Law section 5-311 prohibits any contract that would abrogate the support obligation of any spouse. However, it has been held that merely providing a lump sum in settlement of support does not on its face violate this provision. Rather, the court will look at the facts of the case. In the event that the spouse has dissipated the lump sum and is in danger of becoming a public charge, the court will invalidate the agreement and enforce the duty to support; but not until such an event takes place will the court take this step. **1-1/2 points**

In this case, the facts do not indicate that Christie is in danger of becoming a public charge. There is no showing that she has dissipated the lump sum settlement. Therefore, the court correctly refused to set aside the terms of the separation agreement. **1/2 point**

In addition, New York courts apply general contract principles to separation agreements, to the extent that the agreements do not contradict public policy. While the court may review the agreement to protect a party from "overreaching" by the other party, courts generally will not order rescission of a separation agreement freely entered into by the parties. **1 point**

Here, there is nothing to indicate that either party did not have the benefit of counsel or was the victim of fraud, duress, or misrepresentation. Thus, the court had no cause to order rescission of the agreement. The court's ruling was correct. **1 point**

(2)   The issue is whether a judge may take a child's testimony over her parents' objections.

Where the best interests of the child are at stake, the court may take the testimony of the child over the objections of the parties. [Matter of Lincoln v. Lincoln, 24 N.Y.2d 270 (1969)] However, the wishes of the child are not the sole basis for making a determination as to custody, and it would be improper for the court to rely exclusively upon them. Furthermore, where the court determines the child's preference to be of paramount importance, and has taken the child's testimony out of court, there is no record upon which an intelligent determination may be made upon appeal, and therefore the court's determination must be reversed. [Romi v. Hamdan, 417 N.Y.S.2d 523 (1979)] **1-1/2 points**

In this case, there is no showing that the court relied exclusively on the testimony of Madonna in making its determination. The court did not state that the preferences of Madonna were given undue weight in the court's determination. Therefore, the court had the power to take Madonna's testimony, even out of court and over the objections of the parties. Thus, the court's actions were not improper. **1 point**

(3) At issue is whether the interests of the child required a change in custody. **1 point**

In the area of changes in custody, the interests of the child are deemed to be paramount. An agreement between the parents regarding custody will be given "due regard," but is not controlling. But absent a compelling reason, the courts will not alter custody arrangements. **1 point**

In this case, there has been no showing that the child's interest has been jeopardized by Christie's actions. Madonna's interest is paramount in this instance; therefore, the facts show no basis for a change in custody. Thus, the court acted correctly. **1 point**

ANSWER 61—WILLS/TRUSTS

(1) The issue is what constitutes adequate proof of due execution of a will. **1/2 point**

EPTL section 3-2.1 provides that, in order for a will to be duly executed, the following events must take place: the will must be signed by the testator, at the end of the will; the testator must sign or acknowledge his signature in the presence of each of the attesting witnesses and must declare to the witnesses that this is his will; at least two witnesses must attest the testator's signature and sign their names, within 30 days of one another; and the testator must have testamentary capacity, *i.e.*, be mentally competent and over the age of 18. **1 point**

The burden of proving due execution of a will falls upon the proponent of the will (here, F). [Schillinger's Will, 258 N.Y. 186 (1932)] Due execution is a question of fact to be determined by the fact finder (here, the surrogate). [*See* Estate of Sylvestri, 44 N.Y.2d 260 (1978)] **1/2 point**

While ordinarily the testimony of at least one attesting witness is required to prove due execution [*see* Surr. Ct. Proc. Act §1405(3)], a will may be admitted to probate even though neither witness can remember the circumstances of execution, if the court is satisfied from all the evidence that the will was properly executed [Estate of Collins, 60 N.Y.2d 466 (1983)]. **1/2 point**

Applying the law to these facts, there appears to have been sufficient evidence to support the court's finding of fact that the will of A was duly executed. The testator had testamentary capacity. The witnesses were able to identify their signatures. The presence of an attestation clause, while not dispositive (as a self-proving affidavit would be), supports a finding of due execution. The testimony of both B and the expert witness as to the genuineness of A's signature was uncontroverted. Furthermore, there was no showing of any reason to suspect the genuineness of the will. Hence, the court's ruling was correct. **1-1/2 points**

(2) THE RIGHTS OF F, S, AND N

The general issue is to determine how A's estate will pass under his will and the laws of New York. Specific issues include: whether a testator may make a gift to a former spouse; whether a separation agreement terminates election rights; and whether a trust was established. **1 point**

RIGHTS OF F

F has the right to take under the will of A, notwithstanding her divorce from A. EPTL section 5-1.4 provides that a divorce automatically revokes all dispositions to the divorced spouse unless the will expressly provides to the contrary. Since the facts state that the will was created after the divorce, this section is not applicable. Thus, F will properly take under A's will. **1-1/2 points**

RIGHTS OF S

S is entitled to her elective share. S, as the surviving spouse of A, will be entitled to an elective share under EPTL section 5-1.1 if the distributions to her under A's will amount to less than one-third of A's net estate for elective share purposes. **1/2 point**

S will not be disqualified from exercising her right of election by virtue of the separation agreement entered into between A and S because the separation agreement was neither a final decree of divorce nor a decree of separation rendered against S; neither did the separation agreement by its terms constitute a waiver of the right to elect. Thus, S is still qualified to make an election. [EPTL §5-1.2] **1 point**

S must have exercised her rights within six months of the issuance of letters. Under the facts, she did so, and thus she is not disqualified from exercising her right of election because of a procedural error. **1/2 point**

RIGHTS OF N

N has no right to Whiteacre. Under the law of New York, the settlor (creator) of a trust must show a clear intention to create a trust. Under the facts of this case, A's intent seems to have been to create a landlord/tenant relationship between himself and N, rather than to settle a trust upon N. Consequently, Whiteacre will pass under the terms of A's will to F, subject to S's right of election. **1 point**

Thus, the estate of A will pass as follows: S is entitled to take one-third of A's net estate, including Whiteacre. N has no rights whatsoever under A's will. F will take the remainder of A's estate. **1/2 point**

ANSWER 62—NEW YORK PRACTICE

(1)   The issue presented is whether a claim for "contribution" will enable a third-party plaintiff to recover against a village, in circumstances where the plaintiff would have no right of recovery directly against the village. **1/2 point**

CPLR 9804 provides that no action may be maintained against a village for "damages or injuries" sustained as a result of a defect in or poor state of repair of a street or highway, unless the village clerk was actually given written notice of the defect or poor repair and the village failed or neglected to repair the defect within a reasonable time. Under the facts, it is clear that no notice was given in writing to the village of the defect in Elm Street. **1 point**

CPLR 1401 provides that "two or more persons who are subject to liability for damages for the same personal injury . . . may claim contribution among them whether or not an action has been brought or a judgment has been rendered against the person from whom contribution is sought." The New York Court of Appeals has interpreted this to mean that contribution will lie "when two or more tortfeasors have shared . . . in the responsibility . . . in causing an accident, in violation of the duties they respectively owed to the injured person." [Rogers v. Dorchester Associates, 32 N.Y.2d 553 (1973)] In other words, for an action for contribution to be maintained, it is necessary that each tortfeasor have breached a duty. **1 point**

The village breached no duty to W, plaintiff's decedent, because CPLR 9804 relieves the village of any duty to repair the streets in the absence of written notice. Thus, the village cannot be liable to a claim for contribution, and the court was correct in dismissing D's third-party complaint. **1/2 point**

(2) The issue here is whether the statute of limitations applying to actions for wrongful death will be tolled by the infancy of a beneficiary who becomes the personal representative of the decedent. **1/2 point**

CPLR 208 provides that in the event that a cause of action accrues in favor of an infant, the statute of limitations is tolled until the infant's 18th birthday. The infant may then commence the action within three years of his 18th birthday, unless the applicable statute of limitations is less than three years, in which case the infant must commence the action within the period of the statute of limitations. **1/2 point**

Under EPTL section 5-4.1, the statute of limitations applicable to actions for wrongful death is two years. The statute begins to run when the decedent dies, and not from the date of the appointment of a legal representative. Under the statute, only the duly appointed personal representative may maintain the claim. **1/2 point**

The failure to appoint a personal representative in a timely fashion will not toll the running of the statute of limitations. [Goldberg v. Camp Mikan-Recro, 42 N.Y.2d 1029 (1977)] Nor will the infancy of the beneficiaries suspend the running of the statute. [Mossip v. F. H. Clement & Co., 256 A.D. 469 (1939), *aff'd*, 283 N.Y. 554 (1940)] **1/2 point**

Applying this law to the facts, the statute begins to run upon the death of the decedent, and not upon the appointment of a personal representative. S's infancy will not toll the running of the statute because another personal representative could have been timely appointed. The New York Court of Appeals reached this conclusion in *Ratka v. St. Francis Hospital*, 44 N.Y.2d 604 (1978). Since more than two years have elapsed since W's death, the statute of limitations has run. Hence, the court's ruling was correct. **1 point**

(3)(a) The issue is whether the statute of limitations has run.

The statute of limitations applicable to O's action against B for indemnification is the six-year period provided by CPLR 213(2), which covers actions upon a contractual obligation, whether express or implied. Furthermore, the cause of action does not accrue until the judgment is paid. [Bay Ridge Air Rights v. State, 44 N.Y.2d 49 (1978)] Hence, O's action is within the six-year statute of limitations period and is thus timely. Therefore, the court's ruling was incorrect. **1 point**

(b) The issue is whether a tortfeasor who has been released is subject to a claim for indemnity.

B owes O a duty of indemnity. Section 388 of the Vehicle and Traffic Law of New York states that "every owner of a vehicle used or operated in this state shall be liable and responsible for . . . injuries to person or property resulting from negligence in the use or operation of such vehicle . . . by any person using or operating the same, with the permission . . . of the owner." This is the basis of O's liability. O is vicariously liable by operation of law; he is not liable as a joint or concurrent tortfeasor. O's liability is derivative. As a consequence, B owes O an implied duty of indemnity, arising out of

B's "active" liability as opposed to O's "passive" liability. [Flood v. Re Lou Location Engr., 487 F. Supp. 364 (E.D.N.Y. 1980)] **1 point**

The right of indemnity is not extinguished by release. New York's General Obligations Law section 15-108 provides that a tortfeasor released by the plaintiff may not seek or be subject to a claim for contribution. But it has been held that section 15-108 does not apply to the right of indemnity. "The right of contribution arises among several tortfeasors who share culpability for an injury to the plaintiff and whose liability may be equitably apportioned among them according to fault . . . . Indemnity, however, flows from either a contractual or other relationship between the actual wrongdoer and another, . . . and invokes a complete shifting of the loss." [Riviello v. Waldron, 47 N.Y.2d 304 (1979)] **1 point**

Applying the law to these facts, it can be seen that O may maintain an action for indemnity even though B was previously released by the plaintiff, P, because O's liability to P arises from O's relationship with B, and not from any negligence on the part of O. Therefore, O's action against B is not barred by section 15-108, which applies only when joint and several tortfeasors are independently liable to the plaintiff. Therefore, the court incorrectly dismissed O's action on these grounds. **1 point**

ANSWER 63—CONTRACTS (SALES)/NEW YORK PRACTICE

(1)   The issue is whether a merchant's confirmatory memo is sufficient to bind its recipient under the Statute of Frauds. **1/2 point**

New York applies the U.C.C. Statute of Frauds to a sale of goods. Any contract for the sale of goods of $500 or more is not enforceable unless there is some writing sufficient to indicate that a contract has been made between the parties, and signed by the party against whom enforcement is sought. However, in contracts between merchants, if one party, within a reasonable time after an oral understanding has been reached, sends a written confirmation thereof to the other party which binds the sender, it will satisfy the Statute of Frauds requirements against the recipient as well, if he has reason to know of its contents, unless he objects to its contents within 10 days after it is received. [U.C.C. §2-201] **2 points**

Here, both S and B are merchants. S, on November 8, 1994, sent to B a written confirmation of the verbal order on S's letterhead, which serves as S's signature. Since B did not respond within 10 days, there is an enforceable contract between B and S. **1/2 point**

(2)   The issue is whether the addition of an arbitration provision in an acceptance between merchants will be included in their contract. **1/2 point**

Under U.C.C. section 2-207, a definite acceptance or written confirmation which is sent within a reasonable time is effective as an acceptance, even though it states additional terms for the contract, unless the acceptance is expressly made conditional on assent to the additional terms. As between merchants, the proposed additional terms become part of the contract unless they materially alter the original contract, the offer expressly limits acceptance to the terms of the offer, or the offeror has already objected to the particular terms or objects within a reasonable time after notice of them is received. **1 point**

Here, the written confirmation sent by S contained additional terms, including the arbitration provision. B did not expressly limit the acceptance of his verbal order to its terms, nor did he object to the inclusion of the additional terms after receipt of the confirmation. Thus, it must be determined whether the arbitration clause constitutes a material alteration. In answer to this question, the court of appeals has held that inclusion of an arbitration agreement materially alters a contract for the sale of goods, and thus, pursuant to U.C.C. section 2-207(2)(b), it will not become a part of such a contract unless both parties explicitly agree to it. [Marlene Industries v. Carnac Textiles, Inc., 45 N.Y.2d 327 (1978)] **1 point**

Here, S and B did not explicitly agree to the arbitration clause and thus, the parties cannot be compelled to arbitrate. Accordingly, B may commence a special proceeding to obtain a stay of arbitration. Under the facts at hand, B should be granted such a stay. **1/2 point**

(3)   The issue is what remedies are available to a seller when the buyer repudiates after the goods have already been manufactured. **1/2 point**

Under the U.C.C., when the buyer repudiates or refuses to accept goods, the seller is entitled to recover incidental damages plus either the difference between the contract price and the market price or the difference between the contract price and the resale price of the particular goods. Seller's incidental damages include such expenses as costs of storing, shipping, returning, and reselling the goods which are incurred as a result of the buyer's breach. Where these measures will not make the seller whole, he can recover lost profits. **1 point**

Here, S has resold the suits and therefore, the applicable measure of damages is the difference between the contract price and the resale price. If the seller chooses this measure of damages, he must resell under the provisions of U.C.C. section 2-706. This section requires a good faith, commercially reasonable sale which may be either private or public (auction). Here, it appears that the resale of the suits was commercially reasonable and therefore, S is entitled to the difference between the contract price, $15,000 (200 suits at $75 each), and the resale price, $10,000 (200 suits at $50 each), or $5,000. S is also entitled to recover the storage costs as incidental damages. Alternatively, if S can show that he could have manufactured all that he could sell, the sale to X may not have made S whole because S could have sold 200 different suits to X. Under such facts, S could recover his lost profits from B. **1-1/2 points**

Finally, S may obtain 15% per annum interest on the sums due him. This is so because the additional interest term in the written confirmation—1.25% per month—is reasonable and as such does not constitute a material alteration. Accordingly, under U.C.C. section 2-207, the interest term becomes part of the contract, causing B to be subject to it. **1 point**

ANSWER 64—REAL PROPERTY/NEW YORK PRACTICE/CONTRACTS

(1)   The issue is whether a seller of land can obtain specific performance where there is an incurable defect in title. **1/2 point**

Generally, a seller of real property is entitled to specific performance when there is a curable defect in title, provided that he cures the defect within a reasonable time. However, where the defect in title is such that a buyer "may be obligated to defend [the title] by litigation," the defect is not considered to be curable, and thus the seller may not compel specific performance, and the buyer may recover his down payment. [Chesebro v. Moers, 233 N.Y. 75 (1922)] **1 point**

Even though X cannot enforce his judgment against Whiteacre (see below), a problem with the marketability of title still exists. A significant encroachment on the land constitutes a defect in title. Here, X's garage is a significant encroachment on Whiteacre. S cannot compel X to remove the garage due to adverse possession (*see* below). Therefore, because S cannot remove this cloud on the title, he cannot compel specific performance on the part of Y and Y may recover his down payment. **1 point**

(2)   The issue is whether X gained title to the land on which his garage sits through adverse possession. **1/2 point**

For the purposes of constituting adverse possession by a person claiming title not founded upon a written instrument, land is deemed to have been possessed and occupied where the property has been usually cultivated or improved, or where the property has been protected by a substantial enclosure. Furthermore, to constitute an effective adverse possession, the possession must also be: (i) hostile and under claim of right; (ii) actual; (iii) open and notorious; (iv) exclusive; and (v) continuous for a period of 10 years. [CPLR 212(a); N.Y. Real Prop. Acts Law §521] **1 point**

Under the facts, X's garage extended 10 feet onto S's property for more than a period of 10 years. The fact that neither X nor O was aware of the encroachment does not defeat X's claim. Failure to know that title to property was in another does not preclude acquiring title by adverse possession. Furthermore, possession by mistake may be "hostile and under claim of right," if it consists of use and improvement of land or erection of a building. Finally, as X was in possession of the land and used and improved upon it, O is charged with notice of such possession by the visible facts alone. **1 point**

The conveyance of the property from O to S has no effect on X's acquisition of title through adverse possession. Once adverse possession has begun to run against an owner, it runs against that owner and all of his successors in interest (except holders of future interests). Successive ownerships are tacked on the owner's side as well as on the adverse possessor's side. Thus, since X possessed the 10 feet of Whiteacre for over 10 years, X now owns that portion of Whiteacre. **1 point**

As X meets all the requirements of adverse possession, S cannot compel him to remove the garage.

(3)   The issue is whether O had title to Blackacre or Whiteacre on the date X docketed his judgment. **1/2 point**

Under the law of real property in New York, no conveyance is effective unless title has been both delivered and accepted. The grantor must give up all control over the deed. But it is not necessary that the deed be delivered to the grantee, as long as it is delivered to a third person for the grantee's exclusive use and benefit. Here, O gave up all control over the deed when he delivered it in escrow to L, and L had a duty to deliver the deed only to S. Therefore, the conveyance was effective. **1 point**

The next question is when S became the owner of the properties. While normally a grantee does not become the owner of property deeded to him until final delivery of a deed to him, when title passes upon the death of the grantor, it is presumed to relate back to the time when the deed was absolutely given over to escrow. Thus, S is deemed to have become the title owner of Blackacre and Whiteacre in 1983. On the other hand, courts generally refuse to "relate back" an acceptance where it would defeat the rights of intervening third parties, including attaching creditors of the grantor. However, CPLR 5203(a) provides that a judgment creditor may only execute the judgment against real property owned by the debtor on the date that the judgment was docketed. Since X did not docket the judgment until November 4, 1994, his rights are not ***intervening*** and he has no right to execute against Blackacre or Whiteacre, which belonged to S on that date. **1-1/2 points**

Finally, it should be noted that the recording act does not affect the outcome. The recording act provides that an unrecorded conveyance of real property is void as against subsequent good faith purchasers for value who file first. [N.Y. Real Prop. Law §291] Neither party involved here is entitled to the protection of the recording act; *i.e.*, neither can qualify as a subsequent good faith purchaser for value. Neither a judgment creditor (X) nor a donee (S) is a "purchaser" for purposes of the recording act. Since the recording act does not apply, the result turns entirely on when S took title. As discussed above, S took title to the property before X's lien attached; thus, S takes free of X's lien. **1 point**

ANSWER 65—DOMESTIC RELATIONS

(1) H'S MOTIONS TO DISMISS

(i) The issue is whether W's claim for abandonment may be sustained as a matter of law. **1/2 point**

The Domestic Relations Law section 170(2) provides that an action for divorce may be maintained by a spouse on the grounds of abandonment of the plaintiff by the defendant for a period of one or more years. The term "abandonment" is defined as the voluntary separation of one party from the other with the intention not to return. There must be a showing of a refusal by one spouse to fulfill the basic obligations of the "marital contract." Additionally, the conduct of the "wrongful" spouse must be unjustified and without the consent of the other spouse. **1 point**

In the facts presented, W's claim for abandonment must fail under the Domestic Relations Law. First, abandonment must be for a period of at least one year. W commenced her action in October 1994, and alleged an absence of H from January 1994. W's cause of action falls two months short of the time requirement set by statute. Second, W's claim for abandonment must demonstrate that H's departure was unjustified. The facts state that H was transferred by his employer, and it has been generally held that, absent a showing of intention or lack of good faith, a mandated career move by itself does not constitute abandonment. Last, failure to provide support in and of itself is not a ground for divorce under New York law. Therefore, the court was incorrect in denying H's motion for failure to state a cause of action. **2 points**

(ii) The issue is whether State X had jurisdiction to decree the divorce.

A divorce decree is entitled to full faith and credit if the rendering court had jurisdiction to grant the decree. A court has jurisdiction to grant a divorce if it has jurisdiction over at least one of the spouses and the other spouse is notified of the action. **1 point**

Here, H satisfied the residency requirements of State X, so the state had jurisdiction over H and the marital res, and W was notified of the action. Therefore, the court was incorrect and the divorce decree is entitled to full faith and credit. **1 point**

(2) H'S PETITION FOR CUSTODY

The issue is when a court may modify the custody decree of a sister state court. **1/2 point**

The federal Parental Kidnapping Prevention Act ("PKPA") mandates that full faith and credit be given to child custody determinations of another state if the PKPA's jurisdictional standards are met despite the fact that custody determinations are not final. **1/2 point**

The facts indicate that State X has the same law with respect to custody as New York, which applies the Uniform Child Custody Jurisdiction and Enforcement Act ("UCCJEA"). Under the UCCJEA and the PKPA, if a court of another state has made a custody decree, another court may not modify that decree unless (i) it appears that the court that rendered the decree did not or does not now have jurisdiction or has declined to assume jurisdiction, and (ii) the "modifying" court has jurisdiction. **1 point**

Generally, jurisdiction lies in the "home state" of the child. A child's home state is the state in which the child has lived with a parent at least six consecutive months prior to commencement of the proceeding. If no state has home state jurisdiction, a state may exercise jurisdiction if it is in the best interest of the child that the court assume jurisdiction because the child and his parents, or the child and at least one parent, have a significant connection with the state, and there is within the jurisdiction of the court substantial evidence concerning the child's present or future welfare. A court may also exercise jurisdiction if all other states that would have jurisdiction decline or no other state has jurisdiction under any of these tests. In addition, a court can exercise emergency jurisdiction if the child is physically present in the state, and the child has been abandoned, or it is necessary in an emergency to protect the child. **1-1/2 points**

Although H could argue that because of W's disability an emergency situation exists in which State X should assume jurisdiction of D, there is no indication in the facts that D's physical or mental welfare has been endangered by W's disability. **1/2 point**

Because New York had already rendered a custody decree and had not declined jurisdiction, and because New York's jurisdiction continues by virtue of its being the home state for at least six months prior to the modification proceeding, State X has no jurisdiction under the UCCJEA to modify the custody of D. Thus, the court's ruling was in error. **1/2 point**

(*Note:* Credit will be given to the bar candidate who argues that W's disability constitutes an emergency within the meaning of the UCCJEA, so that the court ruled correctly, provided that the candidate points out that the court ought to make its ruling temporary, so that W may obtain custody once the period of disability has ended.)

ANSWER 66—CONTRACTS (SALES)

(1) The issue is whether a subcontractor's bid, to be used by a general contractor for his bid, is irrevocable. **1/2 point**

Under U.C.C. section 2-205, when a merchant makes an irrevocable offer in writing and signs it, that offer will remain open and irrevocable for the time expressly stated in the writing or for a reasonable time if no specific time is stated. However, under no circumstances can the period of irrevocability exceed three months. No consideration is needed to support the irrevocability of the offer. **1-1/2 points**

In this case, on October 1, 1994, C received a price quote from T as to the price of tile needed for C's project. The offer was in writing, signed by T, and stated that the price quoted was irrevocable. Since T did not specify the length of time the offer would remain irrevocable, under the U.C.C. the offer will remain open for three months. Therefore, C had an irrevocable offer that he had the power to accept within at least three months. On January 1, 1995, the irrevocability of T's offer ended, and T could revoke at any time after that date, unless C accepted the offer prior to revocation. On February 15, C received written notice of revocation. Under the U.C.C., this is a valid revocation of the offer. C had not accepted T's offer in time, and thus, no contract was formed between them. Thus, C cannot recover from T. **2 points**

(2)(a) The issue is whether risk of loss had already passed to C when the doors were destroyed. **1/2 point**

When a contract specifies that delivery is to be F.O.B. a particular destination, the duties, obligations, and risk of loss depend on the destination. If the shipment is F.O.B. seller's place of business, then the seller is responsible for placing the goods, at his own expense and risk, in the hands of a reasonable carrier. The risk of loss passes to the buyer upon delivery to the carrier. If the shipment is to be sent F.O.B. buyer's place of business, then seller is responsible, at his own risk and expense, for tendering conforming goods to the buyer at the destination named in the contract. The risk of loss does not pass until the goods are tendered to the buyer at the named destination. **1-1/2 points**

In this case, C ordered doors from G, F.O.B. Utica. Utica is G's place of business. This means that G is required only to deliver the goods to a reasonable carrier. Based on the facts given, G did not appear negligent in choosing the carrier. At the time of delivery to the carrier, risk of loss passed to the buyer. Thus, while the doors were en route to Buffalo, C had the risk of loss. When the goods were destroyed because of an act of God (lightning striking the truck), it was C who bore the risk. (C should have taken an insurance policy on the goods to be sure of compensation in case of loss.) Therefore, C does not have a cause of action against G for loss of the doors, and thus cannot collect $1,200 from G. **1-1/2 points**

(b)   At issue is a seller's rights to cure prior to the contract's date of performance. **1/2 point**

Under the U.C.C.'s "perfect tender" rule, a buyer may reject goods for "any defect" in the goods or tender in a single delivery contract. However, if the seller can cure the defect within the time originally provided in the contract, he may do so by giving reasonable notice of intent to cure and subsequently tendering conforming goods which the buyer must accept. Failure of the buyer to accept the conforming goods will be a breach of the contract. **1 point**

In this case, G delivered windows to C on May 15, which did not conform to C's specifications. The date of performance under the contract was May 30. On May 18, G sent C notification of his intent to ship conforming goods and on May 28, prior to the expiration of the date set forth in the contract, delivered conforming goods to C. Thus, although G had sent defective goods, he properly cured and tendered conforming goods prior to the expiration of the contract date. C's refusal to accept the conforming goods is a breach of the contract and G may recover. **1 point**

ANSWER 67—WILLS/TRUSTS/FUTURE INTERESTS

RIGHTS OF W

At issue is the amount of a spouse's elective share and the effect the election has on gifts given to the spouse under the decedent's will. **1/2 point**

Under the EPTL, a surviving spouse who files a notice of election is entitled to one-third of the decedent's net estate. A decedent's net estate includes testamentary substitutes, such as survivorship estates (*e.g.*, joint tenancies) and Totten trusts, but a trust created by another is not a testamentary substitute unless the trust gives the decedent a presently exercisable general power of appointment. In arriving at the net estate, the decedent's estate is reduced by debts, administration expenses, and reasonable funeral expenses, but not by estate taxes. Thus, H's net estate includes his $600,000 in assets, but not the $300,000 value of the trust set up by F because the power given to H under that trust is a testamentary power (*i.e.*, exercisable only on H's death) rather than a general power (which would be exercisable any time). Consequently, W is entitled to an elective share of one-third of $600,000, which is $200,000. **1 point**

When a spouse chooses to take an elective share, the elective share amount is reduced by the value of any outright gifts to the spouse under the will or as a testamentary substitute. Here, H's will only gave

W income interests in two trusts. Because the income interests are not outright gifts, they are not set off against the elective share amount. However, as a result of the election, W must forfeit her interest in the trusts. Therefore, W is entitled only to the $200,000 elective share. **1 point**

RIGHTS OF X

At issue is the effect an elective share has on gifts to persons other than the electing spouse. **1/2 point**

Where a spouse takes her elective share, the will is read as if the spouse predeceased the testator, except that beneficiaries of the net estate under the will must contribute ratably to satisfy the elective share. Since W's elective share is 1/3 of H's estate, gifts of the property constituting the net estate under the will will be reduced by one-third. **1 point**

Thus, the corpus of Trust 2 is reduced by 1/3 ($200,000 × 1/3), which would leave $133,333 as the trust corpus. Since the corpus is to be distributed to X and Y in equal shares on W's death and W is treated as predeceasing H, X and Y are each entitled to an outright distribution of $66,667. **1 point**

Trust 3 (the residue) is also read as though W predeceased H. Since this trust was to be distributed to X on W's death, the remainder is accelerated, and X is entitled to immediate distribution of the trust corpus. Once again, that corpus is reduced pro rata by the amount needed to satisfy W's elective share. X is entitled to $400,000 minus one-third, which is $266,667. **1 point**

Thus, X is entitled to half of the principal from the trust created in Paragraph 2 of H's will and to the residue of H's estate.

RIGHTS OF Y

At issue is whether H validly exercised the power of appointment ("POA") created in him by F's will, and the effect of granting Y a remainder contingent on his reaching age 35. **1 point**

H validly exercised the POA. F's will created a general testamentary POA since it provided that the power could be exercised only by H's will, but it could be exercised in favor of anyone. H exercised this power in his will. Thus, the exercise itself was valid. **1 point**

However, the trust H created violates the Rule Against Perpetuities ("RAP") and so will be modified under New York's Perpetuities Reform Act. Under the RAP, no interest in property is good unless it must vest within 21 years after some life in being at the creation of the interest. The EPTL [§§10-8.1, 10-8.2] provides that in the case of a POA, the vesting period starts to run when the POA is created, rather than when it is exercised. Since Y was not alive when the POA was created, he cannot be a measuring life; H is the measuring life. H's will created an interest in Y that could have vested more than 21 years after H's death, since H's will created a trust that gave Y a remainder interest in the POA property only if Y lived to age 35. Such a remainder is not vested because it is contingent on Y's survival, and because the remainder will not necessarily vest within 21 years of H's death (because survival is required for 35 years), it violates the common law RAP. **1 point**

Nevertheless, the trust is valid under New York law. New York has adopted a Perpetuities Reform Act which provides that where an otherwise valid gift would be invalid because an age contingency extends beyond 21 years, that age contingency will be lowered to 21 years in order to save the disposition. Thus, applying the Reform Act, H's will will be reformed so that Y receives the corpus of the trust created by paragraph 1 of H's will when Y reaches the age of 21, and not the age of 35. **1 point**

Additionally, as discussed with regard to X, Y has a one-half remainder interest in the corpus of Trust 2, subject to a ratable contribution to W's elective share.

Thus, Y has a right to income from the trust created by F's will until Y reaches age 21; at that point, Y has a right to the corpus of that trust. Additionally, Y is entitled to one-half of the remainder interest of Trust 2.

ANSWER 68—COMMERCIAL PAPER/FEDERAL JURISDICTION & PROCEDURE

(1)   The issue is whether diversity jurisdiction exists. **1/2 point**

Diversity jurisdiction is sustained when (i) there is complete diversity of citizenship between all plaintiffs and all defendants, provided that such diversity existed at the time that the action was commenced, and (ii) the amount in controversy exceeds $75,000. **1/2 point**

B Bank is chartered in New York, and so is a resident of New York. X, at the time the action was commenced, was a resident of Vermont. Attempts to manufacture diversity as in this case do not destroy diversity, provided that there is a bona fide change of domicile. [Morris v. Gilmer, 129 U.S. 315, 328 (1889); *and see* Peterson v. Allcity Insurance Co., 472 F.2d 71 (2d Cir. 1972)] Hence, (i) above is met. Additionally, the suit is for over $75,000, so (ii) is also met. Therefore, there is proper subject matter jurisdiction and the court's ruling was correct. **1 point**

Note, however, that while the court has subject matter jurisdiction of the claim, B Bank could move to have the case transferred to a district in New York, since Vermont is not a proper forum. Where subject matter jurisdiction is based solely on diversity, the action may be brought only in a judicial district where: (i) all defendants reside; (ii) a substantial part of the claims giving rise to the action occurred; or (iii) all defendants are subject to personal jurisdiction when the case is filed. [Fed. R. Civ. P. §1391(a)] **1/2 point**

Here, the defendant B Bank does not reside in Vermont and the transactions involved did not take place in Vermont. Neither is B Bank subject to personal jurisdiction in Vermont. Personal jurisdiction requires the defendant to: have committed acts within the state, be present or domiciled in the forum, or consent to jurisdiction. None of these requirements are met under these facts at the time the case was commenced. (Although it could be argued that B Bank, by appearing without challenging the court's personal jurisdiction over it, may have consented to personal jurisdiction after the commencement of the suit.) Federal Rules of Civil Procedure section 1406(a) provides that where the initial venue is improper, transfer of the case to a proper venue is more appropriate than dismissal of the case in most actions. Therefore, the court would not dismiss for lack of subject matter but will transfer the case to a federal district court in New York. **1 point**

(2)   The issue is whether the court had ancillary jurisdiction to hear the claim. **1/2 point**

Under Rule 14 of the Federal Rules of Civil Procedure, "[a]t any time after commencement of the action a defending party, as a third-party plaintiff, may cause a summons and complaint to be served upon a person not a party to the action who is or may be liable to him for all or part of the plaintiff's claim against him." Thus, the Federal Rules explicitly authorize third-party actions where the third-party claim is related to the main cause of action. Furthermore, the facts tell us that B Bank "duly commenced the claim," so there is no issue as to timeliness. In addition, the federal court has ancillary jurisdiction over a third-party claim that is related to the underlying action, despite the lack of diversity between the third-party plaintiff and the third-party defendant. When the court asserts its ancillary jurisdiction, no independent jurisdictional basis is required; the original basis of jurisdiction between the plaintiff and the defendant will enable the court to hear the ancillary claim. [Dery v. Wyer, 265 F.2d 804 (2d Cir. 1959)] **1 point**

Thus, B Bank's first related claim against Z is properly before the court, both in terms of the nature of the claim and in terms of the jurisdictional basis by which the court may hear the claim. Therefore, the court ruled correctly. **1/2 point**

(3) The issue is whether the court had ancillary jurisdiction over an unrelated claim.

The second claim by B Bank against Z was unrelated to and independent of the underlying action by X against B Bank. Rule 14 allows third-party practice in federal court only as to related claims. Therefore, B Bank's second (unrelated) claim is properly subject to dismissal. In addition, it should be noted that ancillary jurisdiction does not apply to causes of action unrelated to the plaintiff's claim. Thus, the lack of diversity between B Bank and Z precludes B Bank from maintaining any action against Z in federal court. Hence, the court again ruled correctly. **1 point**

(4) The issue is the extent of B Bank's liability for cashing an altered check. **1/2 point**

Under the Uniform Commercial Code, a bank customer has the obligation to check his statement and his returned checks for errors, and to report any unauthorized alterations promptly after discovery, but in no case more than one year later. [U.C.C. §4-406] X notified B Bank of the alteration 31 days after he received his statement. Therefore, X notified B Bank in a timely manner. Under U.C.C. section 4-401(1), B Bank may charge X's account with those items which are "properly payable." **1/2 point**

However, the court was incorrect in granting judgment in the amount of $81,500. Notwithstanding the alteration to X's check, U.C.C. section 4-401(2)(a) authorizes a drawee bank acting in good faith to charge the account of a customer to the extent of "the original tenor of his altered item"; *i.e.*, the bank can charge the customer's account for the original amount for which the check was drawn. The check in the facts was originally for $1,500: $81,500 - $1,500 = $80,000. Consequently, X can recover only $80,000 from B Bank. Thus, the court's ruling was partially incorrect. **1 point**

(5) The issue is whether Z, as an indorser of the instrument, warranted to B Bank that the instrument has not been materially altered. **1/2 point**

U.C.C. section 3-417 provides:

> (1) Any person who obtains payment . . . warrants to a person who pays in good faith . . . (c) the instrument has not been materially altered . . . .

> (2) Any person who transfers an instrument and receives consideration warrants to his transferee . . . that . . . (c) the instrument has not been materially altered . . . .

B Bank is therefore entitled to judgment against Z because Z indorsed the check and cashed it at B Bank. B Bank is entitled to recover $80,000 from Z, which represents the difference between the original amount for which the check was drawn by X, and what Z received when he indorsed the check and received payment from B Bank. Thus, the court's ruling was in error. **1 point**

ANSWER 69—CONTRACTS (SALES)

(1) At issue is whether any warranties arose in the sale here, and if so, whether the warranties were disclaimed. **1/2 point**

This sale included a number of warranties. Section 2-314 provides that in a sale by a merchant who deals in goods of the kind sold, there is an implied warranty of merchantability. This means that the goods sold must be "merchantable," *i.e.,* must be fit for the purposes for which they are ordinarily used. In this case, there is an implied warranty of merchantability. M is a merchant of burglar alarms, and he sold an alarm to P. Thus, the alarm sold must be "merchantable." **1 point**

Section 2-315 provides that an implied warranty of fitness for a particular purpose exists when a seller, merchant or not, has reason to know the particular purpose for which the goods are to be used and that the buyer is relying upon the seller's skill and judgment to select suitable goods. There was possibly an implied warranty of fitness for a particular purpose here because M knew the alarm was for P's jewelry store, and quite possibly inspected the premises and suggested the type of alarm system. Thus, if P relied on M's skill or judgment in selecting the alarm, a warranty of fitness for the particular purpose of protecting P's store arose. **1 point**

The issue then is whether these warranties were disclaimed. All implied warranties may be disclaimed in one of three ways: (i) by a conspicuous writing included in the contract stating that the product is taken "as is," "with all faults," or any other plain language indicating to the buyer that the seller was disclaiming his warranties; (ii) by inspection or refusing to inspect prior to the making of the contract, in which case there is no implied warranty as to defects that would have been revealed by a reasonable examination; and (iii) by course of dealing, course of performance, or usage of trade. Here, methods (ii) and (iii) seem unlikely, since there is nothing in the facts to indicate that P's inspection would have revealed the defect in the alarm nor anything to show that the course of dealing, course of performance, or usage of trade disclaimed the warranties. As for the language used, there was no disclaimer by the use of "as is" or similar language. Therefore, any disclaimer of fitness for a particular purpose must be conspicuous, and a disclaimer of merchantability must be conspicuous *and* mention the word "merchantability." As for express warranties, these are extremely difficult to disclaim. **2 points**

Here, none of the warranties was effectively disclaimed. The word "merchantability" was not used and thus that warranty was not disclaimed. There is no indication in the facts that the provision in question was different from any other provision in the contract; it was not conspicuous in any way. Therefore, the warranty of fitness for a particular purpose was not disclaimed. And, most likely, the court would not find the express warranty disclaimed. Thus, the court ruled incorrectly. **1 point**

(2)(a) The first issue is whether privity of contract existed between P and Y. The effect of an assignment is to create a privity of contract between the obligor and the assignee, while extinguishing privity between the obligor and the assignor. An assignment that has been given in exchange for consideration is irrevocable. Thus, P's first ground for dismissal should fail because an irrevocable assignment was made between X and Y when consideration passed in exchange for the assignment and the effect of such assignment is to place the assignee and the obligor in privity of contract. Hence, P's motion on this ground fails. **1-1/2 points**

(b) The second issue is whether X could have assigned his contract with P. Contract rights are assignable unless there is a restriction in making such assignment. Restrictions on assignments include assignments prohibited by law or contract terms, assignments of personal services contracts, or assignments that vary the obligor's risk. **1 point**

In this case, the first two restrictions obviously do not apply, and P's risk is not varied by the assignment because Y did not assume X's obligations. Hence, this contract is assignable, and P's motion fails on this ground. **1/2 point**

(c)   P's final ground enables the court to dismiss. Specific performance is available to the purchaser when the seller breaches a land sale contract if the buyer tenders the purchase price. A court will grant specific performance because the legal remedy of money damages is deemed insufficient since land is unique. In this case, Y is willing to tender the purchase price but not in accordance with the terms of the contract. The contract states that P is to receive $50,000 in cash and $50,000 in a bond by X. Y tendered the $50,000 cash but offered a bond made by himself and not by X. Therefore, the court was correct in denying Y the remedy of specific performance because the tendered payment was not in accordance with the contract. Hence, P's motion must be granted on this final ground, and thus the court's ruling was correct. **1-1/2 points**

ANSWER 70—WILLS/TRUSTS

(1)   The issue is whether creditors of a creator of a trust can reach the trust to satisfy claims against the creator. **1/2 point**

P can reach the entire income from the trust, the interest which W had retained, but cannot reach the principal unless the creation of the trust was in frustration of W's creditors. [2 Scott on Trusts (3d ed.) §156] A person cannot frustrate the claims of her creditors by placing her property in trust for herself. EPTL section 7-3.1 expressly provides that a disposition in trust for the use of the creator is void as against existing or subsequent creditors of the creator. The limitations on a creditor to 10% of the income of a trust, under CPLR 5205, and to the excess income over the amount necessary for the education and support of the beneficiary under section 7-3.4 are not applicable here; they apply only when the beneficiary and the creator are not the same person (a spendthrift trust). Thus, the court was partially correct. **1-1/2 points**

Note that if the trust had been revocable by W alone, P could have reached the principal; however, here the trust was silent as to revocation, and so was irrevocable. [EPTL §10-b6; 61 N.Y. Jur. Trust §183] **1/2 point**

(2)   The issue is whether the trust was properly revoked.

If a trust agreement is silent as to revocability, it is deemed irrevocable. However, upon the written consent of all persons beneficially interested in the trust, the creator of the trust may revoke it. The consent must be acknowledged or proved in the manner required for the recording of real property instruments. [EPTL §7-1.9(a)] For the purposes of this section, a disposition "in favor of a class of persons described only as the heirs, next of kin, or distributees (or by any term of like import) of the creator of the trust does not create a beneficial interest in such persons." [EPTL §7-1.9(b)] Thus, W, with the consent of A only, could revoke the trust. H, B, and C were not "beneficially interested" in the trust, and their consent was not necessary. L's advice was correct. **2 points**

(3)   N'S RIGHTS

At issue is whether the gift adeemed by destruction or lapsed by S's death. **1/2 point**

Normally, a specific legacy (here a painting) is to be satisfied only by the delivery of the item specified; if it is not in existence at the date of the testator's death, the gift adeems. [EPTL §1-2.16] However, by statute, when insurance proceeds on property which is the subject of a specific bequest are paid after the death of the testator, the proceeds received by the executor are payable to the specific legatee. [EPTL §3-4.5] Therefore, S, if living, would have been entitled to the $90,000 insurance proceeds. The general rule is that a legacy to a person who predeceases the testator lapses; however, if the deceased legatee is an issue or brother or sister of the testator, the disposition does not lapse but vests in the beneficiary's issue. [EPTL §3-3] N (as S's issue) therefore takes the $90,000 insurance proceeds. **2 points**

RIGHTS OF A, B, AND C

The issue is whether C was "provided for" as a pretermitted child. **1/2 point**

W's children, A and B, were living when W executed her will; if W had made no provision for either A or B in her will, C, the afterborn daughter, would not share in the estate. [EPTL §5-3.2(a)(1)(A)] If C had been "unprovided for," C would have been entitled to share equally with A in the provision of the will for A. [EPTL §5-3.2(a)(1)(B)] **1 point**

But C does not receive this statutory benefit because she received the $25,000 life insurance proceeds and was not "unprovided for by any settlement." [EPTL §5-3.2(a)] The "settlement" need not assume any particular form, as long as some provision has been made for the afterborn child. The intent of the parent is the main factor and the fact that the size of the provision for the afterborn child may be objectively inadequate is of no consequence. [McKinney's Practice Commentary to EPTL §5-3.2] **1-1/2 points**

C takes only the $25,000 life insurance proceeds. A takes the residue of $410,000, and B takes nothing.

ANSWER 71—CONFLICT OF LAWS/FEDERAL JURISDICTION & PROCEDURE/ NEW YORK PRACTICE

(a)(1)   The issue is which state's law should be applied.

When faced with a conflict of law regarding loss distribution rules in a tort case, the New York Court of Appeals has rejected the old vested rights approach, which would mandate the automatic application of the law of the situs of the tort. Now, New York courts apply the ***governmental interest analysis***. This is to ensure that the jurisdiction with the greatest interest in the suit has its law apply. In order to make the determination, the court will look at the factual contacts of each jurisdiction, the differing laws, and the underlying policies for each law; apply the facts to the policies; and apply the greater governmental interest. For tort cases, New York has refined the interest analysis in *Neumeier v. Kuehner*, 31 N.Y.2d 121 (1972). The *Neumeier* rules are a product of the governmental interest analysis. Under the first *Neumeier* rule, if parties are from the jurisdiction then the law of that jurisdiction will apply. **1-1/2 points**

In this case the New York rule allowing the suit should be applied. While the accident took place in State X, each litigant is from New York. State X has very little interest in the litigation because only New York parties are involved and no citizen of State X will be subjected to New York law. New York, which is where all of the interested parties are from, has decided that New York owners of vehicles should be responsible for accidents in their cars. Accordingly, since no interest of State X will be implicated and all of the parties have an expectation that New York law will apply, the court will follow the first *Neumeier* rule and apply the law of New York. The court was correct. **1 point**

(2)   The issue is whether the action can be removed to federal court.

A defendant can only remove a federal action that could have originally been brought by the plaintiff in the federal courts. [28 U.S.C. §1441] Here, the only ground for federal court jurisdiction is diversity.

However, there must be complete diversity between opposing sides for diversity jurisdiction to exist. Complete diversity is lacking here because P, the plaintiff, and O, one of the defendants, are both from New York. **1 point**

Removal can also be accomplished when all defendants join in the petition for removal. If some defendants cannot so join or simply choose not to, removal is not authorized. Here, only E made the removal motion, so it must be denied. **1 point**

Note, however, that whenever a separate and independent claim, which would be removable if sued upon alone, is joined with one or more otherwise nonremovable claims, the entire case may be removed and the federal court may remand all matters not otherwise within its original jurisdiction. **1/2 point**

(3) The issue is whether a release from the plaintiff prevents one from seeking indemnity. **1/2 point**

General Obligations Law section 15-108 provides that a tortfeasor released by the plaintiff may not seek or be subject to a claim for contribution. However, it has been held that section 15-108 does not apply to the right of indemnity. "The right of contribution arises among several tortfeasors who share culpability for an injury to the plaintiff and whose liability may be equitably apportioned among them according to fault . . . . Indemnity, however, flows from either a contractual or other relationship between the actual wrongdoer and another . . . and invokes a complete shifting of the loss." [Riviello v. Waldron, 47 N.Y.2d 297 (1979)] **1 point**

Applying the law to these facts, it can be seen that O may maintain an action for indemnity even though O was previously released by the plaintiff, because O's liability to P arises from O's relationship with D, and not from any negligence on the part of O. Therefore, O's action against D is not barred by section 15-108, which applies only when joint and several tortfeasors are independently liable to the plaintiff. Therefore, the court correctly denied D's motion to dismiss, and correctly granted O's motion for summary judgment. **1 point**

(b) The issue is how to apportion a judgment that has been partially satisfied by pretrial settlement. **1/2 point**

Pursuant to section 15-108, a judgment in favor of the plaintiff against unreleased tortfeasors will be reduced by the greatest of: (i) the amount paid for the release or stipulated in the release, or (ii) the proportionate share of the total injury attributable to the released tortfeasor. Here, the amount paid for the release was $25,000 while O's proportionate share was zero. Therefore, P's $100,000 judgment is reduced by $25,000 to $75,000. Thus, P can collect a total of $75,000 from D and/or E. Should D or E pay more than 50% of that judgment, he could recover the excess against the other in an action for contribution. **2 points**

ANSWER 72—CORPORATIONS

(1) At issue is the fiduciary duty of a promoter to outside investors of the corporation. **1/2 point**

A promoter is a person who provides organizational initiative for the formation of a business and the formation of a corporation to carry on the business. Promoters owe fiduciary duties to the corporation to be formed and to any contemplated outside investors. Thus, promoters must account to the corporation for profits from self-dealing before "outsiders" come in if sale to outsiders was contemplated, unless the "outsiders" had notice of these profits. **1-1/2 points**

Here, Grant is a promoter. He organized Richmond Inc. for the purpose of acquiring ROB, and he made a $200,000 profit in so doing. Given the short time between formation and the sale to outsiders, Grant could be held to have contemplated the sale at formation. Nevertheless, Grant will not have to account to the corporation for the $200,000 profit because Manny, Moe, and Jack examined the books and records of the corporation and therefore they had notice of Grant's profit. **1 point**

(2)   The issue is whether a promoter has a right to be compensated for his services to the corporation. **2/3 point**

Under the BCL, stock may be issued as consideration for labor or services performed for the corporation, including forming the corporation. In the absence of fraud in the transaction, the judgment of the board or shareholders as to the value of the consideration received for shares is conclusive. **2/3 point**

Here, Grant issued 5,000 shares of Richmond, Inc., to himself as compensation for his work in the formation of the corporation. Although the par value of the 5,000 shares is $500,000 and could be viewed as excessive compensation for the formation of a corporation, Manny, Moe, and Jack have no right to have the transaction to Grant canceled. **2/3 point**

(3)   At issue is breach of a director's fiduciary duty for self-dealing. **1/2 point**

Directors owe their corporation a fiduciary duty and will not be allowed to unfairly profit at the corporation's expense. Where a director has an interest in a transaction his corporation is to enter, the director must present all material facts of the transaction to the uninterested directors or the shareholders for approval. Absent such approval, the transaction may be set aside if it is unfair to the corporation. **1 point**

Grant breached his fiduciary duty here through self-dealing. Grant had an interest in the maintenance contract here since he was the sole owner of Maint Co. Since Grant was a director of Richmond, he should have disclosed his interest in the transaction to the board and obtained its approval, disclosed his interest to the shareholders and obtained their approval, or entered into a fair contract. Grant did none of these. Under the facts, Grant did not seek approval from Manny, Moe, and Jack, and the transaction was not fair since the contract called for 5% of the gross receipts of the building and the norm in the area was 2.5%. Thus, the contract can be set aside. **1-1/2 points**

(4)   At issue is whether a director may compete with his corporation. **1/2 point**

In New York, a corporation is entitled to freedom from competition by those charged with the promotion of the corporation's interests. [Robt. Brown Associates v. Fileppo, 38 A.D.2d 515 (1971)] This prohibition extends to directors. Thus, Grant improperly competed. While the noncompetition duty is owed to the corporation, the shareholders would be allowed to recover here because if Grant paid damages to the corporation, as the majority shareholder, he would primarily be benefiting himself. Thus, the corporation's shareholders will be permitted to recover the damages. **1-1/2 points**

ANSWER 73—DOMESTIC RELATIONS

(1)   The issue is whether breach of a separation agreement is a valid ground for a judgment of separation. **1/2 point**

The neglect or refusal of the defendant-spouse to provide for the support of the plaintiff-spouse, where the former is chargeable with such support, is ground for separation. A married person is chargeable with the support of his spouse. [N.Y. Fam. Ct. Act §412] The facts state that H did not make any payments to W. Thus, as stated above, W is entitled to a judgment of separation. **1-1/2 points**

Additionally, a spouse's failure to pay the amount due under the separation agreement entitles the other spouse to the option of either (i) affirming the agreement and bringing an action on the agreement, or (ii) treating the breach as a repudiation, which terminates the agreement, and reasserting statutory rights. **1 point**

By electing the latter option, W gives the court the discretion to determine the level of support in this case, without being limited to the amount set in the agreement. [N.Y. Dom. Rel. Law §236(A)] Thus, the court could properly grant W an award of support in the amount of $350 per week. Hence, the court's ruling on the judgment of separation and the award of support was correct. **1 point**

(2)   The issue is whether the ground of living separate and apart for more than one year can be satisfied under a separation decree. **1/2 point**

The grounds cited by W, also known as a conversion divorce, are available under two distinct circumstances: living apart pursuant to a separation decree and living apart pursuant to a separation agreement. In this case, W is seeking a divorce based on a separation decree. She must prove that the parties have lived separate and apart pursuant to a separation decree for at least one year after the granting of the decree, and that she has substantially performed its terms. The failure of H to perform its terms naturally does not preclude W from obtaining the divorce. The facts state that H and W lived separate and apart for over one year after the separation decree was issued; the facts give no indication that W did not substantially perform the terms of the decree. **2 points**

The reconciliation of the parties does not abrogate the separation decree. Note that a subsequent reconciliation (although not a mere cohabitation) will vitiate a separation agreement and thus preclude a conversion divorce; however, here a decree was in place, which can only be altered or revoked by the court. [N.Y. Dom. Rel. Law §§203, 236] Thus, W would be entitled to obtain a divorce. **1 point**

(3)   The issue is whether the business is marital property to be distributed under the equitable distribution law. **1/2 point**

The Equitable Distribution Law provides that marital property includes all property acquired by either spouse during the marriage, regardless of the form of title prior to the commencement of any matrimonial action, subject to certain exceptions. **1 point**

H's computer business was started in 1985. It was acquired during the marriage and prior to any matrimonial action. It is therefore marital property which the court can distribute. That the judgment of separation did not deal with the business does not preclude the court from doing so, but rather is to be considered along with any other significant factors. **1 point**

Thus, W can get an equitable share of H's computer business.

ANSWER 74—CONTRACTS (SALES)

(1)   The issue is whether an oral contract for services that cannot be performed within one year is enforceable. **1/2 point**

Under the Statute of Frauds, a contract which by its terms cannot be performed within one year of its formation cannot be enforced unless it is in writing. In measuring the applicable period for the Statute of Frauds, the period runs from the date of the agreement and not from the date of performance. Unless it is in writing, an employment contract is terminable at will. **1 point**

Here, although the length of A's employment contract was performable within one year—November 1, 1995, to October 31, 1996—it was not capable of being performed within one year of the date of the agreement, October 1, 1995. Accordingly, it is not enforceable. **1 point**

Since the contract is not enforceable, as an oral employment agreement, it was terminable at will. After C Corp.'s termination of A's employment, C Corp. owed no further duty to A. Accordingly, A cannot collect salary for the last two months of the contract. **1 point**

(2) The issue is whether a perpetual contract is enforceable without a writing. **1/2 point**

In New York, a contract, which by its terms continues indefinitely into the future and which cannot be terminated unless there is a breach, must be in writing to be enforceable. Here, A's agreement to receive commissions indefinitely into the future could only be terminated by C Corp.'s breach—its failure to pay the commissions. Accordingly, it is not enforceable after his termination. **1-1/2 points**

However, A can recover commissions for the period up to his termination. The commissions were part of his compensation for his employment agreement. The agreement was not within the Statute of Frauds, since it was terminable at will. Having fully performed his contract up to his dismissal, A is entitled to receive commissions up to that time. **1 point**

(3) The issues are what type of contract is involved and who bears the risk of loss on it. **1/2 point**

Under the U.C.C., where delivered goods may be returned by the buyer even though they conform to the contract, the transaction is a sale or return contract if the goods are delivered primarily for resale. The facts state that Z is a retailer of camera equipment; thus, the goods delivered to Z were primarily for resale and this constitutes a sale or return contract. **1 point**

Under the U.C.C., if the seller is a merchant (and does not use a common carrier or other bailee), the risk of loss passes to the buyer only when the buyer takes physical possession of the goods. For the purpose of determining the risk of loss, a sale or return contract is treated as an ordinary sale; *i.e.,* the risk of loss passes to the buyer after it takes delivery. If the goods are returned to the seller, the risk remains on the buyer while the goods are in transit. **1-1/2 points**

Here, Z took delivery of the lenses and therefore the risk of loss, as well as the duty of payment, passed to Z. That Z had until August 31, 1996, to return the lenses is irrelevant. C Corp. is entitled to payment for the lenses. **1/2 point**

ANSWER 75—CRIMINAL LAW/CRIMINAL PROCEDURE/CONSTITUTIONAL LAW

(1) The issue is whether a disorderly conduct statute that prohibits "inciteful behavior" is overbroad. **1/2 point**

A person's conduct is protected by the First Amendment of the federal Constitution guaranteeing the right to free speech. It is well recognized that public streets have been associated with citizens being able to exercise their right of free speech. Certain conduct may be restricted by statute if not overbroad or vague. The facts state that a statute prohibiting "inciteful behavior" exists. Since this statute does not specify in sufficient detail the prohibited conduct, it is overbroad or vague. [Terminello v. Chicago,

337 U.S. 1 (1949)] Hence, the statute is unconstitutional and the court will dismiss the disorderly conduct charge. **1-1/2 points**

(2)   The issue is whether the obscenity statute sufficiently defines or has been construed to sufficiently define "obscenity." **1/2 point**

The statute will be found constitutional if the conduct sought to be regulated is sufficiently defined by statute or the state's highest court. [Miller v. California, 413 U.S. 15 (1973)] New York has adopted the standard set forth in *Miller v. California* of what is obscene. [N.Y. Penal Law §235.00] Material is obscene if, when considered as a whole, it: (i) appeals to the prurient interest in sex of the average person; (ii) is patently offensive, as measured by the standards of the community; and (iii) lacks serious literary, artistic, political, or scientific meaning. A child engaging in sexual acts with an adult would satisfy these elements. **1 point**

To be guilty of possession of obscene articles, the defendant must possess the material with the intent to promote. "A person who possesses six or more identical or similar obscene articles is presumed to possess them with intent to promote the same." [N.Y. Penal Law §235.10(2)] Since S possessed approximately 200 identical photos, the presumption would apply. S could rebut the presumption if he conclusively shows that he possessed the material for private use. The ultimate decision of whether material is obscene or the defendant possessed it for his private use is a question of fact for the jury. The defendant's possession of the photos in his van, which is not open to the public, and not offering them to the police officer suggests that they were for his private use. [*See* People v. Marzano, 31 A.D.2d 52 (1968)] **1 point**

S could have been charged with promoting a sexual performance by a child, which does not require that the material be obscene if children are involved. [New York v. Ferber, 458 U.S. 747 (1982)] It is questionable whether "private use" would be a defense where there is obscene activity by a child under 16. The intent of that statute is to protect the child, whereas the intent of the statute S was charged with is to protect the public. [*See* People v. Godek, 113 Misc. 2d 599 (1982)] Hence, the court's decision is a question of fact. **1 point**

(3)   The issue is whether the photographs were obtained in violation of S's Fourth Amendment rights. **1/2 point**

The general rule is that police need a warrant to conduct a search and seizure, and evidence obtained without a warrant will be suppressed. However, warrantless searches are permissible under a number of circumstances, including when incident to lawful arrest and when the evidence is in plain view. **1 point**

Here, the arrest was lawful and pursuant to a proper arrest warrant. There was reasonable cause to issue the warrant based on X's statements, and the warrant was sufficient even though it did not describe S by name. Therefore P was legitimately inside the vehicle. While inside, P saw the pictures in plain view, and, under the general rule, P could seize the pictures. However, articles seized supporting an obscenity charge are to be distinguished from other contraband, such as knives or guns, in considering the reasonableness of their seizure. [Roaden v. Kentucky, 413 U.S. 496 (1973)] **1 point**

A determination of what is obscene cannot be made by a police officer alone. A judicial determination is necessary before the material may be seized. [People v. Gilmore, 120 Misc. 2d 741 (1983)] This rule is to protect persons possessing nonobscene material from unwarranted and unlawful restraints.

[People v. Gilmore, *supra*] Exigent circumstances may justify seizure without such a procedure, but this argument is not supported by the facts here. The police officer had time to get a judicial determination of whether the photos were obscene and then to obtain a search warrant based on that information. There is no evidence that the photos would not be in the van or the van would not be available upon completion of the aforesaid procedure. Thus, based on the above, the court should suppress the evidence. **2 points**

ANSWER 76—COMMERCIAL PAPER/CRIMINAL PROCEDURE/EVIDENCE

(a)   At issue is whether a drawer can recover from the drawee bank when the drawee bank pays out on an instrument containing an unauthorized drawer's signature. **1/2 point**

As a general rule, a drawee bank may pay out on a customer's account only according to the customer's order. [U.C.C. §4-401] Thus, if the bank pays out on an unauthorized drawer's signature, under the general rule the bank must recredit the customer's account because the Code provides that unauthorized signatures are ineffective as the signature of the drawer [U.C.C. §3-404], and so the payment order was not made by the customer. However, there is an exception to this general rule where the drawer's negligence has contributed to the unauthorized signature. [U.C.C. §3-406] In such a case the bank is not required to recredit its customer's account. While what constitutes drawer negligence is not defined in the Code but instead is left as a question of fact for the jury, it is relatively safe to assume that a jury would find it negligent to give an agent the authority to write checks of up to $20,000 without having a second person at least review the checks that are being written. Thus, Allways will be precluded from claiming that the signature was unauthorized and will not be able to force the bank to recredit its account. **2 points**

(b)(1)   At issue is whether the test is the fruit of an unconstitutional arrest. **1/2 point**

Under the exclusionary rule, evidence is inadmissible if it was obtained in violation of a defendant's Fourth, Fifth, or Sixth Amendment rights. Thus, if the breathalyzer test was the fruit of an unconstitutional arrest, the test results must be excluded from evidence. **1/2 point**

The arrest here was unconstitutional because it was not reasonable. Under the Fourth Amendment, which applies to the states through the Fourteenth Amendment, all warrantless arrests in a person's home are deemed unreasonable unless exigent circumstances exist. [Payton v. New York, 445 U.S. 573 (1980)] The government has the burden of proving the exigent circumstances, and the Supreme Court has found that the fact that a defendant's blood alcohol level might dissipate while the police leave to obtain a warrant is not sufficiently exigent where, as here, the crime involved is a misdemeanor traffic violation. [Welsh v. Wisconsin, 466 U.S. 740 (1984)] The fact that the officer was in "hot pursuit" of Harriet is unavailing for similar reasons—sufficient exigent circumstances simply do not exist because of the misdemeanor nature of the violation. **1 point**

The results of Harriet's breathalyzer test are most likely fruit of her unconstitutional arrest and so should be excluded from evidence. The Supreme Court discussed what constitutes the fruit of an unconstitutional warrantless home arrest in *New York v. Harris*, 495 U.S. 14 (1990). There, the Court indicated that any evidence found in the home, as the product of an improper warrantless search, is tainted and as such should be suppressed. However, it is important to distinguish evidence obtained on the premises from evidence obtained subsequently, which because of its "attenuation" to the illegal conduct, is admissible. The determining factor is whether the evidence obtained was an exploitation of the unconstitutional aspect of the arrest. If so, the evidence is suppressed; if not, the evidence is allowed. Here, the result of the breathalyzer test is a direct product of an illegal search, thereby violating the defendant's constitutional rights. As such, the results should be suppressed. **1 point**

(2) The issue is whether tests of physical condition are testimonial or communicative in nature so as to require the issuance of *Miranda* warnings prior to their administration. **1/2 point**

The privilege against self-incrimination of the Fifth Amendment, as applied to the states through the Fourteenth Amendment, bars a state from compelling a person to provide evidence of a testimonial or communicative nature. Evidence is testimonial or communicative when it reveals a person's subjective knowledge or thought processes. Physical performance tests do not do this; rather, they exhibit a person's degree of physical coordination for observation by the police. Therefore, *Miranda* warnings are not required to be given before the administration of such tests. However, once again, any evidence obtained that has been tainted by the illegal arrest would be prohibited from being introduced at trial by the exclusionary rule. **1 point**

Here, Harriet's performance of the physical tests, such as walking a straight line, were not testimonial in nature and so no *Miranda* warnings were required. However, the test results will probably be barred from evidence anyway for the same reasons that justify barring the breathalyzer test results. **1/2 point**

(3) The issue is when may prior bad acts of a defendant be used to impeach the defendant by cross-examination. **1/2 point**

Subject to the discretion of the trial judge, a defendant may be interrogated upon cross-examination with respect to any immoral, vicious, or criminal act of her life that may affect her character and show her to be unworthy of belief. Inquiry into bad acts is permitted even though the defendant was never convicted. Counsel must inquire in good faith, that is, have some reasonable belief that the witness committed the bad act inquired about. In addition, the use of extrinsic evidence is not permitted. The specific act of misconduct can be elicited only on cross-examination. If the defendant denies the act, the use of extrinsic evidence, whether by additional witnesses or otherwise is prohibited. **1 point**

Here, the prosecutor seeks to elicit evidence in regard to the larceny charge as a bad act by the use of cross-examination of Harriet, in order to impeach her credibility. Furthermore, the prosecution is acting in good faith in questioning Harriet in regard to the larceny. The prosecutor may cross-examine Harriet, but is limited to that. Therefore, the court was incorrect in granting Harriet's motion to preclude the cross-examination for purposes of impeachment. **1 point**

ANSWER 77—CRIMINAL LAW/CRIMINAL PROCEDURE

(a)(1) The issue is whether the warrant for video surveillance was properly issued by the judge. **1/2 point**

To be valid, a search warrant must be: (i) issued by a neutral and detached magistrate; (ii) on a showing of probable cause; and (iii) based on an affidavit establishing the veracity and reliability of the person supplying the information. More importantly, to obtain a warrant for a wiretap, or in this case video and audio surveillance, the affidavit must also name the suspects expected to be overheard; describe with particularity the conversations to be targeted; and include a time limit. **1 point**

In this case, the warrant was issued by a supreme court judge who is clearly neutral and detached. John arguably demonstrated probable cause based on his surveillance and experience in gangs and weapons police work. Since the information in the affidavit was based on John's own personal knowledge, the veracity and reliability of the information was established. However, John did not specify the targets of the surveillance, or describe the targeted conversations. Neither did the warrant include a time limit. Moreover, John did not explain why the video surveillance required audio as well. **1 point**

In most states, there is a good faith exception to the warrant requirements. Specifically, if the warrant was executed in good faith by the law enforcement officer, evidence obtained by the police in reasonable reliance on a facially valid warrant may be used by the prosecution. However, unlike the majority, New York does not allow the fruits of a warrant to be admitted into evidence if they are the result of an illegally issued warrant; there is no good faith exception. Thus, the court was incorrect. **1 point**

(2) The issue is whether a defendant may be convicted of conspiracy when the alleged co-conspirators have been acquitted. **1/2 point**

A conspiracy is an agreement between two or more parties to commit a crime. It requires: (i) an agreement between two or more persons; (ii) an intent to enter into the agreement; and (iii) an intent by at least two persons to achieve the objective of the agreement. New York also requires an overt act, which can include an act of mere preparation. Under the traditional view, the acquittal of all persons with whom a defendant is alleged to have conspired precludes conviction of the remaining defendant. However, in New York, a conviction of conspiracy against one defendant is allowed to stand when the alleged co-conspirator is acquitted in a separate trial. **1 point**

In this case, a jury found Squeaky not guilty of conspiring with "the Knife" to sell unlawful firearms, and pursuant to the New York rule, since Squeaky was acquitted in a separate trial, a jury may still find that "the Knife" did indeed conspire with Squeaky. All the elements for conspiracy are present. There was an agreement between "the Knife" and Squeaky, there was an intent to enter into the agreement, and there was an intent between them to sell illegal guns and explosives for money. Consequently, the court correctly denied "the Knife's" motion to dismiss based on Squeaky's acquittal. **1/2 point**

(b)(1) The issue is whether the state or the defendant bears the burden of proving the sanity of the defendant. **1/2 point**

In New York, all defendants are presumed sane; the defendant must raise the insanity issue. The claim of insanity is considered an affirmative defense, and the defendant bears the burden of proving his mental disabilities. The defendant must furthermore give the prosecution advance notice of an insanity defense. **1 point**

In this case, the court instructed the jury that the state needed to prove not only the elements of the crime, but also that "the Knife" had the mental capacity to commit the crime. That is more than the state needed to prove. Thus, the instruction was incorrect. **1/2 point**

(2) The issue is simply what is the correct standard for determining the defendant's sanity. **1/2 point**

New York's insanity defense is based on a combination of two rules: the *M'Naghten* rule and the Model Penal Code ("MPC") test. The *M'Naghten* rule states that a defendant is entitled to acquittal only if he had a mental disease or defect that caused him to either: (i) not know that his act would be wrong, or (ii) not understand the nature and quality of his actions. Under the MPC test, a defendant is insane if he had a mental disease or defect, and, as a result, lacked the substantial capacity to either: (i) appreciate the criminality of his conduct, or (ii) conform his conduct to the requirements of law. In New York, a person is not criminally responsible for conduct if, at the time of the conduct, as a result of mental disease or defect, he lacked capacity to know or appreciate the nature and consequences of his conduct or that his conduct was wrong. **1 point**

In this case, the court instructed the jury that the defendant could be found insane if he could not resist doing wrong. This is the "irresistible impulse test," where a defendant is unable to control his actions or conform his conduct to the law. New York is not an irresistible impulse test jurisdiction. The judge also failed to state that the defendant may be found not guilty if by reason of mental disease or defect, he did not understand the wrongfulness of his conduct. Therefore, the judge's charge to the jury was incorrect. **1 point**

ANSWER 78—DOMESTIC RELATIONS

(1) The issue is what must be shown to justify an award of temporary maintenance. **1/2 point**

Domestic Relations Law section 236-B provides that the court may order temporary maintenance to meet the reasonable needs of a party to a matrimonial action in such amount as justice requires, weighing both the circumstances of the case and the responsibility of the parties. Although the statute lists 10 factors to be considered in determining permanent maintenance, these factors have been held not to be applicable in determining a motion for temporary maintenance. Thus, temporary maintenance is relegated to the same function as temporary alimony and was incorporated into the post-equitable distribution statute [N.Y. Dom. Rel. Law §236-B] to ensure that the needy spouse is provided with sufficient funds to meet her needs pending the disposition of the matrimonial action. **1-1/2 points**

The primary factor the court must consider is the financial need of the applicant. The applicant must show proof of her inability to support herself while the action is pending. Here, W failed to show proof of her need for temporary maintenance. Thus, the court properly exercised its discretion in denying W's application for temporary maintenance. The court, however, was incorrect in denying W's motion on the ground that W had not shown the probability of success on the merits. It is not a prerequisite to obtaining temporary alimony that a spouse show the probability of success. The applicant need merely present pleadings and affidavits from which the court can infer a substantive cause of action. **1-1/2 points**

W's complaint, which was included in her application for temporary maintenance, set forth the substantive cause of action of abandonment of the plaintiff by the defendant for a period of one year or more prior to the commencement of such action. Thus, the court properly denied W's motion but only because W had not shown need. **1/2 point**

(2) At issue is whether the provision in the decree terminating child support upon emancipation was self-executing and whether spousal support can be modified for cohabitation. **1/2 point**

(i) W is entitled to an order directing H to pay W for arrears for support for three months. Although S was 19, H was liable for S's support until S reached 21. The defendant, H, is not entitled to an order retroactively terminating support by reason of S's emancipation. The court is mandated to direct entry of judgment for arrears in support or maintenance "unless the defrauding party shows good cause for failure to make application for relief from the judgment or order directing such payment prior to the accrual of such arrears." [N.Y. Dom. Rel. Law §244] **1 point**

Provisions in a matrimonial decree that provide for support of minor children until they become emancipated generally are not self-executing. H's failure to make a prompt motion for reduction based upon claimed emancipation of S, and H's failure to offer any reason for his failure to make such motion until three months later, preclude the court from making a nunc pro tunc order reducing support for S from the date of the claimed emancipation and canceling the arrears. The reason for the rule barring an automatic and unilateral reduction by H is to allow the court to intervene in order to reevaluate the needs of the unemancipated children and financial condition of the parties. **1-1/2 points**

W was therefore entitled to an order directing judgment for support of S up to the time H cross-moved for a reduction in support based on S's apparent emancipation. In addition, a hearing should be held to determine if, in fact, S is now emancipated and, if so, whether H's total obligation to support should then be reduced. **1 point**

(ii)   As to W's living with F, the Domestic Relations Law gives the court discretion to eliminate maintenance provisions from a divorce decree upon proof that the wife is habitually living with another man and holding herself out as his wife, although not married to such man. Cohabitation alone does not manifest a "holding out." The Court of Appeals has stated that proof of both factors is necessary, and cohabitation alone is insufficient as a matter of law. **1 point**

Even if H had been able to prove both of the factors necessary for relief, Domestic Relations Law section 244 would prevent his obtaining relief retroactively. But, because there are no facts indicating that W has held herself out as F's wife, the court has no discretion to eliminate the maintenance H must pay W. **1/2 point**

The facts suggest no substantial change in circumstances, including financial hardship, which might entitle H or W to a prospective modification of the judgment ordering maintenance. Thus, the court should grant W's motion for arrearages, deny H's cross-motion, and hold a hearing to determine H's future obligations. **1/2 point**

ANSWER 79—CRIMINAL LAW/CRIMINAL PROCEDURE/EVIDENCE

(1)   The issue is whether an accused is entitled to a preliminary hearing when indicted by a grand jury. **1/2 point**

New York Criminal Procedure Law section 180.10 provides a defendant charged with a felony the right to a preliminary hearing. The purpose of a preliminary hearing is to determine whether there is probable cause to prosecute the defendant for the crime charged. At the preliminary hearing both the defendant and prosecutor may present evidence. The right to a preliminary hearing, however, dissipates if a grand jury finds that there is probable cause to prosecute, thereby indicting the defendant. The defendant, although not afforded an opportunity to produce evidence, is not deprived of his due process rights because the underlying purpose of the right to a preliminary hearing (determination of whether probable cause exists) has been satisfied by the grand jury indictment. Additionally, a defendant does not have a due process right to the discovery opportunity otherwise provided by the preliminary hearing. In this case, since a grand jury returned an indictment for burglary and murder, B was not entitled to a preliminary hearing. Thus, the court's decision to deny L's motion to dismiss the indictment on the ground that B had been deprived of his right to a preliminary hearing was correct. **1-1/2 points**

(2)   The issue is whether evidence of the pistol is excludible as the product of an illegal search. **1/2 point**

The Fourth Amendment to the United States Constitution provides that citizens shall not be subject to unreasonable searches and seizures. Any evidence obtained as a result of an unlawful search will be suppressed from use as evidence in any charges against the defendant. **1/2 point**

Absent a lawful search warrant, when a police officer has made a lawful arrest, the officer may search the defendant's person and "grab area" as long as the search is contemporaneous in time and place with the arrest. Therefore, when a police officer lawfully arrests the occupant of a car, he may search the vehicle. The officer, however, must have full probable cause to believe the car contains evidence of a crime before stopping and searching it. **1/2 point**

Alternatively, a police officer can stop a car for "inspection" if he has a reason to believe that a traffic violation has occurred based on his own observation. If the officer has no reason to fear the occupant of the car, he may not conduct a full search of the vehicle. **1/2 point**

In the instant matter, P's search of the car was not pursuant to a valid search warrant. Additionally, P did not have probable cause to believe that a crime was committed, justifying an arrest and search. Rather, P observed B speeding and passing a stop sign, traffic infractions for which he lawfully stopped B. However, an arrest is generally not made for traffic infractions; rather, an appearance ticket would be issued. Therefore, this was an inspection stop, and since there was nothing to indicate that B was dangerous, P had no right to search the duffle bag. Thus, the evidence should be suppressed, and the court's ruling was wrong. **1/2 point**

(3) The issue is whether the dying declaration is an exception to the rule against hearsay. **1/2 point**

As a general rule all statements made out of court by a third party are inadmissible because the statements are hearsay. There are, however, a number of exceptions to this rule. One exception covers dying declarations. A dying declaration is admissible as evidence in a prosecution for homicide if: (i) the statement was made by a homicide victim, who is now deceased, about the circumstances of his impending death, (ii) the victim was aware of the impending death, and (iii) if living, the victim would have been competent to testify. **1 point**

In the present situation, V's statements are admissible as a dying declaration to prove the murder charge: V, the declarant, was a homicide victim; V is deceased; the statement concerned circumstances of his impending death; V was aware of his impending death; and if alive, V would have been a competent witness. Therefore, the testimony was properly admitted to prove the murder charge. **1/2 point**

Although there is some case law suggesting that if the defendant is charged with murder and other crimes, the statements may be used to prove all the charges, the court should have limited use of the dying declaration to prove the murder charge. **1/2 point**

(4) The issue is whether the prosecution made out prima facie causes of action for the crimes charged. **1/2 point**

To convict a defendant of burglary in the first degree, the prosecution must establish, beyond a reasonable doubt, that the defendant knowingly entered a dwelling with intent to commit a crime therein, and while in the dwelling or in flight therefrom he caused physical injury to any person who is not a participant in the crime. [P.L. §140.30] **1/2 point**

There is no admissible evidence establishing that B was in V's store or that B caused injury to V, or any other evidence connecting B to the burglary. Although V's dying declaration would establish B's presence in the store and his causing injury to V, under current New York law the declaration is not admissible as evidence to prosecute the burglary charge. Similarly, the pistol is not admissible because it was obtained during an unlawful search. Therefore the admissible evidence was legally insufficient to support the burglary charge. **1/2 point**

For a conviction of felony murder (*i.e.,* second degree murder) to be sustained, it must be shown that the defendant or a co-felon, during the course of committing or attempting to commit an enumerated felony, killed a third party. There is no element of intent. The felony murder conviction may stand even if the predicate felony charge was dismissed for insufficient legal evidence. **1/2 point**

Had there been intent on the part of B as to killing V, it is only then that B could have been charged with murder in the first degree. A person may be convicted of first degree murder when during the commission of an enumerated felony, of which burglary is one, the perpetrator *intentionally* kills a nonparticipant in the course of the felony or in the immediate flight therefrom. Since the facts indicate that there was no intent on the part of B to kill V during the course of the burglary or flight therefrom, he can be charged only with murder in the second degree. **1/2 point**

Here, there was sufficient admissible evidence to support the murder conviction. V's dying declaration, as discussed above, is admissible to prove the homicide. This evidence is supported by the fact that B was caught speeding near V's store and close in time to the homicide. A jury could find that B wrongfully entered or remained in the dwelling with the intent to commit a crime and in the interim injured V, which resulted in his death. Thus, there is sufficient evidence to establish the second degree murder charge. **1/2 point**

ANSWER 80—REAL PROPERTY/MORTGAGES

(a)(1)   The issue is whether B validly assumed A's mortgage. **1/2 point**

If property subject to a mortgage is transferred to someone who assumes the mortgage, the transferee becomes the primary obligor, and the original mortgagor is only secondarily liable. Assumption of the mortgage requires that the transferee sign a written acknowledgment that he assumed the debt or that he sign the deed reciting assumption of the debt. **1 point**

In this case, B made no written acknowledgment that he assumed the debt. Also, although the deed transferring the property to B contained an assumption clause, B never signed the deed. Therefore, B did not assume the mortgage. A is primarily liable on the loan, and his defense is insufficient. The court should grant O's motion to dismiss A's affirmative defense. **1/2 point**

(2)   MORTGAGE NOT A LIEN

The issue is whether B had actual or record notice of the mortgage. **1/2 point**

New York's recording act protects a subsequent purchaser who records first if he purchased without actual or record notice of a prior conveyance or lien. The failure of a mortgagee to record his mortgage prior to a subsequent conveyance of the mortgaged property does not affect its validity. The mortgagee's lien on the property is still valid and can only be avoided by a subsequent bona fide purchaser for value without notice of the lien. **1 point**

B is not protected by the recording act. The deed from A to B specifically states that the transfer is subject to O's mortgage. Also, B paid A only $40,000 of the $48,000 sales price because of the $8,000 still due on the mortgage. Thus, since B obviously had actual notice of the mortgage, he cannot avoid the lien based on O's delay in recording. The court should grant O's motion to dismiss. **1/2 point**

LIABILITY FOR THE DEFICIENCY

The issue is whether a purchaser of land subject to a mortgage who does not assume the mortgage can be liable for a deficiency judgment. **1/2 point**

As stated in (1) above, to assume the mortgage, B would have had to sign the deed or some other written acknowledgment of assumption. Without an assumption, property transferred subject to a mortgage becomes the primary source for payment of the debt. The original mortgagor is liable on the bond; the transferee of the property is not personally liable on the bond. **1 point**

Since B never agreed in writing to assume the debt, he is not liable for any deficiency. However, the mortgage may be foreclosed, and this would effectively wipe out B's interest in the land. The court should deny O's motion to dismiss. **1/2 point**

(b)   The issue is whether O retained an implied easement. **1/2 point**

If a landowner sells a portion of his land, the existence of a use of the land prior to the sale may give rise to an easement by implication, even if no reference is made to the continuation of that use. To determine whether such an easement exists, the court considers the following factors: (i) whether the previous use had been apparent; and (ii) whether the parties expected that the use would survive division, because it is reasonably necessary to the dominant land's use and enjoyment. **1-1/2 points**

In this case, O's use of the paved road after the sale of the land was the same as his prior use. The prior use of the road was continuous, as O used that road almost exclusively. The use of the paved road would be apparent to someone inspecting the land; the fact that it was paved, maintained, and running across the land would at least put someone on notice of its use. Thus, the only problem is the last factor. O could use the dirt road running to the county highway. Although this is less convenient, it is probably not unreasonable, and thus the court may find no implied easement. **1 point**

No easement by prescription arose in O's favor either, because, as applied to B, O's use of the easement had not continued adverse, open, and notorious for the statutory period of 10 years. **1/2 point**

Therefore, O has no right to use the private road paved across B's property.

ANSWER 81—CORPORATIONS/CONTRACTS/NEW YORK PRACTICE

(1)(a)   The issue is whether a sale of substantially all of a corporation's assets may be approved by 40% of the shares. **1/2 point**

Under the New York Business Corporation Law, any sale, lease, exchange, or other disposition of all or substantially all of the corporation's assets, other than in the usual course of business actually conducted by the corporation, requires shareholder approval. The board of directors must first authorize the sale and then send their decision to the shareholders for approval. Proper notice of the vote must be given and for corporations formed after February 22, 1998, the proposal of sale must then be approved by a majority of all the shares entitled to vote. If the decision is passed by a majority, all dissenting shareholders have the right of appraisal, *i.e.,* to receive the fair market value for their shares. **1 point**

In this case, A, as president of ABC Corp., entered into an agreement with X for the sale of all of the corporation's assets including the corporate name. A brought the agreement before ABC's board of directors, consisting of A, B, and C. Each executed a valid waiver of notice. They decided to go ahead with the proposed sale and seek shareholder approval. **1 point**

A, B, C, and D were present at the shareholders' meeting and executed a valid waiver of notice. A and B, holding 40% of the shares, voted in favor of the sale and C and D, holding 60% of the shares, opposed. This tally does not meet the majority requirement needed to secure the sale under the BCL. **1/2 point**

Under the terms of the agreement, it will only become effective and binding if approved in accordance with the BCL. Here, a majority did not vote in favor of the sale, as is required by the BCL. Therefore, the agreement did not become effective and binding because it did not conform to the requirements of the BCL and the agreement. X has no rights against ABC Corp. **1 point**

(b)   The issue is whether the arbitration clause in the sale agreement is binding. **1/2 point**

The agreement specifically states that any disputes arising under the agreement will be settled by arbitration. A provision also says that the agreement will become effective and binding only if it is "authorized and approved as required by the New York Business Corporation Law." It is clear that the shareholders did not approve the sale by a majority vote, as is required by the BCL, and thus the agreement never became effective and binding. **1 point**

However, X is properly entitled to seek arbitration no matter what the grounds of his claim might be. **1/2 point**

(2)   The issue is when a cancellation is effective and what damages are available for breach of a land sale contract. **1/2 point**

X entered into a valid written agreement with A and B for the sale of their home. A provision in the agreement allowed X to cancel without liability if done within 10 days of execution. To validly exercise the right of cancellation granted within a contract, it must be received during the time period and in the manner set forth in the agreement. **1 point**

Here, the agreement specifically stated cancellation may be made within 10 days by written notice. X had until June 12 to cancel the agreement. His letter of cancellation was mailed to A and B *on* June 12. It could not possibly be received by A and B before the 10-day limitation ran. Thus, X's cancellation was ineffective. **1 point**

Typically, damages are measured by the difference between the contract price and the market value of the land on the date of breach. Under current New York case law, a vendor will be entitled to retain the down payment on the contract as liquidated damages if the down payment does not exceed 10% of the purchase price. **1 point**

In this case, X did not validly cancel the agreement to purchase A and B's house within the 10-day period. This caused X to breach the contract. Thus, A and B are entitled to liquidated damages due to X's breach and may retain the $15,000 down payment made by X. **1/2 point**

ANSWER 82—DOMESTIC RELATIONS/NEW YORK PRACTICE

(1)(a)   The issue is whether grounds for long arm jurisdiction were present. **1/2 point**

The CPLR long arm statute allows the exercise of personal jurisdiction over a nonresident party if: (i) the party to be affected had, at some time in the recent past, a connection with New York, and (ii) the party seeking support is a resident of or domiciled in the state at the time the claim is made. In this case, W, the party seeking support, is a resident of New York; thus, the only issue is whether H, the party to be affected, had a sufficient connection with New York. The statute lists the following sufficient connections: (i) New York was the matrimonial domicile of the parties at or about the time of their separation; (ii) the defendant abandoned the plaintiff in New York; or (iii) the claim accrued under the laws of New York or under an agreement executed in New York. [CPLR 302(b)] **1 point**

Under these facts, although H and W were married in New York, H left W while they were domiciled in New Jersey. They had been living in New Jersey for almost 10 years at the time of the separation. This does not qualify as "at or about" the time of separation. Thus, the court had no basis upon which to assert personal jurisdiction over H. **1/2 point**

Since the court lacked personal jurisdiction, it does not have the power to impose any personal obligations on H. This means that W could not seek and enforce a judgment for maintenance against H. **1/2 point**

(b)   The issue is whether the court had subject matter jurisdiction over the marital res (marital status) of the parties.

In an action for separation, the presence of property within the state at the time the defendant is served out of state is the basis for jurisdiction. The marriage itself is regarded as a res and, for jurisdictional purposes, is deemed located in the state where either party to the marriage is domiciled. Here, W is domiciled within the state and has served H out of state. This provides the court with a jurisdictional basis to determine the status of the marriage, making it improper for the court to dismiss W's entire complaint. The court, however, has no personal jurisdiction over H and cannot award maintenance. **1 point**

A matrimonial action can be heard before a New York court if:

(i)   The parties were married in New York and either party has been a resident for one year immediately preceding the action;

(ii)   The parties resided in New York as husband and wife and either party is a resident for one year immediately preceding the action;

(iii) The cause of action occurred in New York and either party has been a resident for one year prior to commencement of the action;

(iv) The cause of action occurred in New York and both parties are residents at the time of commencement of the action; or

(v)   Either party has been a resident of the state for a continuous period of at least two years preceding commencement of the action. **1 point**

The durational residency requirements are merely substantive elements of the matrimonial cause of action and do not limit the subject matter jurisdiction of the court to adjudicate the dispute. Therefore, although W resided in New York for less than six months, the court may hear W's case. **1/2 point**

(c)   The issue is whether W met the statutory residency requirements to maintain a cause of action for separation.

W's failure to satisfy the residency requirement *is* sufficient for the court to grant H's motion on the ground of failure to state a cause of action. As stated above, to allow a matrimonial action to be heard, a plaintiff must be a resident of New York for one year prior to commencement of the proceeding. Here, W was not a resident of New York for one year, thus her complaint is insufficient to meet the requirements to get to the New York courts. Therefore, the court was correct in granting H's motion. **1 point**

(2)   The issue is whether the motion for change of venue was proper.

Venue rules concern convenience rather than competence to hear the case. This means that improper venue in a court of competent jurisdiction does not affect the validity of the judgment. Also, wherever the plaintiff chooses venue will be deemed proper unless the defendant makes a motion alleging that venue is improper. In a marital action, proper would be a county in which one of the parties resides. Under the CPLR, a defendant may make a motion for change of venue "as of right" by serving prior to or contemporaneously with the answer a demand for a change of venue. If the plaintiff does not respond within five days, the defendant may, within 15 days, make a motion to the court for change of venue. The motion must be made in the original county, but if the plaintiff makes no objection to the demand, the motion may be made in the county to which transfer is sought. **1 point**

Here, W brought the action to the Supreme Court in Queens County. W is a resident of Suffolk County. H is a resident of Albany County. Therefore, under the CPLR, H has a basis for changing venue; he may make a motion "as of right" since Queens County is neither W's nor H's residence. H properly made a demand upon W for a change in venue. W did not respond to H's demand. Thus, H made a motion to the court for a change of venue to Albany County. Although he made the motion in Albany County, and not the county where the action was originally filed, W made no objection to the demand. Therefore, it was proper for H to make his motion for change of venue in Albany County, the place to which he wanted the case transferred. Thus, the court was correct in granting H's motion for change of venue. **1 point**

(3)   The issue is whether adultery is a ground that may be considered when determining maintenance or property distributions.

The Domestic Relations Law sets forth a list of criteria for the court to consider when awarding maintenance and distributing property under equitable distribution. The criteria generally guide the court in considering the "circumstances of the case and of the respective parties" in making its distribution of marital assets to the parties. One of the criteria under the statute is a "catch-all" provision which allows the court to use its discretion in considering additional factors that it deems "just and proper" even though not specifically set forth by the statute. This "catch-all" provision pertains to both maintenance and property distributions. **1 point**

Although the Court of Appeals has held that it is *not* "just and proper" to consider marital fault in awarding property distributions, it has not ruled on this issue with respect to maintenance. The prevailing view is that marital fault can be considered in determining maintenance awards.

In the present case, the court did not award W any property distribution or maintenance because of her adultery. The court erred in considering marital fault in denying W a property distribution. Conversely, the court could properly consider marital fault in determining W's maintenance, although it is unlikely that marital fault, in and of itself, unless egregious, would be upheld as a standard to deny a spouse maintenance entirely. **1 point**

ANSWER 83—COMMERCIAL PAPER/CONFLICT OF LAWS

(1)   At issue is whether a payee's infancy or the drawer's death is a defense to the drawer's duty to pay, and whether a drawee bank owes any duties to a holder to pay a check. **1/2 point**

Otis may recover from Larry's estate because there is no viable defense against Otis, a holder in due course ("HDC") of a negotiable instrument. **1/2 point**

A check is a negotiable instrument under the U.C.C., specifically, a draft. When a negotiable instrument is negotiated to an HDC, the HDC takes the instrument free of "personal" defenses (*i.e.,* most defenses) and is subject only to "real" defenses (*i.e.,* infancy, fraud in the factum, etc.). An HDC is a holder who takes an instrument for value, in good faith, and without notice that the instrument is overdue or has been dishonored, or of any defense or claim to it on the part of another person. A holder is a person in rightful possession of an instrument. Rightful possession requires all necessary indorsements plus delivery. **1-1/2 points**

Here, Otis is a holder of a check (negotiable order paper), since the check was transferred to him by Nancy and it contained all necessary indorsements (Nancy's—the payee). Moreover, Otis is an HDC since he took the check for value (in exchange for records and CDs) and he had no knowledge of any defenses (he had no knowledge of Nancy's defense of infancy because of her poise and demeanor). Therefore, Otis is subject only to real defenses. Death of the drawer is not a real defense; and even though infancy *is* a real defense, it is a defense that may be asserted only by the infant, Nancy. For this reason, Evan has no defense to the check. **1 point**

To hold a drawer liable for a check if the drawee bank refuses to pay, as Bogus Bank did here, the holder must present the check at the bank for payment and give the drawer notice of the bank's dishonor. Here, Otis satisfied these requirements. Therefore, Otis may recover the $600 for the check from Evan—the representative of Larry's estate. **1 point**

Otis cannot recover from Bogus Bank. Even though a bank has a duty to honor its customer's check, the duty is owed to the customer and not to the holder of the check. Thus, Otis has no rights against Bogus Bank. Note also, however, that Bogus Bank's dishonor of Larry's check was proper because a bank may stop honoring a customer's checks upon the customer's death, although it may honor a deceased customer's checks for up to 10 days after obtaining knowledge of the customer's death. Hence, the bank properly refused to honor the check. Thus, Otis can recover $600 from Evan, but nothing from Bogus Bank. **1 point**

(2)   The issue is which state's guest statute should apply. **1/2 point**

When faced with a conflict of law regarding loss distribution rules in a tort case, the Court of Appeals has rejected the old vested rights approach, which would mandate the automatic application of the law of the situs of the tort. Now, New York courts apply the *governmental interest analysis*. This is to ensure that the jurisdiction with the greatest interest in the suit has its law apply. In order to make the determination, the court will look at the factual contacts of each jurisdiction, the differing laws, and the underlying policies for each law; apply the facts to the policies; and apply the greater governmental interest. **2 points**

For tort cases, New York has refined the interest analysis in *Neumeier v. Kuehner*, 31 N.Y.2d 121 (1972). The *Neumeier* rules are a product of the governmental interest analysis. Since under the *Neumeier* rules this is an unprovided-for situation, when the law of the situs does not benefit a citizen of the situs, the law of the situs will control unless that would frustrate or significantly undermine an important policy of the outside jurisdiction. **1 point**

In this case there is no overriding reason why the law of New York should be applied instead of the law of Franklin. Indeed, the accident occurred in Franklin and, more importantly, Rose is from Franklin and would have an expectation that Franklin law would be applied. In addition, no policy of New York is hurt since there is no New York plaintiff. Accordingly, the law of Franklin will be applied and the court should deny Rose's motion. **1 point**

ANSWER 84—FEDERAL JURISDICTION & PROCEDURE/NEW YORK PRACTICE/ TORTS

(1)   The issue here is whether the court had personal jurisdiction over Rocker.

Rocker's pre-answer motion to dismiss Melanie's complaint is proper pursuant to Federal Rule of Civil Procedure 12(b)(ii). Rocker's motion raises two questions: (i) whether there is a basis upon which a New York court could exercise its judicial power over Rocker, and (ii) whether Rocker had proper notice of Melanie's action against him by virtue of proper service. **1 point**

A federal court may acquire personal jurisdiction over parties served outside the state in which the court is sitting under that state's statute and rules for extraterritorial service. [Fed. R. Civ. P. 4] New York's long arm statute [CPLR 302] grants personal jurisdiction to the New York courts over a non-domiciliary as to a cause of action arising from the transaction of any business within New York or contracting anywhere to supply goods or services within New York. The "contracting" provision of the statute is meant to reach one who, though never physically present in New York, agrees to supply goods or render services within New York. **1 point**

Rocker contracted to appear at Club Mystique in New York, thus satisfying the provisions of the long arm statute. That the contract was negotiated and executed in State B is irrelevant. **1/2 point**

As a basis for long arm jurisdiction is present, Rocker may be served with Melanie's summons and complaint outside New York in the same manner as service is made within the state. [CPLR 313] Thus, personal service of the summons and complaint upon Rocker at his home in State B by a State B attorney was proper, and sufficiently provided Rocker with notice of Melanie's suit against him. Consequently, the court improperly granted Rocker's motion. **1 point**

(2)   The issue is whether Melanie has proved tortious interference with a contract. **1/2 point**

A trial court may grant summary judgment only when there is no genuine issue of material fact and the moving party is entitled to judgment as a matter of law. If there are any disputed facts, the case must go to trial. [Fed. R. Civ. P. 56] **1/2 point**

Since the action here is apparently based on diversity, the federal court must apply New York State law—the law of the state in which it is sitting. Under New York law, an action for intentional interference with a contract may be maintained by showing that a person who, with knowledge of a contract, intentionally and without justification induced one of the parties to breach the contract. The person who interferes is responsible to the other party to the contract for any damage suffered as a result of the interference. **1-1/2 points**

Here, the facts show that Steve did not know of Melanie's contract with Rocker; thus, he did not know of Melanie's pecuniary interest in Rocker. Therefore, Melanie cannot prove she has a cause of action, and the court improperly granted her motion for summary judgment. **1/2 point**

(3)   The issue here is whether Sheryl's complaint sufficiently stated a cause of action for negligence. **1/2 point**

Melanie, rather than submit an answer to the complaint, chose to make a motion to dismiss Sheryl's complaint pursuant to CPLR 3211. The ground asserted, that of failure to state a cause of action, proceeds on the theory that even if all of the allegations of the complaint are taken as true, there are no grounds for any relief to the pleader. The focus when this motion is made is on the adequacy of the claim as stated in the complaint. **1/2 point**

Taking all of Sheryl's allegations as true, her complaint does state a cause of action in negligence against Melanie. A cause of action for negligence requires a showing: (i) that the defendant owed a duty of care to a foreseeable plaintiff; (ii) that the defendant breached that duty; (iii) that the breach of that duty was a cause-in-fact and the proximate cause; (iv) of the plaintiff's injuries. **1 point**

Here, Sheryl alleged that Club Mystique was located in a high-crime area. This fact created a duty upon Melanie to provide adequate security measures for the protection of foreseeable customers, such as Sheryl, from harm. Melanie breached that duty by removing the metal detector from the entrance to Club Mystique. But for the fact that the metal detector was removed, Tony could not have slipped the switchblade into Club Mystique concealed under his jacket. As a result, Sheryl sustained personal injuries, a stab wound. Whether or not the intervening criminal act of Tony was sufficient to relieve Melanie of liability is a question for trial and is not relevant in deciding Melanie's motion. Therefore, the court improperly granted Melanie's motion to dismiss. **1-1/2 points**

ANSWER 85—EVIDENCE

(1)   The issue here is whether the New York Dead Man's Act operates to preclude Paula from testifying as to the color of the traffic light and/or David's intoxication. **1/2 point**

Under the New York Dead Man's Act [CPLR 4519], a party or person interested in the action cannot testify to a personal transaction or communication with a deceased when the testimony is offered against the representative or successor in interest of the deceased. This includes every method by which a person can derive impressions or information from the conduct, condition, or language of others. An exception within the Act provides that a survivor of a motor vehicle accident may testify to *facts* concerning that accident pertaining to the negligence or contributory negligence of the deceased. **1 point**

Paula should have been permitted to testify as to the color of the traffic signal at the time of the accident because that information was purely factual in nature. In contrast, Paula was properly not permitted to testify as to David's state of intoxication. Paula's opinion derived from the conduct, condition, or language of David and therefore constituted a "transaction or communication." **1/2 point**

[*Note:* Credit would most likely be given upon demonstrating knowledge of the Act and arguing that the smell of alcohol, slurring of speech, and unsteady gait are factual in nature.]

(2)   The issues here are whether the New York Dead Man's Act prevents Wayne, a nonparty witness, from testifying as to his observations of the accident; and whether Wayne, a lay witness, is competent to testify as to his opinion regarding David's intoxication. **1/2 point**

The New York Dead Man's Act only prevents those persons who are ***interested*** in the action from testifying as to communications or transactions with the deceased. A person is interested in the event if he stands to lose or gain by the judgment at the time the witness seeks to testify. Wayne is not interested in the action because he did not stand to gain or lose by the judgment at the time of trial. Moreover, seeing David's truck enter the intersection against the red light is purely a factual matter. **1 point**

Finally, although a lay witness cannot generally give opinion testimony, exceptions are made when, as a result of the nature of the subject matter, no better evidence can be obtained. In New York, a lay witness may give opinion testimony as to whether a person was intoxicated. The court was correct. **1/2 point**

(3)   The issue here is whether Cathy may presently testify regarding David's former testimony at the prior criminal proceeding, as an exception to the rule against hearsay. **1/2 point**

Former testimony constitutes hearsay. It is a statement, other than one made by the declarant while testifying at trial, offered in evidence for its truth. Such evidence is inadmissible, absent a recognized exception. However, former testimony is admissible if it was given under oath, the declarant is presently unavailable, and there is sufficient similarity of the parties and issues. Identity of the parties requires that the party against whom the testimony is offered must have been a party, or in privity with a party, in the prior action in which the testimony was given. This is to ensure that the party against whom the testimony is presently offered had an adequate opportunity to cross-examine the witness in the prior proceeding. **1/2 point**

The former testimony of David was given under oath. David is presently unavailable, as he is deceased. There is identity of subject matter, as the prior criminal proceeding and the present civil action concern the same motor vehicle accident. However, there is no identity of parties. Paula, the party against whom the testimony is offered, was not a party in the criminal proceeding. Paula did not have an opportunity to cross-examine David's testimony in that proceeding. Therefore, Cathy should not be allowed to testify as to David's prior testimony and the court was incorrect. **1/2 point**

(4)   The issue here is whether Neil is competent to testify regarding Wayne's poor reputation for truth and veracity in the community. **1/2 point**

A witness may be impeached by a showing that he has a poor reputation for truthfulness and veracity. This may be established by asking persons from the same community as the witness about his reputation for truth and veracity in that community. Here, Evelyn's attorney established that Neil was competent to testify as to Wayne's reputation for truth and veracity in the community. Neil testified that he and Wayne lived in the same community, and that Neil knew Wayne's reputation for veracity in that community. The court properly permitted Neil to testify in this regard. **1 point**

(5)   The issue here is whether a reputation witness may testify to prior bad acts of the party being attacked. **1/2 point**

The credibility of a witness may be impeached by inquiring into specific instances of bad acts in which the witness previously engaged. This method of impeachment, however, is limited to cross-examination of the witness. Extrinsic evidence is not admissible to prove that the witness engaged in specific instances of misconduct and is therefore unworthy of belief. Therefore, the court properly precluded Neil from testifying about previous instances during which Wayne had lied to Neil. **1 point**

(6)   The issue is whether the Dead Man's Statute prevents Paula from rebutting her opponent's case. **1/2 point**

A witness who is otherwise prohibited by the New York Dead Man's Statute from testifying to a transaction or communication with a decedent, may so testify when the opponent of the testimony "opens the door" regarding the subject matter of that testimony. Notwithstanding that the court's Ruling (3) was erroneous, Evelyn's attorney, by offering the former testimony of David on behalf of the estate, waived the protection afforded by the statute. The interested party, Paula, may now testify regarding the same subject matter. Thus, the court was incorrect. **1 point**

ANSWER 86—CONTRACTS (SALES)

(1)   The issue presented is whether the contract between Daisy and Rose is void for indefiniteness. **1/2 point**

Under the common law, the essential terms of an agreement must be definite and certain in order to be binding. In this case, the quantity of bulbs being sold is unstated in the letter agreement. Therefore, under the common law the letter agreement would be void for indefiniteness. **1 point**

However, since the transaction between Daisy and Rose involves a sale of goods, the more liberal standards of the Uniform Commercial Code are applicable to this transaction. Section 2-306(a) of the U.C.C. provides that when a purported agreement specifies that the quantity of goods to be sold in a transaction will be measured in terms of "requirements," the term "requirements" is to be interpreted as the actual good faith requirements needed by the buyer, except that no quantity unreasonably disproportionate to any stated estimate or otherwise comparable prior requirements may be demanded. The quantity of tulip bulbs involved in the instant transaction is therefore capable of being made certain by reference to objective extrinsic facts. Therefore, the letter agreement between Rose and Daisy is not indefinite pursuant to the specifications of the U.C.C., and is enforceable. **2-1/2 points**

(2)(a)   At issue are the grounds for unconscionability. **1/2 point**

The basic test for determining the unconscionability of a contract is whether in light of the general commercial background and needs of the particular parties, the clause or clauses involved are so one-sided as to be unconscionable under the circumstances existing at the time of the making of the contract. A contract or contract provision that is held by a court to be unconscionable will not be enforced. **1-1/2 points**

The contract that Rose and Daisy entered into appears to have been reasonable at the time it was made. There was no indication at the time the contract was executed that the price being set for the tulips was unconscionable. Therefore, the agreement is not void for unconscionability. **1 point**

(b)   The issue is whether the mutual mistake as to the nature of the goods being supplied by Daisy renders the agreement void. **1/2 point**

Generally, mistakes as to the value of the subject matter will not be remedied by the court. However, a contract that is based on a fundamental mutual mistake of fact which results in a material effect on the agreed-upon exchange of performance, is voidable by the adversely affected party. The courts will investigate the facts of a particular case to determine whether the parties assumed the risk of the mistake in question when they negotiated their agreement. **1-1/2 points**

In the instant case, both Rose and Daisy were unaware of the nature of the tulips that were being grown at Lily's greenhouse. Since the subject matter of their contract was domestic tulips and the tulips that were in fact being exchanged were an extremely rare breed of tulips from Southern Mongolia, the contract was grounded on a fundamental mutual mistake of fact. Therefore, the contract will be deemed voidable upon Daisy's request. **1 point**

ANSWER 87—CRIMINAL LAW

(1) At issue is what crimes Joe and Hal can be charged with. **1/3 point**

Criminal solicitation occurs when one person solicits another to engage in criminal conduct. Under New York Penal Law section 100.20, a person is not guilty of solicitation if the solicitation constitutes conduct that is necessarily incidental to the commission of the substantive crime. Here, Joe solicited Hal to steal Elsie. Because the solicitation is separate and apart from the attempt to steal Elsie, Joe may be charged with solicitation. **1 point**

Conspiracy occurs when two or more individuals agree to engage in a crime and commit an overt act in furtherance of their conspiracy. A conspiracy charge does not merge into another charge. Joe and Hal agreed to engage in a burglary. In furtherance of their plan, they committed overt acts of driving to Ed's cattle and horse ranch and searching the barn for Elsie. Therefore, they can both be charged with conspiracy. **1 point**

Larceny occurs when a person, with intent to deprive another of property, wrongfully takes such property from an owner. When the property is worth less than $1,000, the individual is guilty of petit larceny. Attempt occurs when an act is done with the intention of committing a crime, but the act falls short of completing the crime. Attempt requires an overt act beyond mere preparation for the offense. Factual impossibility is not a defense to attempt. **1/3 point**

Here, Hal and Joe drove to the ranch and searched for Elsie with the intent to steal her. They were unsuccessful because Elsie was elsewhere. Searching for Elsie was a sufficient overt act for attempt. Because Elsie was worth less than $1,000, the attempted crime was petit larceny. It is no defense that Elsie was elsewhere (and so, in fact, could not be successfully stolen) because this is mere factual impossibility. **1/3 point**

Burglary in the second degree occurs when a person knowingly enters a building with intent to commit a crime, and when he or another participant is armed with a deadly weapon or causes physical injury to any person who is not a participant in the crime. Both Hal and Joe can be charged with burglary. A barn constitutes a building. The fact that Hal was unaware that Joe was armed with a deadly weapon is not a successful defense for Hal, as Hal intended to steal Elsie. Furthermore, it is not a defense that Joe had access to the barn as a part of his job. Joe was only authorized to enter the barn from 9-5 on Monday through Friday. He was not authorized to enter it on the weekend, and the crime here took place on Sunday. **1 point**

One of the several ways a person can be guilty of murder in the first degree is when during the commission of an enumerated felony, of which burglary is one, the perpetrator *intentionally* kills a non-participant in the course of the felony or in the immediate flight therefrom. Joe's shooting of Ed at point-blank range could demonstrate the requisite intent to kill. Therefore, Joe can be charged with murder in the first degree. **1 point**

Hal cannot properly be charged with murder in the first degree. As a result of the wording of the New York statute, an accomplice in the underlying felony would not be guilty of murder in the first degree unless the accomplice also shared the requisite intent to kill the victim. Without a showing of such intent on the part of the accomplice there can be no liability under the statute. The facts indicate that Hal was unaware that Joe was armed and had expressly conditioned his participation on no violence being perpetrated. Thus, it is clear that Hal did not have the intent to kill Ed and accordingly cannot be charged with murder in the first degree. **1 point**

A person is guilty of murder in the second degree when, with intent to cause the death of another, he causes such death. Joe can be charged with murder in the second degree for the intentional killing of Ed. There is enough evidence to conclude that Joe had the requisite intent to kill Ed when he shot him point blank. **1/3 point**

A person is guilty of manslaughter in the first degree when, with intent to cause serious physical injury to another person, he causes the death of such person. Since it is not completely clear whether Joe intended to kill Ed, Joe can properly be charged with first degree manslaughter as a possible alternative to a conviction for murder in the second degree. **1/3 point**

Hal cannot be properly charged with murder in the second degree because there is no basis for concluding that Hal intended to cause Ed's death. Hal was unaware that Joe was armed and had, in fact, agreed to steal Elsie only on the express condition that no violence would be involved in the commission of that crime. **1/3 point**

Felony murder occurs when a person, alone or with another, commits a specified felony and, in the course of the felony, he or another participant causes the death of a person other than a participant. In this case Joe and Hal were engaged in a burglary. Burglary is a specified felony. Since Ed was killed as Hal and Joe attempted to leave the site of the burglary, they can both be charged with felony murder. It is not necessary to show that each participant in the felony had the requisite intent to kill in order to properly charge him with felony murder. It is simply necessary that each felon have the intent to commit the underlying felony. Therefore, it is no defense to Hal that he had no intent to kill Ed, as he intended to commit the burglary. **1 point**

Thus, Joe can be charged with criminal solicitation, conspiracy, attempted petit larceny, burglary, murder in the first degree, intentional murder in the second degree, and felony murder. Hal can be charged with conspiracy, attempted petit larceny, burglary, and felony murder.

(2) The issue is whether Hal has a plausible affirmative defense to the felony murder charge. **1/2 point**

A participant can successfully assert a defense to a felony murder charge if he can establish that he: (i) did not commit or aid in the commission of the homicidal act; (ii) was not armed with a deadly weapon; (iii) did not reasonably believe any of the other participants to be armed with a deadly weapon; and (iv) did not reasonably believe that any other participant intended to engage in conduct likely to result in death or serious physical injury. Here, Hal was unaware that Joe was armed, and only agreed to participate in the felony on the condition that no violence would be used. Therefore, he is entitled to assert a defense to felony murder. **1-1/2 points**

ANSWER 88—CORPORATIONS

ACTION I

The issue presented is whether the directors violated their fiduciary duty to the shareholders when they sold their shares to Bump. **1/2 point**

Controlling shareholders in a corporation who also constitute management have a fiduciary duty to refrain from benefiting themselves at the expense of minority shareholders. In the instant case, Frump's directors succeeded in negotiating a deal whereby Bump modified its original offer from buying *all* outstanding shares of Frump stock for $500 per share to buying only the directors' controlling interest at the higher price of $550 per share. This is indicative of a violation of their fiduciary duty to the other shareholders. The directors were unjustly enriched and must disgorge the $50 per share profit they made over what Bump would have paid them for their shares if they had not diverted a corporate opportunity from the rest of the shareholders. **2 points**

Arguably, the "profit" to be disgorged could be the difference between the $550 per share that was initially paid to the directors and the $450 that was offered to buy the minority shares when the merger was completed. However, if that transaction were to be upheld in court, and the minority shares were worth more than $450, the minority shareholders could also obtain relief by initiating an appraisal proceeding. Any shareholder of a New York corporation entitled to vote who does not assent to a merger or consolidation of the corporation is entitled to exercise her appraisal rights, which require that the shareholder be paid the fair market value of her shares. **1-1/2 points**

ACTION II

(i)   The issue presented is whether a corporation can redeem its stock. **1/2 point**

A corporation may repurchase its stock from shareholders. Repurchase of stock, however, is subject to certain limitations: the corporation may not be rendered insolvent by the repurchase, nor may the repurchase be effected for an improper purpose. In the instant case, there is no reason to believe that the stocks are being repurchased for any improper purpose, such as a greenmail attempt, or that the repurchase will render the corporation insolvent. Therefore, the repurchase of 10,000 shares of Frump stock was proper. **1-1/2 points**

(ii)   The issue presented is what are the requirements for shareholder approval of a merger. **1/2 point**

A merger of two corporations formed after February 22, 1998, must be approved by a majority of each corporation. Here, the shareholders of Bump unanimously approved the merger, and in Frump, the requisite number of votes was received in favor of the merger. The 80,000 shares constituted more than a majority of the outstanding stock of 150,000 shares. (Note that the 10,000 shares that have been redeemed for Frump's treasury cannot be voted.) Thus, the merger was properly approved. **1-1/2 points**

(iii) The issue presented is whether a merger must have a legitimate purpose. **1/2 point**

A merger must have a legitimate purpose, even if approved by the requisite number of shares. A freeze-out of minority voters is not a legitimate purpose. Since the stated purpose for the merger of Frump and Bump was to reduce the number of shareholders in Frump, the merger was unlawful. Additionally, even if the merger were lawful, all shareholders must be treated fairly. In this case, there is a question as to whether the minority shareholders were in fact treated fairly, since they only received $450 per share. **1-1/2 points**

ANSWER 89—EVIDENCE

(1)   The issue is whether a withdrawn guilty plea in a criminal action is admissible in a civil action arising out of the same transaction as the criminal action. **1/2 point**

The plea of guilty is a direct acknowledgment that the defendant committed a crime, whether the one charged or a reduced version thereof. Although New York does not allow a withdrawn guilty plea to be used as an admission in subsequent criminal proceedings, New York does allow a withdrawn guilty plea to be used as an admission in a subsequent *civil* proceeding arising out of the same facts. Therefore, even though Jack's guilty plea was withdrawn, the court should have ruled it admissible. **1 point**

(2)   The issue is whether a statement to a doctor regarding who started a fight that caused injuries is admissible under the business records exception. **1/2 point**

Hearsay is an out-of-court statement offered to prove the truth of the matter asserted. Two levels of hearsay are involved in the records: Don's statements and the records themselves. Both statements must be admissible in order to admit the hospital records. Don's statements are admissions of a party opponent and, therefore, as explained above, are admissible. The hospital record itself, however, does not fall within any exception to the rule against hearsay. **1/2 point**

The most plausible hearsay exception for the hospital entry is the business records exception. The exception permits admission of business records that are made in the regular course of business. In the case of hospital records, only entries related to diagnosis and treatment of the patient are considered to be within the hospital's business. The entries here do not fall within the exception because the manner in which the brawl broke out is irrelevant to Don's treatment. Therefore, the court correctly suppressed the hospital records. **1 point**

(3)   The issue is whether a written record of an admission made by a witness who heard it can be admitted into evidence when the witness cannot independently recall hearing the admission. **1/2 point**

Again, there are two levels of hearsay here, and both levels are admissible. Don's statement is admissible as an admission as discussed above and the hospital record is admissible under the past recollection recorded exception to the rule against hearsay. **1/2 point**

When a witness states that he has insufficient recollection of an event to enable him to testify fully and accurately, even after consulting a writing given to him on the stand to refresh his memory, the writing may be introduced as testimonial evidence if the witness had personal knowledge of the facts recited in the writing and he made or adopted the writing when the matter was fresh in his mind. **1 point**

The necessary elements for this exception are present here. Lance cannot recall Don's statement, but he probably wrote it down in the hospital record as soon as Don made the statement to him. Thus, Lance had personal knowledge of the facts in the record and he made the record when the matter was fresh in his mind. Therefore, the evidence should have been admitted. **1 point**

Note also that Don's statement does not fall within the physician-patient privilege for two reasons: First, Don waived the privilege by putting his physical condition in issue by bringing this action. Second, even if Don had not waived the privilege, it would not apply here because the privilege applies only to information related to diagnosis and treatment, and, as stated above, Don's statements were irrelevant to that issue. **1/2 point**

(4)   The issue is whether a certified transcript of an acquittal from criminal charges is admissible in a civil action arising from the same transaction as the criminal action. Two subissues are involved: Is the transcript within an exception to the hearsay rule (since it is being offered to prove the truth of the matter asserted), and, if so, is it otherwise admissible? **1/2 point**

A transcript is generally admissible under the hearsay exception for official records. Certified records of judgments are admissible as proof that the judgment was entered. Nevertheless, a record of an acquittal is inadmissible because a much stricter standard is used in criminal cases than in civil cases. An acquittal means that the state could not prove guilt beyond a reasonable doubt, and this has little bearing on whether a civil litigant can prove the more lenient burden of guilt (liability) by a preponderance of the evidence. Therefore, the acquittal was inadmissible, as the court ruled. **1 point**

(5)   The issue is whether a witness's specific instances of misconduct can be raised on cross-examination. **1/2 point**

The general rule is that a witness's credibility can be attacked on cross-examination by raising any immoral, criminal, or vicious act of his life that may affect his character and show him unworthy of belief. A conviction resulting from the bad acts is not required; although there must be some reasonable ground to believe that the witness committed the act. Here, Jack was acquitted. Moreover, there were not two brawls and thus the question was not asked in good faith. Furthermore, whether Jack was involved in other barroom brawls does not bear on whether he is worthy of belief. Therefore, the court was correct in sustaining the objection to the question. **1 point**

ANSWER 90—WILLS

RIGHTS OF MARCUS AND SIDNEY IN THE $35,000 BANK ACCOUNT

The issue here is whether Tessa effectively devised the Totten trust account to Marcus in her will. **1/2 point**

Tessa's account at the Spendthrift Savings & Loan is a Totten trust account. The account was opened by Tessa in trust for Sidney. To revoke, modify, or alter a Totten trust by will, the will must refer to the particular trust account as being in trust for a named beneficiary in the named financial institution. These requirements are strictly construed and the courts require full compliance. Assuming the trust is not revoked, modified, or altered, the named beneficiary's rights vest at the time of the depositor's death if the trustee survives the depositor. **1 point**

Here, Tessa's will purported to devise to Marcus the money in the Totten trust account. This purported bequest, however, fails because Tessa's will did not specifically revoke the Totten trust—it did not refer to the specific account, named beneficiary, and financial institution. Mere reference to an account at the Spendthrift Savings & Loan is insufficient. Therefore, Sidney is the lawful beneficiary of the Totten trust account and is entitled to the $35,000 contained therein. Sidney's rights vested at the time of Tessa's death. **1/2 point**

RIGHTS OF PAUL AND DEBBIE IN THE MONET PAINTINGS

The issue is whether Tessa made a valid inter vivos gift of the paintings to Debbie. **1/2 point**

Under New York law, an inter vivos gift is made if: (i) the donor manifests an intent to make an immediate gift (not a gift to take effect upon donor's death); (ii) the gift was actually or constructively delivered to the donee; and (iii) the donee accepted the gift. Each of these elements must be proved by clear and convincing evidence. **1 point**

Tessa manifested the requisite donative intent. The letter makes clear that Tessa intended to make a present transfer of ownership in the paintings to Debbie. The clear intent from the letter is that she wished to retain a life estate in the paintings herself, but immediately transfer the remainder interest to

Debbie. In New York, a life estate and a remainder can be created in a chattel the same as in real property. [*See* Gruen v. Gruen, 68 N.Y.2d 48 (1986)] **1/2 point**

The next issue is whether valid delivery occurred. Since Tessa retained a life estate in the paintings, physical delivery of the paintings to Debbie does not make sense. Thus, we must look to see whether Tessa's actions constituted symbolic or constructive delivery sufficient to divest her of dominion or control over the property. The acts that constitute sufficient delivery depend on the individual circumstances of the case. Here, where the donor retains a life estate and is parting only with title, an instrument of gift, such as the letter, is sufficient delivery. Lastly, Debbie must have accepted the gift. When, as here, the gift is of value to the donee, the law presumes acceptance. **1 point**

Thus, there was a valid gift of the paintings to Debbie (with a retained life estate in Tessa) in June 1994. While the 1996 will is evidence that Tessa may have changed her mind about the gift, it does not change the fact that the gift was made. Nothing in the letter suggests that the gift is revocable. A valid gift was made to Debbie and cannot be changed by an alternate disposition in Tessa's will. Since the paintings were not in Tessa's estate at her death, the specific bequest to Paul is adeemed; *i.e.*, it fails. Paul takes nothing. **1/2 point**

RIGHTS OF JOHN, SIDNEY, AND DEBBIE IN THE STOCK

At issue are the effects of a stock split and stock dividend on stock given as a general legacy. **1/2 point**

For purposes of ademption, a gift of stock in a publicly traded corporation is classified as a general legacy absent language indicating a contrary intention. However, such a gift is treated as a specific bequest (regardless of whether the possessive pronoun "my" is used) in the case of stock splits. Therefore, upon the death of the testator, a devise of stock will include not only the original shares, but also any and all stock acquired through stock splits occurring after the will is executed. However, a bequest of stock does not include stock acquired through stock dividends absent evidence of testamentary intent indicating otherwise. Stock dividends are considered capitalization of accumulated profits. **1 point**

Therefore John is entitled to the 300 shares Tessa purchased in November 1994 and the 300 shares Tessa received in October 1996 as a result of the stock split. The 50 shares received by Tessa in November 1998 as stock dividends become a part of the residuary estate, which will be shared by Sidney and Debbie equally. **1/2 point**

RIGHTS OF LEON, SIDNEY, AND DEBBIE IN THE $75,000 BEQUEST

The issue here is whether the subsequent divorce of a beneficiary who is related to the testator only through marriage affects the gift to the beneficiary under the will. **1/2 point**

Under New York law, if, after executing a will, the testator "is divorced, his marriage is annulled, or the marriage is dissolved on the grounds of absence, incest, or bigamy" any testamentary disposition to the former spouse is revoked. [EPTL §5-1.4] This rule, however, revokes only testamentary dispositions to a person to whom the testator was married. A bequest to the spouse of a sibling or offspring is not revoked if after execution of the will the sibling or offspring and spouse divorce. **1/2 point**

Tessa's description of Leon as her son-in-law cannot be interpreted as a condition precedent requiring Leon to remain married to Debbie to be entitled to the gift. The use of the phrase "son-in-law" is merely descriptive to help identify the intended beneficiary. It is not an expression of intent that the beneficiary must continue to fit that description to receive the bequest. Therefore, Leon is entitled to receive $75,000. **1/2 point**

RIGHTS OF SIDNEY AND DEBBIE IN THE REMAINDER OF TESSA'S ESTATE

The issue is to determine what Sidney and Debbie will receive under the residuary clause of Tessa's will. **1/2 point**

Under the residuary clause of Tessa's will, Sidney and Debbie will share in the remainder of Tessa's $750,000 estate not otherwise bequeathed to the other devisees under the will. **1/2 point**

ANSWER 91—CONTRACTS (SALES)

(a)(1)   The issue is whether the parties' agreement violated the Statute of Frauds. **1/2 point**

When dealing with a contract for the sale of goods, the question of the enforceability of the contract will be governed by the Uniform Commercial Code ("U.C.C."). To be enforceable under the U.C.C. Statute of Frauds, a contract for the sale of goods for the price of $500 or more must be evidenced by "some writing sufficient to indicate that a contract of sale has been made between the parties and signed by the party against whom enforcement is sought or by his authorized agent or broker." [N.Y. U.C.C. §2-201(1)] **1 point**

While Fashion Coordinates wrote a letter stating that a contract had been made between the parties, the letter did not meet the requirements of section 2-201(1) because the letter was not signed by X, the party to be charged. **1/2 point**

However, specially manufactured goods are exempted from the requirements of section 2-201(1) under certain circumstances. A contract may be enforceable if the goods are to be specially manufactured for the buyer and are not suitable for sale to others in the ordinary course of the seller's business, and the seller, before notice of repudiation is received and under circumstances reasonably indicating that the goods are for the buyer, has made either a substantial beginning of their manufacture or commitments for their procurement. **1/2 point**

Here, Fashion Coordinates ordered the material specifically for the manufacture of the sweat suits and manufactured eight of the suits prior to X's repudiation of the contract. Thus, there was an enforceable contract between Fashion Coordinates and X because the requirements of the U.C.C. Statute of Frauds were met. **1/2 point**

(2)   The issue is whether the nondelivery of the goods by October 16 constituted a breach of contract that would prevent Fashion from obtaining damages. **1/2 point**

New York U.C.C. section 2-615(a) provides that delay in delivery or nondelivery by a seller who complies with the statutory notice requirement is not a breach of his duty under a contract for sale if performance "has been made impracticable by the occurrence of a contingency the nonoccurrence of which was a basic assumption on which the contract was made." The seller must notify the buyer "seasonably that there will be delay or nondelivery." [N.Y. U.C.C. §2-615(c)] **1 point**

Fashion's failure to obtain the required material from Y in time to manufacture the sweat suits by October 16 constituted "the occurrence of a contingency the nonoccurrence of which was a basic assumption on which the contract was made." Fashion and X know that Y was the only importer in the United States of the special material and they assumed that Y would be able to supply a sufficient quantity of the material in time for Fashion to complete manufacture by October 16. Fashion complied with the statute by seasonably notifying X that there would be a delay. Therefore, the late delivery did not constitute a breach of the contract. Fashion may recover damages due to X's breach. **1 point**

It should be noted that if X contested the delay in delivery to be material, he could, upon receipt of Fashion's notice, have terminated and thereby discharged any unexecuted portion of the contract by written notice to Fashion. **1/2 point**

(b)   The issue is the amount of damages to which Fashion is entitled. **1/2 point**

X's repudiation of the contract gave Fashion the right to stop manufacture of the additional sweat suits and resell the completed suits and extra material in a commercially reasonable manner. [N.Y. U.C.C. §§2-703(d), 2-704(2), 2-706] **1/2 point**

Upon resale, Fashion was entitled to recover as damages the difference between the resale price and the contract price, plus incidental damages, less any expenses Fashion saved as a consequence of X's breach. [N.Y. U.C.C. §§2-706, 2-710] **1/2 point**

Fashion resold at private sale and gave X "reasonable notification of her intention to resell." [N.Y. U.C.C. §2-706(3)] Since Fashion made the resale in good faith and in a "commercially reasonable" manner, Fashion does not have to show that the resale was made at market price in order to recover the differences between the resale price and the contract price. [N.Y. U.C.C. §2-706(2); *and see* President Container, Inc. v. Patinco, 82 A.D. 879 (1981)] **1 point**

Fashion resold the eight sweat suits (with a contract price of $6,000) for $4,000, incurring $500 in shipping costs due to the resale. Fashion also sold $2,000 worth of material for its scrap value of $100. Fashion saved manufacturing expenses of $2,000 by not manufacturing the four remaining sweat suits after X's repudiation of the contract. **1 point**

Thus, the damages Fashion would be entitled to would be calculated as follows: Fashion is entitled to recover the difference between the resale price ($4,100) and the contract price ($9,000), plus the shipping costs ($500), less the manufacturing expenses saved as a result of the breach ($2,000), for total damages of $3,400. **1/2 point**

ANSWER 92—CRIMINAL LAW/CRIMINAL PROCEDURE/CONSTITUTIONAL LAW

(1)   The issue is whether the elements of the three crimes are met. **1/2 point**

(a)   Burglary is knowingly and unlawfully entering or remaining in a building with the intent to commit a crime therein. Tom and Ned knowingly entered into the museum unlawfully, with the intent to commit the crime of larceny. It is burglary in the second degree because, while in the museum, they injured Wally, a person not a participant in the crime. [P.L. §140.25] Peter, the lookout accomplice, intentionally aided in the commission of the crime and should be convicted as a principal. [P.L. §20.00; People v. Jackson, 44 N.Y.2d 935 (1978)] Thus, the burglary in the second degree charge can be established against Tom, Ned, and Peter. **2 points**

(b)   Robbery is forcible stealing, defined as committing a larceny in which physical force is used upon another against resistance to the taking of the property. [P.L. §160.00] Tom and Ned forcibly stole property by using force to overpower Wally, and tied him up to prevent his resisting the larceny of the paintings and money. It is robbery in the second degree because Tom and Ned each aided the other in the commission of the robbery and because they physically injured Wally. [P.L. §160.10] Peter can be convicted as a principal because he intentionally participated in the crime as lookout. It was foreseeable that the museum would have a watchman who would have to be subdued to prevent resistance to the crime. Thus, the elements of robbery in the second degree can be established from the facts against all three defendants. **2 points**

(c)   Kidnapping in the second degree is the abduction of another person. Abduction is the restraint of a person with intent to prevent his liberation by secreting or holding him in a place where he is not likely to be found. Wally was abducted because he was bound, put in the trunk of Peter's car, and driven away from the museum. The restraint of Wally consisted of moving him from one place to another and confining him against his will with the knowledge that the restriction was unlawful. [P.L. §§135.00, 135.20] There is no merger of the crimes of robbery and kidnapping because the robbery was consummated by the forcible stealing of the money and paintings before the commencement of the kidnapping. [People v. Smith, 47 N.Y.2d 83 (1979)] Hence, the elements of kidnapping in the second degree can be established against all of the accused. **2 points**

Therefore, the elements of all three crimes are met as to all three defendants.

(2)   The issue is whether the court should suppress the leather bag and the five paintings. **1/2 point**

The Fourth Amendment to the United States Constitution and Article 1, section 12 of the New York Constitution protect the privacy interests of the people and require that all searches and seizures be reasonable. For a search by a police officer to be reasonable, it must be conducted pursuant to a warrant or within one of the exceptions to the warrant requirement, such as the "automobile" exception. Warrantless searches under the automobile exception are valid because there is a reduced expectation of privacy with respect to automobiles and their use. [People v. Belton, 55 N.Y.2d 49 (1982)] **1 point**

It is proper to set up a sobriety roadblock as long as every automobile is stopped and the driver checked for signs of intoxication. [Delaware v. Prouse, 440 U.S. 648 (1979); People v. Scott, 63 N.Y.2d 518 (1984)] It is also proper in connection with such a stop to check driver licenses and registrations. [People v. Scanlon, 59 A.D.2d 788 (1977)] **1/2 point**

After Jack had been informed that the museum had been burglarized and seeing that Peter's car had come from the direction of the museum and further seeing the leather bag in plain view, he had a reasonable suspicion that the bag contained the fruits of a crime. When Jack found that the bag was marked "New York Art Museum," he had probable cause to open the bag and examine its contents. [People v. John BB, 56 N.Y.2d 482 (1982)] **1 point**

Once Jack discovered that the bag was filled with cash, it was reasonable to search the rest of the vehicle for other stolen goods. [People v. Coffey, 12 N.Y.2d 443 (1963)] Hence, the five paintings in the trunk should not be suppressed. Therefore, both motions to suppress must be denied. **1/2 point**

ANSWER 93—DOMESTIC RELATIONS

(a)(1)   The issue is whether Jane had a cause of action against Tom for annulment. **1/2 point**

A marriage may be annulled for fraud if the fraud or misrepresentation is material or relates to something vital to the marriage. The fraud must be of the type that would deceive an ordinary person. [Boardman's New York Family Law, §181] These requirements have been held to be satisfied where one fraudulently promises to convert to the religion of the spouse to induce that spouse to enter into the marriage. [N.Y. Dom. Rel. Law §991] However, in this case, Tom had planned on converting when they were married but *later* changed his mind. **1-1/2 points**

A marriage will not be annulled for fraud if the parties voluntarily cohabited as husband and wife with knowledge of the facts constituting fraud. [N.Y. Dom. Rel. Law §140(e)] Before the action was commenced, and after Jane learned of the fraud, Jane and Tom lived together as husband and wife from July 1985 to June 1987. Therefore, based on the above, Jane has no cause of action against Tom for annulment. Hence, the court was correct. **1-1/2 points**

(2) The issue is whether the court has power to equitably distribute the marital property. A court only has this authority when part of the relief granted is a divorce, or the dissolution, annulment, or declaration of the nullity of a marriage. Since the court denied Jane's action for annulment, she is not entitled to equitable distribution. Thus, the court's ruling was correct. **1-1/2 points**

(3) The issue is whether Jane is entitled to temporary maintenance of $350 per week.

During the pendency of an action, a court may order temporary maintenance to meet the needs of a party if the circumstances of the case and the parties warrant. [N.Y. Dom. Rel. Law §236B(6)(a)] Such an award would be justified if the applicant is in genuine need of financial support. However, where the parties have entered into a separation agreement that provides for maintenance, a court may not order temporary maintenance. [N.Y. Dom. Rel. Law §236(6)(9)] It is well settled that alimony pendente lite is not allowed until a separation agreement is set aside or breached by the parties. [N.Y. Dom. Rel. Law §1270] Thus, since Tom has complied with the separation agreement, the court cannot order temporary maintenance. Hence, the court's ruling was correct. **1-1/2 points**

(4) The issue is whether a judgment of divorce is proper.

A spouse is entitled to a judgment of divorce upon proof that the couple has lived separate and apart pursuant to their separation agreement for at least one year. Proof must also be furnished that the terms and conditions of the separation agreement have been substantially complied with. [N.Y. Dom. Rel. Law §107(6)] **1 point**

The only deviation from the terms of the separation agreement here is that Jane and Tom cohabited on one occasion. This will not abrogate the separation agreement since there is no proof of an intention to abandon the agreement, to reconcile, or to permanently resume the marital relationship. [N.Y. Dom. Rel. Law §807] Thus, the court's ruling was correct. **1 point**

(b) The issue is whether child support should be increased. **1/2 point**

It is well settled that the child support provisions of a separation agreement could be disturbed on a showing of unanticipated and unreasonable change in circumstances. Thus, Jane would be entitled to an increase in child support if she could show that Joe's needs are not being adequately met due to a change in circumstances, including financial hardship. However, Jane cannot show that Joe's needs are not being adequately met. Tom's good fortune has no bearing on Joe's needs. Thus, the court should deny Jane's motion to increase Joe's child support. **1 point**

ANSWER 94—CRIMINAL LAW/CRIMINAL PROCEDURE/EVIDENCE

(1) The issue is whether Jerry's waiver of his *Miranda* rights was valid. **1/2 point**

For any statement, including a confession, made during a custodial interrogation to be admissible into evidence, the accused must first be advised of his *Miranda* rights and must validly waive those rights. To be valid, a waiver must be knowing, voluntary, and intelligent. Moreover, in New York, a waiver from an accused actually known to be represented by an attorney is valid only if the waiver is made in the presence of the attorney (the so-called indelible right to counsel), but this rule does not apply to waivers on unrelated charges where the accused is released on the charge on which he is represented and later arrested on the unrelated charge. [People v. Bing, 76 N.Y.2d 331 (1990), *overruling* People v. Bartolomeo, 53 N.Y.2d 225 (1981)] **2 points**

Here, nothing in the facts indicates that Jerry's waiver was involuntary. Moreover, while the police might have known that Jerry was represented on the earlier reckless driving charge, he was released on that charge ("Alan was able to get Jerry cleared"). Thus, his waiver without counsel was valid, and his confession is admissible. **1/2 point**

Alan will not be able to have Betty's confession suppressed, even if it was obtained in violation of *Miranda*. The second issue is whether Jerry has standing to have Betty's confession suppressed. **1/2 point**

Generally, the exclusionary rule prohibits introduction of evidence obtained in violation of a defendant's Fourth, Fifth, or Sixth Amendment rights. Thus, a confession obtained in violation of a defendant's constitutional rights can be suppressed under the rule. However, the Supreme Court has held generally that a person cannot raise the constitutional rights of others. Thus, a person generally cannot exclude evidence merely because it was obtained in violation of another person's constitutional rights. That a defendant may be aggrieved by the introduction of damaging evidence does not give the defendant automatic standing to challenge the evidence based on how it was obtained from another. Thus, since nothing in the facts indicates Betty's confession was obtained in violation of Jerry's constitutional rights, he has no standing to have Betty's confession suppressed. **2 points**

Note, however, that Betty's written confession nevertheless would probably be inadmissible at trial because it constitutes hearsay (an out-of-court statement offered to prove the truth of the matter asserted) and it is not within any exception. **1/2 point**

(2) The issue is whether a defendant has a Sixth Amendment right to have counsel present at precharge line-ups. **1/2 point**

A suspect has a Sixth Amendment right to the presence of an attorney at any *postcharge* line-up or show-up. [Moore v. Illinois (1977)] The purpose of this representation is to ensure that when the witness identifies the defendant at trial, she is identifying the person who committed the crime and not merely the person whom the witness had previously seen at the police station. Since Betty and Jerry were *not* charged with grand larceny until *after* the line-up, this was not a postcharge line-up, and no Sixth Amendment right to counsel has been violated. Hence, Alan's motion to suppress the line-ups and identifications will fail. **1-1/2 points**

(3) The issue is whether the Queens District Attorney can properly use evidence from the Brooklyn scam to help convict Betty and Jerry of the Queens scam. **1/2 point**

In New York when a person is charged with one crime, extrinsic evidence of his other crimes or misconduct is inadmissible if such evidence is offered solely to establish a criminal disposition. The danger in allowing this type of evidence is that the jury may convict the defendant because of past crimes rather than because of his guilt of the offense charged. However, evidence that the accused has committed prior criminal acts that are so distinctive as to operate as a "signature" may be introduced to prove that the accused committed the act in question. **1 point**

Since we are told that Betty and Jerry committed the same scam (going house to house, fraudulently stating that they repair and beautify lawns and gardens, taking cash advances and running away with this money before doing any of the promised lawn work) in Brooklyn and Queens, the evidence will be admissible because this scam acts as Betty's and Jerry's "signature" or modus operandi. Hence, the evidence will be admissible, and Alan's motion to suppress will be denied. **1/2 point**

ANSWER 95—WILLS

(1)   The first issue is whether the will was validly executed. New York requires that the testator be at least 18 years of age and:

(i)   the will must be signed by the testator;

(ii)   the testator's signature must be at the end of the will;

(iii)   the testator must sign the will in the presence of each witness, or acknowledge his previous signature;

(iv)   the testator must publish the will by declaring to the witnesses that the instrument is his will;

(v)   there must be two attesting witnesses who sign at the testator's request; and

(vi)   the witnesses must sign their names within 30 days of each other.

Although elements (i), (ii), (iii), (v), and (vi) above are arguably present in the facts, it appears that Thomas failed to publish his will to the two delivery drivers. Without this publication, the will is not validly executed and Thomas died intestate. **1 point**

The second issue is distribution of Thomas's intestate estate, and whether Donna is included in the distribution. When one dies intestate and is survived by a spouse, the following rules apply:

(i)   If the decedent is survived by a spouse and one or more children or their issue, the spouse takes money or personal property worth $50,000 off the top, and also takes one-half of the balance of the estate. The remaining one-half passes to the decedent's children and the issue of deceased children; and

(ii)   If the decedent is survived by a spouse but not issue, the surviving spouse takes the entire estate. [EPTL §§4-1.1 - 4-1.5]

Since the facts state that Sue and Thomas had no children together, Sue inherits the entire estate. **1/2 point**

Donna, however, could get in Sue's way. A child born out of wedlock has no inheritance rights in the natural father's estate unless paternity can be established. Inheritance rights can be established after the father's death if in probate proceedings paternity is established by clear and convincing evidence **and** the father of the child openly and notoriously acknowledges the child as his own. The letter that Thomas sent to Donna might be enough to prove paternity if it was witnessed, acknowledged before a notary public, and filed with the Putative Father Registry. If it is, Thomas is survived by his spouse, Sue, and his daughter, Donna. In that case, Sue would take personal property or money worth $50,000 plus one-half of the balance of the estate, with the remaining one-half passing to Donna. No one else would take under intestacy laws. **1 point**

If, however, the will was published and is therefore validly executed, the third issue is whether the will was revoked by being found cut in half.

If a will is in the sole possession of the testator and is found cut or otherwise mutilated, there is a presumption that the testator destroyed the will with the intent to revoke it. This presumption may be overcome by adequate proof to the contrary, but such proof does not include declarations of the decedent designed to establish the continued existence of the will unless the declarations are made in connection with some act, under such circumstances as to become part of the res gestae. [Bonner's Will, 17 N.Y.2d 9 (1966)] Therefore, Stanley's statement that Thomas had no intention of revoking the will will not be enough to overcome the presumption that Thomas, in fact, intended to revoke it. Hence, again, intestacy is present and the above intestacy analysis applies. **1 point**

(2)   The issue is distribution of Thomas's estate under the will. Assuming that the will is admitted to probate:

Sue: Sue will receive $200,000. Sue is entitled to an elective share of Thomas's estate. The amount of the elective share is the greater of $50,000 or one-third of Thomas's net estate. Here, Sue's elective share would be $200,000, one-third of Thomas's net estate. However, since Sue received an outright disposition of $100,000 cash in the will, her elective share is reduced. Thus, the net elective share to which she is entitled is $100,000 (plus the $100,000 legacy in the will). **1/2 point**

In making up the net elective share, all other beneficiaries contribute pro rata. The remaining value of Thomas's net estate (the sum of all other dispositions in the will) is therefore reduced by one-fifth:

$$\frac{\$100,000 \text{ (amount to which Sue is entitled as her net elective share)}}{500,000 \text{ (amount remaining in Thomas's net estate subject to ratable contribution)}} = 1/5$$

1/2 point

Since Thomas died after September 1, 1994, the testamentary trust created for Sue would not be credited against her elective share. If Sue files for her elective share, her income interest in the trust will be treated as if Sue predeceased Thomas. The remainder will be accelerated, and the $200,000 would pass to the Red Cross, less a pro rata contribution to Sue's net elective share. **1/2 point**

Larry: Larry will probably retain the $25,000 legacy if he can defeat an inference of undue influence. Larry should have no problem with his appointment as executor.

Generally, the burden of proving undue influence by a preponderance of the evidence is on the person contesting the will. The will contestant must prove: (i) the existence and exertion of influence, (ii) the effect of the influence was to overpower the mind of the testator at the time of the execution of the will, and (iii) that the will or the particular gift would not have been made but for the influence. However, if the will makes a gift to a person who was in a confidential relationship with the testator and who was involved in the drafting of the will, there is an inference of undue influence. Such a beneficiary must provide evidence that the gift was freely made, and the beneficiary's testimony alone is not sufficient to overcome the inference. This is called *Putnam* scrutiny. Even if there is no will contest, a bequest to a person in a confidential relationship with the testator triggers an automatic inquiry into whether the gift was freely made. **1 point**

Larry, as Thomas's lawyer, stood in a confidential relationship to Thomas. Larry also drafted Thomas's will. The bequest to Larry must thus be subjected to *Putnam* scrutiny. Larry will thus have to put forth evidence that the $25,000 bequest was freely made and not the product of his influence. Often, evidence that the testator had a longstanding friendship and social relationship with the beneficiary will support a finding that the gift was not a product of undue influence. Since the facts state that Larry was Thomas's close friend, Larry should be able to produce such evidence. If he cannot, his bequest will be expunged. **1/2 point**

Assuming the bequest to Larry is not expunged for undue influence, Larry will take the $25,000 bequest despite being an interested witness.

A disposition to an attesting witness is void "unless there are, at the time of execution of an attestation, at least two other attesting witnesses to the will who receive no beneficial disposition . . . thereunder." [EPTL §3-3.2] In this case, since two delivery drivers who are disinterested witnesses also witnessed the will, Larry's disposition is not void even though Larry is an interested witness. Thus, Larry receives his bequest, less one-fifth ($5,000), which is his pro rata contribution to Sue's elective share. This is a general bequest since it is a bequest of money. **1/2 point**

If a will nominates the drafting attorney as a fiduciary and the testator/client dies after 1996, a disclosure statement must have been signed by the testator/client acknowledging that (i) any person, not just the attorney, can be named executor, (ii) executors are entitled to statutory commissions, and (iii) the attorney also will be entitled to attorney's fees for any legal services rendered to the estate. As the facts state this was properly executed, Larry may remain executor and collect full commissions. **1/2 point**

The Red Cross: The Red Cross will receive $160,000. Due to Sue's election, the Red Cross takes the accelerated remainder of Sue's income trust, less one-fifth ($40,000) which is its pro rata contribution to Sue's net elective share. This is also a general bequest.

Danny: Danny will receive the remaining $220,000 as a residuary gift. Thomas's net estate was valued at $600,000 at the time of his death. Sue received $100,000 cash as an outright disposition, Larry received $25,000, and the Red Cross received $200,000. This left a remainder of $275,000 for Danny, from which $55,000 went to Sue, as Danny's one-fifth pro rata contribution to her net elective share. Therefore, Danny receives $220,000 as a residuary gift. **1/2 point**

Donna: To take under Thomas's will, Donna must prove that she is Thomas's daughter. A nonmarital child has no inheritance rights in the natural father's estate unless paternity is established. Paternity can be established at a probate proceeding if there is clear and convincing evidence and the father openly and notoriously acknowledged the child as his own. If paternity is established, the child and her kin have full inheritance rights from the father. **1/2 point**

To satisfy this test, Donna's guardian must prove at a probate proceeding that the letter Donna received from Thomas constitutes clear and convincing evidence that Thomas was her father and that he openly and notoriously acknowledged Donna as his child.

If Donna's guardian is able to prove that Donna is Thomas's daughter, and that Donna was born after the will was executed, she will take under the pretermitted child statute. This statute provides that a child who is born after the will is executed and is not provided for by any lifetime settlement, or in any way mentioned in the will, may share in the estate. [EPTL §5-3.2] If the testator had no children when the will was executed, the afterborn child takes an amount equal to the intestate share she would have inherited had the testator died without a will. A child born out of wedlock is included in the term "afterborn child" under this statute. If Donna was born after February 1995, she is an afterborn child and since Thomas had no other children, Donna would be entitled to the intestate share of Thomas's estate she would have inherited had Thomas died without a will. Here, that amount would be $275,000. **1 point**

(As the spouse, Sue's intestate share would be the first $50,000 plus one-half of the balance of the estate; the remaining one-half passes to the decedent's children.) Donna's share would first be taken from the residuary estate, then from general bequests, then from demonstrative gifts, and finally from specific bequests. Donna's share too would be reduced to reflect a pro rata contribution to satisfy Sue's elective share. **1/2 point**

ANSWER 96—TORTS

(1) *Bugs v. Daff (on behalf of Porky):*

The issues are whether a parent can be sued for his child's injuries allegedly caused by the negligence of the parent and whether the elements of negligence have been satisfied. **1/2 point**

Daff is being sued for the injuries caused by his entrusting Porky with a vehicle that can travel 35 miles per hour. Since New York does not have parent-child immunity, this defense will not help Daff. **1/2 point**

The elements of negligence are as follows:

(i)   duty of care to a foreseeable plaintiff;

(ii) breach of this duty;

(iii) actual and proximate causation; and

(iv) harm to the plaintiff. **1 point**

When a person engages in an activity, he is under a legal duty to act as an ordinary, prudent, reasonable person to foreseeable plaintiffs. The facts state that Daff gave his 13-year-old son, who had never driven a vehicle before, the mini-car. This is not how an ordinary, prudent, reasonable person would act. Additionally, since Daff gave his son this mini-car, the son is a foreseeable plaintiff if the son is injured while using the mini-car. Daff did not exercise the proper duty of care to a foreseeable plaintiff. Hence, Daff breached his duty of care to a foreseeable plaintiff. Since Porky's injuries were caused by the mini-car, Daff's actions were the actual cause of the injury. **1 point**

The next issue to determine is whether Daff's act was the proximate cause of the injury. Extraordinary forms of negligent conduct, against which the defendant was under no obligation to take precautions, have been held to be superseding intervening forces. If superseding intervening forces exist, the defendant's conduct is not deemed the proximate cause of the plaintiff's injury. The defendant is not negligent unless he is the proximate cause of the plaintiff's injury. Since the facts state that the accident occurred solely because of the gross negligence of Acme, Acme's extraordinary negligent conduct is a superseding intervening cause. Hence, Daff is not the proximate cause of Porky's injury and is not liable. **1 point**

Yosemite v. Acme Corp. (on behalf of Elmer):

The issue is whether a third party with no privity can sue a manufacturer for injuries caused by its product. Elmer can bring a products liability case against Acme Corp. using a (i) negligence or (ii) strict liability theory. **1/2 point**

(i)   Applying the above discussed elements of negligence, Acme has a duty of care to Elmer since Elmer was injured while using Acme's vehicle. It is irrelevant that Elmer has no privity of contract with Acme. Since the mini-car had a defective part, which was the sole cause of the injury, Acme has breached its duty of care to a foreseeable plaintiff. The defect was also the actual and proximate cause of the injury. Hence, Acme will be held liable for Elmer's injuries. **1 point**

(ii)   If Elmer so decides, strict liability can also be a winning theory. The elements of a strict liability cause of action are:

   (i)   a strict duty owed by the commercial supplier to the user;

   (ii)   breach of this duty;

   (iii)   actual and proximate causation from the breach of duty; and

   (iv)   harm. **1 point**

Since Elmer is a user of Acme's product, and the product was defective, Acme has breached its strict duty of care. Since the defect caused the injury, actual and proximate cause is also present. Since Elmer suffered injuries, all elements are met and Elmer will win. **1/2 point**

(2)   *Daff v. the Day:*

The issue is when can a republisher of an allegedly defamatory article be held liable. **1/2 point**

To be liable for defamation, the following elements must be proven:

   (i)   the material is not true;

   (ii)   publication of falsity;

   (iii)   harm to the plaintiff's reputation; and

   (iv)   malice on the defendant's part if the plaintiff is a public figure. **1 point**

Since the facts state that the story was false and that the *Day* republished the article, elements (i) and (ii) above are clearly present. Because the article represents Daff as an affiliate to the mob and as an unloved father, there is obvious harm to the mayor's reputation and hence element (iii) above is present. **1/2 point**

For element (iv) above to be present, the defendant must have entertained serious doubts as to the truthfulness of the publication. In New York, the republisher of a work may rely on the research of the original publisher, absent proof that the republisher had, or should have had, substantial reasons to question either the accuracy of the article or the good faith of the reporter. [Karaduman v. Newsday, Inc., 51 N.Y.2d 531 (1980)] **1/2 point**

Since the facts do not indicate that the *Day* had any reason to believe that Will's article was defamatory, element (iv) above is not met, and therefore no defamation is present. Daff will lose. **1/2 point**

ANSWER 97—TORTS/WILLS/NEW YORK PRACTICE

(1)   The issue is whether New York recognizes a holographic last will and testament. **1/2 point**

Hap's will is classified as a holographic will since it was handwritten by the testator and since it was neither executed with testamentary formalities nor attested to by two disinterested witnesses. The Estates, Powers & Trusts Law or "EPTL" (the law governing wills in New York) invalidates all holographic wills except those written by a member of the armed services during war or by a mariner at sea. Since Hap does not fall into one of the exceptions, his will is invalid and cannot be admitted to probate. **1-1/2 points**

(2)   The issue is what causes of action survive Haps's death. The following causes of action exist:

    (i)   personal injury and wrongful death: Hap's estate v. John, Mary, and New York State; and

    (ii)   indemnity: Mary v. John

Hap's estate may maintain the personal injury action pursuant to the provisions of EPTL section 11-3.2, which states that no cause of action for personal or property injury is lost because of the death of the person in whose favor the cause of action existed. Instead, the decedent's estate may continue or commence any such actions. Thus, Hap's estate may maintain a cause of action against John, Mary, and New York State for Hap's conscious pain and suffering sustained before his death. **1 point**

The estate may also commence a second cause of action for wrongful death. EPTL section 5-4.1 permits recovery of damages against persons who would have been liable to the decedent had their wrongful conduct not resulted in the decedent's death. The action differs from a personal injury action in a few respects. In a wrongful death action, damages are limited to the pecuniary losses of the distributees; in a personal injury action, the damages are the decedent's damages. There is also a difference in the manner in which recovery under each of these actions is distributed. **1 point**

Damages recovered as a result of pursuing the decedent's personal injury action belong to the estate and are distributed according to the decedent's will or by intestacy depending on whether the decedent died testate or intestate. [EPTL §11-3.3] As discussed above, Hap's attempted will is invalid and he died intestate. Thus, damages recovered in a personal injury action will be distributed to Hap's intestate distributees. Damages recovered by a wrongful death action are not part of the decedent's estate. Rather, the personal representative allocates the award among the distributees who have sustained a pecuniary loss as a result of the decedent's death in proportion to the amount of loss sustained by each. [EPTL §5-4.4] (Note that since wrongful death awards are not part of the decedent's estate, they are not subject to estate tax.) **1 point**

Mary may assert a cross-claim for indemnity from John in the event that she has to pay any part of the judgment awarded to Hap's estate. The rules of indemnity are grounded in contract and provide that when one party satisfies another party's debt, the payor is entitled to reimbursement. In this case, any potential liability accrues to Mary solely due to John's negligent operation of her car. Since she has no actual fault, she is entitled to indemnification from John for money she pays to Hap's estate on John's behalf. **1/2 point**

(3)   The issue is whether the owner of a motor vehicle involved in an accident in New York is subject to the state's jurisdiction solely by virtue of ownership. **1/2 point**

New York's Vehicle and Traffic Law ("VTL") section 253(1) provides that a nonresident owner of a motor vehicle may be subject to action in New York if the use of the vehicle was with express or implied permission. The facts reveal that John had Mary's permission, rendering her amenable to legal action. **1 point**

As for John, VTL section 253(1) also establishes jurisdiction over the vehicle's operator. Additionally, CPLR 302(a)(2) provides for long arm jurisdiction over persons committing tortious acts within New York State. John negligently operated Mary's car and is therefore subject to long arm jurisdiction. Thus, Mary and John are subject to legal action in New York. Notice to both Mary and John may be accomplished by (i) mailing a summons and complaint to the secretary of state and (ii) serving the defendants in person or by mail. **1 point**

(4)   The issue is in what courts should the actions be brought.

The supreme court, New York's court of general jurisdiction, has jurisdiction over all actions, except those where New York State is a defendant. Thus, the administrator of Hap's estate should commence the action against John and Mary in the supreme court. **1 point**

Article 6, section 9 of the New York Constitution provides that the Court of Claims has jurisdiction over all claims against the state. The action against the state of New York must be heard in the Court of Claims. As a prerequisite to maintaining the action, Hap's executor must file a notice of claim within 90 days from his appointment. [Court of Claims Act §10(2)] **1 point**

ANSWER 98—CONTRACTS (SALES)

(1)   At issue is whether seeking modification of a price term in good faith constitutes coercion. **1/2 point**

Coercion arises where a party's free will to contract is overcome by an unlawful use of force or threats of imminent use of force. A party's poor economic condition generally is not a ground for the defense of coercion, although wrongful abuse of poor economic condition caused by the plaintiff sometimes is found to be a defense. Here, Hillary did not threaten Bill with force, and even if poor economic condition is a ground for coercion, it would not be available to Bill here because there was nothing wrongful about Hillary seeking a modification of the price term. The U.C.C. allows a party to seek modifications in good faith, and Hillary exercised good faith here since she: (i) was under no obligation to purchase the plastic when the price was low (Hillary's performance was not due for another month when the price of plastic increased), (ii) truthfully told Bill that she could not make a profit at the current contract price, and (iii) did not threaten to breach if Bill did not agree to a price modification. Thus, Bill was not coerced. **1-1/2 points**

(2)   At issue is whether consideration is required to modify a contract for the sale of goods. **1/2 point**

Under the common law, consideration is required to modify a contract, but this is not true of a contract for the sale of goods. A contract for the sale of goods may be modified by agreement of the parties without consideration as long as the modification is sought in good faith. [U.C.C. §2-209] Here, as discussed above, Hillary sought the modification in good faith. Thus, lack of consideration is not a defense. **1-1/2 points**

(3)   At issue is whether failure to put in writing a modification of a contract for the sale of goods for more than $500 is a defense where a party has materially changed position in reliance on the modified price. **1/2 point**

Generally, to be enforceable under the U.C.C. Statute of Frauds, a contract for the sale of goods for $500 or more must be evidenced by a writing signed by the party to be charged; although between merchants, if one party sends the other a memorandum of the contract sufficient to bind the sender, it will also bind the recipient if the recipient does not object within 10 days of receiving the memorandum. [U.C.C. §2-201] These rules apply to modified contracts as well as unmodified contracts. [U.C.C. §2-209] Thus, under the general rule, the original contract is enforceable against both parties because Bill sent a sufficient memorandum to Hillary. However, the contract modification here would not be enforceable against Bill because the modification was not evidenced by a writing signed by Bill and there was no confirmatory memorandum regarding the modification. **1 point**

Furthermore, none of the U.C.C. exceptions to the Statute of Frauds apply under the facts. The first exception under section 2-201 applies where the contract calls for specifically manufactured goods not generally suitable for sale to others, and nothing in the facts indicates that the plastic here was specially manufactured; rather, Hillary appears to be serving as a broker for ordinary plastic. The second exception applies where the modification is admitted in court, which has not occurred here. The third exception applies where the buyer has paid for or accepted the goods, which also has not occurred here. Thus, the modification is unenforceable under the Statute of Frauds. **1/2 point**

However, even though the Statute of Frauds has not been met, the modification will operate as a waiver here, allowing Hillary to enforce the modified price term. U.C.C. section 2-209 provides that a modification not enforceable under the Statute of Frauds can operate as a waiver to enforce the contract as written. The waiver may be retracted only by reasonable notice given before the other party changes position in reliance on the waiver. Here, Hillary relied on the modified price in purchasing the plastic, and so Bill will be held to have waived his objections to the modified price term. Thus, the modified price term is enforceable. **1 point**

(4)   At issue is whether a party must tender delivery when the other party unequivocally indicates that he will not perform. **1/2 point**

Hillary was discharged from her duty to tender the plastic because of Bill's anticipatory repudiation; thus, Bill may be held liable for his failure to pay. Under the contract, Hillary was required to deliver the plastic to Bill's Albany plant on December 15. Although ordinarily the delivery would be a condition precedent to Bill's duty to pay, the condition will be discharged here because of Bill's anticipatory repudiation. Anticipatory repudiation arises when a contract is executory on both sides and one party to the contract unequivocally indicates that he will not perform. In such a situation, the nonrepudiating party has an option of several remedies, including suspending her own performance. **1-1/2 points**

Here, Bill's statement that he would not purchase the plastic from Hillary constitutes anticipatory repudiation because the statement unequivocally indicates that Bill will not perform and the contract was still executory on both sides since both parties had duties yet to be performed. Thus, Hillary can enforce Bill's duty to pay despite Hillary's failure to deliver the goods according to the terms of the contract. **1 point**

ANSWER 99—REAL PROPERTY/DOMESTIC RELATIONS

(1)   The issue is when failure to strictly comply with the renewal clause of a lease will be excused. **1/2 point**

Failure of a tenant to give timely notice of her option to renew will be excused if it is the result of an honest mistake, the landlord was not unfairly prejudiced by the lateness, and substantial forfeiture would result to the tenant as a result of the loss of her leasehold. [Sy Jack Realty Co. v. Pergament Syosset Corp., 27 N.Y.2d 449 (1971)] **1 point**

Here, Patty sent the required notice within the time prescribed in the lease, but to the wrong party. Patty's mistake in sending the notice to Larry's attorney was an excusable oversight because she had directed all previous correspondence in regard to the lease to the attorney, not Larry. In addition, the facts indicate that Larry had not as of yet relet the premises, and since a year remains on his current lease with Patty, he has failed to demonstrate how this technically "late" notice has unduly prejudiced his position. Finally, Patty, has not been able to find comparable office space and has substantially contributed to the improvement of the premises by the installation of fixtures such as bookcases, plumbing, and electrical work, all of which would result in a substantial forfeiture to Patty for a mistake, which on the face of it, still gives ample notice of renewal to the landlord. Therefore, the court was correct in deciding that Patty had effectively renewed her option. **2 points**

(2)   The issue is whether an equitable property distribution on divorce may be modified. **1/2 point**

Bruce and Patty took title to Fairacre as husband and wife, which means that they took title as tenants by the entirety. Tenants by the entirety may not partition the property unless both agree. Thus, since Bruce did not agree to the partition sale, Patty would be unable to bring an action for partition if the property were still held as a tenancy by the entirety. Divorce, however, converts tenants by the entirety to tenants in common. Therefore, generally, after a divorce and *absent a contrary court order*, a spouse would be entitled to partition. **1 point**

In light of the court order, however, the issue then becomes whether Patty is entitled to partition when that action is contrary to a court decree which sets forth a property distribution. **1/2 point**

In a divorce action, the court may make any award concerning the possession of property (including exclusive possession of the marital residence) as, in the court's discretion, justice requires. [N.Y. Dom. Rel. Law §§234, 236B(5)(f)] Property acquired during the marriage is considered marital property and may be distributed in a divorce decree according to the guidelines for equitable distribution set forth in New York Domestic Relations Law section 236(b). The factors taken into consideration include financial circumstances of each spouse at the time of marriage and commencement of the action; age and health of the parties; duration of the marriage; maintenance awards; and contribution to acquisition of marital property. Unlike awards for maintenance, child support, or child custody, property distribution awards are not modifiable. Thus, there is nothing Patty can do to force the sale of the property. **2 points**

Furthermore, the courts have held where exclusive use and possession of the parties' marital premises is awarded to one spouse, the other is precluded from seeking partition of the premises since the other spouse is neither in present, actual, nor constructive possession of the premises. Here, the facts indicate that Bruce was granted exclusive possession of Fairacre until March 1992. Since Bruce was awarded exclusive occupancy until March 1992, Patty has no standing to commence a partition action until the exclusive occupancy is extinguished. **1-1/2 points**

In conclusion, an equitable property distribution on divorce concerning the marital residence may not be modified. Patty will have to wait until March 1992, at which time Fairacre can be sold with the proceeds of the sale to be divided between Patty and Bruce. Therefore, the court was incorrect in denying Bruce's motion for summary judgment. **1 point**

ANSWER 100—TORTS/NEW YORK PRACTICE/CONFLICT OF LAWS

(1) At issue is whether a retailer can be held liable for defectively designed products on a strict liability tort theory. **1/2 point**

Since Mary has not alleged any negligence, she can recover against HAL only if she can show that HAL was strictly liable. To make out a prima facie case for strict liability in tort, Mary need only prove a strict duty owed by a commercial supplier, breach of that duty, actual and proximate cause, and damages. **1 point**

A retailer can be liable for design defects under a strict products liability theory because the strict duty owed is not limited to manufacturers. All commercial suppliers, which includes a retail seller like HAL, owe a duty to not put unreasonably dangerous goods in the market. No fault need be proved. Thus, HAL's motion to dismiss because HAL is a retail seller was properly denied. **1 point**

(2) At issue is what the statute of limitations is for an injury occurring outside New York in an action brought in New York under a strict products liability theory. Since the cause of action here accrued in State A and the action is being brought in New York, the first issue to be resolved is which state's limitations period will be applied. **1/2 point**

New York will apply its own limitations period under the facts here. As a general rule, statutes of limitations are procedural and states generally apply their own procedural rules. However, New York, like many other states, has a borrowing statute that provides that in actions involving more than one state, the shortest limitations period shall apply. However, the borrowing statute also provides that if the cause of action accrued in favor of a New York resident, the borrowing statute does not apply [CPLR 202] and the appropriate New York statute of limitations will be applied. Thus, the New York statute of limitations will be applied here and not the State A limitations period. **1-1/2 points**

Mary's motion to strike HAL's affirmative defense should be granted because the appropriate New York limitations period has not expired here. **1/2 point**

The limitations period for strict products liability in tort in New York is three years, and the cause of action accrues at the time of the injury. [CPLR 214] Thus, Mary's cause of action is timely since she was harmed on July 1, 1998, and brought this action on October 1, 1999. The limitations period HAL seeks to apply (four years from the date of delivery) is the limitations period for a products liability action under a warranty theory, but Mary's cause of action sounds in tort. Thus, Mary's motion was properly granted. **1 point**

(3) The issue is whether the laws of New York or the laws of State A should be applied in this case. **1/2 point**

When faced with a conflict of law regarding loss distribution rules in a tort case, the New York Court of Appeals has rejected the old vested rights approach, which would mandate the automatic application of the law of the situs of the tort. Now, New York courts apply the ***governmental interest analysis***. This is to ensure that the jurisdiction with the greatest interest in the suit has its law apply. In order to make the determination, the court will look at the factual contacts of each jurisdiction, the differing laws, and the underlying policies for each law; apply the facts to the policies; and apply the greater governmental interest. For tort cases, New York has refined the interest analysis in *Neumeier v. Kuehner*, 31 N.Y.2d 121 (1972). The *Neumeier* rules (below) are a product of the governmental interest analysis. **1 point**

Neumeier #1 states that the law of the domicile applies when the plaintiff and defendant have the same domicile. However, *Neumeier* #2 states that if the plaintiff and defendant have different domiciles, and the tort occurred in the state of the domicile of one of the parties and that state's law favors its domiciliaries, then that state's law will apply. Finally, in all other situations, *Neumeier* #3 applies the law of the place of the accident unless that place is totally fortuitous, in which case basic government analysis applies. **1 point**

In this case, New York has the greatest interest. While State A seeks to limit recovery for strict liability, to protect against unfair awards, New York wants to see its plaintiffs fully compensated for injuries. Although the injury took place in State A, the plaintiff is from New York, a New York corporation sold the mower, and the mower was purchased in New York. Accordingly, the overwhelming interest is New York's. Finally, New York's policy would be frustrated by applying the law of State A, but State A is not impacted by the application of New York law. Accordingly, under *Neumeier* the court will apply the law of New York. Thus, MOW's motion was properly denied. **1-1/2 points**

ANSWER R-1—PROFESSIONAL RESPONSIBILITY/DOMESTIC RELATIONS

(1)   The issue presented is whether an oral retainer agreement in matrimonial actions is valid and whether an attorney is entitled to retain the full amount of a paid retainer fee. **1/2 point**

Under New York's Code of Professional Responsibility and Court Rules, an attorney who undertakes to represent a client in any matrimonial action must obtain a written retainer agreement signed by the attorney and client setting forth in plain language the nature of the relationship and the details of the fee arrangement. The agreement may not include a nonrefundable fee clause. Additionally, in domestic relations matters, a lawyer must provide a prospective client with a statement of the client's rights and responsibilities at the initial conference and prior to the signing of a written retainer agreement. Failure to abide by these rules results in an attorney's preclusion from collecting and recovering a legal fee for services rendered and not paid. However, where a retainer fee has already been paid, an attorney may deduct reasonable fees for services rendered and must return the balance. **1 point**

Parker violated the above rules. Parker and Molly entered into an oral retainer agreement rather than a written agreement, as required. Moreover, Parker had Molly give him a $4,000 nonrefundable retainer fee and failed to provide Molly with a statement of client's rights and responsibilities at their initial conference, both of which were improper. As a result of violating the Professional Responsibility and Court Rules, Parker would ordinarily be precluded from obtaining any fee. However, because he has the $4,000 retainer, as explained above, he will be allowed to keep a reasonable fee for his services and will be required to return the balance to Molly. The $150 per hour fee Parker quoted Molly seems reasonable, so he may keep $1,500 for his 10 hours of work and should return the other $2,500 to Molly. Additionally, Parker may be subject to discipline for failure to comply with New York's Code of Professional Responsibility and the Court Rules. **1 point**

(2)   The issue presented is whether parties executing a separation agreement can obtain a valid conversion divorce. **1/2 point**

Under New York's Domestic Relations Law, a conversion divorce may be granted on the ground that a husband and wife have lived apart for one year or more pursuant to a written, properly acknowledged agreement, if the plaintiff submits satisfactory proof that he has substantially performed all of its terms and conditions. At any time prior to the commencement of a divorce action, the agreement, or a memorandum of the agreement, must be filed in the office of the county clerk where either party resides. **1 point**

In the present case, Molly and Joe's separation agreement was signed and acknowledged in January 1996. Since its signing, Molly and Joe have lived separate and apart with no intent to reconcile and have abided by the terms of their agreement. At the time the divorce action was commenced (June 1997), Molly and Joe's agreement had been filed with the Niagara County Clerk's Office (the county in which both parties reside) since April 1997, and Molly and Joe had been living separate and apart for over one year. Thus, the conversion divorce was properly granted. **1 point**

(3)   The issue is whether a party may request blood testing to determine the paternity of a marital child and deny the spouse's paternity. **1/2 point**

Under New York law, the Family Court ordinarily is to advise parties of their right to one or more genetic marker tests or DNA tests, and on the court's own motion or the motion of any party, the court may order the mother, her child, and the alleged father to submit to one or more genetic marker or DNA tests. No such test is to be ordered, however, upon a written finding by the court that it is not in the best interests of the child on the basis of res judicata, equitable estoppel, or the presumption of legitimacy of a child born to a married woman. Estoppel applies to prevent the enforcement of rights that would work a fraud or injustice upon the person against whom enforcement is sought and who, in reliance upon the opposing party's words or conduct, has been misled into acting upon the belief that enforcement of any purported rights would not be sought. Furthermore, New York courts are more inclined to impose equitable estoppel to protect the status of a child in an already recognized and operative parent-child relationship. **1 point**

In the instant case, the doctrine of estoppel applies to prevent Molly from denying Joe's paternity of Tim and prevents her from securing a blood test to disprove Joe's paternity, as it would not be in Tim's best interest. A recognized and operative parent-child relationship exists between Joe and Tim, as Joe is the only father Tim, now 13 years of age, has ever known. Here, Joe is listed as Tim's father on his birth certificate, Molly has never before told anyone that Joe is not Tim's biological father, and Molly and Joe have always held Tim out as Joe's son in every way. In addition, Molly and Joe's separation agreement recites that Tim was a child of their marriage, and their subsequent divorce recites these terms. Molly had an opportunity in both the separation agreement and divorce action to allege and prove that Joe was not the biological father of Tim and she failed to do so. Also, Tim has continuously resided with Joe since Molly and Joe's separation in 1995. Joe, in maintaining custody of Tim, can be said to have relied upon Molly's representation that he was Tim's father, and injustice will result if Molly is permitted to compel Joe to undergo a blood test and definitively establish that the only father Tim has known throughout his entire lifetime is not in fact his father. Accordingly, the court correctly precluded Molly from denying Joe's paternity of Tim and correctly denied Molly's application for blood testing. **1 point**

(4)   At issue is the standard to be applied when a custodial parent petitions the court for approval to geographically relocate with a child and the relocation will substantially affect the noncustodial parent's visitation rights. **1/2 point**

Under New York law, in order to approve the relocation of a custodial parent and child, the court must determine by a preponderance of the evidence that the proposed relocation will serve the best interests of the child. In determining what is in the best interests of the child, the court may consider factors such as each parent's reasons for seeking or opposing the move, the quality of the relationships between the child and the custodial and noncustodial parents, the impact of the move on the quantity and quality of the child's future contact with the noncustodial parent, the degree to which the custodial parent's and child's life may be enhanced economically, emotionally, and educationally by the move, and the feasibility of preserving the relationship between the noncustodial parent and child through suitable visitation arrangements. **1 point**

Here, the court incorrectly denied Joe's petition on the ground that no exceptional circumstances were presented justifying the relocation to Florida. The proposed relocation should not have been subject to an exceptional circumstances requirement, but rather, determined based on the best interests of the child. Presently, both Joe and Molly are respectively seeking and opposing the relocation in good faith, as neither is doing so with malicious intent towards the other. Also, although Molly would essentially no longer be able to enjoy the frequency of visits she now enjoys with Tim, this factor alone is not determinative. Here, both Joe's and Tim's lives will be enhanced economically, emotionally, and educationally by the move. Economically, the move would afford Joe greater employment opportunities not available in the current area. Next, the move would emotionally benefit both Tim and Joe, as Joe's plans to remarry would provide a more stable home life for Tim, especially since Joe's fiancée has developed a close relationship with Tim and her two sons have also become good friends with Tim. Tim would also benefit educationally from the move, as Joe has made arrangements for Tim to attend an excellent school in Florida. Tim currently attends a school where funding is low and the academic achievement of students is below the state average. Attending a better school would enable Tim to not only receive a better education, but also to increase his opportunities to attend institutions of higher learning in the future (college and beyond). Finally, Joe has stated that he is willing to send Tim for frequent visits with Molly on holidays and school vacations during which she wishes to have visitation, and is willing to cooperate fully in maintaining Molly's continuing nurturing relationship with Tim. Thus, although the quantity of Molly's visits with Tim will be diminished, the quality will be enhanced through extended visits and the relationship between Molly and Tim preserved through suitable alternate visitation arrangements. As a result, since a preponderance of the evidence demonstrates that Joe's proposed relocation would effectively serve Tim's best interests, Joe should succeed on his appeal. **1 point**

ANSWER R-2—WILLS/PROFESSIONAL RESPONSIBILITY

(1)   The issue presented is whether a valid will and codicil have been executed. **1/2 point**

A will is an instrument to take effect on death, that is revocable until death, and that makes disposition of property, directs how property shall be disposed, disposes of testator's body or any part thereof, exercises a power of appointment, and/or appoints a fiduciary. For a will to be validly executed, New York's Estates, Powers, and Trusts Law ("EPTL") provides that: (i) it must be in writing and signed at the end by the testator; (ii) the testator must sign in the presence of each witness (or acknowledge her previous signature); (iii) it must be published by the testator (declaring to each attesting witness that "this is my will"); (iv) there must be two attesting witnesses; and (v) that the witnesses must sign their names within 30 days of each other. Witnesses need not sign in the testator's presence or be present at the same time, but they must sign as attesting witness, not in another capacity, such as a notary public. A codicil is an amendment or supplement to a will that either adds to, takes from, or alters the will's provisions. In New York, a codicil is constructed as part of a will and must be executed with the same formalities. **1 point**

In the present case, Cole's will was in fact in writing, Cole signed in the presence of each witness, she published her will by announcing to Walker and his two secretaries that the instrument she was about to sign was her will, there were two secretaries serving as the two attesting witnesses, and when they signed two days after Cole executed her will, they fulfilled the 30-day requirement; as discussed above, they were not required to sign in the presence of the testator. **1/2 point**

Similarly, Cole's codicil was validly executed. It was in writing, signed by Cole in the presence of each attesting witness, published by her announcement that it was intended to serve as a codicil to her will, and Nelson's two paralegals served as attesting witnesses and signed their names within 30 days of each other. Here, although one attesting witness was also a notary public, that witness did not sign the codicil in her capacity as a notary public, but rather, as an attesting witness. Hence, Cole's codicil was validly witnessed by two persons during the requisite time period. **1/2 point**

As a result, the will and codicil were duly executed and Dave's objection to their probate should not be sustained.

(2) The issue involved is whether a bequest made in a testamentary instrument to an attorney-draftsman is valid. **1/2 point**

Under New York's Code of Professional Responsibility, a lawyer should not suggest to the client that a gift be made to the lawyer for the lawyer's benefit. If a lawyer accepts a gift from a client, the lawyer is peculiarly susceptible to the charge that he unduly influenced or overreached the client. Additionally, under the *Putnam* Doctrine, New York law provides that if a will makes a gift to a person who was in a confidential relationship with the testator and who was directly or indirectly involved in drafting the will, there is an inference that the gift was the product of undue influence. In such a case, the burden of proof of undue influence remains on the contestant, but it is incumbent upon the beneficiary to explain the circumstances and to show in the first instance that the gift was freely and willingly made. Generally, the explanation consists of proof that the beneficiary was a natural object of the decedent's bounty, such as a relative or close friend. If the attorney is a relative or friend of the decedent with a long-standing relationship or friendship, the objective, rational basis of the gift is explained and the bequest allowed to stand. **1 point**

(a) *Walker:* In the instant case, Walker was the attorney-draftsman of Cole's original will. The bequest made to Walker, however, was made in the codicil drafted by Nelson. Walker is not subject to the rules pertaining to an attorney-draftsman because he did not actually draft the testamentary instrument under which the bequest was made to him. As a result, there is no inference of undue influence raised by the bequest made to Walker. However, it should be noted that even with respect to Cole's original will, Walker fully complied with his ethical duties by denying that a bequest be made to him as he was the attorney-draftsman. **1 point**

(b) *Nelson:* Here, Nelson was the attorney-draftsman of the codicil under which a bequest was made to him. As a result, he was obligated to not only refrain from suggesting that a gift be made to him, but also to demonstrate that the gift was freely and willingly made and explain the circumstances of the gift. Ordinarily, the fact that he was a relative would suffice to explain the gift, but in the instant case, it is clear that the gift was not made freely and willingly. Although he is a cousin of Cole's, Cole did not originally intend to leave a bequest to Nelson, as one was not provided under the will prepared by Walker or later when Nelson prepared the codicil. In fact, the bequest was included in the codicil solely because Nelson placed it there himself as payment for his legal services. In other words, the bequest was not made because of Cole's affection for her cousin, but rather, as payment for his professional services. A $10,000 fee for drafting a codicil to a will is unreasonable and excessive and suggests undue influence. Moreover, the fact that Cole was initially suspect of the $10,000 bequest further demonstrates that the bequest was not freely made. Thus, the bequest to Nelson does raise issues concerning its propriety, Nelson is susceptible to a charge that he overreached the client, Cole, and he may be subject to professional discipline for violating an ethical consideration. **1 point**

(3) The issue presented is whether the attorney general has standing to raise an objection in a Surrogate's Court proceeding. **1/2 point**

New York's EPTL provides that the attorney general is to represent the beneficiaries of dispositions for religious, charitable, educational, or benevolent purposes, and it is the attorney general's duty to enforce the rights of such beneficiaries by appropriate proceedings in the courts. **1/2 point**

Here, the residue of Cole's estate was bequeathed for charitable purposes to CO, a properly qualified charitable organization. Consequently, the attorney general is charged with enforcing CO's rights in appropriate proceedings in the courts. Thus, the attorney general has standing to raise objections in this Surrogate's Court proceeding. **1/2 point**

(4) At issue is what share, if any, Ira's children will receive from Cole's estate. **1/2 point**

Under New York's EPTL, distribution by representation (per capita at each generation) is the default statutory distribution. However, if a testator so provides in his will, distribution may be made per stirpes. A per stirpes disposition of property is made to persons who take as issue (children, grandchildren, etc.) of a deceased ancestor and receive in equal shares what the deceased ancestor would have received. **1 point**

Here, Cole's will and codicil were validly executed and provide for a $100,000 bequest to Walker. Further, the will provides for per stirpes distribution to Walker's issue in the event of Walker's death. Having died, Walker's $100,000 bequest will be distributed per stirpes among his issue: Dick, Bryan, Diane, and Ira, as collectively they are entitled to receive an equal share of what Walker would have received. Individually, Dick, Bryan, Diane, and Ira are each entitled to receive one-fourth of Walker's bequest ($25,000 each). However, because Ira has also died, under the per stirpes distribution provided for in Cole's will, Ira's three daughters are entitled to receive what Ira would have received. As a result, Ira's three daughters will each receive an equal share (one-third) of the $25,000 Ira would have received (approximately $8,333 each). Thus, because Cole's will and codicil provide for per stirpes disposition to Walker's issue, Ira's children will collectively receive $25,000 from Cole's estate. **1 point**

ANSWER R-3—WILLS/PROFESSIONAL RESPONSIBILITY

(1) The issue is whether an attorney may accept employment by a prospective client whose interests present a conflict of interest with a current client or with the attorney himself. **2/3 point**

Under the New York Code of Professional Responsibility, a lawyer must not enter into a relationship where there is a potential conflict of interest that is likely to adversely affect his ability to exercise independent and professional judgment. Under Disciplinary Rule 5-105, a lawyer must not accept or continue employment if the exercise of his professional judgment on behalf of a client would be adversely affected by the employment or if it would be likely to involve the lawyer in representing differing interests. Additionally, under Disciplinary Rule 5-101(a), a lawyer must refuse employment when his professional judgment will reasonably be affected by his own financial, business, property, or personal interests. However, in either case, an attorney may accept employment if: (i) a disinterested lawyer would believe that the lawyer can competently represent the clients' interests; and (ii) the clients consent after full disclosure of the potential conflict. **1 point**

Here, Luke had prepared Herb's 2001 will, which revoked Wendy as primary beneficiary and executor of the estate. Herb's new will executed in 2001 gave Herb's entire estate to his son Seth, and named Luke as executor. The 2001 will is adverse to Wendy's interests because her interest in the estate is revoked by implication. This conflict of interest between Herb and Wendy is likely to adversely affect Luke's ability to exercise professional judgment in representing their differing interests. Additionally, the facts indicate that Herb's 2001 will appointed Luke as executor of the estate. As executor of the estate, Luke may not be able to exercise independent, professional judgment on behalf of Wendy because of his conflicting business and personal interests. Thus, Luke may not advise Wendy regarding her rights in Herb's estate. **1 point**

(2)   The issue is whether a separated spouse has any rights in the estate of a deceased spouse. **2/3 point**

Under the Estates, Powers, and Trusts Law, the elective share exists to protect a surviving spouse against disinheritance, by giving the spouse an entitlement to a minimum share of the decedent's estate. When a spouse is provided for minimally in the will, the spouse has the choice of taking the elective share. The amount of the elective share is the greater of $50,000 or one-third of the net estate. She also is entitled to an exempt personal property set-aside. Personal property set aside includes items that come over and above property passing to the spouse by will, intestate share, or elective share (*e.g.*, furniture, car, and appliances). If the elective share applied only to the probate estate (property owned at death), a person who wanted to disinherit a spouse could make nonprobate transfers to others, defeating the protection of the elective share statute. Thus, when calculating the net estate, the augmented estate applies to both property owned at death and certain testamentary substitutes. **1 point**

Testamentary substitutes include Totten trust bank accounts and survivorship estates. A Totten trust is one where the depositor deposits funds in a bank account in his name as trustee for another. The depositor reserves the right to withdraw funds at any time, and, on his death, the account passes to the named beneficiary. A joint tenancy is a survivorship estate in which tenants must take their interests at the same time, by the same title, with identical, equal interests and with identical rights to possess the whole. A joint tenancy (*e.g.*, the investments in Herb's name), is included in the net estate to the extent of the decedent's contributions. If spouses were tenants by the entirety, the statute raises a presumption that the decedent's contribution was one-half. Life insurance proceeds are not testamentary substitutes and do not affect the elective share. **1 point**

Finally, a spouse is disqualified from exercising the right of election if: (i) there is a final divorce decree; (ii) a final decree of separation was rendered against the surviving spouse; (iii) the surviving spouse abandoned the deceased spouse; or (iv) the surviving spouse failed to support the deceased spouse. **1/2 point**

In this case, Herb's 2001 will did not leave any outright disposition to Wendy. Although Herb and Wendy, by mutual agreement, lived separate and apart for many years, there was never a final court-ordered decree of separation. As a result, Wendy is not disqualified from exercising her right of election and has the option of receiving the greater of $50,000 or one-third of Herb's estate. **1/2 point**

Herb's augmented estate includes investments (totaling $300,000), one-half of his joint tenancy with Wendy (one-half of $120,000), and a Totten trust (totaling $90,000). Therefore, Herb's net estate totals $450,000. The elective share is $150,000 (the greater of $50,000 or one-third of the net estate of $450,000). Wendy is entitled to the elective share amount minus the value of all outright dispositions passing to her under the will or as testamentary substitutes. Wendy did not receive any dispositions under the will, but did receive the joint tenancy property valued at $120,000 by virtue of her survivorship. However, she need not subtract the full $120,000 value from her one-third elective share. Because of the presumption (discussed above) that she owned half of the property already, she need only subtract $60,000 from the $150,000 one-third elective share. Therefore, she is entitled to receive $90,000 from the estate plus an exempt personal property set-aside. **1 point**

(3)   The issue is whether an attorney who drafts a will where he is named executor may receive both attorneys' fees and an executor's commission. **2/3 point**

If an attorney drafts a will that names the attorney as executor, he must disclose to the client that: (i) any person, not just an attorney, can be named executor, (ii) executors are entitled to statutory commissions, and (iii) the attorney will also be entitled to attorneys' fees for any legal services rendered to the estate. The client must sign a written acknowledgment of this disclosure in a form set out in the statute (and two witnesses are required). Absent compliance with the statute, the commission of the attorney who serves as executor is to be one-half of the statutory commission. This requirement applies to the estates of decedents dying after 1996, regardless of when the decedent's will was executed, and even if the will was executed in another jurisdiction. The statute thus imposes a duty on attorneys to contact clients who signed their wills before the statute's enactment, but authorizes the court to waive this requirement for good cause shown. **1 point**

In the present case, there is no signed, written acknowledgment between Herb and Luke. Additionally, there are no facts indicating that Luke disclosed to Herb that (i) any person can be named executor and that (ii) Luke is entitled to a statutory commission in addition to his attorneys' fees. As a result, Luke is entitled to attorneys' fees and only one-half of the statutory executor's commission. **1 point**

ANSWER R-4—CONTRACTS/PROFESSIONAL RESPONSIBILITY/CORPORATIONS

(1)(a)(i)   The issue is whether an employee has a valid claim for breach of contract when her employment is terminated before the expiration of her employment term. **1/2 point**

Under the CPLR, a plaintiff states a valid cause of action if, on its face, the plaintiff's complaint states any valid grounds for relief under the substantive law; the standard is liberal. To find that Mal and the Professional Corporation ("the P.C.") breached the contract with Bonnie, the court will first have to find that there was a valid contract between the parties. **1/2 point**

A valid contract requires an offer, an acceptance, and consideration. Here, Mal, as a representative of the P.C., offered Bonnie $60,000 per year to work until the conclusion of the disciplinary proceedings against Mal. Bonnie accepted this offer. Consideration requires that there be a bargained for exchange between the parties to the contract which constitutes a benefit to the promisor or a detriment to the promisee. The consideration in this case takes the form of an exchange of promises. **2/3 point**

Mal and the P.C. promised to employ Bonnie for a stated term, and Bonnie promised to continue working for the P.C. for that term. Therefore, there was a valid contract between the parties. In addition, in New York, unless otherwise stated, employment contracts are "at will," meaning that either party can terminate the contract at anytime for any reason or no reason at all. However, in this case, Bonnie was hired for a specific term—"until the conclusion of any disciplinary proceeding against Mal and during the period of any suspension." Therefore her employment contract was not "at will" because it was for a stated period of time. **2/3 point**

In order to state a cause of action for breach of contract, the non-breaching party must show that the other party breached a material term of the contract. A material breach is one that prevents the non-breaching party from receiving the substantial benefit of her bargain. In this case, the term of the contract is material because it involved the duration of the employment. The P.C. had a duty to retain Bonnie until the completion of the disciplinary proceedings against Mal, provided that Bonnie performed under the contract. The P.C. terminated Bonnie's employment before the completion of the disciplinary proceedings against Mal and, by doing so, breached the contract with Bonnie. **2/3 point**

Therefore, Bonnie has made out a claim for breach of contract, and the court correctly denied the motion to dismiss the action on this basis.

(a)(ii)   The issue is whether compliance with ethical standards is an implied term in legal employment contracts. **2/3 point**

In New York, courts will imply missing terms into contracts when they are necessary to make the contract complete. Attorneys in New York are bound by the Code of Professional Responsibility. Any employment contract for legal employment contains an implied term that lawyers will comply with the rules of professional responsibility. An attorney in New York has a duty to report a violation of the disciplinary rules by another attorney. **1 point**

Here, Bonnie correctly informed Mal that she would not participate in the practice of law with a suspended attorney. Mal had his right to practice law temporarily revoked and should not have been coming into the office and meeting with clients. By practicing law, Mal was violating the Rules of Professional Conduct. Mal was a supervisory attorney whose responsibility was to make sure that other attorneys made reasonable efforts to conform to the disciplinary rules. A law firm must make reasonable efforts to ensure that all attorneys conform to the rules as well. The P.C. continued to allow Mal to work with clients, even though this did not conform to the rules of professional conduct. Bonnie, even though she is a subordinate attorney, was putting herself at risk of penalty by continuing to work with Mal during his suspension. In fact, she had an obligation to report Mal to the New York State Bar Association. Since Bonnie's employment was terminated because she complained about Mal's unlawful activity, Mal and the P.C. breached the contract because the maintenance of ethical standards is an implied term of the contract. **1 point**

The court correctly denied the motion to dismiss the action on this basis.

(b)   The issue is whether an employment contract for a specified yet uncertain term falls within the Statute of Frauds. **2/3 point**

Under New York law, the Statute of Frauds requires certain contracts to be in writing in order to be enforceable. Included in these contracts are service contracts not capable of being completed within one year of entering the contract. The actual amount of time that it takes to complete the contract is irrelevant for the purpose of determining if a service contract falls within the Statute of Frauds. **2/3 point**

Here, the term of the contract between the P.C. and Bonnie was "until the conclusion of any disciplinary proceeding against Mal and during the period of any suspension." That the parties may have expected this period to be greater than a year does not matter. Since the conclusion of the disciplinary proceeding against Mal and the period of suspension, if any, could have been completed in less than a year, the contract does not fall within the Statute of Frauds and does not need to be in writing. **1 point**

Therefore, the court was correct in denying the motion.

(2)   The issue is whether a partner in a professional corporation is personally liable for a breach of contract action against the professional corporation. **1/2 point**

In New York, the designation as a professional corporation limits liability against its partners. Although partners, for public policy reasons, remain liable on tort claims, they are not liable on contract claims. **1/2 point**

Here, Bonnie's claim is for the breach of her employment contract that she had with the P.C. Since Bonnie's claim is for breach of contract, Mal is liable only to the extent of his ownership of the P.C., and he is not independently personally liable on this action. **1/2 point**

Under the CPLR, a party will be granted summary judgment if there is no triable issue of fact and the moving party is entitled to judgment as a matter of law. Here, since Mal cannot be held liable on a breach of contract claim against the P.C., the court was incorrect in denying Mal's motion. **1/2 point**

ANSWER R-5—EVIDENCE/CRIMINAL LAW

(1)   The issue is whether the prosecution can introduce evidence of prior specific acts of the defendant as substantive evidence at trial. **2/3 point**

In general, to be admissible, evidence must be relevant. That is, it must tend to prove or disprove a material issue. To be relevant, the evidence must relate to the time, event, or person involved in the trial. **1/3 point**

Here, Owl's testimony relates to time because Chef approached Owl shortly before the restaurant fire. It relates to the event (the restaurant fire) because Chef purportedly asked Owl to set fire to Chef's house. Finally, it relates to the same person, Chef. **1/3 point**

However, relevant evidence is not always admissible. The courts have broad discretion to exclude relevant evidence if its probative value is substantially outweighed by its prejudicial effect. Under New York law, the general rule is that evidence of specific acts of a defendant that show bad character may not be introduced by the prosecution merely to show that the defendant was more likely to have committed the crime. An exception to this rule exists when the defendant first introduces evidence of his good character. However, when the prosecution proposes to offer such evidence for something other than showing the defendant's propensity to commit the crime, evidence of prior specific acts may be introduced. The prosecution may use prior specific acts to show motive, intent, identity, absence of mistake or accident, or a common plan or scheme. **1 point**

Here, Owl's testimony may be introduced as evidence of a common plan by Chef to burn down the properties that he owns. Chef is accused of hiring Arnie to burn down his restaurant. Owl's testimony that Chef had recently approached him and attempted to hire him to burn down Chef's house tends to prove that Chef hired someone to burn down his restaurant. Although the court has broad discretion in excluding evidence, Owl's testimony should have been admitted. **1 point**

Therefore, the court's ruling was incorrect.

(2)(a)   The issue is whether the prosecution must show that the defendant personally committed the act in order to establish his culpability. **1 point**

In New York, an accomplice is liable for all of the foreseeable acts of all "parties to the crime." An accomplice is one who aids, abets, or encourages another to commit a crime with the intent to encourage the commission of that crime. Accomplices may be held liable for the substantive offenses of the person whose acts constituted the crime itself. An accomplice may avoid liability only if he withdraws from the crime before it is actually committed by the principal. Under New York Penal Law, arson in the third degree requires the intentional burning of a building by intentionally setting fire or using an explosive device. **1-1/3 points**

In this case, Chef is charged with arson in the third degree as an accomplice to Arnie. Arnie's testimony and the evidence, including Arnie's fingerprints on the gasoline can, show that Arnie intentionally burned down Chef's restaurant after Chef hired him to do so. Chef encouraged Arnie's actions by paying him $5,000. Clearly, Arnie's acts in this case were foreseeable in that they were precisely what Chef hired him to do. Since Chef intentionally encouraged Arnie to commit the crime by paying him, Chef is an accomplice of Arnie's; furthermore, Chef did not attempt to withdraw from the crime and took no action to prevent Arnie's act of arson. Thus, Chef can be held liable for the substantive offense. **1-1/3 points**

Therefore, the court should deny Chef's motion to dismiss the indictment on the grounds that Chef could not be convicted of arson without actually setting the fire.

(b) The issue is whether an accused can be convicted of a crime based on the testimony of his accomplice and circumstantial evidence. **1 point**

Under New York law, a person cannot be convicted solely on the testimony of an accomplice. Testimony of an accomplice must be supported by corroborative evidence tending to connect the defendant with such offense. **1 point**

Here, the prosecution based its case on Arnie's testimony that Chef hired him to burn down Chef's building for $5,000. However, the prosecution corroborated this testimony with evidence showing that Chef sold some of his restaurant equipment for $5,000 a few days before the fire and that Chef recently increased his insurance coverage. Both of these facts, although circumstantial, tend to support Arnie's testimony because they are relevant to motive and intent. **2/3 point**

Given that Arnie's testimony is not the only evidence that the prosecution is using to convict Chef, his conviction would not rest solely on the testimony of an accomplice. **1/3 point**

Therefore, the court should deny Chef's motion to dismiss the indictment.

ANSWER R-6—DOMESTIC RELATIONS/MORTGAGES/WILLS

(1) The issue is whether maintenance payments terminate after the paying spouse dies. **2/3 point**

Under New York Domestic Relations Law ("DRL"), spousal support agreements terminate when either party dies, the receiving spouse remarries, or the receiving spouse lives with another and holds herself out as married to that person. This rule, however, applies absent an alternative agreement. **1 point**

In this case, John and Ann entered into a separation agreement that stated that Ann would continue to receive payments until her death or remarriage. This agreement shows the parties' intention to vacate the general rule of the DRL, and provide for a different contractual arrangement. Furthermore, the separation agreement was not merged with the divorce decree; rather its express terms were to survive the divorce decree. Since both John and Ann negotiated and agreed to this agreement, the contract will be binding on John's estate. Therefore, Ann is entitled to continue receiving maintenance payments from John's estate per the separation agreement, even though John predeceased her. **1-1/3 points**

(2)(a) The issue is whether a mortgage survives the death of the mortgagor. **2/3 point**

Under New York law, a valid mortgage survives the death of a party and remains attached to the land. To be valid, a mortgage must comply with the Statute of Frauds, which requires that the mortgage be evidenced by a writing signed by the mortgagor. Here, the mortgage was in writing and signed by John. **1 point**

Furthermore, because separation agreements are governed by contract principles and John gave Ann the mortgage pursuant to a valid separation agreement, this is further evidence of the mortgage's validity. Ann therefore is entitled to the value of the mortgage on Greenacre given to her by John upon the sale of the property by the estate. **2/3 point**

(b)   The issue is whether Ann's mortgage is superior to Lender's mortgage. **2/3 point**

Under New York law, priority in real estate interests is determined based on the race-notice statute. In a race-notice jurisdiction, one who gives valuable consideration and has no actual notice of a prior instrument will prevail over another provided that he records before the prior grantee. **1 point**

Here, Lender was given a duly executed mortgage and recorded it in November of 1997. Ann's mortgage, although valid, was not recorded. Thus, Lender will have priority because he recorded the mortgage before she did. Additionally, Lender did not have notice that anyone else was entitled to Greenacre. **1 point**

Therefore, Ann's rights under her mortgage on Greenacre will be subordinated to the Lender's superior first mortgage.

(3)   The issue is whether someone can either serve as an executrix of or receive as a beneficiary from the estate of an ex-spouse if the will was executed prior to the divorce. **2/3 point**

Under New York law, a divorce terminates all benefits going to a spouse under a will. Furthermore, divorce also terminates a spouse's right of election. Here, Ann and John divorced after John executed his will. Therefore, Ann is not entitled to serve as executrix, receive as a beneficiary under John's will, or receive under her right of election. The court would have to appoint a new executor, treat Ann as predeceasing John and divide the residuary equally between the two children. **1-1/3 points**

ANSWER R-7—NEW YORK PRACTICE/TORTS/EVIDENCE

(1)   The issue is whether the Erie County New York Supreme Court has personal jurisdiction over a foreign corporation. **2/3 point**

For a state to have personal jurisdiction over a defendant foreign corporation, the corporation must have minimum contacts with the state, an opportunity to be heard, and proper service. Under New York law, jurisdiction can be obtained over a corporation if the corporation: (i) is domiciled in the state, (ii) does "sufficiently substantial" business in the state, (iii) performs an act falling under New York's long arm statute, or (iv) consents to jurisdiction. **2/3 point**

Here, Fire Corp. is not domiciled in New York. Additionally, nothing in the facts indicates that Fire Corp. either engaged in activities sufficient to rise to the level of "doing business" or consented to jurisdiction. Therefore jurisdiction over Fire Corp. must be obtained using the long arm statute. **2/3 point**

To qualify for long arm jurisdiction the defendant must: (i) transact business in the state and the claim must arise out of that transaction; (ii) engage in tortuous activity in the state; (iii) engage in tortuous activity outside of the state which causes injury in the state; or (iv) own or lease real estate in the state. "Transaction of business" includes contracting to supply goods or services in New York State. Here, Fire Corp. contracted to supply an alarm system to Dave in New York. In addition, Paul was injured in a hotel located in New York as a result of the defective fire alarm (although also due to the defective wiring). Therefore, jurisdiction may be exercised over Fire Corp. under New York's long arm statute. **1 point**

Furthermore, exercising personal jurisdiction over Fire Corp. will not violate due process. Due process will be satisfied if the defendant could "reasonably anticipate being haled" before a New York court and purposely availed itself of the state. Here, Fire Corp. solicited Dave in New York, and sent a purchase order and shipped a fire alarm to New York. Clearly, Fire Corp. availed itself of the laws of New York, made sufficient minimum contacts, and thus can reasonably expect to be sued in New York based on these activities. Therefore, the court was correct in ruling that it could exercise personal jurisdiction over Fire Corp. **2/3 point**

(2)   The issue is whether a municipality can be sued for negligently failing to comply with its statutory duty. **1 point**

Generally, the violation of a statute is negligence per se with regard to the class of people intended to be protected by the statute and the harms against which the statute was to protect. However, the state and its municipalities are immune from claims arising out of functions that are governmental in nature. The reason for this is that without this immunity, the government, which is responsible for all, would be liable for all. There are exceptions to this immunity for business or non-governmental functions or when there is a special relationship between the class of persons protected by the statute and the municipality. **1 point**

Here, although the statute was clearly intended to protect the people in the county from electrical fires, the inspection by the town's building inspector is a governmental duty. Since the town building inspector was acting in a governmental capacity on behalf of the town and there is no special relationship between the town and Paul, the town cannot be held liable. Therefore, the court was incorrect in denying Erie's motion to dismiss for failure to state a cause of action. **1 point**

(3)   The issue is whether proof of payment by an insurance company of plaintiff's medical expenses is admissible when offered by the defendant. **1 point**

Under New York law, to be admissible, evidence must be relevant. That is, it must tend to prove or disprove a material issue. To be relevant, the evidence must relate to the time, event, or person involved in the trial. **1/3 point**

Here, the material issues at trial relate to liability. The payment by a collateral source, such as an insurance company, of a plaintiff's medical expenses does not tend to prove or disprove the defendant's liability, nor does it relate to the amount of damages suffered by Paul. **1 point**

In this case, the monetary amount of Paul's medical bills can be obtained without broaching the subject of payment by Paul's insurance company and the jury should come to a conclusion about the amount of damages suffered by Paul without knowledge of the insurance proceeds. After the award of damages, the level of insurance proceeds is only relevant in connection with the court, after trial, potentially subtracting the amount from the jury's award for Paul's damages. Therefore, the fact that Paul's bills were paid by his insurance company is irrelevant to any issue at trial and the court was correct in granting Paul's motion. **1 point**

ANSWER R-8—WILLS/PARTNERSHIP

(1)   The issue is whether a relative of the decedent who is an attorney is automatically deemed to be more qualified to receive letters of administration than other, non-attorney relatives of the decedent. **2/3 point**

Letters of administration are those court documents that appoint an administrator for a decedent who dies intestate. An administrator has significant responsibilities in handling a decedent's estate. In New York, the surrogate's court will seek to appoint someone who is familiar with the decedent and the decedent's estate and who can adequately and completely perform the requisite responsibilities. Oftentimes, the person who best suits this position is the decedent's spouse. **2/3 point**

Here, the court granted letters to Win because as Iz's wife she is presumably closely familiar with his estate and there was no evidence to indicate that she would be unable or unsuited to perform the required duties. Sam's status as an attorney does not automatically qualify him as the best candidate to receive the letters. Therefore, the court was correct in granting letters of administration to Win. **2/3 point**

(2)(a) *Rights and liabilities of Win:* The issue is whether an administratrix is liable for any losses to the estate when she acts outside her powers as administratrix. **1/3 point**

Under New York law, an administratrix has a duty to conserve and protect the assets of the estate. In order to fulfill this duty, broad powers are bestowed on the administratrix. However, the administratrix cannot act in a way that would expose the estate to unnecessary risk. If the administratrix breaches her duty, she can be held liable to the estate for any losses sustained as a result of her breach. **1/3 point**

Here, Win was appointed administratrix over Iz's estate and tried to continue "Izquisite Affairs" even though she had never worked with Iz and had no business experience. Carrying on a business in which the administratrix has no experience is a breach of the duty owed to the decedent's estate. Therefore, Win will be liable for the losses that resulted from her actions. **1/3 point**

Under New York law, when a decedent dies intestate leaving a spouse and children, the spouse is entitled to the first $50,000 and half of the balance of the estate, while the children split the remainder. **1/3 point**

Here, Iz's estate consists of $160,000 in cash assets ($10,000 in the "Izquisite Affairs" bank account and $150,000 in a personal savings account) and a one-third interest in PIP Manor. Iz was survived by his wife, Win, and one child, Sam. Win is entitled to $50,000 plus half of the remaining $110,000 and half of Iz's interest in PIP Manor. Thus, Win would receive $105,000 ($50,000 + one-half of $110,000) in cash and one-half of Iz's interest in PIP Manor. However, Win will have to reimburse the estate for $60,000 that she lost as administratrix out of her share of the estate. Thus, Win will receive $45,000 ($105,000 - $60,000) from the estate plus half of Iz's interest in PIP Manor. **2/3 point**

(b) *Rights and liabilities of Sam:* The issue is how to value a son's intestate share, when the value of the estate has been reduced due to the administratrix's breach of duty. **1/3 point**

As discussed above, Iz's estate was valued at $160,000 plus his one-third interest in PIP Manor. Sam was his only son and as such he is entitled to the remainder of Iz's estate ($55,000) after Win takes her share, plus half of Iz's share of PIP Manor (Win gets the other half). Sam has no liabilities with regard to Iz's estate. **2/3 point**

(3) *Pat's and Pete's rights in the partnership/assets:* The issue is whether the remaining partners can recover partnership property (the car) that is in the possession of a deceased partner's estate. **1/3 point**

Under New York law, if partnership money is used to buy assets on behalf of the partnership, it is partnership property, not personal property. Partners have equal rights with respect to partnership property. Upon the death of a partner, his right in specific partnership property vests in the remaining partners. Surviving spouses, heirs and next of kin are not entitled to share in partnership property absent an agreement giving them those rights. **2/3 point**

Here, Iz has died and the facts do not indicate that there was an agreement altering the rights of the partners. As a result, after Iz's death, his right to possess partnership property (the car) vested in Pat and Pete. The car is partnership property regardless of the fact that Iz used it exclusively while he was alive. Therefore, Pat and Pete are entitled to recover the car from Win on behalf of the partnership. **2/3 point**

Pat's and Pete's rights in the partnership: The issue is whether the remaining partners can continue a partnership after the death of a partner. **1/3 point**

There are no formalities needed to create a general partnership. A partnership exists when two or more people operate a business as co-owners for profit. In the absence of a partnership agreement, the partnership and its partners' rights and liabilities are governed by New York statutory defaults. Unless otherwise agreed, a partnership ends with any material change, including the death of one of the partners. **1/3 point**

Here, PIP Manor has no written partnership agreement to alter the statutory defaults. Once Iz died, the partnership dissolved by operation of law. Therefore, Pat and Pete must dissolve PIP Manor. **1/3 point**

When dissolving a partnership, its assets are reduced to cash and its liabilities are paid in the following order: outside creditors, then partner's advances, and then partner's contributions to capital. Here, PIP Manor will be dissolved and Pat and Pete are entitled to any monies due to them according to the above schedule, with the surplus or profits being shared equally among Pat, Pete, and Iz's estate. **1/3 point**

Win's rights in the partnership in her role as administratrix: The issue is what rights Win has as administratrix of the estate in the partnership and its assets. **1/3 point**

As administratrix of Iz's estate, Win is obligated to return all partnership property, including the car, and to ensure that Iz's estate receives the proper distribution of assets upon the dissolution of PIP Manor. In addition, as discussed above, the partnership will be dissolved in accordance with New York law. Thus, in the absence of any agreement thereto, Win has no right to be substituted for Iz as partner of PIP Manor. Win has no other rights to the partnership and its assets. **2/3 point**

The rights of Iz's estate in the partnership: The issue is whether the estate has a right to Iz's interest in the partnership. **1/3 point**

Any assets purchased by a partner with personal funds are transferable by a partner. In addition, a partner's personal share of profits is considered personal property and is freely transferable by that partner. **1/3 point**

As discussed above, Iz's estate is entitled to receive any advances or contributions to capital that Iz made to PIP Manor, provided that there is enough money after the sale of the partnership's assets. If there is additional money, Iz's estate is entitled to share equally with Pat and Pete in any surplus or profit. The estate does not have any other rights in the partnership. **1/3 point**

ANSWER R-9—CONTRACTS/AGENCY/PROFESSIONAL RESPONSIBILITY/CORPORATIONS

(1) The issue is whether oral statements made prior to or contemporaneously with a written contract, which contradict or supplement the written terms, may be admissible as testimony regarding the terms of the contract. **2/3 point**

Oral statements made prior to or at the time of a written contract are parol evidence and as such their admissibility is governed by the Parol Evidence Rule ("PER"). **1/3 point**

The PER bars the admission of any testimony of contemporaneous oral statements to a written contract that is offered to establish terms inconsistent with the contract. When applying this rule, courts look at several factors to determine if there was an expectation that the term would be part of the contract, including: (i) whether the contract was fully integrated, (ii) whether there is any ambiguity in the language, and (iii) whether similarly situated parties naturally and normally would have included the matter in their written contract. A fully integrated written contract is one that is intended by the parties as a final expression of that contract and embodies all the terms of the agreement. **1 point**

In this case, the oral statements in question were made contemporaneously to the written contract and clearly relate to a written term therein, the buyback provision, and are being offered to limit the written term and make the buyback provision only available when the corporation is making a profit. Although there is no merger clause reciting that the agreement is complete on its face, there is nothing to indicate that this contract does not embody all of the terms of the agreement. Therefore, the contract is fully integrated. The contract explicitly addresses the issue of the stock buyback, and any evidence contradicting the written contract is parol evidence. In addition, the court should determine that similar parties would have included the buyback provision in the written contract. The language of the contract is clear and unambiguous, and Major and Min have not alleged any other exceptions to the PER, such as formation defects, the existence of a condition precedent, consideration problems, or subsequent modifications. **1 point**

The oral testimony is parol evidence and it does not fit within any exception of the PER. Therefore, the oral testimony should be inadmissible, and the court's ruling was incorrect.

(2) The issues are whether an attorney may bind a client to a settlement agreement with neither notice to the client nor approval by the client, and whether a third party may then hold the client liable. **1/2 point**

In general, an agent can bind a principal provided that such a relationship exists and there is authority for the agent to act on behalf of the principal. Authority can be actual, apparent or inherent. Actual authority can be express or implied and exists when the agent reasonably believes that he has authority to act. Apparent authority exists when a third party reasonably believes that the agent has authority to act through the third party's dealings with the principal. Inherent authority is created by courts to protect innocent third parties. **2/3 point**

In this case, it was not reasonable for Al to think that he had actual authority to bind Dan to the settlement. Under these facts, Al was not given actual authority to enter into a settlement agreement. In fact, Dan was not present in court and Al was not able to reach him to discuss the settlement. Al should not have apparent authority to enter into the settlement because, although it is reasonable for Dressco's attorney to believe that Al, as Dan's attorney, was acting with Dan's approval, Dressco's attorney did not have any dealings with Dan, who was not in court during the settlement negotiations. Inherent authority may exist, because even though Al exceeded his actual authority, he was conducting himself, as Dan's attorney, in a manner similar to previously authorized conduct. The court, however, should not find that Al had inherent authority because the court usually only does so in cases where an innocent third party will be harmed, and in this case, it is Dan who will be harmed, not Dressco. **2/3 point**

The second issue that needs to be addressed is whether an attorney can bind a client to a settlement without the client's consent. **1/2 point**

The New York Code of Professional Responsibility states that any decision affecting the merits of a case must be made by the client. The attorney has an ethical obligation to ensure that the client is fully informed regarding the matter before making any such decision. Settlement offers affect the merits of the case and therefore fall within this rule. **1/2 point**

In this case, Al did not have the proper authority to settle the case. As Dan's attorney, Al had an ethical obligation to inform Dan that Dressco had made a settlement offer. Al was also obligated to make sure that Dan understood the terms of the offer and how Dan's decision would affect his rights and obligations. The decision whether to accept this offer should have been made by Dan. Al breached his duty by failing to notify Dan of the offer and its specifics, and by accepting the offer without Dan's approval. The fact that Al believed that the offer was in Dan's best interest is irrelevant. Al still had an obligation to discuss the proposed settlement with Dan. **2/3 point**

Thus, because Dan did not accept the offer and Al did not have authority to act as his agent when he accepted, Dan is not bound by the terms of the settlement. Furthermore, if the court binds Dan to the stipulation of settlement, he may have grounds to file a malpractice claim against Al for damages incurred.

(3)(a)   The issue is whether the wasting of corporate assets will produce irreparable harm such that equity would require the issuance of a preliminary injunction. **1/2 point**

A preliminary injunction is a form of equitable relief which is used to preserve the status quo until the underlying judicial proceeding is completed. In order to obtain a preliminary injunction, the moving party must show that: (i) irreparable harm would result if the preliminary injunction is not granted; (ii) there is a likelihood of prevailing at the later trial; (iii) available legal remedies and monetary damages would not be sufficient; and (iv) such party has "clean hands." **1/2 point**

In this case, Major is wasting corporate assets by using the assets to pay personal expenses and neglecting the business in general. Min, a shareholder of the corporation, is seeking to dissolve Dressco. Without the preliminary injunction, Min will suffer irreparable harm because if Major is allowed to continue wasting Dressco's assets, then dissolution of Dressco may prove to be a fruitless victory for Min. Min must also show a likelihood of success on the merits of the underlying case for dissolution of Dressco. The facts clearly indicate that Major has refused to discuss company business with Min, give Min any financial statements or hold any director or shareholder meetings. Min has a strong case for dissolution based on these actions of Major. **1/2 point**

Given that Min has not been involved in the neglect of the business and can show irreparable harm if the preliminary injunction is not granted, that monetary damages would not be sufficient and a likelihood of success on the underlying claim, Min is entitled to a preliminary injunction. Min will be required to post a bond if the preliminary injunction is granted and such injunction may be vacated or modified based on a change in circumstances. **1/2 point**

(b)   The issue is whether a minority shareholder may petition for voluntary dissolution of a corporation. **1/2 point**

Under New York law, a shareholder may move for voluntary dissolution if the shareholder holds at least 20% of the voting shares and the directors or those in control of the corporation have acted to defraud or oppress that shareholder, or if the assets of the corporation are being wasted or diverted by those in control. The court will consider liquidation if it is the only feasible way to achieve a fair return on the petitioner's investment and it is reasonably necessary to protect petitioner or any substantial number of shareholders. **1/2 point**

In this case, Min owns 50 of the 200 shares issued and outstanding. Since Min is a minority share-holder and holds 25% of the voting shares of Dressco, Min meets the threshold 20% ownership test. Major is both a controlling shareholder and a director. Min can show that Major has oppressed Min by refusing to hold meetings, discuss company business and provide her with financial statements and by wasting Dressco's assets. Further, the court can reasonably find that dissolution is the only means of getting Min a fair return and is reasonably necessary to protect Min. The court can, in the alternative, allow Major to purchase the petitioner's shares at their fair market value and on terms approved by the court, rather than effecting a liquidation of the company. **1/2 point**

Min has satisfied the requirements for judicial dissolution and is entitled to have the petition for dissolution of Dressco granted.

ANSWER R-10—CRIMINAL LAW/COMMERCIAL PAPER

(a)(1) *Issuing a bad check.* The issue is whether a person who writes a check with knowledge that the bank account has insufficient funds to cover that check can be found guilty of the crime of issuing a bad check. **2/3 point**

The elements of any crime are a physical act by the defendant, the requisite mental state to commit such act, the concurrence of the act and mental state and a harmful result caused by such act. Issuing a bad check is a specific intent crime. Under New York law, the elements for issuing a bad check are: (i) the drawer puts a check into circulation, (ii) knowing that there are insufficient funds to cover it, (iii) with the belief that payment will be refused by the drawee, and (iv) payment is in fact refused by the drawee. **2/3 point**

In this case, Duke drew a check on his account at B Bank for $10,000 and gave it to Earl as payment for Earl's boat. The criminal act here is the issuance by Duke of the bad check. Duke exhibited the requisite mens rea by issuing the check with the knowledge that his account had insufficient funds. At the time that he drew the check, Duke knew that his balance was only $7,000. Although he hoped for a deposit from an insurance settlement, Duke knew that without that deposit his check would be dishon-ored. B Bank refused payment on Duke's check. The fact that Duke was hoping to get enough money to cover the check is irrelevant. **2/3 point**

Thus, Duke can be convicted of issuing a bad check.

(2) *Larceny.* The issue is whether (i) issuing a bad check and (ii) fraudulently taking money from another constitutes the crime of larceny. **1/2 point**

Larceny is the taking away of the personal property of another with the intent to permanently deprive such person of that property without consent or with consent obtained by fraud. Under New York law, an individual who obtains property by means of issuing a bad check is guilty of larceny. **1/2 point**

In this case, Duke agreed to buy Earl's motor boat for $10,000. Earl delivered the boat to Duke and Duke gave Earl a check for $10,000. Duke knew that his bank account had insufficient funds to cover that check. Therefore, Duke issued a bad check. Duke obtained property, namely Earl's boat, through the issuance of this bad check. Duke is therefore guilty of larceny against Earl for his actions to obtain the boat. **1/2 point**

Duke also is guilty of larceny against Acme. Duke took two checks totaling $5,000 from the offices of Acme through the use of fraud and deposited them in his own account. He intended to permanently deprive Acme of its money, since he used a majority of that money to complete payment to Earl for the boat. **1/2 point**

Therefore, Duke can properly be convicted of larceny.

(3) *Forgery.* The issue is whether a person has committed a forgery when, without authorization, he drafts a check payable from the account of another and signs the name of a party authorized to draw checks on that account. **1/3 point**

Under New York law, forgery consists of the making or alteration of a writing, with apparent legal significance, so that it is false, with the intent to defraud. **1/2 point**

In this case, Duke drafted a check payable from Acme's account for $2,000. Acme's check is a writing with apparent legal significance. Duke, who is not authorized to draw checks, then made it false by signing the Acme treasurer's name to it. Finally, Duke intended to defraud Acme. Therefore, Duke can properly be convicted of forgery for the $2,000 check. **1/2 point**

The second issue is whether a person who falsely prepares a check and obtains a valid signature by fraud can be convicted of forgery. **1/3 point**

If the third party realizes that he is signing a document, forgery has not been committed even if the third party was induced by fraud to sign it. **1/2 point**

Duke did not sign the $3,000 check himself. Even though Duke acted with the intent to defraud by making the check payable to Duke Corp., a non-existent entity, Duke obtained a lawful signature from the treasurer. Therefore, Duke cannot be convicted of forgery for the $3,000 check because Acme's treasurer signed that check knowing that it was a check. In order for Duke to have committed a forgery on the $3,000 check, he would have had to trick the treasurer into signing the check without realizing it was a check. **1/2 point**

Therefore, Duke can only be convicted of forgery for the $2,000 check.

(b)(1) *$3,000 check.* The issue is whether the drawee bank is liable to the drawer for honoring an unauthorized check with a valid signature. **1/2 point**

Under the U.C.C., a bank is not liable to the maker of a check when the bank makes payment on a check which was duly presented for payment, appeared valid on its face and had an authorized signature. **1/2 point**

In this case, B Bank made payment on the check for $3,000 when it was presented for payment. Although the check was unauthorized, since Acme's treasurer was defrauded into signing the check and the payee, Duke Corp., was a fictitious company, it appeared to B Bank that the check was valid on its face because it had the authorized signature of the treasurer. **1/2 point**

Therefore, B Bank cannot be held liable to Acme for the $3,000 check.

(2) *$2,000 check.* The issue is whether the bank, as drawee, is liable to the drawer for honoring an unauthorized check with a forged signature. **1/3 point**

Banks issue periodic statements to its customers, typically monthly, which contain a statement of the account as well as the canceled checks. Under the U.C.C., after receiving such a statement, a customer must use reasonable care to promptly examine that statement for (i) unauthorized signings of the customer's own name and (ii) any alterations in amounts payable. A failure to examine this statement, and report any resulting discrepancies within a reasonable time, is a form of negligence that may preclude the defenses of forgery and alteration. **1/2 point**

However, under the U.C.C., a bank is liable when it makes payment on a check that is duly presented for payment but which contains the forged signature of the maker. Courts will use a negligence standard in determining whether a bank may be held liable on a forged instrument. Under this standard, a bank is required to recognize the signatures of the drawers who hold accounts with it and is liable to a drawer if it pays out funds on a forged instrument. **1/2 point**

Here, Duke forged the treasurer's signature on the check, endorsed the check and deposited it with B Bank. On these facts, it is unclear whether ACME has received any statement which would alert the treasurer of the forged check. Notwithstanding the aforementioned, B Bank is charged with knowledge of the signatures on accounts held with them. If B Bank failed to exercise ordinary care in paying the check, as in a case where a forged signature is sloppy, B Bank would be liable. Although the facts do not indicate how genuine Duke's forged signature appeared, if the signature was an obvious forgery, B Bank could be required to credit ACME's account. **1/2 point**

Therefore, B Bank may or may not be held liable to Acme for the $2,000 check. **1/2 point**

ANSWER R-11—WILLS

(a)   The issue is whether a handwritten amendment to the will made after execution of a will is valid. **2/3 point**

In New York, a will may only be modified or amended by a document (usually as a codicil to the original will) that complies with the same testamentary formalities needed to create a valid will. In other words, it must be signed by the testator, it must be written, and it must be published to two witnesses who must sign it within 30 days of one another. **2/3 point**

In this case, after the will was properly executed and witnessed, Ted attempted to amend it by inserting an additional bequest to Mary. Although this was done immediately following the execution and attestation of his will and published to the same witnesses, neither Ted nor the witnesses subsequently signed the amendment. Therefore, the bequest to Mary is not valid and Mary is not entitled to receive the $25,000. If the additional bequest had been made before the will had been duly executed, it would have been valid. **1 point**

(b)   The issue is whether a beneficiary of a specific bequest of a certain number of shares is entitled to receive shares obtained by the testator in a stock split of those shares. **2/3 point**

A specific bequest is a gift of a specified or identified item of the testator's property. Under New York law, a specific bequest of stock includes additional shares produced by a stock split after the will is executed and before the testator's death. **1 point**

In this case, the gift to Bob is a specific bequest because the language of the bequest states "my 100 shares of C Corp." The use of the word "my" changes what would have been a general bequest of 100 shares of C Corp. into a specific bequest of Ted's 100 shares. At the time of the will's execution, Ted owned 100 shares of C Corp. Subsequent to the execution of Ted's will, but before Ted's death, the shares associated with the bequest to Bob were subject to a two-for-one split and Ted received an additional 100 shares. **1 point**

Therefore, Bob is entitled to receive the full 200 shares of C Corp.

(c)   The issue is whether the beneficiary of a specific bequest can receive the equivalent value of the bequest when the bequeathed property is not in the testator's estate at the time of the testator's death. **2/3 point**

In New York, specific bequests are subject to the doctrine of ademption. The doctrine of ademption states that when specifically bequeathed property is not in the testator's estate at his death, the bequest is adeemed and it fails. The doctrine is applied as an objective test without regard to the testator's probable intent. Ademption does not apply to general dispositions. **2/3 point**

In this case, the bequest to Ann is specific because the language indicates that it is referring to a particular piece of Ted's property (the Tiffany lamp) and includes the use of the word "my." Since Ted sold the lamp a month before his death, it was not part of his estate at the time of his death. Therefore, the specific bequest to Ann fails because the property bequeathed to her was not in Ted's estate at his death. Further, the proceeds of the sale do not fall within any of the exceptions to ademption. There-fore, Ann is not entitled to receive $50,000 (the value of the lamp) from Ted's estate. **2/3 point**

(d)   The issue is whether a pretermitted child has the right to claim an intestate share of a parent's estate if that child is provided for in a testamentary substitute. **2/3 point**

A pretermitted child is a child of the testator born after the execution of a will and not provided for or mentioned in the will. Under New York law, a pretermitted child is entitled to (i) share in bequests to his siblings if substantial gifts were made to them, (ii) take nothing if the other children take nothing, or (iii) take an intestate share, if the other children were given limited provisions. The general rule is that if the testator had no children when the will was executed, the afterborn child takes the intestate share that he would have inherited had the testator died without a will. However, if the afterborn child is otherwise provided for by a lifetime transfer, such as Totten trust or other settlement, he is not entitled to the statute's protection. The size or appropriateness of the settlement is not important. **1 point**

In this case, Debra is Ted's only child. She was born after the execution of Ted's will and was not provided for in the will. However, the facts indicate that Ted provided for Debra by creating a Totten trust in the amount of $75,000. A Totten trust, also known as a bank account trust, is a bank account in the depositor's name "as trustee" for a named beneficiary. In this case, the bank account was created in the name of Ted in trust for Debra. Ted retained all rights over the account, and Debra, as benefi-ciary, had no beneficial interest in the account during Ted's lifetime but succeeded to the amount on deposit when he died. The facts here indicate that after Ted's death, Bank B paid the $75,000 to Debra's duly appointed guardian. **2/3 point**

Therefore, although Debra was an afterborn child and is not provided for in Ted's will, her "pretermit-ted" rights have been satisfied because she received the Totten trust. Debra is not entitled to an intes-tate share of Ted's estate. **1/3 point**

ANSWER R-12—TORTS/NEW YORK PRACTICE/EVIDENCE

(1)(a)   The issue is which causes of action can be asserted on behalf of Nathan in order to file a claim against Martin for the injuries sustained by Nathan in the car accident.

Nathan has a cause of action against Martin based upon negligence. Under New York law, to be successful on a claim for negligence, a plaintiff must show that the defendant owed a duty to the plaintiff, the defendant breached that duty, the defendant's breach was the actual and proximate (legal) cause of the plaintiff's injury and that the plaintiff suffered damages. **2/3 point**

There is a general duty of care imposed on every person to act in such a way as to prevent foreseeable harm to others. The standard of care is that of the reasonable person and thus is an objective standard. Nathan must show that Martin breached his duty of care when he crossed the centerline of the road and collided with Nathan. Nathan will be able to do this because Martin was issued a ticket for his actions (which violated New York State law) and found guilty after a trial. Since Nathan fell within the class of individuals intended to be protected by the statute, the violation is considered to be negligence per se in New York, although we must still establish causation and damages to complete the prima facie case for negligence. **2/3 point**

We will then have to show that Martin's breach was both the actual and proximate cause of Nathan's injuries. An act or omission is the actual cause of an injury when the injury would not have occurred "but for" that act. Here, we can show that but for Martin crossing the centerline, the collision would not have occurred and Nathan would not have sustained his injuries. A defendant's act or omission is the proximate cause of an injury when the injury is a foreseeable harmful result of the act or omission. Here, we can show that a collision with an oncoming car was the foreseeable harmful result of crossing a centerline on a two-way road. Finally, we will need to show damages, which in this case are evidenced by the physical injuries Nathan sustained and for which he underwent surgery. **2/3 point**

Nathan may also have a cause of action against Martin for Scalpel's negligence because a tortfeasor is liable for any foreseeable damages arising from his actions, including the aggravation of the plaintiff's condition caused by the malpractice of plaintiff's treating physician. **1/3 point**

(b)   The issue is whether plaintiff's speeding and failure to wear a seatbelt can be used as affirmative defenses by the defendant to bar the plaintiff's negligence claims. **1/3 point**

Here, Martin may claim that Nathan was contributorily negligent because Nathan was speeding and failed to wear a seatbelt, and he may also raise the statute of limitations as a defense. **1/3 point**

New York is a pure comparative negligence state, which will not bar Nathan's claim. Comparative negligence permits a contributorily negligent plaintiff to recover a percentage of his damages. The trier of fact weighs plaintiff's negligence against that of the defendant and reduces plaintiff's damages accordingly. Additionally, the action will not be barred by the statute of limitations because Nathan has three years from the time of the accident to commence any negligence claim against Martin. **2/3 point**

Thus, if Nathan's action is brought timely, Martin's affirmative defenses will not bar Nathan's claims.

(2)(a)   The issue is whether Nathan can assert a valid cause of action against Scalpel for injuries relating from Scalpel's medical malpractice. **2/3 point**

Nathan may be able to recover under a theory of negligence for Scalpel's medical malpractice. Under New York law, to be successful in a claim for negligence, a plaintiff must show that the defendant owed a duty to the plaintiff, the defendant breached that duty, the defendant's breach was the actual and proximate (legal) cause of the plaintiff's injury, and that the plaintiff suffered damages. **2/3 point**

As a professional, Scalpel is held to a higher standard of care than an ordinary person. Scalpel, as Nathan's treating physician, is required to possess the knowledge and skill of a physician in good standing in similar communities and act accordingly. Nathan can show that Scalpel breached this duty under the theory of res ipsa loquitur. Under the theory of res ipsa loquitur, the very occurrence of an event can be used to establish the breach of a duty. In order to use this theory, the plaintiff must show that the accident causing injury is a type that would not normally occur unless someone was negligent, and the instrumentality causing the injury was in defendant's exclusive control. A "foreign object" such as a sponge being left inside a patient after surgery qualifies as an event that warrants the use of res ipsa loquitur, because it would not otherwise have been left in Nathan's body unless someone were negligent. Scalpel was in sole control of the sponge, and Nathan will be able to use res ipsa loquitur to show Scalpel breached the duty of care owed to him. Causation and damages can be shown through Smith's testimony regarding Nathan's ailments. Thus, Scalpel may be liable to Nathan for medical malpractice. **1 point**

(b)   The issue is whether Nathan's claim against Scalpel is barred by the statute of limitations. **1/3 point**

In New York, the statute of limitations for a medical malpractice claim is two and a half years from the date of the procedure. Nathan's post-surgical visits ended on June 20, 2000. Although Nathan went back to Scalpel in December 2000, that visit was for the removal of a cyst from his arm. Because the December visit was unrelated to the surgery, the continuing treatment theory, under which the statute of limitations would run from the date of the last visit, does not apply, and the statute of limitations would have lapsed. **2/3 point**

An exception is made, however, for situations where a "foreign object" is left in a patient's body by a doctor. The "foreign object" exception allows for the claim to be filed within two and a half years from the date of the operation or from the termination of continued related treatment, or within one year from the date of discovery of facts that would have led to discovery of the object, whichever period is longer. **1/3 point**

In this case, more than two and a half years have passed since the operation and the post-surgical visits. Thus, we will have to use the "foreign object" exception to keep Nathan's claim from being time-barred. Using this exception, Nathan has one year from the date that he knew or should have known about the sponge in order to file his claim. Nathan began experiencing pain and went to Smith, who subsequently discovered the sponge, in October 2002. Therefore, the claim is presently timely, and Nathan had until October 2003 to file his claim. Scalpel does not appear to have any other affirmative defenses. **2/3 point**

(3)   The issue is whether a traffic conviction can be used at a later civil trial associated with the same sequence of events. **1/2 point**

The threshold question in determining the admissibility of evidence is the relevance of that evidence to the case being tried. Relevant evidence is evidence that makes a fact more or less probable than it would have been without the evidence. Generally, if the evidence relates to the time, event, or person involved in the present litigation, it is deemed relevant. **1/2 point**

In this case, Martin's traffic conviction relates to the time, event, and person involved in this litigation, and it is clearly relevant because it shows that Martin violated the statute by crossing over the centerline, which was the principle cause of the accident.

However, relevant evidence may still be excluded if its probative value is outweighed by its prejudicial effect. Generally, prior convictions are only permitted to impeach a defendant or witness in criminal cases or when the conviction is being offered solely to attack the credibility of the defendant or witness. **1/2 point**

In this case, Martin's traffic violation is being offered to prove a fact alleged in the civil case, namely that Martin crossed the centerline, and not to attack his credibility or character. Furthermore, because criminal trials have a higher burden of proof than civil trials, the court will, in the interest of judicial economy, be inclined to allow evidence of the conviction rather than making Nathan reprove what the prosecution has already shown. **1/2 point**

Therefore, Martin's traffic conviction will be admissible in the civil trial.

ANSWER R-13—DOMESTIC RELATIONS/MORTGAGES

(1)(a)   The issue is whether verbal abuse by one spouse qualifies as "cruel and inhuman treatment" and is thereby grounds for a divorce in New York. **1/2 point**

New York Domestic Relations Law provides for five grounds for divorce, one of which is "cruel and inhuman treatment." A divorce will be granted against a spouse whose behavior toward the other spouse is such as to endanger the physical, emotional, or mental well being of the abused spouse. In determining if cruel and inhuman treatment exists, courts will use a subjective test and consider the effect of the defendant's conduct on the particular spouse and the length of the marriage. The sensibility and weakness or strength of the abused spouse will be taken into consideration. Unless the abusive behavior endangers the well being of the abused spouse, the court will not grant a divorce grounded on cruel and inhuman treatment. **1 point**

In this case, the facts do not indicate the emotional, physical, and mental state of Ben as a result of Bonnie's abusive behavior. The lack of a showing of endangerment coupled with Ben's repeated attempts to persuade Bonnie to move back to Albany are strong evidence showing that her behavior did not rise to the level of cruel and inhuman. **1 point**

Therefore, Ben is unlikely to prevail in his cause of action for divorce.

(b)   The issue is whether a spouse can obtain a judicial separation on the ground of abandonment if the other spouse voluntarily leaves. **2/3 point**

Under New York law, a separation grounded on abandonment will be granted if the following are proven: (i) the abandonment was voluntary; (ii) there is no intent to return on the part of the abandoning spouse; and (iii) the abandonment was without justification. Note that for a judicial separation there is no time requirement to constitute abandonment. **1 point**

In this case, Bonnie moved back to Buffalo because she did not like Albany, so her move was voluntary. Bonnie has informed Ben that she will not live in Albany, so she has no intent to return. Bonnie's reason for leaving is that she does not like Albany, so her abandonment of the marriage was without justification. Nothing in the facts contradicts any of the above conclusions. Therefore, Ben will be granted a separation based on the grounds of abandonment. **2/3 point**

(2)(a)   The issue is whether a mortgage will be deemed to contain an acceleration clause even though it is silent with respect to the acceleration of principal on default. **2/3 point**

An acceleration clause permits the mortgagee to declare the full balance due by the mortgagor in the event of default. Under New York law, in the absence of an acceleration clause agreed on by both parties, a default in payment will only give the mortgagee the right to commence an action against the defaulting party to collect on the debt or to foreclose on the mortgage. There is no acceleration clause implied by law. **2/3 point**

In this case, the mortgage and note signed by Owen were silent on the matter of acceleration of the principal. Since the documents did not contain an acceleration clause and the law does not imply one, Mort cannot prevail in claiming the existence of such a clause. Therefore, Mort is incorrect about the effect that the default had on the mortgage debt. **2/3 point**

(b) The issue is whether a buyer who takes property subject to the seller's mortgage and orally agrees to assume the mortgage is personally liable on that mortgage in the event of any deficiency on the foreclosure sale. **2/3 point**

Under New York law, a buyer who takes property subject to a mortgage is not personally liable on that mortgage. By taking subject to the mortgage, the person assumes no personal liability on the debt; however, if the mortgage is not paid, the property may be foreclosed. The property becomes the primary source for the payment of the debt. The original mortgagor continues to be liable on the note. **1 point**

In this case, Ben's deed from Owen stated that the conveyance was subject to Owen's mortgage. Therefore, Owen remains personally liable on the mortgage and Ben assumed no personal liability on the mortgage based on the deed. **2/3 point**

A buyer may also take property and assume a mortgage in which case the buyer becomes primarily responsible on the mortgage and is personally liable. To be valid, however, such an assumption is subject to the Statute of Frauds, which requires that it must be evidenced by a writing and signed by the mortgagor. **1/3 point**

In this case, although Ben agreed to assume Owen's mortgage, that agreement was oral. Because there is no written agreement, the Statute of Frauds is not satisfied and the agreement is unenforceable. **1/2 point**

Therefore, Ben will not be personally liable on Owen's mortgage in the event of any deficiency.

ANSWER R-14—SALES/CONTRACTS

(1) The issue is whether a valid contract exists between two merchants for the sale of goods when the parties intend to determine the purchase price after delivery of the goods. **2/3 point**

The U.C.C. governs this issue because the contract involves the sale of goods. In addition, the Statute of Frauds applies to contracts for the sale of goods at a price of $500 or more. Under the U.C.C., a sale of goods contract must contain a quantity term. Furthermore quantity is the only essential term in a U.C.C. contract. The failure to state the price does not prevent the formation of a contract if the parties intended to enter into a written agreement without the price being settled before delivery of the goods. If the price term is missing, the court will supply a reasonable term for the price. **1 point**

Here, there is a meeting of the minds. Linda agreed to sell and Sarah agreed to buy 10,000 leather heels with the price to be determined by the parties after delivery of the heels to Sarah. Linda and Sarah entered into the contract with the intention that the price would be considered later. Since there was no price in the written agreement and the parties disagreed about the price after the heels had been delivered (Sarah billed Linda for $5,000, while Linda wanted to pay $4,000), the court will determine the price that Sarah needs to pay to Linda. The Statute of Frauds applies to this argument because the goods cost at least $500 or more and is satisfied because the contract is in writing, signed by the parties and the quantity is stated (10,000 heels) therein. **1 point**

Therefore, because quantity is the only essential term and the quantity is defined in the contract, the contract is valid.

(2)   The issue is who bears the risk of loss when a contract states F.O.B. (free-on-board), seller's location, and the goods are destroyed prior to receipt by the buyer. **1/2 point**

Again, this written contract is covered by the U.C.C. The general rule is that in a contract for a sale of goods between merchants that states F.O.B., seller's location, F.O.B. is the delivery point. In the same manner as a shipment contract, the risk of loss shifts to the buyer as soon as the seller completes its delivery obligations (*i.e.,* delivers the goods to a common carrier for transport to a buyer). The seller also must arrange for shipment, including obtaining and tendering all documents necessary for the buyer to take possession of the goods and promptly notifying the buyer of the shipment. If the goods are destroyed while in transit to the buyer, the loss falls on the buyer and the buyer remains liable to the seller for the contract price. **2/3 point**

In this case, the contract states F.O.B., Farmingdale, the location of Sarah's (the seller's) factory. Sarah's obligations with respect to the quality of the goods, therefore, ended as soon as she completed her delivery obligations in Farmingdale. Sarah completed these obligations by delivering the shoes to a licensed carrier in Farmingdale, notifying Anne (the buyer) of the shipment and sending Anne all of the necessary documentation to enable her to take possession of the shoes. Any risk of loss then shifted to Anne. The shoes were then destroyed while on the carrier's truck en route to Anne's store. Anne, therefore, is liable to Sarah for the full amount of the contract, $20,000, even though the goods were destroyed. Accordingly, Anne's claim for $5,000 in damages will be rejected. **2/3 point**

The next issue is what remedies are available to a buyer when the seller does not deliver contracted for goods. **1/2 point**

One of the buyer's basic remedies when the seller does not deliver goods is the difference between the contract price and the cost of buying replacement goods ("cover"). This remedy involves making a reasonable contract for substitute goods in good faith and without unreasonable delay. Here, although Anne entered into a reasonable replacement contract, she bore the risk of loss on the original contract. Sarah, therefore, has no obligation to cover Anne for the difference in price between the original shoes and the replacement shoes. **2/3 point**

Anne is liable for the full $20,000 for the shipment from Sarah and the $25,000 for the shipment of shoes from the other shoe manufacturer. The only claim she may have is against the common carrier for the negligent delivery of the original shipment of shoes. **1/2 point**

(3)(a)   The issue is whether a real estate contract which grants one party the exclusive right to cancel the contract is illusory. **1/2 point**

The general rule is that for a contract to be valid there must be consideration on both sides of a contract; that is, the promises must be mutually obligatory. Agreements in which one party is bound but the other is not lack mutuality and the consideration often fails because the promise is illusory. Consideration is the bargained for exchange between the parties to the contract which constitutes a benefit to the promisor or a detriment to the promisee. The unqualified right to cancel a contract at any time may be an illusory promise. Consideration is valid if the right to cancel is in any way restricted. (For example, the U.C.C. will imply a requirement of reasonable notice even if it is not specified in the contract.) **1 point**

Here, Beth, the buyer, was granted an absolute right to cancel the contract up until the time of closing. Thus, Beth suffered no detriment in making the contract. Sarah, the seller, was not granted a similar right. Thus, she gains no benefit in making the contract given that Sarah can back out of the contract without penalty. The cancellation clause, therefore, makes the contract illusory and the contract is not binding. **1/2 point**

(b)   The issue is whether failure to close on a specified date in a real estate contract that states that "time is of the essence" constitutes a material breach of contract entitling the nonbreaching party to keep the down payment. **1/2 point**

The general rule is that failure to perform by the time stated in a contract is not a material breach if performance is rendered within a reasonable time. However, if a contract specifically provides that "time is of the essence," the failure of one party to perform on time is considered to be a material breach. A material breach is one for which the nonbreaching party does not receive the substantial benefit of her bargain as a result of failure of performance or defective performance. Here, the contract had a closing date of June 9 and provided that time was of the essence. Beth did not appear at the closing on June 9 and so committed a material breach. **2/3 point**

The standard measure of damages for a breach of a land sale contract is the difference between the contract price and the fair market value of the land. However, where a down payment constitutes a valid liquidated damages clause, it is well settled in New York that if a purchaser is not ready or is unwilling to perform, the seller may keep the down payment whether or not she has suffered any damages. For a liquidated damages clause to be valid, at the time the contract is made actual damages that may result from a breach must be difficult to ascertain (which generally is the case with contracts for real property) and the amount must be a reasonable forecast of actual damages. The down payment here of $50,000 was 10% of the contract price and appears to be a reasonable forecast of actual damages. Therefore, Sarah is entitled to keep the $50,000 due to Beth's breach. **2/3 point**

ANSWER R-15—EVIDENCE/CRIMINAL LAW/CRIMINAL PROCEDURE/PROFESSIONAL RESPONSIBILITY

(1)(a)   *Motion to suppress the evidence.* The issue is whether a police officer may enter an apartment with a "strange odor" without a warrant and whether, after doing so, any items or observations obtained therein should be excluded under the exclusionary rule. **1/2 point**

The Fourth Amendment protects individuals against unreasonable searches and seizures. The Supreme Court has interpreted the Fourth Amendment to include a reasonable expectation of privacy in one's home. The police may not enter a private home without cause and a valid search warrant unless one of the warrantless search exceptions applies. Such exceptions include consent or some type of emergency, such as hot pursuit or evanescent evidence. Consent can only be given by a person with apparent equal access to the premises to be searched. Although there is no general emergency exception to justify a warrantless search, if evidence is likely to disappear before a warrant can be obtained or some emergency regarding health or safety exists, a warrantless search and seizure may be justified. **2/3 point**

The exclusionary rule states that a victim of an illegal search can have the product of the illegal search excluded from trial. To qualify for this exclusion there must be a violation of either a federal law or the United States Constitution. **1/3 point**

In this case, Cal, the building superintendent did not have reasonably apparent authority to consent to a search of the apartment because he did not share the premises. He did not have regular access to the apartment as evidenced by his inability to provide Officer Opie with a key to the apartment. The officer was aware that the apartment was rented to a couple who were not home at the time he entered the apartment, as Cal had provided him this information. **1/2 point**

However, Cal called the police to report a smell coming from the apartment in question. Although the apartment was a private dwelling and a warrant would generally have been required before Opie could search it, in this case the exigent circumstances appear to justify the warrantless search. The smell was identified as a "rotting smell" such that a person could reasonably determine that someone or something could have been in trouble. If it could be determined that the officer believed the smell to be of a dead person, a claim could also be made that a warrantless seizure of the property was reasonable to prevent further decomposition (evanescent evidence) and to protect the public health. **1/2 point**

Thus, the court properly denied the motion suppressing the evidence of the knife found and Opie's observations because Max's Fourth Amendment rights were not violated by the search. The appellate court should affirm the lower court's ruling.

(b) *Motion to dismiss.* The issue is whether the prosecution or defense bears the burden of proof with respect to an insanity plea. **1/2 point**

The Due Process Clause requires that in criminal cases the prosecution bear the burden of proving that a defendant is guilty beyond a reasonable doubt. This burden includes proving each element of the crime charged beyond a reasonable doubt, including mens rea (the level of intent required by the crime). However, this burden does not apply to affirmative defenses. **2/3 point**

Under the New York Penal Law, insanity is an affirmative defense. All defendants are presumed sane. All affirmative defenses must be raised by and proved by the defense by a preponderance of the evidence. A defendant is considered insane, if, as a result of his mental illness, he is unable to know or appreciate the nature and consequences of his conduct or that his conduct is wrong. **2/3 point**

In this case, Max was prosecuted for murder. Therefore, the prosecution must prove that Max is guilty beyond a reasonable doubt, including that Max intentionally killed his wife, Veda. The state does not have to prove that Max was sane when he did it. The defense must plead and prove by a preponderance of the evidence that Max lacked the requisite intent to understand the nature or consequences of his actions. The prosecution did not bear any burden to produce evidence with regard to this affirmative defense. The evidence or testimony to substantiate Max's insanity defense must be presented by his attorney. **2/3 point**

Therefore, the prosecution's failure to offer any psychiatric testimony regarding Max's mental state is irrelevant. The court properly denied the motion to dismiss and the appellate court should affirm that ruling.

(2) The issue is whether the judge, at the request of the defense, must inquire into the prosecutor's motivations for exercising her peremptory challenges. **1/2 point**

The racial motivation of a prosecutor is deemed to be state action for the purposes of the Fourteenth Amendment's Equal Protection Clause. Such use of a peremptory challenge is subject to strict scrutiny and will only be held constitutional if it is necessary to achieve a compelling or overriding state interest. In order to make an equal protection-based attack on the prosecutor's use of peremptory strikes, a defendant must show facts or circumstances that raise an inference that the exclusion was based on race. After such a showing, the burden shifts to the prosecutor to provide a race-neutral explanation for the strike, and the judge must then determine whether the prosecutor's explanation was the genuine reason for exercising the peremptory challenge. **2/3 point**

In this case, the prosecutor used her first seven peremptory challenges to excuse jury panel members who were the same race as Max. Although the prosecutor is given broad discretion in the exercise of peremptory challenges, the exclusion of jury members on the basis of race alone is discriminatory and unconstitutional absent a compelling state interest and the means necessary to achieve that interest. A reasonable inference could be made that the strikes were being used in a discriminatory manner since all seven were members and were the same race as the defendant. Therefore, once Max's attorney requested that the judge inquire about the prosecutor's motives, the judge should have questioned the prosecutor to determine if her explanation for the utilization of the strikes was sincere. **1 point**

The judge should have inquired into the prosecutor's motives behind her peremptory challenges. This ruling should be overturned by the appellate court. Furthermore, on this basis, Max's conviction stands to be reversed should the court determine the prosecutor engaged in discriminatory jury selection. **1/2 point**

(3)   The issue is whether a defendant is denied the effective assistance of counsel when the attorney violates a rule of professional responsibility by engaging in an improper fee arrangement. **2/3 point**

Under the New York Code of Professional Responsibility, contingency fees are prohibited in criminal cases. The Sixth Amendment right to counsel includes the right to effective counsel. Effective assistance of counsel is a presumption. A defendant who claims ineffective assistance of counsel must prove deficient performance by counsel, and that but for such deficiency, the result of the trial would have been different. Typically, such claims can be made out only by specifying particular errors of trial counsel, not by showing that the attorney implemented an improper fee arrangement. **2/3 point**

Here, Al, the attorney, violated the rules of professional responsibility by entering into a contingency fee arrangement in his defense of Max. The agreement stated that Al would receive an additional $25,000 if Max were acquitted or found not guilty by reason of insanity. Although Al will be subject to disciplinary proceedings and penalties, Max will not be able to use this violation as the basis for a claim of ineffective assistance of counsel. The fee agreement did not constitute a deficiency in Al's performance in court. Moreover, Max would not be able to prove that but for the contingency fee arrangement, the outcome of the trial would have been different. **1 point**

The appellate court should rule that this ground did not give rise to a claim of ineffective assistance of counsel and Max's conviction should not be reversed.

ANSWER R-16—DOMESTIC RELATIONS

(1)   The issues are whether: (i) adultery committed by the accusing spouse is a defense to a claim of adultery and (ii) an unacknowledged separation agreement can be converted into a divorce decree. **1/2 point**

Pursuant to New York law, adultery is one of the five grounds for divorce. Adultery is the commission of an act of sexual intercourse, voluntarily performed by the defendant with a person other than the plaintiff after the marriage of the plaintiff and defendant. The defenses to adultery are: (i) recrimination; *i.e.,* the plaintiff is also guilty of adultery; (ii) condonation; *i.e.,* the parties voluntarily cohabit with a non-marital party with knowledge of the adultery; (iii) connivance (entrapment); or (iv) the plaintiff fails to commence an action within five years of discovering the offense. **1/2 point**

In this case, Win has claimed divorce on the grounds of adultery. However, Win has been living with her boyfriend, just as Hal has been living with his girlfriend, ever since she and Hal decided to separate. Hal will therefore be able to claim recrimination and condonation as defenses to adultery. Therefore, Win will not be able to use adultery as the ground for divorce. **1/2 point**

A couple may be able to obtain a conversion divorce when they have lived apart for at least one year pursuant to a court order or a valid separation agreement. To be valid, a separation agreement must be freely and voluntarily made, be in writing, signed and acknowledged. The court can then convert the separation agreement into a divorce agreement. **1/2 point**

In this case, Win will not be able to divorce Hal by means of the conversion divorce because they do not have a valid separation agreement. Win and Hal each gave to the other a signed letter agreeing that they have separated stating that neither will be responsible to provide support for the other. Although written and signed, their separation agreement was never acknowledged or filed with the court. Hal can successfully assert a defense that the agreement is not a valid separation agreement pursuant to which a conversion divorce action may be maintained. Thus, the grounds for divorce alleged by Win are not valid. **2/3 point**

(2)(i)   The issue is how the marital property will be distributed if the court issues a default judgment against the defendant spouse. **2/3 point**

The rule is that a default judgment will dissolve a marriage, but it should not have an effect on the distribution of marital property. In New York, marital property is subject to the rules of equitable distribution. In determining the equitable disposition of marital property, the court considers all of the circumstances of the case, including the financial circumstances of each spouse, the age and health of the parties, the length of the marriage, any maintenance awards, the tax consequences to the parties, and the economic fault of the parties. The fact that the party defaulted in the divorce action generally will not be considered in distributing the marital property. **2/3 point**

In this case, Hal did not appear at the divorce trial and a default judgment will be entered after a submission of proof. Hal's default should not affect equitable distribution because a default is not a consideration that factors into property distribution. The court will divide the marital property subject to the equitable distribution rules and criteria. **2/3 point**

Therefore, although Win must prove her cause of action Hal should not be concerned that his default will adversely affect the distribution of marital property.

(ii)   The issue is how the court will set a defendant spouse's child support obligations if such spouse defaults in answering the complaint in a divorce action. **2/3 point**

Child support is the sum paid by either or both parents for the care, maintenance, and education of any unemancipated child under age 21. Parental misconduct is irrelevant when determining child support obligations. Absent an agreement between the parents, the laws of New York require that the courts follow a mechanical formula to determine the financial responsibility of each parent. The formula applies a fixed percentage based on the number of children, and it considers the combined gross incomes of the parents, then prorating the result between the parents based on their respective incomes. The percentage may be modified pursuant to a variety of statutory factors if the court deems the noncustodial parent's pro rata share of support to be unjust or inappropriate. **2/3 point**

In this case, Hal's failure to appear in court for the divorce proceeding will not affect his child support obligations. His obligations, following the divorce order will be based on his percentage of contribution to the combined parental income and certain other factors that the court may deem relevant, such as his financial resources as the non-custodial parent, in comparison to those of Win, the financial needs of their son and visitation expenses. **2/3 point**

Therefore, Hal should not be concerned that his default will adversely affect the amount of child support he must pay.

(3)(a)   *Parcel A.* The issue is whether real property that is owned by one spouse prior to the marriage and was never improved is considered to be marital property. **1/2 point**

Pursuant to the rules of equitable distribution, marital property includes all property acquired by either spouse both during the marriage regardless of the form of title and acquired prior to the commencement of any matrimonial action, unless provided by agreement of the parties. Separate property includes property acquired before the marriage and property acquired through inheritance or gift from a non-spouse. **2/3 point**

In this case, Parcel A was owned by Hal before he married Win and no changes were made to the land to cause an increase in the value of the property. When Hal purchased Parcel A, it was a vacant tract of land. Its value has not changed since Hal purchased it. **1/2 point**

Therefore, since Parcel A was owned by Hal prior to his marriage to Win, for purposes of equitable distribution, Parcel A will not be considered marital property.

(b)   *Parcel B.* The issue is whether real property that is owned by one spouse prior to the marriage and has been improved during the marriage is considered to be marital property. **1/2 point**

As discussed above, separate property includes property acquired before the marriage. However, where there is an increase in the value of the separate property of one spouse during the marriage and prior to the commencement of a separation or divorce proceeding, which is due in part to the contributions (direct or indirect) of the other spouse, the court can consider it to be marital property. The amount of the appreciation in value may be added to the sum of the marital property for purposes of equitable distribution. **2/3 point**

In this case, Hal owned Parcel B prior to his marriage to Win, which was then improved by an apartment building. Hal and Win lived in the apartment building during their marriage, and while living together, Win handled calls from tenants and collected and deposited rent payments, which certainly may be considered direct contributions. **1/2 point**

Therefore, Parcel B will be considered marital property for purposes of equitable distribution because the property increased in value in part due to the contributions of Win.

ANSWER R-17—WORKERS' COMPENSATION/TORTS/NEW YORK PRACTICE

(1)(a)   *The dismissal of the complaint.* The issue is whether a claim for wrongful death can be brought by a decedent's estate against an employer. **2/3 point**

Any employee working in a business, trade, or occupation carried on by the employer for profit is covered by New York's Workers' Compensation Law ("WCL"). If an employee sustains an injury arising out of or in the course of his employment, or if he dies because of such injury, his exclusive remedy against his employer and third parties is the WCL. In other words, the employee does not have a common law tort claim against the employer, and he may only claim benefits as provided under the WCL. Accordingly, wrongful death actions may not be maintained against an employer by the decedent employee's family. However, the injured employee may still maintain a tort claim against a third party that is partially at fault for the accident. **1 point**

In this case, Evan was employed by Apple as a maintenance mechanic at the mill. While working at the mill he was injured and died. Since his injuries were sustained arising out of and in the course of his employment, he is covered by the WCL. Evan's estate may not maintain a wrongful death action against Apple. The estate's only claim will be for death benefits according to statutory schedules and funeral expenses. **2/3 point**

Thus, the court properly granted the motion dismissing the complaint against Apple.

(b) *The dismissal of the cross-complaint.* The issue is whether a third party may obtain contribution from an injured party's employer for an injury arising out of and in the course of employment. **2/3 point**

Under the WCL, the general rule is that a third party is barred from seeking contribution for damages from the employer of an injured employee unless the employee sustains a grave injury. Grave injury is defined in the WCL to include the death of the employee. **2/3 point**

Here, Evan suffered a grave injury while at work at the mill because he died as a result of the explosion. Renee and Carp may therefore seek contribution against Apple, Evan's employer, for any damages they must pay to Evan's estate for his wrongful death. **2/3 point**

Note, however, that where the injured employee accepts benefits under the Workers' Compensation Law and institutes a common law action for the same injuries against such a third party, the workers' compensation insurance carrier has a lien against the proceeds awarded in the third-party action to the extent of benefits paid to the employee pursuant to the Workers' Compensation Law. Hence, any damage award proceeds must first go to reimburse the insurance carrier for the workers' compensation benefits it paid out to the employee. **2/3 point**

Thus, the court incorrectly dismissed their cross-claims.

(2)   The issue is whether a contractor is vicariously liable for a subcontractor's negligence. **2/3 point**

Vicarious liability means that a person will be held liable to a third party for tortious acts committed by another person against such third party. The general rule is that a principal will not be liable for tortious acts committed by her agent if the agent is an independent contractor. A person is an agent and not an independent contractor if: (i) there is assent; (ii) the person is acting for the benefit of the principal; and (iii) the principal maintained control over the alleged agent's activities. A principal will be held liable for the acts of an independent contractor, however, if such contractor is engaged in inherently dangerous activities. **1 point**

In this case, there is assent because Renee and Carp mutually agreed to have Carp lay carpet in exchange for compensation. In addition, Carp was working for the benefit of Renee because laying the carpet will help Renee finish the renovation of the space. Renee, however, did not maintain control over Carp's activities. Although Renee supplied the carpet and determined what hours and where in the store Carp would work, Carp selected and supplied the adhesives to be used in laying the carpet, utilized his own tools and determined the methods to be used in preparing the premises for carpeting. Since Renee did not control his activities, Carp was an independent contractor. Moreover, the laying of carpet is not an inherently dangerous activity for which liability can be construed on Renee. **1 point**

Therefore, Renee will not be liable for Carp's negligence.

(3)   The issue is which parties may recover damages in a wrongful death action and what actual damages may be recovered. **2/3 point**

A wrongful death action may be brought by the personal representative of the decedent's estate within two years of the decedent's death, if the decedent is survived by distributees. The personal representative can recover punitive damages and allocate these damages to the distributees who have sustained pecuniary loss. The damages are awarded in proportion to the amount of loss each distributee sustained. Recovery is allowed only to the extent that the deceased could have recovered in an action had he lived. Loss of consortium is not compensable in a wrongful death action. **2/3 point**

In this case, Evan's wife, Willie, as executrix of Evan's estate, properly commenced a wrongful death action. Willie will be able to receive damages based on her loss of the economic support provided by Evan. Evan's two adult children will not be able to recover for parental support because they are not minors, but they will be able to seek and receive pecuniary damages including loss of economic support for the loss of household maintenance and car repair assistance that Evan provided to them. Evan's sister, Sara, although disabled and dependent on Evan for support, and pursuant to Evan's will a beneficiary of one-half of his estate, will be unable to recover in an action for wrongful death, because she is not a distributee as defined under New York law. **1 point**

Therefore, only Evan's wife and children will be proper beneficiaries of a wrongful death action.

ANSWER R-18—WILLS

(a)   The issue is whether the testator's intent will govern the construction of an otherwise valid will. **1 point**

In New York, if there is no ambiguity, extrinsic evidence is not admissible to show that a provision contained in a will is not what the testator intended. If patent ambiguity exists, that is, a mistake appears on the face of the will, statements made by a testator to her attorney are admissible to cure the ambiguity. Admissible evidence includes evidence about the testator, her family, the claimants under the will and their relationship to the testator and testator's habits and thoughts. **1 point**

Here, the will stated that if Theresa's mother survived Theresa, the remainder of the estate would go to her in trust, and upon her death to Theresa's friend Mary or Mary's issue. Robert claimed that the language of the will created a trust only if Theresa's mother survived her. Theresa's mother predeceased her by almost eight years. In that time, Theresa never changed her will. She accounted for both of her cousins in the event of her death. She left Denise a painting and named her the trustee of the residuary estate. Theresa did not leave Denise any money. Robert was not mentioned in the will but was separately provided for as the beneficiary under Theresa's life insurance policy. This evidence tends to indicate that Theresa did not want to condition the gift on the survival of her mother. Furthermore, it appears that she did not intend to have her estate go into intestacy to be shared by Denise and Robert, thus leaving Mary with no inheritance. **1-1/2 points**

Therefore, the court will attempt to act pursuant to Theresa's intention and the residuary estate should go to Mary or her issue.

(b)   The issue is whether a residuary clause in a will containing "insurance benefits," validly changes the beneficiary under a life insurance policy. **1 point**

A life insurance policy is a private contract between the policy holder and the insurance company, in which the policy holder lists a specific beneficiary of the policy. An insurance company is bound by its agreement with such policy holder, not by the policy holder's will. The beneficiary of a life insurance policy can only be changed by complying with the terms of the policy governing beneficiary designations. **1 point**

In this case, the life insurance policy listed Robert as the beneficiary. If Theresa wanted to make a change of beneficiary under the insurance policy, she had to comply with the terms of the policy. Her policy provided that in order for Theresa to change her designated beneficiary she needed to file a written request with the Home Office of the Insurance Company. Theresa never filed her will or sent any written request regarding a change of beneficiary to the insurance company. The fact that her will specifically listed "insurance benefits" as part of the residuary estate cannot by itself change the beneficiary under the policy. **1-1/2 points**

Therefore, Robert, not Mary, should receive the insurance proceeds.

(c)   The issue is whether an interested witness who attests to a will is entitled to receive a bequest under that will. **1 point**

In New York, a will is validly executed if it is a written instrument, signed by the testator, published to two witnesses that it is the maker's will, and signed by two attesting witnesses. A disposition to an attesting witness never invalidates the will. Under New York law, the rule is that the bequest to an interested witness is void unless at the time of execution of the will, there are two other disinterested attesting witnesses or the interested witness would be a distribute (intestate heir) if testator had died without a will. In the latter case, the witness beneficiary then takes the lesser of the amount given by the will or her intestate share. **1 point**

Here, Denise was one of three witnesses who attested to Theresa's will. The disposition to Denise will be valid, since two uninterested witnesses also attested to the will and her signature was not necessary for Theresa to have a validly executed will. If Denise were one of two witnesses to the will, the will would have been upheld, but Denise would receive the lesser of the bequest or her intestate share. **1 point**

Therefore, despite being an "interested" witness, Denise was able to act as a third witness and will be entitled to receive the portrait of the grandmother from Theresa's estate.

ANSWER R-19—TORTS/CONFLICT OF LAWS/NEW YORK PRACTICE

(1)   The issue is whether a pedestrian hit by a motor vehicle is entitled to reimbursement for medical expenses paid. **1/2 point**

In New York, drivers are required to purchase automobile insurance with both liability coverage and no-fault insurance. No-fault insurance provides benefits to injured parties who, through no fault of their own, are involved in an accident with motor vehicles, including vehicles where the insured denies coverage or disclaims liability. **1 point**

Persons covered under no-fault insurance include persons injured by an insured owner's vehicle, including pedestrians, and coverage extends to accidents resulting from the use or operation of an automobile anywhere in New York or in any other state. Benefits which covered persons are entitled to include necessary medical expenses, such as the recovery of doctors' fees paid out of pocket for injuries incurred as a consequence of the accident. **1 point**

Here, Walker, a pedestrian, was hit by a vehicle driven by Paul, a New York resident, after his car was struck by a car driven by Dan. Under New York law, Paul's automobile insurance is required to have no-fault coverage. Paul is disclaiming liability, having asserted that his car was pushed on to the sidewalk as a result of Dan's negligence, and through no fault of his own. Despite Paul disclaiming responsibility for the accident, Walker is entitled to recovery of his doctor's fee through the no-fault insurance coverage provided under Paul's automobile insurance. **1 point**

(2)   The issue is which state's law should apply in a dispute between a New York resident and an out-of-state insurance company. **1/2 point**

Where a conflict exists as to which state's law should apply, New York generally follows the governmental interest approach. That is, the state with the greatest interest in the outcome of the litigation is the state whose law applies. However, with respect to actions involving the rights and obligations of an insured and insurer, the law of the state where the policy was written controls, regardless of where the accident occurred. **1 point**

Thus, despite Dan being a New York resident and the accident precipitating the dispute having occurred in New York, the law of State X applies because this is where the insurance policy was written. **1 point**

(3)   The issue is whether a court should grant summary judgment for failure to state a cause of action for negligence where Plaintiff's evidence provides no objective testing to support its claim. **1 point**

A motion for summary judgment is used when the pleadings, on their face, state a cause of action, but there is no genuine issue of material fact to be tried. To show there is no genuine issue, the motion will generally be accompanied by affidavits based on personal knowledge, and the court will also consider pleadings, admissions on file and the products of discovery. In turn, the opposing party must file similar evidence in order to defeat the motion. Where the only issue is damages, the court may grant summary judgment and immediately try the damages issue. **1-1/2 points**

In order to plead a cause of action in negligence, a plaintiff must demonstrate that a defendant owed a duty to the plaintiff, he breached that duty, and the breach caused plaintiff's injuries. Here, the only point of contention is whether Paul suffered damages. Although under the facts presented here, a court could grant summary judgment on the issues of duty, breach, and causation, it would still have to submit the issue of damages to a jury. Whether Paul suffered serious injury is a fact in dispute. Dan's doctor has submitted an affidavit based on his knowledge and experience indicating there was no objective finding of physical injury. In turn, Paul has submitted an affidavit from his own doctor testifying as to his observations of Paul and his diagnosis based on his examination and experience. The fact that Paul's doctor has not referenced any objective testing is not dispositive on the issue of damages, but rather is something to be considered by the jury in making its determination. Thus, the court should deny summary judgment on the issue of damages, and submit that matter to a jury. **1-1/2 points**

ANSWER R-20—PROFESSIONAL RESPONSIBILITY/NEW YORK PRACTICE/TORTS/ CONFLICT OF LAWS

(1)(a) The issue is whether an attorney may solicit clients through an agent and pay a referral fee. **1/2 point**

Lawyers are not permitted themselves or through the use of agents to solicit clients through in-person or telephone contact unless the prospective client is a close friend, relative, or former client. **1/2 point**

In addition, referral fees for such solicitations are unethical. Although a lawyer may ethically divide fees with an outside attorney under certain circumstances, a referral fee to a non-attorney is always a violation of the rules of professional responsibility. **1/2 point**

Here Don, an ambulance driver, gave Anne's business card to Fred, promising that Anne would be able to get Fred money for his injuries. In turn, Anne sent Don a check for $500 for the referral. Neither Don nor Anne had a prior relationship with Fred, and thus, Don's actions in soliciting Fred on behalf of Anne are unethical and impermissible. The fee to Don, who is not an attorney, violates the rules of professional responsibility. **1/2 point**

(1)(b) The issue is whether a fee agreement with an attorney for a flat fee or a fair percentage of recovery violates the rules of professional responsibility. **1/3 point**

A lawyer has a duty to fully explain fee arrangements, and such arrangements should be in writing. In the event a fee is projected to exceed $3,000, the attorney must provide the client with a written retainer agreement that explains the scope of the attorney's services, an explanation of fees, expenses and billing practices, and notice of the client's right to arbitrate fee disputes. No agreement is required if the services are of the same general kind previously provided to the client. **2/3 point**

Contingency fees dependent on the successful resolution of a client's case and payable from judgment proceeds must be in writing and explain the method by which the fee is to be determined. Contingency fees are prohibited in criminal and domestic relations matters. **1/3 point**

Anne told Fred that for a flat fee of $1,000 she would get the cancellation of his insurance policy rescinded. The fee agreement was not in writing. Although fee agreements are recommended to be in writing, here the amount agreed to was less than $3,000, and thus the arrangement does not violate the rules of professional responsibility. **1/3 point**

Anne also indicated to Fred that she would file a negligence action on his behalf and that her fee would be a "fair percentage" of any recovery. This is a contingency fee arrangement and is permitted in personal injury lawsuits. Nonetheless, the arrangement neither explains the method by which Anne's fee is to be determined, nor is it in writing. Consequently, the arrangement violates the rules of professional responsibility. **2/3 point**

(2) The issue is whether the Court should grant a motion for summary judgment, and the arguments the parties should make. **1/3 point**

A motion for summary judgment is granted when the pleadings state a cause of action, and there is no genuine issue of fact to be decided by a jury. **1/3 point**

Here, the cause of action is for the negligent operation of a wildlife preserve and the failure to warn of a dangerous condition that caused Fred's accident. **1/3 point**

In order to plead a cause of action in negligence, a plaintiff is required to demonstrate that defendant had a duty of care to a foreseeable plaintiff, the duty was breached, and the breach of the duty was the cause of plaintiff's injuries. In New York, the duty of care owed by possessors of land to those on their premises is one of reasonable care under the circumstances. Plaintiff's status as an invitee, licensee, or trespasser is no longer determinative, although it remains relevant in determining whether the plaintiff was foreseeable and the amount of precautions necessary to be reasonable under the circumstances. **2/3 point**

In the present case, Fred was a visitor to WW and was hiking a well-marked trail. As such, Fred was a foreseeable plaintiff to whom WW owed a duty of care. Fred climbed down a riverbank he knew to be steep and muddy. WW neither fenced off the area where Fred was hurt nor posted warning signs. Whether the failure to fence off the land or provide warning signs is a breach of WW's duty of care or reasonable under the circumstances is a question of fact for the jury to determine. **2/3 point**

Defenses to negligence include contributory negligence or assumption of risk. New York is a pure comparative negligence jurisdiction, whereby a plaintiff's contributory negligence or assumption of risk does not bar recovery. However, it may reduce the amount of damages recovered. **1/2 point**

WW may argue that Fred was contributorily negligent or assumed the risk of injury by hiking down a riverbank he knew to be steep and muddy. In either event, the matter remains a question of fact for the jury. Further, although WW's argument may reduce the amount of damages Fred is able to collect, the argument would not serve as a bar to Fred's recovery. **1/2 point**

Because issues relating to the scope of WW's duty of care, whether such duty was breached by failing to fence in the area or provide warning signs, and the extent to which Fred's own conduct contributed to his injuries remain outstanding, a court should deny the motion for summary judgment and allow the matter to be decided by a jury. **1/3 point**

(3)   The issue is which state's law a court should apply in resolving a dispute with an out-of-state insurance carrier. **1/3 point**

Where a conflict exists as to which state's law should apply, New York generally follows the governmental interest approach. That is, the state with the greatest interest in the outcome of the litigation is the state whose law applies. However, with respect to actions involving the rights and obligations of an insured and insurer, the law of the state where the policy was written controls, regardless of where the accident occurred. **1 point**

Here, Fred, a New York resident, entered into an insurance agreement with an insurance carrier from State X. The insurance policy was written in State X. Irrespective of the interest New York may have in the outcome of the dispute, the law of State X should be applied. **2/3 point**

ANSWER R-21—DOMESTIC RELATIONS/REAL PROPERTY

(1)   The issue is whether a custodial parent can obtain an increase in child support as a consequence of losing a job and being unable to find another. **1/2 point**

Fred's argument that he should not be required to increase payments under the terms of the separation agreement will fail. The general rule is that separation agreements not merged into divorce decrees are contracts governed by general contract principles. However, child support provisions within such agreements are not binding and can be modified on a showing of an unanticipated and unreasonable change in circumstances. Additionally, a request for increased support based on the fact that support is inadequate will be granted upon showing a substantial change in circumstances warranting an increase, and that the modification is in the child's best interests. **1-1/2 points**

Here, the custodial parent, Mary, unexpectedly lost her job and has been unable to find another job despite her best efforts. This could qualify as a showing of a substantial change in circumstances to warrant an increase. Additionally, because Deb's needs are not being met, Mary can show that a modification would be in Deb's best interests. Mary should be able to show this by the fact that she lost her job and therefore there needs to be a redistribution of the burden between the parents. **1-1/2 points**

(2)   The issue is whether a noncustodial parent can obtain custody of a child based on a custodial parent's financial difficulties and the child's expressed desire to live with the noncustodial parent. **1/2 point**

Issues involving the custody of children are governed by the best interests of the child. Agreements of parents as to custody are accorded due regard, but they are not controlling, and neither parent has a prima facie right to custody. Furthermore, courts are reluctant to alter a custody arrangement absent a compelling reason. **1 point**

Here, neither Mary's temporary financial difficulties, nor Deb's expressed desire to live with Fred appear sufficiently compelling to alter the parties' custody arrangement. There is nothing in the facts suggesting that Mary is an incompetent parent or that Deb is not well cared for. Furthermore, Deb is about 10 years old, and while the court may give limited consideration to her expressed preference, it is by no means controlling in ascertaining the "best interests" of the child. Under the facts as presented, there is nothing supporting a change in the custody arrangement. **1-1/2 points**

(3)   The issue is whether a property owner with a covenant limiting property to single-family homes can prevent the conversion of a single-family home into a two-family residence by an owner in the same subdivision. **1/2 point**

A covenant is a written promise to do or not do something on land. Covenants run with the land, which means that subsequent owners may enforce or be burdened by the covenants. Equitable servitudes are covenants that are enforceable against assignees of burdened land that have notice of the covenant either by actual, inquiry, or record notice. Either a covenant or equitable servitude can be enforced by a party benefited by the promise. A breach of a real covenant is remedied by money damages. To obtain an injunction compelling a property owner to do or not do something with the property, the promise must be enforced as an equitable servitude. **1-1/2 points**

Here Phil and Jeff possess lots in the Black Acres subdivision. Each of their deeds contains a restrictive covenant limiting the building of homes to single-family residences. The deed by which Jeff acquired his property was duly recorded in the county clerk's office, thus providing Jeff with record notice of the restriction on building the property. Because Jeff had notice of the restriction, it is enforceable as an equitable servitude. Phil is a party benefited by the restriction to single-family homes because he lives within the same subdivision, and is burdened by the same restriction on his property. Thus, Phil will be able to successfully obtain an injunction preventing Jeff from converting the house into a two-family residence by enforcing the covenant as an equitable servitude. **1-1/2 points**

ANSWER R-22—DOMESTIC RELATIONS/PROFESSIONAL RESPONSIBILITY/REAL PROPERTY

(1)   The issue is whether the court was correct in denying a motion to disqualify an attorney from

representing the defendant on the ground that he previously acted as a mediator in the same dispute between the plaintiffs and defendants. **1/2 point**

Attorneys employed as mediators work as neutral arbiters, in an attempt to resolve disputes without litigation. Mediators gather information, which can be confidential, from both sides in an attempt to bring parties to a mutually satisfactory resolution. An attorney who has acted as mediator in a dispute may not represent either side in litigation that arises from the dispute, because one client's interests are necessarily materially adverse to that of the other side. Attorneys are not permitted to use a former client's confidential information against that person. Representation of one client in a matter whereby the client's interests are materially adverse to those of another client, without that former client's consent, violates the rules of professional responsibility. **1-1/2 points**

Here, Art acted as a mediator in a dispute between Nancy and Harry and Wanda. In his role as mediator he represented the interests of both sides in the dispute. Harry and Wanda have objected to Art representing Nancy in litigation that has arisen from the dispute, and, thus, Art would be in violation of the rules of professional responsibility if he persisted in representing Nancy. Thus, the court was incorrect in denying Harry and Wanda's motion. **1 point**

(2)   The issue is whether the plaintiffs have acquired by adverse possession a 50-foot strip of land, which they did not own, on which they planted a vegetable garden. **1/2 point**

Title to real property may be acquired by adverse possession. Gaining title by adverse possession results from the operation of the statute of limitations for trespass to real property. If an owner does not, within the statutory period, take legal action to eject a possessor who claims adversely to the owner, the owner is therefore barred from bringing suit for ejectment, and title to the property vests in the possessor. To acquire property by adverse possession under New York law, the possession must have been (i) hostile and under claim of right, (ii) actual, (iii) open and notorious; (iv) exclusive; and (v) continuous for a period of 10 years. **1-1/2 points**

Here, Harry and Wanda have cultivated and improved the 50-foot strip of land into a vegetable garden. They protected the strip of land by installing posts and a six-foot fence without Nancy's permission, thus acting in a manner that was hostile and under claim of right. They acted in a manner that was actual and exclusive because they did not share the land with Nancy, the true owner—the fact that Nancy picked vegetables in the garden from time to time is not demonstrative of sharing possession, particularly because she did so only with Harry and Wanda's permission. The use was open and notorious in that the garden was not covert and was sufficiently apparent to put Nancy on notice of their occupancy, and they did so continuously for more than 10 years. The fact that neither Harry and Wanda nor Nancy knew that the property was being acquired by adverse possession is not relevant. Thus, the court was incorrect in its ruling denying Harry and Wanda an ownership interest in the 50-foot strip by adverse possession. **1 point**

(3)   The issue is whether a deed citing an ownership interest as that of "husband and wife" creates a tenancy by entirety even though the parties to the deed were not married until after the property was acquired. **1/2 point**

When a disposition of real property is made to unmarried persons whom the conveyance describes as "husband and wife," a joint tenancy is created unless a tenancy in common is expressly declared. Subsequent marriage to each other by the parties does not convert the joint tenancy to a tenancy by the entirety absent a new conveyance. **1/2 point**

Harry and Wanda acquired the property as "husband and wife" prior to being married, and a tenancy in common was not expressly declared. Thus, the property was acquired in joint tenancy with right of survivorship. Their subsequent marriage did not convert the property into a tenancy by the entirety. Therefore, the court was incorrect in finding that Harry and Wanda owned Blueacre as tenants by the entirety. **1 point**

(4)   The issue is whether an individual who acquired property as "husband and wife" prior to marriage is entitled to partition and sale of that property. **1/2 point**

A tenancy by the entirety cannot be terminated by involuntary partition. It can be terminated only by the death of a spouse, divorce, mutual agreement, or execution by a joint creditor of the husband and wife. However, as discussed above, Harry and Wanda do not own Blueacre as tenants by the entirety. Instead they are joint tenants. **1/2 point**

Unlike a tenancy by the entirety, a joint tenancy with right of survivorship can be terminated by a voluntary or involuntary partition. Partition can be brought by any joint tenant. Here, it should be determined that Harry possessed Blueacre as a joint tenant with a right of survivorship and therefore would be entitled to partition and sale of Blueacre, irrespective of any objection from Wanda. **1 point**

ANSWER R-23—DOMESTIC RELATIONS/REAL PROPERTY/NEW YORK PRACTICE

(1)   The issue is what grounds exist for divorce in New York and whether the facts support any of these grounds. **1/3 point**

New York Domestic Relations Law provides five grounds for divorce, one of which is adultery. A divorce will be granted against a spouse for adultery where the spouse has sexual relations outside of the marriage. In order to plead a cause of action for adultery, the spouse making the claim must have some proof other than her own accusation, and may not have condoned the adultery or also committed adultery. The spouse bringing the cause of action must do so within five years of discovering the adultery. **2/3 point**

Here, Ann has a valid cause of action against Bill for divorce based upon adultery. She has proof other than her own accusation in that Bill and Dawn are sharing an apartment. She did not condone the adultery, having separated from Bill after discovering the affair, and nothing in the facts suggests that Ann committed adultery herself. She is bringing the action within five years of discovering the adultery, and thus is not precluded by the statute of limitations. **2/3 point**

New York Domestic Relations Law also permits an action for divorce where the spouses have lived separate and apart for a period of one year or more pursuant to a written separation agreement, if the plaintiff spouse has substantially performed all of its terms. For the separation agreement to serve as grounds for the divorce (known as a conversion divorce), the spouses may not cohabitate with intent to reconcile after the agreement is executed and before the divorce is granted. **2/3 point**

Here, Ann and Bill entered into a separation agreement that was executed, acknowledged, and filed on December 30, 2005. Ann and Bill have not cohabitated with one another with an intent to reconcile since entering into the agreement, and have lived separate and apart for more than a year. Moreover, nothing in the facts indicates that Ann did not perform the agreement's terms. Thus, Ann will be able to obtain a conversion divorce as well. **1/3 point**

(2)(a) The issue is what jurisdiction is necessary to grant a divorce in New York, and how it may be obtained by a New York court. **1/3 point**

In order for a New York court to have jurisdiction to grant a divorce, one of the parties to the marriage must be present within the state so that the court has a basis to determine the status of the marriage. Here, Ann presently resides in New York, which satisfies the first jurisdictional requirement. **1/2 point**

In addition, durational residency requirements must be satisfied. This can be achieved in two ways: (i) either party has resided in New York for at least one year prior to commencing the proceeding and the parties were married in New York, resided in New York as husband and wife, or the cause of action arose in New York; or (ii) either party has resided in New York for a continuous period of at least two years preceding the commencement of the action. **1/2 point**

Here, the parties satisfy New York's durational residency requirements because they resided in New York as husband and wife, and the cause of action arose in New York. Ann has resided in New York for more than a year prior to commencing the proceeding. Also, she has continuously resided in New York for a period of more than two years, which alone would be sufficient for the court to consider the cause of action for divorce. **1/2 point**

Finally, in order for a court to have jurisdiction to grant a divorce, personal service must be made on the defendant, on his appointed attorney, or by court order. In order for Ann to commence a divorce proceeding, she will have to personally serve Bill or his attorney, or obtain a court order allowing for service of process in an alternative manner. **1/3 point**

(b)   The issue is what jurisdiction is necessary to incorporate a separation agreement into a divorce judgment in New York, and how this jurisdiction may be obtained by a New York court. **1/3 point**

In order for a New York court to effect property distribution by incorporating the separation agreement into the divorce judgment, the court must have personal jurisdiction over a nonresident defendant. The long-arm statute allows the exercise of personal jurisdiction over a nonresident if: (i) the party to be affected had, at some time in the recent past, a connection with New York; and (ii) the party seeking support is a resident of or domiciled in the state at the time the claim is made. **2/3 point**

In this case, Ann, the party seeking to have the separation agreement incorporated into the judgment of divorce, is a resident of New York. Further, Bill has a marital connection to New York in that New York was the matrimonial domicile of the parties at or about the time of their separation. Under these facts, a New York court has a basis upon which to assert personal jurisdiction and incorporate the separation agreement into the divorce decree. **2/3 point**

(3)(a)   The issue is whether the plaintiff has acquired the five-foot strip of land by adverse possession. **1/3 point**

Title to real property may be acquired by adverse possession. Gaining title by adverse possession results from the operation of the statute of limitations for trespass to real property. If an owner does not, within the statutory period, take legal action to eject a possessor who claims adversely to the owner, the owner is therefore barred from bringing suit for ejectment and title to the property vests in the possessor. In order to acquire property by adverse possession in New York, the possession must have been: (i) hostile and under claim of right, (ii) actual, (iii) open and notorious, (iv) exclusive, and (v) continuous for a period of 10 years. **1 point**

Here, Ann has a valid claim in adverse possession for the five-foot strip. Possession was hostile in that the five-foot strip was enclosed by a fence without the owner's permission. The fact that neither Ann and Bill nor Carl knew that Ann and Bill were taking possession is irrelevant. The possession was open and notorious in that the possession was apparent and not covert to Carl, and he knew that Ann and Bill had erected the fence. Possession of the five-foot strip was actual and exclusive in that Ann and Bill occupied the parcel by building a tool shed, planting a garden, and mowing the lawn. They did so continuously for more than 10 years. Thus, Ann has acquired the five-foot strip by adverse possession. **2/3 point**

(b) The issue is whether an adverse possessor, by agreeing to pay rent to the owner, terminates her rights in the property acquired by adverse possession. **1/3 point**

Title by adverse possession results from the operation of the 10-year statute of limitations. If an owner does not, within the statutory period, take action to eject a possessor who claims adversely to the owner, title vests in the possessor. It is not necessary for the adverse possessor to quiet title. A decree would only confirm the title the adverse possessor has acquired. **1/2 point**

Here, more than 10 years have passed since Ann's claim in adverse possession began to run. The fact that Ed, himself, owned the property possessed for less than the 10-year statute of limitations has no effect on the time period, as the statute of limitations continues to run through successive owners. Ed did not give notice to Ann that her possession constituted trespass until more than 10 years after Ann took possession of the property. The fact that Ann paid rent after the statutory period and before a decree has no bearing. Thus, Ed's actions are ineffective to terminate Ann's interest in the property by way of adverse possession. **2/3 point**

ANSWER R-24—CONTRACTS

(1) The issue is whether a contract with a 21-year-old is enforceable if made under "suspect" circumstances. **1/2 point**

Contracts are enforceable when there is mutual assent, consideration, and no defenses to enforcement. Here there is a contract, notwithstanding the fact that Mike did not know what he was assenting to, other than the fact that Alice would be his manager. Mike was 21 at the time the contract was entered and thus had capacity. Also, the parties mutually assented to Alice being Mike's agent for 10 years in consideration of Mike paying 60% of all his gross income to Alice. **1 point**

However, defenses to a contract include unconscionability. A contract may be voidable where the clauses are so one-sided as to be patently unfair. Whether a contract is unconscionable is tested at the time the contract was made. Unconscionability is often found where one party has substantially superior bargaining power, or in contracts of adhesion whereby an offeree is told "take it or leave it." **1 point**

Here, the contract between Alice and Mike was unconscionable, and, thus, is voidable at Mike's discretion. Alice is an experienced sports agent. She presented the contract to Mike, a young basketball player with little or no experience in contracting with agents. When Mike asked for an opportunity to review the contract, Alice insisted that if he did not sign immediately the contract would be withdrawn, creating a "take it or leave it" situation. Finally, the terms of the contract are grossly one-sided and patently unfair—binding Mike to a 10-year term and forcing him to pay Alice 60% of his earnings when a standard contract in the industry is for three years and 20% of earnings. **1 point**

Thus, the contract is voidable based on the defense of unconscionability and unenforceable by Alice. **1/2 point**

(2) The issue is the rights and liabilities of a contractor who breached but substantially performed a construction contract. **1/2 point**

To sue for breach of contract, a party must demonstrate that a valid contract exists and that he has performed all conditions precedent to the promisor's duty to perform. A party who fails to perform all of his conditions precedent generally cannot bring a suit for breach. However, in common law contracts there is an exception to the general rule when the first party's failure to perform constitutes only a minor breach—*i.e.*, where the promisor has received the substantial benefit of her bargain. In such cases, the party who has rendered the substantial performance may sue the promisor for breach, but the promisor is entitled to damages caused by the minor breach, often assessed as a setoff against the substantially performing party's damages. In determining whether a breach is material or minor, courts consider the benefit received, the adequacy of the compensation, the extent of the part performance, hardship to the breaching party, whether the breach was willful or negligent, and the likelihood that the breaching party will perform the remainder of the contract. **1-1/3 points**

Here, Ben and Mindy entered into a contract whereby Ben agreed to construct an addition to Mindy's home that would include a gym with hardwood floors and a basketball hoop, and the remainder of the addition would be carpeted. Ben breached the contract by failing to provide hardwood floors and a basketball hoop. However, this breach will probably be deemed minor. Mindy bargained for an addition to her home and she received an addition to her home. While the addition was not quite to contract specifications in that it had carpeting where it was supposed to have wood floors and a basketball hoop was not installed, these flaws seem relatively minor. It would be unfair and a hardship to allow Ben to forfeit half of his agreed-upon compensation for lack of a hardwood floor and basketball hoop, especially when it appears that the flaws were caused inadvertently and can be remedied. Thus, the court is likely to allow him to recover for breach of contract if Mindy refuses to pay. However, Mindy will be able to offset the cost of installing hardwood floors and a basketball hoop against what she owes Ben. **1-1/2 points**

(3)   The issue is whether a builder may terminate his offer before it is accepted. **1/2 point**

An offer may be accepted so long as it has not been terminated. It may be terminated by (i) an act of either party or (ii) operation of law. The offeror terminates an offer if he directly communicates the revocation to the offeree. Upon revocation, an acceptance cannot be used to create a contract. **1/2 point**

Under the facts presented here, Ben advised the School District of his error and communicated the withdrawal of his bid to the School District prior to its acceptance, thus effectively withdrawing the bid before creating a contract. **1/2 point**

Because School District's purported acceptance of Ben's offer (*i.e.,* the bid) came after Ben's withdrawal of the bid, no contract was formed and Ben is not bound. School District's purported acceptance in awarding the contract based on the submitted bid will be ineffective to create a contract.

Neither can the School District successfully make a claim for quasi-contractual relief. Quasi-contractual relief is available when there is reasonable detrimental reliance on a promise or when a failed contract results in unjust enrichment. Under the facts presented here, there is nothing to suggest that Ben was either unjustly enriched having made the bid, or that School District relied on the bid to its detriment before receiving notice that the offering bid was revoked. Thus, Ben is not bound by the bid he submitted under contract law or quasi-contract principles. **1/2 point**

ANSWER R-25—CORPORATIONS

(1)   The issue is whether a special meeting of a corporation's board of directors can be held without notice. **1/2 point**

Special meetings of a board of directors require notice. The notice need not state the purpose of the meeting, but must provide directors with notice of the place and time of the meeting. However, notice may be waived by (i) a signed, written waiver before or after the meeting or (ii) attendance without protest prior to commencement of the meeting. Where proper notice is neither provided nor waived, actions taken at the meeting are invalid. **1 point**

Al, Bob, and Cal were the only directors at the time of the meeting. Al and Bob held a special directors' meeting for the purpose of terminating Cal as an employee and director. No notice of the meeting was provided. Nonetheless, Cal walked into the meeting and attended without protesting about the lack of notice prior to the commencement of the meeting, and then participated in the vote. Thus, the special meeting of the board of directors was validly held, and Cal waived his ability to contest the validity of the meeting by attending without protest. **1 point**

(2)   The issue is whether a majority of the board of directors may terminate an employee and remove a fellow director. **1/2 point**

Generally, the business of the corporation is managed under the direction of the board of directors. The board's management authority may be restricted or transferred to another provided it is allowed under the certificate of incorporation. The board of directors has authority to take action provided that proper notice of the meeting has been provided, no less than a quorum is present, and a majority of those present approve the action. **1/2 point**

The decision to terminate an employee falls within the scope of managing a corporation's business and, thus, would be an appropriate decision for the board of directors to make. There is nothing in the facts suggesting that the certificate of incorporation restricted the board's ability to terminate an employee or made it the responsibility of another authority. All of the members of the board were present, notice was waived, and a majority of those present approved the dismissal of Cal. Thus, the board acted within the scope of its powers in removing Cal as an employee. **1 point**

The board meeting technically was not a proper forum for removing Cal as a director. Shareholders elect directors and generally directors can be removed only by a vote of the shareholders at a shareholders' meeting called for that purpose. However, given that all of the shareholders were present at the board meeting and this is a closely held corporation, a court might dispense with this technicality and uphold Cal's removal as a director despite the lack of a specially called shareholders' meeting. **1/2 point**

(3)   The issue is under what circumstances a disgruntled shareholder of a closed corporation can bring an action against the corporation. **1/2 point**

Holders of 20% or more of outstanding shares of a corporation, no shares of which are listed on a national securities exchange or are otherwise publicly traded, who are entitled to vote in an election of directors, may present a petition of dissolution on the grounds that those in control of the corporation have been guilty of illegal, fraudulent, or oppressive action towards the complaining shareholder. **1 point**

Here, Cal holds more than 20% of Builder's shares, Builder is not a publicly traded corporation, and he is entitled to vote in elections of directors. Thus, he may bring an action for dissolution of Builder on the ground that Builder's act in terminating his employment is oppressive conduct. **1/2 point**

(4)(a)   The issue is whether upon proceeding for dissolution, a shareholder can be compelled to sell his shares in the corporation back to the corporation. **1/2 point**

Where a shareholder applies for dissolution of a corporation based on fraudulent or oppressive conduct, any other shareholder of the corporation may, within 90 days after filing of the petition, prevent dissolution by purchasing the petitioner's shares at their fair market value upon terms approved by the court. If the prospective purchaser and petitioner cannot agree on a fair price, the court, on motion by the prospective purchaser, may stay the proceeding and set a fair value of the shares as of the day before filing the petition. **1/2 point**

Here, should Cal move for dissolution of Builder based on a claim that terminating his employment constituted oppressive conduct, the dissolution could be prevented by either Al or Bob moving to purchase Cal's shares at fair market value upon terms fixed by the court. In such a case, Cal could be compelled to sell his shares as an alternative to dissolving the corporation. **1/2 point**

(b)   The issue is whether the court should enforce the "right of first refusal" on shares which are part of an employment agreement. **1/2 point**

New York law prohibits unreasonable restraints on alienation of shares. However, reasonable share transfer restrictions are valid. Restrictions requiring a selling shareholder to first offer his shares to the corporation generally are valid. However, any restrictions on the price at which a selling shareholder must sell must be reasonable. Restraints on alienation are strictly construed and will not be inferred where not otherwise expressly provided for. **1/2 point**

In the present case, Cal's agreement with the corporation provided Builder an option to purchase Cal's shares for $20,000 in the event Cal voluntarily terminated his employment. Although the option to purchase is valid, the price restriction would only be enforceable if the price were a reasonable estimation of the shares' fair market value. In either event, because the right to purchase Cal's shares is contingent on Cal voluntarily terminating his employment, and Cal was involuntarily terminated, Cal will not be required to accept the $20,000 for his shares. He may rely on the court to determine the fair market value of the shares in a dissolution proceeding. **1/2 point**

ANSWER R-26—TORTS/NEW YORK PRACTICE/CONTRACTS

(1)(a) The issue is whether a court should grant a motion to dismiss a cause of action for damages to the product based on a theory of strict liability. **1/3 point**

A court will grant a motion to dismiss for failure to state a cause of action in instances where, viewing the facts as stated in a light most favorable to the nonmoving party, the pleadings fail to state a cause of action for which relief may be granted. **1/2 point**

A cause of action for strict products liability requires a demonstration of (i) a strict duty owed by a commercial manufacturer, retailer, supplier, (ii) a breach of that duty, (iii) actual and proximate causation; and (iv) damages. Damages can include physical injury or property damage. However, if the sole claim is for economic loss (*e.g.,* the product requires repairs), recovery under strict products liability will be denied. **1 point**

Here, Move-It was the manufacturer of the hydraulic lift. As such, Move-It owed a strict duty to users, consumers and bystanders for defects in its hydraulic lift that existed when the hydraulic lift left Move-It's control, and is liable for damages caused by the defective product. Whether the defect existed when the hydraulic lift left Move-It's control will be a question of fact for a jury to decide. The scope of damages for which a tortfeasor can be held responsible in a strict products liability action includes property damage, but it does not include damage to the product itself. Hence, the cost of repairing the conveyor system damaged by the hydraulic lift is not recoverable in a strict products liability action. Thus, the court should grant Move-It's motion to dismiss for failure to state a cause of action. **1 point**

(b)   The issue is whether the plaintiff's cause of action for strict products liability is barred by the statute of limitations. **1/3 point**

In New York, the statute of limitations for strict products liability is three years from the occurrence of the injury complained of. Here, the conveyor system was damaged in January, 2002. Shortly thereafter, and within three years, Punch commenced an action for recovery. The fact that Move-It originally manufactured the product 12 years earlier has no effect on the statute of limitations. Thus, the court should deny the motion to dismiss on the grounds that the statute of limitations had expired. **1-1/2 points**

(2)   The issue is whether a modification of a contract for services is enforceable absent new consideration. **1/3 point**

Under the common law, in order for a contract modification to be enforceable, the modification was required to be supported by new consideration. Under New York law, a modification without new consideration is binding provided that the modification is in writing, the consideration from the original agreement is expressly stated and can be proven, and the writing is signed by the promisor. **2/3 point**

Here, Punch and Gen contracted for Gen to install a conveyor system in consideration for $350,000. Subsequently, the parties entered into a revised written contract reciting the parties' original consideration, promising that Gen would install the system even though it would require additional labor beyond that which had been originally contracted for, and signed by both parties. Because the modification was in writing, recited the past consideration, and was signed by Gen, it is enforceable against Gen irrespective of the fact that Gen received no additional consideration for the promise to provide additional labor. **1 point**

(3)   The issue is whether an employer can recover against a subcontractor for breach of contract for failure to do installation work in accordance with a contract that the employer had with the general contractor. **1/2 point**

For an individual to sue for breach of contract, the individual generally must be in privity of contract with the party being sued. In this instance, Punch is in privity with Gen, but has no contract with Sub. Punch is merely a third-party beneficiary to the Gen-Sub subcontract. **1/2 point**

Third-party beneficiaries have a right to recovery when they are the intended beneficiaries of the contract. Third-party beneficiaries who provide consideration for the benefits they receive under a contract are creditor beneficiaries with contractual rights. A third-party beneficiary will also be considered to be a creditor beneficiary if the promisee's primary intent in contracting was to discharge an obligation owed to the third party. **1-1/3 points**

In this instance, Punch provided consideration to Gen to be benefited under this agreement. Gen's primary intent in contracting with Sub was to discharge Gen's obligation to Punch to install the system. Consequently, Punch has a right to sue Sub for breach of contract because Punch is a third-party creditor beneficiary of the contract between Gen and Sub. **1 point**

ANSWER R-27—CORPORATIONS/CONTRACTS

(1)   The issue is whether a president of a corporation can bring a lawsuit on behalf of that corporation without express authorization from the board of directors. **1/2 point**

Unless provided for in the certificate of incorporation or bylaws, and in the absence of a direct prohibition by the board, the president of a corporation has apparent authority to bring suit on behalf of the corporation. **1 point**

Here, the president of Best commenced a lawsuit on behalf of Best against Comparison without consulting with the board of directors. Nothing in the facts indicates that there is anything in the certificate of incorporation or bylaws prohibiting a president of the corporation from filing a suit on behalf of the corporation. Neither do the facts indicate that there has ever been a directive from the board prohibiting such action. Thus, the president of Best was acting within the scope of his powers in commencing the lawsuit on behalf of Best. **1 point**

(2) The issue is whether a contract entered into on behalf of a corporation prior to incorporation is enforceable against that corporation absent express authorization from the board of directors. **1/2 point**

A contract entered into on behalf of a corporation prior to that corporation coming into existence is not binding on the corporation unless the corporation adopts the contract, either expressly or impliedly. Implied adoption can be inferred from a knowing acceptance of the contract's benefits. **1 point**

Here, plaintiff Best entered into an agreement with an owner of Comparison prior to Comparison being incorporated. Comparison never expressly adopted the contract at a meeting of the board of directors. Nonetheless, Comparison accepted the benefit of Best's payroll services under the contract and paid three invoices while incorporated without objection. Comparison's actions are an implied adoption of the agreement, and, thus, Comparison's affirmative defense that the corporation had not expressly authorized the contract will not prevent Comparison from being liable under the contract. **1 point**

(3) The issue is whether the Statute of Frauds precludes enforcement of a services contract which, by its terms, cannot be performed within one year of its making, but which has been partially performed. **1/2 point**

Under the Statute of Frauds, a contract which by its terms cannot be performed within one year of its formation, cannot be enforced unless it is evidenced by a writing containing the material terms of the agreement and signed by the party to be charged. In measuring the applicable period for the Statute of Frauds, the period runs from the date of the agreement and not from the date of performance. **1 point**

Here, the parties' agreement was within the Statute of Frauds as it could not be performed within a year of its making—the agreement was made on June 1, 2001, and by its terms performance was to extend to June 30, 2002. The agreement was memorialized in a writing signed by an officer of Best, and so is enforceable against Best, but Comparison did not sign a writing sufficient to satisfy the Statute. The facts indicate that Comparison (through its president, Early) signed a credit application referring to the parties' agreement, but the application did not contain the material terms of the agreement, such as the nature of the work to be performed, the duration of the work, the compensation for the work, etc. **1 point**

Best might argue that the agreement should be taken out of the Statute of Frauds by Comparison's part performance. However, generally, only full performance of a contract not performable within a year of its making will take such a contract out of the Statute of Frauds. Thus, because there was neither a sufficient writing signed by Comparison nor full performance by Best, the contract is unenforceable against Comparison. **1 point**

Nevertheless, Best could recover from Comparison for the four unpaid invoices under a quasi-contract theory. Where, as here, a contract fails and a party to the failed contract will be unjustly enriched as a result, an action may be brought to recover the unjust enrichment. Here, the parties' contract failed because of the Statute of Frauds. However, Best rendered accounting services to Comparison for seven months under the failed contract and has been paid for only three of those months. Comparison would be unjustly enriched if it did not have to pay for all seven months of services. Thus, Best may bring an action against Comparison to recover the unjust enrichment—the fair market value of four months of accounting services. **1-1/2 points**

ANSWER R-28—CONSTITUTIONAL LAW/CRIMINAL LAW/CRIMINAL PROCEDURE

(1)(a) The issue is whether a demonstrator is protected by the First Amendment when she urges other demonstrators to "fight the cops." **1/2 point**

Freedom of speech is protected by the First Amendment. While it is presumptively unconstitutional for the government to place burdens on speech because of its content, the Supreme Court has determined that certain categories of speech generally are proscribable despite the First Amendment. Restrictions on the content of speech must be narrowly tailored to achieve a compelling government interest. The courts allow these restrictions to prevent grave injury. The following are the cases in which a court will allow content-based restrictions on speech: (i) speech that presents a clear and present danger of imminent lawless action; (ii) fighting words; (iii) obscenity; (iv) defamation; (v) false or deceptive advertising; and (vi) where the government can demonstrate a compelling interest. **1/2 point**

Fighting words are those words which, when addressed to the ordinary citizen, are inherently likely to incite immediate physical retaliation. In addition, words that cause a clear and present danger of imminent lawlessness must meet a two-prong test. First, they must be directed to producing or inciting imminent lawless action, and second, they must be likely to produce such action. **1/2 point**

In the instant case, as police were instructing the crowd to disperse, Clare climbed atop the barricades and screamed, "Don't let the cops stop you . . . . We will fight if they try to stop us . . . . Let's go . . . . Fight the cops if you have to." The words first qualify as fighting words in that on two separate occasions Clare tells the crowd of protestors to "fight." Second, the words also qualify as words that cause a clear and present danger of imminent lawless action, in that they are directed at inciting imminent lawless action (fighting the cops), and they were likely to produce such action (crowd was likely to follow Clare's command to fight cops to get to the State Capitol). Therefore, Clare's words were not protected by the First Amendment and the charge of inciting to riot will not be dismissed. **1 point**

(b) The issue is whether PL section 120.05(3) requires intent to cause physical injury to the victim. **1/2 point**

According to the facts, Penal Law section 120.05(3) provides that a person is guilty of assault in the second degree when with intent to prevent a police officer from performing a lawful duty, he causes physical injury to that police officer. In this statute, the intent element goes to preventing a police officer from performing his lawful duty. The defendant need not intend to cause physical injury to the police officer. As such, the prosecutor need not prove that defendant intended to cause physical injury. **1 point**

In the instant case, Paul, the police officer, was performing his lawful duty by attempting to place Clare under arrest for inciting to riot. As part of the lawful arrest procedure, Paul attempted to place handcuffs on Clare, at which time Clare screamed, "no way" and pulled away. Clare's behavior of pulling away and screaming "no way" demonstrated an intent to prevent Paul from performing his lawful duty of arresting Clare and placing cuffs on her. In addition, Clare's action of pulling away caused the handcuffs to fly up and cut Paul on the head. As such, while she did not intend the resulting injury, Clare did intend the act to prevent Paul from arresting her, which resulted in the injury to Paul's head. Therefore, the assault charge should not be dismissed. **1 point**

(c) The issue is whether the defendant's Fourth Amendment rights were violated by searching her backpack after her arrest. **1/2 point**

The Fourth Amendment provides that people should be free from unreasonable searches and seizures. Probable cause is required in order to arrest a person. Once there is probable cause to arrest someone, the police may conduct a warrantless search incident to the lawful arrest. The scope of this search is the defendant's wingspan. The police need not actually fear for their safety or believe that they will find evidence of a crime, so long as the suspect is placed under arrest. The police may also search an arrestee's personal belongings before incarcerating her after a lawful arrest. **1 point**

In the instant case, there was probable cause to arrest Clare for her behavior of inciting a riot and assaulting Paul. Once she was placed under lawful arrest for those crimes, Paul was permitted to conduct a warrantless search of her wingspan. Furthermore, before incarcerating Clare, Paul was permitted to search Clare's personal belongings, which included her backpack. As such, the marijuana recovered from Clare's backpack as a result of the search will not be suppressed. **1 point**

(2) The issue is whether justification should be charged as a defense to resisting arrest by a police officer. **1/2 point**

Under certain circumstances, the commission of an act is justified and not appropriate for criminal punishment. Justification is an affirmative defense that must be raised by the defendant. As a general rule, an individual who is without fault may use nondeadly force as reasonably appears necessary to protect herself from imminent use of unlawful force on herself. However, in New York a person may not use force to resist arrest, lawful or unlawful, made by a peace officer when it reasonably appears that he is such. If the police officer uses excessive force, then the defendant may resist the assault, relying on general rules of self-defense. **1 point**

In the instant case, as discussed above, Clare was being placed under lawful arrest for the crime of inciting to riot. While attempting to place Clare under arrest and place cuffs on her, Clare resisted arrest, by a known officer, Paul. Under the above rules, Clare cannot use justification as a defense for injuring officer Paul when she pulled away from him even though she believed the arrest to be unlawful, as it is not relevant whether she believed it to be a lawful or unlawful arrest. Moreover, nothing in the facts indicates that Paul used excessive force in the arrest. Therefore, a justification charge would be improper. **1 point**

ANSWER R-29—CRIMINAL PROCEDURE/CRIMINAL LAW

(1) The issue is whether a defendant's Fourth Amendment right against unreasonable search and seizure is violated when a police officer, after arresting the defendant, opens a locked glove compartment in the defendant's car and recovers contraband. **1/2 point**

The Fourth Amendment provides that people should be free from unreasonable searches and seizures. Probable cause is required in order to arrest a person. Once there is probable cause to arrest someone, the police may conduct a warrantless search incident to a lawful arrest. The scope of this search is the defendant's wingspan. With regard to automobiles, an officer may conduct a warrantless search of the passenger compartment (not the trunk) of an automobile, including containers, after arresting occupants. **1 point**

New York law affords a defendant broader protection than the United States Constitution and requires an officer to suspect that a defendant is armed in order to search containers in the wingspan, but once a defendant has been removed from the vehicle, police may not remove closed containers or bags to look for weapons. However, if police have probable cause to believe contraband is inside of a vehicle, they can search the entire vehicle, including all containers and the trunk. **1 point**

In the instant case, Drew was under lawful arrest for possession and sale of narcotics. Incident to that arrest, Udall was able to conduct a search of Drew's person and the area within his wingspan. As such, Udall's recovery of the two bullets from Drew's pocket was lawful. While under the Fourth Amendment, Udall would have been able to search the containers within Drew's wingspan, which would have included the glove compartment, under New York law, because Drew was safely removed from the vehicle with handcuffs on, Udall would need a warrant in order to search the containers in the vehicle incident to the arrest. However, as Drew handed officer Udall a packet of cocaine from inside the car, the officer had probable cause to believe that the car contained more cocaine. Thus, he could search the entire vehicle on that basis. Therefore, the opening of the locked glove box was permissible and the court properly denied Drew's motion to suppress the handgun found within it. **1-1/2 points**

(2)   The issue is whether PL section 220.06(5) requires knowledge of the weight of the controlled substance defendant possessed. **1/2 point**

As per the facts, PL section 220.06(5) provides that a person is guilty of criminal possession of a controlled substance in the fifth degree when he knowingly and unlawfully possesses cocaine that weighs 500 milligrams or more. The word "knowingly" in this statute goes to the possession element and not the weight—*i.e.,* the prosecution must show that the defendant knowingly possessed the cocaine; the defendant need not know that the amount he possesses is at or over the 500-milligram threshold. Therefore, the court properly denied Drew's motion. **1-1/2 points**

(3)   The issue is whether a defendant is entitled to the charge of entrapment even though he denied the crime charged. **1/2 point**

The charge of entrapment requires two elements: (i) the criminal design must have originated with law enforcement; and (ii) the defendant must not have been predisposed to commit the crime prior to the initial contact by the government. Providing the opportunity for commission of the crime to a defendant who is otherwise ready and willing to commit it is not entrapment. The predisposition of a defendant to commit the crime must exist before the government's initial contact. **1 point**

Under the common law, the defense is not available if the defendant denies having committed the crime. However in New York, a defendant is entitled to the entrapment charge if a reasonable view of the evidence supports the charge, even if defendant's testimony is inconsistent and denies the crime charged. **1 point**

In the instant case, one can argue that the criminal design of the sale for which Drew was charged originated within law enforcement, specifically Udall. In support of this is the fact that Udall approached Drew on several occasions before October 21, and on each occasion Drew refused to sell to Udall. Furthermore, while Drew's prior conviction for possession of cocaine shows a predisposition to possess narcotics, it does not show a predisposition to sell narcotics. **1 point**

Furthermore, under the New York rule, the fact that the defendant denied the underlying crime during his testimony does not preclude the judge from charging the jury with the defense of entrapment. Therefore, based upon the above, the court should charge the jury on the defense of entrapment with respect to the charge of criminal sale of a controlled substance. **1/2 point**

ANSWER R-30 CRIMINAL PROCEDURE

(1)   The issue is whether the search warrant based on a reliable police informer's statements was valid. **1/2 point**

In order to be valid, a search warrant must: (i) be issued by a neutral and detached magistrate; (ii) be based on probable cause; and (iii) particularly describe the place to be searched and the items to be seized. When dealing with probable cause based on informers, New York applies the *Aguilar-Spinelli* test, which provides that a search warrant application must demonstrate: (i) reliability of the source; and (ii) basis of informer's knowledge. In addition, New York does not recognize the good faith exception to defective search warrants. **1 point**

In the instant case, assuming the warrant was issued by a neutral and detached magistrate, there was sufficient probable cause, as Nick, the informer, heard Dom, the defendant, say that the tractor was stolen and knew that Dom still had the key. Furthermore, Nick meets the requirements of New York's *Aguilar-Spinelli* test because he is both reliable (as per the facts) and his basis of knowledge was first hand. However, while the search warrant particularly described the place to be searched (Dom's house), it failed to particularly describe the items to be seized. While it particularly describes the tractor ignition key to be searched for, the portion that states, "any other property which would be considered contraband" is too broad and invalidates that portion of the search warrant. Therefore, the portion of the search warrant pertaining to the ignition key will be valid, but the portion pertaining to contraband will be invalid. **1 point**

(2)   The issue is whether any of the "contraband" seized notwithstanding the invalidity of part of the search warrant will be suppressed. **1/2 point**

As stated above, the only valid portion of the warrant was as to the keys. Therefore, any other evidence seized outside of the keys will be suppressed. However, the plain view doctrine provides an exception to this rule. The police may make a warrantless seizure when they are legitimately on the premises and discover contraband in plain view. As a result of this exception, the police may seize unspecified property while executing a search warrant. **1 point**

Here, the police recovered two guns while executing the search warrant. The first gun was found alongside the tractor key in a clear plastic bag. As it was contraband and in plain view in a place the police could legitimately be looking pursuant to the search warrant, it should not be suppressed. **1 point**

The second gun, on the other hand, should be suppressed. It was recovered under a bathroom sink, sometime after the tractor keys were found. Because, as stated above, the search warrant was valid only as to the tractor keys, once the keys were found the police had no additional authority to continue to search the house. Thus, they had no right to look under the bathroom sink for anything, and clearly a gun wrapped in cloth and hidden under the bathroom sink will not be considered to have been in plain view of a place the police had a right to be. Moreover, because New York does not recognize a good faith exception for a defective search warrant, as is permitted under federal law, the police cannot rely on the invalid search warrant as a basis for admitting the second gun, even if they thought the warrant was valid. Therefore, the second gun—found under the sink and wrapped in cloth—will be suppressed. **1 point**

(3) The issue is whether the wiretap warrant was properly issued and the effect that the phone number changing has on its validity. **1/2 point**

Wiretapping is protected under the Fourth Amendment and requires a valid warrant based on probable cause to believe that a specific crime is being committed. The warrant must: (i) state the names of the persons whose conversations are to be overheard; (ii) describe with particularity the conversations that may be overheard; (iii) be limited in duration to no more than 30 days; and (iv) provide for early termination once the information sought is obtained. A return must be made to court showing what conversations have been intercepted. **1 point**

In the instant case the reasons for believing Nick committed a crime and the type of communications sought was included in the warrant. Also Nick, the target, was specifically named. However, there is no mention as to the length of time the wiretap is limited to, the provisions for termination, or a return to the court. If the warrant complied with those requirements, the wiretap was valid. However, if there was no compliance with those requirements, then the wiretap was invalid. The fact that the number changed has no affect on the validity of the warrant. **1 point**

(4) The issue is whether the defendant's admissions obtained pursuant to the wiretap should be suppressed. **1/2 point**

Assuming the wiretap warrant was properly issued, in New York, a warrant is only good for 30 days. Furthermore, within 90 days after the termination of the warrant, the person whose conversations were seized must be informed of the wiretap, but the period preceding disclosure can be extended. **1/2 point**

In the instant case, the communication was intercepted 40 days after the warrant was issued. This is beyond the time period statutorily provided for in New York. Therefore, the admission made by Nick will be suppressed. **1/2 point**

ANSWER R-31—PROFESSIONAL RESPONSIBILITY/WILLS

(1) The issue is whether a conflict of interest exists when an attorney serves as both executor of a decedent's estate and legal advisor to the decedent's spouse, who is contesting the will. **1/2 point**

According to the New York Code of Professional Responsibility, a lawyer is prohibited from entering into a relationship where there is a potential conflict of interest that is likely to adversely affect his ability to exercise independent professional judgment. Employment must be refused where such judgment will or reasonably may be affected by the lawyer's own financial, business, property, or personal interests, unless (i) a disinterested lawyer would believe that the representation of the client will not be adversely affected thereby, and (ii) the client consents to such employment after full disclosure of the potential conflict. **1 point**

In this case, Len has been Hub's attorney since at least 2001, when he prepared the will in question. To represent Win might jeopardize Len's ability to exercise his own independent professional judgment as the executor of the estate. As executor, it is Len's responsibility to distribute Hub's estate as Hub intended. These duties conflict with Win's interests because she was omitted from Hub's will. It is unlikely that a disinterested lawyer would believe that Len's ability to serve as executor would not be adversely affected by representing the testator's spouse, who is contesting the will and could be seeking to take a significant portion of the estate. Therefore, Len cannot give Win any legal advice regarding her rights in Hub's estate. **1 point**

(2)   The issue is whether an oral contract to execute mutual wills is enforceable in New York. **1/2 point**

In New York, the mere execution of mutual wills (*i.e.*, separate wills executed by two or more testators that contain substantially similar or reciprocal provisions) is not evidence of a contract. A contract to make a testamentary gift is unenforceable unless it is in writing and signed by the party to be charged therewith. **1 point**

Here, Hub and Win's agreement to execute mutual wills was merely oral and not in writing. Therefore, Win does not have any rights under the agreement to execute mutual wills. **1/2 point**

(3)   The issue is what a spouse is entitled to when she is not named in her deceased spouse's will. **1/2 point**

New York has an elective share statute designed to protect a surviving spouse from being disinherited by the deceased spouse's will. Under the statute, the surviving spouse is entitled to the greater of: (i) $50,000 or (ii) one-third of the net estate. The net estate includes testamentary substitutes, in addition to the spouse's probate estate. Testamentary substitutes include certain lifetime transfers, survivorship estates, Totten trusts, "pay on death" accounts, property over which the decedent held a presently exercisable general power of appointment, and some pension benefits. **1 point**

Survivorship bank accounts are testamentary substitutes to the extent that the decedent made the deposits in the account. However, if the joint account is created before marriage between the decedent and a third party and the decedent made the only deposits, only one-half of the balance is a testamentary substitute. Where the joint account is between spouses, there is a presumption that the decedent's contribution was one-half. **1 point**

Totten trust bank accounts are bank accounts that are opened by one party "as trustee for" another party. The amount on deposit at the testator's death is a testamentary substitute, regardless of when the account was established or when the deposits were made. **1/2 point**

In this case, Hub's net estate consists of the Vermont condo valued at $180,000, as well as certain testamentary substitutes. One-half ($45,000) of the joint savings account in the names of Hub and Mona should be added to the net estate, as it is a survivorship bank account between the deceased spouse and a third party, it was created before the marriage, and Hub made the only deposit. One-half ($15,000) of the joint checking account in the names of Hub and Win should also be added to the net estate, regardless of the fact that Hub made the only deposit. **1 point**

Finally, the Totten trust account in the name of Hub, in trust for Mona, is included in the estate, in its entirety ($120,000). The net elective share estate totals $360,000. One-third of that amount is $120,000, which is greater than the alternative of $50,000 under the elective share statute. Therefore, Win is entitled to receive $120,000 as her elective share. However, because $15,000 passes to Win by survivorship rights in the joint checking account with Hub, her net elective share is $105,000. **1 point**

It should be noted that the spouse is also entitled to certain pieces of exempt property that are not deemed part of the decedent's estate and are not subject to administration. These items include: (i) furniture, appliances, computers, and other household items up to $10,000 total in value; (ii) books, video tapes, and software worth up to $1,000 total, (iii) domestic animals, farm machinery, one tractor, and one lawn tractor, not exceeding a total value of $15,000; (iv) one car not exceeding $15,000; and (v) a $15,000 allowance. However, these items are taken "off the top" of the estate, before the estate is distributed under the decedent's will, as an elective share, or by inheritance. **1/2 point**

SUBJECT INDEX OF ESSAYS

NOTE: MOST ESSAYS COVER MORE THAN ONE SUBJECT.

BAR REVIEW

Released Exam
Questions and Answers

JULY 2001

NEW YORK STATE

BAR EXAMINATION

RELEASED QUESTIONS AND ANSWERS

QUESTION 1

You are an associate with an upstate New York law firm. A senior partner seeks your assistance concerning a matter presented by a new corporate client, Chips, Inc. ("Chips"). Chips manufactures two different computer chips, one designed for laptop computers and one designed for handheld computing devices.

The partner shares with you that on October 28, 1999, Devices Corp. ("Devices") faxed Chips an offer to buy 1,000 chips for handheld computing devices. The offer provided for payment in the sum of $500,000 on delivery, which was to take place by December 15, 1999.

One day later, Chips faxed Devices written confirmation that Chips would provide the 1,000 computer chips as specified, but "would suggest shipment in the year 2000 on or before January 16, 2000, to avoid Y2K problems."

On January 9, 2000, Devices faxed Chips instructions for shipping the computer chips. That same day, Chips forwarded 1,000 computer chips to Devices. On January 10, immediately upon receiving the lot of 1,000 computer chips, Devices overnighted a check to Chips in the amount of $500,000. The following day, on inspecting the shipment, Devices noticed that the chips received were for laptop computers, not handheld devices. That same day, Devices received word that the ultimate purchaser of the handheld devices for which the chips were to be utilized was canceling its order. Devices immediately stopped payment on its $500,000 check, and notified Chips that, because the shipment was nonconforming, it was canceling the order. On that same day, but following receipt of the notice advising that the wrong chips had been delivered, Chips called Devices and said it would cure the problem immediately. Chips then forwarded the correct chips, which were received by Devices on January 15, 2000.

Devices inspected that shipment and found it to conform with the order. Nevertheless, Devices returned the entire shipment to Chips, accompanied by an acknowledgment of receipt form, which included an unequivocal general release of Devices for any and all claims Chips might have against Devices. The receipt form was signed by the supervising clerk in the shipping department of Chips and returned to Devices. When Chips presented the $500,000 check for payment, Devices's bank refused to honor it due to the stop payment order. On January 31, 2000, Chips brought suit against Devices seeking full payment for the chips.

Upon proof of the foregoing facts, Devices moved for summary judgment. The court granted the motion dismissing Chips's claim. The court found that there was a valid contract, but that Chips had breached the contract by initially delivering nonconforming goods and, in any event, Chips's representative had signed a release of all claims. The attorneys previously representing Chips have advised that an appeal is not worth pursuing.

The partner would like you to prepare a memorandum discussing:

(1)   Whether a valid contract was formed.

(2)   Whether, assuming a valid contract, Chips's nonconforming delivery afforded Devices the right to cancel.

(3)   Whether the general release bars a successful claim by Chips.

QUESTION 2

At about 2:00 p.m. on Sunday, May 20, 2001, Paul, a Suffolk County police officer, was patrolling in a commercial area. He suddenly heard the shattering of window glass from a closed store, Ann's Antiques, and the ringing of the store's alarm. When Paul looked across the street, he saw a woman running out of the antique store, carrying a lamp. Paul immediately chased the woman, but before he reached her, she accidentally ran into Mark, an elderly pedestrian, who fell and severely injured his head on the sidewalk. The woman ran away, but the lamp she had been carrying was lying on the street with a tag on it which read, "Ann's Antiques, $150."

Shortly after Mark fell, an ambulance drove him to a local hospital. There, the doctor told Mark, who was conscious, that there was internal bleeding in his head, that his condition was serious, and that Mark would require prompt surgery. Before losing consciousness, Mark told Paul, who was questioning him at the hospital, that the woman who knocked him down was Denise, a waitress who worked at a nearby restaurant. Mark's final words to Paul were, "The doctor said my condition is serious, and surgery will be required to save my life. Don't let Denise get away with this." Despite surgery, Mark died later that night from the injuries he sustained when Denise ran into him.

Thereafter, Paul arrested Denise, and on May 24, a Suffolk County grand jury returned an indictment charging Denise with burglary and felony murder.

At Denise's trial, Ann, the owner of Ann's Antiques, testified that on May 20, her store was closed and that Denise had no right to be in the store. Paul then testified to the pertinent foregoing facts, and began to testify to Mark's statement to him at the hospital. Over the objection of Denise's attorney that Mark's statement to Paul at the hospital constituted inadmissible hearsay, the court (1) permitted Paul to testify to Mark's statement.

When the jury returned a guilty verdict against Denise on the charge of felony murder, her attorney moved to set aside the verdict on the ground that the facts proved at trial failed, as a matter of law, to constitute the crime of felony murder. The court (2) denied the motion.

After the verdict, Jan, a juror, advised Denise's attorney that one afternoon during the trial, she had walked past Ann's Antiques to see for herself whether Paul could really have seen Denise run from the store. Jan said that she thought Paul could have seen Denise, and that while she had discussed her visit to the area with two other jurors during deliberations, the discussion had not affected the jury's verdict. On the basis of Jan's statement, Denise's attorney timely moved for a mistrial. The court (3) denied the motion.

Were the numbered rulings correct?

QUESTION 3

Bob, a resident of State X, died and his will was duly probated in State X. Al, Bob's son, a resident of New York, is executor of Bob's estate. Bob had owned Greenacre, a summer home located on a large lake in Washington County, New York, which he had occupied each summer. Greenacre is now an asset of Bob's estate. On May 1, 2000, Carl, a house painter and resident of Washington County, met with Al at Greenacre. Carl and Al agreed that Carl would paint the exterior of the summer home, finishing by June 30; that Carl would furnish ladders, brushes, and other necessary equipment; and that Al would furnish the paint and would pay Carl $20 per hour for his work. Al also told Carl that he could use Bob's rowboat, which was pulled up on shore, to view the paint job from the water, but warned Carl that he should be careful. Carl began work on May 8, and Al did not return to Greenacre until after June 20.

On June 20, Carl decided to go out in the rowboat to view the paint job. When Carl was about 100 feet from shore, the boat suddenly capsized, throwing Carl into the water. Carl, who was a poor swimmer, attempted to swim to shore but soon sank below the surface and drowned. An investigation revealed that the boat did not leak and was not otherwise defective, but that there were no life preservers or other flotation devices in the boat or in the vicinity of the boat when Carl placed it in the water.

Dot, Carl's widow and the personal representative of his estate, duly commenced an action in Supreme Court, Washington County, on behalf of herself, her children, and Carl's estate against Al as executor of Bob's estate, for negligence and wrongful death. Dot's complaint sought damages of $1 million. The complaint alleged that the defendant was negligent both as a matter of common law and because the defendant breached Navigation Law section 40(1)(a), which requires that every rowboat shall have at least one wearable, personal flotation device (life preserver) for each person on board, "while underway or at anchor with any person aboard . . . ."

Al duly filed a notice of removal in federal district court to remove the action to that court, and Dot promptly moved in federal district court for remand of the action to the state supreme court. The court (1) granted Dot's motion.

After issue was joined, Al moved, upon proof of the pertinent foregoing facts, for summary judgment dismissing the complaint on the separate grounds that (a) Carl was an employee of Bob's estate and the plaintiff's exclusive remedy is pursuant to the Workers' Compensation Law, and that (b) Bob's estate had breached no duty owed to Carl, and Carl's own negligence caused his death. The court (2) denied the motion as to (a), and (3) granted the motion as to (b).

Were the numbered rulings correct?

QUESTION 4

In 1999, Bob, a widower, duly executed a will, which had been drafted by Linda, his attorney. The will provided as follows:

FIRST: I leave Blackacre, my home in Erie County, to my son, Jeff.

SECOND: I leave Greenacre, my hunting lodge in Warren County, to my friend, Mitch.

THIRD: I leave the balance of my estate to Trust Co., in trust, to pay the income to my sons, Jeff and Patrick, for their lives, and upon their deaths, to pay the principal to any children of Jeff and Patrick who shall reach age 30.

FOURTH: I name Linda, my attorney, executrix of my estate.

On January 2, 2001, Greenacre, which was insured by I Co. for $100,000, was destroyed by fire. Bob filed a claim against I Co. for the loss.

Bob died on March 15, 2001, survived by his sons, Jeff and Patrick, neither of whom has any children, and by Mitch.

After his death, Bob's original will was found in his desk drawer. The "FIRST" provision of the will, leaving Blackacre to Jeff, was crossed out. In the margin was written, "I hereby leave Blackacre to my son, Patrick. [signed] Bob. January 20, 2001."

In April 2001, Linda presented a petition in Surrogate's Court, Erie County, for the probate of Bob's will. After a hearing, the Surrogate admitted Bob's will to probate.

The insurance proceeds for the loss of Greenacre have now been paid by I Co. to Linda, as executrix of Bob's estate.

(1) To whom should the insurance proceeds be distributed?

(2) Who will inherit Blackacre?

(3) Was the residuary gift of the principal of the trust valid?

BAR/BRI MODEL ANSWERS

MODEL ANSWER TO QUESTION 1—CONTRACTS/AGENCY

Memorandum
To: Partner
From: Associate

(1)   The first issue is whether a contract is created when the terms in a purported acceptance do not match the terms in the offer. **1/2 point**

It should first be noted that the issue is controlled by Uniform Commercial Code ("U.C.C.") section 2-207. U.C.C. Article 2 applies to all sales of goods (*i.e.*, things that are moveable when they are identified under the contract), and computer chips would qualify as goods. U.C.C. section 2-207 controls contract formation issues. It abandons the common law mirror image rule and provides that an acceptance, or written confirmation that indicates an intent to be bound, will be effective as an acceptance even if it states additional or different terms. Here, Devices sent a fax on October 28, 1999, offering to purchase 1,000 computer chips, and Chips sent a confirmation containing a clear intent to be bound (*i.e.*, "Chips will provide the 1,000 chips"). The fact that Chips proposed a different delivery date than the one in the offer (*i.e.*, on or before January 16, 2000, instead of December 15, 1999) does not prevent formation of a contract. Therefore a contract was formed. **1 point**

The next issue is whether the delivery date stated in the offer or a different delivery date stated in an acceptance will control in a contract between merchants. **1/2 point**

U.C.C. section 2-207(2) states that between merchants, additional terms become part of the contract unless: (i) the offer expressly limits acceptance to its terms; (ii) the additional terms materially alter the contract; or (iii) objection has already been given or is given within a reasonable time. The U.C.C. definition of a merchant includes persons who regularly deal in goods of the kind sold in the transaction in question. Here, the offer and acceptance each include different delivery dates. Section 2-207 is silent on the effect of different terms. If the different delivery dates are treated like additional terms, the January 16 delivery date will be deemed controlling, because both parties appear to be merchants with respect to computer chips (Chips regularly sells them and Devices regularly purchases them to use in its computerized devices), the offer did not expressly limit acceptance to its terms, the January 16 delivery date does not appear to materially alter the contract, and Devices did not object to the later delivery date (indeed, it initially accepted the goods on the later delivery date). Thus, the January 16 delivery date will be included in the contract. **1-1/2 points**

(*Note:* A "knockout" rule argument could also be made. Because the terms of the offer and acceptance were different regarding the delivery date, and the U.C.C. does not say what to do in such a case, a court might find that the delivery dates knock out each other, leaving a contract with no delivery date. Under the U.C.C., when a delivery date is not included in a contract, a reasonable delivery date is implied. Delivery on January 10 (or even January 15—when the replacement goods were received) seems reasonable, especially given the fact that Devices did not complain about delivery on that date.)

(2)   At issue is a seller's right to cure and a buyer's right to cancel a delivery of nonconforming goods. **1 point**

Under the U.C.C.'s "perfect tender" rule, a buyer may reject goods for "any defect" in the goods or tender in a single delivery contract. However, if the seller can cure the defect within the time originally provided in the contract, he may do so by giving reasonable notice of intent to cure and subsequently tendering conforming goods that the buyer must accept. Failure of the buyer to accept the conforming goods will be a breach of the contract. **1 point**

In this case, Chips delivered laptop computer chips on January 10, 2000, rather than the handheld computer chips ordered by Devices. As established above, the delivery date under the contract was January 16, 2000, or some other, reasonable delivery date. Upon receiving notice of the defect, Chips notified Devices of the intent to cure the problem immediately. Devices received conforming chips on January 15, 2000, one day prior to the expiration date set forth in the acceptance and probably within a reasonable time for acceptance. Thus, whether the court follows the rule for additional terms or the knockout rule, Chips cured the defect in a timely manner, and Devices had no right to cancel. **1-1/2 points**

(3) At issue is whether a shipping clerk has authority to bind his employer to an agreement releasing another from liability for breach of contract. **1 point**

When determining whether a principal will be bound by an agent's contract, it must be determined if the agent had actual, apparent, or inherent authority to act on behalf of the principal. Actual authority is authority the agent reasonably believes he possesses based on the principal's dealings with him. It may be express or implied. There are no facts here indicating that the shipping clerk was given authority to bind Chips to agreements relating to contractual commitments. Apparent authority arises from the reasonable belief of a third party, based on the principal's holding the agent out, that the agent has authority to bind the principal. Here, no facts indicate that Devices could reasonably believe that a company shipping clerk had authority to waive the right to sue for breach of contract. Finally, inherent authority results in the principal being bound even though the agent had no actual authority to perform the particular act. It arises in circumstances where the agent exceeds his actual authority, but the conduct is similar to acts authorized. The responsibilities of a shipping clerk are neither similar nor related to making determinations regarding whether its employer will release another from contractual commitments. **1-1/2 points**

Thus, Chips's shipping clerk lacked actual, apparent, and inherent authority to release Devices from liability. Chips will not be bound by the release and can maintain a cause of action for breach of contract against Devices. **1/2 point**

MODEL ANSWER TO QUESTION 2—CRIMINAL LAW/CRIMINAL PROCEDURE

(1) The issue is whether the out-of-court statement constituted a dying declaration, an exception to the hearsay rule. **1 point**

Hearsay is a statement, other than one made by the declarant while testifying at trial, offered into evidence to prove the truth of the matter asserted. Hearsay must be excluded upon appropriate objection unless a hearsay exception applies. A dying declaration is an exception to hearsay. In New York, a dying declaration is admissible as evidence if the statement was: (i) made by the victim of a homicide; (ii) the declarant was dying when he made the statement and knew he was dying; (iii) the declarant would have been a competent witness and the statement is pertinent to the action; and (iv) the statement is offered in the victim's homicide prosecution. **1 point**

Here, Mark is a victim of a homicide and the statement is being offered in his homicide prosecution. Additionally, it appears Mark would have been a competent witness if he were still alive, and the statement concerned the circumstances of his death. However, the facts do not indicate that Mark knew he was dying when he made the statement. Mark told Paul his condition was serious and that surgery was required to save his life. The statement indicates that although Mark knew his condition was serious, he believed he would survive. Thus, the offered testimony does not meet the conditions of a dying declaration. Therefore, the statement is inadmissible and the court was incorrect when it overruled the objection. **1-1/2 points**

(2) The issue is whether the prosecution made out a prima facie case for felony murder. **1/2 point**

For a conviction of felony murder (second degree murder in New York) to be sustained, it must be shown that the defendant or a co-felon, during the course of committing or attempting to commit an enumerated felony, or in immediate flight, causes the death of a nonparticipant. The killing in a felony murder need not be intentional. **1/2 point**

Burglary is one of the enumerated felonies for which a defendant may be held responsible for felony murder. Burglary in the second degree requires a showing that the defendant (i) knowingly entered or remained unlawfully, (ii) in a building, (iii) with intent to commit a crime, (iv) along with one of the following aggravating factors: (a) the building is a dwelling; or (b) defendant injures a nonparticipant during the commission or in immediate flight; or (c) the defendant is armed. **1 point**

Ann, the owner of Ann's Antiques, testified that her store was closed when Denise was observed and that Denise had no permission to be in the store. Ann's testimony established that Denise knowingly entered or remained unlawfully in the store. Ann's store constitutes a building. Paul is able to testify that he heard glass shatter and observed Denise running from Ann's Antiques carrying a lamp, which he later observed had one of Ann's price tags attached to it. Paul's testimony establishes Denise's intent to commit the crime of larceny—taking with intent to permanently deprive. Paul is also able to testify that he chased Denise and observed her knock down Mark, who in turn, injured his head. This testimony establishes the aggravating circumstance of the defendant injuring a nonparticipant while in immediate flight from the burglary. Thus, the facts are sufficient as a matter of law to prove the under-lying felony of burglary in the second degree and support a felony murder charge. **1 point**

Mark died as a result of the injuries sustained while Denise was in immediate flight from the burglary. If Denise intended to kill Mark, Denise could have been charged with and convicted of murder in the first degree. Since the facts indicate that Denise did not intend to kill Mark, a conviction for felony murder in the second degree is supported as a matter of law. **1/2 point**

(3) The issue is whether an unauthorized visit by a juror to the crime scene and subsequent discussion with other jurors violate a defendant's due process rights to a fair trial, and whether discovery of such visit and jury discussion after the verdict is grounds for a mistrial. **1 point**

Every defendant has a due process right to a fair trial by an impartial judge or jury. If a jury is exposed to influences favorable to the prosecution, due process is violated. The trial must be conducted in such a manner that the jury gives the evidence presented reasonable consideration. **1 point**

Here, Jan made an unauthorized visit to the crime scene and discussed it with other jurors. Despite her insistence that the visit had no influence on her determination, the visit threatens to influence the way she, or the jurors with whom she discussed the visit, considered the evidence presented at trial by bringing in extraneous material for consideration. Furthermore, since the visit was disclosed after the verdict, the jury acted without benefit of judicial admonition. Thus, Denise has a valid argument that her due process rights to a fair trial were violated, and the judge should have granted her motion for a mistrial. **1 point**

MODEL ANSWER TO QUESTION 3—TORTS/NEW YORK PRACTICE/FEDERAL JURIS-DICTION/WORKERS' COMPENSATION

(1)   The issue is whether an action may be removed to federal district court based on diversity jurisdiction. **1/2 point**

First, a federal court has subject matter jurisdiction over causes of action (i) arising out of a federal question or (ii) where there is complete diversity among the parties and the amount in controversy exceeds $75,000. **1/2 point**

Here, complete diversity among the parties exists. Carl's widow, Dot, filed a wrongful death action on behalf of her deceased husband, a resident of New York. The defendant, Bob's estate, is a resident of State X. The fact that the executor, Al, is a resident of New York is irrelevant. Additionally, the amount in controversy ($1 million) exceeds $75,000. Therefore, the federal district court has subject matter jurisdiction. **1 point**

Second, section 1441(b) of the United States Code provides that where complete diversity exists between parties, and the amount in controversy exceeds $75,000, an action originating in state court may be removed to the appropriate United States district court. Such removal is permitted unless one of the defendants is a citizen of the state where the action was originally brought. **1/2 point**

Here, the action was originally brought in New York State Supreme Court. The defendant is Bob's estate, and Bob was a citizen of State X. Therefore, under section 1441(b) of the United States Code, removal to federal district court was appropriate, and the case was incorrectly remanded to state court. **1/2 point**

(2)   At issue is whether New York's Workers' Compensation Law bars recovery for wrongful death by a contractor's estate. **1/2 point**

Under the New York Workers' Compensation Law, if an employee is injured on the job and the employer provides workers' compensation coverage, the injured employee finds his exclusive remedy under the provisions of the Workers' Compensation Law. Recovery under workers' compensation replaces tort liability arising out of accidental injuries, and death resulting from such injuries, that occur in the course of employment. **1 point**

The facts indicate that Carl was not an employee of Bob's estate, but rather was an independent contractor hired to paint his house. Carl's status as an independent contractor is supported by the fact that he was hired to do a single job and provided his own tools to complete the job. Further, even if Carl were considered to be an employee of Bob's estate, there is no indication that the estate provided Carl with workers' compensation insurance. Thus, Carl's estate, Dot, and her children are not barred by the Workers' Compensation Law from recovering for Carl's wrongful death. Therefore, the court correctly denied summary judgment. **1 point**

(3)   The first issue is whether the defendant breached a duty to the plaintiff in violation of a state statute. **1/2 point**

To sustain a cause of action in negligence, the plaintiff must prove: (i) that the defendant had a duty to conform to a specific standard of conduct for protection of the plaintiff against an unreasonable risk of injury; (ii) that the defendant breached that duty; (iii) that the breach is the actual and proximate cause of the plaintiff's injury; and (iv) that the plaintiff sustained damages. **1/2 point**

In New York, violation of a state statute constitutes negligence per se. This means that there is a conclusive presumption of duty and breach so long as the plaintiff can establish (i) that the accident that occurred was within the class of harms the statute was designed to prevent, and that (ii) the plaintiff was within the class sought to be protected by the statute. **1 point**

Here, the statute, Navigation Law section 40(1)(a), requires all boats to carry flotation devices. The purpose of the statute is to protect individuals from drowning. The protected class is individuals using boats. **1/2 point**

In this case, Bob's estate failed to equip the boat Carl used with the estate's permission with a flotation device. Additionally, drowning is within the class of harms the statute is designed to prevent. Thus, Carl was within the protected class. Therefore, Bob's estate violated the state statute, and the violation constitutes negligence per se. **1/2 point**

The next issue is whether the plaintiff's negligence caused his own death, thus precluding recovery from the defendant's estate for negligence. **1/2 point**

New York is a "pure" comparative negligence state. A plaintiff may recover even when his culpability exceeds that of the defendant, provided the risk taken is not so great that it is effectively the sole proximate cause of the injury. **1/2 point**

Here, Carl knew that he was not a strong swimmer, yet he proceeded to use the boat anyway. By doing so, he assumed some risk. A jury will consider this when they assign equitable fault, but it is not enough to make his conduct the sole proximate cause of the injury. Thus, the court erred in deciding, as a matter of law, that Carl's own negligence was the sole proximate cause of Carl's death. **1/2 point**

MODEL ANSWER TO QUESTION 4—WILLS/TRUSTS

(1)   The issue is the status of a specific bequest if the subject matter no longer exists. **1/2 point**

Under the Estates, Powers, and Trusts Law ("EPTL"), a specific bequest is a gift of a specified or identified item of the testator's property. Under the doctrine of ademption, when specifically bequeathed property is not part of the testator's estate at death, the bequest is adeemed; *i.e.*, it fails and the devisee takes nothing. **1/2 point**

Here, Greenacre was specifically bequeathed to Mitch. Additionally, Greenacre was destroyed so it was not in Bob's estate at death. Thus the doctrine of ademption applies. **1/2 point**

However, the EPTL further provides that in spite of the doctrine of ademption, casualty insurance proceeds for a specific bequest will be paid to a specific devisee, where the proceeds are not paid until after the death of the testator. Here, the insurance company issued a check covering the loss of Greenacre a month after Bob died. Thus, Mitch will be entitled to the proceeds. **1 point**

(2)   At issue is whether a testator's act of crossing out one beneficiary's name and inserting another beneficiary's name after the initial execution of a will will be given effect. **1/2 point**

New York does not recognize partial revocations by physical act. Striking or mutilating a clause in a will or interlineating additions to the will cannot change the will unless made with the same formalities as are required for the execution of a will. For example, the testator must sign, or acknowledge his signature, at the end thereof, in the presence of two witnesses. If, however, the striking or interlineation was made before the testator executed the will, it will be given effect, for the changes are part of the will that was duly executed. However, any attempted partial revocation without testamentary formalities (in effect creating a codicil—an amendment to the original will) will be disregarded and the will probated as executed. **1 point**

Here, the "FIRST" provision was crossed out and an addition was interlineated. Bob placed his signature at the end of the attempted partial modification. However, he did not sign in the presence of two witnesses, which is one of the testamentary formalities. Therefore, the modification was not made with the same formalities required for the execution of a will. Note that the alteration occurred on January 20, 2001, after the 1999 will was duly executed. Therefore, Bob's attempt to change his will is treated as a partial revocation and will be disregarded. Thus, the original clause stands, and Jeff will inherit Blackacre. **1 point**

(3)   The issue is whether a remainder interest in a trust that is bequeathed to beneficiaries "not in being," upon their attaining age 30, violates the Rule Against Perpetuities and the New York Suspension Rule. **1 point**

New York follows the common law rule that the validity of interests created by will are determined as of the date of the testator's death. Here, the interests created as of Bob's death are: (i) a life estate in Patrick; (ii) a life estate in Jeff; and (iii) contingent remainders in the children of Patrick and Jeff. Bob's estate holds a reversion in fee simple, and the remainder interest would revert to Bob's estate in the event that neither Patrick nor Jeff had children. **1 point**

The Rule Against Perpetuities holds that no interest in property is valid unless it must vest, if at all, not later than 21 years after some life in being at the creation of the interest. If there is any possibility that the interest might vest more than 21 years after a life in being, the interest is void. In this case, Bob's instructions provide that the principal of the trust be paid to any children of Jeff and Patrick who reach age 30. Patrick and Jeff can still have children, and those children, not yet born, may reach age 30 more than 21 years after the death of all lives in being. Therefore, the principal might not vest within the perpetuities period and, thus, the remainder interest violates the Rule Against Perpetuities. **1 point**

At common law, this defect would have voided the interest. However, the New York Perpetuities Reform Statute automatically reduces all age contingencies to 21 years, thereby saving the gift. Thus, any children of Jeff or Patrick would inherit the principal at age 21. **1/2 point**

The next question is whether Bob's trust also violates the New York suspension rule. The suspension rule provides that every present or future interest is void in its creation if it suspends the absolute power of alienation for a period longer than lives in being plus 21 years. In other words, to be valid under the suspension rule, there must be persons in being who could join together in a conveyance of the full fee simple title within lives in being plus 21 years. Remainder interests are alienable, even when they are contingent, immediately upon the birth of the remaindermen. Therefore, since Bob's trust creates a remainder interest in Jeff and Patrick's children, the New York suspension rule is not violated. **1-1/2 point**

SAMPLE CANDIDATE ANSWERS

**PLEASE NOTE THAT THE SAMPLE CANDIDATE ANSWERS ARE REPRINTED WITH-
OUT CHANGE EXCEPT FOR MINOR EDITING, AND NO REPRESENTATION IS MADE
THAT ANY ANSWER IDENTIFIES OR CORRECTLY RESPONDS TO ALL OF THE IS-
SUES RAISED BY THE QUESTION.**

SAMPLE ANSWER TO QUESTION 1 (CANDIDATE A)

Issue 1: The issue is whether the two companies entered into a binding contract such that a breach by either party entitles the other to adequate remedies. A valid contract is formed where there is an offer, namely a manifestation to enter into a valid contract by one party, and an acceptance of that offer by the other party, which indicates a commitment to be bound. In addition to a valid offer and acceptance, there must be adequate consideration or a bargained-for legal detriment or, as in New York, a bargained-for legal benefit. Finally, there must be no defenses to formation that would invalidate an otherwise valid contract entered into by the parties, such as the Statute of Frauds. In this case, the transaction involves the sale of goods. For this reason, Article 2 of the U.C.C. is controlling. The computer chips represent goods, and Chips was selling them to Devices. Because Article 2 is controlling, the faxed offer must only set out the quantity term, which it did here of 1,000 units, and the writing must be signed by the person to be charged. Devices's offer and Chips's acceptance (confirmation) by fax represent signed offers and acceptances under New York law. Chips is a merchant under the facts presented because it is in the business of selling the laptop and handheld computers (it is a manufacturer). The offer by Devices was thus sufficient because the quantity term was set out and Devices manifested an intent to be bound on its offer. The acceptance by Devices was similarly valid because it indicated an intention to be bound and because it was faxed on Devices's paper. The additional terms added by Chips's acceptance became part of the contract as well under the U.C.C. rules relating to contracts between merchants. It is unclear whether Devices is also a merchant, a corporation in the business of buying and selling these types of goods. But whether Devices Corp. was a merchant, the additional term, whether it needed to be considered separately or not, became a part of the contract because no objection was made to its inclusion within 10 days by Devices. Given a valid offer and acceptance, there was adequate consideration because there was a bilateral contract and both sides promised to perform, Chips in exchange for $100,000 and Devices agreed to pay for the computer chips sent by Chips. Finally, since this is a sale of goods for over $500, the contract is within the Statute of Frauds. The Statute was satisfied because there was a written offer signed by Devices (the fax). Thus, there was a valid contract between Chips and Devices. The term added was acceptable because there was no mutual alteration, no objection, and no acceptance conditional upon the additional term.

Issue 2: The issue is whether Chips was capable of curing the contract or whether its actions constituted a breach sufficient to allow Devices the right to cancel. Under Article 2, merchants are normally required to deliver a perfect tender to the other party. Few exceptions are made to this rule. Here, as a merchant, Chips was under an obligation under the U.C.C. to deliver perfect goods (chips for handheld devices, not for laptop computers). Because the contract stated that performance was not due until January 16, 2000 (the additional term had become a part of the contract), Chips was entitled to an opportunity to cure the contract, and it had until January 16, 2000, to do so. Chips should have been given the opportunity to send Devices the proper goods until that date, and Devices was not entitled to cancel. This cure rule is specific to Article 2, where the party to be charged is a merchant. Thus, assuming a valid contract, Chips's nonconforming delivery on January 10, 2000, and its cure on January 15, 2000, prior to receiving notice of a valid reason for cancellation by Devices (for nonconformity is insufficient here) and prior to the date of performance contained in the contract of January 16, 2000, Chips had a right to cure, and Devices could not cancel for the reason given.

Issue 3: The issue is whether Chips's employee had authority to return the acknowledgment form of his own volition on Chips's behalf. A principal is liable on all contracts entered with its authority. Here, it could be argued that Chips's employee had implied authority to return the acknowledgment because he was an employee in Chips's shipping department. However, the employee was only a supervising clerk in the shipping department who was probably not familiar with the terms or details of Devices's order, nor what was going on with it. Thus, he probably did not have sufficient authority to bind Chips without the consent of someone in a management position or position of authority. The employee may have had apparent authority because he was cloaked with authority given his position, but at this point it is unclear if Devices reasonably relied on the form's return with respect to the contract. Furthermore, the release may not represent a contract, thus its ability to bind the principal in this situation is not adequate. Even though Chips was a merchant, such a release without more should be insufficient to bind Chips. Chips can still proceed with its claim.

SAMPLE ANSWER TO QUESTION 1 (CANDIDATE B)

(1)   The issue is whether Devices's offer on October 28 and Chips's written confirmation met the requirements outlined in the U.C.C. for a sale of goods contract. Between merchants (a merchant is one who regularly deals in the sale of specific goods or has specialized skill pertaining to goods) a contract may be formed by a written confirmation. All the requirements for contract formation are met: there is consideration in that 1,000 chips are to be exchanged for $500,000, there is an agreement or meeting of the minds, and there is bargained-for exchange or detriment. A valid contract was formed between Devices and Chips.

The central question is whether Chips's change of date for delivery entered the contract. Under the U.C.C., a contract for the sale of goods between merchants does not have to comply with the common law mirror image rule. In other words, the acceptance may contain additional terms. These terms will become part of the contract if they do not materially alter the terms of the contract, if the contract does not limit acceptance expressly to its terms, or if the other party does not object to their addition in a timely manner (*i.e.,* within 10 days of receipt). In this case, the offer did not limit acceptance to its terms. As to whether a change in delivery date materially altered the contract, one can infer from the fact that time was not of the essence, that a one-month delay was unlikely to be material. This is supported by the fact that Devices did not object to the new date. Devices impliedly accepted or acknowledged the new date when it faxed instructions for delivery on January 9 after the time of delivery proposed in the offer had passed. Because the delivery date was not objected to by Devices, it became part of the contract between the parties despite the fact that it conflicted with the original delivery date specified in the offer.

(2)   Chips's nonconforming delivery did not give Devices the right to cancel the contract because performance was not yet due and a seller has the right to cure a nonconforming shipment before performance is due. The general rule for buyer's rights on receipt of nonconforming goods is that a buyer may reject the goods entirely, retain units that conform to the contract, or accept the nonconforming goods. However, there is an exception to the general rule when a seller ships nonconforming goods before performance is due. In this case, a seller may notify the buyer upon learning of the nonconformity of its intent to cure. The buyer must accept conforming goods tendered when performance is due and may not cancel the contract before then. In this case, Chips breached its contract when it shipped the wrong chips. However, because it notified Devices of its intent to ship the correct chips and did so by January 16, 2000, Devices had no right to cancel the contract, even though Chips's first shipment was in breach of the contract. (It should be noted that the first shipment was not an accommodation, so the seller was in breach.)

(3)   The issue is whether the release signed by a supervising clerk binds Chips from pursuing its claims. The first issue is whether the supervising clerk had the authority as an agent or employee of Chips to execute such a release. An agent can have express, implied, apparent, or necessary authority to act on behalf of the principal. Here, it is highly unlikely that an agent in shipping would have the actual or express authority to sign such a release. Express authority is authority that has been explicitly given. In this case, the release was not a separate document, but part of the acknowledgment of receipt. A supervisor in shipping would have authority to sign a receipt of acknowledgment but not a release. Signing the release appears to have been necessary to acknowledge receipt.

The next question is whether the supervisor's signature binds Chips. It is likely that it does not bind because it is doubtful that a supervisor would be thought to have the apparent authority to bind the corporation. Devices, as a merchant participating in the chip market, would not have relied on the apparent authority of a person working in shipping to release any rights the company would have to make any subsequent legal claims. Industry custom and course of dealing should have informed Devices that the release obtained as part of the acknowledgment of receipt was not executed by an agent with the authority to bind Chips. Therefore, Chips is free to pursue its claims.

SAMPLE ANSWER TO QUESTION 2 (CANDIDATE A)

Issue 1: The issue is whether Mark's statement was hearsay and whether it fit within any exception permitting its admission at trial.

A statement is hearsay if it was made out of court and is being offered to prove the truth of the matter asserted in the statement. Here, Mark's statement was made out of court while he was in the hospital before surgery. The matter asserted in his statement was that Denise was the person who injured him. The statement is being offered to prove that Mark identified Denise as his assailant. Because the out-of-court statement is being offered to prove the truth of the matter asserted, it is hearsay.

To admit hearsay in court, the statement must fit within one of the exceptions to the hearsay rule, which have developed at common law. The only possible exception applicable to this statement is the exception for dying declarations. To be admissible under this exception, the declarant must be unavailable because he is dead, it must be offered in a homicide prosecution, and the declarant must have made the statement while under the belief that he was in imminent danger of dying (and the statement must be relevant to the cause of his death).

In this case, Mark has died and his statement is being offered in a homicide prosecution (felony murder is murder in the second degree, which constitutes a homicide prosecution). Mark's statement identifying his assailant also clearly pertained to the cause of his injuries. The issue is whether Mark made the statement while under the belief that his death was imminent.

Mark was not sufficiently convinced of the imminence of his own death for his statement to fit within this exception. First, the doctor told Mark his condition was "serious," not life-threatening or certain to cause death. Second, Mark's own description of his condition to Paul indicated that he held out hope for his own recovery since he said that surgery could save his life. Mark's statement reveals that he did not actually believe that he would die when he identified Denise as his assailant. The purpose of the dying declaration exception to the hearsay rule is that statements made in contemplation of death bear sufficient indicia of reliability to warrant their admission, despite the fact that the declarant is not on the witness stand for the jury to evaluate his credibility. Dying declarations are believed to be especially reliable because people generally do not want to die with a lie on their lips. That reliability stems from an actual belief on the declarant's part that he will die very soon. Mark simply did not have that belief, so his statement is not reliable enough to warrant its admission as an exception to the hearsay rule.

Issue 2: The issue is whether the facts proved at trial constituted the crime of felony murder.

The elements of (second degree) felony murder are that the defendant caused the death of a nonparticipant victim while in the course of, or in immediate flight from, the commission of one of the enumerated felonies in the New York penal law. One of the enumerated felonies in the penal law is burglary. To constitute a felony under the felony murder statute, it can be any degree of burglary (for second degree felony murder). The elements of burglary are the breaking and entering of a dwelling or place of business with the intent to commit a crime therein. It is not required to occur at night.

In this case, the facts proved that Denise caused Mark's death by running into him and causing him to fall and hit his head. Denise caused Mark's injury while in immediate flight from Ann's antique store. She had not yet reached a place of safety, so the immediacy of her flight was sufficient to fit within that element of the statute. Clearly, Mark was a nonparticipant in Denise's crime. These facts were all established by Paul's testimony at trial.

The next question is whether Denise was in immediate flight from an enumerated crime. Since we don't know from these facts whether Denise was convicted of burglary at trial, we must determine whether the facts at trial were sufficient to prove the elements of that crime.

Denise broke into Ann's Antiques on May 20. This fact was proven by Ann's testimony that her store was closed and that Denise had no right to be in the store that day. Ann's Antiques was a place of business.

The facts at trial proved that Denise broke in and entered Ann's Antiques with the intent to commit a felony therein. Paul testified that he observed Denise running out of the store carrying a lamp. After running into Mark, Denise dropped and left the lamp bearing a tag, which read "Ann's Antiques." Since Denise actually committed and completed the crime of larceny, and absent facts to the contrary, her intent to commit that crime upon entering Ann's Antiques may be inferred.

Therefore, since all of the elements of burglary and felony murder were proved by the prosecution at trial beyond a reasonable doubt, the court correctly denied Denise's motion to set aside the verdict on felony murder.

Note: The standard for the court to determine whether to grant a motion to set aside the verdict would be whether the prosecution presented sufficient evidence for a jury to reasonably find that the defendant committed each element of a crime beyond a reasonable doubt.

Issue 3: The issue is whether a juror visiting the crime scene, deliberating prior to the close of the evidence and/or discussing the case with fellow jurors constitute sufficient grounds for a mistrial.

A trial judge should grant a mistrial if a juror visits the crime scene on his own initiative, does not limit his deliberations to evidence presented at trial, deliberates prior to the close of the evidence and/or deliberates with fellow jurors prior to the closing arguments and instructions. In this case, Jan did all of the above acts. Because any one of her actions probably affected the verdict, the judge should have granted a mistrial. Because all of her actions combined certainly affected the verdict, the trial judge was definitely incorrect to deny the motion.

SAMPLE ANSWER TO QUESTION 2 (CANDIDATE B)

(1)   The issue is whether Mark's statement constitutes a dying declaration sufficient to except it from the general rule preventing the admission of hearsay.

Under the New York rules of evidence, hearsay is an out-of-court statement offered for the truth of the matter asserted. Hearsay is inadmissible unless it falls within an exception or is excluded from the definition of hearsay. A "dying declaration" is an exception to the rule against hearsay and may be admitted for the purposes of establishing its truth. To be admissible, (i) the statement must be made under a sense of impending death, (ii) it must concern the circumstances that put the declarant in the position of impending death, (iii) the declarant must thereafter die, (iv) the declarant must have been competent to testify at trial, and (v) in New York, the exception may only be used in a homicide case.

Under the facts, the statement by Mark meets requirement (ii) because he explained that his position was caused by Denise. It meets requirement (iii) because Mark died after the surgery. It also meets requirement (v) because it is being offered in a homicide (felony murder) case. However, the statement does not meet requirement (i) because the facts suggest that Mark had at least some hope that he would survive. The statement arguably fails to meet requirement (iv) also because a person with internal bleeding in the head would probably not be considered competent to testify at trial. Thus, the court ruled improperly when it permitted Paul to testify as to Mark's statement.

(2)   The second issue is whether there were sufficient facts to support a felony murder verdict against Denise (enough so that a denial of Denise's attorney's motion was proper).

Under New York penal law, the crime of felony murder arises where the defendant causes the death of a nonparticipant during the commission of an enumerated felony or during the immediate flight therefrom. The prosecution must prove the crime beyond a reasonable doubt in order to sustain a guilty verdict.

Under the facts, the prosecution has proven that the enumerated felony burglary occurred and that a nonparticipant, Mark, died during the perpetrator's/felon's immediate flight from the felony. These elements can be proven without regard to the out-of-court statement made by Mark. Assuming that the declaration constitutes inadmissible hearsay, there would not be sufficient evidence to warrant a guilty verdict against Denise (*i.e.*, without the statement, there would be no identification of Denise as the felon. Neither the police officer nor Ann, the owner of the antiques store, actually saw Denise herself commit the crime of burglary or the accidental contact with Mark). Assuming the admissibility of the statement, there would be sufficient evidence. It should be noted that third degree burglary in New York arises where the defendant knowingly enters or unlawfully remains behind in a building with the intent to commit a crime therein. It can be aggravated to second degree where there is injury to a nonparticipant. Again, under the facts, the requisite elements of burglary were met, except that there is no identification of Denise without the hearsay statement.

(3)   The issue is whether a juror's visit to the scene of a crime, unaccompanied by a judge, during the trial is grounds for a mistrial.

Under New York law, jurors may not visit the scene of a crime of their own accord during trial or deliberations. The fact that the verdict is not affected as a result of such a visit is not sufficient to prevent the granting of a motion for mistrial. Here, Jan made an unaccompanied, "unofficial" visit to the scene of the crime. It does not matter that the verdict was not ultimately affected. The court incorrectly denied Denise's attorney's motion for a mistrial.

SAMPLE ANSWER TO QUESTION 3 (CANDIDATE A)

(1)   The issue is whether Al can remove Dot's claim to federal court based on diversity jurisdiction.

To remove a claim to federal court, the plaintiff's claim must have been capable of initially being brought in federal court. Presuming Navigation Law is a matter of state law, Al would have to remove the case based on diversity. If Navigation Law is federal, federal jurisdiction might have given the district court subject matter jurisdiction arising out of a federal question. At that point the state law issue would be remanded to state court. Diversity jurisdiction exists when there is complete diversity of citizenship between all plaintiffs and all defendants. This means no plaintiff can be from the same state as any defendant. In addition, the amount in controversy must exceed $75,000.

In this case, Al is being sued as an executor of Bob's estate. As such, New York law requires that the domicile of the decedent be used to determine diversity. Because Bob was a domiciliary of State X and Carl and his widow of New York, there is complete diversity. In addition, the claim exceeds $75,000. As such, Dot could have brought the action initially in federal court, so Al is entitled to remove it. Therefore, the court was incorrect in granting Dot's motion, because diversity jurisdiction allowed the federal district court to hear this case.

(2)   The issue is whether Carl was an employee of Bob's estate and therefore limited to workers' compensation recovery.

Summary judgment is granted when there is no genuine issue of material fact. In this case, Carl might very well have been an employee of Bob's estate, but he could also have been an independent contractor. In fact, the facts seem to suggest an independent contractor relationship existed because Al hired Carl for a specific job at an hourly rate. Likely, Carl was not on any employee payroll of Al's. Assuming Carl was an independent contractor, his damages are not limited to workers' compensation. Workers' compensation is a damages remedy that limits an employer's liability to a preset contractual amount. There are no pain and suffering damages and no punitive damages under the workers' compensation system. Workers' compensation excludes independent contractors, teachers, clergy, and domestic part-time help from its coverage.

Because Carl's status as an employee is not conclusive, and a jury could find a genuine issue as to whether Carl was an independent contractor or an employee subject to workers' compensation, the court was correct in denying Al's motion for summary judgment.

(3)   The issue is whether Al, as representative agent of Bob's estate, owed a duty to Carl to protect him from his eventual death.

Under New York common law negligence, landowners (or representative agents of landowner, *i.e.,* executors of estates) owe a duty of reasonable care. The majority of states apply different standards depending on the injured party's status as an invitee, licensee, or trespasser. However, New York simply relies on a reasonably prudent standard. Under the facts of this case, Al warned Carl to be careful. This is a genuine issue of material fact as to whether this warning constitutes reasonable prudence under the circumstances, depending on whether "be careful" was a general warning or whether it represented a knowledge of lack of life vests by Al. As such, there could have been a breach of duty for which Al is liable to Carl.

Additionally, Al owed Carl a statutory duty of care under the Navigation Law. Where the injury that results is in the class of risk the statute intended to protect and the injured party is in the class of persons intended to be protected, courts will find a breach of duty, or negligence per se. Here, the law was enacted to prevent users of boats from drowning. Carl is in both the class of persons and the class of risk. As such, the jury not only could, but should find a breach of duty by Al. Al might try to argue that he did not personally owe any duty, but as agent to Bob's estate, he takes on that duty.

The court was incorrect in granting summary judgment, on the basis that Carl's own negligence caused his death. The issue is whether contributory negligence bars a claim for negligence recovery in New York.

New York uses a pure comparative negligence standard. This means a plaintiff may recover for a defendant's negligence no matter how negligent the plaintiff was, even if the plaintiff was more than 50% negligent (which is a bar in a modified comparative negligence jurisdiction). This means that even if Carl was negligent, if a jury could find that Al and Bob's estate was even 1% negligent, Al cannot be granted summary judgment.

Therefore, the court was wrong in granting summary judgment to Al because Bob's estate breached no duty and Carl's own negligence caused his death.

SAMPLE ANSWER TO QUESTION 3 (CANDIDATE B)

(1)   The issue is whether there is jurisdiction of the federal district court. Under federal rules of civil procedure, in order for a case to be tried in federal court, the court must have subject matter jurisdiction. Subject matter jurisdiction is obtained when a federal question is at issue or there is diversity of citizenship and the amount in controversy is over $75,000.

In this case, the causes of action are for negligence and wrongful death, so there is no federal question. As for the second method for obtaining jurisdiction, the two prongs are met.

For purposes of diversity, an executor or personal representative is deemed to have the residence of the decedent. In this case, Al, as executor, is a resident of State X. Dot, as Carl's widow and as personal representative, is from New York (assuming she lived with Carl in Washington County on the issue of her residence in suing on behalf of herself). Therefore, because the plaintiffs are residents of a different state than the defendant, diversity exists. Moreover, because damages are being sought for $1 million, the amount in controversy requirement is met.

Thus, removal by Al was proper. The defendant can choose to remove when jurisdiction is proper. A plaintiff can only seek to remand if removal was improper. Here, it was proper removal, so Dot's motion to remand should have been denied.

(2)   The issue is whether the workers' compensation laws apply.

In New York, workers' compensation law is the sole remedy for employees injured on the job. This law applies to all employees and employers with limited exceptions. Independent contractors are not covered by the laws. The issue then becomes whether or not Carl was an independent contractor.

The relevant inquiry centers on who had the control. Factors considered are the type of work, the pay rate (hourly or for the whole job), who supplied the equipment, and how much supervision or discretion was given.

In this case, Al paid by the hour and furnished the paint, which point in favor of an employee/employer relationship. However, the nature of the job, specifically the painting of a house, is a job tending toward an independent contractor position. Moreover, Carl furnished all the equipment including brushes, ladders, etc. Seemingly also the right to use the boat "to view the paint job from the water" gives an indication of control and discretion on Carl's part. It was up to Carl to make sure he did a good job. Thus, Carl was an independent contractor and outside the scope of the workers' compensation laws.

Thus, the summary judgment motion should be denied because there is a genuine issue of material fact to be tried.

(3) The issues are whether the Navigation Law should be used to replace the reasonably prudent person standard (as negligent per se) and also if Carl's negligence should bar recovery under the pure comparative negligence statute.

A statute can be used to demonstrate a duty of care. In a negligence action, four elements must be shown: a duty, a breach of that duty, causation (in fact and proximate cause) and damages. When a statute's standard is substituted for the reasonably prudent person standard, if a defendant breaches the statute's standard, the two first elements are found and the plaintiff need only prove causation and damages. To use negligence per se, the statute's purpose must be to prevent the type of injury that the plaintiff has suffered and the plaintiff must fall into the category of persons sought to be protected.

In this case, the statute requiring life preservers to be on board is seemingly for the reason of preventing drowning. Since Carl drowned, the statute seems appropriate.

Thus, if the court applies the statute, Dot need only show causation and damages, which she can probably do. Thus, the motion for summary judgment should not have been granted because there are issues of triable fact that need to be determined.

The issue as to whether Carl's negligence caused his own death should go to a jury. In New York, the pure comparative negligence statute does not bar recovery if the plaintiff is partially at fault. Rather, the trier of fact determines the percentages and allocates the damages accordingly.

Thus, even if Carl was a bit at fault for using the boat, despite Al's warnings to be careful, this does not bar recovery and the issue should be decided by the trier of fact, *i.e.*, the issue should survive summary judgment.

SAMPLE ANSWER TO QUESTION 4 (CANDIDATE A)

(1) At issue is whether the EPTL makes an exception to the general ademption rules for casualty insurance paid after the testator's death.

The general rule of ademption is that a distributee is only entitled to the actual bequest if the bequest is a specific bequest. Thus, if the subject of the bequest is sold or destroyed prior to the testator's death, the beneficiary takes neither the bequest nor compensation equal in value.

Absent exceptions, the general rule would apply because the gift of Greenacre was a specific bequest (that is, it named a particular property).

However, the EPTL makes three exceptions to the general rule of ademption. Specifically, casualty insurance paid after the testator's death is paid to the beneficiary of the otherwise specific bequest.

The insurance proceeds were for casualty loss because they were paid after a fire destroyed the property. The proceeds were paid after the testator's death because the facts state that the proceeds were paid to Linda "as executrix." Had Bob been alive, the proceeds would have been paid to him. Thus, Mitch will take the insurance proceeds.

(2) At issue first is whether partial revocation by physical act is valid.

The rule is that a testator may revoke his or her will in its entirety by physical act (*i.e.,* burning, cutting, destroying). However, a testator may not partially revoke a will by physical act.

Here, the revocation was only partial because the cross-out merely crosses out one entry, rather than the entire document or signature. Thus, the revocation was only partial, and thus invalid.

At issue secondly is whether an attempted codicil, which is unattested, may serve as a revocation. Generally, partial revocation by codicil is permissible. However, codicils, like wills, are only valid if they meet the following requirements: (i) signed by testator, (ii) at the end, (iii) the codicil must be publicized to attesting witnesses, (iv) there must be two attesting witnesses, (v) the attesting witnesses must sign after publication, and (vi) each witness must sign within 30 days of the other.

Here, the first requirement was met because the testator signed. The second requirement was met because he signed at the end of the codicil. However, the third, fourth, fifth and sixth requirements were not met because there were no attesting witnesses (or at least none who signed). Furthermore, New York does not recognize holographic wills, except for members of the armed forces and mariners at sea. Thus, the codicil was invalid. There was no revocation, and Jeff will take Blackacre.

(3) At issue is whether a gift to people not in being at the execution of the will is valid if those contingent remainderman do not take until the age of 30.

The general rule is that a gift must vest, if at all, within 21 years of the death of any life in being at the execution of the instrument. Otherwise, the gift violates the Rule Against Perpetuities.

The residuary gift of the principal of the trust will not vest within the perpetuities period because it is possible that either Jeff or Patrick will have children and then die within less than nine years. The result would be that those children would turn 30, which is the vesting age, more than 21 years after the death of the relevant life in being.

However, New York has modified the common law Rule Against Perpetuities such that the courts will reduce any age contingencies that violate the rule to 21. Here, the age 30 requirement will be reduced to 21 because it otherwise violates the Rule Against Perpetuities. Thus, as modified, the residuary gift of the principal of the trust is valid.

SAMPLE ANSWER TO QUESTION 4 (CANDIDATE B)

(1) The issue is who receives insurance proceeds for property left in a will.

Under the doctrine of ademption, if property left in a will to a survivor is destroyed or no longer with the testator at his death, the beneficiary gets nothing. An exception is casualty insurance proceeds paid out after the death of the testator. Proceeds paid out after death are given to the beneficiary.

In this case, Greenacre was destroyed before Bob died, but the insurance proceeds were not paid out until after his death (as evidenced by payment to Linda, the executrix). Therefore, Mitch will receive the insurance proceeds.

(2) The issue is whether a testator can make valid handwritten changes to a will without any witnesses present. A testator can revoke a will by physical act, such as tearing or burning. He can cross out a will but only if he makes it evident that he is destroying the whole will, such as by complete cross-outs. There is no partial physical revocation. In addition, a cross-out with new words added is not valid because New York does not recognize holographic wills (except in the case of mariners at sea or soldiers during war—neither of which applies here). A modification must be made by a codicil or new will and signed by the testator with publication in front of two witnesses who both sign within 30 days of each other. A holographic will (or written alteration) is handwritten and signed by the testator but not witnessed, so it is therefore invalid in New York.

In this case, Bob's crossed-out writing is akin to a holographic will and therefore not valid. The will will be honored as though no changes had been made. His partial cross-outs do not qualify as full physical revocation. Therefore, the original beneficiary, Jeff, will inherit Blackacre.

(3) The issue is does a clause leaving the residuary to children "who shall reach age 30" violate the Rule Against Perpetuities in New York.

No estate interest shall be valid if it does not vest or fail within a life in being plus 21 years from the date of creation of the interest. The income to Jeff and Patrick is valid and they will be considered "lives in being," or measuring lives, because their existence affects the trust outcome.

The clause that states that the principal will go to any children of Jeff and Patrick who shall reach age 30 would normally be invalid. Under the common law Rule Against Perpetuities, the clause would be struck because Jeff and Patrick could both die and leave young children (under the age of nine) that would not allow the interest to vest within 21 years.

In New York, however, the court applies an Age Contingency Doctrine that would reduce the age to 21 years old if it would save the gift. Here, the clause in New York would thus be valid, and if Jeff or Patrick had children, they would get the gift at age 21. Since there are no children, there is a reversion back to Bob's estate.

Note that Linda was made executrix of the estate. An attorney must not write herself into a will as an executrix unless she explains that she will be paid for both attorneys' fees plus executor commissions and that anyone can be an executor. She must also get a signed separate consent from the testator. If she fails to do so, her commission will be cut in half.

barbri®

BAR REVIEW

Multiple Choice by Subject

AGENCY QUESTIONS

1.   An instrument granting a power of attorney states that it will not be effective until the holder of the power of attorney declares the principal incompetent. The principal will be considered incompetent when:

(A) A court declares the principal incompetent.

(B) The holder of the power of attorney in fact declares the principal incompetent in writing.

(C) The holder of the power of attorney petitions the court to declare the principal incompetent.

(D) The provision is invalid as a matter of law because the relationship always terminates on the incapacity of the principal.

2.   Joe hired Ashley to sell his mansion. They signed a nonexclusive listing contract. Ashley was still attending real estate brokers' school and hoped to have her license in a few months. Ashley called Joe to inform him that she had someone who wanted to make an offer on the mansion. Joe said he would get back to her. Five days later Joe called Ashley to tell her he found someone on his own to buy the mansion. Knowing she missed out on a $200,000 commission, Ashley brought a claim against Joe for breach of contract. Which of the following statements is correct?

(A) Ashley will prevail because she had an exclusive power of sale.

(B) Ashley will prevail because she had someone ready, willing, and able to purchase the house.

(C) Ashley may not enforce a claim for commission.

(D) Ashley may not prevail because she did not consummate the sale.

Questions 3 and 4 are based on the following situation:

3.   Dr. Rugin had been working as a proctologist for 10 years when he decided to expand his practice and hire another doctor to join his office. Dr. Rugin interviewed many prospective candidates and finally decided to hire Dr. Find. During the final interview, Doctor Rugin told Dr. Find that her salary would be based on the number of patients she saw every week and that she would be considered an independent contractor. Dr. Find agreed to these terms. While Dr. Find was still employed with Dr. Rugin, she was involved in an automobile accident. Dr. Find was returning to the doctor's office after doing her rounds at the city hospital. Before Dr. Find reached the office, she pulled into a convenience store to buy a can of soda and a candy bar. As Dr. Find was backing out of the parking lot, she failed to see a small child behind her and hit and killed the child. The parents of the child seek damages from Dr. Rugin and Dr. Find. If their action against Dr. Rugin is unsuccessful it is because:

(A) Stopping at the convenience store was not in Dr. Find's normal course of employment.

(B) Doctors cannot be held vicariously liable for each other.

(C) Dr. Find was an independent contractor.

(D) The child's parents were contributorily negligent.

4. Assume for purposes of this question that Dr. Rugin's employee of 10 years, Nurse Vaivo, was returning home from the hospital. Before Nurse Vaivo left, her friend Nurse Williams, nurse for Doctor Chest, asked for a ride back to Dr. Chest's office. Before they reached the office, Nurse Vaivo fell asleep at the wheel, her car crashed, and Nurse Williams was seriously injured. Nurse Williams brings an action for her injuries against Nurse Vaivo and Dr. Rugin. If Nurse Williams's action is unsuccessful against Dr. Rugin it is because:

(A) Dr. Rugin did not know that Nurse Vaivo was at the hospital.

(B) Dr. Rugin did not expressly authorize Nurse Vaivo to give Nurse Williams a ride.

(C) Nurse Vaivo's travel from the hospital was not within her scope of employment.

(D) None of the above.

AGENCY ANSWERS

1. **(B)**

A power of attorney, being an agency power, generally terminates on the incapacity of the principal unless it specifically provides otherwise. However, by statute, a power of attorney can be made to survive the disability or incapacity of the principal if the power so states. [N.Y. Gen. Oblig. Law §5-1601] The power of attorney granted here is called a "springing power of attorney" [N.Y. Gen. Oblig. Law §5-1602] because the instrument has been drafted so as to become effective only on the happening of a specified future event—the principal's incapacity. Under the terms of this springing power, for the power of attorney to become effective, the power-holder must declare in writing that the event has occurred. Thus, (B) is the correct answer.

2. **(C)**

Ashley may not enforce a claim for commissions because in New York, only a licensed real estate broker may enforce a claim. This applies to full- or part-time brokers.

3. **(C)**

In general, a principal may be liable to third parties for torts committed by her agent under the doctrine of respondeat superior. For respondeat superior liability to attach, there first must be an employment relationship and then the tortious conduct must have been within the scope of employment. The principal is not generally liable for torts committed by an agent functioning as an independent contractor. An agent will generally be found to be an employee only if the principal exercises control over how the agent performs. An employee generally works full-time, is compensated on a time basis, and is subject to the supervision of the principal in the details of his work. It was clear by the terms of the employment agreement that Dr. Find was an independent contractor, and thus Dr. Rugin will not be liable for the torts committed by Dr. Find.

4. **(B)**

The master is not liable for the torts of the servant unless the tort occurred within the scope of the servant's employment. At the time of the act, the servant must be motivated by a desire to serve the purposes of the master. However, when the situation arises that the servant invited a third person to ride in her vehicle without the express authorization by the master, this is considered to be outside the scope of the employment relationship. Thus, the master is not liable for the injury to the third person. Accordingly, (B) is the correct answer.

COMMERCIAL PAPER QUESTIONS

1.   A holder is precluded from holder in due course status if the instrument is:

(A) Purchased for less than its legal value by the holder.

(B) Negotiated as security in the regular course of business.

(C) Vested in the holder.

(D) Purchased as part of a bulk transaction not in the regular course of business.

2.   An instrument (1) is postdated, (2) states two rates of interest applicable to different periods, and (3) provides for payment "on my Father's death." The instrument is not negotiable because of:

(A) (1).

(B) (2).

(C) (3).

(D) The instrument is negotiable.

3.   Mrs. Levy borrowed $25,000 from the First Bills Bank & Trust. The bank required her to sign the following writing and return it to the bank in 10 days: "60 days after date, I promise to pay to the First Bills Bank & Trust the sum of twenty-five thousand dollars ($25,000) plus interest at the rate of fifteen percent (15%)." This writing is:

(A) Not negotiable, because the time for payment is indefinite.

(B) Not negotiable, because it is not for a definite sum.

(C) Negotiable, because it is signed by Mrs. Levy.

(D) Negotiable, because it is a promise to pay.

4.   D was the holder and payee of a 60-day note signed by M as evidence of a $10,000 debt owed by M to D, payable July 1. C, G, and S had signed the note as co-guarantors of collectibility and had, without D's knowledge, agreed among themselves that in the event they became liable on the note, they would contribute 25%, 25%, and 50%, respectively, toward payment thereof. On June 1, M advised S that he would be unable to pay any part of the debt when it became due. S therefore obtained a letter signed by D in which D said that he released S from liability on the debt. On July 1, D demanded payment from M and received the bad news. In an action by D to recover $10,000 from C and G as co-defendants, D will recover:

(A) $10,000.

(B) $2,500 only.

(C) $5,000 only.

(D) None of the above.

5.   S fraudulently induces R to buy a phony gold watch for $350 on June 1. R gives S a check for $350. On June 15, S negotiates the check to T for a refrigerator. T negotiates the check to U on July 1 for a television set. On July 15, T and U discover the fraud S had perpetrated on R.

Who can collect the check?

(A) T only.

(B) U only.

(C) Both U and T.

(D) Neither U nor T.

COMMERCIAL PAPER ANSWERS

1.   (D)

Even though the holder may satisfy the requirements that he take for value, in good faith, and without notice, he still does not become a holder in due course of an instrument if he (i) purchases the instrument at judicial sale or takes it under legal process; (ii) acquires the instrument in taking over an estate; or (iii) purchases the instrument as part of a bulk transaction not in the regular course of business of the transferor. [U.C.C. §3-302(3)] (A), (B), and (C) are incorrect statements of the law. (D) is the correct answer.

2.   (C)

An instrument is negotiable if it is in writing and signed by the maker or drawer, containing an unconditional promise or order to pay a sum certain, and to be payable on demand or at a definite time, to order or bearer. [U.C.C. §3-104] (A) and (B) do not affect the negotiability of the instrument. A post-obituary note is not negotiable since the time for payment is uncertain. [U.C.C. §3-102(2)] (C) is the correct answer.

3.   (A)

This instrument is not negotiable because the time for payment is indefinite. To be negotiable, a writing must be (a) signed by the maker or drawer; (b) contain an unconditional promise or order to pay a sum certain in money; and (c) be payable on demand to order or bearer. To be payable at a definite time, an instrument by its terms must be payable on or before a stated date or at a fixed period after a stated date. Here, the time for payment is indefinite because it is tied to the date of the writing, which is undated. Thus, (A) is the correct answer. (Note that the instrument will be treated as an incomplete instrument and can become negotiable by the authorized filling in section of the missing date under U.C.C. section 3-115.)

4.   (D)

One who guarantees collection of an instrument is not liable to the holder of the note until the holder has exhausted his remedies against the debtor or has shown such an effort to be futile. Here, D has not exhausted his remedies against M or shown that such efforts would be futile. Thus, he may not recover the amounts specified in (A), (B), or (C).

5.   (B)

S is a "holder" of the check given to him by R since he is in the possession of an instrument drawn to his order. [U.C.C. §1-201(20)] A holder of an instrument may negotiate it. [U.C.C. §3-301] Here, it appears that T was a holder in due course when he accepted the check as payment, since he took the check in good faith, for value, and without notice of the fraud. [U.C.C. §3-302] U also became a holder in due course when he accepted the check as payment from T. Since T has given up title to the check by negotiating it to U, only U can collect on the check. U, as a holder in due course, will not be subject to the personal defense of fraudulent inducement, which would be asserted by R. [U.C.C. §3-305] Thus, U can collect on the check.

CONFLICT OF LAWS QUESTIONS

1.   Darby Dinosauropolis, a citizen of Ontario, is on his way to a camping trip in Lechworth State Park in New York. While driving through Ohio, Darby stops at the famous Williams Neanderthal Man Brew Pub. While in the pub, Darby imbibes shots of William's Grain Alcohol. After his sixth shot, Darby leaves the pub and continues on his way. When he reaches East Aurora, New York, Darby accidentally swerves to the left and hits Alfred Brodsky, the mayor of East Aurora, in a head-on collision. After getting out of the hospital, Mayor Brodsky brings an action in the New York state court against Darby and Todd, the owner of the pub. Ohio does not have a Dram Shop Act. The applicable law should be:

(A)   New York, because that is where the injury occurred.

(B)   New York, because a New York plaintiff has a vested right to have apply the law of the state in which the injury took place.

(C)   Ohio, because the law of the defendant's domicile is controlling.

(D)   Ohio, because when one state has a Dram Shop Act and the other does not, the law of the state with the Dram Shop Act would not apply.

2.   Brandon, a resident of State A, while vacationing in State B, is injured in a motorcycle accident with Dillon, a resident of State C. Brandon brings an action against Dillon in State B. In determining what state's law the forum state should apply to determine whether Dillon's conduct was negligent, which of the following statements is incorrect?

(A)   This is a question of "procedure" and the forum state always applies its own procedural rules.

(B)   The law of the place of the wrong may be applied in personal injury cases unless some other state has a more significant interest in the outcome of the case.

(C)   If Dillon's conduct was privileged in State B, this would not be an absolute defense to the application of any other state's law.

(D)   A litigant does not have a vested right to have the law of the state in which the event took place applied.

3.   Leland and Douglas enter into a contract which states that all issues arising under the contract shall be decided by the laws of New York. Neither party resides in New York. Which of the following is a true statement?

(A)   The designation of New York as controlling will be given effect if suit is filed outside New York, because jurisdiction springs from the law.

(B)   The parties' agreement that the laws of New York shall govern the construction of their contract will be generally respected.

(C)   The parties' designation of New York as controlling will be given effect even if it violates some fundamental policy of the state in which the parties were domiciled.

(D)   If there is no reasonable basis for the parties' choice because the chosen state bears no substantial relationship to the parties or the transaction, nevertheless, the provision will be applied.

4. **Which of the following is not a defense to the forum state's application of a foreign law?**

(A) **The law is procedural.**

(B) **The law is a penal law.**

(C) **The law violates a fundamental principle of justice.**

(D) **The law is substantive.**

CONFLICT OF LAWS ANSWERS

1. **(D)**

A conflict of law or choice of law problem may arise in any case involving multistate contacts or elements. When this occurs, the New York court will have to decide whether to apply the law of New York or the law of some other jurisdiction. In this case, the plaintiff was a New York domiciliary and the defendants were Ontario and Ohio domiciliaries. The forum state is New York. Under the New York Dram Shop Act [Gen. Oblig. Law §11-101], New York imposes statutory liability on the vendor of liquor if his drunken customer injures another. Where the liquor was served in a state without a Dram Shop Act and the injury occurred in a state having such an act, the question arises as to which state's laws will apply. In this true conflict situation, the court will generally follow the rule that the state with the Dram Shop Act will not apply its own law because it would be extremely unfair to the defendant who would not be held liable in the state where the conduct is legal. Thus, (D) is the correct answer.

2. **(A)**

The law determining the ultimate outcome of the case is regarded as substantive and the forum court may decide to apply foreign substantive law to a given case. (A) is untrue and thus the correct answer because while the forum court will apply its own procedural rules, the rule here was substantive. (B), (C), and (D) are true statements.

3. **(B)**

When parties draw a contract, they intend to be bound and, with regard to the construction of the contract, the parties can always choose the desired law. This is a shorthand reference to the intention of the parties. (A) is incorrect because jurisdiction does not spring from the law, but rather the courts look to whether there is a sufficient nexus with the law chosen, even when the parties do not reside in the state whose law was chosen. (C) is incorrect because if the application of the law of the chosen state would be contrary to a fundamental policy of a state that has a materially greater interest than the chosen state in the determination of the particular issue, the provision will not be applied. (D) is an incorrect statement. Accordingly, (B) is correct.

4. **(D)**

Three defenses that should be considered when determining a choice of law issue are whether the law to be applied is procedural, the foreign law is against public policy, and the foreign law is a penal law. The forum court may apply the foreign substantive law to a given case but will follow its own procedural laws. (D) is the correct answer.

CONSTITUTIONAL LAW QUESTIONS

1.   A law enacted by the state of New York to allow couples to divorce each other without a judicial proceeding would be:

(A) Unconstitutional under the federal Constitution.

(B) Unconstitutional under the state constitution.

(C) Unconstitutional under both the state and federal constitutions.

(D) Constitutional under both the state and federal constitutions.

2.   In the state of New York, the right of employees to organize and bargain collectively to representation of their own choosing is a right:

(A) Expressly created under the federal Constitution.

(B) Expressly created under the state constitution.

(C) Expressly created under both the state and federal Constitutions.

(D) Not a constitutional right.

3.   The defendant, an African-American woman named Donnie, and two Caucasian men robbed a man named Charles outside a grocery store using a razor. Two weeks later, Donnie attempted to rob another person, Nicky, outside the same store. Store security guards chased Donnie until the police successfully apprehended her. Donnie was indicted on one count of robbery in the first degree and on one count of robbery in the second degree based on the first incident, and on one count of attempted robbery based on the second incident.

During voir dire, the prosecutor used two peremptory challenges to remove the only two African-American people from the jury; two peremptory challenges to remove two out of four women from the jury; and three peremptory challenges to remove three out of five Hispanics from the jury. During voir dire, the defense attorney accused the prosecutor of using his peremptory challenges in a prejudicial manner. The judge called a *Batson* hearing. During the hearing, the defense attorney concentrated on the dismissal of an African-American woman named Mary. The prosecutor gave a neutral explanation for Mary's dismissal. The defense attorney claimed that this explanation was pretextual. However, the judge ruled in favor of the prosecution. Donnie was later convicted, and her defense counsel appealed on the basis of the *Batson* challenge. The appeals court ruled that the challenges were not reviewable on appeal.

Which of the following statements is true with regard to the appellate court's ruling:

(A) The ruling is incorrect only as to the African-American people dismissed in the case.

(B) The ruling is incorrect only as to the women dismissed in the case.

(C) The ruling is incorrect as to all dismissals made on the basis of race or gender in the case.

(D) The ruling is incorrect only as to Mary.

CONSTITUTIONAL LAW ANSWERS

1.   (B)

The New York State Constitution, Article 1, section 9(1), provides that there can be no divorces except by judicial proceeding. There is no analogous provision under the federal Constitution.

2.   (B)

The New York State Constitution, Article 1, section 17, creates the right of employees to organize their collective bargaining arrangements. There is no analogous provision under the federal Constitution. Accordingly, (B) is the correct answer.

3.   (D)

In making a *Batson* challenge, the moving party must make specific objections to the exclusion of a juror, or jurors, in order to properly preserve the challenge for review. The moving party must establish a prima facie case that its opponent is using peremptory challenges to exclude a certain individual, or group, from the jury. If a prima facie case is made, the burden then falls to the nonmoving party to provide a race neutral or gender neutral reason for the exclusion. The moving party must then assert that the reason given is merely pretextual, in order for the specific challenge to be preserved. Consequently, (A), (B), and (C) are incorrect answers, as *Batson* challenges were not raised at the requisite time during the case.

CONTRACTS QUESTIONS

1.   Tiffany duly executed her will, "I bequeath to Steve my new Nagasaki XL1000 speed boat to remember our speedy love affair." The remainder of her $10 million estate is left to her cat, Morris. Tiffany died three months later in a parachuting accident.

The speed boat needs extensive repairs and Steve brings the boat to Alan Mechanic. Alan and Steve agree in a written work requisition that Alan will repair the boat for $5,000, with all repairs to be completed within six months. A week later, Steve decides that to impress the ladies, he must have the boat in time for his next party. In a telephone conversation, Steve and Alan agree that Alan will complete the repairs in five months for an extra $1,000. At the end of the five months, Alan delivers the completely repaired boat to Steve who pays Alan $5,000. If Alan sues Steve, Alan may recover:

(A) $5,000 only.

(B) $6,000 only.

(C) $1,000 only.

(D) Nothing.

2.   Carla and Melinda went to college together in a small Amish town in New York. After graduation, Carla moved to western New York and purchased a large, prosperous poppy field. Melinda moved to New York City and bought a greenhouse and made a paltry living growing carnations. Two years later, Carla, who was lonely, called Melinda and told Melinda to sell her greenhouse and move to western New York. Carla told Melinda that she would let Melinda use 25 acres from another field Carla owned for no charge, so Melinda could make a start in the poppy business. Melinda sold her greenhouse and moved to western New York to take Carla up on her offer. When Melinda arrived, Carla told Melinda that Carla had needed the extra cash to buy a new evening gown and had sold off her spare fields. If Melinda brings an action against Carla for breach of contract, she will:

(A) Not prevail, because of the Statute of Frauds.

(B) Prevail, because she accepted Carla's offer by performing the acts which Carla requested.

(C) Prevail, because she relied to her detriment upon Carla's promise to let her use the field, and her reliance was foreseeable.

(D) Not prevail, because Carla's promise was gratuitous, not supported by consideration.

3.   On January 1, 2005, John and Katie entered into a one-year written lease which also contained an option to purchase the property on or before January 1, 2006. John believed Katie would not exercise her option, and so offered the property for sale during the month of December 2005. John received an acceptance from Jason, by telegram, on December 31, 2005. On January 1, 2006, Katie mailed her acceptance of the option to John, who received it on January 2, 2006. Who is entitled to buy the property?

(A) Katie, because of the mailbox rule.

(B) Either Katie or Jason, because both made valid acceptance.

(C) Jason, because his acceptance arrived first.

(D) Jason, because Katie's acceptance arrived after the option had expired.

4. Elissa, age 14, and Kevin, age 15, were married on July 27, 2006. Shortly after they were married, Kevin signed a one-year furniture lease with Woods Furniture, Inc. Three months later, Elissa died in childbirth. Now Kevin wants to get out of his furniture lease because he is moving back home with his mother and has no need for the excess furniture. If Kevin breaks the lease, will Woods have a valid cause of action against him?

(A) Yes, because Kevin was married at the time the lease was signed.

(B) Yes, if the residential furniture is a necessity.

(C) No, because the lease became invalid when Elissa died.

(D) No, because Kevin was a minor at the time the lease was signed.

5. Dr. Rugin had been working as a proctologist for 10 years when he decided to expand his practice and hire another doctor to join his office. Dr. Rugin interviewed many prospective candidates and finally decided to hire Dr. Find. Four weeks after Dr. Find had been working in Dr. Rugin's office, Dr. Rugin gave Dr. Find an agreement to sign which stated that in the event that Dr. Find left Dr. Rugin's employment, she would agree not to practice proctology within a two-mile radius, nor would she treat or solicit Dr. Rugin's patients for a period of two years. Dr. Find signed the agreement. Two years later, Dr. Find ended her relationship with Dr. Rugin and went to work for the prominent proctologist, Dr. Chest, whose office was 1.5 miles from Dr. Rugin's. Dr. Rugin filed an action to enjoin Dr. Find from working in Dr. Chest's office based on the noncompete clause. The court should:

(A) Not grant the injunction, because the noncompete agreement is unenforceable because there was no additional consideration in exchange for the promise.

(B) Grant the injunction, because Dr. Find could have been discharged for not signing the contract; this was the additional consideration needed for the restrictive covenant.

(C) Not grant the injunction, because the restrictive covenant is unconscionable.

(D) Grant the injunction, because to restrict the movement of doctors would be against public policy.

6. A and B own adjoining farms. In 2001, the town assessor advised A and B that the deed descriptions for their two farms overlapped and gave each of them a freehand sketch of the area, which showed an overlap of five acres. A agreed to convey to B his interest in the land in question for $1,500. Neither A nor B had the land surveyed. B's attorney proposed a deed which described the land in question based on the freehand sketch and recited that the lands described conferred "by estimate five acres of land." In 2002, A executed the deed and delivered it to B, who paid A the $1,500 and recorded the deed. In 2005, B had his property surveyed and learned that the deed from A actually conveyed to B a parcel which was 50 acres in size and which did not in any way overlap any of the lands described in the original deed to B's farm. B did not tell A about these survey findings. Last month, A had his remaining property surveyed and learned that he actually conveyed 50 acres to B. A duly commenced an action against B to rescind the contract and deed to B. Which of the following statements is correct?

(A) A is entitled to recover judgment because the contract was based on a substantial mutual mistake of fact.

(B) A is entitled to recover judgment because B fraudulently concealed his discovery of A's mistake in executing and delivering the deed.

(C) A is not entitled to recover because the contract is no longer executory because both parties fully performed their obligations.

(D) A is not entitled to recover because A was negligent in not having the property surveyed prior to executing and delivering their obligations.

7.   On April 1, P entered into a contract with X for the sale of Blackacre. Under the terms of the agreement between P and X, at the closing X would give to P a down payment of $50,000, with the balance of $50,000 to be given as a 25-year bond with 10% interest per annum, and a purchase money mortgage to secure the bond. Closing was set for May 15.

On May 1, X assigned his right in the contract for sale of Blackacre to Y. Y assumed all the rights of X, but did not assume X's obligations. X and Y gave notice to P of the assignment. Y paid $2,000 to X for the assignment.

On the appointed date set for closing, Y appeared and tendered to P $50,000 cash and a bond made by himself, but otherwise in accordance with the agreement. P refused to perform, and sued X for breach of contract. Is X liable to P under a theory of breach of contract?

(A) Yes, because Y did not accept any of X's obligations.

(B) No, because P had notice that Y had assumed all the rights of X with regard to the contract.

(C) Yes, because contracts for the sale of real property are not assignable.

(D) No, because Y performed the terms of the contract.

8.   After winning the "American Idol" competition, Kelly goes to a recording studio in New York and makes a set of master recordings for which her production company, Simon, Inc., wants to secure ownership rights. Simon, Inc.'s, attorney draws up a contract stating, "I, Kelly Clarkson, assign all rights to my April 1999 master recordings on a work for hire basis to Simon, Inc., for $250,000." Kelly and her attorney read and signed the contract in May 1999.

For the next three years, Simon, Inc., exclusively uses those master recordings to sell CDs, tapes, and DVDs. In May 2003, Kelly, while strolling through a sound and equipment exposition, discovers that a few of the tracks she had recorded during the April 1999 session were available on new state of the art technology, the "cerebral headset." The headset allows all music created by an artist to be downloaded directly on the headset by simply entering the artist's name into the headset. Kelly feels that she did not give Simon, Inc., the right to use the music in this new format.

Kelly asserts a claim for breach of contract and seeks to get an injunction. The court will most likely find that Kelly will:

4. NEW YORK CONTRACTS QUESTIONS

(A) Not prevail, because the contract was silent as to third-party licensing.

(B) Not prevail, because the contract was complete on its face and unambiguous.

(C) Prevail, because this format was not contemplated by the contracting parties.

(D) Prevail, because this contract has an ambiguous term that will be construed in favor of the nondrafting party.

CONTRACTS ANSWERS

1. **(C)**

Alan is only entitled to the additional $1,000. If a contract is subsequently modified by the parties, this will serve to discharge those terms of the original contract that are the subject of the modification. Generally, consideration is needed to modify a contract, although in New York no consideration is needed if the modification is in writing and signed by the party against whom enforcement is sought. Here, the New York rule is irrelevant because there was consideration on both sides of the modification: Steve agreed to pay an extra $1,000 and Alan agreed to complete the work a month sooner. Thus, the original $5,000 price term is discharged and a $6,000 price term is substituted. Since Steve has already paid $5,000, Alan is entitled to the additional $1,000. Thus, (C) is the correct answer.

2. **(C)**

Melinda will prevail, at least to the extent necessary to prevent injustice, because her foreseeable detrimental reliance is a sufficient substitute for consideration. To be enforceable, a contract must ordinarily be supported by consideration (a bargained-for exchange of a benefit to the promisor or a detriment to the promisee), and Melinda's selling her greenhouse is not sufficient consideration here because it was not sold as part of a bargained-for exchange between Carla and Melinda; rather, it is clear that Carla intended to give Melinda a gift. Nevertheless, New York follows the majority view that holds that detrimental reliance on a promise to make a gift can serve as a substitute for consideration where, as here, the promisor should reasonably expect to induce action of a definite character and such action is in fact induced. Here, Carla should have expected Melinda to sell her greenhouse and Melinda did sell the greenhouse. Thus, detrimental reliance applies and a contract was formed.

3. **(D)**

New York follows the rule in the Restatement (Second) for the acceptance of an option contract. An acceptance under an option contract is effective only upon receipt rather than upon dispatch. Thus, Katie's acceptance arrived one day after the option expired. Thus, Jason will be able to buy the property rather than Katie.

4. **(B)**

There are certain protected classes that are legally incapable of incurring binding contractual obligations. An infant (a person under 18) lacks the capacity to enter into a contract binding on themselves. Thus, the contract is voidable by the infant but binding on the adult. However, in certain situations, the infant cannot choose to avoid the contract entered into by him. One situation is where the infant contracts for necessities. Here, based on Kevin's station in life, the furniture was deemed a necessity and Kevin is bound to the terms of the contract. Note that New York General Obligations Law section 3-101 does not validate the contract here as (A) would suggest, because the statutory exception is for real estate contracts, not furniture leases.

5. **(B)**

A covenant not to compete is an agreement by a person to refrain from exercising his trade. Frequently an employee promises his employer that upon the completion of the employment he will not compete with his employer either in his own business or by working for another. The restrictive covenant will generally be upheld if the terms of the agreement are not overbroad regarding length and distance. Here, the employee claims that the covenant is unenforceable because there was no additional consideration offered in exchange for the promise not to compete. Unless there is consideration, there will not be a binding contract. There was consideration here because a condition of Dr. Find's continued employment was her execution of this noncompete agreement, and continued employment is adequate consideration where discharge is the alternative. On the other hand, where an employer has the right to discharge an employee without cause, forbearance of that right is a legal detriment which can stand as consideration of the restrictive covenant.

6. (A)

When a contract is entered into under a mutual mistake of fact, the contract is void. [First Regional Securities, Inc. v. Villella, 84 Misc. 2d 790 (1975), *aff'd,* 88 Misc. 2d 81 (1976)] To understand the answer to this question it is important to look to the formation of the contract. Here, both A and B were under the belief that a certain parcel of land, approximately five acres between A's land and B's land, overlapped, and they entered into a contract of sale based on that belief. Apparently, their belief was untrue. Therefore, rescission is available. (B) is incorrect because fraud would require knowledge of the mistake at the time the contract was entered into, and here B did not discover the error until three years later. (C) is incorrect because the contract was invalid from its inception. If (D) had any merit at all, it would be a reason for denying A a judgment (a court would not rescind in favor of the negligent party), but in any case, negligence of a party will generally not invalidate a contract.

7. (A)

The assignment of rights alone will not relieve the assignor of the obligations he incurs under the contract. For the duties of a contract to be transferred to the assignee, the duties must be specifically delegated. In this case, while Y assumed all of the rights of X with regard to the contract, Y specifically did not accept any of X's obligations, and therefore there was not a valid delegation of duties. Thus, (B) is incorrect. (C) is incorrect because generally, all contractual rights may be assigned, including those for the sale of real property. (D) is incorrect because the contract states that P is to receive $50,000 in cash and $50,000 in a bond by X. Y tendered the $50,000 cash but offered a bond made by himself and not by X.

8. (B)

In New York, an artist's transfer of master recording ownership rights gives a producer the unconditional right to redistribute those performances in any technological format, absent the artist's explicit contractual reservation of rights. Although the contract was silent as to the issue of new recording technology and third-party licensing, it was complete on its face and unambiguous. When a contract is unambiguous, extrinsic evidence will not be considered, and only the plain language of the contract will be operative; as such, (A), (C), and (D) are incorrect.

CORPORATIONS QUESTIONS

1.   David is a director of the Morris Canning Corporation. The corporation is in the business of canning rare fish eggs. David's wife Kris, also a director, was starting her own boutique geared toward conservative clothing for the politically conscious woman. At the next meeting of the board of directors, all the directors were in attendance except for David. Kris asked the board of directors to grant her a corporate loan for $10,000. The board voted and passed the loan by all in attendance. No one submitted a dissent and Kris had the money three days later. Who is liable to the corporation for the loan?

(A) No one, because the loan was properly approved by two-thirds of the board.

(B) The entire board, because the loan was not properly approved.

(C) The board except for David.

(D) Kris, because as a director she breached her fiduciary duty by voting.

2.   Bandage Corporation has decided to mortgage substantially all of its assets so that it may participate in a new lucrative joint venture. Chairman of the Board Ace calls the other two directors separately and gets their permission for the mortgage. Then 60% of the shareholders ratify the proposal. Shareholder Stan, a record shareholder, does not approve of the decision and seeks to prevent the mortgage. The mortgage is:

(A) Proper, because either the board of directors or the shareholders could approve this action.

(B) Proper, because it was approved by the board.

(C) Not proper, because it was not properly approved by the board.

(D) Not proper, because at least two-thirds of the shareholders had to approve.

3.   Buyer Corporation is in the business of bicycle manufacturing. Target Corporation, a wholly owned subsidiary, is in the business of bicycle tire manufacturing. Buyer Corp. owns 91% of the stock of Target Corp. and the board of directors believes that a merger between Buyer Corp. and Target Corp. would prove beneficial. In a validly held meeting, the board of directors of Buyer Corp. approves the merger. Notice is sent to the outside shareholders of the subsidiary, and Target Corp. is duly merged into Buyer Corp. Is the merger valid?

(A) No, because the shareholders of Buyer Corp. did not vote on the merger, which is a fundamental corporate change.

(B) No, because the shareholders of Target Corp. did not vote on the merger, which is a fundamental corporate change.

(C) No, because the board of directors of Target Corp. did not vote on the merger.

(D) Yes.

4.   A, B, and C form a corporation under the laws of New York and each is a director. The stated purpose of the corporation as recited in the certificate of incorporation is to "sell, rent,

and repair lawnmowers." A, the president of the corporation, enters into a contract to purchase helicopter parts in order to broaden the scope of the corporation's business. The contract is with H Corp. and requires H Corp. to deliver $10,000 worth of helicopter parts on June 1, payment to be made within 30 days after delivery. B and C first learn of the contract when the helicopter parts are delivered. Must the corporation purchase the helicopter parts?

(A) No, because it was an ultra vires act.

(B) No, because the agreement with H Corp. was an extraordinary contract beyond the scope of A's apparent authority as president of ABC Corp.

(C) No, because B and C did not vote on the contract.

(D) Yes.

5. On June 1, S enters into a written subscription agreement to buy 500 of the 1,000 shares of XYZ Corp. at $10 per share and pays $3,000. On July 10, S defaults on the balance. On July 15, the corporation makes a demand for payment. On August 20, XYZ Corp. sells all 500 shares at $50 per share for $25,000. If there is no expense incurred in the resale, how are the proceeds from the sale distributed?

(A) S gets nothing and XYZ keeps the initial $3,000 paid by S and the $25,000 from the sale of the stock.

(B) S gets $3,000 and XYZ Corp. gets $22,000.

(C) S gets $23,000 and XYZ Corp. gets $2,000.

(D) S gets $10,000 and XYZ Corp. gets $15,000.

6. Bandage Corporation has decided to mortgage all of its assets so that it may participate in a new lucrative joint venture. Chairman of the Board Alice meets with the corporation's other two directors and gets their permission for the mortgage. Then 25% of the shareholders ratify the proposal. Shareholder Sue, a record shareholder, does not approve of the decision and seeks to prevent the mortgage.

Sue objects to the mortgage and immediately files an action on behalf of the corporation. The board of directors then files a motion to dismiss. The motion should be:

(A) Denied, because Sue filed the action before the board of directors could act on their own behalf.

(B) Granted, because the board may authorize any mortgage, all or in part, of the corporate property, without the consent of the shareholders.

(C) Granted, because Sue must first wait to see if any harm comes to the corporation.

(D) Denied, because Sue must file an action on behalf of herself first before the board can file a derivative suit.

7. At a special meeting of the shareholders of X Corp., the shareholders by a two-thirds majority passed an amendment to the bylaws, expanding the board of directors from five to seven

directors. By the same margin, the shareholders voted to remove Adam as a director, without cause. The certificate of incorporation and the bylaws are silent as to the number of directors and removal of a director. At the meeting of the board of directors immediately following the shareholders' meeting, the four remaining directors may:

I. Elect a new director to complete Adam's term.
II. Elect two new directors pursuant to the amended bylaws.

(A) I. but not II.

(B) II. but not I.

(C) Both I. and II.

(D) Neither I. nor II.

8. A, B, and C set up X Corp., each purchasing 100 shares of the corporation's 300 authorized shares. A, B, and C elected themselves as the three directors, and, as directors, elected A as president, B as vice president, and C as secretary. The certificate of incorporation was silent on voting and election, tenure, and removal of officers and directors. Some months later, A and C began to have disagreements with B. Thereafter, at a duly noticed and held meeting of the directors, a resolution was adopted by A and C (with B dissenting) in which it was decided that B would be removed as officer and director. B wants to be reinstated, and he has come to you, his attorney, for advice. Can X Corp. be compelled to reinstate him as officer and director?

(A) Yes.

(B) X Corp. can be compelled to reinstate him as officer, but not as director.

(C) X Corp. can be compelled to reinstate him as director, but not as officer.

(D) No.

9. A and D were competitors in the retail ski equipment business, both owning and operating independent retail stores in the county of Nassau. In November of 1991, A and D entered into an agreement in which D agreed to sell his store to A for $100,000. As part of the acquisition agreement, D agreed not to compete with A in Nassau County for a period of 10 years. The agreement provided for liquidated damages in the sum of $10,000 in the event of a breach. In November of 2000, D became bored with his early retirement and opened a new ski equipment store in Nassau, in direct competition with A. A instituted an action for, amongst other things, liquidated damages in the amount of $10,000. Will A prevail?

(A) Yes, irrespective of whether A suffered any actual damages.

(B) Yes, if A can prove that she suffered actual monetary damages.

(C) No, because D substantially complied with the noncompetition agreement.

(D) No, because A has alternative remedies available, including an injunction.

10. R Inc. is wholly owned by D Corp. and conducts its business of repairing and reconditioning used drills acquired from D Corp. for sale on the second-hand market from its office in New York City. In March 2001, P delivered a drill worth $8,000 to R Inc. for extensive repairs. After the work was finished, the drill was laid aside for delivery but by mistake was placed with a number of reconditioned drills that were being held for resale. X, a retailer of second-hand drills, purchased 10 second-hand drills from R Inc. including the drill delivered by P for repair. In May 2001, a plan to merge R Inc. into D Corp. was executed, and on May 24, a certificate of merger was filed in the office of the New York secretary of state. In June 2001, P sought the return of his drill and discovered that it was sold. P comes to you for advice. You advise him that he may seek recovery from:

(A) R Inc., because a merger does not extinguish the company's liabilities.

(B) D Corp., because the surviving company in a merger assumes the liabilities of the merged entity.

(C) Neither R Inc. nor D Corp., because once R Inc. ceased to exist, its liabilities were extinguished.

(D) R Inc. and D Corp. are joint and severally liable.

11. A, B, C, and D formed X Corp. A, B, C, and D each received 100 of the authorized 500 shares at $100 each. The certificate of incorporation and the corporate bylaws were silent as to the number of votes needed for board action. Prior to the first shareholders' meeting, A, B, C, and D agreed in writing that any director action would require a unanimous vote. Thereafter, at the first shareholders' meeting, A, B, C, and D elected themselves as directors. Two years later, a directors' meeting of X Corp. was called and due notice to all directors was given. The purpose of the meeting was to decide a resolution proposed by A to move the corporation's office from Syracuse to Buffalo. C asked for an adjournment of the meeting because B was sick and unable to attend. A and D refused to adjourn the meeting. The meeting was continued. A and D voted for the resolution and C abstained. A and D announced that the resolution was binding and the corporate offices would be moving. C comes to you seeking to avoid the resolution. You advise her that:

(A) C can avoid the resolution based upon the ground that the shareholder agreement requiring unanimous votes of the directors was violated and is binding on the board.

(B) C can avoid the resolution because the two directors voting for the resolution failed to comprise a quorum.

(C) C cannot avoid the resolution because she failed to vote at the meeting.

(D) C cannot avoid the resolution because the shareholder agreement is not binding on the board and a quorum voted for the resolution.

12. John purchased an office building for $500,000 and conveyed his entire interest in the building to John's Corp., a corporation he formed in the state of New York. John's Corp. was authorized to issue 100,000 shares of common stock at $100 par value per share. Immediately thereafter, Bob and Pete each purchased 1,000 shares in John's Corp.; they each paid $100,000 for their shares. A week later, John had John's Corp. issue him 10,000 shares of common stock in consideration for the maintenance services he had rendered to the office building. Then John, who remained a director and president of John's Corp., entered into a contract on behalf of the corporation with J Corp., a maintenance company he wholly owned. The contract provided that J Corp. would clean and maintain the office building owned by John's Corp. for an annual fee of 5% of gross receipts. The customary fee for maintenance contracts in the area was 2.5%. Bob and Pete are very unhappy to learn about these transactions, and have come to you, their attorney, to see if they can set aside the issuance of 10,000 shares to John and the maintenance contract with J Corp. How will you advise them?

(A) The transactions are both valid and cannot be set aside.

(B) They can set aside the 10,000 shares issued to John, but will be unable to set aside the maintenance contract entered into with J Corp.

(C) They can set aside the maintenance contract entered into with J Corp., but they will be unable to do anything about the 10,000 shares issued to John for valid consideration.

(D) They can have both transactions set aside.

13. Pat was the Chief Financial Officer ("CFO") of a major corporation, Chuie Financial. In her capacity as CFO, she was joined as a defendant in a class action suit, alleging multiple acts of securities fraud and waste of corporate assets. The action was filed in the United States District Court, Southern District of New York. The suit named Chuie Financial, an affiliated trading house, various officers, and directors of the corporations. Ultimately, all claims against Pat were dismissed by stipulation. Pat, who had hired an attorney and incurred reasonable expenses in defending herself in this action, has requested reimbursement from Chuie Financial.

The recently elected board of directors voted to refuse Pat's reimbursement request. Pat subsequently moved in the district court for indemnification from Chuie Financial. Included in the motion was a request for attorneys' fees for making the motion. Pat based her motion on the director/officer indemnification provisions of the New York Business Corporations Law.

In regard to this motion, the court would most likely decide that:

(A) A corporate officer has no right to indemnification for attorneys' fees.

(B) A corporate officer has an absolute right to indemnification for attorneys' fees.

(C) A corporate officer has a right to recover attorneys' fees, so long as the officer is successful in the underlying action, within the meaning of New York Business Corporation Law section 723(a).

(D) A corporate officer does not have a right to recover attorneys' fees for expenses incurred in a proceeding to force the corporation to indemnify the officer.

14. With regard to a shareholder's derivative action, which of the following is false?

(A) The plaintiff must have been a holder when the action was brought and from the time of the transaction at issue.

(B) The action must be brought on the corporation's behalf.

(C) A demand always must first be made on the board of directors before pursuing the claim in court.

(D) The action may not be settled without the approval of the court.

Questions 15 through 16 are based on the following situation:

Zorn was the majority shareholder, the president, and a director of Best Corp. Zorn and Best Corp. were indicted for tax fraud for actions Zorn caused Best Corp. to take. After Zorn was indicted, he pled guilty, admitting in court that he knew his actions were unlawful when he took them. Subsequently, the board of directors of Best Corp. decided to indemnify Zorn for his legal fees and expenses in defending himself against the charge.

15. Shareholder, who was a Best Corp. shareholder at the time of Zorn's illegal act and who still is a shareholder, asks you whether the board's indemnification of Zorn is permissible. How would you advise Shareholder?

(A) The board's action was inappropriate because the decision whether to indemnify an officer or director for legal fees must be made by shareholders.

(B) The board's action was inappropriate because Zorn admitted that he knew his actions were unlawful when he took them.

(C) The board's action was appropriate because an officer or director has an absolute right to indemnification for legal fees and expenses incurred as a consequence of action taken on behalf of a corporation.

(D) The board's action was appropriate provided Zorn acted in good faith and reasonably believed his actions were in the best interest of the corporation.

16. If Shareholder wants to bring a shareholders' derivative action against Best Corp., arguing that Best Corp.'s financing of Zorn's legal fees was a breach of fiduciary duty and a waste of corporate assets, must you make a demand on the corporation before filing the action?

(A) Yes, because a demand must always be made on the board of directors before bringing a shareholder's derivative action.

(B) Yes, because a demand must always be made on the shareholders before bringing a shareholders' derivative action.

(C) No, because demand would be futile.

(D) No, because Shareholder is protected by the business judgment rule.

CORPORATIONS ANSWERS

1.   (B)

Under Business Corporations Law section 714, a corporation may lend money to a director if the loan is approved by the vote of majority of the shares entitled to vote, not counting the shares owned by the borrower. For corporations formed after February 22, 1998, the loan can also be approved by the board of directors if the board finds that the loan benefits the corporation. Directors who approve unlawful loans violate their duty to the corporation and are jointly and severally liable for any loss that results. [BCL §§714, 719] A director who is present at the meeting is deemed to concur unless the director sends a dissent within a reasonable time after the meeting. Here, the loan did not benefit the corporation, therefore shareholder approval was required. Since the board approved the loan without such approval and no one dissented, the entire board is liable.

2.   (C)

While a mortgage of substantially all of a corporation's assets is not a fundamental change and so may be approved by board action alone [N.Y. Bus. Corp. Law §911], there was no proper board action here. A valid act of the board requires a majority vote at a meeting at which a quorum of directors is present. [N.Y. Bus. Corp. Law §708(d)] A teleconference meeting will do if all participants can simultaneously hear one another and the articles or bylaws allow such meetings. [N.Y. Bus. Corp. Law §708(c)] There was no meeting here, and even if the articles or bylaws provided for teleconference meetings, there was no valid teleconference meeting here because Ace called each of the other directors separately. Thus, there was no valid board approval.

3.   (D)

Under the Business Corporations Law section 905, in a merger between a parent corporation and its subsidiary where the parent owns 90% or more of the outstanding voting shares of each class of stock of the subsidiary, the subsidiary may be merged into the parent without the authorization of the shareholders of either corporation. The only requirements are that the board of the parent corporation adopt the plan, a copy or outline of the plan of merger be given to outside shareholders of the subsidiary, and the certificate of merger be filed not less than 30 days after notice to the outside shareholders.

4.   (B)

Officers of a corporation are agents of the corporation, and ordinary agency rules govern the officers' agency power to bind the corporation. Under agency principles, a principal can only be bound if the agent acted with authority, and here A did not have any authority to buy helicopter parts. A had no actual authority to buy helicopter parts since an officer can get actual authority only from the articles, bylaws, or a vote of the directors. Here, the articles limit corporate activities to repairing lawn mowers, there is no bylaw provision given on the president's scope of authority, and the directors did not vote to allow A to purchase helicopter parts. Thus, there is no actual authority here. Neither is there any apparent authority. In New York, a corporation's president has apparent authority to make ordinary contracts required or justified by the customs or necessities of the business. The president does not have apparent authority to make unusual or extraordinary contracts. Here, the corporation's business was lawn mower repair. A $10,000 contract for helicopter parts is both extraordinary and unusual for such a corporation. Thus, A did not have apparent authority to make the purchase. Finally, the corporation clearly is not seeking to ratify. Therefore, there is no authority for the contract here, and the corporation will not be bound.

5. (C)

When the subscriber defaults on payment, the corporation may proceed as in collecting any other debt, or 30 days after a written demand is made for payment, the board may declare a forfeiture. If the board declares a forfeiture and the subscriber has paid at least 50% of the subscription price before defaulting, the corporation must attempt to sell the subscribed shares for cash, and the delinquent subscriber gets any proceeds in excess of the amount due the corporation minus selling expenses. [N.Y. Bus. Corp. Law §503]

6. (B)

Under New York Business Corporations Law section 911, the board of directors may authorize any mortgage or pledge of, or the creation of a security interest in, all or part of the corporate property. Shareholder consent is not required unless otherwise noted in the certificate of incorporation. There is no such provision in the facts.

7. (B)

Under Business Corporations Law section 706, the shareholders may remove a director without cause, but only if the certificate of incorporation or the bylaws so provide. Because the certificate and the bylaws are silent on this issue, the shareholders may not remove Adam unless first they have amended the certificate or passed a bylaw. Furthermore, a vacancy caused by removal of a director without cause may be filled only by a vote of the shareholders, unless this power is granted to the board in the certificate or a shareholder-adopted bylaw. Thus, the directors could not fill the vacancy and could not perform I.

Business Corporations Law section 702 governs changes in the constitution of the board of directors. The number of directors may be increased or decreased by (i) an amendment to the bylaws; (ii) action of the shareholders; or (iii) action of the board, if pursuant to a shareholder-adopted bylaw. Therefore, the shareholders properly expanded the number of directors from five to seven. Newly created directorships may be filled by a vote of the board; thus, the board could perform II.

8. (C)

B has no remedy for his removal as an officer of X Corp. An officer of a corporation may be removed at any time, with or without cause, by a majority of the board of directors, unless the officers are elected directly by the shareholders pursuant to a provision in the certificate of incorporation. In this case, the officers are not elected by the shareholders. Therefore, B may be removed as an officer by a simple majority of the directors, with or without cause. However, B's removal as director was ineffective, and B may be reinstated as a director. When a director is elected by the shareholders, absent a provision in the certificate of incorporation or a bylaw adopted by the shareholders, the director may be removed for cause by the shareholders at any time. A director may be removed by the shareholders without cause only if the certificate of incorporation or a shareholder bylaw so provides. In other words, to remove a director without cause, the shareholders must first insert an enabling provision into the certificate or the bylaws, and only then may they proceed. In the absence of such provision, a director may be removed only for cause. In this case, the certificate of incorporation is silent as to removal of directors. Therefore, B may be removed only for cause. B was removed, without apparent cause, by the directors at a meeting of the board. Therefore, B may compel X Corp. to reseat him as director for failure to comply with the requisite formalities. It follows that (A), (B), and (D) are wrong.

9.   (A)

Liquidated damages are generally recoverable where actual damages are difficult to ascertain, and the amount contained in the agreement is not so unreasonable as to constitute a penalty. Clearly, in this case both of these requirements are met. Therefore, D will recover the amount stipulated in the contract as liquidated damages, even if he has not actually suffered any monetary damages. This is because where there is a liquidated damage clause, actual damages are irrelevant. Thus, (B) is wrong. (C) is wrong because there was a year remaining on the noncompetition agreement, and this is not insignificant. (D) is wrong because the availability of injunctive relief does not preclude the recovery of liquidated damages, nor does the availability of liquidated damages preclude injunctive relief unless expressly agreed to in an agreement. Here, there is nothing to indicate that either party gave up the right to seek injunctive relief or liquidated damages.

10.   (B)

P may not proceed directly against R Inc., as R Inc. has ceased to exist as an independent entity. Thus, (A) and (D) are wrong. Under the Business Corporations Law of New York, the surviving company in a merger assumes the liabilities of the merged entity. Therefore, P may proceed against D Corp. as the successor in interest of R Inc. D Corp. legally effected a merger of its subsidiary, R Inc., into D Corp. Consequently D Corp. assumed all the liabilities of R Inc. Thus, (C) is wrong and (B) is right.

11.   (D)

Under Business Corporation Law section 708, the vote of a majority of the directors present (if a quorum is present) constitutes an act of the board. A provision for a supermajority voting requirement must appear in the certificate of incorporation. Here, there is no indication that X Corp.'s certificate of incorporation contained such a provision. That the "written agreement" contained a supermajority voting agreement is irrelevant. Thus, (A) is wrong. In the absence of specific provisions in the certificate of incorporation, a majority of the "entire board" constitutes a quorum. The vote of a majority of the directors present (if a quorum is present) constitutes an act of the board. Here, S Corp.'s certificate of incorporation was silent on quorum requirements. The directors' meeting was called after due notice to all of the directors. There was a quorum of the board present since three of the four directors attended. The resolution was validly passed because a majority of the directors present (A and D) voted for it. Accordingly, C cannot assert that the resolution is not effective because only two directors voted for it. Thus, (B) is wrong. (C) is also wrong. Nothing in the Business Corporations Law requires a director to vote on a matter in order to be able to contest it.

12.   (D)

With respect to the 10,000 shares issued for one week's worth of maintenance services, in New York, par value shares must be issued for consideration worth at least the par value. Proper forms of consideration include money, property, and services. Where, as here, services are exchanged, the board of directors must value those services and the board's determination of value will be conclusive absent fraud. Here, John's Corp. issued 10,000 shares of $100 par value stock to John in exchange for one week of cleaning services. While a director may charge his corporation for services rendered to the corporation outside the director's official duties, the valuation here is clearly fraudulent, and thus can be set aside. With respect to the maintenance contract with J Corp, John breached his fiduciary duty here through self-dealing. John had an interest in the maintenance contract since he is the sole owner of J Corp. Since John was a director of John's Corp., he should have disclosed his interest in the transaction to the board and obtained its approval, disclosed his interest to the shareholders and obtained their approval, or entered into a fair contract. John did none of these. Under the facts, John did not seek approval from Bob or Pete, and the transaction was not fair since the contract called for 5% of the gross receipts of the building and the norm in the area was 2.5%. Thus, this contract can be set aside. It follows that (A), (B), and (C) are wrong.

13. (D)

Attorneys' fees are recoverable under section 723 to the extent that they are incurred in connection with the defense of a derivative action. Attorneys' fees incurred in a proceeding to force the corporation to indemnify the officer (so-called fees on fees) are not incurred in defense of a derivative action, and so are not recoverable. (A) is incorrect because New York Business Corporation Law section 723(a) provides for recovery of attorneys' fees. (B) is incorrect because it overstates the officer's rights. (C) is incorrect because Pat is seeking "fees on fees" and not merely indemnification.

14. (C)

A shareholder's derivative action requires that the plaintiff was a shareholder: (i) when the action was brought and (ii) when the complained-of transaction took place. Additionally, the shareholder must be pursuing a corporate right, as opposed to an individual right. Thus, (A) and (B) are true statements. Furthermore, a shareholder's derivative action may not be compromised without court approval, making (D) a true statement. Finally, a demand for relief ordinarily must be made before bringing suit; however, this requirement is excused when a majority of the directors is interested in the challenged transaction or when the majority of directors failed to exercise independent judgment as directors in restraining the self-interested minority.

15. (B)

Under the BCL, if an officer or director unsuccessfully defends an action brought against him in relation to his corporate position, the corporation generally has discretion to indemnify him for expenses of the litigation. However, indemnification is prohibited when a director or officer acts in bad faith or, in a criminal case, has no reason to believe actions were lawful. Here, Zorn admitted in court that he knew that his actions were unlawful when he took them. Therefore, indemnification would be prohibited and (B) is correct. (A) is incorrect because by statute [BCL 722] the decision to indemnify may be by resolution of the shareholders or directors. No adverse presumption is created by a conviction or plea. (C) is incorrect because indemnification is only discretionary when the officer or director is unsuccessful in defending. (D) is incorrect because it fails to note the additional requirements applicable in a criminal case.

16. (C)

Normally, prior to commencing a shareholder derivative action, a plaintiff is required to make a demand on the board of directors to cure the problem unless demand would be futile. Thus, (A) and (B) are incorrect. Demand is futile when, among other instances, a majority of the board of directors is interested in the transaction, a self-interested director controls the board, or the challenged transaction was so egregious that it could not have been the result of sound business judgment. Here, Shareholder should not be required to make a demand because Zorn's control of the board is evidenced by the board's continued financial support even after Zorn admitted guilt. (D) is incorrect because the business judgment rule protects the decisions of officers and directors and is inapplicable to Shareholder under the facts given.

CRIMINAL LAW QUESTIONS

1.   Having graduated from business school and not being able to find a job, Todd found himself extremely frustrated and bored. One afternoon, at the height of his boredom, Todd approached Keith and Ollie and convinced them to go with him to rob Old Man Rubin's gas station. Todd got his car and the three men drove over to the gas station to figure out when the owner would be alone. Unbeknownst to Todd, Keith is an undercover police officer and Ollie has been declared incompetent. Todd can be convicted of entering into a conspiracy with:

(A) Keith only.

(B) Ollie only.

(C) Both Keith and Ollie.

(D) Neither Keith nor Ollie.

Questions 2 and 3 are based on the following situation:

Prince, Sprout, Twerp, and Duff all agreed that they hated King and wanted him killed. In furtherance of this agreement, they devised a way to murder him. After following through with their plans, all four were charged with conspiracy to murder King and the murder of King.

2.   Prince and Sprout were acquitted of both the conspiracy and the murder charges. Twerp was acquitted of the conspiracy charge, but was convicted of murder. Duff's trial on the charges is now pending. Can Duff now be convicted of conspiracy to murder King?

(A) Yes, because Twerp has been convicted of murder.

(B) No, because Twerp has been convicted of murder.

(C) No, because Duff's conspiracy charge merges into the murder charge.

(D) Yes, because conspiracy requires one guilty mind.

3.   If Duff asserts an insanity defense to the murder charge, he must show at the least:

(A) That at the time of the conduct, as a result of mental disease or defect, he lacked substantial capacity to know or appreciate either the nature and consequence of the conduct or that the conduct was wrong.

(B) That he lacked the ability at the time of his action to control his actions or to conform his conduct to the law.

(C) That he had a disease of the mind that caused a defect in his ability to reason.

(D) That a disease of the mind caused a defect of reason such that he lacked the ability at the time to know the wrongfulness of his actions or to understand the nature and quality of his actions.

4.   A New York police officer may use deadly force to arrest a fleeing felon where:

(A) The officer reasonably believes his action is necessary to prevent the felon's escape.

(B) The officer reasonably believes that the felon will attempt to resist arrest and that his actions will involve a death or serious bodily injury to another.

(C) The officer reasonably believes the felon's actions will involve a death or serious bodily injury to another.

(D) The officer reasonably believes the felon has committed a crime involving the infliction or threatened infliction of serious harm to another person's property.

5. Which of the following is an accurate statement about the defense of entrapment?

(A) The prosecution may introduce evidence of the defendant's past criminal acts in its direct case, if the defendant raises the issue of entrapment.

(B) The defendant must prove entrapment by a preponderance of the evidence.

(C) A person cannot be entrapped by a private citizen.

(D) All of the above.

6. Karen, age 18, and Stacey, age 15, agreed to rob a local grocery store. Karen drove Stacey to the store and instructed her to contact Karen by cell phone if the police arrived. Karen entered the store, drew her gun, and ordered the cashier to hand over the cash. The cashier handed Karen a bag of money, and then tripped an alarm. Karen fled, and upon leaving the store was met by four police officers with their guns drawn. Karen fired her gun, and a fierce firefight erupted, leaving one police officer dead and Karen under arrest. Stacey watched the entire sequence of events unfold and simply drove away undetected. Shortly after Karen's arrest, the police received information that Stacey was also involved in the robbery, and they placed her under arrest. An autopsy revealed that the police officer killed during the robbery was actually killed by a bullet fired from a fellow officer's gun. Assuming the above facts were proven, what crimes can Stacey and Karen be convicted of?

(A) Both Karen and Stacey can be convicted of second degree murder and first degree robbery.

(B) Karen can be convicted of first degree murder and first degree robbery, but Stacey can be convicted of neither since she effectively withdrew from the crime.

(C) Karen and Stacey can be convicted of first degree robbery, but only Karen can be convicted of second degree murder.

(D) Both Karen and Stacey can be convicted of first degree murder and first degree robbery.

7. Squeaky and Dinky were separately indicted on charges of conspiracy to sell illegal weapons. At trial, Squeaky was acquitted on the conspiracy charge. As a result, Dinky moved to dismiss his conspiracy charge since there was no one with whom he could conspire and based on the impossibility of the district attorney being able to prove an agreement between him and Squeaky. How should the court rule?

(A) Grant the motion because acquittal of persons with whom a defendant is alleged to have conspired precludes conviction of the remaining defendant.

(B) Grant the motion because acquittal of one party to a conspiracy is proof that an element of the conspiracy charge is not present.

(C) Deny the motion.

(D) There is not enough information in the facts presented to determine how the court should rule.

8. David and Victor were best friends who worked out together and dated a pair of sisters, Amy and Beth. Victor had been going out with Amy for almost 10 years and David had been dating Beth for a little over a year. While celebrating Amy's birthday, harsh words were exchanged between Victor and David. Victor implied that David was unfaithful to Beth. There were three eyewitness accounts of the incident: Steve's, Bob's, and Erica's.

Erica testifies that, "As they were screaming at each other, David abruptly turned around and pulled out a gun and pointed it in the direction of Victor." Bob testifies that, "As they were screaming at each other, David abruptly turned around with a gun in his hand and I could not see much else." Steve testifies that "As they were screaming at each other, David abruptly turned around with a gun in his hand and a brief struggle ensued, during which the gun discharged and Victor was wounded."

Forensic evidence shows that a bullet perforated Victor's left lung, causing severe internal bleeding that ultimately resulted in his death. Gunpowder residue from around the hole in Victor's shirt, corresponding to the chest entrance wound, indicates that the shot was fired 12 to 18 inches from Victor's chest.

Of which of the following could a rational jury convict David?

(A) First Degree Murder.

(B) Second Degree Murder.

(C) Criminally Negligent Homicide.

(D) None of the above.

9. Joe came home late one night from the pub after he was out with his co-workers. He went to the alcove of his apartment building to pick up his mail. After he had collected his mail and was walking up the stairs, John came running up after him yelling racial obscenities. Joe recognized John as the former boyfriend of Josephine, Joe's girlfriend. Josephine had broken up with John in order to start dating Joe. Consequently, John has had several breakdowns. Apparently, the thought of Josephine and Joe together has made John very unstable.

Joe started yelling back. John subsequently pulled out a knife and screamed, "I am going to gut you like a fish!" Joe pulled out his licensed handgun and shot John in the head, killing him instantly.

Which of the following statements is most correct?

(A) Joe could use deadly force because a person who is not the initial aggressor can always repel deadly force with deadly force.

(B) Joe could use deadly force because deadly force can always be met with deadly force.

(C) Joe had a duty to retreat if he was able to do so safely.

(D) Joe did not have a duty to retreat because he was in his dwelling.

10. Lisa and Leeann were arrested in an undercover buy-and-bust operation. Bob, an undercover police officer, approached Lisa and asked for four $25 bags of crack cocaine. Lisa replied that, "All her clients know she only sells $50 bags." Bob replied, "I'll just take two then." Lisa asked Bob if he was a police agent or informant. He remained silent. Lisa then walked over and spoke with Leeann, who was seated in a parked car. Lisa told Bob to speak with Leeann. Bob asked Leeann for two $50 bags, and Leeann replied, "Give me the money and I will get you the stuff." Bob handed Leeann a marked $100 bill.

Instead of turning over the crack, Leeann held out a crack pipe and told Bob to "take a hit." Bob, being an officer, refused and asked for the drugs he had paid for. Leeann replied, "You'll get it as soon as you take a hit, so I know that you're not a cop!" As the standoff continued, Bob's backup team became concerned and moved in. Leeann was arrested at the scene, and Lisa was arrested several blocks away, but the police officers were unable to find the crack pipe or the buy money.

Lisa and Leeann were later convicted based on their offer to sell to a police officer. Defense counsel appealed, stating that the convictions were not supported by sufficient evidence to convict on an "offering for sale" theory.

Under these facts the court will most likely:

(A) Affirm, because in order to reverse, the court would have to make a new finding of fact.

(B) Affirm, because the intent and ability to sell was established by the defendants' conduct.

(C) Reverse, because there was not sufficient evidence of a bona fide offer to sell.

(D) Reverse, because Lisa and Leeann both had prior drug convictions, demonstrating that they had the ability to complete the transaction.

11. T walked into the Bar Review Cafe and quickly noticed V sitting at a table. T left quickly, but came back, pulled out a gun, and shot V in the chest. T then leaned over V, who was lying on the floor, and fired multiple shots from extremely close range. T waved the gun at the witness, warned him not to say anything, and left the cafe. After his arrest, T claimed that he had been afraid of the victim, who he said had repeatedly threatened him, and that he panicked when he saw V at the cafe. What is the most serious offense for which T could be convicted?

(A) Intentional murder.

(B) Depraved indifference murder.

(C) Manslaughter in the second degree.

(D) T cannot be convicted because he was acting in self-defense.

12. Defendant Sam stabbed his girlfriend Joanne three times—once in the throat, once in the chest, and once in the abdomen. Sam fled without summoning assistance, and Joanne bled to

death. Sam told police that he slapped Joanne during an argument, and that she lunged at him with a knife. Sam wrested the knife away from her and lunged back in outrage. He testified that he never intended to kill Joanne.

Assuming the facts as stated, which of the following best reflects the crimes of which Defendant may be convicted?

(A) Intentional murder in the second degree or depraved indifference murder in the second degree.

(B) Depraved indifference murder in the second degree or intentional manslaughter in the first degree.

(C) Intentional manslaughter in the first degree or reckless manslaughter in the second degree.

(D) Intentional manslaughter in the second degree or intentional murder in the second degree.

13. Defendant attempted suicide in his 12th floor Manhattan apartment. Sealing the apartment door with tape, he blew out the pilot lights of his stove, turned on the gas, took tranquilizers, and fell asleep in front of the oven, expecting the gas to kill him. Several hours later, a spark, apparently from the refrigerator compressor, ignited the gas, causing an explosion that wrecked the walls of his apartment and heavily damaged a number of neighboring apartments. Defendant survived the blast.

Which of the following is the most serious crime of which Defendant could be convicted?

(A) First degree reckless endangerment.

(B) Second degree reckless endangerment.

(C) First degree criminal mischief.

(D) Attempted murder in the second degree.

14. Defendant and Victim lived next door to one another in an apartment building. The two argued through a shared bedroom wall. Victim then left his apartment with a knife and argued with Defendant in the hallway. Fearing that he was going to be stabbed, Defendant struck Victim in the head with a metal pipe while standing in his doorway. Victim died as a result.

Can Defendant raise the affirmative defense of justification?

(A) Yes, because a doorway between an apartment and the shared hall is part of a dwelling, so Defendant was not under a duty to retreat.

(B) Yes, provided Defendant can establish that Victim initiated the argument.

(C) No, because Defendant was not actually inside his apartment when confronted by Victim and so had a duty to retreat.

(D) No, because a person is required to abandon or retreat from his home before causing the death of another.

CRIMINAL LAW ANSWERS

1. (C)

Conspiracy is an intentional agreement between two or more persons to commit a crime. New York law also requires the conspirators to make an overt act in furtherance of the conspiracy. Under the common law, conspiracy is a specific intent crime, and there is no conspiracy unless there is a meeting of two or more "guilty minds." However, New York does not follow the common law rule. Under New York Penal Law section 105.30, a person has no defense to conspiracy based upon a co-conspirator's irresponsibility, incapacity, or failure to have requisite culpability for the crime. Thus, in New York a person may be guilty of conspiracy even though he conspires with one who is a police officer or an incompetent. Accordingly, (C) is the correct answer.

2. (D)

Conspiracy is an intentional agreement between two or more people to commit a crime. New York also requires that there must have been an overt act committed by one of the conspirators in furtherance of the conspiracy. (D) is the correct answer because New York has adopted the unilateral approach to conspiracy, under which a person may be found guilty of conspiracy notwithstanding the lack of intent or capability of his co-conspirator.

3. (A)

Under Penal Law section 40.15, insanity is an affirmative defense which must be proved by a preponderance of the evidence by the defendant. The New York insanity defense is a compromise between the *M'Naghten* Rule and the approach of the Model Penal Code. (A) is a correct statement of this rule. (B) is the Irresistible Impulse Test, (C) is the Durham Test, and (D) is the *M'Naghten* Rule.

4. (B)

The use of force by a police officer to apprehend a fleeing felon constitutes a seizure. The force used to effectuate the seizure must be reasonable. Deadly force is reasonable only when the felon threatens death or serious bodily harm and deadly force is necessary to prevent his escape. (A) and (C) are incorrect because they are not complete statements of the rule. (D) is wrong because deadly force may not be used merely to prevent harm to property. Thus, (B) is the correct answer.

5. (D)

Penal Law section 40.05 provides that the defense of entrapment will be sustained if the defendant can prove that he was actively induced or encouraged to commit the offense either by a public servant or by someone who was acting in cooperation with a public servant, and the defendant must not have been in any way predisposed to commit the crime. New York law provides that where the defendant raises a defense of entrapment, the prosecution need not wait for rebuttal to offer proof of the defendant's prior crimes but may do so on its direct case, in order to show the defendant's disposition to commit the crime in question.

6. (A)

Robbery consists of: (i) a taking of personal property of another, (ii) from the other's person or presence; (iii) by force or threats of immediate death or physical injury to the victim, a member of the victim's family, or some person in the victim's presence; (iv) with the intent to permanently deprive the victim of it. In New York, a defendant is guilty of first degree robbery if she: (i) caused a nonparticipant serious physical injury; or (ii) was armed, threatened the use of a dangerous instrument, or displayed what appeared to be a firearm. In this case, Karen robbed the store and threatened the storekeeper with a firearm. She took personal property from the storekeeper's person or presence by threatening immediate death or physical injury, with the intent to permanently deprive him of it. Therefore, Karen should be convicted of first degree robbery. With respect to Stacey, New York law allows the prosecution of defendants age 14 or 15 who are responsible for serious offenses against person or property. They need not be brought up on juvenile delinquency charges in Family Court. Furthermore, under the general rule of modern accomplice liability, a person who intentionally aids or encourages a principal to commit a crime is liable for the principal crime. Moreover, while withdrawal can be raised as an affirmative defense, the accomplice must voluntarily withdraw and renounce her criminal purpose prior to commission of the crime, and make a substantial effort to prevent the crime. In this case, although Stacey left the scene, she did not affirmatively withdraw in any manner recognized in New York. Thus, (B) is wrong. Under New York law, a defendant who is 13, 14, or 15 years of age may be prosecuted for second degree murder. Any death caused in the commission of, or in an attempt to commit, a felony is felony murder. The killing must have been a foreseeable result of the felony, and the death must have been caused during the commission or immediate flight from the crime. Robbery is included in the list of felonies to which the felony murder rule applies. Stacey should be convicted of second degree murder under New York's felony murder rule since she was an accomplice to the robbery. Thus, (C) is wrong. Karen cannot be convicted of first degree murder. While the New York felony murder rule applies to first degree murder as well as second degree murder, for first degree murder, the victim must have been killed intentionally by the defendant during the course of the robbery or in immediate flight. That is not the case here. The autopsy showed that Karen did not actually kill the police officer; instead, the officer was killed by a bullet from a fellow officer's gun. Consequently, a first degree murder charge could not be sustained, and thus, (D), as well as (B), is wrong.

7.   (C)

A conspiracy is an agreement between two or more parties to commit a crime. It requires (i) an agreement between two or more persons; (ii) an intent to enter into the agreement; and (iii) an intent by at least two persons to achieve the objective of the agreement. New York also requires an overt act, which can include an act of mere preparation. Under the traditional view, the acquittal of all persons with whom a defendant is alleged to have conspired precludes conviction of the remaining defendant. However, in New York a conviction of conspiracy against one defendant is allowed to stand when the alleged co-conspirator is acquitted in a separate trial. Thus, (A) is wrong. Furthermore, while a conviction is evidence of the elements of a crime, an acquittal is not. An acquittal means that the prosecutor has not proven beyond a reasonable doubt that all the elements are present; it does not mean that the elements are not there. In a separate trial, the prosecutor may very well be able to prove the element that is lacking. Thus, although Squeaky was acquitted of the conspiracy charge, the assistant district attorney may still pursue the same charge against Dinky. Therefore, (B) is wrong. The forgoing is sufficient for the court to deny the motion, and thus, (D) is wrong.

8.   (B)

A rational jury could harbor reasonable doubt that a murder was intentional, while finding that David demonstrated an indifference to human life so depraved as to deserve the same punishment as intentional murder. Once the jury rejected intentional murder, it could reasonably conclude that David's conduct was so manifestly destined to result in Victor's death as to deserve the same societal condemnation as purposeful homicide. Therefore, (B) is the correct answer, and (D) is an incorrect answer. (A) is incorrect because the facts do not show sufficient intent. (C) is also incorrect because a reasonable person would perceive drawing a gun as having a substantial and unjustifiable risk of death; it is a foreseeable risk.

9.   (C)

A person may not use deadly force if he can safely retreat. An exception to this rule applies when the person is in his dwelling and is not the initial aggressor. Here, however, Joe was in the alcove and stairwell area of his apartment lobby. These areas are not part of his dwelling. Thus, (D) is incorrect. (A) and (B) are incorrect because they are too broad.

10.   (B)

To support a conviction under an offering for sale theory, there must be evidence of a bona fide offer to sell—*i.e.*, that the defendant had both the intent and the ability to proceed with the sale. Under the facts, the intent and ability to sell may be inferred from the defendants' conduct. Consequently, (A) and (C) are incorrect. (D) is incorrect because it relies on evidence that is inadmissible to prove the ability to complete the transaction, and a former conviction does not imply the ability to complete the current transaction given the circumstances.

11.   (A)

Depraved indifference murder occurs when an individual kills another recklessly under circumstances showing a depraved indifference to human life. Here, there was nothing highly reckless about T's conduct—the conduct was intentional. Likewise, manslaughter in the second degree requires reckless conduct. Intentional murder requires a specific, conscious intent to cause death. Firing multiple shots at a victim at close range establishes a specific, conscious intent to kill. Thus, (A) is correct, and (B) and (C) are incorrect. (D) is incorrect because, in New York, a person may not use deadly force if he can safely retreat. Because T had safely left the cafe, it is obvious that he could have safely retreated.

12.   (D)

Defendant's acts in stabbing Joanne in the throat, chest, and abdomen did not, as a matter of law, constitute depraved indifference murder. Depraved indifference murder arises in circumstances when the defendant intends neither to kill, nor to cause serious injury, but nevertheless abandons a helpless and vulnerable victim in circumstances where the victim is highly likely to die. Here, Defendant acted with the intent either to kill or to cause serious injury, and thus his crime is not one of depraved indifference, even though he fled without summoning assistance. Thus, (A) and (B) are incorrect. Reckless manslaughter is conduct that is not intentional, but rather, disregards substantial risk which causes the death of another. Because Defendant acted with intent to kill or cause serious injury, (C) is incorrect. Whether Defendant will be convicted of intentional manslaughter or intentional murder will depend on whether a jury determined defendant intended to injure or kill Joanne.

13.   (B)

A person is guilty of reckless endangerment in the first degree when under circumstances evidencing a depraved indifference to human life, he recklessly engages in conduct that creates a grave risk of death to another person. A person is guilty of reckless endangerment in the second degree when a person recklessly engages in conduct that creates a substantial risk of serious physical injury to another person. Depraved indifference is an utter disregard for the value of human life—a willingness to act not because one intends to harm, but because one simply does not care whether or not harm results. First degree reckless endangerment can be distinguished from second degree reckless endangerment in that it requires a culpable state of mind that is absent from second degree reckless endangerment. Because under the facts as presented, there is no indication that Defendant possessed the required state of mind regarding risk to his neighbors, (B) is a more appropriate answer than (A). (C) is incorrect because first degree criminal mischief is a malice crime for using an explosive to damage property. Although appropriate to the circumstances as stated here, it does not account for the risk of injury or death to individuals and thus, is a less serious crime than (A) or (B). (D) is inappropriate because an attempt crime requires specific intent, which is lacking under the facts as presented.

14. (C)

New York recognizes a justification defense to homicide in instances where a person is in his own home. Thus, (D) is incorrect. The justification defense makes no distinction over which party initiated the confrontation. Thus, (B) is incorrect. Nonetheless, the justification defense and the absence of a duty to retreat applies to a person's dwelling only where the person exercises exclusive possession and control, and does not extend to a doorway which straddles an apartment and a hallway, since Defendant is capable of closing a door rather than resorting to violence. Thus, (A) is incorrect.

CRIMINAL PROCEDURE QUESTIONS

1. Harvey Harpman has been a security guard at Columbia University for the past 25 years. One night he responded to a call from the Computer Library that there was an unauthorized person in the building. Harvey responded to the call and, once there, immediately called his supervisor who was a Special Police Officer. Harvey did not have the authority to arrest anyone but his supervisor did. Harvey and his supervisor located the intruder, established that he was trespassing, and then detained him until the City Police arrived. While waiting, they searched the intruder and found what appeared to be stolen credit cards. Based on this evidence, the intruder was charged with criminal possession of stolen property. Intruder's attorney moved to suppress the stolen credit cards. The court should:

(A) Grant the motion because the search was unlawful without a search warrant.

(B) Deny the motion because the search was lawful as a search incident to a lawful arrest.

(C) Deny the motion; Intruder does not have a Fourth Amendment right because there was no state action.

(D) Grant the motion because there was no probable cause to search Intruder.

Questions 2 and 3 are based on the following situation:

Jimbo Rodriques, leader of the Gumbo Gang, broke into Vern Victim's home one evening, pushed Vern's wife to the ground, and forced Vern to open his safe and give Jimbo the contents. Three months later, Vern's wife, Velma, saw Jimbo's picture in a mug book and was able to identify Jimbo as the person who broke into their home. Based on this information, the police found Jimbo and brought him to the station for a lineup. Jimbo was told that he was a suspect in a crime and he requested to call his attorney. The police granted the request. Jimbo's attorney then spoke to the police and informed them that he wanted to be present at the lineup but could not be there until 6:00. The police agreed to try to accommodate the attorney's request and scheduled the lineup for 6:00. At 6:15 the attorney called and said he would be there at 7:00. Because the witness had to be at a 7:00 Bingo game, the lineup was conducted without Jimbo's attorney and it consisted of the defendant and five other males with similar physical features. The defendant was picked out of the lineup by the witness as the person who broke into her home. The attorney arrived at 7:00.

2. Before trial, the attorney moved to suppress any evidence regarding the witness's identification of the defendant at the lineup because Jimbo was denied his constitutional right to counsel. If the motion is granted it is because:

(A) A person always has a right to counsel during a lineup.

(B) A person has a right to counsel during any type of interrogation.

(C) This was a critical stage of the criminal proceeding.

(D) A person has a right to counsel during an identification proceeding if the person is represented by counsel and the police are aware of this representation.

3. Assume for this question only that Jimbo had a right to counsel, of which he was deprived. Which of the following is a true statement?

(A) The witness may not testify about the identification of the defendant in the lineup.

(B) The witness may not make an in-court identification of the defendant.

(C) The witness may testify about the identification in the lineup provided that the jury is instructed that the relevance of the testimony is circumstantial.

(D) The witness may make an in-court identification of the defendant provided that the jury is instructed that the relevance of the testimony is circumstantial.

4. Dwayne was arrested on July 15 and on August 1 was charged by indictment with murder. Dwayne was being held with no bail. On December 15, Dwayne received notice that his trial would be held on March 15. On the day of the trial, Dwayne moved to dismiss for failure to observe the speedy trial rule.

(A) Dwayne's motion should be denied, because he has been charged with homicide.

(B) Dwayne's motion should be granted, since he will not be tried within six months of his arrest.

(C) Dwayne's motion should be granted, since he will not be tried within six months of his indictment.

(D) Dwayne's motion should be denied, since by his appearance at trial he has waived any objection to the state's failure to try him within the speedy trial time limit.

5. Through a properly filed discovery motion, a defendant is entitled to receive from the prosecution all but one of the following. Which one is he not entitled to receive?

(A) Tapes or recordings of wiretapped or bugged conversations intended to be used at trial by the prosecution.

(B) Reports of physical, mental, or scientific tests or experiments.

(C) A copy of all grand jury minutes that relate to the accused or the incidents from which this offense arose.

(D) All specific instances of a defendant's prior uncharged criminal, vicious, or immoral conduct that the prosecutor intends to use at trial to impeach the defendant's credibility.

6. D was on trial for robbing a liquor store. At trial, when the jury was excused from the courtroom, a spectator shouted out, "It looks like that bum is going to get off like all the other robbers, rapists, and murderers in town." D thought to himself, "Gee, I'd better come clean about that rape I did," and blurted out that he had also committed a rape. Can the defendant's in-court confession be admitted in a subsequent trial for rape?

(A) Yes.

(B) No, because the statement is hearsay.

(C) No, because D was not provided *Miranda* warnings prior to making the statement.

(D) No, because the confession would not have been made without the inducement, provocation, or encouragement of the spectator.

7.   On November 10, 1998, as Alan was driving 80 m.p.h., he attempted to pass Ben at a blind curve in the road, and struck and killed Vic, a pedestrian who was crossing the road. Alan remained at the scene. Police arrived, and Jerry, a police officer, suspected that Alan was intoxicated. Jerry escorted Alan to the police station where he asked Alan to take a sobriety test, consisting of walking a straight line and standing on one leg. When Alan said no and refused to take the test, Jerry placed Alan under arrest and then gave Alan the *Miranda* warnings. Alan was thereafter indicted for driving while intoxicated and criminally negligent homicide. Prior to the start of his trial, Alan moved to suppress Jerry's testimony of Alan's stated refusal to take the sobriety test on the ground that he had not received the *Miranda* warnings prior to his refusal. How should the court rule on Alan's motion?

(A) Grant the motion because Jerry's testimony would violate Alan's Fifth Amendment right against compelled self-incrimination.

(B) Grant the motion because Alan was in custody and subject to interrogation.

(C) Deny the motion because a sobriety test is not incriminating.

(D) Deny the motion because Alan was not subject to interrogation.

8.   Joe killed Ed in the course of burglarizing Ed's home. Based upon Joe's fingerprints lifted off of Ed's desk and information from an eyewitness who saw Joe running from Ed's house, Detective Clark developed probable cause to believe that Joe had killed Ed. Without obtaining a warrant, he drove to Joe's apartment. When he got there, he drew his gun and knocked on Joe's door. Joe looked out the peephole and asked the detective what he wanted. Detective Clark responded that he was investigating Ed's murder. Joe opened the door and was immediately placed under arrest. Joe then blurted out a confession (1). After hearing the confession, Detective Smith read Joe his *Miranda* rights and searched the apartment where he found a gun that was later determined to be the weapon that killed Ed. Joe was then taken to the police station where he was read his *Miranda* rights again. Once again, Joe confessed to Ed's murder (2). Are Joe's confessions admissible against him?

(A) Both confessions are admissible.

(B) The first confession is admissible, but the second will be excluded.

(C) The second confession is admissible, but the first will be excluded.

(D) Neither confession is admissible.

9.   On November 13, shortly after dark, Thug was walking on the public sidewalk in the theater district of the city, an area frequented by drug peddlers. There was nothing in Thug's appearance or in his actions to suggest that he might be engaged in criminal activity. Gum, a rookie detective investigating drug trafficking in the area, stopped Thug, and after identifying himself as a police officer, questioned Thug concerning Thug's presence in the area. As they were talking, a plain, sealed envelope that Thug had been carrying in a folded newspaper under his arm fell to the ground. Before Thug could retrieve the envelope, Gum picked it up, opened it, and found that it contained two packets of heroin. Gum then placed Thug under arrest on a charge of criminal possession of a controlled substance and took Thug to the police station. Is Thug entitled to an order suppressing the evidence of the two packets of heroin contained in the envelope picked up by Detective Gum?

(A) No, because Gum merely stopped Thug to ask him questions in an area known to be frequented by drug peddlers and the subsequent seizure of the envelope was of an object in the officer's plain view.

(B) No, because even if Gum's stop of Thug were deemed to be arbitrary and capricious, the subsequent seizure of the envelope was an object in the officer's plain view.

(C) Yes, because even though Gum's stopping Thug to ask him questions in an area known to be frequented by drug peddlers was valid, there was no probable cause to seize the envelope.

(D) Yes, because Gum's stop of Thug was arbitrary and capricious, and the subsequent seizure of the envelope was without probable cause.

10. The NYPD received an anonymous tip indicating that a man named Josh was involved in a recent shooting. The anonymous tip provided a description of Josh, a tall, skinny, African-American, with a distinctive Bon Jovi tattoo on his face. The tip also indicated the location where Josh could be found and that he was armed and accompanied by two women. After this information was dispatched, an officer spotted a person he knew as Josh Lucas with two companions, one of whom is the defendant, Leslie.

Because Josh matched the description given in the anonymous tip, the officer approached the group. Josh was dressed in orange shorts and a lime green tank top, under which he could easily conceal a weapon. The officer told Josh to place his hands on the police car to be frisked. A plainclothes officer approached Leslie and ordered her to face his unmarked car. Instead, Leslie fled. Leslie was ultimately apprehended by police, and a search of her backpack revealed a quantity of marijuana and drug paraphernalia.

At trial, Leslie moved to suppress the evidence. Which of the following would be the best argument in support of her motion?

(A) The tip did not mention her.

(B) Josh did not have a weapon in plain view.

(C) The tip did not have sufficient indicia of reliability.

(D) The police did not know the identity of the tipper.

11. Erica was pulled over by a police officer for driving a new Lamborghini Murcielago at 210 miles per hour on the Henry Hudson Parkway. The officer ran the license plates on the car and the registered owner, Steve Thompson, had reported the car missing two days earlier. The officer asked Erica where she had gotten the car, and she stated that she had borrowed it from a friend. The officer subsequently arrested Erica for grand larceny and numerous other driving infractions. Erica was eventually charged with the crime of unauthorized use of an automobile. There is a statutory presumption in the New York Penal Law that a person who "rides in or otherwise uses a vehicle . . . without the express consent of the owner is presumed to know that he does not have such consent." At trial, the officer testified as to the above mentioned facts and further stated that, "The driver was an adult, and that nothing in the appearance of the automobile indicated that it was stolen." No other facts were admitted into evidence, and at trial the court found Erica guilty beyond a reasonable doubt.

Is this holding proper?

(A) Yes, because the presumption has not been rebutted.

(B) Yes, because the presumption is irrebuttable on the underlying charge.

(C) No, because the presumption alone is not sufficient to prove guilt beyond a reasonable doubt.

(D) No, because the mere presumption is rebutted by the officer's testimony stating that "nothing in the appearance of the automobile indicated that it was stolen."

12. While conducting a roadblock in Manhattan, the NYPD stopped the defendant's car. Dawn, the defendant and owner of the car, had two passengers with her. While a sergeant spoke to the driver, another officer directed his flashlight into the car and saw a clear plastic bag containing a hard white substance, packaged as if it were cocaine. The officer also spotted a brown paper bag on the floor near the other passenger's feet. The officer signaled to the sergeant that he had seen something, and all three individuals were removed from the car. The officer picked up the bags he had seen, and after confirming his identification of the substance in the first bag, arrested the defendant and both passengers.

Dawn was indicted for criminal possession of a controlled substance in the first and third degrees, and moved to suppress the evidence seized from the vehicle.

What additional evidence would best support the motion to suppress?

(A) The roadblock was set up with the sole objective of checking for seat belts.

(B) The roadblock was set up in order to stop a recent carjacking spree.

(C) The roadblock was set up in order to search for illegal drug trafficking and use.

(D) The roadblock was set up in order to protect city roads from recent terrorist activities and threats.

13. Joe, an overworked accountant, was called in for jury duty and was looking forward to serving. He was not motivated by a sense of civic responsibility, but rather, he needed a good excuse to get out of work for a few days. However, when he got to voir dire, he realized that one of the questions would be a major obstacle to getting selected. The jurors were asked whether they had any family members or friends who worked either at the District Attorney's office or for the Public Defender.

Joe immediately realized that Tom, who was a friend of his college roommate, Brian, recently became an Assistant District Attorney, but was not assigned to this particular case. In college, Joe and Brian socialized often. Tom was present at many of those social gatherings. However, since their graduation 10 years ago, Joe had no contact with Tom.

Joe said that he did not know anyone who worked at either office, and crossed his fingers that he would be a juror. He was selected and the jury on which he sat rendered a guilty verdict. After the verdict was rendered, the defendant discovered that Joe knew someone at the prosecutor's office. The defense moved to set aside the verdict, asserting that the defendant was denied his right to a fair and impartial jury.

The motion should be:

(A) Granted, because Joe's acquaintance with an assistant district attorney would be presumptively prejudicial.

(B) Granted, because Joe's misrepresentation on the voir dire questionnaire should disqualify him from serving on the jury.

(C) Granted, because Joe is guilty of perjury.

(D) Denied.

14. Bill, an experienced lawyer, spent years at the district attorney's office and gained a good reputation through his loyal service as an adept prosecutor. Recognizing Bill's abilities as a skilled litigator, a large law firm attempted to lure him away with a major salary increase as bait. The firm concentrated its practice in areas in which Bill wanted more exposure. At the same time, Bill was assisting in the prosecution of an accountant, Ted Swindler, in a white-collar crime case. The appeal of a more stable financial future finally swayed Bill into accepting an associate position at the firm.

Because of his expertise as a prosecutor, one of the first cases to which Bill was assigned was the case involving Ted. Having just started his new job, Bill did not want to make any waves and dutifully prepared his defense. The jury found Ted guilty, and, while serving time in prison, Ted learned that Bill used to work for the prosecutor's office. Ted immediately moved for a reversal of his conviction, citing Bill's conflict of interest.

How should the court rule?

(A) Ted's conviction should be reversed, because there was an attorney conflict of interest.

(B) Ted's conviction should be reversed, as Ted was denied effective assistance of counsel.

(C) Ted's conviction will not be reversed, because Ted was not denied effective assistance of counsel.

(D) Ted's conviction will not be reversed, because there was no conflict of interest.

15. Defendant shot and killed two people. When the indictment was handed down, the defendant was charged with multiple counts of first degree murder and second degree murder. The second degree murder charges consisted of intentional murder and depraved indifference murder. Before the case was submitted to the jury, the judge advised the parties that there was not enough evidence to prove intentional murder and that he did not intend to submit the charge of intentional murder to the jury at the conclusion of the trial. After both sides had presented their arguments, the only charges submitted to the jury were depraved indifference murder and second degree manslaughter. The defendant did not attempt to dismiss the intentional murder charges against him. The jury found the defendant not guilty of the second degree murder charges but was unable to reach a verdict on the second degree manslaughter charges. The judge then declared a mistrial. The defendant was subsequently indicted for counts of manslaughter in the first degree and manslaughter in the second degree.

If Defendant moves to dismiss the second indictment for first degree manslaughter, would double jeopardy apply?

(A)   No, because the first trial did not result in an acquittal because defendant never sought a trial order for dismissal of the first degree murder charges.

(B)   No, because first degree manslaughter is not a lesser included offense of second degree murder.

(C)   No, because double jeopardy does not apply when there is a hung jury.

(D)   Yes, double jeopardy would apply.

16.   Manny was a sophomore at Derek Jeter High School where he was arrested for armed robbery of Mariano's ring. Prior to placing him in a lineup, the investigating officer called Manny's mother to ask whether she could attend the identification lineup. At a hearing to suppress the lineup, Manny's mother testified that she told the officer that she was unable to attend the lineup because she had to take care of Pedro, her baby, but that Manny had a lawyer. She said that she asked the police officer if he wanted the telephone number of Manny's attorney. As it happened, the police were already aware that Manny was represented by counsel in a pending, unrelated matter. (Manny had previously attempted to steal Donnie's baseball at the playground.) The police officer did not attempt to contact Manny's attorney, nor did he afford counsel the opportunity to attend the lineup at which Manny was identified by two eyewitnesses as the perpetrator of the crime at issue.

Can Manny's lawyer have the lineup suppressed?

(A)   No, a third party cannot invoke counsel on behalf of a defendant.

(B)   Yes, the police were already aware that defendant had counsel on a pending unrelated matter.

(C)   Yes, because a defendant is automatically entitled to counsel at investigatory lineups.

(D)   No, the mother needed to specifically request that counsel be present.

17.   Carl, a known member of a hate group, was arrested as a suspect in a physical attack against an illegal immigrant. He had lured the immigrant into his car with the false promise of work. Upon arriving at an abandoned building, Carl launched an unprovoked and brutal attack on the victim. Carl later turned himself in with counsel present but refused to make any statements. When questioned about the attack, Carl invoked his Fifth Amendment right against self-incrimination. Over defendant's objections, the police, who were aware of defendant's tattoos from a previous investigation, took photographs of defendant's tattoos. The tattoos, which the victim did not see during the attack, included symbols of religious hatred and words promoting anarchy. In order to get the photographs admitted into evidence, the prosecution would like to call an expert witness, who would testify about the customary meaning of the images depicted by Carl's tattoos, and someone who saw the defendant with the tattoos before the crime was committed.

Are the photographs admissible in the defendant's trial?

(A)   No, they are inadmissible because the Fifth Amendment protects the contents of preexisting documents.

(B) No, they are inadmissible because the photographs violate defendant's privilege against self-incrimination.

(C) No, they are inadmissible because they are not relevant, given that the victim did not see them during the assault.

(D) Yes, they are admissible as evidence of motive for committing a hate crime.

18. Defendant has been acquitted of second degree murder. Prosecutor wishes to retry Defendant on a charge of first degree manslaughter arising from the same transaction that was involved in the first trial. Does the first degree manslaughter charge violate Defendant's rights under the Double Jeopardy Clause?

(A) Yes, because first degree manslaughter is a lesser included offense to second degree murder.

(B) Yes, because first degree manslaughter has at least one additional fact which needs to be proven apart from second degree murder.

(C) No, because first degree manslaughter is a lesser included offense to second degree murder.

(D) No, because first degree manslaughter has at least one additional fact which needs to be proven apart from second degree murder.

19. The attorney general issued a subpoena commanding the custodian of records for a small partnership to produce records relating to the partnership's business. May the partnership refuse to produce records based on a right against self-incrimination?

(A) Yes, because the partnership is not an entity separate from its individual partners.

(B) Yes, because every legal entity possesses a Fifth Amendment right against self-incrimination.

(C) No, because a partnership is not an individual with a Fifth Amendment right against self-incrimination.

(D) No, because the Fifth Amendment right against self-incrimination applies to testimony and not records.

20. During arrest processing, law enforcement officials—over Defendant's objection, without providing *Miranda* warnings or having Defendant's counsel present—forced Defendant to remove clothing and photographed his various tattoos. Defendant's tattoos included the phrase "All Cops are Bastards," a Nazi swastika, and a depiction of a skinhead. Defendant moved to have the photographs excluded from evidence, claiming a violation of his Fourth, Fifth, and Sixth Amendment rights.

Which of the following statements is a correct statement?

(A) The photographs violate Defendant's Fourth Amendment expectation of privacy during his arrest processing.

(B) The photographs violate Defendant's Fifth Amendment right against self-incrimination because by forcing Defendant to remove his clothing to reveal his tattoos, Defendant was compelled to reveal thoughts and beliefs without the benefit of *Miranda* warnings.

(C) The photographs did not violate Defendant's Fifth Amendment right against self-incrimination because the photographs depict Defendant's physical characteristics.

(D) The photographs violate Defendant's Sixth Amendment right to have counsel present during a critical stage of proceedings against Defendant.

21. Defendant was 15 years old when he was arrested for robbery. Prior to placing Defendant in a lineup, the officer called Defendant's mother to ask whether she could attend the identification procedure. The mother told the officer that she was unable to attend, but added to the officer that Defendant had a lawyer, and she asked, "Do you want a number?" The officer did not attempt to contact Defendant's lawyer or otherwise afford counsel an opportunity to attend the lineup, at which Defendant was identified.

Was Defendant's right to have counsel at the investigatory lineup violated?

(A) Yes, because Defendant's mother communicated a request to have counsel present on behalf of her son.

(B) No, because there is no right to counsel at an investigatory lineup.

(C) No, because a third party cannot invoke the right to counsel on behalf of another.

(D) No, because a suggestion that counsel may be desired is insufficient to invoke a defendant's right to counsel.

CRIMINAL PROCEDURE ANSWERS

1.   (B)

The security officers had reasonable cause to approach the intruder based on their belief that he was trespassing. The rule in New York is that a forcible stop is authorized where a police officer reasonably suspects that a particular person has committed a crime. [People v. DeBour, 40 N.Y.2d 210 (1976)] In this case, the security officers were entitled to inquire into the legality of Intruder's presence in the library. When his presence was shown to be unlawful, the issue becomes whether the police had probable cause to arrest the intruder. Since the intruder's presence was unauthorized, the officers had probable cause to arrest him. "A search incident to the arrest of a suspect based on probable cause requires no additional justification." [People v. Belton, 50 N.Y.2d 447 (1980)] Once it is established that there was a valid arrest, it follows that the seizure of Intruder's wallet was valid as a search incident to a lawful arrest. (B) is the correct answer. (C) is incorrect because even though the security officer had no power to arrest, his supervising officer did have the power to detain and arrest and thus, his conduct is considered state action. This conduct then is subject to Fourth Amendment analysis.

2.   (D)

A person is entitled to counsel at any critical stage of a criminal proceeding. A criminal proceeding generally is deemed to commence upon charging. Thus, the right to counsel generally does not apply to a precharge "investigatory lineup" held prior to formal prosecutorial action. However, in New York an attorney may not be excluded from the identification proceeding when the defendant is represented by counsel, explicitly requests counsel, and the police are aware of the representation. The police must notify defendant's counsel and provide an opportunity for counsel to appear before they proceed with the lineup. The right to counsel had attached here because the defendant did have counsel and that counsel had conveyed his intention to be present during the lineup. The attorney must have been given a reasonable opportunity to attend the lineup. Thus, the defendant was deprived of his right to counsel and (D) is the correct answer.

3.   (A)

The remedy for an unconstitutional identification is exclusion of the identification. Thus, the witness will not be able to testify as to the identification at the lineup. However, where, as here, the witness had other opportunity to observe the defendant, the witness will be allowed to make an in-court identification of the defendant despite the unconstitutional identification. Thus, (A) is correct and (B) is incorrect.

4.   (A)

Under the speedy trial requirements of Criminal Procedure Law section 30.30, if the People are not ready for trial, the defendant may be entitled to either release from custody or dismissal of the charge, depending upon the amount of the delay. Criminal Procedure Law section 30.30(1) and (2) provide the time periods for dismissal for felonies (six months), misdemeanors (90 or 60 days), and violations (30 days). The time starts to run from the filing of the accusatory instrument and, in computing the time within which the People must be ready for trial, the statute sets exceptions for reasonable delay. However, Criminal Procedure Law section 30.30(3) provides for an exception to dismissal—if homicide is the charge, dismissal will not be granted. Accordingly, (A) is the correct answer.

5. (C)

(A), (B), and (D) are accurate statements as to what the defendant is entitled to obtain for inspection and copying upon demand. The defendant is only entitled to grand jury minutes of his or his co-defendant's testimony, not all grand jury minutes that relate to the offense charged. However, after the jury has been sworn and before the prosecutor's opening statement, the prosecutor must turn over to the defense any written, recorded, or videotaped statement, including any grand jury testimony made by a person whom the prosecutor intends to call as a witness and relating to the subject matter of the witness's testimony.

6. (A)

The oral confession can be admitted. Any confession made without inducement, provocation, or encouragement of police officers is admissible. D's statement was a spontaneous, unprovoked utterance. As such, it is no bar to admissibility that D was not given his *Miranda* warnings before he made the statement. Thus, (C) is wrong. The statement was "blurted out" and may be used against D. (D) is wrong because the spectator was not a police officer. In addition, as the party defendant to the rape action that will be instituted against him, D's statement constitutes the admission of a party, and thus is an exception to hearsay, and (B) is wrong.

7. (D)

Jerry's testimony should not be suppressed. The Fifth Amendment to the United States Constitution, applicable through the Fourteenth Amendment, provides that no person shall be compelled to give self-incriminating testimony. The Fifth Amendment privilege only protects statements or acts that are testimonial or communicative in nature. To protect this right, the United States Supreme Court requires the police to inform detained persons of their rights to remain silent and to an attorney (*Miranda* warnings) before conducting a custodial interrogation. A person is considered to be in custody when the person's freedom of action is denied in a significant way. The more constrained the person feels, the more likely the Court will consider the involuntary detention to be custody. Interrogation refers to any words or actions on the part of the police that the police should know are reasonably likely to elicit an incriminating response from the suspect. Here, Jerry, a police officer suspecting Alan of being intoxicated, asked Alan to take a sobriety test that consisted of walking a straight line and standing on one leg. Alan refused. The sobriety test was a physical performance test used by the police officer to observe and determine Alan's coordination. The test was not likely to elicit an incriminating response because it was not testimonial in nature. Therefore, *Miranda* warnings were not required at that point and there is no ground on which to suppress Alan's refusal. Thus, (A) and (B) are wrong. (C) does not make sense.

8. (D)

Joe's initial confession will be suppressed on the ground that it was a product of an illegal search and seizure. The warrantless arrest of a person in his home constitutes a seizure. Absent exigent circumstances, the Fourth Amendment of the Constitution, which is made applicable to the states by the Fourteenth Amendment, prohibits the seizure of a person or property without a warrant. In this case, Detective Smith did not have a warrant for Joe's arrest, and there are no exigent circumstances. Furthermore, despite the fact that spontaneous statements are admissible as evidence even though a *Miranda* warning was not made prior to their declaration, the fact that Joe blurted out his confession has no impact on its suppression. Joe's confession will be suppressed because it was acquired as the direct result of an illegal search and seizure. Thus, (A) and (B) are incorrect. Joe's confession at the precinct house will be suppressed on the same ground as stated above. The receipt of *Miranda* warnings subsequent to an illegal search and seizure is only a threshold requirement to a determination of whether a confession that is obtained subsequent to the *Miranda* warnings is admissible. In the instant case, although the confession made at the police station may be deemed to have been made under circumstances sufficiently attenuated from the initial illegal search and seizure, the fact is that it was merely a repetition of Joe's original confession. Having made the first statement, there was little incentive for Joe to refrain from repeating it at the precinct house. Thus, the facts do not present any intervening circumstance to outbalance the purposeful violation of Joe's Fourth Amendment rights when he was initially arrested. Thus, Joe's confession at the precinct house will also be suppressed, and (C) is incorrect.

9. (D)

Thug is entitled to an order suppressing the evidence of the two packets of heroin contained in the envelope picked up by Detective Gum. The Fourth Amendment protects people from unreasonable searches and seizures. New York uses a sliding scale to determine the reasonableness of a detention. Detentions to request information are on the first level of the scale. They involve the least amount of intrusion and are valid if they are based on anything more reasonable than whim or caprice. The detainee has a right not to respond, and may even run away, without giving the police probable cause for an arrest. In this case, Gum stopped Thug while he was walking on a public sidewalk in the theater district. Although drug peddlers frequent the area, there was nothing in Thug's appearance or his actions that would suggest that he was involved in criminal activity. Gum randomly selected Thug, approached him, and inquired into the reason he was in the area. Gum did not question any other pedestrian. Gum's actions were arbitrary and thus would be considered whimsical and capricious. There was no articulable reason for detective Gum to select Thug, approach him, and inquire into why he was on that street. Therefore, Gum had no right to stop and detain Thug. Thus, (A) and (C) are wrong. Furthermore, the Fourth Amendment protects individuals from unreasonable searches and seizures. Police may not search a person or his belongings if the person has a reasonable expectation of privacy in the thing or place searched, unless they have a warrant or the search falls into one of the six recognized exceptions to the warrant requirement. A warrant will be issued only if there is probable cause to believe that seizable evidence will be found on the person or premises being searched. Here, Thug had a reasonable expectation of privacy in the contents of the envelope. The envelope was sealed and on his person. Although he dropped it in plain view of the detective, the detective was only able to see a sealed plain white envelope. There was no probable cause to believe that the envelope contained contraband. Furthermore, the seizure of the sealed envelope does not fall within any of the recognized exceptions to the warrant requirement. Thus, (B) is wrong too.

10. (C)

Police may stop a person for investigative purposes if they have a reasonable suspicion that criminal activity is afoot. Such suspicion can be based on an informer's tip. Whether the informer's tip is sufficient to give rise to reasonable suspicion is judged by a totality of the circumstances. While the identity of the informer is not required (making (D) incorrect), the tip must include sufficient indicia of reliability. The tip here did nothing more than indicate a particular person could be found at a particular place; it did not include any indication of how the informer knew that Josh was involved in the shooting, give any predictive information about Josh, etc. Therefore, it did not include sufficient indicia of reliability. (A) is incorrect because defendants do not need to be named in a tip if an underlying search based on the tip is indeed warranted. (B) is not relevant. If the police had reasonable suspicion of criminal activity, they could stop Josh and Leslie to investigate; there is no requirement that a weapon be in plain view.

11. (A)

The statutory presumption created by New York Penal Law section 165.05(1) establishes a "light burden" of explanation that may be placed on the defendant. The presumption can require that an alternative explanation or theory be offered placing the driver within the stolen automobile. The fact finder is given the discretion to reject the presumption even if the underlying predicate is established, as not to punish someone who is merely an ignorant passenger. Here, the fact finder could reasonably require a full explanation for why Erica was driving the car, not just "I borrowed it from a friend." Consequently, (A) is correct, and (B), (C), and (D) are incorrect.

12. (C)

Generally, police may not stop a car unless they have a reasonable suspicion, specific to that person, that a law has been violated. However, the Supreme Court allows police to set up roadblocks to stop cars without individualized suspicion. To be valid, the roadblock must stop cars on the basis of some neutral, articulable standard (*e.g.*, every car) and be designed to serve purposes closely related to a particular problem related to automobiles (*e.g., drunk driving, failure to wear a seat belt*). A roadblock to search cars for general illegal drugs and trafficking is not valid, because the purpose of such a checkpoint is to look for evidence of ordinary criminal wrongdoing. Consequently, (C) being a purpose closest to a general crime is the answer that best helps the defendant's motion.

13. (D)

A court may grant a defendant's motion to set aside a verdict if juror misconduct that was unknown to the defendant affected one of the defendant's substantial rights prior to the verdict. Absent a showing of prejudice to a substantial right, proof of juror misconduct does not entitle a defendant to a new trial. The court must examine the particular facts of each case and weigh the nature and extent of juror misconduct against the potential for impermissible prejudice. Joe's concealment of his relationship with the assistant district attorney was remote and was done to serve as a juror in order not to go to work. Therefore, (A) and (B) are incorrect. (C) is incorrect because Joe was not testifying and cannot be guilty of perjury.

14. (C)

An attorney conflict of interest is usually sufficient to reverse a conviction only when there is an identifiably negative consequence arising from the alleged conflict. Here, Bill served in a prosecutorial role in the defendant's case, but the defendant was not denied effective assistance of counsel, and the conflict did not operate to negatively affect the representation. During the trial, the defendant never indicated any dissatisfaction with Bill's representation. Thus, (A), (B), and (D) are incorrect.

15. (D)

In New York, a defendant has to be charged with all offenses arising from a single transaction except when, for example, the offenses have substantially different elements. Here, first degree manslaughter is a lesser included offense of second degree murder, because second degree murder requires an intent to cause the death of another and first degree manslaughter requires the intent to cause serious bodily harm to another. Logically, if one has the intent to cause the death of another, he must have the intent to cause serious bodily harm also. Thus, for double jeopardy purposes, first degree manslaughter is a lesser included offense of second degree murder, making (B) an incorrect answer and (D) the correct answer. (C) is incorrect because it is not applicable here because the first degree manslaughter charge was never submitted to the jury in the first case. The hung jury pertained to the second degree manslaughter charge. (A) is incorrect because the refusal of a judge to submit a case to a jury because of insufficient evidence is tantamount to an acquittal for double jeopardy purposes.

16. (D)

In this case, the mother only asked the police if they wanted the lawyer's number. She needed to specifically request that the attorney be present prior to the investigatory lineup occurring. Thus, (D) is the correct answer. (A) is incorrect because a parent or legal guardian may invoke counsel on behalf of a juvenile. (C) is incorrect because the right to counsel generally attaches upon the commencement of a criminal action. Pre-accusatory, investigatory lineups do not fall within this rubric. (B) is incorrect because the right to counsel at an investigatory lineup attaches in two circumstances: (i) when counsel has actually entered the matter under investigation and (ii) the defendant in custody invokes the right by requesting counsel.

17. (D)

The Fifth Amendment does not protect the contents of preexisting documents. The creation of those documents (similar to tattoos) was not compelled by the prosecution or the police. Thus, (A) is incorrect. Furthermore, the privilege against self-incrimination does not necessarily bar compelling the disclosure of evidence that a criminal defendant created voluntarily in the past, even if the evidence betrays incriminating assertions of fact or belief. Here, the expert did not give his opinion about what the defendant might have been thinking during the attack, nor did the police compel the defendant to give such testimony. Rather, the expert testified about what the tattoos meant. Thus, (B) is incorrect. The fact that one holds racist beliefs makes it more likely that he would have the motive to commit an assault against a minority, making the evidence of the tattoos relevant. This makes (C) incorrect and (D) correct.

18. (A)

Two crimes will not be considered the same if each requires proof of an element that the other does not require. Second degree murder can be proven by showing that the defendant caused a death with the intent to kill or through highly reckless conduct. First degree manslaughter can be proven by showing that the defendant caused a death while intending serious bodily injury. Because it is impossible to intend to kill a person without simultaneously intending to cause serious physical injury to that person, proof of second degree manslaughter does not have any elements in addition to those needed to prove second degree murder. Therefore (A) is correct and (B), (C), and (D) are incorrect.

19. (C)

Although individual partners are individually liable for the activities of a partnership, the Fifth Amendment right against self-incrimination is concerned with protecting individual civil liberties and does not apply to organizations, including partnerships. Thus, (A) and (B) are incorrect. (D) is incorrect because the statement is overbroad; records can be communicative in nature so as to fall within the Fifth Amendment right against self-incrimination.

20. (C)

Defendants do not have a legitimate Fourth Amendment expectation of privacy during the arrest process, and, thus, (A) is incorrect. The Fifth Amendment privilege against self-incrimination protects an accused only from being compelled to testify against himself, or otherwise provide the state with evidence of a testimonial or communicative nature. Tattoos are not testimonial, and, thus, (B) is incorrect. (D) is incorrect because processing a defendant after arrest is not a point in the proceeding during which there has been any significant judicial activity.

21. (D)

(B) is incorrect because while there is no automatic entitlement to counsel at a pre-charge lineup, the right to counsel will attach if either counsel has actually entered the matter under investigation, or a defendant requests his attorney to be present. (C) is incorrect because although a third party cannot invoke counsel on behalf of an adult, the considerations are different when a juvenile is involved. Nonetheless, although a parent or legal guardian can invoke the right to counsel on behalf of a child, the invocation of the right must be unequivocally communicated. The suggestion that counsel might be desired, the notification that counsel exists, or a query as to whether counsel ought to be obtained is insufficient, thus (A) is incorrect.

DOMESTIC RELATIONS QUESTIONS

1.   Marvin and Nannette want to get married. Marvin is 19 and Nannette is 17. Although Nannette's parents agree to the marriage, Nannette and her entire family are currently living in Hawaii and Marvin is in New York. Marvin is afraid that Nannette will fall for someone else and insists that they marry immediately. Marvin gets Mayor Dingleberry to perform the marriage ceremony because Nannette's parents have provided their sworn, written consent and Nannette's best friend Missy has agreed to stand as substitute for Nannette in the ceremony. The marriage between Marvin and Nannette is:

(A) Valid.

(B) Invalid, because Nannette is under 18 years of age.

(C) Invalid, because a mayor cannot perform a marriage in New York.

(D) Invalid, because New York does not recognize proxy marriages.

2.   In December 1997, Kelly James and Honey Amber became engaged and Kelly moved into Honey's apartment. In February 1998, because they were fighting too much, Kelly moved out and ceased all contact with Honey. Honey then discovered that she was pregnant but she did not tell Kelly. She made arrangements for her Uncle Smitty and Aunt Tasker to adopt the baby. In October 1998, Honey gave birth to a baby boy who was delivered to Honey's aunt and uncle upon Honey's discharge from the hospital. Honey then duly executed a judicial consent and the adoption was finalized six months later. During this entire time, Kelly made no attempts to contact Honey.

In March 2000, Kelly and Honey reconciled and subsequently married. Honey then informed Kelly that a baby boy had been born and that she had given it up for adoption. After this discovery, Kelly commenced a proceeding seeking to vacate the final order of adoption and to assert his rights as the father. The court should:

(A) Vacate the order of adoption solely because Kelly is the biological father; his parental rights have priority.

(B) Uphold the order of adoption because Kelly did not promptly hold himself out as willing to assume custody.

(C) Vacate the order of adoption because as soon as he knew of the child, he sought to assert his parental rights.

(D) Uphold the order of adoption because it is in the best interests of the child not to remain with the father.

3.   Glory was addicted to crack cocaine and on March 10, 1995, gave birth to a four-pound baby boy whom she named Tim. When Tim was born, his biological father, Shadow, was serving a prison sentence. Shortly after his birth, Glory placed Tim in the care of Frank and Freda, foster parents. Glory died three months later. Shadow was released from prison when Tim was two. After his release, Shadow only visited Tim occasionally because Shadow was frequently in and out of prison on other charges. When Tim was seven, Frank and Freda sought to adopt him, but

Shadow would not agree and also sought to gain custody of Tim. In determining who shall have custody of Tim, the court's sole basis for an award of custody is the best interests of the child. This standard requires the court to:

(A) Be most concerned with the child's psychological bonding with the foster parents.

(B) Be most concerned with the fitness of the biological father.

(C) Be most concerned with who has spent more time with the child.

(D) None of the above.

Questions 4 through 7 are based on the following situation:

Julio and Sarah were married in 1979. Because Sarah always had dreamed of having a storybook wedding, they were married at Le Cordon Bleu, in Queens, New York. The couple lived in Aberdeen, New Jersey, for the entire duration of their marriage. In 1997, Sarah could no longer stand Julio's disgusting lack of personal hygiene and moved to Lancaster, Pennsylvania, to live among the Amish. In 1999, Julio moved to a new house in Muttontown, New York. Later that year he resigned himself to the fact that Sarah was not coming back and filed for divorce in New York Supreme Court, on the grounds of cruel and inhuman treatment and abandonment. They had no children, but Sarah had worked for seven years while Julio finished his education. Sarah had also taken care of the marital home which allowed Julio to start his own business.

4.   The durational residence requirement is:

(A) None.

(B) One year and six months.

(C) One year.

(D) New York may not hear this action.

5.   The divorce decree was issued in August 2001. The court awarded Sarah the marital home and, because of her contribution to the marriage which enabled Julio to start his own business, the court also awarded Sarah $700 per month maintenance. In March 2002, Sarah began seeing Sean. Because Sarah was very lonely, Sean would usually spend Wednesday, Friday, and Saturday at Sarah's home. In August 2002, Julio filed a petition to terminate his maintenance obligation, arguing that Sarah was living with Sean and she had essentially "remarried." The court should rule:

(A) To terminate Julio's maintenance obligation because Sarah's standard of living has changed.

(B) That Julio will only have to pay $350 a month because Sarah is living with Sean.

(C) That Julio must continue to pay $700 if the court finds that he has the ability to pay that amount.

(D) Julio's maintenance obligation cannot be terminated because Sarah has merely entered into a de facto marriage.

6. Assume for the purposes of this question that Julio stopped paying the maintenance to Sarah. The statute of limitations on a claim to enforce payment of the arrears is:

(A) Three years.

(B) Six years.

(C) Twenty years.

(D) None of the above.

7. Which of the following is not marital property?

(A) 100 shares of General Cinema stock left to Sarah by her mother's will.

(B) Julio's Ph.D. from the Wharton Business School.

(C) The dividends from the 100 shares of General Cinema stock left to Sarah by her mother's will put into a bank account held jointly by Sarah and Julio.

(D) As a gift for their 10th anniversary, Julio bought Sarah a 1954 red Corvette, with the title in Sarah's name only.

8. H and W were married in Brooklyn in 1998. In 2003, W brought an action for separation in state supreme court. During the pendency of the action, H and W agreed upon and executed a separation agreement that provided that H pay W $500 per week for her support and maintenance. The agreement was silent as to its survival after the entry of a decree of divorce or separation. At the trial of the separation action, W was awarded a judgment of separation. The judgment, dated June 1, 2004, explicitly incorporated the separation agreement by reference. In January 2005, H moved to the state of New Jersey and embarked on a new business venture, whereupon he ceased making support payments. In August 2005, H instituted an action for divorce in New York, based upon living separate and apart pursuant to a judgment of separation, in which he alleged that because of business reverses, he was now without funds or income and sought judgment reducing the amount, if any, payable by him to $100 per week. W objected to the proposed reduction and applied for an order granting counsel fees to aid her in the prosecution of the action. How should the court rule with respect to H's request for reduction in support payments and W's application for counsel fees?

(A) It is up to the trier of fact to determine whether business reversal constitutes extreme hardship sufficient for modification of the separation agreement and whether sufficient cause exists to warrant W's application for counsel fees.

(B) With respect to modification of the separation agreement, it is up to the trier of fact to determine whether business reversal constitutes extreme hardship sufficient to warrant modification, but W is entitled to counsel fees in her action to compel payment under the matrimonial judgment.

(C) The parties' separation agreement is a contract between the parties that survived the divorce decree and cannot be modified, but an award of counsel fees is dependent on whether the trier of fact finds sufficient cause to warrant an award of counsel fees.

(D) The parties' separation agreement is a contract that survived the divorce decree and cannot be modified, and W is entitled to counsel fees in her action to compel payment under the matrimonial judgment.

9.   H and W were married in May 1992. They lived happily until 1998 when they decided they should separate. In February 1998, H and W entered into a separation agreement providing for maintenance and support, and H removed his belongings from their Long Island home and moved to Queens. In August 1999, H and W ran into each other at a party. After spending an enjoyable evening together, they decided that they would go away for a week to their favorite resort with the intent of reconciling their marital relationship. Nevertheless, after spending the week together, they agreed that it would be better if they remained apart, and they did not see each other again. In September 1999, H filed for divorce in the supreme court alleging that he and W had lived separate and apart pursuant to the separation agreement. W, in her answer, set forth an affirmative defense based on their week-long stay at the resort, and counterclaimed for divorce, setting forth several allegations of acts of adultery by H, which took place on specific dates from January 1999 up to and through the commencement of the divorce action. H timely moved to dismiss W's affirmative defense and counterclaim. The court granted both motions. Were the court's rulings correct?

(A) Yes.

(B) Yes with respect to H's motion to dismiss W's affirmative defense; no with respect to H's motion to dismiss W's counterclaim.

(C) Yes with respect to H's motion to dismiss W's counterclaim; no with respect to H's motion to dismiss W's affirmative defense.

(D) No.

10.   H and W were married in New York on October 6, 1992. Their only daughter was born shortly thereafter. They lived together in New York until March 1995. At that time, they separated and entered into a separation agreement, which they duly executed and filed in the supreme court of the county in which they resided. The agreement provided, amongst other things, that H would have custody of their daughter; and W would pay $100 per week for child support. At the time the parties separated H was making $20,000 a year as a painter, and W was making $35,000 a year as an actress. The agreement stated that it would be incorporated but would not merge into any divorce that either party might obtain in the future. In March 1999, W started a divorce action in a New York supreme court in the county of her residence, based on the separation agreement, which alleged that the parties had lived separate and apart for a period of one year in accordance with the terms of the agreement. H filed an answer, and made a motion to increase child support from $100 per week to $1000 per week, based upon the fact that W had become a movie star, and was now making $2 million per year, while H was now making $30,000 per year. W opposed H's motion for an increase in child support. Which statement most accurately describes how the court should rule?

(A) The parties' separation agreement is a contract that survived the divorce decree and cannot be modified.

(B) Although the parties' separation agreement is a contract that survived the divorce decree, the court will modify the agreement based on either party's changed financial circumstance.

(C) Absent an unforeseen change in circumstances together with a showing of true need, the court may enforce the terms of a separation agreement that survives the divorce decree.

(D) The best interests of the child require that the separation agreement be modified to require W to pay a greater proportion of her income towards child support.

11. H and W were married in 1985 in Buffalo, New York. In 1990, W gave birth to a child, D. In January 1999, H's employer transferred him to State X. W refused to accompany H to State X and remained in Buffalo with D when H moved. In June 2000, having satisfied the residency requirements of State X, H commenced an action in State X for divorce on grounds of irreconcilable differences, and W was properly served. In August 2000, after W failed to appear or respond, H procured a decree of divorce together with an order providing that H pay no maintenance to W. Thereafter, W commenced an action in the New York State Supreme Court for divorce based upon grounds of abandonment. W also moved for an order providing for maintenance for her and support for D, as well as for custody over D. H moved to dismiss W's action and her motion for maintenance and support on the grounds that it was barred by the decree and order of State X. Which of the following is the best statement concerning how the court should rule?

(A) The court should give full faith and credit to the divorce granted by State X and its order concerning maintenance.

(B) The court should give full faith and credit to the divorce granted by State X, but disregard the order concerning maintenance.

(C) The court should disregard the divorce granted by State X because State X lacked jurisdiction, but give full faith and credit to the order concerning support because W failed to timely respond to the State X action.

(D) The court should disregard the divorce granted by State X and the order concerning support because State X lacked jurisdiction.

12. H and W were married in New York in January 1986. They have one child, S, born in February 1987. In April 2001, following marital differences, H and W separated, and entered into a separation agreement that was fair and reasonable in all respects to W and H when it was made. Pursuant to the agreement, H gave W custody of S, then 14, and H was obligated to pay the sum of $300 per week until S attained the age of 25, at which time the payment was to be reduced to $150. The agreement did not allocate any specific portion of the $300 weekly payment to S's support. The agreement also provided that it would survive any subsequent judgment of divorce. H made the required support payments until May 1, 2002, when S, over W's opposition, went to live with H, with whom S continued to reside. Although W was a fit mother and wanted to retain custody of S, S refused to return to W's home. Thereupon, H informed W that he would no longer pay her $300 a week because S was no longer living with W, and instead offered to pay $150. W duly instituted an action against H in a New York supreme court for a judgment of separation on the grounds of nonsupport. The complaint alleged the foregoing facts and asserted that H's conduct constituted a repudiation by H of the separation agreement. In the event that the court finds for W, which of the following best states the amount of support and maintenance the court should award W?

(A) W is entitled to $150 per week in maintenance, as agreed in the separation agreement.

(B) W is entitled to recover $300 per week until S attains the age of 25, at which time the payment should be reduced to $150, as agreed in the separation agreement.

(C) W is entitled to receive whatever amount the court determines is reasonable, without being limited to the amount set in the agreement.

(D) W is entitled to receive nothing so long as S resides with H.

13. After 17 years of marriage to W in New York, H moved out of the marital residence due to marital difficulties. Thirteen months later, W commenced a divorce action for abandonment by properly serving H with a summons and complaint. The court granted W a divorce on the grounds of abandonment, and gave W 80% of the marital property and H 20% of the marital property based solely on H's abandonment of W. Was the court's distribution of the marital property correct?

(A) Yes, because the court may distribute marital property in any way it finds just and proper.

(B) Yes, because while marital fault generally may not be considered, abandonment of a spouse is considered so egregious that the court may consider the conduct in distributing assets.

(C) No, because marital fault generally may not be considered, and abandonment alone is not sufficiently egregious to permit a court to deviate from a more equal distribution of assets.

(D) The facts are insufficient to allow a definite determination respecting the court's distribution of marital property.

14. In 1970, Harry met Sally, and they fell madly in love. They wanted to get married, but, Harry, being a realist and an attorney, decided that he should protect his assets. Although he had only recently graduated from law school, Harry had a feeling that his earning potential would far exceed Sally's, who had a high school diploma and showed no signs of wanting to pursue a career of her own. Harry drew up a prenuptial agreement in which Sally waived her spousal property and elective rights.

Specifically, in pertinent part, Sally agreed to "WAIVE AND RENOUNCE ANY AND ALL RIGHTS that, and to which, she would otherwise be entitled to because of such marriage, whether present or future rights, to any and all property which Harry has now, or which he may acquire in the future, whether the same be real, personal, or mixed property, or of any kind or nature and wherever situated."

Thirty years later, Harry filed for divorce on the grounds of Sally's alleged adultery. Sally argued that the prenuptial agreement should not be valid after 30 years of marriage and demanded equitable distribution. The parties do not dispute that the defendant was not represented by counsel in the negotiating, drafting, and signing of the document, nor that she signed the document.

How should the court rule?

(A) The prenuptial agreement should be voided, because it violated execution requirements of current New York equitable distribution statutes.

(B) The prenuptial agreement should be voided, because a spouse cannot waive equitable distribution rights.

(C) The prenuptial agreement should be voided, because Sally and Harry were married for 30 years, and because of Sally's alleged adultery, she will receive no maintenance.

(D) The prenuptial agreement should stand, and Sally will receive some maintenance.

15. In 1981, Terrance met Patty, and they fell madly in love. Because of Terrance's two prior unsuccessful marriages, Patty wished to protect her real property and other assets in the event that the marriage failed. Patty insisted that Terrance enter into a postnuptial agreement, the provisions of which described a distribution of assets upon divorce. At the time, each spouse earned approximately $40,000 annually. Both Terrance and Patty signed the agreement, which had been drafted by an attorney friend of Patty, but the agreement was never acknowledged.

The agreement provides that the parties waive any rights of election pursuant to the Estates, Powers, and Trust law "and other rights accruing solely by reason of the marriage" with regard to property presently owned or subsequently acquired by either party. It further specifies that "neither party shall have nor shall such party acquire any right, title, or claim in and to the real and personal estate of the other solely by reason of the marriage of the parties."

Throughout their marriage, Terrance and Patty maintained substantially separate finances and filed individual tax returns. Twenty years after their marriage, Terrance had become incredibly wealthy, after returning to school to complete an MBA and having worked for a software company from its inception 15 years before. In 2002, Terrance commenced a divorce action. At the time, his annual salary had risen to over $3 million, while Patty continued to earn $40,000. Terrance sought to enforce the terms of the postnuptial agreement. How will the court rule?

(A) The postnuptial agreement is unenforceable.

(B) The postnuptial agreement is enforceable, regardless of whether it remains unacknowledged.

(C) The postnuptial agreement is enforceable, because intent is admissible under Domestic Relations Law section 236B(3).

(D) Postnuptial agreements are not valid in New York.

16. H and W filed for divorce on various grounds, including cruel and inhuman treatment whereby W pled various instances of assault, battery, and intentional infliction of emotional distress. Accordingly, a divorce was granted and issues related to marital property were resolved. Subsequently, W brought a tort action against H for the instances of assault, battery, and intentional infliction of emotional distress originally pled in the divorce proceeding. H brought a motion to dismiss under the doctrine of res judicata, claiming that the issues had been decided as part of the divorce.

How should the court rule?

(A) Motion to dismiss will be granted because the tort action is barred by res judicata, as the tort claim was raised in the divorce action.

(B) Motion to dismiss will be granted because the tort action is barred by interspousal tort immunity.

(C) Motion to dismiss will be denied because to require joinder of interspousal personal injury claims with the matrimonial action would complicate and prolong the divorce proceeding.

(D) Motion to dismiss will be denied because assault, battery, and intentional infliction of emotional distress under tort law are necessarily defined differently from domestic relations law.

17. **In New York, can a child be removed from a home based solely on the child witnessing domestic violence against one parent by the other?**

(A) **Yes, because it is neglect to permit a child to witness domestic abuse.**

(B) **Yes, because domestic violence in the household makes it possible that the child will be the victim of violence.**

(C) **No, because witnessing the abuse of a parent is not abuse to the child.**

(D) **No, because the harm caused by removal of the child may outweigh the harm caused by remaining in the premises.**

DOMESTIC RELATIONS ANSWERS

1.   (D)

The Domestic Relations Law in New York provides that parties to a marriage must declare that they take each other as husband and wife in the presence of a person qualified to solemnize the marriage. Thus, New York does not recognize proxy marriages (*i.e.*, a marriage where a prospective spouse appoints a representative agent as a substitute in the ceremony). Therefore, the marriage is invalid. (B) is incorrect because a person under 18 may marry in New York with the sworn, written consent of one parent. (C) is incorrect because a mayor may perform a marriage ceremony in New York.

2.   (B)

Both the federal rule and the New York rule grant unwed fathers constitutionally protected parental rights if fathers "grasp the opportunity to form a relationship with their child." The unwed father of a newborn has a right to veto an adoption if he promptly manifests a willingness to establish a relationship with the child. (A) is incorrect because this right does not arise merely from the biological tie, but rather from the effort the father makes to establish a relationship between himself and the child. (C) is incorrect because the promptness with which the father establishes the relationship is measured in terms of the baby's life, not by the onset of the father's awareness. Under similar facts, the court found the fact that the father did not know of the child unavailing. [Matter of Robert O. v. Russell K., 590 N.Y.S.2d 37 (1992)] (D) is not a good answer because there are no grounds here to believe that this is a correct statement. Accordingly, (B) is the correct answer.

3.   (B)

In New York, strong deference is given to the parental relationship between a biological parent and his or her child. Thus, when a dispute arises involving the custody rights of a biological parent and a foster parent, the biological parent will be held to have a superior right to custody of the child unless the parent has abandoned the child or is proved unfit. A parent will be deemed to have abandoned the child when the parent has not visited the child for six months when able to visit. Thus, as long as Shadow visited Tim when Shadow was out of prison, he will not be deemed to have abandoned Tim, and the sole remaining issue is whether Shadow is a fit parent.

4.   (C)

Because the marriage was entered into in New York, a matrimonial action can be heard in a New York court after Julio has resided in New York for one continuous year. Thus, (C) is the correct answer and (D) is incorrect. Choice (A) is the residency requirement if both spouses are New York residents and the cause of action arose in New York.

5.   (C)

Maintenance payments are support payments to be paid at fixed intervals for either a definite or indefinite period. The amount of maintenance awarded is based on the reasonable needs of the parties. A maintenance award terminates upon death of either party, marriage by the recipient, or modification of the final judgment. [N.Y. Dom. Rel. Law §236B] For post-equitable distribution maintenance awards and where there was no separation agreement or agreement merged into the divorce decree, the paying spouse would have to petition the court and show a substantial change of circumstances to get an upward or downward modification of the support. (A) is incorrect because Sarah's standard of living during the marriage was one factor that the court used to determine the amount of the maintenance. This factor will not affect a request for modification unless Sarah would become a burden on the state. (B) is incorrect because the maintenance award generally terminates only upon marriage of the recipient, not merely if the recipient spouse is seeing another person or periodically living with another. Domestic Relations Law section 248 provides discretion for the court to annul or modify maintenance upon proof that the wife is "habitually living with" another man and "holding herself out as his wife" even though they are not married. The court has determined that cohabitation alone is insufficient, absent a determination that the former wife is **holding herself out** as the other man's wife. Here, Sean and Sarah were spending time together but there was no proof that they were habitually living with each other or holding each other out as spouses. Thus, Julio will not be entitled to termination of maintenance solely because Sarah is spending a great deal of time with another man. (D) is incorrect because a de facto marriage is not a "marriage" and does not constitute a marriage for the purpose of termination of maintenance. Sarah has not taken on all the accoutrements of married life, nor is she holding herself out to be Sean's wife. Therefore, Julio has not met the standard set by Domestic Relations Law section 248 for termination of maintenance. (C) is the correct answer.

6.   (C)

Under CPLR 211-(e), there is a 20-year statute of limitations period for the enforcement of maintenance and child support arrears, regardless of whether they have been reduced to a money judgment.

7.   (A)

For all matrimonial actions on or after July 19, 1980, the equitable distribution rule applies. This rule separates the property of the parties either into marital property or separate property. Separate property is that which was owned by one of the spouses prior to the marriage and is not subject to equitable distribution. Marital property is subject to equitable distribution and includes all property acquired by either spouse during the marriage, regardless of the form of title, prior to the commencement of any matrimonial action, unless otherwise provided by agreement of the parties. Certain property has been deemed by the statute as separate property, including property acquired by bequest, devise, descent, or gift from a nonspouse. Thus, (A) is separate property. (C) is separate property which became marital property when placed in a joint bank account. (B) is marital property because a professional license or degree obtained by a spouse during marriage and to which the other spouse contributed financially or by other means is marital property. (D) is incorrect because the car was acquired during the marriage despite the title being in Sarah's name, and thus is deemed marital property.

8.   (B)

Under New York Domestic Relations Law, if a separation agreement is incorporated and survives the divorce decree, the court may modify the provision relating to maintenance only if the petitioning party makes a showing of extreme hardship. Whether business reversal constitutes extreme hardship is up to the trier of fact. Thus, (C) and (D) are wrong. However, with respect to W's application for counsel fees, Domestic Relations Law section 238 states that counsel fees may be awarded in an action to compel payment of any sum of money required to be paid by a matrimonial judgment. Here, W is enforcing a sum due under the judgment of separation and is therefore entitled to counsel fees. Hence, (A) is also incorrect.

9.   (D)

Under the Domestic Relations Law of New York, a decree of divorce is available when the spouses have lived separate and apart for a period of one year, pursuant to a written separation agreement. For the separation agreement to serve as grounds for the divorce, the spouses may not cohabit after the agreement is executed and before the decree is granted. Here, H and W cohabited with the intent to reconcile, and thus, the separation agreement was rescinded by the parties' actions, and the divorce cannot be granted on the basis of the agreement. Thus, (A) and (B) are wrong. Furthermore, (C) is incorrect, because the court should not have granted H's motion to dismiss W's counterclaim based on adultery. Although a counterclaim for adultery based on acts committed after the date of separation is improper in an action for divorce based upon a separation agreement, if the separation agreement is rescinded by voluntary cohabitation, the statutory bar to a counterclaim grounded in adultery is removed, and W should be allowed to present her proof on the merits.

10. (C)

The contract between the parties does not limit the court's power to change child support, and thus (A) is wrong. The standard that New York courts generally apply to modification of child support is whether there is an unanticipated and unreasonable change in circumstances since the time of the original award. While qualifying factors a court might consider include the increased needs of the child due to special circumstances or additional activities, increased costs of living resulting in greater childhood expenses, a parent's loss of income or improved financial condition, and the current and past lifestyle of the children, one party's improved financial condition alone does not require an increase in support, and thus, (B) is not the best answer. Furthermore, while the court applies the "best interests of the child" in determining whether to modify child support, there is nothing in the facts that indicates that daughter has been required to endure a lower standard of living since the parties separated; H has not lost any income, and thus, there has been no change in daughter's circumstances that would require an increase in child support. Thus, (D) is not the best answer.

11. (B)

The court should give the divorce decree from State X full faith and credit in New York because H satisfied the residency requirements of State X, so the state had jurisdiction over H and the marital res, and W was notified of the action. However, State X lacked personal jurisdiction over W since she had no contact with that state. Therefore, the New York court is properly able to award support and maintenance. Thus, (A), (C), and (D) are incorrect.

12. (C)

Separation agreements are governed by ordinary contract principles to the extent that there is no conflict with public policy. A separation agreement, properly executed, must be enforced according to its terms without regard to altered conditions not provided for in the agreement and not attributable to the party seeking to enforce the agreement. H's obligation to W did not provide for a reduction if S should no longer reside with W, nor did it specify explicitly the amount to be allocated to child support. The fact that the agreement provided for a future reduction affords no basis for implying the amount of support intended for S. Thus, (A) and (D) are incorrect. Additionally, a spouse's failure to pay the amount due under the separation agreement entitles the other spouse to treat the breach as a repudiation, which terminates the agreement, and allows for a reassertion of statutory rights. Thus, by electing to treat the breach as a repudiation, W gave the court the discretion to determine the level of support in this case, without being limited to the amount set in the agreement, and thus, (B) is not the best answer.

13. (C)

The court's distribution of the marital property was incorrect. In determining the equitable disposition of marital property, Domestic Relations Law section 236 part B(5) requires the court to consider all the circumstances of the case, including: (i) the financial circumstances of each spouse at the time of the marriage, at the commencement of the action, and as predicted in the future; (ii) the duration of the marriage; (iii) the age and health of the parties; (iv) the needs of the parties regarding both occupancy and ownership of the marital residence; (v) the loss of inheritance and pension rights due to the divorce; (vi) maintenance awards; and (vii) direct or indirect claims to marital property by the party without title. Although the equitable distribution statute further states that "the court may consider any other factor which the court finds just and proper," the court of appeals has held that marital fault generally may not be considered—only in those "rare and extraordinary cases where the marital conduct is so egregious or unusual as to shock the conscience of the court." The facts do not indicate any egregious or unusual conduct by H. Thus, H's abandonment of W is not a factor that the court may consider. Therefore, the court was incorrect and should have ordered a more equal distribution of the assets.

14. (D)

The language of the prenuptial agreement did not amount to a waiver of support or maintenance. Sally waived her right to the distribution of property that Harry owned at the time and later acquired, but the agreement did not contain a waiver of support. Maintenance payments are support payments. Absent a written agreement, a court may order maintenance to meet the reasonable needs of a party as determined by the parties' preseparation standard of living. While marital fault is generally not a proper consideration in determining the equitable distribution of marital property upon dissolution, it may be considered when determining maintenance provisions. (A) is incorrect because equitable distribution did not exist in 1970. (C) is also incorrect. The duration of the marriage may be a factor in determining support, which may also be affected by Sally's wrongdoing. However, the mere passage of time does not make an agreement invalid. A spouse can waive equitable distribution rights in New York; thus, (B) is incorrect.

15. (A)

Domestic Relations Law section 236B(3) provides that a nuptial agreement made before or during the marriage must be: (i) in writing, (ii) signed by the parties, and (iii) acknowledged by a public notary. Here the postnuptial is not enforceable because it was not acknowledged. Thus, (B) and (C) are incorrect answers. (D) is also incorrect, as such agreements are valid in New York.

16. (C)

The New York Court of Appeals has held that requiring joinder of interspousal personal injury claims with matrimonial actions would complicate and frustrate divorce cases, delay resolution of custody and support, and force the parties to resolve their tort differences in a forum—divorce court—that is not conducive to such actions. Tort claims require different types of relief and different types of proof; matrimonial actions are tried by a judge while most personal injury actions are tried by a jury. Personal injury lawyers routinely charge a contingency fee while matrimonial lawyers are barred from doing so. For all these reasons, in New York, interspousal tort actions initiated subsequent to a divorce are not precluded by res judicata. Thus, (C) is correct and (A) is incorrect. (B) is incorrect because New York does not follow the common law rule barring interspousal tort actions. (D) is an incorrect statement.

17. (D)

The Court of Appeals has set forth a two-part test that the Family Court must apply in order to find that a child has been neglected and thus should be removed from the home. There must be a showing:

(i) of near or impending danger—not merely the possibility of danger—and (ii) that the parent did not act as a reasonable parent would under the circumstances. Courts must balance the harm that removal will cause against the risk to the child remaining in the parent's care. (A), (B), and (C) are incorrect because they do not articulate the test established by the court.

EVIDENCE QUESTIONS

1. Ellen was taking Judi for a drive around town to show off her brand new Lamborghini when she noticed union picketers outside Hot Rocks Café. Hoping to land a good job with a pro-management law firm, Ellen was particularly enraged by the picketers' signs that day. Ellen told Judi that these days people should be grateful they have a job. Judi agreed that she hated the picketers too.

Wanting to have a little fun, Judi suggested to Ellen that they try to scare the picketers by driving and swerving at them with the car and then pulling away at the very last moment. Ellen agreed that this would be fun and pulled around the block to have a go at the first picketer. However, Ellen was not used to the feel of her new car and instead of swerving away ran head on into the crowd of people. Luckily the brakes were good and she only hit and killed two people.

Police Officer Ray arrived a half hour later and saw the crowd around the two dead picketers and Ellen's damaged car. Ray then took statements from the witnesses, examined Ellen's car, and noted that there were two-foot skid marks on the pavement. Ellen, obviously upset because this could really hurt her chances of being admitted to the bar, told Ray that she didn't mean to hurt anyone, they were just having some fun. Ray included all this into his report at the end of the day. At trial, the prosecutor asked Ray about Ellen's role in the accident and the report he wrote regarding the accident. Which of the following are correct statements?

I. The report may be admissible under the public record exception to hearsay.
II. The report may be admissible under the business record exception to hearsay.
III. The report may be admissible as an excited utterance.

(A) I. and II. only.

(B) II. and III. only.

(C) II. only.

(D) III. only.

2. Defense attorney Gail Frasier called defense witness Margyt Smalgyt to the stand. During the questioning, Gail realized that Margyt's testimony directly contradicted what Margyt had stated in a previous deposition. Gail wanted to impeach Margyt's testimony. What can Gail do?

(A) Gail can only impeach Margyt if she is hostile, an adverse party, or required to be called by law.

(B) Gail can never impeach her own witness.

(C) Gail can impeach her own witness if she uses a prior inconsistent statement which was signed by Margyt or taken under oath.

(D) Gail cannot impeach Margyt unless she admits that her prior deposition was true.

3.   **Edwina wants to sell her boat and asks her friend Mitchell if he wants to buy it for $35,000. Mitchell agrees to buy the boat as long as it passes inspection by a marine surveyor. Mitchell's attorney, Able, prepares a written contract of sale which Mitchell executes and forwards to Edwina. Edwina signs the contract. Three days later, Edwina dies in a plane crash in Syracuse. The inspection of the boat shows that the boat is unseaworthy because of extensive rot. Mitchell notifies Agamemnon, the executor of Edwina's estate, that he does not intend to close on the sale of the boat because it did not pass inspection. Agamemnon then sues Mitchell for specific performance and damages. Agamemnon testifies that the contract has been lost, but states that he had read the contract and that it provided for the sale of the boat to Mitchell for $35,000. As part of the defense's case in chief, Able calls Mitchell to testify as to the contract term concerning the inspection. Agamemnon objects on the grounds of the Dead Man Act. The trial court should rule the testimony:**

(A)   Inadmissible under the Dead Man Act.

(B)   Admissible, despite the Dead Man Act.

(C)   Inadmissible, because of the best evidence rule.

(D)   Admissible, because New York has abolished the Dead Man Act.

4.   **S, a student attending a bar review lecture in a crowded theater, was severely injured when the entire balcony fell on him. In an action against P, Inc., the sponsor of the bar review course, lawyers for P, Inc. introduced as part of its direct case testimony by B, the director of the bar review course, to the effect that the balcony "looked all right" at the beginning of the lecture. S's lawyer cross-examined B with respect to his capacity for observation. On the rebuttal case of S, the attorney representing S then attempted, over P, Inc.'s objection, to introduce evidence that B said, "That balcony's rocking so much, it makes me feel sorry for the poor sailors at sea on a night like this!"**

The evidence of B's statement is:

(A)   Admissible evidence as to B's credibility.

(B)   Admissible evidence as to the condition of the balcony.

(C)   Admissible for purposes (A) and (B) above.

(D)   Inadmissible.

5.   **D was indicted for the crime of rape of V. At D's trial, D's attorney offered to introduce evidence on D's direct case that (1) V had voluntarily engaged in specific prior acts of sexual intercourse with D; and (2) V had been convicted of prostitution two years prior to the alleged rape by D.**

Over objection of the prosecution, the court may properly admit evidence of:

(A)   (1), but not (2).

(B)   (2), but not (1).

(C)   Both.

(D)   Neither.

6.   B sued A to recover damages for his serious personal injuries resulting from a car accident with A. At the trial X, B's attorney, offered proof showing that A, on his plea of guilty, had been convicted in the City Court of Syracuse of the traffic offense of driving with unsafe tires at the time and place of the accident, in violation of the Vehicle and Traffic Law. On A's defense case, Y, A's attorney, offered proof showing that B had been convicted in the same city court of the traffic offense of failing to keep to the right at the time and place of the accident in violation of another section of the law. B had pled not guilty in this action, and his conviction had followed a trial in which the only evidence offered and received was the testimony of A and B. Is the evidence offered by X and Y admissible?

(A) The evidence offered by X and Y is inadmissible.

(B) The evidence offered by X is admissible, but the evidence offered by Y is inadmissible.

(C) The evidence offered by X is inadmissible, but the evidence offered by Y is admissible.

(D) The evidence offered by X and Y is admissible.

7.   In 1998, Mary purchased a new riding lawn mower recently manufactured by MOW, Inc., a New York corporation. A few months later, while Mary was operating the mower on her lawn, the blade on the machine spun out of control and severely injured her. Mary instituted an action against MOW, Inc. in New York supreme court. At trial, she made an offer of proof that other riding mower manufacturers made design modifications to their mowers in 1991, correcting the alleged design defect that she claimed caused her injuries. She stated that this offer of proof would establish that MOW, Inc. knew of these changes prior to manufacturing her mower and for the purpose of establishing that the blade design in her mower was defective. Should the court admit the evidence offered?

(A) Yes, because it is relevant and not subject to any exclusionary rules.

(B) No, because it violates the exclusionary rule against admitting evidence of subsequent remedial measures in strict liability cases involving design defects.

(C) No, because it is more prejudicial than probative.

(D) No, because changes made by other manufacturers are not relevant in a case against MOW, Inc.

8.   Amanda, a defense attorney, had a client, Joshua, who was on trial, accused of participating in an armed robbery. Joshua claimed that he was merely a bystander and that he has been mistakenly identified by a traumatized shop merchant at a pre-trial lineup. Joshua told Amanda that a friend of his, Carlos, was with him at the time the robbery took place and that the friend could be an alibi for him and support his version of events. Carlos was the only witness who could corroborate Joshua's story. When Amanda contacted Carlos, he confirmed Joshua's story but also explained that he was afraid of testifying in court because he was an illegal immigrant and feared deportation.

At trial, Amanda called Joshua to the stand to testify on his behalf, but did not call Carlos. Carlos was never subpoenaed. The judge addressed the jury and gave an adverse inference instruction with respect to Amanda's unavailable witness.

Was the judge's instruction to the jury proper?

(A) No, because the fear of deportation is a valid excuse.

(B) No, because the friend is an unavailable declarant, and his statements fall under an exception to the hearsay rule.

(C) Yes, because the fear of deportation is not a valid excuse.

(D) Yes, because the conditions for a "missing witness" charge have been met.

9. David, the defendant, was arrested for the murder of a friend committed when he was a teenager. A number of witnesses from the defendant's past came forward, as did Lisa, David's wife. Lisa told the police that, while defendant was choking her and screaming obscenities at her, he threatened her and he told her about the crime. She said that David stated that he was so angry he could kill her just like he did his friend. When David's wife was called by the prosecution to testify in court against her husband, David's attorney objected to any questioning of her.

What should the judge rule with respect to the objection?

(A) Sustained, because a spouse is incompetent to testify against the other spouse in a criminal matter.

(B) Overruled, because Lisa may waive the privilege.

(C) Sustained, regardless of whether the action is civil or criminal.

(D) Overruled, because the communication must be made in reliance upon the intimacy of marriage.

10. Officer came to the aid of Victim, who had been stabbed twice in the eye. Victim was taken to the hospital, and approximately one hour after the stabbing, while still agitated and excited, Victim described to police the events that led up to the encounter whereby Defendant stabbed Victim. Soon thereafter, Victim died of unrelated causes. Prosecutor seeks to have Victim's description of the events leading up to the stabbing admitted over Defendant's objection.

How should the court rule?

(A) Victim's description is inadmissible hearsay and no exception applies.

(B) Victim's description is hearsay but is admissible as an excited utterance.

(C) Victim's description is hearsay but is admissible as a dying declaration.

(D) Victim's description is hearsay but is admissible as a present sense impression.

11. While in the midst of a vehement argument during which Defendant tried to choke his wife, Defendant stated that he was so mad he could kill her, just like he killed Sam. Subsequently, Defendant was on trial for murdering Sam. Wife indicated a willingness to testify as to what Defendant told her about killing Sam. Defendant objects to Wife's testimony on the basis of marital privilege.

The court should find Wife's testimony is:

(A) Inadmissible, based on the marital communications privilege.

(B) Inadmissible, because Defendant relied on the marriage confidentiality in making the statement.

(C) Admissible, because communications or threats made during physical abuse are not covered by the marital privilege.

(D) Admissible, at the discretion of the witness spouse.

EVIDENCE ANSWERS

1.   (C)

Hearsay is an out-of-court statement offered to prove the truth of the matter asserted in the statement. Hearsay can be written or spoken, but in any case it is inadmissible into evidence unless it falls within an exception. The police report of the accident is hearsay but it will fall within the business records exception. To fall within the business records exception, the record must be made in the regular course of business; at the time of the act, transaction, or occurrence or within a reasonable time thereafter; and consist of matters within the personal knowledge of the entrant. The report here meets these requirements. However, an accident report prepared by a police officer does not meet the requirements of the public records exception. Under CPLR 4520, the public records exception applies where a public officer is required to make a certificate or an affidavit to a fact ascertained, or an act performed by him in the course of his official duty, and to file or deposit it in a public office of the state. Accordingly, the police report does not meet all the criteria of the public record exception to the hearsay rule and answer (C) is the only possibility. (A) is wrong for the reasons just stated. (D) is wrong because an excited utterance is a statement made during or soon after a startling event. Too much time has elapsed here before the statement was made, and Ellen had time to reflect upon the event.

2.   (C)

There is no impeachment of one's own witness permitted in New York except by use of a prior inconsistent statement, either in writing and signed by the witness or under oath. [CPLR 4514] Thus, (C) is the correct answer.

3.   (B)

The Dead Man Act provides that a person interested in the event is incompetent to testify to a personal transaction or communication with a deceased when the testimony is offered against the representative or successors in interest of the deceased. In other words, death having silenced one party, the statute closes the mouth of the living person who, being interested in the outcome of the litigation, wishes to testify on her own behalf against someone who is suing or defending in a representative capacity. Note that the act applies even when the decedent's estate is suing, as it is here. Since Mitchell is clearly interested in the outcome of the suit, all requirements for the Dead Man Act have been met. Thus, Mitchell will be permitted to testify only if an exception to the statute applies to these facts. Luckily for Mitchell one does. If the protected party or an agent of the deceased testifies to a transaction with an interested person, the interested person may testify about the same transaction. Protected parties are executors, administrators, heirs, legatees, and devisees. Agamemnon is the executor, a protected party. Since he testified to the transaction, he opened the door for Mitchell's testimony.

4.   (B)

Admission by an employee made in the ordinary scope of employment against the interest of the employer is receivable in evidence of the facts submitted. Sufficient foundation indicating inconsistent statements by B has not been laid.

5.   (C)

Under the Federal Rules of Evidence, evidence of the victim's prior sexual activity is inadmissible except, inter alia, to show prior sexual intercourse with the defendant. Thus, D can properly introduce (1). The New York law expands upon the evidence admissible in a sex crime case. Evidence that tends to show that the victim was convicted of prostitution within three years prior to the time of the alleged rape is admissible. Thus, (2) is admissible. Therefore, (C) is the correct choice.

6. (B)

Although A's guilty plea is hearsay because it is an out-of-court statement offered to prove the truth of the matter asserted, it is admissible because it is an admission by a party, and therefore is within an exception to the hearsay rule. Thus, the court would admit the evidence offered by X, and (A) and (C) are wrong. Note that this is not a record of criminal conviction, within the meaning of the hearsay exception. Records of prior criminal conviction do not include traffic infractions. Like A's guilty plea, B's conviction is hearsay because it is an out-of-court statement offered to prove the truth of the matter asserted. Unlike A's guilty plea, however, B's conviction does not fall within any exception to the rule against hearsay. It is not an admission by a party since B pleaded not guilty and was convicted at trial—unlike A, who pleaded guilty. And as established above, B's conviction is not admissible under the prior recorded conviction exception because that exception does not extend to traffic convictions. Therefore, the court would have to exclude B's conviction. Thus, (D) is wrong too.

7. (A)

Mary's evidence is admissible because it is relevant and it is not subject to any exclusionary rules. Evidence is relevant if it tends to prove or disprove a fact of consequence to the determination of the cause of action. The proffered evidence here is relevant because it tends to show that the mower was unreasonably dangerous, since evidence that other manufacturers knew that the old design was dangerous in 1991 tends to show that it was possible for MOW, Inc. to design a nondefective mower prior to 1998, and tends to show that the MOW, Inc. mower was unreasonably dangerous. Thus, (C) and (D) are wrong. The evidence also does not violate any exclusionary rule of evidence. Generally, New York has an exclusionary rule against admitting evidence of subsequent remedial measures in strict liability cases involving design defects. However, the proffered evidence here does not violate the rule for two reasons: First, the evidence offered is not evidence of a subsequent remedial measure, but rather is evidence of a ***prior*** design change by the industry. Second, the prohibition against subsequent remedial measures extends only to measures by the defendant, and here Mary is trying to show changes made by other manufacturers. Thus, the evidence is admissible.

8. (D)

An adverse inference instruction allows a jury to draw an unfavorable inference based on a party's failure to call a witness who would normally be expected to support that party's version of events. There are three preconditions for the "missing witness" charge: (i) the witness in question must have knowledge material to the trial, (ii) the witness must be expected to give testimony favorable to the party against whom the charge is brought, and (iii) the witness must be available to testify. Upon learning of Carlos's reluctance to testify, Amanda did nothing to mitigate Carlos's absence. Amanda could have requested leniency for the witness, or could have gotten a subpoena issued. (B) is incorrect, because a declarant is unavailable if he refuses to testify concerning a hearsay statement despite a court order or is absent (beyond the reach of a court's subpoena).

9. (D)

The communication in question must be made in reliance upon the intimacy of the marital relationship. Abusive language and misconduct directed at the spouse are thus not privileged. New York also does not recognize spousal immunity except with regard to confidential communications, and certain adultery and nonaccess situations. Thus, (A) and (C) are incorrect. (B) is incorrect because both spouses hold the privilege, and either can prevent the other from disclosing the confidential communication. Thus, both David and Lisa need to waive the privilege for the communication to come into evidence.

10. (A)

Hearsay is an out-of-court statement offered to prove the truth of the matter asserted. Here, Victim's out-of-court description of the events that led to the stabbing is being offered to prove the events of the stabbing and, thus, is inadmissible. (B) is incorrect because an excited utterance must have been made before there has been time to contrive and misrepresent, and although there is no definite measure of seconds or minutes, an hour was more than enough time for reasoned reflection. Similarly, (D) is incorrect because a present sense impression is a statement made contemporaneously with the event. (C) is incorrect because in New York a dying declaration must relate to the cause of death, the victim must have died, and the statement must have been made by the declarant knowing that death is imminent. The elements of a dying declaration are not satisfied here. It should be noted that even if Victim's statement qualified for admission under a hearsay exception, it still would be inadmissible here under the Confrontation Clause.

11. (C)

A spouse may not be required to disclose a confidential communication made to a spouse during marriage. The privilege belongs to the defendant spouse, and, thus, (D) is incorrect. The privilege is designed to protect and strengthen the marital bond. It encompasses only those statements that are confidential and that are induced by the marital relation and prompted by the affection, confidence and loyalty engendered by such relationship. Communications or threats made during the course of physical abuse are not entitled to be cloaked in the privilege, because the maker of the statement is not relying on any confidential relationship to preserve the secrecy of his acts and words. Thus, (A) and (B) are incorrect.

FEDERAL JURISDICTION & PROCEDURE QUESTIONS

1.   Peter, a citizen of New Jersey, brings a personal injury action arising in Connecticut against Jody, a citizen of New York, in the Federal District Court of Massachusetts. Peter is claiming $100,000 in damages. On which ground may the court sustain Jody's motion to dismiss?

(A) Lack of subject matter jurisdiction.

(B) Failure to meet the jurisdictional amount.

(C) Improper venue.

(D) No federal question.

2.   Alan resides in New York and Michael resides in New Jersey. Alan and Michael own their own construction company and for two years did all their work repairing homes in New York. Knowing that Michael wanted to get out of the business, Alan offered to buy Michael's tools and equipment. Michael accepted but later changed his mind and started a new business in New Jersey, leaving Alan with no equipment and all the expenses. Alan filed an action in federal district court for breach of contract and alleged $85,000 damages. In which federal district may Alan bring this action?

(A) Where the plaintiff resides.

(B) Where either the plaintiff resides or the defendant resides.

(C) Where the defendant resides.

(D) Whichever district is most convenient for plaintiff to travel to.

FEDERAL JURISDICTION & PROCEDURE ANSWERS

1.   (C)

Under section 1332 of the Federal Rules of Civil Procedure, the district court has diversity jurisdiction (since the parties reside in different states), but venue is improper because section 1391, the general venue statute, requires that actions founded solely on diversity be brought either in the judicial district where the defendant resides, the district where the claim occurred, or the district where the defendant is subject to personal jurisdiction. Since Massachusetts fits none of these allowed venues, the court may sustain a motion to dismiss for improper venue.

2.   (C)

Federal venue rules determine the judicial district in which an action may be brought. Where subject matter jurisdiction is based solely on diversity of citizenship, the action may be brought in any judicial district where (i) all defendants reside; (ii) a substantial part of the events giving rise to the claim occurred or a substantial part of the property that is the subject of the action is situated; or (iii) all defendants are subject to personal jurisdiction. Accordingly, (C) is the correct answer.

MORTGAGES QUESTIONS

1. Al gave a $25,000 mortgage on Blackacre to B Bank in 1987. In 1990 Al dies. Blackacre passes to Charlie under Al's will. Charlie does not renounce the gift. Blackacre is still encumbered by the mortgage to B Bank. The will that left Blackacre to Charlie is silent as to how the mortgage is to be satisfied. Who is personally liable on the mortgage?

(A) Al's estate.

(B) Charlie.

(C) The executor of Al's estate.

(D) No one.

2. A buys a building for $100,000 and gives B a mortgage for $75,000. Thereafter, A sells the building to C for $100,000 subject to B's mortgage. If C fails to make the mortgage payments to B:

(A) B may foreclose on the property and hold C personally liable for any deficiency.

(B) B may foreclose on the property and hold A personally liable for any deficiency.

(C) B may foreclose on the property and hold both A and C personally liable for any deficiency.

(D) B may no longer foreclose on the property, but may commence an action for breach of contract against A.

3. Owen gives A Bank a mortgage on Blackacre for $100,000. Two years later, Owen gives a second mortgage to B Bank for $20,000. Two years later, Owen defaults on the mortgage held by A Bank. A Bank, not knowing that B Bank holds a second mortgage, forecloses on the property without joining B Bank as a party to the action. What are B Bank's rights in the property?

(A) B Bank's mortgage interest was terminated when A Bank foreclosed on Blackacre.

(B) B Bank may hold A Bank personally liable for the money owed by Owen.

(C) Blackacre is still subject to B Bank's mortgage.

(D) B Bank has no rights.

MORTGAGES ANSWERS

1.   (D)

When property subject to a mortgage passes to a devisee or distributee, the property continues to be subject to the mortgage. However, neither the personal representative nor the devisee or distributee is personally liable or responsible for satisfaction of the mortgage. The testator may, by will, impose upon his estate the burden of satisfying the mortgage, but he must do so expressly. [EPTL §3-3.6] Since the facts do not state that Al clearly expressed his intention that his estate satisfy the mortgage, no one is personally liable for the debt.

2.   (B)

If mortgaged property is transferred "subject to the mortgage," the property becomes the primary source for the payment of the debt; the original mortgagor continues to be liable on the note. The grantee is only personally liable if he has expressly assumed the mortgage. The facts do not indicate that C expressly assumed the mortgage; therefore (A) and (C) are wrong. B may foreclose even if C is not personally liable; therefore (D) is wrong.

3.   (C)

Every person whose interest is claimed to be subordinated to the plaintiff's mortgage lien is a necessary party to a foreclosure action. The effect of omitting a necessary party is to preserve her interest despite foreclosure and sale. Therefore, Blackacre remains subject to B Bank's mortgage.

NEW YORK PRACTICE QUESTIONS

1.   Plaintiff serves defendant with a summons with notice. The defendant still may object to personal jurisdiction:

(A) After his attorney responds by serving a notice of appearance and demand for the complaint.

(B) After his attorney moves to dismiss based solely on a statute of limitations defense.

(C) After his attorney appears at a proceeding to contest the merits on his behalf.

(D) At any time.

2.   A bill of particulars must be verified when:

(A) The responding party objects to the propriety of the demand.

(B) Only if the bill may not be responded to within the 20-day time limit.

(C) An action by an infant for breach of contract.

(D) The cause of action is for negligence.

3.   A plaintiff is not entitled to a jury trial for:

(A) An action for an annulment from a spouse.

(B) An action against a doctor for malpractice.

(C) An action to enjoin and recover damages from a slaughterhouse behind the plaintiff's house for dumping animal wastes into a pile within 25 yards of plaintiff's back door.

(D) None of the above.

4.   On July 15, 2002, Barnabus Collins slipped down the stone stairs in his castle and was taken to the Mercy Medical Center for a hip replacement operation performed by Dr. Reyes. Barnabus saw Dr. Reyes three times after the operation. His last appointment was scheduled for January 15, 2003. On August 17, 2005, Barnabus went in to see Dr. Reyes because his back was bothering him and he still could not walk correctly. Barnabus then discovered that the hip replacement operation was faulty. What is the latest date on which Barnabus can commence a malpractice action against Dr. Reyes?

(A) Two years and six months from the date of the operation.

(B) Two years and six months from the January 15, 2003 appointment.

(C) One year after discovery of the problem.

(D) Two years and six months from the August 17, 2005 appointment.

5. Which of the following statements is (are) correct?

I. The court can compel a former employee of a corporation to be deposed.
II. A deposition may never be obtained prior to the service of the complaint.
III. The court can compel a party to respond to a deposition after the trial has begun.

(A) I. and III.

(B) II. and III.

(C) I. only.

(D) I., II., and III.

6. Buffalo Chips Corp., incorporated in New York, invites Thurman to come to New York to interview for a job in its research and development division. Thurman, who has lived in Arizona for the past 20 years, arrives in New York at 9 a.m. for the interview. At the end of the day, Thurman signs a contract to represent Buffalo Chips Corp. in Arizona. He returns to Arizona that same day. Thurman works in the Arizona office of Buffalo Chips Corp. for three years and is then fired for revealing corporate secrets. The corporation then brings an action against Thurman for breach of contract. Jurisdiction in New York is:

(A) Not proper, because Thurman did not do business in New York.

(B) Not proper, because there is no personal jurisdiction over Thurman.

(C) Proper, because Thurman's act caused injury in New York.

(D) Proper, because Thurman transacted business in New York.

7. In September 1994, N and P were the passengers in a car involved in a one-car accident. The accident, which occurred in State X, was allegedly caused due to failed brakes. State X had a two-year statute of limitations for negligence and products liability. On July 6, 1997, N and P brought separate actions in New York Supreme Court against A Corp, the manufacturer of the brakes. P is a resident of State X. N is a resident of New York. A Corp, a New York corporation, moves to dismiss both actions on the grounds of untimeliness of the claim.

A Corp's motion should be granted against:

(A) N, but not P.

(B) P, but not N.

(C) N and P.

(D) A Corp's motion should be denied.

8. X commenced an action against Y by causing Y to be personally served in New York with a summons that included the following recital: "The object of this action and the relief sought herein is the recovery of damages in the amount of $5,000. In the event that you fail to appear in this action, judgment will be entered against you by default in the amount of $5,000."

After an appearance by M, Y's attorney, X served M with a complaint specifying that X sought to recover $5,000 as damages for fraud and an additional $1,000 as damages for breach of warranty of merchantability. M and Y decided to ignore the complaint as being legally insufficient, and did not submit an answer or otherwise participate in the proceedings thereafter. Upon proof of the foregoing facts and application to the clerk of the court, and without giving Y further notice, which of the following statements is correct?

(A) X is entitled to a default judgment against Y in the amount of $5,000 only.

(B) X is entitled to a default judgment against Y in the amount of $6,000.

(C) X is not entitled to a default judgment because the application should have been directed to the court itself.

(D) None of the three statements above is correct.

9.   P brought an action in the New York Supreme Court against D, a resident of State X, for damages resulting from a breach of contract. The contract, which was entered into in State X, provided for the delivery of goods and services within New York State. No delivery had been made. P's attorney had a summons and complaint served on D by certified mail, a manner of service permitted in State X. D moved to dismiss the complaint on the ground that the New York court had not acquired jurisdiction over him.

D's motion should be:

(A) Granted because the method of service was improper.

(B) Granted because D had no contacts with New York.

(C) Denied because another state's method of process can be adopted by New York.

(D) None of the above.

10. In 1994, H, a physician, entered into a written lease with O, the owner of an office building in New York, to lease a suite of medical offices for 10 years. In July 1996, H decided suddenly to move his residence and medical practice to Utah, and H left New York without informing O of his departure. H did not pay O any more rent for the office suite, which remained vacant until January 1, 1997, when O was able to secure another tenant. O wrote to H in Utah, demanding that H pay rent due from August 1 through December 31. H ignored O's letters. H returned to New York briefly in April for a medical convention. There he told several persons who knew O that O was a "money-hungry, scheming thief." In May, O's attorney prepared a summons and complaint in an action by O against H, asserting: (1) a cause of action for damages for breach of the lease, and (2) a cause of action for damages for slander. A copy of O's summons and complaint was personally served upon H in Utah by a Utah attorney. H has duly moved in New York to dismiss both causes of action against him on the ground of lack of personal jurisdiction.

The court should properly dismiss:

(A) (1) only.

(B) (2) only.

(C) Both.

(D) Neither.

11. H sued D for injuries H sustained in a car accident with D. Five days after H's summons and complaint were served upon D, D moved to have the action dismissed and served a notice of examination before trial. H promptly moved to strike the notice of examination on the ground that it was premature. With his motion to strike, H served D with a notice to produce for inspection any and all accident or liability policies possessed by D. D immediately moved to strike the notice to produce as improper. The court denied both H and D's motions. Was the court's ruling correct?

(A) Yes.

(B) Yes with respect to denying H's motion to strike the notice of examination as premature, but no with respect to denying the motion to strike the notice to produce accident and liability policies possessed by D.

(C) Yes with respect to denying D's motion to strike the notice to produce accident and liability policies possessed by D, but no with respect to denying H's motion to strike the notice of examination as premature.

(D) No.

12. F sued A and P in the Rochester Supreme Court. After trial but before the judgment in the action between F, A, and P, P settled with F for $30,000. F prevailed in the judgment. The court awarded $100,000, finding P and A each 50% liable. A's assets equal only $10,000. How much must P pay, and how much can F collect from A?

(A) P must pay $30,000 and F can collect $50,000 from A.

(B) P must pay $30,000 and F can collect $30,000 from A.

(C) P must pay $30,000 and F can collect $10,000 from A.

(D) P must pay $90,000 and F can collect $10,000 from A.

13. H was the sole shareholder of S Co., a New York corporation. In June, U Co., also a New York corporation, S Co., and H executed a contract whereby U Co. would acquire all the shares of S Co. in return for paying H a monthly salary of $3,000, and H would be employed in a supervisory capacity for no less than five years. After a year, economic downturns caused the business to suffer huge losses, and U Co. was forced to let H go and ceased paying him his $3,000 per month. U Co. was on the brink of insolvency. H brought an action in a New York supreme court, and in his complaint demanded an order of attachment against U Co.'s assets, or, in the alternative, an order that U Co. be placed into receivership for the benefit of its creditors. Which, if any, of these remedies would be appropriate for the court to order?

(A) Either attachment or receivership.

(B) Attachment, but not receivership.

(C) Receivership, but not attachment.

(D) Neither attachment nor receivership.

14. P rented a lift machine from C. The machine was manufactured by M and bought by C in 1996. On June 1, 1997, P was injured when the machine cable gave way, and struck him in the head. On May 1, 2000, P sued C for his injuries under theories of negligence and strict liability in tort. On July 1, 2000, C impleaded M by serving a third-party summons and complaint upon M. On August 15, 2000, C settled with P for $50,000, and thereafter M moved to dismiss C's third-party action. How should the court rule on M's motion?

(A) The court should grant the motion because C's impleader claim against M is based on a claim for contribution for shared responsibility, and thus is barred as a matter of law because of the settlement.

(B) The court should grant the motion because C's impleader claim against M is based on a claim for indemnification, and thus is barred as a matter of law because of the settlement.

(C) The court should deny the motion because C has a right to seek contribution from M based upon a theory of shared responsibility for the injury.

(D) The court should deny the motion because it is impossible to tell on the facts whether C is seeking contribution or indemnification.

15. After Beth and Pat were married in 1981, they moved to Whiteacre, property in Broome County. Lisa, their only child, was born in 1982. After 17 years of marriage, Beth and Pat began to experience marital difficulties and decided to separate. On May 1, 1998, they entered into a written agreement providing that Pat and Beth would live separate and apart. The agreement also provided that Pat would pay Beth maintenance and support, along with Lisa's college tuition. On September 10, 1999, while Beth was away from home on an errand, Lisa was served at Whiteacre with a summons and complaint in an action by Pat against Beth seeking a divorce. On September 13, 1999, Beth received in the mail an envelope with the return address of Pat's attorney, which contained copies of the papers served on Lisa. Has Beth been properly served in the divorce action?

(A) No, because Lisa is not a person of suitable age and discretion.

(B) No, because service in a matrimonial action must be by personal service.

(C) Yes, because service in a matrimonial action can be by personal or substituted service, and is within the discretion of the plaintiff's attorney.

(D) Yes, if substituted service was authorized by court order.

16. Patty, who had been an associate in a law firm, decided to start her own practice in 1989. Needing office space, she entered into a written lease with Larry, who owned an office building in Queens. The lease period was for 10 years beginning June 1, 1989, and ending May 31, 1999. The rent was to be paid monthly at $1,500 per month. The lease also included an option to renew for another 10-year period upon written notice mailed to Larry at a specified address no later than one year prior to the expiration of the lease. The rent for the renewal term would be $2,000 per month.

Happy with her surroundings, on May 15, 1998, Patty sent, by certified mail, a written notice of her intent to exercise her option to renew the lease. Patty sent this notice to Larry's attorney whom she knew professionally and to whom she had sent all other communications regarding the lease for the past several years. Upon reviewing her lease in June, Patty realized her error and sent written notice directly to Larry, who refused to renew the option, stating that it had not been exercised on time.

Due to the refusal, Patty commenced an action in supreme court, Queens county, seeking a declaratory judgment that she had effectively exercised her option to renew. Larry moved to dismiss, stating that the action was premature because the lease had not yet expired. How should the court rule?

(A) The court should deny the motion because a justiciable controversy exists.

(B) The court should grant the motion because no justiciable controversy exists.

(C) The court should deny the motion because the lease has effectively expired.

(D) The court should grant the motion because the supreme court does not have the power to hear actions for declaratory relief.

17. Defendant moved to New Jersey from New York three weeks before getting into a car accident in New Jersey with a New York resident. Defendant had not changed his driver's license and vehicle registration from New York to New Jersey prior to the accident. Plaintiff sought to bring an action in a New York court.

Does a New York court have long arm jurisdiction over Defendant?

(A) No, because Defendant's possession of a New York license and registration is too insubstantial to warrant a New York court's exercise of personal jurisdiction.

(B) No, because the state with the greatest interest in the outcome of litigation arising out of an automobile accident is the state in which the accident occurred.

(C) Yes, because Defendant's license and registration demonstrated that Defendant transacted business within New York, thus subjecting himself to New York's long arm jurisdiction.

(D) Yes, because a condition of possessing a New York driver's license is subjecting oneself to the jurisdiction of a New York court in matters relating to automobile accidents.

NEW YORK PRACTICE ANSWERS

1. (A)

In New York, an appearance is not a waiver of jurisdictional defects or a form of consent to the court's jurisdiction. Even after an appearance, under CPLR 320 a defendant can raise a jurisdictional defect either by a preanswer CPLR 3211 motion to dismiss on jurisdictional grounds or by interposition of an answer containing the affirmative defense of lack of jurisdiction. However, if a defendant makes a motion to dismiss on any ground other than lack of jurisdiction and fails to join the jurisdictional defense in the motion, the defense is waived. Similarly, a defendant who contests on the merits without having objected to jurisdiction waives the jurisdictional objection. Thus, (A) is correct because a defendant who has merely appeared and demanded a complaint can still object to jurisdiction.

2. (D)

A bill of particulars is the process by which a party seeks to particularize the general statements in the pleadings. The bill of particulars for any pleadings with respect to a cause of action for negligence must always be verified. [CPLR 3044] (D) is the correct answer. Note that a bill of particulars must also be verified whenever the pleading it particularizes is verified.

3. (D)

In New York, there is a right to trial by jury in actions seeking a judgment for money only, actions to abate and recover damages for a nuisance, and actions where the constitution or a statute so provides, such as annulment proceedings. (A), (B), and (C) are all correct statements of the law and, accordingly, (D) is the correct answer.

4. (B)

Statutes of limitations are arbitrary, fixed periods of time within which an action must be commenced. If an action is not commenced within the applicable time, the defendant may bar the suit. The statute of limitations for medical malpractice is two years and six months. CPLR 214-a provides that the statute of limitations for a medical malpractice suit commences to run when the malpractice occurs, rather than when it was discovered. However, when the doctor commits malpractice but continues to treat the patient for the same injury, the statute of limitations runs from the last treatment. This exception extends the running of the statute of limitations to two years and six months from the time of the last treatment. Here, Barnabus continued to be treated by Dr. Reyes and thus, the statute of limitations would not begin to run until the treatment for the operation has ended. In this case, it was the January 15, 2003, appointment. The continuous treatment exception does not include examinations undertaken at the patient's request for the sole purpose of ascertaining the state of his condition such as the August 17, 2005, appointment here. Thus, the latest date for bringing the action is two years and six months from January 15, 2003, and (B) is the correct answer.

5. (A)

I. is correct. Under CPLR 3101(a)(4), a court can compel a nonparty such as a former employee to make disclosures by whatever device is appropriate. One need not be a party to be subject to disclosure. II. is incorrect. CPLR 3102 permits the use of depositions prior to suit where the potential plaintiff can show that he has a cause of action but is uncertain as to the details. III. is correct. CPLR 3102 allows depositions after trial has begun upon motion to the court. Thus, (A) is correct.

6. (D)

New York has personal jurisdiction over Thurman because Buffalo Chips Corp.'s cause of action arises out of a business transaction in New York. One single transaction is sufficient if the plaintiff's claim is based on this transaction. A court must have both personal jurisdiction over the parties and subject matter jurisdiction over the claim to render a valid judgment. To have personal jurisdiction, there must be some "minimum contact" between the forum and the party. The New York long arm statute limits jurisdiction over nondomiciliaries to certain minimum contact cases, including: (i) doing business in the state [CPLR 301]; (ii) transacting business in the state or contracting anywhere to provide goods or services in the state [CPLR 302(a)(1)]; and (iii) committing a tortious act outside the state that causes injury to a person or property within the state, except for defamation [CPLR 302(a)(3)].

(A) is incorrect because Thurman's in-state activities do not constitute doing business, which contemplates having a corporate-type presence in New York conducting continuous business activities within the state. (B) is incorrect because pursuant to CPLR 302(a)(1), Thurman's in-state activities rise to the level of transacting business. Accordingly, the court does have personal jurisdiction. (C) is incorrect because while Thurman did commit a tortious act (revealing trade secrets) that had an effect in New York, Buffalo Chips Corp. is not suing on that claim but rather on a breach of contract claim. (D) is the correct answer, because Thurman's interviewing and signing a contract in New York is sufficient activity to constitute transacting business.

7. (B)

CPLR 202 states that when a cause of action arises outside of the state of New York the shorter of the two statutes of limitations shall be the controlling time period in which to bring the action, "except that where the cause of action accrued in favor of a resident of the state [of New York] the time limited by the laws of the state [of New York] shall apply."

Almost three years have passed since the cause of action arose in favor of N and P. State X has a two-year statute of limitations in negligence and products liability actions, and New York has a three-year statute. [CPLR 214]

Since the cause of action arose in State X and its statute of limitations is only two years, State X's statute is applied to P's action, and the cause of action is barred.

However, N is a resident of New York. Thus, N's cause of action is not barred since the three-year statute applies to N.

8. (C)

Under CPLR 3215(a), a default judgment may be entered by the clerk only for a sum certain (*e.g.,* on a contract for the sale of goods at a set price), or for a sum that can be made certain in each of the causes of action in the complaint. In other cases the moving party must apply to the court for a judgment by default. Damages arising from fraud or breach of warranty are not for a "sum certain." Thus, the default is not for a sum certain. Therefore, (A) and (B) are incorrect because in these two cases plaintiff must make application to the court for judgment by default within one year after the default. (D) is wrong in light of the foregoing.

9. (A)

CPLR 302(a)(1) provides in part as follows:

Rule 302. Personal jurisdiction by acts of nondomiciliaries.

> (a)   Acts which are the basis of jurisdiction. As to a cause of action arising from any of the acts enumerated in this section, a court may exercise personal jurisdiction over any nondomiciliary, or his executor or administrator, who in person or through an agent:
>
> > 1.   transacts any business within the state or contracts anywhere to supply goods within New York.

Thus, there was a basis for long arm jurisdiction over D, who contracted to supply goods within New York. CPLR 313 provides in part as follows:

> Rule 313. Service without the state giving personal jurisdiction.
>
> A person domiciled in the state or subject to the jurisdiction of the courts of the state under sections 301 or 302, or his executor or administrator, may be served with the summons without the state, in the same manner as service is made within the state, by any person authorized to make service within the state who is a resident of the state or by any person authorized to make service by the laws of the state, territory, possession, or country in which service is made or by any duly qualified attorney, solicitor, barrister, or equivalent in such jurisdiction.

Here, service was made by certified mail, which is not a manner specified in CPLR 308 (although some courts have allowed certified mail service pursuant to CPLR 308(5) in matrimonial actions where service was otherwise impracticable). Here, no court order directing long arm service by certified mail was obtained by P. Thus, the motion to dismiss should be granted because the method of service was improper.

10.   (B)

CPLR 302 governs the court's ability to obtain personal jurisdiction over a nondomiciliary. Briefly, the section permits the court to obtain personal jurisdiction when the nondomiciliary "transacts business within the state or contracts anywhere to supply goods or services in the state," "commits a tortious act within the state, except . . . defamation," "commits a tortious act without the state causing injury . . . within the state," or owns, uses, or possesses any real property situated within the state.

In this case H contracted (leased) for the use of an office suite in New York. The cause of action arose from his obligation under the agreement to pay rent for a set period of time. H's failure to pay gives rise to a cause of action stemming from his action within the state and thus falls under the long arm statute. Thus, service upon H in Utah is valid for this cause of action and (1) should not be dismissed. This answer also eliminates choice (C).

O's second cause of action is for slander. Slander is defamation made orally. As indicated above, if the tort is defamation, personal jurisdiction cannot be properly obtained through use of the long arm statute. Thus, the court can properly dismiss O's second cause of action. Therefore, (B) is the only correct choice.

11.   (A)

With respect to H's motion to strike the notice of examination on the ground that it was premature, the issue is whether a defendant must wait for any period of time before giving notice to the plaintiff for a deposition. While the CPLR requires the plaintiff to secure leave of the court if he wishes to depose a party before the party's time to serve an answer to the complaint has expired [CPLR 3106], no such restriction applies to the defendant. Thus, the court was correct in denying H's motion, and (C) and (D) are incorrect. With respect to D's motion to strike the notice to produce accident and liability policies possessed by D, the issue is whether a plaintiff may notice the defendant to provide insurance policy records before the defendant has served an answer to the complaint, or if, in fact, the plaintiff may inspect such records at all. CPLR 3120 provides that any party may notice another party to produce records at any time after commencement of the suit. Furthermore, the CPLR specifically mentions the contents of an insurance policy as being within the scope of disclosure of the policies. Thus, (B) is also incorrect.

12. (C)

F cannot collect anything from P beyond the $30,000 settlement. Clearly, fundamental contract law indicates that once a plaintiff and defendant have bargained for a settlement, the plaintiff's acceptance of the proffered settlement releases the defendant from any further liability. The facts state that F and P settled for $30,000. Accordingly, P must only pay F $30,000, as stated above. Thus, P would be released from any liability over $30,000. Therefore, (D) is wrong. With respect to how much F can collect from A, under General Obligations Law section 15-108(a), since F settled with one tortfeasor, P, recovery against the remaining tortfeasor, A, will be reduced by the highest of these three figures: (i) $30,000 (the amount P agreed to pay in settlement of F's claim); (ii) $30,000 (the amount P actually paid); or (iii) $50,000 (the apportioned damages that P would have had to pay had he not settled). Thus we reduce the $100,000 award by $50,000, and A's liability would be limited to the $50,000 remaining. Therefore, (B) is wrong. However, A actually has only $10,000 under the facts. Therefore, F can collect no more than the $10,000 and can seek no additional contribution from P, notwithstanding the reduction in his recovery caused by the settlement and A's impoverished condition. Thus, (A) is also wrong.

13. (D)

When a plaintiff's claim is for money damages, either in whole or in part, attachment is an available remedy. Under CPLR 6201, an order of attachment will be granted when one of the following grounds is established: (i) the defendant is a nondomiciliary and nonresident or is an unauthorized foreign corporation; (ii) the defendant resides in or is a domiciliary of New York but cannot be personally served (*i.e.,* cannot be located, not in state, etc.); (iii) the defendant has secreted, disposed of, or removed property from the state with intent to defraud creditors or frustrate enforcement of a judgment; or (iv) the action is based on a judgment, decree, or order of a court of the United States or of any court entitled to full faith and credit in New York or according to the provisions in article 53 (recognition of money judgment from foreign courts). H seeks the provisional remedy of attachment to secure payment to him of monies still owed under the June contract with U Co. In the present action, U Co. is a domestic corporation. Thus, the first ground cannot be established. As for the second ground, service upon a corporation can either be made upon an officer, director, agent, or, in the alternative, the secretary of state. Given these alternative methods of service, it does not appear that H would be unable to properly serve U Co. Thus, the conditions pertaining to impossibility of service are not met. Additionally, H's claim for recovery has not been reduced to a judgment in this or any other state. Therefore, the fourth ground is not available. Finally, there is nothing in the facts to show that the third ground can be established. Therefore, H's request for attachment will be denied because he cannot establish any of the requisite grounds for attachment. Furthermore, under CPLR 6401, receivership is available only when the claim involves a specific subject matter, and there is a danger that the subject matter will be (i) removed from the state; (ii) lost; (iii) materially damaged; or (iv) destroyed. Actions solely to recover sums of money are excluded from this remedy. In this action, H is seeking to obtain the amount of money owed to him by U Co. under his contract. H does not claim that any specific subject matter is owed to him; his claim is only for money damages. Therefore, the remedy of receivership is also unavailable to him. It follows that (A), (B), and (C) are incorrect.

14. (D)

The court should deny M's motion. The issue is whether C's settlement with P bars C from bringing an action against M for contribution or indemnity. General Obligations Law section 15-108 provides that when a tortfeasor such as C settles an action prior to trial, he thereby relinquishes any right to contribution from any other joint tortfeasor, such as M. Thus, to the extent C's impleader claim against M is based on **contribution** for shared responsibility, it is now barred as a matter of law because of the settlement. Thus, (C) is incorrect. However, section 15-108 **does not** apply to claims for **indemnification**, and thus (B) is also incorrect. If C's liability to P is based solely on strict products liability for leasing a defective product, such liability would be the result solely of M's sale of a defective product. Such a 100% shifting of responsibility to M constitutes indemnification; a settlement, therefore, would have no effect on C's rights against M. C could seek full reimbursement of the $50,000 settlement from M. In that event, M would have a right to assert against C whatever defenses C would have had against P. The court might find, for example, that P had no cause of action against C to begin with, thereby rendering the settlement improvident in retrospect. In any case, since it is impossible to state whether C's claim against M sounds in contribution or indemnity, C's third-party action should not be dismissed on the facts, and thus, (D) is a better answer than (A).

15. (D)

Service in a matrimonial action must be made by personal delivery unless the court authorizes substitute service. Leave and mail service is complete when delivery of the summons is made to a person of suitable age and discretion at the defendant's actual place of business, dwelling, or usual place of abode, and by mailing to either the defendant's last known residence or actual place of business. The delivery and mailing must occur within 20 days of each other. Leave and mail is appropriate here so long as authorized by the court. Thus, (D) is the correct answer, and (B) and (C) are incorrect. (A) is incorrect because while the statute requires that the person who does the "leaving" of the service be at least 18 years old, there is no such requirement for the person with whom the papers are left. Lisa is a 17-year-old college bound student. Lisa would be considered a person of suitable age and discretion.

16. (A)

CPLR 3001 grants the supreme court the power to hear actions for declaratory relief as long as a justiciable controversy exists. Thus, (D) is wrong. To be justiciable, the time for performance need not have passed; all that is required is that the controversy be genuine. Here, there is a genuine controversy. Patty believes that she effectively renewed her lease and Larry believes the renewal is ineffective. The fact that the first lease period has not yet lapsed does nothing to change the controversy. Thus, a real controversy over the parties' rights under the option exists, and the supreme courts have jurisdiction over the controversy. Thus, (B) is wrong. (C) is wrong because the lease has not expired.

17. (A)

New York has long arm jurisdiction over a nondomiciliary if: (i) the nondomiciliary transacts business within the state, and (ii) the cause of action arises from that transaction of business. A "substantial relationship" must be established between the nondomiciliary's transactions in New York and a plaintiff's cause of action in order to satisfy the nexus requirement of the statute. Mere possession of a license and registration alone is too insubstantial to warrant a New York court's exercise of personal jurisdiction. Thus, (C) is incorrect. (B) and (D) are incorrect statements of law.

NO-FAULT INSURANCE QUESTIONS

1.   Under the New York No-Fault Motor Vehicle Law, which of the following statements is not correct?

(A) The statute of limitations begins to run on the date of the accident, not when the plaintiff discovers his serious injury.

(B) First party benefits include pain and suffering.

(C) Basic economic loss includes medical expenses and lost earnings.

(D) A person will be excluded from coverage if injured while operating a motor vehicle in a race or a speed test.

NO-FAULT INSURANCE ANSWERS

1.   (B)

(B) is not a correct statement of the law. First party benefits do not include noneconomic loss (*i.e.,* pain and suffering). (A) is a correct statement of the rule because the period of limitation on a plaintiff's claim begins to run on the date of the accident, not when the plaintiff discovers his "serious injury" or when "basic economic loss" is exceeded. (C) is correct because "basic economic loss" includes recovery of all necessary medical expenses, including psychiatric care. Also included is loss of earnings from work that the insured person would have performed had he not been injured. Recovery for lost earnings is limited to $2,000 per month for not more than three years from the accident. (D) is a correct statement of the rule.

PARTNERSHIP QUESTIONS

1.   **A partnership is terminated on which of the following?**

(A) **Bankruptcy of a partner.**

(B) **Incapacity of a partner.**

(C) **The business can only be carried on at a loss.**

(D) **All of the above.**

2.   **Merlyn and Dave were both land surveyors and decided to form a partnership. They each contributed $5,000 in assets. One day when Dave was out in the field measuring for a new satellite tower, his tripod fell over and injured Debbie.**

Tory later joins the partnership and contributes $5,000. The partnership now has a total of $15,000 in assets. Debbie files an action against the partnership for her injuries caused by Dave's tripod and all the partners were duly served. Debbie obtains a $20,000 judgment. Debbie can satisfy the judgment against:

(A) **The partnership property and liability for the remainder is split evenly among Merlyn, Dave, and Tory personally.**

(B) **The partnership property and liability for the remainder from Merlyn and Dave personally.**

(C) **The partnership property only.**

(D) **None of the above.**

3.   **Mike and Bill form a partnership to which each contributes $1,000. Mike is 16 years old; Bill is 22 years old. The partnership incurs debts of $3,000. What is the liability of each partner?**

(A) **Each is liable only to the extent of his capital contribution.**

(B) **Mike and Bill are equally liable for all the debts.**

(C) **Bill is solely liable for the debts.**

(D) **Mike is only liable to the extent of his capital contribution.**

4.   **John and Mary form a partnership for the purpose of making wagers on dog racing. Such an enterprise is prohibited under the penal law. The money secured by the enterprise is deposited in National Bank under Mary's name. Mary is not sharing the profits earned with John. John commences an action to compel an accounting of the partnership funds held by Mary. The court will:**

(A) **Grant John's petition and compel Mary to give an accounting of the funds held in her name since John is a partner.**

(B) **Refuse to grant the accounting on the grounds of illegality of the partnership.**

(C) Grant the accounting on principles of equity.

(D) Refuse to grant the accounting since the funds became Mary's personal funds when they were deposited in her name.

5.   Joe and Pat are partners. The partnership owns Blackacre. Joe borrows money from Sam and gives Sam a mortgage on his interest in Blackacre. Joe defaults on the loan. What is Sam's remedy?

(A) Sam may foreclose on Blackacre.

(B) Sam may hold Joe and Pat personally liable on the note secured by the mortgage.

(C) Sam may hold Joe alone personally liable on the note secured by the mortgage.

(D) Sam may hold only the partnership liable for the note secured by the mortgage.

6.   A, B, C, and D form a partnership. C goes to Africa and is killed on January 1. On January 2, without notice of C's death, A contracts on behalf of the partnership to build a house. On January 3, after he has notice that C is dead, B contracts to purchase lumber on behalf of the partnership. Both contracts result in a loss to the partnership.

C's estate will be liable on:

(A) A's contract.

(B) B's contract.

(C) Both.

(D) Neither.

PARTNERSHIP ANSWERS

1. **(D)**

When there is a change in the relationship of the partners caused by any partner ceasing to be associated in the carrying on of the business, the partnership will dissolve. Dissolution may be caused either by (i) an act of the parties; (ii) operation of law; or (iii) a court decree. (A), (B), and (C) each fit one of these categories. (A) is correct because the bankruptcy of any partner will dissolve the partnership. [Partnership Law §62(5)] (B) is correct because the court may find sufficient reason to dissolve the partnership where a partner has been declared incompetent in a judicial proceeding or is shown to be of unsound mind. [Partnership Law §63(1)(a)] (C) is correct because the court may issue a decree of dissolution if, with sufficient reason, it finds that the business can only be carried on at a loss. [Partnership Law §63(1)(e)] Accordingly, (D) is the correct answer.

2. **(B)**

For torts committed by any partner or employee of the firm in the ordinary course of partnership business, partners will be jointly and severally liable. Where there is joint and several liability, an action may be brought against any one or more of the partners or the partnership. The judgment is personally binding only if a partner has been served. Each partner is personally and individually liable for the entire amount of all partnership obligations. An incoming partner's liability for obligations that arose before becoming a partner, however, can be satisfied only out of partnership property. Thus, Debbie's judgment can be satisfied out of the entire partnership property with the remainder from Dave and Merlyn personally. Tory is not personally liable for any obligation incurred by the partnership before he became a member. (B) is the correct answer.

3. **(D)**

If a would-be partner lacks capacity, such as nonage, he is not personally liable for the obligations of the partnership. However, such a partner is bound to the extent of his capital contributions. Since Mike is a minor, he is liable for the partnership debts only to the extent of his $1,000 capital contribution.

4. **(B)**

The purpose for which the partnership is formed must be legal. The illegality of the enterprise will cause the partnership to be void. Where a partnership is formed for an illegal purpose, the court will compel neither an accounting nor a settlement of partnership affairs.

5. **(C)**

A partner's ownership interest in any specific item of partnership property is not that of outright ownership but merely that of a tenant in the partnership. An attempted mortgage of a partner's interest in specific partnership property has no effect upon the passing of title to the property. Sam, the mortgagee, has no rights against the property. Further, since the loan was personal to Joe, Sam has no rights against Pat or the partnership.

6. **(A)**

Unless there is a specific agreement to the contrary, death of a partner will dissolve the partnership by operation of law. However, the authority of a partner to act for the partnership ceases only when he receives knowledge or notice of the partner's death. Here, the January 2 contract came before notice of

C's death, so it binds the partnership and consequently C's estate. B's contract, however, came after notice. Since the partnership was dissolved, B had no power to bind the partnership on this contract. Thus, (A) is the correct answer.

PERSONAL PROPERTY QUESTIONS

1.   Mike and Gillie drove their new Honda Accord to the Bronx to visit Mike's father. They decided to park their car in a pay lot instead of parking on the street. After visiting Mike's father for about three hours, Mike and Gillie returned to the lot to pick up their car. The parking lot attendant informed them that he could not locate their keys so Mike had no choice but to leave the car in the lot and take a cab home. The next day Mike returned to the lot to retrieve his car. Unfortunately the night before, vandals broke into Mike's car and stole everything in his glove compartment and his car radio. If Mike brings an action for damages against the parking lot, he will:

(A) Not prevail, because he did not transfer title, only possession, to the parking lot.

(B) Not prevail, because he was parking his car at his own risk.

(C) Prevail, because he surrendered his keys, thus creating a bailment situation in which the bailee must exercise a duty of ordinary care.

(D) Prevail, because the parking lot owed him an absolute duty of care.

PERSONAL PROPERTY ANSWERS

1.   (C)

When goods have been lost, destroyed, or damaged during a bailment, the burden is on the bailee to prove that such loss was caused without a breach of his duty of care. A bailment is the relationship created by the transfer of possession of an item of personal property by one called the bailor to another called the bailee, for the accomplishment of a certain purpose. In the situation of a parking lot, a bailment will occur if the owner of the automobile surrenders the keys to the vehicle to the parking lot attendant. A bailee owes a duty of ordinary care and, to establish a prima facie case, the bailor need only show that a bailment was created, he made proper demand for the return of the goods, and the goods were returned in a damaged state. Thus, (C) is the correct answer.

PROFESSIONAL RESPONSIBILITY QUESTIONS

1.   Plaintiff Ava and Brian married in 1975. Under Brian's employee benefit plan, a surviving spouse would be eligible to receive either retirement benefits or survivorship benefits. The couple separated in 1990, after Brian's interest in the plan had vested. In 1991, Ava hired the law firm TopFirm, Inc., defendants, to represent her in the divorce. In 1992, TopFirm, Inc., and Brian's lawyer entered the following stipulation of settlement: "It is agreed that Ava will receive a portion of Brian's pension plan and the figures shall be divided as indicated by recourse to an order, which TopFirm, Inc.'s, office will prepare and submit to the court either simultaneously with or shortly after the judgment of divorce."

TopFirm, Inc., never prepared the order. The stipulation of settlement was incorporated but not merged into the judgment of divorce. Ava remained unaware that the order was never prepared or filed, until 2002, upon Brian's death. TopFirm, Inc., sought unsuccessfully to obtain for Ava the preretirement death benefits payable under Brian's employee benefit plan. The plan administrator ultimately determined that because there was no order naming Ava as the surviving spouse under the plan, Ava was ineligible to receive preretirement death benefits.

TopFirm, Inc., also represented Ava in a family court support action against Brian that concluded in 2000, and in various real estate dealings concluding in 2001. There is no record evidence that Ava had further contact with TopFirm, Inc., regarding the stipulation, divorce judgment, order, or employee benefit plan until 2002.

In 2002, Ava brought a legal malpractice claim, alleging malpractice on the part of TopFirm, Inc. Is this claim time barred?

(A) Yes, because the statute of limitations for legal malpractice is three years from the date of discovery of the malpractice.

(B) Yes, because the actionable wrong, giving rise to the injury, occurred on or before the date that the final judgment was entered.

(C) No, because TopFirm, Inc., had continuously represented Ava both in the same court and on other related matters.

(D) Both (A) and (B).

PROFESSIONAL RESPONSIBILITY ANSWERS

1.   (B)

The New York Court of Appeals held "what is important is when the malpractice was committed, not when the client discovered it." Under the facts, the accrual date would be either the date that the stipulation was entered into or the date on which the stipulation was incorporated into the judgment. Both of these dates are more than three years prior to the commencement of this action. The statute of limitations on a malpractice claim is tolled by the "continuous representation" doctrine only when the attorney further represents the client on the same specific matter that gave rise to the malpractice claim. Thus, (A) and (C) are incorrect answers and (B) is the correct answer.

REAL PROPERTY QUESTIONS

1.   Horace and Wanda marry in 1981. Wanda gives birth to Socrates the following year. In 1991, Aunt Hilda conveys Blackacre to Horace and Wanda as tenants in common. Horace dies in 2001 and leaves all his property to Socrates. Who owns Blackacre?

(A) Wanda, because there was a tenancy by the entirety by operation of law.

(B) Socrates and Wanda, because there was a tenancy in common.

(C) Socrates and Wanda, because there was a joint tenancy by operation of law.

(D) Socrates, because the will is controlling.

2.   Frank purports to convey a 100-acre tract of land, known to those in the community as Billy Hills, to Jack by means of a defective deed. Frank does not own Billy Hills, which is an un-occupied forested area. Believing that he now owns the property, Jack occupies 35 acres of the tract and continues in possession for 12 years. What does Jack have title to by adverse posses-sion?

(A) Nothing.

(B) 35 acres.

(C) 100 acres.

(D) 50 acres.

3.   Dave conveys Redacre to Simon, Alvin, and Theodore as joint tenants with rights of survi-vorship. Subsequently, Simon dies leaving a will which states: "I leave all my interest in Redacre to my son Joe." Which of the following is true?

(A) Alvin, Theodore, and Joe each have an undivided 1/3 interest in Redacre.

(B) The bequest to Joe is invalid because it violates the Rule Against Suspension of Alienation.

(C) Alvin and Theodore each have an undivided 1/2 interest in Redacre.

(D) Redacre reverts to Dave.

4.   Bambi conveys Blueacre to Flower and Thumper as joint tenants. Thereafter, a creditor of Flower sues him for breach of contract and obtains a judgment. There is no other action taken. Flower then dies. Which of the following is true?

(A) Thumper owns Blueacre.

(B) Thumper and the creditor are joint tenants in Blueacre.

(C) Thumper and the creditor are tenants in common in Blueacre.

(D) The creditor may levy on Blueacre to satisfy the judgment.

5. Lola leases her warehouse to Tom for an indefinite term at $1,500 per month. Tom takes possession on June 1, 2000. On November 1, 2002, Tom informs Lola that he will be renting another warehouse and that he plans to vacate Lola's warehouse on January 1, 2003. On January 1, 2003, Tom's new warehouse is not ready for use, and Tom holds over in Lola's warehouse until March 30, 2003. How much rent does Tom owe Lola?

(A) $4,500.

(B) The fair market value of three months' rent.

(C) $9,000.

(D) Nothing if Lola failed to commence eviction proceedings.

6. Sam executed a contract of sale with Bill to convey Sam's house and property in Queens, New York. Prior to the closing and before Bill takes possession, the house is destroyed by fire without the fault of either Sam or Bill. Who bears the risk of loss?

(A) Sam.

(B) Bill.

(C) Sam and Bill share the loss.

(D) The financing lender of Bill.

7. On June 1, 1993, F and H entered into an agreement whereby H would assist F in maintaining Acreacre, F's farm, for five years, during which H would receive free room and board from F and at the end of which F would convey Acreacre to H and herself as joint tenants. On June 1, 1998, H completed the term of employment and received from F a deed to Acreacre, drafted in accordance with the agreement. The next day H recorded the deed and returned to Acreacre, whereupon F shot herself dead for various reasons, including her distress concerning her previous financial transactions.

One such transaction was the sale of Acreacre by F to O in 1988, accomplished by receiving the purchase price from O and delivering to O a deed that O recorded as soon as she learned of F's death. Another was the mortgage F executed on Acreacre in 1989, with B as mortgagee, in consideration of B's postponing until 2001 the payment of a debt owed by F to B since 1987. B recorded the mortgage just before telling O about F's death. Title to Acreacre is held by:

(A) O only.

(B) O, subject to the mortgage.

(C) H only.

(D) H, subject to the mortgage.

8. In 1970, X died leaving Farmacre, a prosperous apple orchard, to W, his wife, for life, with his children Charlie and Donald to take as joint remaindermen. In that same year, Donald left for the West Coast to seek his fortune as an orchardist in Washington state. Charlie stayed on

Farmacre, operating the orchard and taking care of W. In 1981, W died, after which Charlie continued to live on Farmacre and operate the orchard. At all times Charlie paid all expenses, including real estate taxes and insurance premiums. In 2001, half of Donald's Washington state apple orchard empire was destroyed by ash from an explosion of the Mt. St. Helens volcano. In 2002, after a 32-year absence, Donald showed up at Farmacre and demanded that Charlie cut him in on the operations and profits. Charlie refused, saying that he owns the property himself now.

Does Donald have any rights in Farmacre?

(A) No, because Charlie obtained title in his own right in 1990.

(B) Yes.

(C) No, because Charlie obtained title in his own right by 2002.

(D) No, because Donald has effectively abandoned his rights by being absent for 32 years.

9.   S owns a number of properties that are subject to a restrictive covenant which limits development on this land to single family homes. S recently leased a portion of one of the properties to a telecommunications company for the purpose of constructing an antenna and equipment storage shed to provide cellular telephone service in the surrounding area. After considering multiple sites, the town approved a special permit for the construction of the antenna on S's property and construction began. D, the owner of a number of lots in the subdivision, commenced an action for permanent injunction against the building of the antenna based on the restrictive covenants. S believes that the restrictive covenant is unenforceable because: (1) the town's issuance of a special permit to construct the antenna precluded enforcement of the covenant; and (2) it unreasonably restricts land use and is therefore void as against public policy.

The restrictive covenant may not be enforced by D because of:

(A) (1) but not (2).

(B) (2) but not (1).

(C) Both (1) and (2).

(D) The restrictive covenant may be enforced by D.

REAL PROPERTY ANSWERS

1. (B)

Under the New York Estate, Powers, and Trusts Law, a grant by anyone to a husband and wife results in the creation of a tenancy by the entirety unless the grantor declares the tenancy to be a joint tenancy or a tenancy in common. Here, since Blackacre is a tenancy in common, there is no right of survivorship. Horace and Wanda each have a distinct and undivided interest in Blackacre which is freely alienable. Thus, from the testamentary transfer, Socrates becomes the owner of Horace's interest in Blackacre, and Socrates and Wanda own Blackacre as tenants in common. (B) is the correct answer.

2. (C)

Under the doctrine of ***constructive adverse possession***, where the claimant enters into actual possession of some portion of the property under color of title, such as a defective deed, she is deemed to be in ***possession of the entire property*** described in the instrument, provided that the following conditions are met: (i) the adverse possessor enters the property under a ***good faith belief*** that the instrument of conveyance is valid; (ii) the adverse possessor occupies a ***significant portion*** of the property as compared to the whole; and (iii) the property described in the deed is ***understood in the community*** to be a single parcel. Jack meets the first requirement because he has a good faith belief in the validity of the deed. The second condition merely requires occupation sufficient to put members of the community on notice of the adverse possessor's existence on the single parcel. The third condition is met by the facts; the tract is known as Billy Hills.

3. (C)

Alvin and Theodore each have an undivided 1/2 interest in Redacre. The right of a surviving joint tenant to the whole property takes precedence over any devisees under the will of a deceased joint tenant.

4. (A)

Thumper owns Blueacre in its entirety as the surviving joint tenant. The right of survivorship takes precedence over any creditors of a deceased joint tenant. To satisfy a judgment out of a joint tenant's property interest, a judgment creditor must sever the tenancy by levy execution prior to the debtor-joint tenant's death.

5. (C)

Under New York law, Tom owes double rent for each month that he held over. Where a tenant holds a lease of indefinite duration, notifies the landlord of an intention to quit the premises, and then fails to deliver possession at the specified time, the tenant must pay the landlord double the rent otherwise payable, for as long as he continues in possession. [N.Y. Real Prop. Law §229]

6. (A)

Sam bears the risk of loss. New York has adopted the Uniform Vendor and Purchasers Risk Act. [N.Y. Gen. Oblig. Law §5-1311] Under this statute, prior to the conveyance of title or the transfer of possession to the purchaser, all loss falls on the vendor if the purchaser is without fault.

7.   (C)

Pursuant to Real Property Law section 291, a subsequent bona fide purchaser will prevail if and only if he is the first to record. Here, H prevails over O and the mortgage because he recorded his interest prior to them. Thus, (A), (B), and (D) are incorrect.

8.   (C)

The 20-year adverse possession statute for co-tenants does not run against the holder of a future interest (*e.g.,* a remainder) until that interest becomes possessory. This is because until the prior present estate terminates, the holder of the future interest has no right to possession and thus no cause of action against a wrongful possessor. Here, the statute could not have begun to run in Charlie's favor until W's death in 1981. Actual possession of property held in concurrent ownership by one concurrent owner for the statutory period is sufficient to give that possessor title to the whole estate to the exclusion of his co-tenant when the other concurrent owner is absent (this is implied ouster). Accordingly, (C) is correct.

9.   (D)

The issuance of a special permit is separate and distinct from the right to enforce the restrictive covenant. Other sites not subject to the covenant were available. Restrictive covenants will be enforced when the intention of the parties is clear and the limitation is reasonable and not offensive to public policy. The balancing of the equities favors enforcement of the restrictive covenant limiting development to single family homes. The hardship here was largely self-created since the landowner proceeded with the construction with knowledge of the covenant and of the other landowner's intention to enforce the covenant. Because the restrictive covenant may be enforced, (A), (B), and (C) are incorrect.

SALES QUESTIONS

1.   Jerry owns a home improvement store. Jerry usually orders most of his plumbing materials from Kramer. On February 29, Jerry ordered 20 white sinks from Kramer. Twenty blue sinks were delivered to Jerry's store three days later. Accordingly, Jerry immediately called Kramer to tell him that he delivered the wrong sinks. Kramer informed Jerry that he would send replacement sinks and pick up the blue sinks the following week. Jerry agreed to set the blue sinks aside in his storeroom. Later that day, Jerry received a phone call from George who asked Jerry to pick out 20 sheets of oak paneling to be picked up and paid for the next day. Jerry selected the paneling for George and set it aside. After Jerry closed the store for the evening, a fire started in the basement. The fire was caused by vandals and not due to any negligence on Jerry's part. Jerry's store was completely destroyed along with the blue sinks and oak paneling. Which of the following statements is correct?

(A) Jerry bears the risk of loss on the sinks only.

(B) Jerry bears the risk of loss on the paneling only.

(C) Jerry bears the risk of loss on both the sinks and the paneling.

(D) Jerry bears the risk of loss on neither the sinks nor the paneling.

2.   On September 6, B went to S's offices in Troy and examined a catalog for transistor switches. Before leaving, B signed a purchase order for 500 transistor switches, and requested shipment to his office in Rome as soon as possible. B agreed to pay the catalog price of $10 per switch, F.O.B. Troy. Upon returning to his offices in Rome on September 7, B discovered that he could obtain the same transistor switches from T for $9 per switch. On that same day, B wrote to S to cancel his order. S received the letter of cancellation on September 9. On the previous day, S had delivered the 500 switches to Motor Express, a trucking carrier, for shipment to B in Rome. When S received B's letter he immediately telegraphed B to reject B's cancellation and informed him that the switches had already been shipped. Through the fault of the telegraph company, B did not receive S's telegram until September 12. On that same day, Motor Express delivered the switches to B in Rome, but B refused delivery. S was unsuccessful in an attempt to resell the switches in Rome and directed Motor Express to return them to Troy. Motor Express charged S $500 for the round trip from Troy to Rome. If S seeks to recover the $500 delivery charge, he can successfully seek recovery from:

(A) B.

(B) The telegraph company.

(C) B and the telegraph company.

(D) Neither B nor the telegraph company.

3.   G and C entered into a written agreement whereby G agreed to provide windows to C's specifications no later than May 30 for $12,000. G's profit on the sale was to be $2,000. On May 15, G delivered windows to C; however, the windows did not conform to C's specifications. C refused the windows and notified G in writing that day. On May 28, G delivered new windows that conformed to C's specifications, but C had already purchased the windows he needed from another supplier for $13,000 and refused to accept G's second shipment. G sold the windows to another

buyer for $12,000. G buys windows from A. A can supply G with as many windows as G needs, at anytime. G has sued C on a theory of breach of contract, and C has counterclaimed on the same theory. As between the parties:

(A) C is entitled to recover $1,000, which is the difference between the amount C contracted to pay G and the amount C was forced to pay for conforming goods.

(B) G is not entitled to recover because he resold the windows for the amount contracted with C.

(C) Neither party has a right of recovery against the other under a theory of unclean hands.

(D) G is entitled to $2,000 lost profits.

4.   On January 1, P, the owner of a jewelry store, bought a burglar alarm from M, a manufacturer of security systems. The burglar alarm was installed by M, and P signed M's standard contract of sale, which stated that, ". . . M has no responsibility for any losses arising from failure of the burglar alarm system. However, if the burglar system fails to function, P will receive the sum of $50 as his sole remedy."

On March 15, P's store was broken into, and P sustained a loss of $50,000 as a result of the alarm system failing to operate properly. P commenced an action against M for the sum of $50,000. M interposed an affirmative defense based upon the quoted term of the agreement. As between the parties:

(A) P is entitled to recover $50,000 based on breach of an express warranty that the alarm would function properly.

(B) P is entitled to recover $50 based on breach of an express warranty that the alarm would function properly.

(C) M is not entitled to limit recovery to $50 because such a limitation is unconscionable.

(D) M is not entitled to limit recovery to $50 because liquidated damages clauses are prohibited in contracts governed by the U.C.C.

5.   X manufactures unique camera lenses. X agrees with Y on May 1, to manufacture specially, to Y's specifications, 100 lenses at $100 each, delivery to be August 31, and payment to be made 10 days thereafter. X immediately begins to manufacture the lenses. Subsequently, X learns on June 1 that he will be unable to manufacture the goods at the agreed upon price. X calls Y to tell him of his dilemma and asks that the price be increased to $150 per unit. Y tells X that he is not happy about the change, but really needs the lenses, and thus agrees in a signed memo. X does not sign the memo. X delivers the goods on time and bills Y for $15,000. Y responds that X is only entitled to $10,000 and that he will pay only that amount. X is entitled to recover:

(A) $10,000 because the modification fails for lack of consideration.

(B) $10,000 because the modification fails to satisfy the Statute of Frauds.

(C) $10,000 because the modification was obtained under duress, and thus, is unenforceable.

(D) $15,000.

6. Iris and Violet entered into a requirements contract whereby Iris would provide Violet with her monthly rosebud requirements for Violet's flower shop at a set price for a period of one year. The contract was terminable upon 30 days written notice to Violet from Iris. It did not grant Violet a similar right of termination. Both Iris and Violet duly executed the contract. Is the contract valid?

(A) Yes, because both parties duly executed the contract.

(B) No, it is void due to lack of mutuality.

(C) No, it is void due to unconscionability.

(D) No, it is void due to the terms being illusory.

7. In September, Hillary, a manufacturer of toy missiles in Albany, telephoned Holly, a large volume plastics wholesaler who was also located in Albany. Hillary ordered 6,000 sheets of plastic at an agreed upon price of $2 per sheet for a total of $12,000. Delivery was to be made by truck at Hillary's plant on December 15. The parties executed a written contract setting forth the forgoing terms. In November, Hillary determined that the market for toy missiles had bottomed out, and she switched over her business to manufacturing wooden toy boats. Hillary contacted Holly on November 15, and informed her that she was no longer interested in purchasing the plastic from her. Holly made no attempt to deliver the plastic to Hillary, and resold the 6,000 sheets to George, a regular customer and manufacturer of plastic coffee mugs, for $2 per sheet on February 15. Holly has contacted you to see what rights, if any, she has against Hillary. You inform her that she has a right to recover:

(A) Nothing, because she has suffered no damages due to her ability to resell the plastic at $2 per sheet.

(B) Nothing, because she failed to deliver the plastic to Hillary as agreed to under the contract.

(C) The difference between the contract price and market price plus incidental and consequential damages.

(D) Lost profits and incidental damages.

SALES ANSWERS

1.   (B)

The general rule is that if the seller is a merchant, risk of loss passes to the buyer only when the buyer has taken physical possession of the goods. Jerry clearly is a merchant here (one who deals in goods of the kind sold), and so the risk of loss for the paneling had not yet passed to the buyer when the paneling was destroyed because the paneling was still in possession of the seller, Jerry. Thus, Jerry bears the risk of loss on the paneling. The rule for nonconforming goods is different. If a seller sends a buyer nonconforming goods (the blue sinks) and the buyer (Jerry) informs the seller that the buyer is rejecting because of the nonconformity, risk of loss remains with the seller even though the buyer has possession of the goods. Thus, Jerry would not bear the risk of loss of the sinks.

2.   (A)

S may recover the $500 freight charge from B. The issue is whether a seller can recover damages for nonacceptance of shipped goods. U.C.C. section 2-708 provides that a seller's damages for nonacceptance of goods shall include incidental damages, defined in section 2-710 to include shipping charges. B and S had a valid contract for the transistors, which B breached by nonacceptance. Although S's catalog cannot be construed as an offer because of the lack of an identified offeree, it was a general offer to the public, and B's signed order to S could be construed as an offer from S to B. An ambiguous offer for the purchase of goods may be accepted by a promise to ship or by prompt shipment. Thus, S accepted by promptly shipping. B's attempt to cancel his offer was not effective because revocations are not effective until received, and S did not receive the revocation until after he accepted the contract by shipping the transistor switches. B's telegram rejecting S's revocation and its delayed transmission are immaterial because S was under no duty to reject B's rejection, and thus, (B) and (C) are wrong. By not accepting the goods, B was in breach. Thus, S may recover the $500 from B, and (D) is wrong.

3.   (D)

G is entitled to recover lost profits from C. G is a "lost volume" seller; that is, he had enough windows to supply all comers, including C. His remedy is to recover the profit he would have made had C not breached. Because he can sell the same windows to someone else, G's only loss is his profit, and (B) is wrong. (A) is incorrect because, although G initially sent windows that did not conform to C's specifications, the date of performance under the contract was May 30, and G properly cured prior to the expiration of the contract date. G was thus not in breach of contract, but C's refusal to accept the conforming goods is a breach of the contract. (C) has no application to the present fact pattern.

4.   (B)

Under section 2-313, when a buyer relies upon any affirmation of fact or promise made by the seller, an express warranty is created if the statement is the basis for the bargain. Also, the Magnuson-Moss Act provides that when a seller undertakes in writing to replace, repair, refund, or take other remedial action in the event that its product does not meet the specifications set forth in the agreement, the writing becomes a basis of the bargain for purposes other than resale of the product. Thus, the contract provision in question may have created an express warranty. By promising to pay $50 if the alarm failed, M was warranting that the alarm would function properly. However, the U.C.C. allows contract provisions limiting damages for breach of warranty to be enforced provided that limitation is not unconscionable. Thus, (D) is wrong. Liquidated damages for breach of warranty are valid if reasonable in light of anticipated or actual harm, difficulties of proof, and inconvenience or feasibility of other remedies. Under these facts, the $50 limitation is reasonable and will be enforced. Thus, (A) and (C) are wrong.

5.   (D)

Under the U.C.C., contract modifications sought in good faith are binding without consideration. Here, X sought the modification in good faith, so lack of consideration is no defense, and thus, (A) is wrong. Contract modifications must meet the Statute of Frauds requirement if the contract as modified is within the Statute of Frauds. Under the Statute of Frauds, contracts for the sale of goods at a price of $500 or more are not enforceable unless there is some writing signed by the party to be charged or that party's agent. However, a writing is not required if the goods are to be specially made for the buyer and are not suitable for sale to others in the ordinary course of the seller's business. Here, Y signed a memo containing the modified term. Moreover, Y was bound on the original and modified contract even absent a writing since the contract here falls into the exception to the Statute of Frauds for specially manufactured goods. Thus, (B) is wrong. Finally, there is nothing in the fact pattern that indicates the use of force, or threat of force which would constitute duress, and thus (C) is wrong.

6.   (A)

The contract is valid. The issue is whether a requirements contract cancelable on 30 days' notice is enforceable. A contract will not be binding unless there is consideration on both sides. Each party must be mutually bound to the terms of a valid agreement. Agreements pursuant to which one party is bound and the other is not will be deemed illusory by a court. However, pursuant to U.C.C. section 2-306, requirements contracts generally present adequate consideration on both sides of the contract because one party is bound to supply the goods, and the other has lost her right to buy goods from another source. Thus, (D) is wrong. Furthermore, although an unqualified right to terminate a contract could also render a contract illusory, if the right to terminate is restricted in any way, the consideration will be valid and the contract will be upheld. In the instant case, Iris has agreed to give Violet 30 days' notice of her intention to terminate the contract. Since her right to terminate is restricted, there is mutuality of obligation between the parties to the contract, and it is valid. Thus, (B) is wrong. Finally, (C) is wrong because there is nothing in this fact pattern that would indicate that the contract is so one-sided as to be unconscionable.

7.   (D)

When there is an anticipatory repudiation of a contract by the buyer, the seller is under no duty to perform and thus, (B) is wrong. Ordinarily, the seller is entitled to recover incidental damages plus the difference between the contract price and the market price on the date performance was due. The seller is also entitled to recover the difference between the contract price and the resale price of the goods. If damages based on these calculations do not put the seller in as good a position as performance by the buyer would have, then the seller may recover lost profits plus incidental damages. U.C.C. section 2-703, which provides these remedies, does not demand an election of remedies, but considers them cumulative in nature. The facts of each case determine whether the pursuance of one remedy will bar the pursuit of another. Here, Holly has resold the goods for the same price as the contract price, and it would be unjust to allow her double recovery for goods that she has already been able to sell at the contract price, and thus (C) is wrong. However, it took Hillary an additional period of two months from the date of performance of the contract to sell at that price. Therefore, Holly is entitled to incidental damages for the resale and costs for the period that she held the goods, and thus, (A) is wrong. In addition, since Holly is a volume seller, Hillary may be liable to her for lost profits since Holly would have been able to make that additional sale of plastic but for the fact that Hillary breached. Thus, Holly is also entitled to her lost profits.

SECURED TRANSACTIONS QUESTIONS

1.   On May 1, Dan applies for a $10,000 loan from Bank A. Dan signs a financing statement and a security agreement granting a security interest in Dan's equipment. On May 2, after checking the files and finding no competing interests, Bank A files the financing statement. On May 3, Dan borrows $20,000 from Bank B, giving Bank B a security interest in the same equipment. Bank B loans the money and immediately files a financing statement covering the equipment. On May 10, Bank A loans Dan $10,000 from the loan application he submitted on May 1. Who has priority to the equipment?

(A) Bank A.

(B) Bank B.

(C) Neither.

(D) If a conflict over priority arises, Banks A and B must divide their interests.

SECURED TRANSACTIONS ANSWERS

1.   (A)

When there are conflicting perfected security interests in the same collateral, priority goes to which-ever party was the first to either file or perfect. Although perfection occurs upon the actual lending of the money to Dan, Bank A has priority to the equipment under the "first to file or perfect" rule [U.C.C. §9-322(a)(1)] since Bank A was the first to file, notwithstanding the fact that Bank B filed and perfected its security interest before Bank A perfected its security interest.

TORTS QUESTIONS

1.   Rocco was playing in an amateur soccer game and was injured when a ball hit him in the head. Maurizio kicked the ball that injured Rocco. Prior to the game, Maurizio had approached Rocco and said, "today is your day to bleed." Maurizio will not be liable in tort for a battery to Rocco if:

(A) Rocco breached his duty of care.

(B) Rocco assumed the risk by playing in the game.

(C) Rocco hit Maurizio in the head with a ball earlier.

(D) Rocco consented to the injury merely by playing in the game.

2.   At the annual beer bash at the Steer, Dennis told his friends that Christine sleeps with all the guys in his band. The next day, Dennis wrote to his sister Pam, and told her that Christine sells cocaine to all his friends. Christine discovers from Ray what Dennis has been saying about her and brings an action against Dennis for libel and slander. Christine can recover for:

(A) The letter.

(B) The statement.

(C) Neither the letter nor the statement.

(D) Both the letter and the statement.

3.   Matt and Bob were owners of the Battleship Carpentry Company of Rochester, the most reputable home construction company in western New York. Their latest job was to construct the new Starship Enterprise Apartment Complex in Brighton for the Ready Made Realty Company. Matt and Bob had been on the job about three weeks and nearly had the foundation and walls complete. Before they could continue, scaffolding had to be erected and Bob volunteered to climb the ladder to attach the structure. Bob climbed the ladder and, to Matt's dismay, the side of the ladder broke away from the rungs and Bob plunged to the ground. Bob commenced an action against the Ready Made Realty Company who had supplied the ladders. If Bob prevails it will be because:

(A) The defendant did not meet the ordinary due care of a reasonably prudent person.

(B) The defendant did not meet the special statutory standard of care to protect construction workers.

(C) The defendant failed to warn Bob that climbing the ladder was inherently dangerous.

(D) Bob will not prevail because the injury was not foreseeable.

4.   Which of the following correctly states the law in New York?

(A) To establish a prima facie case for intentional infliction of emotional distress or negligent infliction of emotional distress, the plaintiff must prove he suffered physical impact or physical manifestation of psychological trauma.

(B) To establish a prima facie case for intentional infliction of emotional distress, but not for negligent infliction of emotional distress, the plaintiff need not prove he suffered physical impact or physical manifestation of psychological trauma.

(C) To establish a prima facie case for negligent infliction of emotional distress, the plaintiff must prove he suffered physical impact or psychological trauma.

(D) None of the above.

5.   The *Get Up and Shout!*, a weekly sports tabloid, learned that Bryce Kretzer, a well-known football player, was hospitalized with a rare, genetic disease. Bryce died 10 days later. The next day, the *Get Up and Shout!* carried the following front-page headline: "Football Player Bryce Kretzer Hospitalized—AIDS to Blame?" If Bryce's personal representative sues the tabloid for defamation, he will:

(A) Not prevail, because defamation of a deceased person is not actionable.

(B) Not prevail, because the public has a First Amendment right to know.

(C) Prevail, but only if Bryce would have a cause of action against the tabloid if he were alive.

(D) Prevail, but only if the matter is deemed not to be of public concern.

6.   Gillie and Mike gave their son, Adonis, a beautiful red 10-speed bicycle for his seventh birthday. Adonis was told that he was not to ride his bike unless one of his parents was running alongside him. One spring afternoon, Mike, Gillie, and Adonis were in their front yard enjoying the weather and Adonis wanted to ride his bicycle. Gillie and Mike were too tired to run along-side Adonis and told him to wait. They then fell asleep, taking a brief cat-nap. Seeing that his parents were not watching him, Adonis got on his bike and rode off into the street. Mike and Gillie woke up and saw their son headed into the path of Carrie Cabdriver and both began running after him. Carrie Cabdriver swerved to miss the boy and drove into a tree. Carrie Cabdriver's sister, Constance, was sitting in the front seat because Carrie was bringing her to visit their mother before he went to work. When Carrie swerved to miss hitting Adonis, Constance was thrown through the windshield and broke every bone in her face. In the action by Constance against Mike, Mike seeks to use evidence that Constance was not wearing her seat belt. Which of the following statements is correct?

(A) Mike may plead failure to use the seat belt as an affirmative defense.

(B) Mike may introduce evidence that Constance failed to use an available seat belt to mitigate the damages.

(C) Mike may not use failure to use an available seat belt on the issue of liability.

(D) All of the above.

7.   W mailed a check to one of her creditors, S, in the amount of $200. A mail carrier took W's letter and, while on an authorized coffee break, left his bag unattended in a high crime area. The bag was taken by H, a thief. H took W's check made payable to the creditor, and indorsed it, "Pay to the order of H. [Signed] S." He then presented it for payment, and received $200 from the bank from which the check was drawn. Assuming that H cannot be apprehended, W's rights against the United States Postal Service are:

(A) The Postal Service is liable to W for the $200 because of the negligent act of its servant.

(B) The Postal Service is not liable to W for the $200 because the check was stolen while the mail carrier was on break.

(C) The Postal Service is not liable to W for the $200 because the theft of the bag was a superceding, intervening force.

(D) The Postal Service is not liable to W for the $200 because of the doctrine of sovereign immunity.

8.   B sued A to recover damages for his serious personal injuries resulting from a car accident with A. At the trial X, B's attorney, offered proof showing that A, on his plea of guilty, had been convicted in the City Court of Syracuse of the traffic offense of driving with unsafe tires at the time and place of the accident, in violation of the Vehicle and Traffic Law. Assume the court admitted the evidence about A's conviction. After both sides had rested, X requested that the jury be instructed as follows:

> A's violation of the Vehicle and Traffic Law constituted negligence per se and would justify your finding a verdict in B's favor.

How should the court rule with respect to X's request for the jury instruction?

(A) The court should permit the instruction because the plaintiff was within the class sought to be protected by the statute.

(B) The court should permit the instruction because the accident that occurred was within the "class of harms" the statute was designed to prevent.

(C) The court should deny using the instruction because the statute was not intended to protect against personal injury actions.

(D) The court should deny using the instruction because it does not follow that violation of the statute was inevitably the proximate cause of B's injuries.

9.   Jennifer was injured as she left Club Mystique when a railing on the outside stairway broke away from the building wall, causing her to fall. She duly commenced an action against Club Mystique to recover damages for personal injuries suffered in her fall, alleging negligence on the part of the club in maintaining the stairway. Club Mystique interposed a timely answer to Jennifer's complaint consisting of a general denial. At the trial of the action, Jennifer presented evidence that (i) Club Mystique owned and occupied the entire building in which the club was located, and (ii) Jennifer had grasped the railing in a normal manner before it broke away from the outside wall. Club Mystique presented evidence that (i) the railing had been inspected at regular intervals prior to the incident and that it had been found free from defect, (ii) the stairway was on the outside of the building and was accessible to the general public, and (iii) Club Mystique was open six nights each week, and approximately 450 people used the stairway on each night that Club Mystique was open. Would it be appropriate for the court to submit Jennifer's case to the jury on the theory of res ipsa loquitur?

(A) Yes, because the accident would not have occurred absent Club Mystique's negligence.

(B) Yes, because the stairway was within the sole control of Club Mystique.

(C) No, because the stairway was not within the sole control of Club Mystique.

(D) No, because Jennifer was the proximate cause of the railway breaking away from the building.

10. Stevie, 17 years old, and his younger brother Joey, age 15, climbed over the airport fence to watch airplanes land. On the fence were signs that read, "Danger, No Trespassing." Once over the fence, the boys started running across the runway. Joey tripped and twisted his ankle. Stevie started to head back to help Joey, but then saw a plane heading toward him. The pilot saw Joey, but was unable to avoid hitting him. Joey was propelled through the air. Stevie ran to Joey, who was conscious for a few moments before dying in Stevie's arms. Stevie's parents have come to you to find out whether they may bring an action for negligent infliction of emotional distress on behalf of their son Stevie against the airport. You tell them:

(A) Yes, because Stevie was an immediate family member.

(B) Yes, because Stevie was within the "zone of danger."

(C) No, because Stevie assumed the risk by climbing over the fence.

(D) No, because there is no evidence of physical injury suffered from the distress to Stevie.

11. Robert had had a difficult week. He and his wife were not seeing eye to eye; his boss was a tyrant who did not care whom he stepped on in order to advance politically; and creditors were calling Robert night and day to encourage him to pay his overdue bills. After work on Friday, he went home to watch the baseball game and proceeded to become intoxicated. He ran out of beer and decided to go to the store to buy some more. Not surprisingly, he ended up on the 11 o'clock news, after he left an exit ramp and collided with a utility pole. Robert died.

Investigators learned that Robert's blood alcohol level exceeded the limits set forth in the Vehicle and Traffic Law. They also discovered that Robert's car's floorboard buckled upward during the collision. They noted that the vehicle did not have adequate subframe reinforcement, and the resulting buckling caused the decedent to be thrown forward. This resulted in severe thoracic and abdominal injuries that caused Robert's death. An expert concluded that, if the vehicle had certain safety features that were readily available and in common use in the automobile industry, Robert would have survived the crash with minimum injury.

Upon receiving this news, Robert's widow and family initiated a wrongful death and products liability lawsuit against the car manufacturer for producing an unsafe vehicle. The car manufacturer moved to dismiss the case on public policy grounds.

How should the motion to dismiss be decided?

(A) The motion should be granted, because drunk driving is a serious infraction and recovery is prohibited on public policy grounds.

(B) The motion should be granted, because the facts show that but for Robert's intoxication the accident would not have occurred.

(C) The motion should be denied, because there is a serious design defect that caused Robert's death.

(D) The motion should be denied, because plaintiff contends that her husband's intoxication was not the direct cause of the injuries for which recovery is sought.

12. Starting in June 2002, an editorial news columnist posted an article on his journal's website stating that a local businessman had countless extramarital affairs and was an incurable drunk. The columnist wrote the piece because he felt that the businessman portrayed a "holier-than-thou" public persona, which was completely the opposite of his personal life.

By September 2003, the article had gained widespread circulation and notoriety. The businessman, who had been involved in negotiations for a proposed buyout, was getting more press coverage related to his alleged womanizing and boozing than to his business deal. Although he was wary of more attention, he felt that a decisive move was required in order to restore his reputation. He sued the columnist and the journal.

In his complaint filed in September 2003, the businessman alleged that the "journal repeatedly published the defamatory piece," as the webpage underwent regular content changes. The publisher moved for the suit to be dismissed because the statute of limitations had already run.

Should the lawsuit be dismissed?

(A) Yes, because the term "publication" refers to newspapers and printed materials and not the Internet.

(B) Yes, because under the single publication rule, alterations to the website that are not related to the article do not constitute republication.

(C) No, because the businessman did not learn about the publication until September 2003.

(D) No, because the journal continually edited the website. Each repetition is a separate publication; therefore, the statute of limitations has not expired.

13. Early one morning in mid-November 2001, it began to snow unexpectedly. BuildCo Corp. had hired NoSno Corp. to remove snow from the sidewalks in front of its corporate office building. The service contract stated that NoSno would respond within 30 minutes of being notified by the client of snow accumulation, and would ensure that all of the public walkways in front of BuildCo's offices were clear of snow. The contract also stated that BuildCo must inspect the property within 12 hours of the snow removal, and any defect in performance must be communicated immediately.

On the date in question, NoSno did respond within 30 minutes, but, due to the sudden and severe weather conditions, NoSno had to go to other client locations as well and did a hasty job for BuildCo before moving on. The other clients had similar contracts to the one that existed between BuildCo and NoSno.

The following day, Betty, an elderly lady, walked by BuildCo to get to her workplace across the street and slipped on a patch of snow and ice that remained on the pavement. Betty broke her hip and tailbone and later sued BuildCo and NoSno under general tort principles.

Which of the following statements is correct?

(A) BuildCo is liable to Betty for her injuries.

(B) BuildCo is secondarily liable and NoSno is primarily liable to Betty for her injuries.

(C) BuildCo is primarily liable and NoSno is secondarily liable to Betty for her injuries.

(D) Both BuildCo and NoSno are comparatively at fault.

14. A few weeks ago, Timmy received a promotion to a managerial sales position at an insurance company, All Insurance, Inc. He was extremely pleased with himself and has been bragging to everyone he knows about his newly acquired status. With this promotion, one of the fringe benefits given to Timmy is the use of a company car. Sales in Timmy's region have been very competitive, so the company leased some new cars to project a strong image of stability to the public.

Upon returning home with a new company car, Timmy was eager to show it off. Timmy's live-in girlfriend of six years, Mary, asked Timmy if she could take the car to the video store to drop off some movies. Timmy agreed. Rather than going to run this errand as she had said, Mary went to Madison Avenue to go shopping for shoes. As she drove down the avenue, checking out the store windows as she drove by, Mary accidentally ran a stop light and hit pedestrian, Beth, crossing the street.

All Insurance, Inc.'s, employee handbook contains a rule that forbids the use of leased company vehicles by third parties, but makes an exception for spouses. Beth later sues.

Where will the court most likely place liability?

(A) On Mary only, as she was the person driving the car.

(B) On All Insurance, Inc., because there was implied permission.

(C) On Timmy and Mary, because they did not have the company's consent.

(D) On Mary, because she only had Timmy's consent to go to the video store.

15. Eddie owns Bailey, a german shepherd-doberman mixed breed dog that he keeps as a family pet. Eddie customarily keeps Bailey confined to the kitchen area of the house behind a gate. Eddie did this whenever he was not at home or if he had visitors because Bailey barked at people with whom she was not familiar, and she would get excited and jump around. However, Eddie did not know of any incident in which Bailey had previously bitten anyone. One day, Justin, an eight-year-old boy, and his sister, Hayley, were visiting Eddie; in fact, they had been guests with their parents many times before. Justin was playing outside and came into the house to use the bathroom and the dog began to bark. Eddie placed Bailey on a leash, and when Justin emerged from the bathroom, Eddie invited Justin to play with the dog. He believed that Bailey knew Justin from prior visits to the house. As Justin approached, however, Bailey jumped up and bit him on the arm.

Should the owner be found liable?

(A) Yes, the owner should have known of the dog's vicious propensities.

(B) Yes, under the doctrine of strict liability.

(C) No, because her owner did not consider her to be a guard dog.

(D) No, because barking and jumping around do not constitute vicious propensities.

16. Shirley was eight months pregnant when she called her midwife to tell her that her she was going into labor and that there was a large amount of blood. The midwife advised Shirley to meet her at the "We Help Deliver Babies Birthing Center" with whom the midwife is affiliated. One hour later, Shirley arrived at the birthing center and again experienced similar bleeding. The Abrigo Pregnancy Pavilion was located in a hospital across the street from the center, but when the midwife called the pregnant woman's doctor, he directed that she be transported to a different hospital that was 45 minutes away. After another 45 minutes, the doctor arrived. In the interim, the midwife did not contact the on-call doctor. When the doctor arrived, he conducted some general fetal examinations, but did not perform a caesarean section until one-half hour later, at which time he delivered a stillborn child.

Can Shirley prevail in a medical malpractice action against the doctor?

(A) Yes, she can recover damages for emotional distress.

(B) No, because there was no independent physical injury distinct from that to the fetus.

(C) Yes, because she was in the zone of danger.

(D) No, because the doctor did not violate any duty of care to the expectant mother.

17. Defendant's dog bit Plaintiff while Plaintiff was visiting Defendant's home. The dog had not threatened or bitten anyone before, but had frequently barked at people. The dog was always enclosed in the kitchen or chained in the backyard.

Can Plaintiff prevail in an action against Defendant sounding in either negligence or strict liability?

(A) No, because Defendant had no reason to believe the dog would bite Plaintiff.

(B) No, because New York law does not recognize strict liability claims for injuries caused by animals.

(C) Yes, in strict liability, because dog owners are strictly liable for injuries caused by their dogs.

(D) Yes, because keeping the dog chained or indoors demonstrated that Defendant was on notice the dog might bite someone.

TORTS ANSWERS

1.   (D)

The harm that occurred here was a battery. Battery is the intentional and unpermitted physical contact to the plaintiff's person. The harm must have been intended and the defendant will be liable as long as he set in motion a force that brought about the harmful or offensive contact to the plaintiff's person. Here, all of the elements appear to be in place. However, when the plaintiff consents to the contact, the defendant is privileged to make it and there will be no tort. Consent may be express or implied. Implied consent arises where the contact is inevitable, customary, and reasonably necessary. Thus, where someone voluntarily engages in a body contact sport, it would be implied that he has consented to the ordinary contacts inherent in playing it. Thus, consent would be the proper defense here and (D) is the correct answer.

2.   (D)

A plaintiff may recover for defamation if the defendant used defamatory language regarding the plaintiff, the language was communicated to at least one other person who understands it, and the language causes damage to the plaintiff's reputation. Since Christine is not a public figure, she does not also have to prove the additional elements of falsity and fault. The first three elements for a defamation action have been met. Dennis used language or statements about Christine that would adversely affect Christine's reputation and the language was communicated to Dennis's friends and sister. The issue is whether the language caused damage to Christine's reputation. Thus, it is necessary to distinguish between libel and slander.

Libel is a written defamatory statement and general damages will be presumed by law. Thus, Christine can make out her libel action. Slander is spoken defamation and injury to reputation generally is not presumed. Ordinary slander is not actionable in the absence of special damages; *i.e.*, a specific pecuniary loss that resulted from the defamatory statement. However, special damages need not be proved if the slander falls within the category of slander per se. Dennis's statement about Christine's sexual promiscuity falls within the libel per se category of imputing unchaste behavior to a woman. Thus, Christine would meet the elements of a prima facie case for slander. Therefore, Christine can recover for both the letter and the statement, and (D) is the correct answer.

3.   (B)

To prevail in his action, Bob must establish a prima facie case for negligence by proving that the defendant owed him a duty to conform to a specific standard of conduct for his protection against an unreasonable risk of injury; defendant's breach of that duty; the breach of that duty was the actual and proximate cause of his injury; and damage to his person or property. The issue here is the applicable standard of care that defendant owed to the plaintiff, and generally, the defendant's conduct will be measured against the reasonable, ordinary, prudent person. Here, however, New York provides for special statutory protection for construction workers. [Labor Law §241—strict liability for failure to comply with statutorily mandated safety precautions; Labor Law §240—statutory standard for injuries sustained when a scaffold or ladder fails] This statutory standard of care will replace the more general duty of care and (B) is the correct answer.

4.   (B)

To state a prima facie case for ***intentional*** infliction of emotional distress, a plaintiff need ***not*** allege physical impact or physical manifestation of psychological trauma. However, to state a prima facie case for *negligent* infliction of emotional distress, plaintiff *must* allege physical impact or physical manifestation of psychological trauma. Only answer (B) correctly states this distinction. Answer (C) is incorrect because the statement is only partially correct—*mere* psychological trauma is insufficient.

5. (A)

To establish a prima facie case for defamation, the plaintiff must be able to prove that the defendant used defamatory language of or concerning the plaintiff, there was publication, and damage to the plaintiff's reputation. In addition, where the defamation refers to a public figure or involves a matter of public concern, the plaintiff must also be able to prove the falsity of the defamatory language and fault on the part of the defendant. However, only a living person may be defamed, and defamation of a deceased person is not actionable. Thus, plaintiff will not prevail in his action. (A) is the correct answer.

6. (D)

As a defense to negligence, where a plaintiff is injured in a motor vehicle accident and has failed to make use of an available seat belt, the trier of fact may consider such nonuse in mitigation of damages, but not as evidence on the issue of liability. New York Vehicle and Traffic Law section 1229-c(8) requires that defendant plead failure to use the seat belt as an affirmative defense before evidence in mitigation of damages may be introduced. Thus, (D) is the correct answer.

7. (A)

The Postal Service is liable to W for the $200 because of the negligent act of its servant. A master is liable for the negligent acts of his servant. Since the mail carrier was an employee of the United States Postal Service acting within the scope of his employment, the Postal Service is liable for his negligent acts. (B) is wrong because while the carrier was on a break, it was authorized, and he was still operating within the scope of his employment when the bag was stolen. (C) is wrong because the theft of the bag was not a superceding, intervening act since the area where the crime occurred is a high crime area, and thus criminal acts of a third party in the area were foreseeable. (D) is wrong because while historically the doctrine of sovereign immunity precluded litigants from asserting an otherwise meritorious cause of action against a sovereign or a party with sovereign immunity, the Federal Tort Claims Act waived such immunity for, amongst other things, "ministerial" acts such as delivering the mail.

8. (D)

If A is shown to be negligent per se, there will be a conclusive presumption of negligent conduct on A's part. However, to establish liability, it still must be proved that A's negligence *caused* B's injuries. For A's conduct in violation of the Vehicle and Traffic Law to constitute negligence per se, it is necessary (i) that the accident that occurred be within the "class of harms" the statute was designed to prevent, and (ii) that the plaintiff be within the class sought to be protected by the statute. While as to (i) it is certainly true that the statute in question (driving with unsafe tires) was designed to prevent accidents, and (ii) B, as a user of the road, is within the class of persons sought to be protected, it does not follow that violation of the statute was inevitably the proximate cause of B's injuries. This is a question for the jury to decide. Thus, (A) and (B) are wrong. (C) does not make sense.

9. (C)

Res ipsa loquitur is a doctrine of circumstantial evidence dealing with those situations where the fact that a particular injury occurred may itself tend to establish a breach of duty owed. Where the facts are such as to strongly indicate that the plaintiff's injuries resulted from the defendant's negligence, the trier of fact may be permitted to infer the defendant's liability. Res ipsa loquitur requires that the plaintiff show that: (i) the accident would not have occurred absent someone's negligence; (ii) the instrumentality causing the injury was in the sole control of the defendant; and (iii) the plaintiff is free from fault on her own part. The rule in New York is that if more than one person may have been in control of the instrumentality, res ipsa loquitur may not be used to establish a prima facie case of negligence against any individual party. The crucial element not proven here by Jennifer is sole control of the handrail. Club Mystique presented evidence that the stairway was accessible to the general public, and that approximately 450 people used the stairway on each of the six nights of the week. Thus, (B) is wrong. (A) and (D) are wrong because while they address causation, they do not address the elements required to establish a cause of action based on a theory of res ipsa loquitur.

10. (D)

Generally, there is a duty to avoid causing emotional distress to another, and this duty is breached when the defendant creates a foreseeable risk of injury to the plaintiff through physical impact or threat thereof and the plaintiff suffers a physical injury from the distress. In New York, recovery is limited to a plaintiff who is an immediate family member, exposed to immediate harm, and who suffers physical injury from the distress. *Note:* Most courts do not require that the plaintiff actually be subjected to physical impact in order to recover, but the plaintiff must have been within the "target zone" or "zone of danger" of physical injury from the defendant's negligent conduct. In this case, Stevie was Joey's brother, Stevie was present at the scene and watched Joey get struck by the plane. More importantly, Joey died in Stevie's arms. However, there is no evidence of a physical injury to Stevie; Stevie will state a prima facie case for negligent infliction of emotional distress only if a physical injury from the distress is established. Thus, (A) and (B) are wrong. (C) is not as good an answer as (D) because whether or not Stevie assumed the risk will ultimately be a question of fact for a jury, while the inability to prove physical injury is an essential element that will cause the action to fail before it gets to a jury.

11. (D)

Perpetrators of serious violations of the law may not recover for another's negligence if their injury results directly from their own illegal activity. This is known as the Barker-Manning rule. However, the Court of Appeals has held that this rule is limited in scope: It applies only to situations in which the parties to the suit were involved in the underlying criminal conduct or where a criminal plaintiff sought to impose a duty arising out of a criminal act. The court determined that the rule was never intended to indemnify against any negligence simply because the injured party was in the wrong. Here, the motion should be denied because it is contended that specific thoracic and abdominal injuries caused by the manufacturing defect—and not the intoxication—led to Robert's death. Consequently (A) is a wrong answer. (B) and (C) are incorrect because they are not the questions of law or fact at issue in this motion.

12. (B)

The New York Court of Appeals has held that the single publication rule (the publication of a defamatory statement in a single issue of a newspaper, or a single issue of a magazine, although such publication consists of thousands of copies widely distributed, is, in legal effect, one publication, which gives rise to one cause of action, and the applicable statute of limitations runs from the date of that publication) applies to alleged defamatory materials posted on the Internet and that website alterations unrelated to the offending article do not constitute republication for statute of limitations purposes. Therefore, (D) is incorrect. (A) is incorrect because defamatory language is defined as language tending to adversely affect one's reputation, regardless of the mode of communication. Other papers were gossiping about the businessman's personal life; therefore, his reputation was negatively affected. (C) is incorrect because the statute of limitations does not start running upon the plaintiff's discovery of the offending article.

13. (A)

In New York, contractual obligation alone will generally not give rise to tort liability in favor of a third-party plaintiff. NoSno does not owe a duty of care to third-party beneficiaries like Betty. New York recognizes three situations in which tort liability will run contractually to third-party beneficiaries: (i) where the contracting party, in failing to exercise reasonable care in the performance of his duties, "launch[es] a force or instrument of harm"; (ii) where the plaintiff detrimentally relies on the continued performance of the contracting party's duties; and (iii) where the contracting party has entirely displaced the other party's duty to safely maintain the premises. Although NoSno undertook to provide snow removal services under specific circumstances, BuildCo at all times retained its landowner's duty to inspect and safely maintain the premises. NoSno does not fit into any of the above-mentioned categories imputing liability. Therefore, (A) is correct and (B), (C), and (D) are incorrect.

14. (C)

Vehicle & Traffic Law section 388(1) creates a rebuttable presumption that a vehicle is operated with the owner's consent, thus making every owner of a vehicle liable for injuries resulting from the negligent operation of the vehicle by anyone using it with either the owner's express or implied permission. Here, the employee handbook has an express provision forbidding the use of leased company cars by third parties, and the company may expect employees to comply with the restriction. Consequently, answers (A) and (B) are incorrect. (D) is incorrect because Mary still had general consent from Timmy to use the car.

15. (D)

The owner of a domestic animal is strictly liable for any injury caused by the animal *if the owner has knowledge of that particular animal's vicious propensities*. The rule applies even if the animal never actually injured anyone. Here, Eddie had no reason to know of Bailey's vicious propensities; as a result, he cannot be liable for Bailey's attack on Justin. This makes (A) and (B) incorrect. (C) is incorrect because an owner of a dog with vicious propensities may be liable even if he did not use the dog as a guard dog. (However, use of a dog as a guard dog may show that the owner knew of the dog's vicious propensity.)

16. (A)

Even in the absence of an independent injury, medical malpractice resulting in a miscarriage may be construed as violation of a doctor's duty of care to an expectant mother, thus entitling her to damages for emotional distress. This makes (A) correct and (B) incorrect. (C) is incorrect because the "zone of danger" requirement applies when the plaintiff's distress is caused by threat of physical impact to someone in the plaintiff's immediate presence—if the plaintiff is outside the "zone of danger," she cannot recover damages. Clearly, that requirement is inapplicable here. (D) is factually incorrect.

17. (A)

Dogs are domestic animals. Owners of domestic animals are only liable for injuries caused by their pets where negligence can be proven. Thus, (C) is incorrect. Owners in possession of wild animals are subjected to a strict liability standard, and thus (B) is incorrect. An owner is negligent in possessing a domestic animal in instances where the owner knows that the animal has a propensity to cause injury. Notice of a propensity to bite is not demonstrated by virtue of the dog being chained or kept inside. Thus, (D) is incorrect.

TRUSTS QUESTIONS

1.   Sarah Settlor, a widow, created an inter vivos trust in 2007. The trust provided that it could be revoked by Sarah by an instrument delivered to Truman Trustee. The trust also provided that it was to pay income to Sarah for her life, and at Sarah's death, to pay the income to Sarah's daughter, Dolly Dailey, for life. Upon Dolly's death, the remainder of the trust was to be paid to Dolly's issue as designated in Dolly's will.

Which of the following statements is (are) not true?

I.   During Sarah's life, Sarah could revoke the trust over Dolly's objections.
II.   During Sarah's life, Sarah could revoke the trust over Truman's objections.
III.   Sarah's creditors could reach her entire income interest.

(A) I. only.

(B) III. only.

(C) I., II., and III.

(D) None of the above.

2.   In 2000, Connie Shanelan transferred 500 shares of her Xerox stock to Scrapper Attorney, in trust, to pay the income to Orchard Parker until Orchard reaches age 30 and then to transfer the shares to Orchard. In 2002, Orchard, age 24, requested Scrapper to terminate the trust of the Xerox stock and transfer the 500 shares to Orchard. Scrapper refused to do so. Which of the following statements is correct?

(A) Orchard may compel Scrapper to transfer the shares because she is the sole beneficiary.

(B) Orchard may compel Scrapper to transfer the shares but only if Orchard agrees not to sell the shares.

(C) Orchard may compel Scrapper to transfer the shares if Connie joins in her request.

(D) Orchard may not compel Scrapper to transfer the shares because the trust may never be terminated.

3.   Spade Settlor created a trust of $300,000 that provides "income to Spade Settlor for life, principal to his children on his death." Spade Settlor then borrows $100,000 to open up a new bar review course. Because his materials are too voluminous and no one is going to law school anymore, Spade's business fails and he loses his entire $100,000 investment. Spade owes his book publisher, Crispy Creditor, $50,000 and Crispy wants to reach the trust as payment for what Spade owes him. Creditor can reach:

(A) 10% of the principal and all interest.

(B) All principal and all interest.

(C) No principal but all interest.

(D) Cannot reach anything.

4. In August 1995, G, pursuant to a written agreement, transfers $300,000 to T, as trustee, to invest the principal and to pay the income to G during her lifetime, and on G's death to pay the principal equally to G's children. The trust agreement was silent concerning G's right to revoke the trust. On May 1, 1996, G borrowed $100,000 from C, and G gave C a promissory note due May 1, 1997, for that amount. G invested the $100,000 in a business venture, which soon failed.

When G did not pay the note on May 1, 1997, C recovered a judgment against G for $100,000. C duly petitioned the court for an order requiring T to apply both the interest and the principal of the trust created by G to the satisfaction of C's $100,000 judgment.

The court should properly grant an order directing T to pay C:

(A) 10% only of the income trust.

(B) All the income but no principal.

(C) All the income and sufficient principal to satisfy the judgment.

(D) The court should not grant an order directing T to pay C any part of the income or principal of the trust.

TRUSTS ANSWERS

1. (D)

Generally, trusts are irrevocable unless the settlor expressly reserves the right to revoke, alter, or amend the trust. Here, the settlor expressly reserved the right to revoke the trust and thus, I. and II. are correct. New York has a statutory spendthrift rule that generally prohibits voluntary or involuntary transfer of a beneficiary's interest. However, the statutory spendthrift rule does not apply and a creditor can reach the trust income if the settlor retains the power to revoke, because the settlor remains the absolute owner of the property disposed of so far as the rights of his creditors are concerned. Thus, III. is also correct.

Note: If the trust were irrevocable and the settlor retained some but not all of the beneficial interest in the trust, his creditors could reach the full amount of the interest retained by the settlor, but no more.

2. (C)

When a beneficiary wants to terminate a trust, the rule is that the trust may be terminated only if (i) all beneficiaries consent; and (ii) the termination will not interfere with a material purpose of the settlor. Since Orchard is the only beneficiary and she wishes to terminate the trust, the first requirement has been satisfied. However, when a trust is created to pay the income to the beneficiary until she reaches a certain age and to then distribute the principal to the beneficiary, the court will not allow the termination by the sole beneficiary because the court assumes that the purpose of the trust is to keep the principal out of the beneficiary's hands until reaching the designated age. Thus, Orchard cannot compel Scrapper to transfer the trust and (A) and (B) are incorrect. However, if Connie joins Orchard in asking that the trust be terminated, then Orchard can compel the transfer of the shares. Where all the beneficiaries request the termination of the trust and the settlor joins in the request for termination, the courts will waive the purpose and permit the beneficiaries to compel termination. Thus, (C) is correct and (D) is incorrect.

3. (C)

In New York, trust income interests are given spendthrift protection by statute. This means that an income beneficiary cannot sell or transfer his trust income, nor can the beneficiary's creditors reach that interest. However, where the settlor is the beneficiary, the spendthrift rule does not insulate the interest of the trust from his present or future creditors. Here, since Spade has retained some beneficial interest in the trust, his creditors can reach the full amount of the interest retained by him, but no more. Accordingly, (C) is the correct answer.

4. (B)

In New York, all trusts are irrevocable and unamendable unless the settlor specifically retains the power to revoke or amend. However, a disposition in trust for the use of the creator is void as against the existing or subsequent creditors of the creator. This provision is to insure that settlors will not create trusts merely to escape their debts to creditors.

When an irrevocable trust is created and the settlor retains an interest in the trust (in this case, the income), the creditors can reach the full amount of the interest retained by the settlor. This is the sole remedy that the creditor has as to the settlor's trust. Therefore, (B) is the proper answer.

WILLS QUESTIONS

Questions 1 and 2 are based on the following situation:

Hiram and Wynonna were married in 1994, a second marriage for both. Hiram had two sons from his first marriage, Andrew and Bob. Wynonna had two daughters from her first marriage, Carolyn and Darlene. Two months after their marriage, Hiram and Wynonna executed a contract following all the formalities required for a duly executed will. "This is a contract to make a joint will. We leave all our property to the survivor of us; and then to Andrew, Bob, Carolyn, and Darlene in equal shares. This document constitutes a contract and is to be legally binding on the survivor of us." Their total estate was worth $200,000.

The family was then struck by tragedy when they were all severely injured in a car crash. Wynonna died in August 1995. Andrew died in September 1995 without issue. Carolyn died in October 1995 without issue but with a will leaving everything to her spouse. Hiram was miraculously nursed back to health by Nancy. In December 1995, Hiram married Nancy and duly executed a will leaving all his property in trust to Nancy for life. Hiram then died in 1997 leaving an estate worth $300,000.

1. Darlene is entitled to:

(A) One-third of Hiram's estate because New York does not recognize contracts to make a testamentary provision.

(B) One-third of Hiram's estate because joint wills are invalid in New York.

(C) One-fourth of Hiram's estate because all beneficiaries are entitled to a share of the estate.

(D) Nothing unless the contract was supported by consideration.

2. Nancy seeks to have Hiram's second will probated. Which of the following are true statements?

I. The second will should be probated even though it is in breach of the first.
II. Darlene is entitled to a suit to enforce the first will contract.
III. The second will should be denied probate.

(A) I. only.

(B) II. only.

(C) II. and III. only.

(D) I. and II. only.

3. In 1979, Testator executes a will. In 2003, Testator executes a codicil that changes the alternate executor. Two weeks later Testator dies. What effect does the codicil have on the will?

(A) No effect since changing the alternate executor is a minor change.

(B) The will is now deemed to have been executed in 2003.

(C) The will is still deemed to have been executed in 1979.

(D) The will is deemed to have been executed in 1979, but as to the designation of a new alternate executor, the will of 2003 will apply.

4. In 1985, Chaim and Kate got married. They remained married, without children, until 2000 when they separated. In June 2005, they entered into a formal separation agreement and divorced one year later.

The agreement stated in part that each party would "relinquish any and all rights to the property of the other, real or personal, with full power to dispose of the same as fully and effectually in all aspects and for all purposes as he or she desires . . . [T]he parties agree and acknowledge that any and all bank accounts, held jointly or otherwise, not specifically mentioned in this agreement, have been divided equitably to the mutual satisfaction of both parties prior to the execution of this agreement."

During the marriage, Kate established several bank accounts "in trust for Chaim" and deposited funds into these accounts. After they separated, Kate continued to maintain the funds in the accounts and pay income tax on the interest generated. In Kate's final will, she left her entire estate to her brother and sister. There was no express mention of the trust accounts in her will. The will was never revoked. Kate died in 1998, and Chaim now contests his former in-laws' interpretation of the separation agreement.

How should the funds be disposed of that are held in the trust?

(A) To the brother and the sister, because Chaim waived his right to the trust funds in the separation agreement.

(B) To the brother and the sister, because the Totten trusts pass to them, as per the testator's will.

(C) Chaim should receive the funds in the trusts, because he never waived his right to the accounts and Kate never validly revoked them.

(D) Chaim, because a Totten trust is a testamentary substitute that should not be included in a net estate against which the elective share applies.

WILLS ANSWERS

1. (D)

New York recognizes joint wills as valid. EPTL section 13.2.1(b) provides that joint wills executed on or after September 1, 1983, can be established only by an express statement in the will that the instrument is a joint will and that the provisions thereof are intended to constitute a contract between the parties. Thus, (A) and (B) are incorrect. (D) is the correct answer because all contracts to make a will must be supported by consideration.

2. (D)

A new will executed in breach of a contract is not denied probate. In this instance, the beneficiary of the contract has only one remedy—to bring a suit to enforce the contract. Accordingly, (D) is the correct answer.

3. (B)

In cases in which it is important to determine the date on which the will is deemed to have been executed, the will is treated as having been executed on the date of a validly executed codicil thereto. Consequently, the will is deemed to have been executed in 2003.

4. (C)

Chaim did not waive his right to the Totten trusts. The language used in this separation agreement was too broad to effectuate a waiver. A beneficiary may waive his right so long as the waiver is explicit, voluntary, and made in good faith. Thus, (A) is incorrect. Kate did not validly revoke the Totten trusts while she was alive. She could have done this by: (i) withdrawing funds, (ii) expressly revoking it in a will, or (iii) instructing the bank to revoke via an acknowledged writing. Answer (B) is an incorrect statement. A Totten trust passes by law on the death of the depositor, and not by disposition. Answer (D) is an incorrect statement of the law.

BAR REVIEW

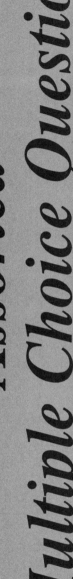

Assorted

Multiple Choice Questions

Celebrating

XL

years

one million students

NEW YORK MULTIPLE CHOICE—ASSORTED QUESTIONS

TABLE OF CONTENTS

1.   Doctor, a licensed physician, resided in her own home. The street in front of the home had a gradual slope. Doctor's garage was on the street level, with a driveway entrance from the street. A few days ago, at two in the morning, Doctor received an emergency call. She dressed and went to the garage to get her car and found a car parked in front of her driveway. That car was occupied by Parker, who, while intoxicated, had driven to that place and now was in a drunken stupor in the front seat. Unable to rouse Parker, Doctor pushed him into the passenger's side of the front seat and got in on the driver's side. Doctor released the brake and coasted the car down the street, planning to pull into a parking space that was open. When Doctor attempted to stop the car, the brakes failed to work, and the car crashed into the wall of Owner's home, damaging Owner's home and Parker's car and injuring Doctor and Parker. Subsequent examination of the car disclosed that the brake linings were badly worn. A state statute prohibits the operation of a motor vehicle unless the brakes are capable of stopping the vehicle within specified distances at specified speeds. The brakes on Parker's car were incapable of stopping the vehicle within the limits required by the statute. Another state statute makes it a criminal offense to be intoxicated while driving a motor vehicle.

If Parker asserts a claim against Doctor for his injuries, Parker will probably:

(A) Recover, because Doctor was negligent as a matter of law.

(B) Recover, because Doctor had no right to move the car.

(C) Not recover, because his brakes were defective.

(D) Not recover, under the New York Comparative Negligence Statute.

2.   A, a mentally competent but otherwise incompetent attorney, executed a will purporting to dispose of all his property. At the time of execution and in the presence of subscribing witnesses, A added a handwritten provision underneath all the signatures, in which A made a specific bequest and designated an executor. With the possible exception of this last clause, the will was duly executed in all respects.

After A's death, the will:

(A) Cannot be admitted to probate.

(B) May be admitted to probate entirely.

(C) May be admitted to probate, except for that portion of the handwritten clause that purports to make a specific bequest.

(D) May be admitted to probate, except for the handwritten clause.

3.   In January 2005, C gave D a duly executed promissory note in which C promised to pay D $1,000 on June 1, 2005. In February 2005, C placed all his property in trust, payable to C for life, the remainder to be disposed of in accordance with his will. In March 2005, C gave O a duly executed promissory note in which C promised to pay O $1,000 on June 1, 2005. D and O were not paid and, in July 2005, obtained separate judgments against C. The trust corpus may be levied on by:

(A) **D only.**

(B) **O only.**

(C) **D and O.**

(D) **Neither D nor O.**

4.   Q, D, and A, who were employed as powder stuffers in B Bomb Factory, had finished half a day's work and were driving in A's automobile through the bomb shed on the way to their lockers when J, a second-story bomb handler, accidentally dropped a bomb from the second story of the shed onto A's automobile. Q, A, J, and everyone else were injured.

Q is entitled to:

(A) **Institute an action for personal injuries against A only.**

(B) **Institute an action for personal injuries against J only.**

(C) **Institute an action for personal injuries against B Bomb Factory.**

(D) **File a claim for workers' compensation, but institute no action for personal injuries.**

5.   F, who was robbing a bank by pointing a loaded gun at the teller and threatening to shoot, became bored and decided to terrify a bank guard by pointing a water pistol at him. When F pointed the water pistol at him, the guard was terrified. F's action, with respect to the bank guard only, constituted:

(A) **Menacing.**

(B) **Harassment.**

(C) **Third degree assault.**

(D) **Second degree assault.**

6.   On the afternoon of October 31, Q and A broke into the house of G, an archaeologist who was away on a field trip. Their intention was to steal mummy bones. Q was armed with a loaded rifle; A, without Q's knowledge and contrary to his instructions, had hidden a dagger in her boot. Upon removing the bones from their casket, Q and A were mysteriously paralyzed and then were apprehended by the police. The following person or persons may properly be convicted of burglary in the first degree:

(A) **Q and A both.**

(B) **Q only.**

(C) **A only.**

(D) **Neither Q nor A.**

7. A law enacted by the state of New York, providing for arraignment and trial on felony charges without grand jury indictment in cases where the defendant waives such indictment, would be:

(A) Constitutionally permissible, provided the crime charged is not punishable by death or life imprisonment.

(B) Constitutionally impermissible, solely by virtue of federal law.

(C) Constitutionally impermissible, solely by virtue of state law.

(D) Constitutionally impermissible, because of the state and federal constitutions.

8. A owns all the stock of C Co., which is engaged solely in the manufacture of rubber tires, which it sells to automobile manufacturers. E Co. is a corporation engaged in the manufacture of rubber trees, which it sells to wholesale interior decorating showrooms. A is a member of the board of directors of E Co. and asks E Co. to sell him one of its rubber research laboratories and take a purchase money security interest in C Co.'s inventory to the extent of the fair market value of the laboratory.

In the absence of any applicable express provision in its bylaws, E Co. is:

(A) Not empowered to accept A's proposal.

(B) Empowered to accept A's proposal.

(C) Empowered to accept A's proposal only pursuant to a majority vote of E Co.'s shareholders.

(D) Empowered to accept A's proposal only pursuant to a two-thirds majority vote of the shareholders.

Questions 9 and 10 each describe an offense. Select from the choices (A)-(D) the *most serious offense* of which the defendant could be properly convicted.

(A) Second degree manslaughter.

(B) First degree manslaughter.

(C) Highly reckless murder.

(D) None of the above.

9. Defendant, an avid fan of his hometown football team, shot at the leg of a star player for a rival team, intending to injure his leg enough to hospitalize him for a few weeks, but not to kill him. The victim died of loss of blood.

10. Defendant, a worker in a metalworking shop, has long been teasing Vincent, a young colleague, by calling him insulting names and ridiculing him. One day Vincent responded to the teasing by picking up a metal bar and attacking Defendant. Defendant could have escaped from the shop. He parried the blow with his left arm, and with his right hand picked up a crowbar and struck Vincent a blow on his head from which the young man died.

11. In an action by D against R to compel specific performance of an oral contract for the conveyance of a camel ranch, R pleads the Statute of Frauds as a defense. D can overcome this defense:

(A) Upon showing that D had been in possession for more than one year subsequent to the alleged agreement.

(B) Upon showing that D made a down payment for the ranch to R.

(C) Upon showing both of the above.

(D) Only by showing facts other than those in (A) and (B) above.

12. U is entitled to more than $3,000 in unpaid arrearages arising under a divorce decree that required P, U's former husband, to make alimony and support payments to U. U's claim against P will abate:

(A) When U or P dies.

(B) Only when U dies.

(C) Only when P dies.

(D) Only when satisfied by P or P's estate.

13. On May 1, A and G, two New York City merchants, entered into a contract for the sale to G of tea leaves that had been packed in boxes marked with A's name (Alphonse) and were then being shipped to New York via Boston on a slow boat from China. Prior to the execution of the contract, A held title to the tea. The contract provided for delivery of the tea to G at dockside in New York City on May 17, which was the date on which the parties expected the ship would arrive in New York. Payment was due on or before June 17.

On May 2, A gave G a written order instructing the shipper to tender the tea leaves to G. On May 12, G learned that the ship had arrived in Boston and was being detained there pursuant to a declaration of martial law. On May 20, G went to the office of the shipper in New York City and was informed that the ship, which was still in Boston, had been seized and its cargo destroyed on the previous day by "hostile elements."

In an action by A against G to recover the purchase price of the tea leaves:

(A) G is entitled to assert as a complete defense that the tea was destroyed prior to June 17.

(B) A will prevail on the ground that G bore the risk of loss on May 1 and at all times thereafter.

(C) A will prevail on the ground that G bore the risk of loss at all times subsequent to May 1.

(D) G will prevail if it was not commercially reasonable for G to take delivery in Boston, instead of New York, prior to May 19 upon learning that the ship was being detained.

14. In 1991, plaintiff P met in New York City with D, an officer of defendant corporation. Both P and the corporation do business in New York. P arranged the meeting to interest the corporation in constructing, in Saudi Arabia, a plant that would convert natural gas into fertilizer. After a series of meetings in New York, P and his associates negotiated with Saudi officials at the corporation's request. P contends that as a result of these negotiations, the corporation was removed from an Arab blacklist, and in 1996 was awarded the sought-for contract. The plant was completed in 2001.

P brings an action to be paid 5%, or $2.5 million, of the contract for his services under an agreement P alleges he had with the corporation. Which of the following defenses made by the corporation is valid?

(A) The agreement violated the one-year provision of the Statute of Frauds since there was no writing evidencing the agreement.

(B) The alleged agreement fell within the scope of the provision of the Statute of Frauds requiring a writing to evidence an offer of compensation in exchange for services rendered in negotiating a business opportunity.

(C) P is not entitled to any fee until the contract with Saudi Arabia is consummated; and under Saudi law, this does not come about until the plant begins operations (which has yet to occur).

(D) None of the above.

15. A, a theatrical booking agent, manufactured snake oil at home in her spare time. A entered into an agreement with P, a high school principal, whereby P would find customers to make wholesale purchases of oil and execute sales contracts with such customers on behalf of A. It was mutually understood that P would receive a commission proportionate to the amount of snake oil that he sold in this manner; and that the oil was useful only as a lubricant for automobile parts.

P thereupon induced S, a wholesale druggist, to purchase A's entire oil output on the basis of P's false representation that the oil was effective in the treatment of whiplash injuries. The contract of sale, which was signed by S and by "P, as agent for A," recited that it reflected the entire agreement and that no representations had been made as to the medical effectiveness of the oil. A believed at all times that no such representations had been made.

S soon learned that he could sell the oil only to automobile mechanics, at a fraction of the price he had paid for it. S is entitled to recover damages for fraud against:

(A) A only.

(B) P only.

(C) A and P.

(D) None of the above.

16. G Inc., a not-for-profit corporation formed by radio listeners with the purpose of perpetuating classical music broadcasts that had been terminated by the owners of a license to operate radio station WINO, made an appeal for funds in which the public was invited to submit written pledges in the following form:

> At such time as G Inc. commences legal proceedings to compel resumption of classical music broadcasts by WINO, I promise to pay G Inc. (amount) to be applied first toward its legal fees and then, if G Inc. is unsuccessful in such proceedings, to be applied to any other expense of G Inc. reasonably related to the continuation of classical music broadcasting by other means. (Signature)

F, a particularly wealthy contributor, pledged $50,000 pursuant to the above terms. On the basis of pledges in the total amount of $200,000, G Inc. succeeded in retaining counsel who was paid $100,000 for litigation that eventually proved unsuccessful. The remaining $100,000 was used to purchase two-thirds of the WINO classical record collection, which was then transferred gratuitously to a not-for-profit broadcasting corporation, thereby restoring classical music broadcasts on another station. At the commencement of the litigation and thereafter, F declined to pay G Inc. the $50,000 he had pledged.

In an action by G Inc. against F to enforce the pledge, F is:

(A) Not liable, because he received no consideration.

(B) Liable to the extent of $50,000.

(C) Liable to the extent of $25,000 only.

(D) Liable for nominal damages only.

17. On March 11, N Inc. offered C the job of giving bar review lectures on contracts and sales at a salary of $30 per hour during the summer bar review course, and advised C in writing that N Inc. would keep the offer open until July 1. On March 12, N Inc. completed its review of student evaluation forms for the preceding bar review course in which C had taught and therefore hired D instead of C. In an action by C against N Inc. to compel N Inc. to reopen the offer:

(A) C will prevail on the ground that the offer was not kept open for a reasonable time.

(B) C will prevail on the ground that the offer was not kept open until July 1.

(C) N Inc. will prevail on the ground that it received no consideration from C.

(D) N Inc. will prevail on the ground that C did not accept the offer on or before March 12.

18. As a result of exposure to asbestos during his employment by Doorco, Peter, a resident of Erie County, New York, contracted asbestosis. Doorco is incorporated in Ohio, where it maintains its corporate offices and plant. Doorco does substantial business in New York state. Peter brought an action against Doorco to recover $80,000 in damages in the New York Supreme Court for Erie County. Erie County is within the geographical jurisdiction of the United States District Court for the Western District of New York. Peter's action against Doorco may be removed from the New York State Supreme Court for Erie County to the United States District Court for the Western District of New York by:

(A) Peter only.

(B) Doorco only.

(C) Either Peter or Doorco.

(D) Neither Peter nor Doorco.

19. Late one night in a tavern in Tucson, Arizona, A and P duly entered into a contract whereby A would pay P $1,000 for converting some of A's desert properties in Tucson into swamps suitable for alligators. A and P were residents of New York City at the time the contract was made; but by the time P had completed performance of the contract, A had established a domicile in Arizona and had decided not to pay P.

Upon returning to New York City, P duly obtained an order of attachment against A's five alligators, which had been boarded temporarily in P's apartment and whose fair market value was $100 each. P then caused a Tucson marshal to personally serve A with a copy of a summons and complaint alleging breach of contract. A's attorney duly filed an answer that contained a defense based on lack of jurisdiction. The court is empowered to:

(A) Dismiss the complaint.

(B) Hear the case on the ground that it has personal jurisdiction over A.

(C) Hear the case on the ground that it has quasi in rem jurisdiction over A.

(D) Hear the case on both of the above grounds.

20. M was born in 1970, and W was born in 1982. In 1999, M proposed to W that if W would marry him, he would give her title to his guava plantation in Hawaii and all the proceeds thereof. W, who detested M, consented, and later that year they duly underwent a marriage ceremony. M thereafter gave W a deed to the property in Hawaii; and they cohabited ever after as husband and wife until 2005, when W visited Hawaii and learned that in 1971, the property had fallen into the Pacific Ocean. M admitted to W that he had always known this. W therefore moved out of M's house and instituted an action for annulment. The court is empowered, in its discretion, to render judgment in favor of W:

(A) On the ground of nonage, without reaching any other ground for decision.

(B) On the ground of fraud, without reaching any other ground for decision.

(C) On both of the above grounds.

(D) On neither of the above grounds.

21. Householder hired Contractor to remodel her kitchen. She had learned of him through a classified advertisement he placed in the local newspaper. During the telephone conversation in which she hired him, he stated he was experienced and qualified to do all necessary work. Because of his low charge for his work, they agreed in writing that on acceptance of his job by Householder, he would have no further liability to her or to anyone else for any defects in materials or workmanship, and that she would bear all such costs.

Householder purchased a dishwasher manufactured by Elex Co. from Dealer, who was in the retail electrical appliance business. The washer was sold by Dealer with only the manufacturer's warranty and with no warranty by Dealer; Elex Co. restricted its warranty to 90 days on parts and labor. Contractor installed the dishwasher.

Two months after Householder accepted the entire job, she was conversing in her home with Accountant, an acquaintance who had agreed to prepare her income tax return gratuitously. As they talked, they noticed that the dishwasher was operating strangely, repeatedly stopping and starting. At Householder's request, Accountant gave it a cursory examination and, while inspecting it, received a violent electrical shock which did him extensive harm. The dishwasher had an internal wiring defect which allowed electrical current to be carried into the framework and caused the machine to malfunction. The machine had not been adequately grounded by Contractor during installation; if it had been, the current would have been led harmlessly away. The machine carried instructions for correct grounding, which Contractor had not followed.

If Accountant asserts a claim based on strict liability against Elex Co. for damages, the probable result is that Accountant will:

(A) Recover, because the dishwasher was defectively made and because liability extends to any foreseeable plaintiff user, occupier, or bystander.

(B) Recover, because Elex Co. is vicariously liable for the improper installation.

(C) Not recover, because he assumed the risk of inspecting the machine.

(D) Not recover, because he was not the purchaser.

22. K, a 10-year-old child, was attacked and seriously injured in New York City by D, a dog owned by O. G, K's guardian, brought a negligence action against O in the Supreme Court for New York County. During the trial, H, G's attorney, asked the court to take judicial notice of a New York City ordinance that imposed certain regulations on dog owners. The court:

(A) Is not permitted to take judicial notice of a municipal ordinance.

(B) Is empowered to grant or deny H's request, in its discretion.

(C) Is required to grant H's request.

(D) Is required to deny H's request on the ground that H failed to notify O's attorney of H's intention to make the request.

23. Daughter was born in 2000, and several years later her parents were divorced, with Father and Mother both demanding custody. The court intends to apply the "best interest of the child" test in determining custody. Under that test as applied in New York, which of the following statements is true?

(A) The admission by Father that he is a homosexual is presumptive evidence that he is an unfit parent and that, accordingly, there is a presumption in favor of the other spouse.

(B) The intention of Father to leave New York and his position with a large company in Big City in favor of farming in Idaho creates a presumption in favor of the spouse that intends to remain within the state of New York.

(C) The fact that the child is of tender years gives rise to a presumption in favor of the mother's having custody.

(D) None of the above.

24. If, on the foregoing facts, the court had decided to give custody to Father, who properly supported daughter until she turned 19, when did his obligation of support end?

(A) It ended when she turned 18.

(B) It ended when she turned 21, even though she became a recipient of public assistance six months thereafter.

(C) It ended under all circumstances when she married.

(D) It ended under all circumstances when she became emancipated at age 17.

25. Alan, Ben, and Charlie bring a breach of contract action against Dale, Ellen, and Ferdi. Alan and Dale are citizens of New York, Ben and Ellen are citizens of Florida, and Charlie and Ferdi are citizens of Texas. In which court may the action be commenced?

(A) The federal district court in Florida.

(B) The federal district court in New York.

(C) The federal district court in Texas.

(D) The claim must be brought in a state court.

26. D is an employee of AB Co., a partnership of which A and B are partners. D is involved in an accident with P. P sues A, B, AB Co., and D by serving three copies of the summons and complaint naming A, B, AB Co., and D as defendants on A in his office and then serving D at his home.

Assuming no defendant appears in the action and P obtains a default judgment, against whose assets may P execute the judgment?

I.   A's assets.
II. B's assets.
III. AB Co.'s assets.
IV. D's assets.

(A) I., III., and IV.

(B) I., II., and III.

(C) I. and IV.

(D) None of the above.

27. H and W, residents of New York City, argue constantly. H leaves W and moves to California. W sues H in New York for divorce and maintenance. Pursuant to court order, H is served in California by certified mail sent to his mother's house, since H's exact address was unknown.

H was properly served for:

(A) Divorce only.

(B) Divorce and maintenance.

(C) Maintenance only.

(D) None of the above.

28. Gillie and Mike were married in July, and Gillie gave birth to their son, Adonis, a year later. For his seventh birthday, Gillie and Mike gave Adonis a beautiful red 10-speed bicycle. Adonis was told that he was not to ride his bike unless one of his parents was running alongside him. One spring afternoon, Mike, Gillie, and Adonis were in their front yard enjoying the weather and Adonis wanted to ride his bicycle. Gillie and Mike were too tired to run alongside Adonis and told him to wait. They then fell asleep, taking a brief cat-nap. Seeing that his parents were not watching him, Adonis got on his bike and rode off into the street. Mike and Gillie woke up and saw their son headed into the path of Carrie Cabdriver, and both began running after him. Just as they were about to reach the boy, Mike turned and tripped Gillie, who fell and broke her ankle. Carrie Cabdriver swerved to miss the boy and drove into a tree. Adonis, frightened by his father's yelling, fell off the bike and broke his arm. Adonis and Carrie bring an action against Mike for negligent supervision, and Gillie brings an action against Mike for battery. Who is not precluded from bringing an action?

(A) Adonis.

(B) Gillie.

(C) Carrie.

(D) All of the above.

29. B testifies that she was a victim in the following situation:

A came up to her, accosted her, held a knife to her throat, raped her, grabbed her necklace, and ran away. B testifies to this at trial. The defendant offered no evidence and rested.

The jury may properly find the defendant, A, guilty of:

(A) Robbery.

(B) Rape.

(C) Rape and robbery.

(D) Neither robbery nor rape.

30. Testator's will is found cut in two among his papers after death. It is in a large envelope, also cut in two, bearing the legend "Last Will and Testament of Testator." The will and the envelope are found in a larger envelope bearing the legend, in Testator's handwriting: "My Will." All these are found in Testator's home. Will proponents offer testimony that Testator had mentioned to them that he cut the will by accident. Will opponents offer testimony that Testator had told them that he cut the will with an intention to revoke it. Is the will valid?

(A) No, because mutilation of the will is conclusive evidence of its revocation.

(B) No, because evidence that the will was mistakenly cut in two is insufficient to explain the mutilation.

(C) Yes, because evidence the will was mistakenly cut in two is sufficient to explain the mutilation.

(D) Yes, because there is sufficient evidence to establish that Testator did not intend to revoke his will.

31. The charter and bylaws of a corporation are silent as to the quorum and voting requirements for the board of directors. There are 15 directors on the board. Eight show up for a scheduled meeting. How many directors are required to pass a resolution?

(A) 15.

(B) 8.

(C) 5.

(D) 4.

32. A, a resident of Albany County, lends his tools to D, a resident of Schnectady County. D then takes the tools and goes to Saratoga County where he works on his summer home. The agreement was that the tools would be lent for a period of one month. One month later, A asks D for his tools back and D refuses to return them. Where can a suit to recover the tools be brought?

(A) Albany County only.

(B) Albany or Saratoga County only.

(C) Albany or Schnectady County only.

(D) Albany, Schnectady, or Saratoga County.

33. C, a contractor, contracts with H, a homeowner, to make improvements on H's house. The total cost is to be $15,000, payable in five equal installments of $3,000 each. C supplies all materials and labor. Work progresses at a satisfactory pace and two payments are made at a total of $6,000. The third payment is, without any legal justification, not made by the homeowner. The work so far has involved labor and materials for $5,000, and to finish the remainder of the house would cost C approximately $4,000. The damages that C can sue for are:

(A) $1,000.

(B) $3,000.

(C) $5,000.

(D) $6,000.

34.   C's children live in a house owned by C in Orleans County, New York, which C has never visited. C resides in New York City and has no other property in Orleans County. W has obtained a judgment against C for $5,000 for personal injury arising out of an accident that occurred when C was driving through Orleans County on a vacation trip in an attempt to visit his children; and W has caused the judgment to be docketed in Orleans County. C owns real property in New York County.

W has a lien against:

(A)   C's house in Orleans County.

(B)   C's real property in New York County.

(C)   All of C's real property.

(D)   None of the above.

35.   A sold explosives to D knowing that D intended to use the explosives to blow up V's house and kill V.

A is guilty of:

(A)   Arson.

(B)   Murder.

(C)   Facilitation.

(D)   Being an accomplice to murder.

36.   A bill of particulars must be verified:

I.   When the pleading it particularizes is verified.
II.   When it pertains to a negligence lawsuit.
III.   All the time.

Which is correct?

(A)   I. only.

(B)   None of the above.

(C)   I. and II.

(D)   III.

37. T, a widower, died last month and was survived by S, his adult son, and D, his 14-year-old daughter—his sole heirs.

T's duly probated will leaves $90,000 to C Charity and the residue of T's estate to T's friend, F. T's estate, after payment of debts, is $100,000 and expenses of administration will be $5,000.

The gift to charity may be contested as excessive by:

(A) Neither S nor D.

(B) Both S and D.

(C) S only.

(D) D only.

38. S and B entered into a written contract pursuant to which B agreed to buy from S a printing press at $10,000. The contract provided that "any controversy or claim arising out of or relating to this contract may be settled by arbitration at the option of S only." B claims that the press is defective and has refused to pay S.

A right to arbitration upon a duly filed demand exists in:

(A) Either S or B.

(B) S only.

(C) B only.

(D) Neither S nor B.

39. A lease stated that "tenant shall make all inside and outside repairs and replacements and shall keep the building in as good a condition as at present." The lease was silent about fire damage. The building was destroyed by fire.

Which of the following statements is correct?

(A) Tenant must rebuild the premises.

(B) Tenant has no obligation to rebuild or restore the building.

(C) Tenant has the option to rebuild the premises.

(D) None of the above.

40. P brought an action against D for breach of contract. The case proceeded to trial, where P introduced documentary evidence on his direct case. At the close of P's case, D moved for dismissal of P's complaint, which was granted by the court.

Dismissal of P's complaint was:

(A) On the merits.

(B) Not on the merits.

(C) Improper because D's motion was untimely.

(D) None of the above.

41. X Inc. has a 12-member board of directors. X's board adopted a resolution designating an executive committee of three directors and vested in the committee the authority to fill vacancies of and set compensation for company officers who are not directors.

The delegation to the committee was:

(A) Improper because the committee should have had four members.

(B) Proper.

(C) Improper because the powers given were too broad.

(D) None of the above.

42. Boobie University's Medical School ran short of cadavers for its first-year students to dissect. Dr. Vile, a staff professor, called Sleaze Funeral Home and asked Slime, the funeral director, if he knew of any corpses. Slime replied, "Sure, a fresh one just came in," and shipped a body which was supposed to be embalmed. The relatives of the decedent found out about this dastardly deed and suffered great emotional distress. They brought a suit alleging intentional infliction of severe emotional distress and sought punitive damages. The defendants moved to dismiss the complaint on the following grounds:

I. Failure to state a cause of action.
II. Inability to prove physical damages.
III. Punitive damages are not allowable.

The court should:

(A) Grant the motion on ground I. only.

(B) Grant the motion on ground II. only.

(C) Grant the motion on all three grounds.

(D) Deny the motion.

43. Detective Sharp went to the home of Snort, a well-known drug dealer, and after identifying himself as a police officer, asked Snort's mother, Mary, who owned the house, whether he could search Snort's room. Mary said, "O.K. Go ahead." In Snort's room, Sharp found a padlocked trunk marked with Snort's name which he pried open with a crowbar and hammer. There were 30 pounds of cocaine inside. Snort was charged with various crimes relating to the cocaine. Snort's lawyer moves to suppress the cocaine.

Which statement best describes the proper disposition of the motion?

(A) The motion should be granted because Sharp probably exceeded the scope of the authority to search granted by Mary and, in any event, Mary could not have consented to the search of the trunk.

(B) The motion should be granted because Mary had no right to consent to a search of Snort's room.

(C) The motion should be denied because Sharp seized the cocaine within the bounds of the search allowed by Mary.

(D) None of the above.

44. Andy and Bill plan to rob Joe's gas station. While Bill is driving them to the gas station, Andy shouts, "Stop the car, I don't want to do time, I'm getting out," whereupon Andy bolts out of the car. Bill continues on and robs the gas station.

Andy is guilty of:

(A) Nothing.

(B) Robbery.

(C) Conspiracy to rob.

(D) Conspiracy to rob and robbery.

45. X breaks into Y's house and steals silverware. X leaves the house and is about to put the silverware into his car when W, Y's neighbor, spots him and screams, "Police." X decides that taking the silverware is not worth the trouble so he reenters Y's house and returns it to the room he had taken it from. Upon leaving the house the second time (this time, empty-handed), the police arrive and he is arrested.

What crimes may X be charged with?

I.   Criminal trespass.
II. Second degree burglary.
III. First degree burglary.

(A) II.

(B) I. and II.

(C) III.

(D) I.

46. Which of the following cannot be used to show that a letter was signed by Peter?

(A) Testimony by John that he saw Peter sign the letter in his presence.

(B) Testimony by Sam, a handwriting expert, that he compared Peter's signature on the letter with Peter's signature on his divorce settlement agreement, which he signed in the presence of two lawyers and a Supreme Court Justice, and that both signatures are identical.

(C) A determination by a jury of genuineness, after the jurors compared the letter with a signed and notarized application by Peter to take the New York bar exam, which was admitted in evidence.

(D) Proof that the letter was at least 20 years old, free from suspicion concerning its authenticity, and found in a place where, if authentic, it would have been kept.

47. Brat's driver's license suspension for reckless driving has just been lifted. Brat would like to borrow Dad's car to go to the beach. Dad says, "O.K., provided you stay away from those miscreants Stoned and Useless." Brat nevertheless picks up Stoned and Useless and allows Useless to drive the car. On the way, Useless carelessly causes Dad's car to sideswipe the car owned by Jones, causing it to run off the road. Brat tells Stoned to drive instead. Near the beach, Stoned sees the Corvette owned by Kool, a cocaine dealer who recently sold Stoned a substance which turned out to be 100% glucose. Stoned intentionally rams the Corvette to get back at Kool. Jones and Kool sue Dad. Dad's lawyer moved to dismiss both lawsuits.

The court should:

(A) Dismiss both lawsuits.

(B) Dismiss Kool's lawsuit but not the lawsuit of Jones.

(C) Dismiss the lawsuit of Jones but not the lawsuit of Kool.

(D) Allow both lawsuits to stand.

48. While waiting for his commuter train, Sam heard moans. Upon looking in the direction of the moans, Sam saw a semiconscious man lying on the side of the tracks perilously close to the third rail. Sam jumped on the tracks and attempted to pull the man across the roadbed to a safe area. To Sam's great surprise, the commuter train for which he was waiting approached the station on schedule for the first time in months. Sam panicked, dropped the man in the center of the tracks, and climbed to the platform. Unfortunately, the train did not stop in time. The estate of the man killed sued Sam.

Which of the following statements is correct?

(A) Sam is liable because he breached a duty of care owed to the man.

(B) Sam is not liable because he owed no duty to aid the man.

(C) Sam is not liable because the train should have stopped in time.

(D) None of the above.

49. While driving his car, A negligently crashes into B's car, which was traveling in an opposing lane of traffic. C, seeing that B is trapped in the car, goes to offer him assistance. While C is doing so, gasoline from B's car catches fire, causing C severe injuries. C sues A and B. A moves to dismiss C's complaint on the ground of failure to state a cause of action.

The court should:

7/23/07   NY MC

(1)	B ×D	(21)	A ✓	(41)	C ×B
(2)	A ×D	(22)	B ×C	(42)	D ✓
(3)	C ✓	(23)	D ✓	(43)	A ✓
(4)	D ✓	(24)	B ✓	(44)	D ×C
(5)	D ×A	(25)	D ✓	(45)	B ✓
(6)	A ✓	(26)	B ×A	(46)	D ✓
(7)	A ✓	(27)	D ×B	(47)	B ✓
(8)	C ×B	(28)	C ×B	(48)	A ✓
(9)	C ×B	(29)	B ×C	(49)	C ✓
(10)	D ×B	(30)	D ×B	(50)	A ×D
(11)	A ×C	(31)	C ✓		
(12)	D ✓	(32)	D ✓		
(13)	B ×A	(33)	D ×C		
(14)	B ✓	(34)	A ✓		
(15)	C ✓	(35)	D ×C		
(16)	A ×B	(36)	C ✓		
(17)	B ✓	(37)	D ×A		
(18)	B ✓	(38)	D ×B		
(19)	B ×A	(39)	C ×D		
(20)	B ✓	(40)	B ×A		

$$\frac{25}{50}$$

(A) Grant the motion because C should have minded his own business.

(B) Grant the motion because B may have been negligent as well.

(C) Deny the motion because C was a foreseeable plaintiff.

(D) None of the above.

50. While driving a car belonging to the city of New York, Joe, a 25-year-old city employee, strikes and injures Elderly, an 80-year-old man. Elderly sues Joe and the city.

Who may obtain a trial preference?

(A) The city.

(B) Joe.

(C) All parties.

(D) Elderly and the city.

51. Joan injured herself during her meal of baked beans when she bit into a piece of metal which had been packed into XYZ Co.'s can of baked beans. Joan sues XYZ Co. on a strict liability claim. At trial, Joan seeks to introduce evidence that after her accident, XYZ Co. changed the construction and metal used in its cans.

Such evidence:

(A) Can be admitted if Joan seeks to recover under a design defect theory.

(B) Can be admitted if Joan seeks to recover under the theory of a manufacturing defect.

(C) Can be admitted regardless of the theory of recovery used by Joan.

(D) Should not be admitted because to do so would be against the public policy of New York state.

52. H and W are married in 1992 and have child C in 1998. W discovers that H was married in 1988 and never divorced his first wife, who is still alive.

Which of the following is true?

(A) W can get a divorce and C is illegitimate.

(B) W cannot get a divorce and C is illegitimate.

(C) W can get a declaration of nullity and C is legitimate.

(D) W can get a declaration of nullity and C is illegitimate.

53. On March 29, 2000, while driving a car owned by his father, Oscar, Dennis collided with an auto driven by Alice that belongs to her fiance, Barry. In February 2003, Oscar sued Alice and

Barry. Barry immediately attempted to bring a third-party action against Dennis but was unable to serve him. At the conclusion of the trial, the jury awarded judgment against both defendants. In June 2003, a month after the entry of the judgment, Barry served Dennis with a summons and complaint. Dennis moved to dismiss Barry's complaint. The court should:

(A) Grant the motion because res judicata bars the action.

(B) Grant the motion because the statute of limitations has run.

(C) Deny the motion because the statute of limitations has not run.

(D) None of the above.

54. John, a general contractor, is building a house for Paul. Paul executes and delivers to John a promissory note which states "I promise to pay to the order of John $100,000 in 2006 if John finishes building my house." In September 2003, John finished building the house and obtained all necessary certificates of occupancy and inspection certificates from the local building department. In October 2003, John indorsed the note over to his subcontractor, Ken, in payment of substantial past due bills. Ken demands payment from Paul, but is refused. Ken sues Paul on the note. Paul moves to dismiss Ken's complaint. The court should:

(A) Deny Paul's motion because Ken is a holder in due course of the note.

(B) Grant Paul's motion because the note contains a conditional promise to pay.

(C) Grant Paul's motion because the note is not payable at a definite time.

(D) Deny Paul's motion because Ken is an assignee for value of the note.

55. George guarantees David's note payable to the order of Jean by placing his indorsement on the back. Jean indorses the note over to Kevin, a good faith purchaser for cash. Kevin demands payment from David, but David refuses to pay and flees the country. Kevin then sues George for payment. George asserts in his answer (1) an affirmative defense that Jean fraudulently induced David to issue the note, and (2) an affirmative defense that David, a 15-year-old, had no legal capacity to make the note. Which affirmative defense will withstand Kevin's motion to dismiss?

(A) (1).

(B) (2).

(C) Both.

(D) Neither.

56. Defendant is charged in the state of New York with a crime not punishable by death or life imprisonment. Defendant signs a waiver of grand jury indictment with the prosecution's consent. Which of the following statements is correct?

(A) The New York State Constitution expressly permits this waiver.

(B) The federal Constitution expressly permits this waiver.

(C) The New York State Constitution expressly prohibits this waiver.

(D) The federal Constitution expressly prohibits this waiver.

57. T leases Blackacre from L. The lease states that all nontrade fixtures shall remain with the leasehold upon its termination. When the lease terminated, T had (i) a track lighting system throughout the premises which had been installed three years earlier, (ii) a washer and dryer in the basement, and (iii) a darkroom which included an enlarger and projector which were glued to the floor. Of the aforementioned, which of the following must stay with Blackacre?

(A) Only (i) and (iii).

(B) Only (i) and (ii).

(C) Only (ii).

(D) Only (i).

58. While walking across Fifth Avenue in Manhattan, P, a New York resident, was injured by a car running a red light. The car was driven by D, a Manhattan resident and Italian citizen, and owned by D's employer, R Co. R Co. is an Ohio corporation with its headquarters located in Cincinnati. It does substantial business in New York because of the efforts of D, its New York regional salesman. P commences a lawsuit in the United States District Court for the Southern District of New York. P may properly serve:

(A) R Co.

(B) D.

(C) Both R Co. and D.

(D) Neither R Co. nor D.

59. Tom's will gives all of his property "to my beloved wife Joan, if she survives me. If she does not survive me, then my estate shall be distributed in equal shares to my beloved son, Richard, and my beloved daughter, Carrol." Carrol has two sons, Ned and Paul. Carrol and Joan predecease Tom. Upon Tom's death, how should his estate be distributed?

(A) Richard gets one-half; Ned and Paul each get one-quarter.

(B) Richard, Ned, and Paul each get one-third.

(C) Richard gets the whole estate.

(D) Joan's sister Kate takes the whole estate.

60. Defendant is charged with driving while intoxicated and injuring a small child. Prosecutor calls Witness to the stand who will testify that Defendant has a reputation in the community for being a heavy drinker. Witness's testimony:

(A) Is admissible as relevant to a trait of the crime.

(B) Is inadmissible, because not relevant to the crime.

(C) Would be admissible only if Defendant had introduced evidence of his reputation for sobriety.

(D) Would be admissible only if Witness's testimony included specific incidents that he had seen Defendant intoxicated to a substantial degree.

61. In his will executed on July 1, 2003, Charlie, a widower, left $100,000 to his current lover, Sophie, and $20,000 to his only son, Bruce. This will contained a clause stating, "Should any beneficiary named herein contest this will or any part thereof, he shall forfeit all interests given to him by this will." On August 26, 2003, Charlie died. The next day, Bruce went to Charlie's home and found what appeared to be another will executed by Charlie. In this will, Charlie "revoked" all prior wills and left his whole estate to Bruce. Although the date of this will was obscured by water damage, it appeared to be either July 7, 2003, or July 7, 2002. Both wills were offered for probate. Bruce contested the June 1, 2003 will on the ground that it had been revoked by a subsequent will. Thereafter, Sophie filed a timely motion with the surrogate to deny Bruce's legacy under the June 1, 2003 will.

The surrogate should:

(A) Grant Sophie's motion.

(B) Deny Sophie's motion.

(C) Deny Sophie's motion because her legacy was revoked by a subsequent will.

(D) None of the above.

62. Dick and Jane were married in New York in 1995. In 2002, Dick and Jane separated; Dick relocated to Maryland. For over a year, Dick and Jane lived apart pursuant to a written, filed, properly executed separation agreement. Jane now seeks a divorce and, as plaintiff, will submit satisfactory proof that she has performed and complied with all agreement terms and conditions.

Jane:

(A) Cannot obtain personal jurisdiction in New York over Dick in this action.

(B) Can meet the requirements for long arm jurisdiction and must serve Dick with a summons and verified complaint to commence the action.

(C) Can meet the requirements for long arm jurisdiction and need only serve a summons to commence the action because only Jane's name will appear on the summons.

(D) Can meet the requirements for long arm jurisdiction only if she has been domiciled in New York for two years.

63. Bill Tenant rents warehouse space from Land Corp. Bill Tenant is a resident of Connecticut and owns and operates a business confined exclusively to the state of Connecticut. Nevertheless, Bill stores some business-related items in a New York City warehouse owned and maintained by Land Corp. Bill was in New York City to supervise the deposit of goods and has not been in New York for 12 months. Bill has been delinquent in paying rent on a duly executed three-year lease, and Land Corp. seeks to recover three months' unpaid back rent. Land Corp:

(A) Will not be able to obtain in personam jurisdiction over Bill.

(B) Can obtain in personam long arm jurisdiction because Bill uses real property in New York.

(C) Must serve Bill within New York state.

(D) None of the above.

64. Decedent, a Florida resident and domiciliary, owned a large tract of land in upstate New York. Decedent visited New York only once since 1990. In 2000, he was in New York to sign the appropriate deed papers to the tract of land. Decedent died intestate. The manner in which this property shall descend:

(A) Is determined by Florida law.

(B) Is determined by New York law.

(C) Is determined based on evidence of Decedent's intention.

(D) None of the above.

65. Same facts as 64. above, except that the property in question is a painting presently loaned to the Metropolitan Museum in New York City. The manner in which this property shall descend:

(A) Is determined by Florida law.

(B) Is determined by New York law.

(C) Is determined based on evidence of Decedent's intention.

(D) None of the above.

66. On June 1, X Bank loans Joe's Hardware Store money and takes a security interest in Joe's existing inventory and all after-acquired inventory. A financing statement is filed. On July 1, Y Bank promises to loan Joe's $10,000 to purchase hammers and obtains a security agreement from Joe's granting Y Bank a security interest in the hammers. Y Bank immediately files a financing statement and notifies X Bank of the impending loan and its purchase money interest. The loan is then made to Joe's, which endorses the Y Bank check over to the hammer distributor in exchange for the hammers. Who has priority in the security interest in the hammers?

(A) X Bank, because it has priority in all after-acquired property.

(B) X Bank, because it filed its financing statement first.

(C) Y Bank, because it has an inventory purchase money security interest in the hammers.

(D) Y Bank, because X Bank did not object to the loan.

67. Byron held 8% of the outstanding shares of Snap Corp. On February 12, Byron wrote Snap Corp. a letter which said, "On February 20, I shall come to the corporate offices for the purpose of inspecting the corporation's books and financial records." On February 20, Byron appeared at the corporation's offices and demanded the right to inspect the following items:

I. The shareholders' minutes and the record of shareholders.
II. The financial records of the corporation, including the most recent financial statement of the corporation.

Byron may inspect:

(A) I. but not II.

(B) II. but not I.

(C) Both I. and II.

(D) Neither I. nor II.

68. On January 1, 2004, Sam and Lola agreed that Sam would paint Lola's house starting on June 1, 2004. Lola gave Sam a check for $5,000, the amount agreed upon, dated May 31, 2004. On February 1, 2004, Sam indorsed the check in blank to Artie, in payment of a debt Sam had owed to Artie since the previous year. With regard to the check:

(A) Artie is *not* a holder in due course, because the check is subject to a condition precedent.

(B) Artie is *not* a holder in due course, because the check was postdated.

(C) Artie is *not* a holder in due course, because Artie received the check in payment for an antecedent debt.

(D) Artie *is* a holder in due course.

69. On April 15, 2005, P commenced an action against D to enforce an easement agreement granting P the right to use a driveway owned by D adjacent to P's real property in Erie County. After service of summons and complaint, P filed a notice of pendency and the complaint on May 20, 2005, in the Erie County Clerk's office. On July 1, 2007, before P's action was ready for trial, D moved to cancel P's notice of pendency.

D's motion should be:

(A) Granted, because a notice of pendency could not be properly filed in P's action.

(B) Granted, because the notice of pendency was not filed before P's action was commenced.

(C) Granted, because the notice of pendency has expired.

(D) Denied.

70. P contracted in writing to purchase a standard model boat from D, a boat dealer, for $15,000. P paid D a deposit of $5,000 for the boat, which was to be delivered to P a week later.

The next day, P suffered a stroke, and P's attorney immediately sent a letter to D rescinding the contract and demanding a refund of the deposit. Although the contract contained no express provision as to the liquidated damages, D refused to refund P's deposit. P then commenced an action to recover the $5,000 deposit. D counterclaimed, alleging that P had breached the contract and was seeking to retain the $5,000 deposit as liquidated damages. At the trial, it was proved that D had resold the boat to another buyer for $15,000 and that D's profit on the sale to P would have been $3,000. D also proved that he had incurred incidental expenses of $500 for the storage, upkeep, and insurance between the time the boat would have been delivered to P and the time that it was ultimately sold.

P is entitled to recover his $5,000 deposit less an offset to D of:

(A) $500 only, as liquidated damages.

(B) $3,000 only, for D's lost profit.

(C) $3,500 for D's lost profit and incidental expenses.

(D) D is entitled to retain the entire $5,000 deposit as liquidated damages.

71. P duly commenced an action to enjoin D from demolishing a building on property which P allegedly owned. P moved for a preliminary injunction, and, in support of his motion, P submitted affidavits establishing that the demolition of the building by D during the pendency of the action would result in irreparable injury to P and that P would likely succeed on the merits. P also submitted proof that his personal net worth was in excess of $1 million.

The court, in its discretion, may properly grant P's motion if the motion were made:

(A) On notice to D, without requiring P to give an undertaking.

(B) On notice to D, but requiring P to give an undertaking in an amount fixed by the court.

(C) Without notice to D, and without requiring P to give an undertaking.

(D) Without notice to D, but requiring P to give an undertaking in an amount fixed by the court.

72. On January 15, C loaned his friend D the sum of $8,000, and D signed and delivered to C an unsecured note for that amount. Unknown to C, D subsequently became insolvent and remained so at all times afterwards. When D failed to make the payment due on the note on March 15, C insisted that D provide security for the loan. On March 16, D executed and delivered to C a security agreement covering D's office furniture. C immediately perfected his security interest. On April 30, C loaned D an additional $5,000. On the same day, as collateral for the new loan, D executed and delivered to C a security agreement covering D's manufacturing equipment. C immediately perfected his security interest. D filed a voluntary petition in bankruptcy on June 30, scheduling $15,000 in assets and $100,000 in debts. T was duly appointed trustee and now wishes to avoid both security interests as voidable preferences.

T will be successful in avoiding:

(A) Neither security interest.

(B) Both security interests.

(C) Only the security interest in the office furniture.

(D) Only the security interest in the manufacturing equipment.

73. P, a New York resident, went to New Jersey to negotiate a contract with D, a New Jersey resident, and E, a New York resident, for the purchase of certain shares of stock from D and E. P paid D and E $50,000 for the shares but, a short time later, P learned that the actual value of the shares was only $10,000. At P's request, P's attorney prepared a summons and complaint in an action by P against D and E, seeking $40,000 damages for fraud. P's attorney delivered copies of the summons and complaint to S, a process server. S learned that D had come from New Jersey to New York to give testimony voluntarily before a New York grand jury, which was investigating the possible criminal fraud of D and E in the sale of securities to New York residents. S delivered a copy of P's summons and complaint to D in the courthouse parking lot as D was about to go back to New Jersey. S then went to E's residence in New York. When no one answered the doorbell, S affixed a copy of P's summons and complaint to the door and the same day mailed another copy of the summons and complaint to E at E's residence. P's attorney duly filed S's affidavits of service upon D and E. D and E each moved to set aside the service on each of them as invalid.

The court should properly set aside the service on:

(A) D only.

(B) E only.

(C) Both D and E.

(D) The court should deny the motions of both D and E.

74. At the selection of the jury in an action by P against T Town to recover damages for P's personal injuries, J, the first prospective juror, states that she is (1) a clerical employee of T Town, (2) a property owner and taxpayer of T Town, and (3) a shareholder of an insurance company that issues liability insurance policies. J knows that T Town does not carry any liability insurance.

P's attorney may successfully challenge J for cause on the basis that J is:

(A) (1), (2), and (3).

(B) (1) and (3), but not (2).

(C) (1), but not (2) or (3).

(D) (3), but not (1) or (2).

75. The certificate of incorporation of C Corp., a New York business corporation, provides for the election of directors and the election of the president, but no other office, by the shareholders. The certificate of incorporation and the bylaws of C Corp. are silent concerning removal of officers and directors. At the annual meeting of the 50 shareholders of the corporation held on December 10, 2005, A and B were among seven persons elected as directors and A was duly elected

president. At the meeting of directors, immediately following the meeting of shareholders, B was elected treasurer. On July 17, 2006, A and B were convicted of embezzling funds belonging to C Corp. Due notice has been given of a regular meeting of the directors of C Corp. to be held today to vote upon a resolution to remove A and B for cause as directors and officers of C Corp.

At today's meeting a majority of the directors will be sufficient to remove:

(A) B as officer, but not as director.

(B) Both A and B as officers and directors.

(C) Both A and B as officers only.

(D) Neither A nor B as officers or directors.

76. A certificate of incorporation of a proposed New York business corporation was delivered to the secretary of state for filing. The certificate of incorporation: (1) did not designate the secretary of state for service of process; (2) did not designate a registered agent for service of process; and (3) stated that one of the corporate purposes was to carry on a commercial banking business.

The secretary of state may properly refuse to file the certificate because it:

(A) (1) and (2), but not (3).

(B) (1) and (3), but not (2).

(C) (1), but not (2) or (3).

(D) The secretary of state may not properly refuse to file the certificate because of (1), (2), or (3).

77. A hired B, the operator of a boatyard, to repair A's boat for $5,000. B gave a signed written assignment of his right to receive the $5,000 to L Co., a loan company to which B owed $5,000. Neither L Co. nor B gave notice of the assignment to A. When the repairs were completed, A paid $5,000 to B, who used the money to pay gambling debts. L Co. was not paid, and it commenced an action against A for $5,000. A served an answer asserting as defenses that: (1) A paid B in full prior to receiving notice of the assignment; (2) the assignment by B was invalid because the contract between A and B involved the performance of personal services; and (3) the assignment was unenforceable because it was given in consideration of an antecedent debt. L Co. has moved to dismiss all of A's affirmative defenses as insufficient as a matter of law.

The court may properly grant L Co.'s motion with respect to defense(s):

(A) (2), but not (1) or (3).

(B) (3), but not (1) or (2).

(C) (2) and (3), but not (1).

(D) (1), (2), and (3).

78. On opening day of the NFL season, the First Bank of Winecta, New York was robbed at 1:30 p.m. The bank's video scanner recorded the perpetrator as a male with a large build, scar on his left cheek, wearing a Giants football helmet, and carrying a black doctor's valise. After viewing the tape, Police Officer Pete recognized the perpetrator to be Harry, the season ticket holder in the seat next to his. Pete and Harry have both been season ticket holders for the past 20 years and neither has ever missed a home game until this year, when Harry did not attend the opening day game. Surprised that Harry returned home at 2 p.m. on opening day, Wilma, Harry's wife, asked why he wasn't at the game. Harry answered that he "had business to do that day."

Based on Pete's identification, Harry was charged with robbing the First Bank of Winecta, New York.

As its first witness, the prosecution called Wilma. After establishing Wilma's identity, the prosecutor asked Wilma what time Harry returned home on the day the bank was robbed and whether he was carrying a Giants football helmet and a valise when he came home. Harry's attorney objected to any questioning of Wilma. The objection should be:

(A) Sustained, because a spouse is incompetent to testify against the other spouse in a criminal matter.

(B) Overruled, because testimonial privileges do not apply to physical actions.

(C) Overruled, because the only matters privileged are confidential communications.

(D) Sustained, regardless of whether the action is civil or criminal.

79. D was indicted for the crime of robbery in the first degree and duly waived his right to a jury trial. At trial, both the prosecution and the defense informed the court that they wished to waive opening statements.

Opening statement(s) must be made by:

(A) The prosecution, but not the defense.

(B) The defense, but not the prosecution.

(C) Neither.

(D) Both.

80. A, an art dealer, desired to serve as the exclusive agent to market paintings of P, a young painter. On January 5, 2002, A and P agreed in a signed writing that A would be P's exclusive agent for a period of two years. Since that date, A has actively marketed P's paintings, but many remain unsold. On March 15, 2003, P died, survived by his wife, W. W believes that P's unsold paintings will become more valuable because of P's death and does not want to continue with A's agency.

A's agency is terminated:

(A) Immediately upon P's death.

(B) Only when the prospective purchasers with which A is dealing on behalf of P become aware of P's death.

(C) Upon A's receipt of written notice from W that A's agency is terminated.

(D) A's agency is not terminated.

81. D was indicted for the crime of burglary in the second degree and was tried before a jury last week. One of the jurors died during the jury deliberations. There are no alternate jurors available and only 11 are left to deliberate.

The court may allow the jury to complete its deliberation and render a verdict with 11 jurors:

(A) On the court's own motion without the consent of either D or the district attorney.

(B) With consent of D alone.

(C) Only with the consent of D and the district attorney.

(D) The court must declare a mistrial.

82. D shot a gun into a crowd and killed V. D was indicted and tried for the crime of murder in the second degree. At a conference before summation outside the presence of the jury, neither party requested the submission of any lesser-included offense, and the court stated that it would not charge lesser-included offenses. Following summations, the court charged the jury, over D's objections, that D could be found guilty of murder in the second degree or of manslaughter in the first degree. The jury found D guilty of manslaughter in the first degree. On appeal, D argues that the court erred with respect to charging manslaughter in the first degree because: (1) as a matter of law it cannot be a lesser-included offense of murder in the second degree; and (2) the court was bound to inform the parties of its intent to change the summation.

D is correct as to:

(A) (1), but not (2).

(B) (2), but not (1).

(C) Both.

(D) Neither.

83. A and B were partners in an unsuccessful real estate venture. For them to reduce their losses, B proposed to A that they set fire to their building. A agreed to the proposal and purchased the device to be used to start the fire. A has now had a change of heart.

The minimum conduct which A must demonstrate to establish the defense of renunciation with respect to the crime of conspiracy is:

(A) Withdrawal from participation with B before the arson is committed.

(B) Substantial, but unsuccessful, effort to prevent commission of the arson.

(C) Prevention of the arson.

(D) A cannot establish the defense of renunciation with respect to the crime of conspiracy, because it is already a completed crime.

84. P commenced an action against R to recover damages for injuries P sustained when she slipped and fell in front of R's restaurant. In her bill of particulars, served pursuant to R's demand, P stated that the only physical injury she suffered in the accident was a broken leg. After discovery had been completed, P filed a note of issue, placing the action on the trial calendar, and trial is now scheduled for January. P now wishes to serve a supplementary bill of particulars setting forth: (1) that she also suffered an injury to her back in the accident; and (2) continuing special damages as a consequence of her broken leg.

P may now, without leave of the court, serve a supplemental bill of particulars setting forth:

(A)   Both (1) and (2).

(B)   (2), but not (1), and R may, without leave of the court, depose P as to (2).

(C)   (2), but not (1), and R may not, without leave of the court, depose P as to (2).

(D)   P may not now serve a supplemental bill of particulars alleging (1) and (2) without leave of the court.

85.   On June 10, in an action by P against D to recover damages for false arrest, P mailed by certified mail to D, at D's home, a summons with notice of the nature of the action and the relief sought. D timely served a demand for P's complaint. When P failed to serve a complaint in response to D's demand, (1) D moved to dismiss P's action for P's failure to timely serve the complaint. Thereafter, pursuant to a conditional order of dismissal, P served her complaint on D on July 10. On July 15, (2) D served a notice to take P's deposition. On July 20, (3) D moved to strike from P's complaint certain scandalous and prejudicial allegations.

D first appeared in P's action when:

(A)   (1).

(B)   (2).

(C)   (3).

(D)   D has not made an appearance in P's action.

86.   In 1995, D purchased a large tract of land in Erie County, New York, on which he planned to develop a residential subdivision. D subdivided the tract of land into 50 lots and offered the lots for sale. By June 2002, all but five lots had been sold, and single-family residences had been erected on all but lot No. 45, on which a day-care center had been erected in 2001 without objection by the owners of any other lots in the subdivision. B, a builder, has now purchased the remaining five lots and is about to begin construction of two-family residences on them. The deeds to all of the subdivision lots contain a covenant restricting land use in the subdivision to the erection of single-family residences. N, who has been the owner since 1997 of a subdivision lot adjoining one of B's lots, has commenced an action seeking to enforce the restrictive covenant common to the deeds to all lots in the subdivision. B believes the restrictive covenant is unenforceable because: (1) N did not object to the prior violation of the restriction by the construction of the day-care center; and (2) it unreasonably restricts land use and is therefore void as against public policy.

The restrictive covenant may not be enforced by N because:

(A) (1), but not (2).

(B) (2), but not (1).

(C) Both.

(D) The restrictive covenant may be enforced by N.

87. In July 2000, C obtained a judgment for $50,000 against W. W had no money and made no payments on C's judgment. In January 2001, W was struck and seriously injured by a car operated by D, when W was crossing a street. W died three days after the accident. W's duly appointed executor, E, commenced an action against D for damages for W's pain and suffering and for W's wrongful death. In June 2002, the court awarded $15,000 for W's pain and suffering and $35,000 for W's wrongful death. C, who has been paid nothing on her judgment against W, claims the entire $50,000 proceeds. W was survived by her adult daughters A and B. Excluding any recovery from D, the assets of W's estate are sufficient only to pay W's funeral and administrative expenses. W had no creditors other than C.

C is entitled to receive from the $50,000 proceeds:

(A) $15,000.

(B) $35,000.

(C) $50,000.

(D) Nothing.

88. A lawyer, T, in Buffalo, takes a position in Albany to begin on September 1, 2002. In Buffalo, T lives in a one-family dwelling under a written lease which expires on May 1, 2003. Since T is moving to Albany, he wishes to assign the lease to S. The landlord, LL, unreasonably refuses to allow T to assign the lease to S. The lease is silent as to assignments. T now brings an action against LL claiming either: (1) LL must make the assignment; or (2) T must be released from the lease in 30 days.

T will most likely be successful in which claim?

(A) (1), but not (2).

(B) (2), but not (1).

(C) Both.

(D) Neither.

89. H and W buy Blackacre in New York in 1984, as tenants by the entirety. Blackacre is their marital home. In 1986, H and W begin to experience marital difficulties and enter into a written agreement, duly signed and acknowledged, to separate. The agreement states that W is to remain in possession of the marital residence until 1990. In 1990, the house is to be sold and the money is to be divided equally between them. There is no decree of either separation or of divorce; however, W has brought an action for divorce against H, which is still pending. W has died.

Prior to W's death, H and W held the property as:

(A) Tenants in common.

(B) Joint tenants.

(C) Tenants by the entirety and H gets all the proceeds.

(D) Tenants by the entirety and H gets half the proceeds.

90.   In 1995, W and H married in New York. They had a child, C, in 1997. In 2001, H and W divorce. The divorce decree states that W gets custody of C and must live within a 100-mile radius of New York City. H is to pay $150 per week maintenance to W and $100 per week child support for C. H has visitation rights with C every other weekend. In 2002, W moved to Florida and took C with her. H immediately stopped paying maintenance and child support. W, in Florida, brought an action for arrears in New York. H claimed he did not have to pay after W violated the decree and moved to Florida. H moved for: (1) canceling the maintenance arrears to W; (2) suspending future maintenance payments to W; and (3) suspending future child support to C. H wishes for (2) to be suspended for so long as W remains in Florida.

The court may properly grant:

(A) (1), but not (2) and (3).

(B) (2) and (3), but not (1).

(C) (1) and (2), but not (3).

(D) The court may not properly grant any of H's motions.

91.   In 2000, H and W married in New York. After the wedding, H developed a habit of getting drunk and beating W on occasion. In 2002, W tells H she committed adultery with M in November and December of 2001, but that she stopped seeing M in December of 2001. They continued to live together voluntarily until May 1, 2002, when W moved out. On July 1, 2002, W brought an action for divorce on the grounds of cruel and inhuman treatment. H denies W's claims and in his own defense claims: (1) W voluntarily cohabitated after the alleged beatings; and (2) W committed adultery. W moves to dismiss H's claims as insufficient as a matter of law.

The court should grant W's motion to dismiss as to defense(s):

(A) (1), but not (2).

(B) (2), but not (1).

(C) Both.

(D) Neither.

92.   In May, O, the owner of Blackacre, leased to T, by written lease signed by both T and O, a one-family dwelling. The tenancy was to begin on July 15 at $750 to be paid in advance on the 15th of the month. T gave O a $750 security deposit when he signed the lease. On July 15, O refused to allow T to enter Blackacre. O informed T that he must wait until August 15 to take possession.

T is entitled to rescind the lease and:

(A) Recover the security paid plus damages.

(B) T's only remedy is to rescind the lease.

(C) Recover that portion of the security deposit not used to procure another tenant.

(D) T may not rescind the lease and must move in on August 15, but will not be responsible for the July rent.

93. **Which of the following is not true about a grand jury hearing?**

(A) Twelve votes are needed to indict.

(B) A witness may waive immunity only in writing.

(C) A grand jury may hear only criminal matters.

(D) The witness may be accompanied by his attorney provided he has waived immunity.

94. **V, from Vermont, claims $500,000 damages for personal injuries against N, from Buffalo. The injuries resulted from an auto accident which occurred on the Connecticut Turnpike. V wants to bring the action in federal court.**

The proper venue for this case is:

(A) New York only.

(B) Vermont only.

(C) New York or Connecticut.

(D) New York or Vermont.

95. **On May 26, 2003, P, then 14 years old, was injured in a ditch owned by the S School District. On August 19, 2003, P's attorney, Z, filed a notice of claim against S School District on behalf of F, P's father, for P's medical expenses and loss of P's services and P for his injuries. S denied the claim. On May 1, 2007, Z served a summons and complaint upon S, claiming P's injuries, F's expenditure for P's medical treatment, and F's loss of P's services. S moved to dismiss on the grounds of the statute of limitations.**

S's motion to dismiss should be granted as to:

(A) F and P.

(B) F.

(C) P.

(D) S's motion should not be granted.

96. **P's attorney, A, prepared a summons and complaint in an action in Bronx County by P against D for $100,000 damages for slander. On June 10, A went to D's home and asked to see D. D's wife, W, who answered the door, told A that D would not be home for several hours. Thereupon, A delivered a copy of P's summons and complaint to W. W gave the copy of P's summons and complaint to D several hours later. D immediately consulted his attorney. A mailed a copy of P's summons and complaint to D at D's home the same day, but A made no other attempts to personally deliver the summons and complaint to D. On June 15, A filed proof of service with the clerk of the court of Bronx County. On July 10, D moved to dismiss P's complaint on the ground of lack of personal jurisdiction over D.**

D's motion to dismiss P's complaint was timely:

(A) And the court has personal jurisdiction over D.

(B) But the court has no personal jurisdiction over D.

D's motion to dismiss P's complaint was not timely:

(C) But the court has personal jurisdiction over D.

(D) And the court has no personal jurisdiction over D.

97. **On February 2, T's attorney prepared T's will according to T's directions and mailed it to T. On February 4, when T's father, F, was visiting Y, T told F that he was going to sign his will. T then signed his will at the end in F's presence, and at T's request F signed it as a witness. On February 24, T showed his adult son, A, the will and T told A that the signature on it was T's. At T's request, A then signed the will as a witness. T died on June 1, and E, the executor designated in T's will, has offered T's will for probate. Both F and A testified before the surrogate of the above facts concerning the execution of the will. T's will gives A the sum of $100,000 and gives the remainder of T's estate equally to his other two sons, B and C. T, a widower, was survived by A, B, C, and F. T's net estate is $150,000.**

T's will should not be admitted to probate because:

(A) A did not actually witness T sign the will.

(B) F and A are witnesses to the execution of the will.

T's will should be admitted to probate because:

(C) An attorney properly prepared the will in accordance with the testator's wishes.

(D) F and A are witnesses to the execution of the will.

Questions 98 and 99 are based on the following situation:

Ellen was taking Judi for a drive around town to show off her brand new Lamborghini when she noticed union picketers outside Hot Rocks Cafe. Hoping to land a good job with a pro-management law firm, Ellen was particularly enraged by the picketers' signs that day. Ellen told Judi that these days people should be grateful they have a job. Judi agreed that she hated the picketers too.

Wanting to have a little fun, Judi suggested to Ellen that they try to scare the picketers by driving and swerving at them with the car and then pulling away at the very last moment. Ellen agreed that this would be fun and pulled around the block to have a go at the first picketer. However, Ellen was not used to the feel of her new car and instead of swerving away ran head on into the crowd of people. Luckily the brakes were good and she only hit and killed two people.

Police Officer Ray arrived a half hour later and saw the crowd around the two dead picketers and Ellen's damaged car. Ray then took statements from the witnesses, examined Ellen's car, and noted that there were two-foot skid marks on the pavement. Ellen, obviously upset because this could really hurt her chances of being admitted to the bar, told Ray that she didn't mean to hurt anyone, they were just having some fun. Ray included all this in his report at the end of the day.

98.   At Ellen's trial, Ray took the witness stand. The prosecutor asked Ray about what Ellen told him immediately after the accident. If Ellen's attorney objects to this question, the testimony is:

(A)   Admissible, because it is nonhearsay.

(B)   Inadmissible, because it is hearsay, not within an exception.

(C)   Inadmissible, because it is extrinsic.

(D)   None of the above.

99.   Of what crimes can Judi be convicted?

(A)   Criminally negligent homicide.

(B)   Felony murder.

(C)   Battery.

(D)   All of the above.

100.   Witness selected defendant's picture from photographs viewed at the police station. Witness testified at a pre-trial hearing that when she first saw defendant's photograph she thought it might be the person who committed the crime, but she was uncertain. However, when the officer put a piece of paper on the photo to simulate a cap, the defendant became sure the photograph depicted the defendant. Subsequently, Witness picked out defendant at a post-charge lineup, but at a pre-trial hearing the results of the lineup were determined to be inadmissible due to failure to have defendant's attorney present at the lineup.

At the trial, defense counsel requested an *in limine* ruling from the trial judge to determine if counsel were to question Witness about the identification procedures at the police station, would that open the door to testimony concerning the post-charge lineup?

How should the court rule?

(A)   Testimony concerning the post-charge lineup should be held inadmissible as violating the defendant's Sixth Amendment right to counsel.

(B) Testimony concerning the post-charge lineup should have been held admissible to correct a misleading impression from the police station identification.

(C) Testimony concerning the post-charge lineup should be held inadmissible because it had no relevance to issues relating to the identification at the police station.

(D) Testimony concerning the post-charge lineup should have been held admissible, but only with an instruction to the jury that it had been obtained in violation of defendant's Sixth Amendment right to counsel.

BAR REVIEW

Assorted
Multiple Choice Answers

1. (D) (TORTS)

Parker will not recover under New York's "pure" comparative negligence statute because, under the facts, he was 100% negligent whereas Doctor was free of any culpability for same.

2. (D) (WILLS)

Pursuant to New York Estates, Powers, and Trusts Law ("EPTL") section 3-2.1, no effect is given to material following testator's signature and will not affect material preceding testator's signature if validly executed and comprehensible. Thus, A's will may be admitted for probate except for the handwritten clause. Clearly, (A), (B), and (C) are incorrect.

3. (C) (TRUSTS)

EPTL section 7-3.1: A disposition in trust for the use of the creator is void as against existing or subsequent creditors of the creator. Thus, D and O, as existing and subsequent creditors, respectively, may levy on C's trust, a trust created by C for his own use. For the foregoing reasons, (A), (B), and (D) are incorrect.

4. (D) (TORTS)

An aggrieved employee cannot sue his fellow employees for their negligence arising out of and during the course of employment, nor can he hold his employer vicariously liable for its negligence because of the workers' compensation statute. (A) and (B) are wrong because Q cannot sue his fellow employees, A and J, respectively. (C) is wrong because Q cannot sue his employer, B Bomb Factory.

5. (A) (CRIMINAL LAW)

Menacing is intentionally placing or attempting to place another in fear of imminent serious physical injury. Here, F intentionally placed the bank guard in fear of serious physical injury. (B) is incorrect because harassment requires an intent to harass, annoy, or alarm the victim. Here, F had the intent to put the bank guard in fear of serious bodily injury. (C) and (D) are incorrect because criminal assault requires that the victim suffer physical injury. Here, the bank guard did not suffer physical injury.

6. (A) (CRIMINAL LAW)

First degree burglary is the burglary of a dwelling in which any one of four special aggravating circumstances occurs. One of those circumstances is being armed with explosives or a deadly weapon (it need not be displayed). Here, Q and A entered the dwelling of G and both were armed with deadly weapons. Accordingly, both are guilty of first degree burglary. Thus, (A) is correct.

7. (A) (CONSTITUTIONAL LAW—FEDERAL AND STATE)

The Fifth Amendment of the United States Constitution guarantees use of a grand jury in accusing a defendant of capital or infamous crimes. (This federal guarantee has not been held applicable to the states through the Fourteenth Amendment.) Article 1, section 6 of the New York Constitution is similar in effect, but permits the defendant to waive indictment by the grand jury with the prosecutor's approval if the crime charged is not punishable by death or life imprisonment. Thus, (C) and (D) are incorrect. (B) is incorrect because there is no prohibition against waiver of jury indictment in federal constitutional law.

8. (B) (CORPORATIONS)

Under Business Corporations Law section 713, a corporate contract involving an interested director will not be voidable if (i) the board approves the transaction by a sufficient vote without counting the votes of the interested directors; or (ii) the board approves the transaction by a unanimous vote of the disinterested directors, where votes of the interested directors must be counted in order to constitute action of the board; or (iii) the shareholders approve the transaction by vote *and provided* in each case that the "material facts as to the director's interest or of the common directorship, officership, or financial interest are disclosed or known to those voting on such approval." If none of the foregoing occurs, the contract is voidable unless the parties thereto affirmatively establish that the contract was fair and reasonable to the corporation at the time A's proposal was approved. Thus, for the foregoing reasons, (A) is obviously incorrect. (D) and (C) are incorrect because the board of directors may approve the contract.

9. (B) (CRIMINAL LAW)

Under New York criminal law, if the defendant causes the death of another individual with the intent to cause serious physical injury, he is guilty of first degree manslaughter under section 125.0.1.

10. (B) (CRIMINAL LAW)

Defendant would be convicted of first degree manslaughter. In New York, a person is guilty of first degree manslaughter when, with intent to cause serious physical injury to another person, he causes the death of such person. Defendant could not argue self-defense since he had a duty to retreat. Choice (A) is not the best answer because second degree manslaughter turns on a reckless act, as opposed to an intentional act. Similarly, choice (C) is not the best answer because the defendant did not act with depraved indifference.

11. (C) (REAL PROPERTY/CONTRACTS)

Under the doctrine of part performance, a purchaser may compel specific performance of an oral sale of land, notwithstanding the Statute of Frauds, if the purchaser proves that he made at least partial payment *and* shows possession of the land by the purchaser, valuable improvements, or performance of valuable services. Mere possession of land is not sufficient, and thus, (A) is wrong. Mere payment of the purchase price (or a portion thereof) is not sufficient and thus (B) is wrong. (C) is correct because under New York law, partial payment of the purchase price coupled with possession or possession with improvements is sufficient to overcome the Statute of Frauds.

12. (D) (DOMESTIC RELATIONS)

Death of either party, remarriage, or cohabitation of the wife does not affect arrears. Thus, (A) is incorrect because U's estate will be entitled to prosecute the arrearage claim and P's estate will be liable for same. For similar reasons, (B) and (C) are also incorrect.

13. (A) (CONTRACTS)

Pursuant to U.C.C. section 2-322, agreement to deliver via carrying vessel to a named port keeps the risk of loss on the seller until the goods are properly unloaded. Thus, (B) and (C) are incorrect because A had the risk of loss until the goods were properly unloaded, in this case in New York on or before June 17. (D) is incorrect because commercial reasonableness does affect the risk of loss.

14. (B) (CONTRACTS)

Under General Obligations Law section 5-701(10), the Statute of Frauds applies to contracts to pay a fee for negotiating a business opportunity. Thus, P should have put the contract for his negotiating services in writing. (A) is incorrect because if performance by the terms of the contract is possible within one year, the contract is not within the Statute. Here, P could have performed his duties within a few days of the date of contracting. (C) is incorrect because under conflict of laws principles, New York has the most contacts and "governmental interest" in the contract. Thus, Saudi law does not apply.

15. (C) (TORTS/AGENCY)

A principal is liable for the acts performed by her agent in the scope of her agency. Thus, A is liable for the tortious conduct of P because P committed the fraud within the scope of and during the course of his employment. P is also separately liable for his own tortious conduct. For the foregoing reasons, (A), (B), and (D) are incorrect.

16. (B) (CONTRACTS)

F's promise is in the nature of a pledge or charitable subscription which induced detrimental reliance on the part of G Inc. Thus, the promise here may be considered equivalent to consideration and is enforceable for $50,000. (A) is wrong because the New York courts consider a pledge as the equivalent of consideration. (C) and (D) obviously are incorrect.

17. (B) (CONTRACTS)

Pursuant to General Obligations Law section 5-1109, when an offer to enter into a contract is made by the offeror and states that the offer is irrevocable during a fixed period, the offer shall not be revocable because of a lack of consideration. Thus, the offer was irrevocable until July 1. (A) is incorrect because C will prevail on the ground that the offer could not be revoked until July 1. (C) is incorrect because the statute expressly precludes this ground. (D) is wrong for the same reason as (A).

18. (B) (FEDERAL JURISDICTION & PROCEDURE)

The procedure for removal of an action from state court to federal court is covered by 28 U.S.C. sections 1441 *et seq*. Only a defendant may remove an action. A defendant may remove an action only if the federal court had original jurisdiction over the action both at the time the action was commenced and at the time that removal is sought. For the federal court to have original jurisdiction over the case at hand, there must be complete diversity between plaintiff and defendant, and the jurisdictional amount (more than $75,000) must have been alleged. For diversity purposes, a corporation is considered to be the citizen of every state in which it is incorporated, and is also a citizen of the state in which it has its principal place of business. A corporation's principal place of business will be presumed to be where its corporate offices are located, unless the corporation has its entire manufacturing facilities in another state. (This is not the case here.) If an opposing party is a citizen of any state in which the corporation is considered to be a citizen, diversity will be destroyed. [28 U.S.C. §1332] Finally, it should be noted that venue for a removed action lies in the federal district court "embracing the place where such action is pending." Applying the law to this question, it is clear that the defendant, and only the defendant, may remove the action to federal court. Thus, (B) is the best answer.

19. (A) (NEW YORK PRACTICE)

P was unable to obtain long arm personal jurisdiction pursuant to CPLR 302. None of the jurisdictional requirements of CPLR 302(a) are satisfied. Thus, (A) is correct. For the foregoing reasons (B) is incorrect. (C) is incorrect because *Shaffer v. Heitner* abolished the exercise of jurisdiction predicated solely upon the attachment of defendant's New York property; *i.e.*, quasi in rem jurisdiction cannot be exercised here.

20. (B) (DOMESTIC RELATIONS)

Domestic Relations Law section 140(b) allows the party who was an infant at the time of the marriage to obtain an annulment on the ground of lack of legal consent, only if the infant, after reaching the age of lawful consent, does not freely cohabit with the spouse. Section 140(e) allows an action to annul a marriage on the ground that the consent of one of the parties thereto was obtained by fraud, which may be maintained at any time by the party whose consent was so obtained. The rule on annulment of marriage for fraud based on misrepresentation has been broadened to include facts other than those relating directly to cohabitation and consortium. Therefore, (B) is correct because M's failure to tell W about the destruction of the Hawaiian property while possessing such knowledge constitutes a failure to disclose a vital fact which concerned the essence of the marital contract between M and W. (A) is incorrect because W freely cohabited with M after 2000, the year she attained the age of lawful consent, 18. For the reason above, (C) and (D) are also incorrect. *Note:* Contrast general misrepresentations about wealth (not grounds for annulment) with misrepresentations about facts going to the essence of the marital contract (is a ground for an annulment).

21. (A) (TORTS)

This is the correct statement of the law in New York state. (B), (C), and (D) are not correct statements of the law in New York.

22. (C) (EVIDENCE)

Under CPLR 4511(a), judicial notice of a New York City ordinance is mandatory. Thus, (C) is the correct answer and (A), (B), and (D) are wrong.

23. (D) (DOMESTIC RELATIONS)

Pursuant to Domestic Relations Law section 240, in actions to obtain custody, the court must give "such direction, between the parties, for the custody, care, education, and maintenance of any child of the parties, as in the court's discretion, justice requires, having regard to the circumstances of the case and of the respective parties and the best interests of the child." Thus, the presumptions set forth in (A), (B), and (C) are not the law of New York.

24. (B) (DOMESTIC RELATIONS)

Domestic Relations Law section 32(2) provides that parents are liable for support of children under 21 years of age. After age 21, the support obligation ceases, even if the child later becomes a public charge. Thus, (A) and (D) are incorrect. (C) is incorrect because marriage does not affect the support obligation for children under 21.

25. (D) (FEDERAL JURISDICTION & PROCEDURE)

Where there are multiple parties on either or both sides of the controversy, there must be complete diversity between the opposing sides. Whenever one defendant and one plaintiff are co-citizens of the same state, there is no diversity jurisdiction. Consequently, because each plaintiff is a citizen from a state from where a defendant is a citizen, there is no diversity jurisdiction, and the claim must be brought in state court.

26. (A) (NEW YORK PRACTICE/PARTNERSHIP)

The assets of A, AB Co., and D are subject to execution of the default judgment. To gain jurisdiction of a partnership, service need only be made on one of the general partners, here A. [CPLR 310] Thus, the assets of AB Co. are available to satisfy the judgment. To gain jurisdiction of each individual partner, each partner must be named and served. Failure to name and serve a partner will make his individual assets unavailable for satisfaction of the judgment. [CPLR 5018(a)] Here, A but not B has been served, thereby subjecting A's but not B's individual assets to execution. [CPLR 5018(a)] A separate action may be brought against B for that part of the judgment unsatisfiable out of partnership assets. [CPLR 1502] Of course, since D has been served, his assets are subject to execution.

27. (B) (NEW YORK PRACTICE/DOMESTIC RELATIONS)

CPLR 302(b) permits the exercise of personal jurisdiction over a nonresident defendant in any matrimonial action or family court proceeding involving a demand for support, alimony, maintenance, distributive awards, or special relief in matrimonial actions, provided that the plaintiff is a resident of New York, and New York was the matrimonial domicile before separation. Furthermore, under Domestic Relations Law section 232(a)(2), service on a defendant in a matrimonial action may be personally delivered to the defendant, or served on the defendant pursuant to an order directing method of service of summons in accordance with CPLR 308 or 315. While CPLR 308(5) provides for the court to allow substituted service in such manner as the court deems fit, which may include certified mail, this method of service is only available if personal delivery [CPLR 308(1)], leave and mail [CPLR 308(2)], or nail and mail [CPLR 308(4)] is impracticable.

28. (B) (TORTS)

New York has abolished all intra-family tort immunity of any kind. [N.Y. Gen. Oblig. Law §3-313] Under the former traditional view of intra-family tort immunity, one member of a family unit could not sue another in tort for personal injury. Since New York does not recognize the immunity, Gillie is not precluded from bringing action against her husband and (B) is the correct answer. (A) is wrong because in New York, a parent does not owe a duty to his child to exercise due care in supervision of the child's day-to-day activities. (C) is wrong because this also includes the parent's duty to third persons.

29. (C) (CRIMINAL LAW)

A is guilty of rape under Penal Law section 130.35 and robbery under Penal Law sections 160.00 *et seq.* There is no merger of offenses.

30. (B) (WILLS)

The presumption of revocation is not overcome. If the will has been in the custody of the testator and is found among his personal effects, after his death, cut or otherwise mutilated, there is a presumption that the cutting or mutilation was effected by the testator with the intention to revoke the will. This presumption may be overcome by adequate proof to the contrary, but such proof does not include declarations by the decedent designed to establish the continued existence of the will, unless they are made in connection with some act and under such circumstances as to become a part of the res gestae. Therefore, the only remaining evidence is the fact that the will was cut in two, and there is no evidence to overcome the presumption of revocation.

31. (C) (CORPORATIONS)

In New York, a majority of the "entire board" constitutes a quorum unless the certificate of incorporation or bylaws provide for a lesser quorum (not less than one-third). Here, a quorum is present since eight directors are in attendance. A vote of a majority of the directors present (if a quorum is present) constitutes an act of the board. Here, a majority of the quorum constitutes five directors. Thus, (C) is correct.

32. (D) (NEW YORK PRACTICE)

Under CPLR 508, venue in a replevin action is properly laid in the county of residence of any party or in the county where the personal property to be replevied is located. Thus, (D) is correct since the suit may be brought in Albany, Schnectady, or Saratoga county.

33. (C) (CONTRACTS)

Where a construction contract is breached by the owner during the construction, the measure of damages to be recovered by the contractor is the contract price minus the cost of completion and any payments which have been made by owner. Here, C recovers the contract price, $15,000, minus the cost of completion, $4,000, and the two payments, $6,000, or $5,000. Thus, (C) is the correct answer.

34. (A) (NEW YORK PRACTICE)

A judgment docketed with the county clerk of a particular county only imposes a judgment lien on the judgment debtor's real property within that county. Here the judgment was not docketed in New York County, the situs of C's other real property. Thus, (A) is correct.

35. (C) (CRIMINAL LAW)

Under the facts, (C) is the correct answer. The offense of criminal facilitation reaches a defendant who does not have the requisite intention to be classified as an accomplice, but who has knowingly aided in the commission of a crime.

36. (C) (NEW YORK PRACTICE)

A bill of particulars must be verified whenever the pleading it verifies is verified. By special provision of CPLR 3044, all bills of particulars in negligence actions must be verified.

37. (A) (WILLS)

Until 1981, EPTL section 5-3.3 provided that a testator's issue or parents could set aside testamentary gifts to charity. However, effective July 7, 1981, the legislature repealed that provision. Thus, there is no longer any restriction on testamentary gifts to charity and, accordingly, neither S nor D can challenge the bequest to C Charity.

38. (B) (NEW YORK PRACTICE)

Mutuality of remedy is no longer required in arbitration contracts. If there is consideration for the entire agreement, that is sufficient. The consideration supports the arbitration option as it does every other obligation in the agreement.

39. (B) (REAL PROPERTY)

In the absence of an express covenant to rebuild demised premises destroyed by fire, upon such destruction through no fault of the tenant, the tenant is under no obligation to rebuild or restore them.

40. (A) (NEW YORK PRACTICE)

CPLR 5013 provides as follows:

> Rule 5013. Effect of judgment dismissing claim.
>
> A judgment dismissing a cause of action before the close of the proponent's evidence is not a dismissal on the merits unless it specifies otherwise, but a judgment dismissing a cause of action after the close of the proponent's evidence is a dismissal on the merits unless it specifies otherwise.

Thus, (A) is correct.

41. (B) (CORPORATIONS)

If the certificate or bylaws so provide, the board may designate one or more directors to constitute a committee of the board. A resolution adopted by a majority of the entire board is required. A committee has all the powers of the board subject to limitations in the bylaws or certificate and the following limitations imposed by BCL section 712: (i) submissions to shareholders of actions needing shareholder approval, (ii) filling vacancies on boards or committees, (iii) fixing compensation of directors, (iv) adoption, amendment, or repeal of the bylaws, and (v) amendment or repeal of board resolutions expressly not amendable or repealable by the committee. Thus, (B) is correct and (A), (C), and (D) are incorrect.

42. (D) (TORTS/NEW YORK PRACTICE)

In New York, when mental distress results from the intentional mishandling of a corpse, New York courts recognize a cause of action in favor of the next of kin. Actual damages are not required. It is not necessary to prove physical injuries to recover. It is, however, necessary to establish severe emotional distress (*i.e.*, more than a reasonable person could be expected to endure). Punitive damages are allowable, where defendant's conduct was improperly motivated. Here, all the grounds alleged for dismissal of the complaint had no basis in law.

43. (A) (CRIMINAL PROCEDURE)

Any person with an equal right to use or occupy property may consent to a search, and any evidence found may be used against the other owners or occupants. Here, Mary, as the owner of the house, had the right to enter her son's room (he was not a paying boarder—in which case Mary could not consent to a search) and thus she had a right to consent to the room's search. However, Mary did not have a right to consent to a breaking of the trunk, which was clearly Snort's property. Thus, Sharp's search of the trunk was illegal, and accordingly the cocaine should be suppressed under the fruits of the poisonous tree doctrine.

44. (C) (CRIMINAL LAW)

Andy is only guilty of conspiracy. A defendant has an affirmative defense to conspiracy only if he voluntarily renounces and he prevents commission of the object crime. If the object crime occurs, the defendant has no defense to liability as a conspirator, no matter what efforts he has made. Here, Andy and Bill were co-conspirators, and although Andy voluntarily renounced, Bill nevertheless committed the robbery. Thus, Andy is guilty of conspiracy. Andy, however, is not guilty of the robbery itself, because in New York if a defendant is solely a conspirator and does not participate in the execution of the crime, he is not liable for the substantive offense committed by the co-conspirator. Here, Andy did not participate in the actual robbery, and accordingly, he cannot be liable for it. Therefore, (A), (B), and (D) are incorrect.

45. (B) (CRIMINAL LAW)

X completed two distinct crimes here: second degree burglary and criminal trespass. Second degree burglary is defined as knowingly entering or remaining unlawfully in a building with the intent to commit a crime therein when an additional aggravating element is present. One of those elements, as defined in the statute, is that the "building" is a dwelling. Here, X satisfied the requirements for second degree burglary when he went into the house the first time. Criminal trespass consists of knowingly entering or remaining unlawfully on the premises. The second time X returned to Y's house, he committed a criminal trespass because, although he did not return to the house to commit another crime therein (he was returning stolen goods), he nevertheless had knowledge of the unlawful character of his reentry. X did not commit first degree burglary because that crime entails the burglary of a dwelling and at least one of four aggravating factors; *i.e.*, display of firearms, physical injury to non-participant, threat or use of dangerous instrument, or being armed with explosives or a deadly weapon. Here, none of these aggravating factors is present.

46. (D) (EVIDENCE)

Direct evidence of genuineness or authorship may take the form of: testimony by a witness who was present when the author signed or made the writing (choice (A)); proof of handwriting by testimony of an expert witness who compares questioned handwriting with genuine specimen (choice (B)); or proof of handwriting by allowing the jurors themselves to compare questioned handwriting with a genuine specimen which is placed in evidence [CPLR 4536] (choice (C)). Thus, choices (A), (B), and (C) are incorrect. (D) is correct because in New York, the ancient document rule requires that a writing be more than 30 years old, unlike the federal rule [Fed. R. Evid. 803(13)], which uses 20 years as the norm. Here, there was proof that the letter was only at least 20 years old.

47. (B) (TORTS)

Vehicle and Traffic Law section 388 provides that "every owner of a vehicle used or operated in this state shall be liable and responsible for death or injuries to person or property resulting from negligence in the use or operation of such vehicle, in the business of the owner or otherwise by any person using or operating same, with the permission, express or implied, of such owner." It is not necessary that the person to whom the owner granted permissive use actually operate the vehicle. If such person is present in the vehicle while it is being operated by someone else, he is "using" it within the meaning of the statute and any negligence of the operator will bind the owner. Here, Brat, the individual who received permission to use Dad's car, was present even though he was not driving. Thus, Dad's car was being "used" with his permission as meant by the statute. However, in this case, Dad is only vicariously liable for the damages suffered by Jones because the statute only applies to negligence. The owner is not vicariously liable for intentionally tortious operation by the driver, and therefore, Dad is not liable for the intentional ramming of Kool's Corvette by Stoned.

48. (A) (TORTS)

As a general matter, no legal duty is imposed upon any person to act to rescue another person in a position of peril. However, as an exception to this rule, one who gratuitously acts for the benefit of another, although under no duty to do so in the first instance, is then under a duty to act as would an ordinary, prudent, reasonable person. Here, Sam gratuitously decided to aid the semiconscious man, even though he was under no duty to do so. Having done so, Sam assumed a duty of care which he breached by leaving the man in a more dangerous position in the center of the tracks.

49. (C) (TORTS)

A rescuer, as a matter of law, is a foreseeable plaintiff so long as the rescue is not wanton. Here, C, a rescuer, was a foreseeable party within the scope of the risk created by A's negligent conduct. Thus, (C) is the correct answer.

50. (D) (NEW YORK PRACTICE)

The ordinary rule is that cases are to be tried in the order in which the notes of issue have been filed. However, a case may be advanced for trial in certain cases, including where the party requesting the preference is age 70 or older. Here, Elderly may seek a preference if he wishes. Also, suit brought by or against the state, a state officer, a political subdivision, or an officer thereof is entitled to a preference if requested by the latter parties. Accordingly, (D) is correct.

51. (B) (TORTS/EVIDENCE)

Ordinarily, evidence of repairs or remedial measures taken after an accident is not admissible as an admission of culpability or negligence. However, in a products liability case where plaintiff seeks to recover under the theory of a manufacturing defect, evidence of a post-accident modification in design may be received in evidence against the manufacturer. On the other hand, in a products liability case where plaintiff seeks to recover under a design defect theory, evidence of a post-accident modification in design may not be admitted.

52. (C) (DOMESTIC RELATIONS)

Under Domestic Relations Law section 6, a marriage is void by reason of bigamy. Thus, W is entitled to a declaration of nullity. Notwithstanding the nullity of his parents' marriage, C is nevertheless legitimate, because under Domestic Relations Law section 24, legitimacy is unaffected by the fact that the parents' marriage is void, voidable, annulled, or judicially declared void. Accordingly, (C) is the correct answer.

53. (C) (NEW YORK PRACTICE)

Barry's claim against Dennis appears to be one of contribution. Contribution differs from indemnity in that it is not founded on contract and only ratable or proportional reimbursement is sought. Pursuant to CPLR 1401, a defendant may assert his claim for contribution prior to the payment of any amount to a plaintiff. However, such a claim does not entitle a defendant to contribution until payment by such defendant to plaintiff of an amount in excess of his proportionate share of the judgment is actually made, at which point in time the six-year statute of limitations will begin to run.

54. (D) (COMMERCIAL PAPER)

The promissory note which Paul gave John was not a negotiable instrument under the U.C.C. This is so because, by its terms, the note is not unconditional nor is it payable on demand or at a definite time.

Since the note is not negotiable, Ken cannot be a holder of it. As Ken is not a holder, he cannot be a holder in due course. However, notwithstanding that the instrument is not negotiable, it remains a promissory note which was assigned to Ken for value, and therefore Ken still has a right of payment as an assignee. Accordingly, Ken may sue as an assignee for value and his complaint should not be dismissed. For this reason, only answer (D) is correct. The failure of the note to come under Article 3 of the U.C.C. does not abrogate Ken's underlying contractual rights as an assignee. Thus, answers (A), (B), and (C), which pertain to requisites of negotiability under Article 3, are incorrect.

55. (D) (COMMERCIAL PAPER/NEW YORK PRACTICE)

Kevin is a holder in due course ("HDC"), and George, an accommodation indorser, is a surety. If an HDC knew prior to his acquiring a negotiable instrument that some of the prior parties were sureties (accommodation parties), the HDC takes subject to the right of these parties to raise their suretyship defenses; *i.e.*, these defenses are "real" defenses with respect to the HDC. On the other hand, if the HDC did not know that a prior party signed as a surety, the suretyship defenses—being personal—cannot be raised against him. In this question, Kevin probably knew that George was an accommodation indorser since his signature was not necessary to transfer title (the signature of Jean was). Here, George's suretyship defense is that Jean fraudulently induced David to issue the note. Under suretyship law, the defense that the principal was induced to enter into a contract by fraud is available to the surety only if the principal exercises his right to disaffirm the contract with the creditor. In this case, the principal, David, has not done so. Thus, George cannot assert this affirmative defense as a surety. Moreover, if Kevin did not know that George was a surety, fraud by inducement is a personal defense which cannot be asserted against an HDC. Accordingly, for the foregoing reasons, the first affirmative defense has no merit. Infancy is a defense assertable only by the infant and may not be used by another party to avoid payment. Thus, the second affirmative defense has no merit. For these reasons, (D) is the correct answer.

56. (A) (CONSTITUTIONAL LAW)

The Fifth Amendment of the United States Constitution guarantees the use of a grand jury in federal cases where a defendant is accused of a capital or an infamous crime. This provision does not apply to the states. Article 1, section 6 of the New York Constitution is similar in effect to the Fifth Amendment, but permits a defendant to waive indictment by the grand jury with the prosecutor's approval if the crime charged is not punishable by death or life imprisonment.

57. (D) (REAL PROPERTY)

Under the concept of fixtures, a chattel which has been annexed to real property is converted from personalty to realty. Whether a chattel becomes a fixture is a matter of intent of the annexor at the time of the annexation. The greater the degree of annexation to the realty, the stronger is the indication that the annexor intended to permanently improve the freehold. Hence, only the track lighting system is clearly a fixture. The other items are easily removable.

58. (C) (FEDERAL JURISDICTION & PROCEDURE/NEW YORK PRACTICE)

To bring a suit in federal court, there must be either federal question or diversity jurisdiction. Here, only diversity would be a basis of jurisdiction since there is no federal question involved. In diversity cases, there must be complete diversity of citizenship between the plaintiff and all the defendants. Here, P, a New York resident, has diversity with R Co. because the latter's corporate charter and principal place of business are located in Ohio. Moreover, notwithstanding that D is a New York resident, P also has diversity with this defendant, an Italian citizen, because under 28 U.S.C. section 1322(a)(2), a non-United States citizen may sue and be sued within diversity jurisdiction. Although D is a New York resident, there is no indication that he is a **permanent** resident. If D were a permanent New York resident, this would divest the court of diversity jurisdiction because P is also a New York resident. Thus, there is complete diversity between P and D and R Co. Under Federal Rule of Civil Procedure 4, a federal district court acquires personal jurisdiction over out-of-state defendants pursuant to the long arm statutes of the state where the court sits. Here, service of process on R Co. is governed by New York's statute, CPLR 302. CPLR 302(a)(1) provides for long arm jurisdiction over a defendant who in person or through an agent commits a tortious act within New York. In this case, D, R Co.'s employee and driver of its car, is clearly an agent of R Co. Thus, there is long arm jurisdiction over R Co. With respect to D, as a New York domiciliary, he can be served. Therefore, since both defendants can be properly served, answer (C) is correct and the other answers are incorrect.

59. (A) (WILLS)

Where no provision is made for what should happen if a beneficiary predeceases the testator, New York's anti-lapse statute comes into play. That statute provides that "unless the will provides otherwise, whenever a testamentary disposition is made to the issue or to a brother or sister of the testator and such beneficiary dies during the lifetime of the testator leaving issue surviving such testator, such disposition does not lapse but vests in such surviving issue, per capita at each generation." Here, Tom has made provision for his wife's predeceasing him, but has failed to do so with respect to his children, Richard and Carrol. In this case, Carrol is covered by the statute since she is "issue" of Tom. Had Carrol lived, she would have received one-half of the estate, the other one-half going to Richard. Now, her one-half is shared equally by her two surviving children, Ned and Paul. Thus, Richard gets one-half of the estate while Ned and Paul receive one-quarter each. Accordingly, answer (A) is correct and answers (B), (C), and (D) are wrong.

60. (C) (EVIDENCE)

In New York, a prosecutor may not initiate bad character evidence. If defendant introduces such reputation evidence, then only defendant's reputation in the community, not specific acts, is admissible as rebuttal evidence. Thus, (C) is correct. (A) is incorrect because even though the testimony may be relevant, the prosecutor is precluded from initiating it. (B) is incorrect because it states the wrong reason for the inadmissibility of the evidence. (D) is incorrect because regardless of the purported merit of this testimony, the prosecutor is prohibited from initiating this evidence.

61. (B) (WILLS)

EPTL section 3-3.5 permits "in terrorem" clauses, *i.e.*, "no contest clauses." However, the statute states that a contest based on a ground that the will was forged or revoked—provided that the contest is based on probable cause—does not result in the forfeiture of the legacy of the contesting legatee. Here, Bruce had probable cause to believe that the will giving Sophie $100,000 was revoked by a subsequent will. Thus, the surrogate should deny Sophie's motion. Accordingly, answer (B) is correct and (C) and (D) are wrong. Answer (A) is wrong because the surrogate would deny the motion on the ground that Bruce had probable cause to make the contest.

62. (B) (NEW YORK PRACTICE/DOMESTIC RELATIONS)

CPLR 302(b) extends personal jurisdiction in any matrimonial action, if, among other grounds, New York was the matrimonial domicile of the parties before their separation. CPLR 302(b) is applicable where the defendant is a nonresident. Conversion divorce is available pursuant to Domestic Relations Law section 170 where the separation is for one year or more by agreement. Here, Jane has met the statutory requirements for conversion divorce and thus can serve Dick in Maryland. Thus (B) is correct. For the foregoing reasons, (A) is incorrect. (C) is wrong because service of a mere summons will not suffice; if a summons is served without a complaint, the nature of the action must be endorsed on the summons and it must contain notice of any ancillary relief sought. (D) is incorrect because where the parties have married in New York as here, only one year's continuous residence by one party is required. [N.Y. Dom. Rel. Law §230] In any case, Jane has lived in New York for many years.

63. (B) (NEW YORK PRACTICE)

CPLR 302(a)(4) provides that use of real property situated in New York (hereinunder a lease) subjects the owner or lessee to in personam jurisdiction as to any lawsuits *arising out of such* use. (A) is wrong because Land Corp. can obtain in personam jurisdiction. (C) is wrong because in personam jurisdiction can be obtained under CPLR 302 if Bill is served in Connecticut.

64. (B) (WILLS)

(B) is correct. The situs rule disposes of the property by the law of the jurisdiction in which the land is situated. [EPTL §3-5.1(b)(1)]

65. (A) (WILLS)

(A) is correct. The disposition of personal property (when not disposed of by will) is determined by the law of the jurisdiction in which the decedent was domiciled at death. [*See* EPTL §3-5.1(b)(2)]

66. (C) (SECURED TRANSACTIONS)

A purchase money security interest in inventory collateral has priority over a conflicting security interest in the same collateral if: (i) it is perfected at the time the debtor gets possession of the collateral; and (ii) any secured party who has perfected her security interest on the same collateral receives authenticated notification of the purchase money security interest before the debtor receives possession of the inventory, and the notification states that the purchase money party has or expects to take a purchase money security interest in the inventory of the debtor described by kind or type. Y Bank, having taken all these steps, has priority over X Bank's after-acquired property interest.

67. (C) (CORPORATIONS)

Business Corporations Law section 624 provides that any shareholder of a corporation has the right to examine the "shareholders' minutes and record of shareholders," provided that the shareholder furnishes an affidavit that his purpose is not adverse to the corporation's interest, and that he has not participated in an attempt to sell a list of shareholders within the past five years. In the absence of facts to the contrary, Byron is thus entitled to I. In addition to a shareholder's statutory right of inspection, shareholders have a common law right to inspect the corporate books and records at a proper place and reasonable time and for a proper purpose. [Matter of Steinway, 159 N.Y. 250 (1899); Sivin v. Schwartz, 22 A.D.2d 822 (1964)] Thus, Byron is also entitled to II.

68. (D) (COMMERCIAL PAPER)

Artie is not a holder in due course if the check is not a negotiable instrument. For the instrument to be negotiable, it must contain an unconditional promise. [U.C.C. §3-105] Here, the agreement to paint Lola's house is not a condition precedent to negotiability of the check, for it is not an express condition noted on the check, but is a separate contract. Thus, the agreement does not impair negotiability. (A) is wrong.

Under U.C.C. sections 3-108 and 3-109, in order for an instrument to be negotiable, it must be payable on demand and at a definite time. The check in question is payable on demand; and it is payable at a definite time, but not until the date stated—May 31, 2004. The postdating of the check does not destroy its negotiability, but merely limits the date from which enforcement may be sought. Thus, (B) is wrong.

To be a holder in due course, Artie must take the instrument for value. [U.C.C. §3-202] The U.C.C. specifically provides that payment of an antecedent debt constitutes value. [U.C.C. §3-303] Thus, (C) is wrong.

69. (D) (NEW YORK PRACTICE)

A notice of pendency may be filed by a plaintiff in any action in which the title, possession, use, or enjoyment of premises is to be determined. The notice of pendency acts as constructive notice to a purchaser or encumbrancer of real property that the defendant's property is the subject of a lawsuit. Therefore, since this is an action which will affect the title, etc., of D's premises, it is proper for P to file. Thus, (A) is incorrect. (B) is not correct because a notice of pendency may be filed "before or after service of summons and at any time prior to judgment." [*See* CPLR, Article 65] A notice of pendency, when filed prior to the service of summons, is effective as long as the summons is served within 30 days. Thus, (C) is incorrect.

70. (C) (CONTRACTS)

This case involves a sales contract in which the seller is a merchant. The U.C.C. governs sales contracts involving merchants. U.C.C. section 2-708 provides that when the buyer repudiates, the seller's remedy is either: (i) the difference between the market price and the unpaid contract price, plus incidental damages less expenses saved; or (ii) if that is not sufficient in making the seller "whole," the seller's lost profit plus incidental damages. Here, the market value of the boat and the unpaid contract price (both $15,000) plus incidental damages ($500) does not make the seller whole since he lost out on his profit. The seller's profit, had the buyer not repudiated, would have been $3,000. Thus, to make D whole, the lost profit plus the incidental damages, equalling $3,500, must be paid by P.

71. (B) (EQUITY/NEW YORK PRACTICE)

A preliminary injunction may be granted only upon notice to the defendant [CPLR 6311(1)]; so (C) and (D) are wrong. Under CPLR 6312, all parties seeking preliminary injunctive relief must give an undertaking "in an amount fixed by the Court" before such relief will be granted. Only the state of New York, a domestic municipal corporation, or a public officer on behalf of the state or a municipal corporation are exempt. Thus, (A) is incorrect and (B) is correct.

72. (A) (SECURED TRANSACTIONS)

A trustee can avoid a preference if the transfer was to, or for, the benefit of a creditor *and* it was made for or on account of an antecedent debt *and* while the debtor was insolvent *and* the transfer was made within 90 days prior to the date of the filing of the bankruptcy petition *and* the transfer will increase the amount that the creditor would receive if the preference was not made. The first security interest was made on March 16. D filed for bankruptcy on June 30, more than 90 days after the security interest in D's office furniture was given and perfected. Thus, (C) is incorrect. The security interest given on April 30, while within the 90-day avoidance period, is not an interest made on an antecedent debt. Here, D gave the security at the time the loan was made as collateral for the second loan. Thus, it is not for or on account of an antecedent debt and cannot be avoided. Therefore, (D) is incorrect. *Note:*

The security given on the first loan *was* for or on account of an antecedent debt but could not be avoided because it was made prior to the requisite 90 days. Since both security interests will survive, (A) is the correct choice.

73. (C) (NEW YORK PRACTICE)

Service upon D is invalid even though S served D personally within New York, because D is "immune" from service. Under New York common law, a nonresident who is voluntarily in the state to attend a judicial hearing or proceeding as a party or a witness is immune from process during his stay in the state as long as he travels to the court and leaves the state from the courthouse. Here, D was served while in the parking lot of the courthouse and was immune at the time he was served. Thus, service was invalid.

S's attempted service upon E is also invalid. S attempted to use "nail and mail" service, and nail and mail service cannot be used unless, with due diligence, the plaintiff first attempts personal service or service by leaving a copy of the summons with a person of suitable age and discretion. Proof of service is then filed within 20 days of service with the clerk of the court. Ten days after the filing is made service is deemed complete. Here, S went to E's residence, rang the doorbell, found no one at home, and proceeded to use "nail and mail" service. S's one attempt to serve E is insufficient to show due diligence, and thus, the nail and mail service will not be considered valid service. Additionally, the proof of service, though served by P's attorney upon D and E, was never filed with the clerk of the court designated in the summons. Thus, service was never "complete." Therefore, service on both D and E was invalid.

74. (B) (NEW YORK PRACTICE)

CPLR 4110(a) states that a juror may be challenged for cause if: (i) the juror is an employee of one of the parties; (ii) a shareholder in a corporate party; or (iii) in an action for damages, a shareholder, director, officer, or employee of an insurance company issuing policies for protection against liability for damages for injury to persons or property. The section goes on to state that a juror may *not* be challenged for cause merely because she is a resident in or pays taxes to a town, city, county, or village which may be a party to the action. In this case, J is an *employee* of T Town. Thus, (1) is a valid challenge for cause. J is also a shareholder in an insurance company that issues liability insurance. That makes (3) a valid challenge. (2) is not a valid challenge because merely being a resident and liable for taxes in the town is not "cause" under the CPLR.

75. (A) (CORPORATIONS)

Under the Business Corporations Law, the basic rule when dealing with removal is that officers or directors can be removed only by those who put them in their position in the first place, unless otherwise stated in the certificate of incorporation. In this case, the certificate of incorporation only provides for the election of the president and is silent as to removal of officers and directors. A was elected by the shareholders to the positions of director and president. Because the certificate of incorporation is silent, the Business Corporations Law is the controlling law. Since A was elected by the shareholders to both positions, the shareholders may remove him. Thus, (B) and (C) are incorrect. B was also elected to the board by the shareholders, and for the same reasons as stated above, he can only be removed by the shareholders. However, B was appointed to the position of treasurer by the board and can thus be removed by the board with or without cause. Thus, (D) is not a correct choice.

Therefore, since A cannot be removed by the board and B can only be removed by the board from his position as treasurer, (A) is the correct answer.

76. (B) (CORPORATIONS)

Under the Business Corporations Law, the certificate of incorporation must include a designation of the secretary of state as agent for service of process and must be created for a lawful purpose, except for those purposes reserved for corporations formed under other state statutes (*i.e.*, railroad, banking, insurance, etc.). The designation of a registered agent other than the secretary of state is optional.

In this case, the certificate of incorporation failed to designate the secretary of state as agent for service of process. Thus, (1) and (3) are proper reasons for refusal, but (2) is not.

77. (C) (CONTRACTS)

Where an obligor, **prior** to notice of the assignment, either performs the obligation, secures a discharge of the obligation for consideration, or acquires any other good defense for value against the assignee, the assignee takes subject to that defense. Here, A has fully performed by paying B the full amount of the obligation. A never had notice of the assignment. Thus, (1) is a valid defense.

The defense of personal service exists when the services to be performed to the assignee are "unique." While B's services might be considered unique, it is not his performance that is looked to in this case. A's performance is that which has been assigned. A is to pay money. That is a "routine" performance and not "unique." Thus, (2) is not a valid defense.

No consideration is required for an assignment. One may assign rights gratuitously. Thus, (3) is not a valid defense.

78. (C) (EVIDENCE)

In New York, either spouse, whether or not a party, has a privilege to refuse to disclose, and to prevent another from disclosing, a confidential communication made between the spouses while they were husband and wife. This is the only marital testimonial privilege recognized in New York. Both spouses jointly hold this privilege and either may refuse to disclose any communication made during a valid marriage. For the communication to fall within this privilege, it must be made in reliance upon the intimacy of the marital relationship. Accordingly, (C) is the correct answer. (B) is incorrect because the confidential communication may be by conduct and need not be spoken. (A) is a correct statement of an old rule—spouses were absolutely incompetent to testify for or against each other during the period of marriage.

79. (C) (CRIMINAL PROCEDURE)

In a nonjury trial, the court has discretion as to whether it will permit opening statements. The court cannot grant permission to one party and not the other. [N.Y. Crim. Proc. Law §350.10] Thus, it is not required that any party make an opening statement in a nonjury trial. Therefore, (C) is the correct answer.

80. (A) (AGENCY)

The general rule is that death of either the principal or the agent terminates the agency relationship at the time of death. Therefore, (B), (C), and (D) are incorrect.

81. (D) (CRIMINAL PROCEDURE)

Under Criminal Procedure Law section 270.35, when a juror, prior to verdict, is unable to continue as a juror, one of the alternative jurors must fill the vacancy. If there are no alternative jurors available, the court must declare a mistrial because it is "physically impossible to proceed with the trial in conformity with the law." [N.Y. Crim. Proc. Law §28.10] It should be noted that if a vacancy appears on the jury after deliberations have begun, but prior to verdict, an alternative juror must fill the vacancy *only upon the written consent of the defendant*. Here, there were no jurors to fill the vacancy; thus, the court must declare a mistrial. Thus, (A), (B), and (C) are incorrect.

82. (B) (CRIMINAL LAW)

Criminal Procedure Law section 300.10(4) states that the court must inform the parties as to the charge it will make to the jury "***prior to the summations.***" In this case, the court did not inform the parties as to its charge prior to summation; thus, D is correct as to (2). That eliminates (A) and (D) as possible choices. Penal Law section 125.20(2) states that the defendant is guilty of manslaughter in the first degree when ". . . with intent to cause the death of another person, he causes the death of such person or of a third person under circumstances which did not constitute murder because he acts under the influence of emotional disturbance . . . The fact that homicide was committed under the influence of extreme emotional disturbance constitutes a mitigating circumstance reducing murder to manslaughter in the first degree and need not be proved in any prosecution initiated under this subdivision . . ." Therefore, D cannot correctly state that as a matter of law manslaughter cannot be a lesser-included offense of murder in the second degree.

83. (C) (CRIMINAL LAW)

For A to establish the defense of renunciation, he must voluntarily renounce the conspiracy and prevent the commission of the crime. Thus, (C) is correct and (D) is incorrect. Merely withdrawing from participation is not sufficient. Thus, (A) is incorrect. The crime must be prevented from occurring; therefore, (B) is incorrect.

84. (B) (NEW YORK PRACTICE)

CPLR 3043(b) states that a supplemental bill of particulars may be served at any time without leave of the court for the purpose of showing claims of "continuing special damages and disabilities," but not less than 30 days prior to trial. The party serving the supplemental bill of particulars may not assert a new cause of action or claim new injuries. The responding party has the right to full discovery but only as to the continuing special damages and disabilities. In this case, P has attempted to claim a new injury in her bill of particulars. This is in direct contradiction to the CPLR and will not be allowed. Thus, (1) is incorrect. (2) sets forth special continuing damages and is allowed under the CPLR. Therefore, answer (B) is correct.

85. (C) (NEW YORK PRACTICE)

CPLR 320 provides that a defendant appears when the answer is served, when the defendant serves a notice of appearance, or when the defendant makes a motion which has the effect of extending the time to answer.

D's first motion did not constitute an appearance because he did not file a notice of appearance or make a motion that would extend the time to answer. The complaint was never served on D, so he could not answer, nor could his motion extend his time to answer. Therefore, (1) does not constitute an appearance.

(2) is not an appearance because it is not an answer; there is still no notice of appearance, and D's notice to take depositions does not extend D's time to answer.

D's motion to strike certain allegations in P's complaint will serve to extend D's time to answer while the court decides whether P's allegations are valid. Therefore, D appeared at the time that he made the motion to strike. Answer (C) is correct.

86.   (D)   (REAL PROPERTY)

The court will not enforce a servitude if it could not in good conscience do so. The court will look to see if it is against public policy, if the plaintiff has acquiesced to similar violations, or if the plaintiff has "unclean hands" or is estopped from enforcing the servitude.

Here, N did not object to the construction of the day-care center. However, this is not the type of violation that will bar the plaintiff from making a claim. The plaintiff must have failed to enforce the covenant against a third party for the same or similar violation which the plaintiff claims against the defendant in the instant case, and such a claim must have a significant effect on the plaintiff's interests. The day-care center can be an asset to the community without affecting the interests of the other owners. The construction of the two-family dwelling on the lots *adjoining* N's lot will, however, have a significant effect on N's interest in the property. Thus, N's failure to enforce the covenant against the day-care center is not a valid defense.

B purchased the remaining five lots with the covenant in the deed restricting the use of the land to one-family houses. All of the lots but No. 45 have a one-family house on it. Courts are reluctant to permit relief from restrictions on the use of land in this type of situation for fear that adjoining neighbors will complain that it is unfair to them and will eventually lead the entire plan to become undone. Thus, the court will enforce the restriction.

87.   (A)   (TORTS)

EPTL section 11-3.3 states that the damages recovered for injuries accruing *before*, but not including, death become part of the estate of the deceased. Damages recovered for wrongful death ". . . are exclusively for the benefit of the decedent's distributees . . . ." [EPTL §5-4.3(a)]

In this case, the court awarded $15,000 for W's pain and suffering. That recovery is for the damages incurred *prior* to death, so it is recoverable by C.

The award for $35,000 is for wrongful death and belongs exclusively to W's daughters, A and B.

C has a valid claim against the estate. Under EPTL section 13-1.3(a)(1), the payment of the decedent's debts, administration of the estate, funeral expenses, and taxes have priority over any other distribution of the decedent's assets.

Thus, C will be able to recover only the $15,000 award for pain and suffering that has become part of W's estate.

88.   (B)   (REAL PROPERTY)

Under Real Property Law section 226-b, when the lease is silent as to assignability, the tenant must obtain the written consent of the landlord in order to make a valid assignment. The landlord may unconditionally withhold consent without cause, as long as the landlord releases the tenant from the lease after the tenant gives 30 days' notice of the desire to be released. Release is the tenant's sole remedy. Thus, (B) is correct.

89. (D) (DOMESTIC RELATIONS)

Domestic Relations Law section 236B(3) states, "An agreement by the parties made before or during the marriage, shall be valid and enforceable in a matrimonial action if such agreement is in writing, subscribed by the parties, and acknowledged or proven in the manner required to entitle a deed to be required."

When a married couple purchases real property, they take title as tenants by the entirety. This is a joint tenancy with right of survivorship that is unique to married couples. The only way to destroy the title held by tenancy by the entirety is to partition the property or to end the marriage.

Prior to W's death, H and W were still legally married and still held the premises as tenants by the entirety. Under the Domestic Relations Law, W's divorce action will not have any effect on the agreement regarding the marital property.

Therefore, prior to W's death, H and W held the property as tenants by the entirety, and, under the agreement, H is entitled to half the proceeds from the sale of the property in 1990.

90. (C) (DOMESTIC RELATIONS)

Domestic Relations Law section 241 states that when a custodial parent who is the recipient of maintenance wrongfully interferes with the visitation rights of the other spouse, ". . . the court in its discretion, may suspend such payments or cancel any arrears that may have accrued during the time that visitation rights have been or are being interfered with or withheld." Wrongful interference with visitation rights is *never* a defense to failure to pay child support.

91. (C) (DOMESTIC RELATIONS)

The basic premise of the ground of "cruel and inhuman treatment" is that the defendant has engaged in a course of conduct that so endangers the plaintiff so as to render it "unsafe or improper for the plaintiff to cohabit with the defendant." [N.Y. Dom. Rel. Law §170(1)] Cohabitation is not an issue when this ground is set forth. The mere fact that W resides with H does not negate the ground of cruel and inhuman treatment. Thus, H's first defense is groundless.

[*Note:* There is a five-year statute of limitations on a claim for cruel and inhuman treatment. It is not an issue in this case, but it is something to be aware of.]

H's second defense is W's adulterous acts during the marriage. The affirmative defense of adultery is available only when the ground for divorce alleged is adultery. W's action against H is based on cruel and inhuman treatment, and thus H's defense of W's adultery is invalid. Additionally, adulterous acts of a spouse are deemed "forgiven" if the spouse continues to cohabit with the adulterous spouse. H knew of W's adultery yet continued to live with her. Therefore, adultery is a nonissue under two separate theories.

92. (A) (REAL PROPERTY)

Real Property Law section 223-a states that when the lessor refuses to deliver the premises to the lessee at the commencement of the lease term, ". . . the lessee shall have the right to rescind the lease and recover the consideration paid. Such right shall not be deemed inconsistent with any right of action he may have to recover damages." Thus, (A) is correct.

93. (C) (CRIMINAL PROCEDURE)

A grand jury in New York consists of between 16 and 23 persons and 12 votes are needed to indict. (A) is a correct statement of the law and an incorrect answer choice. Criminal Procedure Law section 190.45 provides that a written waiver of immunity is required by grand jury witnesses and thus, (B) is an incorrect choice. Under Criminal Procedure Law section 190.05, a grand jury may hear and examine evidence concerning crimes and the conduct of public officers, whether or not it is criminal. Thus, (C) is an incorrect statement of the law and a correct answer choice. (D) is a wrong choice because a witness who has waived immunity may be accompanied into the grand jury room by counsel, but the witness's counsel may only advise the witness; counsel may not take part in the proceeding in any other way.

94. (C) (FEDERAL JURISDICTION & PROCEDURE)

In a diversity action, venue is no longer proper in the judicial districts where all plaintiffs reside. According to 28 U.S.C. section 1391(a), suits in which subject matter jurisdiction is based on diversity alone may be brought in the judicial district where all defendants reside, where a substantial part of the acts or omissions on which the claim is based took place, or where the defendants are subject to personal jurisdiction when the case is commenced. Therefore, (A) is incorrect. Connecticut is also a proper venue because the claim is based on an act that took place in Connecticut. (B) and (D) are also incorrect since it does not appear that N has any ties with Vermont that would subject him to personal jurisdiction there.

95. (B) (NEW YORK PRACTICE)

The statute of limitations for bringing an action against a city, town, county, village, or fire or school district is one year and 90 days. The plaintiff must serve a notice of claim on the defendant within 90 days of the occurrence. This is a condition precedent to bringing an action. Failure to serve the notice of claim properly and timely will result in a loss of claim.

If a cause of action accrues in favor of an infant, the statute of limitations is tolled; that is, it does not start to run until the infant reaches his 18th birthday. Once the infant reaches 18, the action must be commenced within three years after his 18th birthday if the otherwise applicable limitations period is three years or more, or within the otherwise applicable period of the statute of limitations if it is less than three years, such being the case in this instance. Although in this case the notice of claim was timely filed, the infancy toll applies both to the statute of limitations and the time limit for a motion to serve a late notice of claim.

In this case, P was 14 years old at the time the cause of action arose. Because of P's infancy, the statute of limitations for P's claim is tolled until P turns 18. Once he turns 18, P has one year and 90 days, or until 90 days after his 19th birthday, to bring the action. P's injury occurred on May 26, 2003. On May 1, 2007, when the claim was filed, P could not have been older than 18; therefore, the claim was timely filed and is not barred by the statute of limitations.

On the other hand, P's father, F, is precluded from bringing his derivative action because his claim is made after the expiration of the statutory time period. F does not benefit from P's infancy. In other words, while P's claim is protected due to his "disability," F cannot preserve his own claim on that basis. The statute of limitations on F's case never tolled. F lost his action one year and 90 days after the cause of action arose.

Therefore, F's action against S should be dismissed on the grounds of the statute of limitations.

96. (A) (NEW YORK PRACTICE)

D was properly served. CPLR 308 sets forth the proper manner in which the court can obtain personal jurisdiction over the defendant, including by personally delivering it to the defendant and by delivering it to a person of suitable age and discretion at the defendant's actual place of residence or business and mailing.

In this case, A served D's wife at D's actual place of residence and then served another copy by mail. Assuming W is of suitable age and discretion (the fact pattern did not hint otherwise), personal service has been made upon D. CPLR 308(2) provides that proof of service must be filed within 20 days of the delivery or mailing, whichever is later. Service becomes complete 10 days after filing. A subsequently filed within the 20-day statutory period. Ten days after A's filing, service was complete.

Note: The service is valid even though it was served by A, attorney for P. The CPLR states that an interested party may not serve the summons and complaint; however, an attorney is not considered an interested party under the CPLR and may properly serve.

D's motion is timely. CPLR 320 states that a defendant has 20 days to serve and answer or make an appearance. However, if the defendant is served in any manner other than delivery to him personally, then the defendant has 30 days from the date of service in which to respond. On June 15, proof of service was filed. On June 25, service was complete. D responded on July 10, well before the 30-day period had expired, and thus made a timely motion. [CPLR 320(a)] Therefore, (A) is the correct answer.

97. (D) (WILLS)

For a will to be valid in New York, it must be in writing, signed at the end by the testator in the presence of at least two witnesses, and the testator must declare the instrument to be his will. The testator need not necessarily sign his name before each of the attesting witnesses, but must merely declare the signature to be his own to the witnesses and have the witnesses sign their names within 30 days of each other.

T, after telling F that the instrument he was holding was his will, signed it at the end in front of F who signed as a witness. He then went to A and repeated his actions. Therefore, F and A are valid witnesses to T's will. However, because they are named beneficiaries under the will, they are classified as "interested witnesses." Under the EPTL, the mere fact that a witness is an "interested witness" does not negate his ability to be a witness, and neither will it prevent the will from being probated. However, the disposition to F and A may become void.

Therefore, since F and A are valid witnesses to the execution of T's will, the surrogate may properly admit the will to probate.

98. (D) (EVIDENCE)

The statement made by Ellen to the police officer was an admission because it was a statement made that amounts to a prior acknowledgment by one of the parties to an action of one of the relevant facts. Under the Federal Rules of Evidence this type of statement is considered nonhearsay. However, New York still treats this as a traditional exception to the hearsay rule. Thus, (A) is wrong and (D) is the correct answer.

99. (A) (CRIMINAL LAW)

Under New York Penal Law section 125.10, a person is guilty of criminally negligent homicide if, with criminal negligence, she causes the death of another. Here, Judi engaged in some "serious blameworthy conduct" creating or contributing to a substantial and unjustifiable risk of death. Judi was an accomplice because she encouraged Ellen to commit the crime and thus can be found guilty of the criminal offense. (B) is wrong because in New York, the felony murder rule only applies if someone commits burglary, robbery, arson, kidnapping, rape, or sexual abuse, none of which occurred here. (C) is incorrect because there is no crime of battery in New York. There is only the crime of assault, which encompasses common law battery. Accordingly, (A) is the correct answer.

100. (B) (CRIMINAL PROCEDURE/EVIDENCE)

Here defense wanted to bring out for the jury the suggestive nature of the photo identification and witness's initial uncertainty. The point of doing this was to attack the reliability of the identification of defendant as the perpetrator. If evidence of the photo identification were admitted but not the lineup, defense would have been free to argue that Witness was able to identify defendant only due to a suggestive identification process, thus, misleading the jury. Use of the identification procedures in the police station opens the door to testimony concerning the post-charge lineup evidence because it would have directly contradicted the impression given by the evidence, and, thus, is relevant and should be available for use by the prosecution, irrespective of any initial violation of defendant's Sixth Amendment right to counsel.

SUBJECT INDEX OF NEW YORK ASSORTED MULTIPLE CHOICE QUESTIONS

SUBJECT	QUESTION NUMBER
AGENCY	15, 80
COMMERCIAL PAPER	54, 55, 68
CONSTITUTIONAL LAW	7, 56
CONTRACTS	11, 13, 14, 16, 17, 33, 70, 77
CORPORATIONS	8, 31, 41, 67, 75, 76
CRIMINAL LAW	5, 6, 9, 10, 29, 35, 44, 45, 82, 83, 99
CRIMINAL PROCEDURE	43, 79, 81, 93, 100
DOMESTIC RELATIONS	12, 20, 23, 24, 27, 52, 62, 89, 90, 91
EQUITY	71
EVIDENCE	22, 46, 51, 60, 78, 98, 100
FEDERAL JURISDICTION & PROCEDURE	18, 25, 58, 94
NEW YORK PRACTICE	19, 26, 27, 32, 34, 36, 38, 40, 42, 50, 53, 55, 58, 62, 63, 69, 71, 73, 74, 84, 85, 95, 96
PARTNERSHIP	26
REAL PROPERTY	11, 39, 57, 86, 88, 92
SECURED TRANSACTIONS	66, 72
TORTS	1, 4, 15, 21, 28, 42, 47, 48, 49, 51, 87
TRUSTS	3
WILLS	2, 30, 37, 59, 61, 64, 65, 97